Equity-Based Career Development and Postsecondary Transitions

A volume in
Contemporary Perspectives on Access, Equity, and Achievement
Chance W. Lewis, *Series Editor*

Contemporary Perspectives on Access, Equity, and Achievement

Chance W. Lewis, *Series Editor*

Recruiting, Retaining, and Engaging African-American Males at Selective Public Research Universities: Challenges and Opportunities in Academics and Sports (2018)
Louis A. Castenel, Tarek C. Grantham, and Billy J. Hawkins

Engaging African American Males in Community Colleges (2018)
Ted N. Ingram and James Coaxum III

Advancing Equity and Diversity in Student Affairs: A Festschrift in Honor of Melvin C. Terrell (2017)
Jerlando F. L. Jackson, LaVar J. Charleston, and Cornelius Gilbert

Cultivating Achievement, Respect, and Empowerment (CARE) for African American Girls in PreK–12 Settings: Implications for Access, Equity and Achievement (2016)
Patricia J. Larke, Gwendolyn Webb-Hasan, and Jemimah L. Young

R.A.C.E. Mentoring Through Social Media: Black and Hispanic Scholars Share Their Journey in the Academy (2016)
Donna Y. Ford, Michelle Trotman Scott, Ramon B. Goings, Tuwana T. Wingfield, and Malik S. Henfield

White Women's Work: Examining the Intersectionality of Teaching, Identity, and Race (2016)
Stephen Hancock and Chezare A. Warren

Reaching the Mountaintop of the Academy: Personal Narratives, Advice and Strategies From Black Distinguished and Endowed Professors (2015)
Gail L. Thompson, Fred A. Bonner II, and Chance W. Lewis

School Counseling for Black Male Student Success in 21st Century Urban Schools (2015)
Malik S. Henfield and Ahmad R. Washington

Exploring Issues of Diversity within HBCUs (2015)
Ted N. Ingram, Derek Greenfield, Joelle D. Carter, and Adriel A. Hilton

Priorities of the Professoriate: Engaging Multiple Forms of Scholarship Across Rural and Urban Institutions (2015)
Fred A. Bonner II, Rosa M. Banda, Petra A. Robinson, Chance W. Lewis, and Barbara Lofton

Autoethnography as a Lighthouse: Illuminating Race, Research, and the Politics of Schooling (2015)
Stephen Hancock, Ayana Allen, and Chance W. Lewis

Teacher Education and Black Communities: Implications for Access, Equity and Achievement (2014)
Yolanda Sealey-Ruiz, Chance W. Lewis, and Ivory Toldson

Improving Urban Schools: Equity and Access in K–16 STEM Education (2013)
Mary Margaret Capraro, Robert M. Capraro, and Chance W. Lewis

Black Males in Postsecondary Education: Examining their Experiences in Diverse Institutional Contexts (2012)
Adriel A. Hilton, J. Luke Wood, and Chance W. Lewis

Yes We Can! Improving Urban Schools through Innovative Educational Reform (2011)
Leanne L. Howell, Chance W. Lewis, and Norvella Carter

Equity-Based Career Development and Postsecondary Transitions

An American Imperative

edited by

Erik M. Hines
Florida State University

Laura Owen
San Diego State University

INFORMATION AGE PUBLISHING, INC.
Charlotte, NC • www.infoagepub.com

Library of Congress Cataloging-in-Publication Data

A CIP record for this book is available from the Library of Congress
http://www.loc.gov

ISBN: 978-1-64802-865-6 (Paperback)
978-1-64802-866-3 (Hardcover)
978-1-64802-867-0 (E-Book)

Printed in the United States of America

I would like to dedicate this book to several individuals. First, my beloved wife who shares the same passion and commitment to helping the most vulnerable population of students achieve academic success and postsecondary opportunities. Second, my two sons, Erik Michael and Harper who I labor for as Black boys to ensure they have an optimal environment to succeed and thrive. Third, to my mother who taught my sisters and I the value of hardwork and her tireless work ethic to provide opportunities for her three children. Last, I dedicate this book to my mentors and the ancestors in which I have the privilege to stand on their shoulders to advance the work of improving academic and postsecondary outcomes for Black students and other students of color.

—Erik M. Hines

I would like to dedicate this book to my colleagues, friends and family who inspire and motivate me to see the gifts and talents every individual brings to this world. To my brother Kevin, who went to work every day even though his developmental level stopped at 10 months old. To the staff at the Trudeau Center who believed he could contribute in meaningful ways to society. To all the school counselors, district counseling directors and counselor educators who work so diligently to help students find their passion and their why. To my children who are each uniquely navigating their own postsecondary path and who make me proud to be their mom. To my partner Steve, I could not do this work without your continuous support and love. Finally, thank you to all the mentors and teachers in my life. Not a single day goes by without thinking about the collective wisdom, compassion, and support you so freely share with me. May this book be an inspiration to all who hope for a more just, equitable and compassionate world.

—Laura Owen

CONTENTS

ix

FOREWORD

Like many young people in the United States, when I began my college journey in the early 1990s at Delaware State University, I was not sure exactly what I wanted to do with my life beyond playing football in the National Football League (NFL). What I did know was that I wanted to help young people like me, who grew up in working-class, middle- and low-income communities, obtain optimal life success. I also knew that I would never see outside the bright lights of the NFL, without outlined career goals and actionable steps to achieve them.

Personally, I believe that a strong career plan steers an individual's vocational orientation and behaviors, quest for mastering new skills and completing tasks, and motivation for overcoming challenges aligned with career goals. Without a formidable career plan, achieving one's career aspirations could take a lifetime, especially when they do not include an accurate assessment of self and the needed skills, experiences, connections, and opportunities to reach career goals. After much input and research, my career plan or path led me to education. From an early age, I believed that mentoring and nourishing young people through the important decisions that can shape their destinies was a just, noble, and important calling. Nearly 3 decades removed from my undergraduate days and now with a PhD in counselor education from Virginia Polytechnic Institute and State University, I still feel that way today.

As I became an academic focused on researching students' education and career aspirations and the many equity-based issues surrounding them, I noticed, through evidence-based models, how truly impactful school

Equity-Based Career Development and Postsecondary Transitions, pages xiii–xiv
Copyright © 2022 by Information Age Publishing
www.infoagepub.com

counselors and other education professionals could be. As the United States reorients its perspectives after an unprecedented global pandemic, the role of school counselors in career development has never been more important. The truth is that there has never been a greater need in the world for human talent than there is today. The stakes have never been higher for humankind. The nation needs to tap sharpened minds from every zip code to solve the world's most vexing problems.

The greatest challenges that lie ahead for humankind—how to best adapt to climate change, turn toward renewable energy, and feed an increasingly crowded planet—will only be answered by highly-trained minds. It only happens if society can widen the pipeline from high school to the postsecondary world—an imperative for the United States and for continued economic growth. To understand how to create, support, and implement equity-based career development and postsecondary successes, I believe that the editors, Drs. Erik Hines and Lauren Owen, have gathered some of the leading minds in the country for this edited volume.

While many chapters focus on different student populations with first generation students, Black student athletes, LGBTQ+ students, immigrant and refugee students as well as the gifted student population all represented, a common thread of proven strategies and best practices for improving postsecondary readiness, enrollment, and retention runs throughout. Whether you are a student studying to become a school counselor, a trained professional counselor currently in the field, a counselor educator, or an academic researcher, the presented chapters offer a variety of new tools and fresh perspectives around age-old issues of how best to prepare young people for career success in an uncertain future. I hope that this edited volume fuels the readers' creative juices and allows them to reimagine and reorient how counselor educators and other education professionals prepare students for the postsecondary world and career development.

—James L. Moore III

James L. Moore III, PhD, vice provost for diversity and inclusion and chief diversity inclusion; executive director for Todd Anthony Bell National Resource Center on the African American Male; and EHE Distinguished Professor of Urban Education at The Ohio State University. E-mail: moore.1408@osu.edu Twitter: @DrJLMooreIII

ACKNOWLEDGMENT

We would like to acknowledge Vania Silva, school counseling graduate student (2020–2022), San Diego State University for designing the book cover.

Equity-Based Career Development and Postsecondary Transitions, page xv
Copyright © 2022 by Information Age Publishing
www.infoagepub.com
All rights of reproduction in any form reserved.

CHAPTER 1

ADVOCATING FOR SCHOOL COUNSELORS' ROLE IN STUDENTS' CAREER DEVELOPMENT AND POSTSECONDARY TRANSITIONS

Mary Edwin
University of Missouri–St. Louis

Diandra J. Prescod
University of Connecticut

ABSTRACT

Changes in America have resulted in a shift in the requirements for success in high skill, high wage jobs (Achieve, 2012) and employers report a lack of highly skilled workers needed to fill positions (Business Roundtable, 2014; Pearson, 2016). Many students who enroll in college do not have clear career goals and often drop out, making the United States the nation with the high-

Equity-Based Career Development and Postsecondary Transitions, pages 1–26
Copyright © 2022 by Information Age Publishing
www.infoagepub.com

est rate of college dropouts in the industrialized world (Coalition for Career Development [CCD], 2019). Of the students who do graduate from college, only about 1 in 3 are confident they will graduate with the skills they need to be successful in the workforce (Strada-Gallup, 2018) and 58% wished they had more career-focused support (CCD, 2019). School counselors' training makes them highly qualified to help prepare students for their future careers through school-based career development interventions. School-based career development interventions are effective in enhancing students' career development skills and school success (Choi et al., 2015). This chapter describes the role of school counselors in developing and implementing interventions that foster students' career development and postsecondary transitions. We highlight the importance of career development throughout PK–12 education for supporting students' career development and postsecondary transitions. We also explore factors impacting school counselors' ability to implement career development interventions and offer strategies for various school stakeholders in advocating for school counselors' roles in students' career development and postsecondary transitions.

Career development is defined as "the life-long psychological and behavioral process as well as the contextual influences shaping one's career over the lifespan" (Niles & Harris-Bowlsbey, 2017, p. 12) and includes the ideas of life roles, decision-making, and values. The Cambridge dictionary (n.d.) defines career development as "the process of learning and improving your skills so that you can do your job better and progress to better jobs." The Career Development Institute (2017) defines career development as "a unique and life-long process for each individual of managing learning, work, and transitions to move forward and participate effectively in work and society" (para. 2). Each definition describes some sort of movement or journey for individuals; the words "life span," "progress," "transition," and "moving forward" each lend themselves to going from one stage to the next.

K–12 career development involves activities that allow students to explore and gain awareness of their skills, abilities, and various careers/occupations. The American School Counselor Association (ASCA) describes the school counselor's role in the career development process in detail. The roles include, but are not limited to,

- introducing careers and the world of work beginning in lower elementary grades (preK–3);
- helping students understand the connection between school and the world of work;
- working with teachers to integrate career education learning in the curricula;
- collaborating with administration, teachers, staff, and decision-makers to create a postsecondary-readiness and college-going culture; and

- providing and advocating for individual pre-K through postsecondary students' college and career awareness through exploration and postsecondary planning and decision making, which supports students' right to choose from the wide array of options after completing secondary education" (ASCA, 2019, p. 7).

Career development at the K–12 level is important because of the many challenges that students face on their career and life journey. Career decision-making proves difficult for many students (Bullock-Yowell et al., 2014; Edwin et al., 2019; Morgan & Ness, 2003) and that difficulty may stem from lack of information, dysfunctional beliefs, and lack of readiness (Gati et al., 1996). Going together with career decision-making, career uncertainty is also a challenge for young people. Uncertainty about the future, options, or possibilities makes it challenging to make career decisions. Penrod (2001) defines *uncertainty* as

> a dynamic state in which there is a perception of being unable to assign probabilities for outcomes that prompts a discomforting, uneasy sensation that may be affected (reduced or escalated) through cognitive, emotive, or behavioral reactions, or by the passage of time and changes in the perception of circumstances. (p. 241)

Thinking about the future and the change that comes along with it can be scary. Uncertainty about the future may also cause negative career thoughts, or negative beliefs and attitudes regarding career decision-making and planning (Sampson et al., 1996). Career interventions at the undergraduate level help decrease negative career thoughts and increase retention and career decision-making skills (Belser et al., 2017, 2018; Prescod et al., 2018). Career development activities are positively linked to students' academic achievement, lower dropout rates, enhancing student attitudes towards school, and increasing school engagement (Castellano et al., 2003; Kenny et al., 2003; Perry et al., 2010). Evidence exists that links career development to self-regulated learning in students (Lapan et al., 2002; Turner & Conkel, 2010), and research shows that self-regulated learning predicts school success (McClelland & Cameron, 2011). Perry et al. (2006) reported that children who are self-regulated learners believe that challenging tasks are an opportunity to practice their learning and better understand the subject matter; and when the effort is put into facing these challenges, it results in academic success. As leaders in the schools, school counselors are charged with leading career development interventions and activities at the K–12 level.

Paying very close attention and detail to what this process should entail, ASCA (2014) also created *ASCA Student Standards: Mindsets and Behaviors for Student Success: K–12 College-, Career-, and Life-Readiness Standards for*

Every Student to describe social/emotional, college, and career readiness development necessary for student success. Mindsets and behavior include building self-confidence, a sense of belonging in school and demonstrating creativity, study skills, and self-discipline. The discussion of career development during K–12 years is an important one due to the knowledge we have of when children begin thinking about themselves within the framework of career. Although we do not stand by her more recent publications around intelligence quotient (IQ) and affirmative action, Gottfredson (1981, 2005) discussed the idea that children begin to accept or reject careers at a young age. According to Gottfredson, the process of accepting or eliminating careers involves ideas around gender, values, and prestige. Lent et al.'s (1994) social cognitive career theory posits that self-efficacy beliefs, outcome expectations, and personal goals influence our career choices. Incorporating career development interventions that allow students to explore their learning style, job skills, money management, and wants/needs can increase their desire to go to college and college and career readiness standards (Mariani et al., 2016). A focus on college and career readiness allows students to be more prepared for their postsecondary transition.

Postsecondary transition is defined as the transition of high school students to their next stage in life, whether it be a 2- or 4-year college or technical school, the workforce, an assisted living facility, or other options (Palmon et al., 2017, p. 1). According to ASCA, every student should have access to counseling and advising services that help prepare them to make decisions for their postsecondary careers and/or education. School counselors help students explore the options available to them in hopes that they will be able to make more knowledgeable and informed decisions. Making choices about one's postsecondary life can be difficult and school counselors play a large role in making that process more manageable for students.

SCHOOL COUNSELORS: LEADERS IN K–12 CAREER DEVELOPMENT AND POSTSECONDARY TRANSITIONS

School counselors are uniquely positioned to effect systemic change from a position of leadership. With their training in human and career development theories, school counselors are the most qualified professionals in school buildings to implement developmentally appropriate interventions that support students' career development (Hines & Lemon, 2011). Organizations such as ASCA, National Career Development Association (NCDA), and the College Board National Office for School Counselor Advocacy (NOSCA) emphasize the critical role school counselors play in providing students with the resources and supports they need to be successful in school and life, including fostering students' career development and successful postsecondary transitions.

According to NOSCA (2010), school counselors are advocates who can influence students' career decisions and plans by providing students with information for successful postsecondary transitions. Hines and Lemon (2011) asserted that school counselors are in a position that allows them to help students by detecting students who are on a path to success and students who are on a "dead-end path" (p. 1). Patricia Martin former vice president of NOSCA (2010)—further maintained that school counselors' interactions with multiple stakeholders allows them to be advocates and leaders in supporting students' career development by connecting students to information and resources to support their postsecondary transition plans.

> It is time to "own the turf." If not you, who? Who in the school is responsible for helping students nurture their dreams for bright futures and for helping them create successful pathways to those dreams? All of our students need school counselors to champion their cause. Each one of them is entitled to a rigorous education that prepares them to successfully attain their college and career goals. (NOSCA, 2010, p. 6)

Indeed, there is an increasing call for school counselors to take a leadership role in preparing students for life after high school. In 2015, then First Lady, Michelle Obama, launched The Reach Higher Initiative (TRHI). The First Lady's mission was to encourage all American students to complete a form of postsecondary education which can include a community college, professional training program, or 4-year university (Obama White House, 2015). TRHI articulated four action plans to aid students in acquiring the necessary information to engage in postsecondary education. These four action plans were to (a) understand ways financial aid can make attending college a feasible option, (b) encourage students in academic planning and learning opportunities outside of the regular school year, (c) engage students in activities that expose them to college and career opportunities, and (d) support school counselors who can help students gain college admission. The final goal of TRHI and the First Lady's 2014 speech on school counselors' role in college and career readiness further emphasized school counselors' important role in facilitating students' career development.

> We forget that an engaged school counselor can be the deciding factor in whether a young person attends college or not...Because if we are going to reach my husband's North Star goal, if we're going to once again have the highest proportion of college graduates in the world by 2020, then good school counseling and advising can't just be a luxury for school systems that can afford it. Instead, we need to ensure that school counselors have what they need to help all our young people reach their full potential. (Obama, 2014, 0:37)

Furthermore, the implementation of the new ASCA standards—*ASCA Student Standards: Mindsets & Behaviors for Student Success* (ASCA, 2014)—highlight the profession's focus on ensuring that all students are ready for successful postsecondary transitions (ASCA, 2014). According to ASCA (2012), it is the school counselor's responsibility to provide students with concrete career development opportunities, in collaboration with other stakeholders. The *ASCA Student Standards: Mindsets & Behaviors for Student Success* (ASCA, 2014) lists standards that guide school counselors as they promote students' career development. School counselors can implement developmentally appropriate career programs that are effective at promoting the career development and postsecondary transitions of all students.

Researchers have found that establishing a comprehensive school counseling program results in an improvement in students' career development skills (Lapan et al., 2012; Wilkerson et al., 2013). School counselors that implemented the ASCA national model in their programs had higher student graduation rates in career and technical education programs (Carey et al., 2012). Additionally, high school students who work with their school counselors to apply and gain admission to postsecondary education or training have stronger aspirations to pursue postsecondary education (Poynton & Lapan, 2017). However, to develop aspirations that are a balance between their idealistic and realistic expectations, students must engage in career development activities that expose them to information about the world of work and as well as career planning. School counselors can serve as a source of social capital in providing students with the necessary information for making sound career decisions.

Social capital refers to the norms and information channels available to students through their social networks (Bryan et al., 2017). McKillip et al. (2012) maintain that access to social capital during the K–12 years is important for students to have successful postsecondary transitions. Students from ethnic minority backgrounds, especially African American students, often have limited access to social capital. Limited access to information about the career development process can create barriers to postsecondary transitions for students, especially students of color (Avery & Kane, 2004; Bryan et al., 2011; Bryan et al., 2017; Engberg & Gilbert, 2014; Farmer-Hinton & Adams, 2006; Holland, 2014; Hurtado et al., 1997; Klasik, 2012).

School counselors are important sources of social capital and can bridge any information gaps for students from marginalized backgrounds by helping students navigate their postsecondary transitions (Bryan et al., 2011; Bryan et al., 2017). School counselors can account for students' social context by observing socio-emotional and community factors that might be barriers to their career development and postsecondary transitions and implement targeted career development interventions that address those barriers (Edwin & Hussman, 2020). Indeed, students from marginalized backgrounds may not be prepared for postsecondary transitions since their families have not experienced it. This lack of access to social support presents as a barrier to the successful career development and postsecondary transitions for students who may lack the family knowledge and support about the application process, how to prepare academically and socially, and how to approach school counselors to get help in the process. School counselors can implement developmentally appropriate and equitable career development interventions to support students' postsecondary transitions.

School-Based Career Development

School-based career development interventions are programs and activities that are aimed at preparing students for postsecondary decision-making and transitions. School counselors must help students engage in self-reflection and exploration of the world of work and pathways to achieving their postsecondary goals through career development interventions to foster successful postsecondary transitions for students. School counselors can support students' future career attainment and prepare students to meet the demands for more skilled workers in the workforce by implementing effective career development interventions that foster career exploration, exposure to the world of work, and ultimately successful career and postsecondary outcomes. Helping students successfully transition into their postsecondary choices is an important role that school counselors have.

Career development activities have been shown to predict and positively impact students' career development, work readiness behavior, and career aspirations (Lapan et al., 2007; Turner & Conkel, 2010). In a 3-year longitudinal study, Lapan et al. (2007) found that engaging in career development activities had a positive impact on high school students' career development as measured by their career aspirations, work readiness behaviors, career expectations, and so on. Additionally, Turner and Conkel (2010) found that students who engaged in career development activities that included career exploration, identification of social supports, learning prosocial and work readiness skills, and group discussions were better able to identify career goals that matched their interests and had higher scores on measures of work readiness skills when compared to a group of peers who did not engage in career development interventions.

Postsecondary transitions signal a phase where adolescents are emerging into adulthood when entering the world of work which can be challenging as students navigate the development of new roles and identities. School counselors can support students' postsecondary transitions by implementing career development interventions that help students make connections between school and their career plans. Blustein et al. (1997) found that students who received school-based career development reported smoother postsecondary transitions and higher job satisfaction in adulthood. Career development activities that emphasize face-to-face contact with a counselor, development of personal relationships, assessing career information, exploring career options, and work experience activities have been shown to impact students' career readiness, career certainty, career development skills, and postsecondary transitions.

FACTORS IMPACTING SCHOOL COUNSELORS' ABILITY TO IMPLEMENT CAREER DEVELOPMENT INTERVENTIONS

Though school counselors are expected to facilitate students' career development through the implementation of a comprehensive school counseling program (ASCA, 2019), Anctil et al. (2012) found that school counselors do not spend as much time on career development and planning as they do on academic and social/emotional development. In one state, school counselors reported recognizing the need for career counseling and their preference to spend more time on career counseling (Osborn & Baggerly, 2004). However, Radford and coauthors (2016) found that when asked, principals who ranked their priorities for school counselors selected spending time helping students with their careers after college as the lowest priority. In a recent study, Edwin and Hussman (2020) found that structural and geographical factors present as barriers to school counselors' ability to implement career development interventions in their school. School counselors in city schools were more likely to spend less time on career planning compared to their counterparts in suburban schools, highlighting the challenges and barriers school counselors in city schools face around implementing a comprehensive school counseling program (Bemak & Chung, 2005; Militello & Janson, 2014). Additionally, school counselors in charter schools spent more time on career planning compared to school counselors in regular public schools and school counselors in public schools spent significantly more time on career planning than school counselors in private schools. Furthermore, Edwin and Hussman (2020) found that in schools with more non-White students, school counselors spent more time on career planning. Moreover, they posited that the finding may reflect school counselors' beliefs that non-White students are not college-bound. Previous studies have also shown that students from some racial minority groups (e.g., African American students) were more likely to contact the school counselor for college and career information (Bryan et al., 2009; Cholewa et al., 2015).

School counselors' ability to implement comprehensive programs, including career counseling, is negatively affected by high student-to-school counselor ratios (Perna et al., 2008). The National Association for College Admission Counseling (NACAC) and ASCA published a report in 2017 that tracked student-to-school counselor ratios by state and found that the national average was 482:1; the recommended ratio is 250:1. Only three states in the United States have the recommended 250:1 ratio or lower (NACAC & ASCA, 2017). High caseloads put school counselors in a position of having to make difficult choices about how to best use their time—meaning that some counselors might have to limit time and resources dedicated to career development to adequately support students' academic and social/emotional development. As per Plank and Jordan (2001), affluent White students have better access to low student-to-school counselor ratios and are better able to access guidance and information. Furthermore, Johnson and Rochkind (2010) maintained that students from racial minority backgrounds are more likely to be underprepared for their future careers compared to their White peers who receive greater academic and career counseling. Dimmitt and Wilkerson (2012) found that higher poverty schools were less likely to use comprehensive school counseling services and less likely to offer career planning resources to students.

Global issues such as the COVID-19 pandemic of 2020 have impacted educational spaces. During the pandemic, many school districts took a hybrid approach to instruction, having some online learning along with face-to-face instruction. Other districts pivoted to fully online formats while some stayed fully in-person. Approximately 54% of parents/guardians were very satisfied with fully in-person instruction, 30% were very satisfied with fully online formats, and 27% with a hybrid approach (Horowitz & Igielnik, 2020). However, while the mode of instruction changed, students' home environments have changed as well. COVID-19 has caused many parents/guardians to lose employment and see an increase in financial and food insecurity (Parker et al., 2020). Additionally, violence against women and girls has also increased which impacts the way students are learning in the home (Vaeza, 2020). Not only do these issues affect learning, but it becomes difficult for school counselors to engage in career development with students when basic needs (i.e., food, shelter, safety) are compromised or not being met.

FRAMEWORKS AND COMPETENCIES TO GUIDE SCHOOL COUNSELORS' IMPLEMENTATION OF CAREER DEVELOPMENT INTERVENTIONS

School counselors can support the career development and postsecondary transitions of students using comprehensive models and student standards dedicated to postsecondary success. Using the *ASCA Student Standards: Mindsets and Behaviors for Student Success* and career development and postsecondary transition models like the *National Career Development Guidelines* (2004) and NOSCA's (2010) *Eight Components of College and Career Readiness Counseling*, school counselors can determine what students should know and be able to do at various developmental stages and use that information to guide the implementation of appropriate interventions that support students' career development and postsecondary transitions.

ASCA Student Standards: Mindsets & Behaviors for Student Success: K–12 College-, Career-, and Life-Readiness for Every Student

ASCA (2014) released their *ASCA Student Standards: Mindsets and Behaviors for Student Success* in an explicit focus on college and career readiness for all students. According to ASCA (2014), these standards were created to establish the knowledge, skills, and attitudes students need, not just for college and career readiness, but also for academic and social development. ASCA (2014) describes the mindsets and behaviors as "the next generation of the ASCA National Standards for students" (p. 1). The mindsets and behaviors were developed from extensive survey research conducted by organizations dedicated to identifying strategies that improve students' achievement and academic performance. These ASCA mindsets and behaviors are organized into three main domains—career, personal-social, and academic—with 35 standards that apply to all three domains.

The 35 standards—summarized in Table 1.1—are categorized into mindset and behavior standards. Mindset standards are defined as beliefs students should possess for the development of their college and career

TABLE 1.1   The ASCA Mindsets and Behaviors for Student Success K–12 College- and Career-Readiness Standards for Every Student

Mindset Standards		
M 1. Belief in development of whole self, including a healthy balance of mental, social/emotional, and physical well-being		
M 2. Self-confidence in ability to succeed		
M 3. Sense of belonging in the school environment		
M 4. Understanding that postsecondary education and life-long learning are necessary for long-term career success		
M 5. Belief in using abilities to their fullest to achieve high-quality results and outcomes		
M 6. Positive attitude toward work and learning		
Behavior Standards		
Learning Strategies	**Self-Management Skills**	**Social Skills**
B-LS 1. Demonstrate critical-thinking skills to make informed decisions.	B-SMS 1. Demonstrate the ability to assume responsibility.	B-SS 1. Use effective oral and written communication skills and listening skills.

(continued)

TABLE 1.1   The ASCA Mindsets and Behaviors for Student Success K–12 College- and Career-Readiness Standards for Every Student

Behavior Standards		
Learning Strategies	**Self-Management Skills**	**Social Skills**
B-LS 2. Demonstrate creativity.	B-SMS 2. Demonstrate self-discipline and self-control.	B-SS 2. Create positive and supportive relationships with other students.
B-LS 3. Use time-management, organizational, and study skills.	B-SMS 3. Demonstrate ability to work independently.	B-SS 3. Create relationships with adults that support success.
B-LS 4. Apply self-motivation and self-direction to learning.	B-SMS 4. Demonstrate ability to delay immediate gratification for long-term rewards.	B-SS 4. Demonstrate empathy.
B-LS 5. Apply media and technology skills.	B-SMS 5. Demonstrate perseverance to achieve long- and short-term goals.	B-SS 5. Demonstrate ethical decision-making and social responsibility.
B-LS 6. Set high standards of quality.	B-SMS 6. Demonstrate ability to overcome barriers to learning.	B-SS 6. Use effective collaboration and cooperation skills.
B-LS 7. Identify long- and short-term academic, career, and social/emotional goals.	B-SMS 7. Demonstrate effective coping skills when faced with a problem.	B-SS 7. Use leadership and teamwork skills to work effectively in diverse teams.
B-LS 8. Actively engage in challenging coursework.	B-SMS 8. Demonstrate the ability to balance school, home, and community activities.	B-SS 8. Demonstrate advocacy skills and ability to assert self, when necessary.
B-LS 9. Gather evidence and consider multiple perspectives to make informed decisions.	B-SMS 9. Demonstrate personal safety skills.	B-SS 9. Demonstrate social maturity and behaviors appropriate to the situation and environment.
B-LS 10. Participate in enrichment and extracurricular activities.	B-SMS 10. Demonstrate ability to manage transitions and ability to adapt to changing situations and responsibilities.	B-SS 10. Demonstrate cultural awareness, sensitivity and responsiveness

Source: https://www.schoolcounselor.org/getmedia/7428a787-a452-4abb-afec-d78ec77870cd/Mindsets-Behaviors.pdf

readiness. The behavior mindsets are outwardly visible behaviors that are said to contribute to a student's success. These behavior standards are subcategorized into learning strategies, self-management skills, and social skills (ASCA, 2014). The learning strategies and self-management skills categories each have 10 standards, and the social skills category has nine standards. ASCA (2014) asserted that these standards can serve as a foundation for classroom lessons, group sessions, and any other developmental activities for students. School counselors can select competencies that align with any specific standard and establish interventions that help improve and support students' career development.

NOSCA's *Eight Components of College and Career Readiness Counseling*

NOSCA is another organization that provides a model advocating for the role of school counselors as leaders in fostering students' career development and postsecondary transitions. NOSCA's (2010) *Eight Components of College and Career Readiness Counseling* provides a framework for counselors to develop a comprehensive school counseling program consisting of developmentally appropriate career development interventions that promote college and career readiness for all students at all levels. This model outlines eight components that school counselors should integrate into their comprehensive school counseling programs to foster the successful career development of all students, especially students from marginalized and disadvantaged backgrounds. The eight components are outlined in Table 1.2. Additionally, NOSCA provides three level-specific guides—elementary, middle, and high—with activities and interventions that school counselors can implement for each of the components to meet the aligned goal.

The National Career Development Guidelines

The National Occupational Information Coordinating Committee (NOICC) created the *National Career Development Guidelines* ([Guidelines] 1989, rev. 2004) to offer a framework for helping all individuals acquire the skills necessary for a successful career development process. According to NOICC, the *Guidelines* can help school counselors improve students' understanding of the need for lifelong learning in career development, promote students' understanding of themselves, increase program accountability through process and outcomes evaluations, and expand stakeholders' awareness of the benefit of career development for students. The *Guidelines* are organized into three domains—personal-social development, educational achievement, and lifelong learning, and career management—with goals (see Table 1.3). The indicators and learning stages for each goal highlight the skills and knowledge students must possess to achieve each goal. The three learning stages—knowledge acquisition, application, and reflection—are derived from Bloom's taxonomy and can be used by school

TABLE 1.2	NOSCA's Components of College and Career Readiness	
1.	College Aspirations	**Goal:** Build a college-going culture based on early college awareness by nurturing in students the confidence to aspire to college and the resilience to overcome challenges along the way. Maintain high expectations by providing adequate supports, building social capital, and conveying the conviction that all students can succeed in college.
2.	Academic Planning for College and Career Readiness	**Goal:** Advance students' planning, preparation, participation, and performance in a rigorous academic program that connects to their college and career aspirations and goals.
3.	Enrichment and Extracurricular Engagement	**Goal:** Ensure equitable exposure to a wide range of extracurricular and enrichment opportunities that build leadership, nurture talents and interests, and increase engagement with school.
4.	College and Career Exploration and Selection Processes	**Goal:** Provide early and ongoing exposure to experiences and information necessary to make informed decisions when selecting a college or career that connects to academic preparation and future aspirations.
5.	College and Career Assessments	**Goal:** Promote preparation, participation, and performance in college and career assessments by all students.
6.	College Affordability Planning	**Goal:** Provide students and families with comprehensive information about college costs, options for paying for college, and the financial aid and scholarship processes and eligibility requirements, so they can plan for and afford a college education.
7.	College and Career Admission Process	**Goal:** Ensure that students and families have an early and ongoing understanding of the college and career application and admission processes so they can find the postsecondary options that are the best fit for their aspirations and interests.
8.	Transition From High School Graduation to College Enrollment	**Goal:** Connect students to school and community resources to help the students overcome barriers and ensure the successful transition from high school to college.

Souce: htto://nosca.collegeboard.org/eight-components

counselors to develop outcomes for classroom lessons, small group sessions, and workshops.

School counselors can use this framework to evaluate their existing career development programs to ensure students are developing the competencies they need for successful postsecondary transitions. Additionally, school counselors can use the framework to develop competency-based career development programs, create a program evaluation plan, develop community, and staff development workshops to ensure that other school stakeholders can support students' career development and postsecondary transitions.

TABLE 1.3 National Career Development Guidelines (NCDG) Framework	
Personal Social Development Domain	*Goals:* • PS1: Develop an understanding of self to build and maintain a positive self-concept. • PS2: Develop positive interpersonal skills including respect for diversity. • PS3: Integrate growth and change into your career development. • PS4: Balance personal, leisure, community, learner, family, and work roles.
Educational Achievement and Lifelong Learning Domain	*Goals:* • ED1: Attain educational achievement and performance levels needed to reach your personal and career goals. • ED2: Participate in ongoing, lifelong learning experiences to enhance your ability to function effectively in a diverse and changing economy.
Career Management Domain	*Goals:* • CM1: Create and manage a career plan that meets your career goals. • CM2: Use a process of decision-making as one component of career development. • CM3: Use accurate, current, and unbiased career information during career planning and management. • CM4: Master academic, occupational, and general employability skills to obtain, create, maintain, and/or advance your employment. • CM5: Integrate changing employment trends, societal needs, and economic conditions into your career plans.

Source: https://www.ncda.org/aws/NCDA/asset_manager/get_file/3384?ver=16587

As school counselors leverage the above-mentioned frameworks to support the postsecondary transitions of students, it is important that counselors are aware of how college and career readiness frameworks can often adopt a color-blind approach and omit consideration of the structural inequities and racism that limit the opportunities of students of color. As per Castro (2013), college and career readiness frameworks often focus solely on the skills and knowledge students of color need for college entry and success. However, school counselors cannot effectively support students' postsecondary transitions without advocating for the dismantling of inequitable policies and structural inequities that puts all the onus on students and families of color to navigate postsecondary transition in a system that provides fewer opportunities for them. As mentioned earlier, school counselors must adopt an anti-racist lens when leading partnerships to support students' career development and postsecondary transitions. School counselors' postsecondary interventions must incorporate critical pedagogy to increase students' critical consciousness and teach them about how structural racism impacts their postsecondary transition and how to navigate that racism and racial relations (Majors, 2019).

RECOMMENDATIONS SECTION FOR RESEARCH, PRACTICE, AND POLICY

Recommendations for Career Development Research

K–12 career development is an area that needs more research to add to the knowledge base. We know that career development and college and career readiness should be important aspects of K–12 education but more research on the impact of these interventions is needed. Much research has been done focusing on undergraduate students, but career development conversations need to start sooner. Four in 10 college students take remedial courses because of inadequate preparation for postsecondary education (Chen, 2016). Adding remedial courses to one's schedule amounts to more courses being taken overall and equates to much more money being spent. Remedial courses cost taxpayers an estimated $2.3 billion annually and have a direct cost to students of $3.6 billion annually (Alliance for Excellent Education, 2011). Additionally, students who take remedial courses in college graduate at much lower rates; 43% of those who start their undergraduate studies will not complete their degree after 6 years.

Those with a high school diploma, those who dropped out of high school, and those with no postsecondary education or training have unemployment rates more than double those with a bachelor's degree (Alliance for Excellent Education, 2011). During challenging times such as the coronavirus (COVID-19) pandemic, the Pew Research Center reported that unemployment rose from 3.8% to almost 15% in the United States; the increase was more than the increase caused by the Great Recession (Kochhar, 2020). Those with higher levels of education were more likely to telework (47%) than those with a high school diploma (4%; U.S Bureau of Labor Statistics, n.d.). 25% of young adults ages 16–24 were unemployed during the first few months of the pandemic (U.S Bureau of Labor Statistics, n.d.), many of which were dealing with postsecondary transitions.

These challenges faced by students are reasons why more research and insight are needed to explore areas of career development and postsecondary transitions for students. School counselors can help prepare students for college, career, technical education, and life. The many students taking remedial courses in college, the unemployment rate of emerging adults during a pandemic, and the benefits of completing postsecondary education are all reasons for school counselors to be at the forefront of working with students and engaging in impactful research. Learning more about evidence-based career development interventions allows for clearer ideas for practical application of findings.

Evidence-based career development interventions have taught us that comprehensive school counseling programs improve students' career development skills (Lapan et al., 2012; Wilkerson et al., 2013), and increase college and career readiness standards and desire to go to college (Mariani et al., 2016). We also know that graduation rates in career and technical education programs tend to be higher for students who had the ASCA national model implemented in their school (Carey et al., 2012). Engaging in career development activities at the undergraduate level can increase retention and decrease negative career thoughts (Belser et al., 2017, 2018; Prescod et al., 2018). For students to continue to benefit from their connections with school counselors and for the profession to move forward, more research is needed. Research keeps school counselors and stakeholders informed on best practices and helps counselors navigate through the ever-changing world of K–12 education and beyond.

Recommendations for Educators and Education Policy

ASCA (2014) mindsets state the importance of collaborations between school counselors, administrators, and teachers for effective school counseling. In order for any initiatives to see success, support and collaboration is necessary. For example, during the COVID-19 pandemic of 2020, school counselors reported having little to no direction from the administration on how to proceed during the pandemic and were rarely involved in school planning during that time (Savitz-Romer et al., 2020). More collaborative efforts during a global pandemic could have impacted learning, connectedness, and sense of support for students, teachers, staff, administrators, and so forth. Whether the world is dealing with a global pandemic or schools are working on implementing new initiatives, support and collaboration are essential from leadership in the schools.

For school counselors to remain leaders in their respective schools, they need to be visible to their students, parents/guardians, and administrators. ASCA recommends an ideal student-to-school counselor ratio of 250:1 and only three states in the United States have the recommended ratio (NACAC & ASCA, 2017). Ratios are as high as 1000:1 in Arizona and California (Gagnon & Mattingly, 2016) which can make it incredibly difficult for school counselors to be effective in their work. The United States has over 111,000 school counselors supporting more than 50.5 million students with a national ratio of 482:1 (NACAC & ASCA, 2017). With three main responsibilities to focus on academic achievement, personal/social learning, and college and career readiness, school counselors are faced with the challenge of juggling many responsibilities and choosing where to place their efforts.

With ratios ranging from 250:1 (or less), to double or triple that amount, effectiveness will be impacted. Mandated ratios would allow for more school counselors to be hired and would show a strong commitment to K–12 student success. The Council for Accreditation of Counseling and Related Educational Programs (CACREP) requires a full-time student to full-time faculty ratio of 12:1 in their counseling programs (CACREP, 2016). The standard exists to help ensure a quality learning experience for students and the same reasoning should exist for the school counselor to student ratio. Fye et al. (2018) found that variables affecting school counselors' level of implementing the ASCA national model were non-counseling responsibilities, perceived support from the principal, and principal knowledge of school counseling. Perceived principal support and knowledge of school counseling were positively associated with implementation and non-counseling responsibilities were negatively associated with model implementation (Fye et al., 2018). Non-counseling duties may include lunch duty, clerical tasks, or bus duty, and are not in line with the ASCA model (Moyer, 2011). If a school counselor has 500 students to engage and has to worry about non-counseling related tasks, it is almost impossible for them to do their job effectively. They would need to choose between meeting students individually or in a group setting, implementing career activities, or needing to substitute teach. As leaders in schools, school counselors should not face the daily challenge of choosing between counseling responsibilities and non-counseling responsibilities.

Recommendations for School Counseling Practice

School counselors can utilize individual career planning, small group counseling, classroom guidance, and collaboration with other school stakeholders to support students' career development and postsecondary transitions. Career planning has been described as the final stage of the career development process for students, with career awareness and exploration preceding planning (Arrington, 2000). Inadequate career planning in adolescent years has been connected to limited future career choices, lower adulthood wages, and lower career and life satisfaction in adulthood (e.g., Arrington, 2000; Ashby & Schoon, 2010). Although research has shown that large caseloads often present barriers to school counselors working with individual students, school counselors must create opportunities to engage students in career planning activities that support students' career development and postsecondary transitions. School counselors can plan and block off time on their calendar over the semester to meet with students individually. Even meetings as short as 15-minute can be beneficial for helping build connections with students and fostering their career development. Some examples of individual career planning activities include having conversations with students about their educational and career goals and creating an action plan that includes courses and co-curricular activities, evaluating students' current skills and creating a plan to develop additional skills, and evaluating all postsecondary options available to students and making collaborative decisions.

Additionally, school counselors can develop group counseling interventions and classroom guidance units and lessons using student competencies shared earlier in this chapter (e.g., *Mindsets & Behaviors*) as target student outcomes. School counselors can leverage small and large group sessions to disseminate postsecondary transition information that may not require much personalization for students. For example, information about graduation requirements, admissions requirements, financial aid opportunities, internship, and job shadowing opportunities can be shared in large group settings with students. Setting up large group sessions can often be difficult for school counselors who do not have regularly scheduled time on the calendar. Collaborations with teachers can be effective in creating time to connect with students in larger groups. For example, during my time as a school counselor, I (first author) partnered with the technology teacher in my school to guide students through using technology to find college-related information. I was able to help students develop technology skills and engage in career development interventions at the same time.

For school counselors working with students in earlier grades (elementary and middle school) where classroom guidance is commonplace, school counselors can use these lessons to teach students skills that will support their career development and postsecondary transition while including teachers, parents, and other school stakeholders. For example, I (first author) implemented a career development unit (see Edwin & Prescod, 2018) where fifth-grade students were able to engage in self-exploration and career research activities. The classroom unit culminated in students creating career research tri-fold display projects that were all exhibited in the school and parents were invited to view them all at the end of the semester. Implementing this intervention involved collaboration with teachers, the principal, and parents. School counselors can use classroom guidance lessons to teach skills like time management, goal setting, and study skills that are important for college and career readiness. It is important to note the importance of building partnerships (explored later in this text) to successfully support students' career development and postsecondary transition. School counselors are often unable to meet the needs of all students due to various barriers. Partnerships with teachers, parents, colleges, community members, and other stakeholders allow school counselors to more effectively meet the career development needs of all students. Finally, school counselors can leverage resources that provide developmentally appropriate career development interventions for all grade levels (e.g., Curry & Milsom, 2017) to better support their students.

STRATEGIES FOR ADVOCACY

As mentioned earlier, school counselors often face various barriers to implementing career development interventions. Barriers such as lack of resources, large caseloads, and nonschool counseling-related tasks can prevent school counselors from effectively supporting the career development and postsecondary transitions of students. School counselors can use the *ASCA National Model's Use of Time Assessment* (ASCA, 2019) to track their time spent on various counseling and non-counseling tasks and utilize this data to advocate for spending less time on non-counseling duties and more time on career development interventions in their schools. Additionally, school counselors can disaggregate student data such as graduation rates and college enrollment rates to determine which groups of students need the most support around career development intervention. School counselors should also ensure that they collect data for any interventions they implement, and their data can be used to advocate for more time spent on career development interventions or more school counselors being hired.

Counselor education programs must dedicate targeted efforts toward preparing school counselors to advocate for themselves and implement career development interventions in their school buildings. Amid the contextual factors impacting school counselors' abilities to implement career development interventions (see Anctil et al., 2012; Edwin & Hussman, 2020; Schenck et al., 2012), a lack of knowledge about interventions to implement may also keep school counselors from engaging in career planning with their students. Bridgeland and Bruce (2011) maintained that most high school counselors receive more training in mental health issues than in college and career planning, leaving a gap in their readiness to engage in career planning with their students. Counselor educators can ensure that school counselors in training receive information across multiple courses about ways to engage students in career exploration and planning. Further, school counselor educators must teach their students creative ways to leverage partnerships and their time to ensure that they are equitably addressing all three components of students' development.

DISCUSSION QUESTIONS

1. What are some strategies that school counselors can use to infuse critical race pedagogy in preparing students of color for their postsecondary transitions?
2. What can school systems do to support school counselors' efforts in implementing career development interventions in school?

3. Thinking about your current or future role (e.g., school counselor, counselor educator, administrator, etc.), how will you integrate anti-racist principles into your school counseling and career development work?

ACTIVITIES

1. Select a grade level and create a career development unit with at least four classroom lessons that include standards from all three frameworks discussed in the chapter—ASCA, NOSC, NCDG.
2. Using the demographic options provided below (select one from each: race, gender, SES, grade level) create a student profile and develop an individual career development plan for the student for that school year. Consider how the students' current grade level fits into their overall postsecondary transition plans and what milestones the student will need to reach for a successful transition. How will each of the student's identities influence your decision-making and counseling?

    a. Race
        i. Black
        ii. Asian
        iii. Hispanic
        iv. Native American
        v. Multiracial
    b. Gender
        i. Male
        ii. Female
        iii. Gender nonconforming
        iv. Transgender
    c. Household Income
        i. Low (Less than $40,100)
        ii. Middle ($41,000–$120,400)
        iii. Upper (More than $120,400)
    d. Grade Level
        i. 8th
        ii. 9th
        iii. 10th
        iv. 11th

REFERENCES

Achieve, Inc. (2012). *College and career readiness and economic competitiveness*. http:// si2012leadertools.ncdpi.wikispaces.net/file/view/College-and-Career-Ready -Competitiveness.pdf

Alliance for Excellent Education. (2011). *Saving now and saving later: How high school reform can reduce the nation's wasted remediation dollars*. https://all4ed.org/wp -content/uploads/2013/06/SavingNowSavingLaterRemediation.pdf

American School Counselor Association. (2012). *The ASCA national model: A framework for school counseling programs* (3rd ed.).

American School Counselor Association. (2014). *ASCA student standards: Mindsets and behaviors for student success: K–12 college-, career-, and life-readiness standards for every student*. https://www.schoolcounselor.org/getmedia/7428a787-a452 -4abb-afec-d78ec77870cd/Mindsets-Behaviors.pdf

American School Counselor Association. (2017). *The school counselor and career development*. https://schoolcounselor.org/Standards-Positions/Position-Statements/ ASCA-Position-Statements/The-School-Counselor-and-Career-Development

American School Counselor Association (2019). *The ASCA national model: A framework for school counseling programs* (4th ed.).

Anctil, T. M., Smith, C. K., Schenck, P., & Dahir, C. (2012). Professional school counselors' career development practices and continuing education needs. *The Career Development Quarterly, 60*(2), 109–121.

Avery, C., & Kane, T. (2004). Student perceptions of college opportunities. The Boston COACH program. In C. Hoxby (Ed.), *College choices: The economics of where to go, when to go, and how to pay for it*. University of Chicago Press.

Belser, C. T., Prescod, D. J., Daire, A. P., Dagley, M., & Young, C. (2017). Predicting undergraduate retention in STEM majors based on career development factors. *The Career Development Quarterly, 65*, 88–93.

Belser, C. T., Prescod, D. J., Daire, A. P., Dagley, M., & Young, C. (2018). The influence of career planning on negative career thoughts with STEM-interested undergraduates. *The Career Development Quarterly, 66*, 176–181.

Bemak, F., & Chung, R. C. Y. (2005). Advocacy as a critical role for urban school counselors: Working toward equity and social justice. *Professional School Counseling*, 196–202.

Blustein, D. L., Phillips, S. D., Jobin-Davis, K., Finkelberg, S. L., & Roarke, A. E. (1997). A theory-building investigation of the school-to-work transition. *The Counseling Psychologist, 25*(3), 364–402.

Bryan, J., Farmer-Hinton, R., Rawls, A., & Woods, C. S. (2017). Social capital and college-going culture in high schools: The effects of college expectations and college talk on students' postsecondary attendance. *Professional School Counseling, 21*(1), 1096–2409.

Bryan, J., Holcomb-McCoy, C., Moore-Thomas, C., & Day-Vines, N. L. (2009). Who sees the school counselor for college information? A national study. *Professional School Counseling, 12*(4), https://doi.org/10.1177/2156759X0901200401

Bryan, J., Moore-Thomas, C., Day-Vines, N. L., & Holcomb-McCoy, C. (2011). School counselors as social capital: The effects of high school college counseling on college application rates. *Journal of Counseling & Development, 89*(2), 190–199. https://doi.org/10.1002/j.1556-6678.2011.tb00077.x

Bryan, J., Farmer-Hinton, R., Rawls, A., & Woods, C. S. (2017). Social capital and college-going culture in high schools: The effects of college expectations and college talk on students' postsecondary attendance. *Professional School Counseling, 21*(1), 1096–2409. https://doi.org/10.5330/1096-2409-21.1.95

Bullock-Yowell, E., McConnell, A. E., & Schedin, E. A. (2014). Decided and undecided students: Career self-efficacy, negative thinking, and decision-making difficulties. *NACADA Journal, 34*(1), 22–34.

Business Roundtable. (2014). *Business Roundtable/Change the Equation survey on U.S. workforce skills.* Retrieved January 10, 2020 from https://www.ecs.org/wp-content/uploads/2014-BRT-CTEq-Skills-Survey-Slides_0.pdf

Cambridge Dictionary. (n.d.). *Online Cambridge dictionary.* Retrieved May 4, 2021 from https://dictionary.cambridge.org/us/dictionary/english/career-development

Career Development Institute. (2017). *Definitions: Career development and related roles.* https://www.thecdi.net/write/CDI_Definitions_FINAL.pdf

Carey, J., Harrington, K., Martin, I., & Hoffman, D. (2012). A statewide evaluation of the outcomes of the implementation of ASCA national model school counseling programs in rural and suburban Nebraska high schools. *Professional School Counseling, 16*(2), 100–107. http://www.jstor.org/stable/profschocoun.16.2.100

Castro, E. L. (2013). Racialized readiness for college and career: Toward an equity-grounded social science of intervention programming. *Community College Review, 41*(4), 292–310.

Choi, Y., Kim, J., & Kim, S. (2015). Career development and school success in adolescents: The role of career interventions. *The Career Development Quarterly, 63*(2), 171–186. https://doi.org/10.1002/cdq.12012

Cholewa, B., Burkhardt, C. K., & Hull, M. F. (2015). Are school counselors impacting underrepresented students' thinking about postsecondary education? A nationally representative study. *Professional School Counseling, 19*(1), 1096–2409. https://doi.org/10.5330/1096-2409-19.1.144

Coalition for Career Development. (2019). *Career readiness for all.* https://irp-cdn.multiscreensite.com/81ac0dbc/files/uploaded/Career%20Readiness%20for%20All%20FINALV.pdf

College Board National Office for School Counselor Advocacy. (2010). *Eight components of college and career readiness counseling.* https://secure-media.collegeboard.org/digitalServices/pdf/nosca/11b_4416_8_Components_WEB_111107.pdf

Council for Accreditation of Counseling & Related Educational Programs. (2016). *2016 CACREP Standards.* http://www.cacrep.org/wp-content/uploads/2017/08/2016-Standards-with-citations.pdf

Curry, J. R., & Milsom, A. D. (2017). *Career and college readiness counseling in P–12 schools.* Springer Publishing Company.

Dimmitt, C., & Wilkerson, B. (2012). Comprehensive school counseling in Rhode Island: Access to services and student outcomes. *Professional School Counseling, 16*(2), 2156759X0001600205.

Edwin, M., & Prescod, D. (2018). Fostering elementary career exploration with an interactive, technology-based career development unit. *Journal of School Counseling, 16*(13), n13.

Edwin, M., & Hussman, M. D. (2020). Factors influencing school counselors' time spent on career planning with high school students. *Professional School Counseling, 23*(1), 2156759X20947724.

Edwin, M., Prescod, D. J., & Bryan, J. (2019). Profiles of high school students' STEM career aspirations. *The Career Development Quarterly, 67*(3), 255–263. https://doi.org/10.1002/cdq.12194

Engberg, M. E., & Gilbert, A. J. (2014). The counseling opportunity structure: Examining correlates of four-year college-going rates. *Research in Higher Education, 55*(3), 219–244.

Farmer-Hinton, R. L., & Adams, T. L. (2006). Social capital and college preparation: Exploring the role of counselors in a college prep school for black students. *Negro Educational Review, 57.*

Fye, H. J., Miller, L. G., & Rainey, J. S. (2018). Predicting school counselors' supports and challenges when implementing the ASCA national model. *Professional School Counseling, 21*(1), 2156759X18777671.

Gagnon, D. J., & Mattingly, M. J. (2016). Most U.S. school districts have low access to school counselors: Poor, diverse and city school districts exhibit particularly high student-to-counselor ratios. *Carsey Research School of Public Policy. 108*, 1–6.

Gati, I., Krausz, M., & Osipow, S. H. (1996). A taxonomy of difficulties in career decision making. *Journal of Counseling Psychology, 43*(4), 510.

Gottfredson, L. S. (1981). Circumscription and compromise: A developmental theory of occupational aspirations. *Journal of Counseling Psychology, 28*, 545–579.

Gottfredson, L. S. (2005). Using Gottfredson's theory of circumscription and compromise in career guidance and counseling. In S. D. Brown & R. W. Lent (Eds.), *Career Development and Counseling: Putting Theory and Research to Work* (pp. 71–100). Wiley.

Hines, P., & Lemon, R. (2011). *Poised to lead: How school counselors can drive college and career readiness.* The Education Trust.

Holland, M. M. (2014). Navigating the road to college: Race and class variation in the college application process. *Sociology Compass, 8*(10), 1191–1205.

Horowitz, J. M., & Igielnik, R. (2020, October 29). *Most parents of K–12 students learning online worry about them falling behind.* Pew Research Center. https://www.pewresearch.org/social-trends/2020/10/29/most-parents-of-k-12-students-learning-online-worry-about-them-falling-behind/

Hurtado, S., Inkelas, K. K., Briggs, C., & Rhee, B. S. (1997). Differences in college access and choice among racial/ethnic groups: Identifying continuing barriers. *Research in Higher Education, 38*(1), 43–75.

Johnson, J., & Rochkind, J. (2010). *Can I get a little advice here? How an overstretched high school guidance system is undermining students' college aspirations.* Public Agenda.

Kenny, M. E., Blustein, D. L., Haase, R. F., Jackson, J., & Perry, J. C. (2006). Setting the stage: Career development and the student engagement process. *Journal of Counseling Psychology, 53*(2), 272–279. http://doi.org/10.1037/0022-0167.53.2.272

Klasik, D. (2012). The college application gauntlet: A systematic analysis of the steps to four-year college enrollment. *Research in Higher Education, 53*, 506–549.

Kochhar, R. (2020). *Unemployment rose higher in three months of COVID-19 than it did in two years of the great depression.* Pew Research Center. https://www.pewresearch.org/fact-tank/2020/06/11/unemployment-rose-higher-in-three-months-of-covid-19-than-it-did-in-two-years-of-the-great-recession/

Lapan, R., Aoyagi, M., & Kayson, M. (2007). Helping rural adolescents make successful postsecondary transitions: A longitudinal study. *Professional School Counseling, 10*(3), 266–272.

Lapan, R. T., Kardash, C. M., & Turner, S. (2002). Empowering students to become self-regulated learners. *American School Counselor Association, 5*(4), 257–265. http://static.pdesas.org/content/documents/ASCA_National_Standards_for_Students.pdf

Lapan, R. T., Whitcomb, S. A., & Aleman, N. M. (2012). Connecticut professional school counselors: College and career counseling services and smaller ratios benefit students. *Professional School Counseling, 16*(2), 117–124.

Lent, R. W., Brown, S. D., & Hackett, G. (1994). Toward a unifying social cognitive theory of career and academic interest, choice, and performance [Monograph]. *Journal of Vocational Behavior 45*, 79–122.

Majors, A. T. (2019). From the editorial board: College readiness: A critical race theory perspective. *The High School Journal, 102*(3), 183–188.

Mariani, M., Berger, C., Koerner, K., & Sandlin, C. (2016). Operation occupation: A college and career readiness intervention for elementary students. *Professional School Counseling, 20*(1), 65–76. https://doi.org/10.5330/1096-2409-20.1.65

McClelland, M. M., & Cameron, C. E. (2011). Self-regulation and academic achievement in elementary school children. *New Directions for Child and Adolescent Development, 2011*, 29–44. https://doi.org/10.1002/cd.302

McKillip, M. E. M., Rawls, A., & Barry, C. (2012). Improving college access: A review of research on the role of high school counselors. *Professional School Counseling, 16*(1), 49–58.

Militello, M., & Janson, C. (2014). The urban school reform opera: The obstructions to transforming school counseling practices. *Education and Urban Society, 46*(7), 743–772.

Morgan, T., & Ness, D. (2003). Career decision-making difficulties of first-year students. *The Canadian Journal of Career Development, 2*(1), 33–39.

Moyer, M. (2011). Effects of non-guidance activities, supervision, and student-to-counselor ratios on school counselor burnout. *Journal of School Counseling, 9.* http://jsc.montana.edu/articles/v9n5.pdf

Niles, S. G., & Harris-Bowlsbey, J. E. (2017). *Career Development Interventions* Pearson.

Obama White House. (2015). *Reaching the "North Star" by 2020.* https://obamawhitehouse.archives.gov/reach-higher

Obama, M. (2014, July 28). *First lady Michelle Obama's address to the Harvard/White House college opportunity agenda* [Video]. YouTube. https://youtu.be/A51cjr_yPSY

Osborn, D. S., & Baggerly, J. N. (2004). School counselors' perceptions of career counseling and career testing: Preferences, priorities, and predictors. *Journal of Career Development, 31*(1), 45–59. https://doi.org/10.1177/089484530403100104

Palmon, S., Hoff, N., Heifner, A., & Peterson, R. L. (2017). *Postsecondary transition planning* [Strategy brief]. Student Engagement Project, University of Nebraska–Lincoln and the Nebraska Department of Education. https://k12engagement.unl.edu/strategy-briefs/Postsecondary%20Transition%20Planning%204-14-17.pdf

Parker, K., Minkin, R., & Bennett, J. (2020, September 24). *Economic fallout from COVID-19 continues to hit lower-income Americans the hardest.* Pew Research Center. https://www.pewresearch.org/social-trends/2020/09/24/economic-fallout-from-covid-19-continues-to-hit-lower-income-americans-the-hardest/

Pearson. (2016). *Employability skills gap.* Retrieved January 10, 2020 from https://www.pearson.com/content/dam/one-dot-com/one-dot-com/us/en/pearson-ed/downloads/Skills-Gap-Infographic-2-3-16.pdf

Penrod, J. (2001). Refinement of the concept of uncertainty. *Journal of Advanced Nursing, 34*(2), 238–245.

Perna, L. W., Rowan-Kenyon, H. T., Thomas, S. L., Bell, A., Anderson, R., & Li, C. (2008). The role of college counseling in shaping college opportunity: Variations across high schools. *The Review of Higher Education 31*(2), 131–159. http://doi.org/10.1353/rhe.2007.0073.

Perry, J., Iu, X., & Pabian, Y. (2010). School engagement as a mediator of academic performance among urban youth: The role of career preparation, parental career support, and teacher support. *The Counseling Psychologist, 38*(2), 269–295. http://doi.org/10.1177/0011000009349272

Perry, N. E., Phillips, L., & Hutchinson, L. (2006). Mentoring student teachers to support self-regulated learning. *The Elementary School Journal, 106*(3), 237–254.

Plank, S. B., & Jordan, W. J. (2001). Effects of information, guidance, and actions on postsecondary destinations: A study of talent loss. *American educational research Journal, 38*(4), 947–979.

Poynton, T. A., & Lapan, R. T. (2017). Aspirations, achievement, and school counselors' impact on the college transition. *Journal of Counseling and Development.* http://doi.org/10.1002/jcad.12152

Prescod, D. J., Daire, A. P., Young, C., Dagley, M., & Georgiopoulos, M. (2018). Exploring negative career thoughts between STEM-declared and STEM-interested students. *Journal of Employment Counseling, 55*(4), 166–175.

Radford, A., Ifill, N., & Lew, T. (2016). *A national look at the high school counseling office.* National Association for College Admission Counseling. https://www.nacacnet.org/globalassets/documents/publications/research/hsls_counseling.pdf

Sampson, J. P., Peterson, G. W., Lenz, J. G., Reardon, R. C., & Saunders, D. E. (1996). *Career thoughts inventory: Professional manual.* PAR.

Savitz-Romer, M., Rowan-Kenyon, H. T., Nicola, T. P., Carroll, S., & Hecht, L. (2020). *Expanding support beyond the virtual classroom: Lessons and recommendations from school counselors during the COVID-19 crisis.* Harvard Graduate School of Education & Boston College Lynch School of Education and Human Development.

Schenck, P. M., Anctil, T. M., Smith, C. K., & Dahir, C. (2012). Coming full circle: Reoccurring career development trends in schools. *The Career Development Quarterly, 60*(3), 221–230.

Strada-Gallup. (2018). *2017 College student survey: A nationally representative survey of currently enrolled students.* https://news.gallup.com/reports/225161/2017-strada-gallup-college-student-survey.aspx

Turner, S. L., & Conkel, J. L. (2010). Evaluation of a career development skills intervention with adolescents living in an inner city. *Journal of Counseling & Development, 88*(4), 457–465. https://doi.org/10.1002/j.1556-6678.2010.tb00046.x

U.S. Bureau of Labor Statistics. (n.d.). *Supplemental data measuring the effects of the coronavirus (COVID-19) pandemic on the labor market.* https://www.bls.gov/cps/effects-of-the-coronavirus-covid-19-pandemic.htm

Vaeza, M. N. (2020, November 27). *Addressing the impact of the COVID-19 pandemic on violence against women and girls.* United Nations. https://www.un.org/en/addressing-impact-covid-19-pandemic-violence-against-women-and-girls

Wilkerson, K., Pérusse, R., & Hughes, A. (2013). Comprehensive school counseling programs and student achievement outcomes: A comparative analysis of RAMP versus non-RAMP schools. *Professional School Counseling, 16*(3), 172–184.

CHAPTER 2

USING DATA AND ACCOUNTABILITY STRATEGIES TO CLOSE COLLEGE AND CAREER READINESS GAPS

Anita A. Young
Johns Hopkins University

Ileana Gonzalez
Johns Hopkins University

ABSTRACT

The call to action to close the college readiness gap and increase career choices has been given and is not debatable. Yet, gaps remain, and in some cases, have widened especially for students of color. The racial reckoning and global pandemic have increased opportunity gaps that will result in decreased college attainment and have a domino effect on stifling educational, economical, and civic capital for today and tomorrow's youth. The potential catastrophic impact of marginal college readiness and limited attainment for

Equity-Based Career Development and Postsecondary Transitions, pages 27–45

students challenges our nation's positionality to compete in a global economy. The complexity to address and resolve the issue lies in collective commitments and collaborative actions to invest in our youth and society for the betterment of all. Using data and accountability strategies have proven to lead to outcome results. More importantly, there must be intentionality to use the data to close gaps for students of color.

In the current educational and economic climate, sustaining and advancing college access for P–12 students is an imperative for a global society. Students in the United States must be prepared and counseled toward entrepreneurial thinking, developing resilient protective factors, and exploring uncharted career professions with public school districts often bearing the brunt of the responsibility to prepare them for postsecondary success and sustainability. Research suggests that access to academic rigor and college exposure interventions correlate with college readiness and sustainability (Castleman & Page, 2014; Clinedinst, 2019; Clinedist et al., 2011; McDonough, 2006). Challenging the preparatory path to college readiness are institutional, affordability and social barriers to access that equate to ill-reputed achievement gaps and deficits.

In the year 2020, a confluence of events occurred to reshape the mission of college counseling and the manner in which educational professionals guide students towards postsecondary plans. Firstly, the global Covid-19 pandemic has brought to light the racial inequities that exist in American systems of healthcare, employment, and education. Research shows that Black, Indigenous, and other People of Color (BIPOC) have been disproportionately impacted by the pandemic (Tamene et al., 2020). This crisis has highlighted the impact of critical funds needed to provide equitable access to resources such as food security, childcare, and educational technology and internet services. Researchers estimate that school closures due to the COVID-19 pandemic will have a lasting "learning loss" effect on schools serving predominantly low-income, Black, and Hispanic students thus predicting increases in high-school dropout rates which have the potential for lifelong earning impact (Dorn et al., 2020). Second, the continued murders of innocent Black citizens such as Breonna Taylor, George Floyd, and Ahmaud Arbery at the hands of law enforcement furthered the call for racial reckoning, systemic accountability, and social action. These events are coupled with the 2020 presidential election season that witnessed American citizens tout notions of White supremacy, falsehoods, and violence veiled as patriotism peaking in an insurrection at the U.S. Capitol building on January 6, 2021. These historic events must serve as the mechanism to advance the mission of equitable college and career readiness practices for BIPOC students to include accountability, advocacy, and social justice.

In the current examination of postsecondary success, there continues to be racial opportunity gaps and deficits, especially for Black and Brown students, to whom access to college, college enrollment rates, college selectivity and attainment affect an individual's long-term earning potential (Espinosa et al., 2019). Students from lower socioeconomic (SES) status, when enrolled in college are less likely to attend a selective 4-year university and more likely to select programs that do not lead to a bachelor's degree. For students in upper and middle-class families, familial support and social capital propel students to postsecondary attainment, yet for students from low socioeconomic families or first-generation students, schools bear the responsibility of imparting the social capital needed to prepare for postsecondary transition (Weinstein & Savitz-Romer, 2009; Welton & Williams, 2015).

Adding to the complexity, despite having high expectations for their children, parents of students from low SES and students of color have access to information that is helpful in the college admissions process (Torrez, 2004). Yet, when these parents do engage with schools to obtain the information, they may encounter negativity or become disenchanted with school personnel (Holcomb-McCoy, 2010). Using data and accountability strategies must be inclusive of all stakeholders to revolutionize college and career readiness in a post Covid 2020 world.

Racial inequities coupled with the unprecedented pandemic, will have a far-reaching impact on today's youth and it is not a surprise that using data and accountability strategies continue to be the catalyst to college readiness. The purpose of this chapter is to explore the use of data and accountability strategies in promoting college readiness through optics focused on systemic inequities and racialized outcomes to address the inconceivable challenges that continue to occur. Throughout the chapter, the readers are encouraged to probe their beliefs and apply accountability strategies through an anti-racist lens by presenting theoretical constructs and practical application. Specifically, this chapter provides a cursory review of the historical context of using data to promote college access, extend traditional views of college readiness from an anti-racist lens, and identify appropriate accountability strategies and interventions intended to focus on the needs of BIPOC students.

RESEARCH AND HISTORICAL CONTEXT

Let's begin by examining generalized beliefs and research that are frequently used in the literature pertaining to college access. Education reform played a pivotal role in the call to action for all educators to use data and accountability strategies through the mandate of No Child Left Behind Act (NCLB) of 2001. There have been mixed reviews about the intent and impact of the federal mandate, NCLB. Controversial or not, NCLB held all educators accountable and became the backdrop for continued school counseling transformation initiatives toward college readiness for all students (Pool et al., 2015). Current rhetoric would lead one to believe that college-access numbers are promising because reports have suggested more students are attending college, which may be true (Espinosa et al., 2019). Yet, opportunity and access gaps remain and are striking, especially for students of color (National Center for Education Statistics [NCES], 2020). According to the NCES (2020), there are major college admission gaps by race and socioeconomic status. Latinx students are less likely to attend selective colleges than their White peers (NCES, 2020). A White student is two times more likely to attend a selective college than a Black or Latinx student (NCES, 2020). The gap between White and Black students does not dissipate even when looking only at students in the highest SES quintile. A White student in this group is two times more likely to attend a highly selective college than a Black student in the highest SES quintile (NCES, 2020).

The evolution of the transformation of the school counseling profession has been well documented and we will not chronicle the details in this chapter (American School Counselor Association [ASCA], 2003; Haycock, 1999; National Office for School Counselor Advocacy, 2011). Yet, a cursory review and recognition of the progress that has occurred and how far we must go to ensure every child has optimal college-going opportunities will be discussed. The Reach Higher Initiative of First Lady Michelle Obama highlighted what students need for college and career readiness through the delivery of comprehensive school counseling programs. In 2009, President Barack Obama charged every American to commit to at least 1 year of postsecondary education by the year 2020. While the charge may not be accomplished, we know that a postsecondary education is the only option to leverage economical, civic, and social equity. School counselors must provide academic, social/emotional, and career counseling for all students to increase college access and attainment. Realistically, students may not always choose a 4-year university for various reasons. It is not the role of school counselors to determine which students attend 2-year institutions, 4-year colleges, or elect a gap year, but rather it is the ethical imperative of the school counselor to maximize academic opportunities and prepare them for postsecondary institutions. The motto "college begins in kindergarten" resonates more today than ever before in the current climate of social injustices (Garcia & Barker, 1997).

LET'S GET STARTED

Achievement gaps remain rampant across race, ethnicity, gender, and socioeconomic groups (NCES, 2020). A school counseling program should address all gaps, be comprehensive in scope and grounded in data driven

TABLE 2.1 Sample High School Data Profile						
School Year Enrollment	#	%	9th #	10th #	11th #	12th #
Total Enrollment	2,020	100%	636	416	495	473
Advanced Placement or Honors Courses	929	46%	210	255	249	215
English for Speakers of Other Languages	580	29%	145	180	166	89
Students With Disabilities	511	25%	145	161	140	65
Ethnicity	#	%	9th #	10th #	11th #	12th#
Asian or Pacific Islander	93	4%	23	23	20	27
Black	978	48%	275	235	255	213
Latinx	640	31%	247	88	142	163
White	233	11%	67	52	59	55
Other	76	3%	24	18	19	15
Free and Reduced Meals	#	%	9th #	10th #	11th #	12th #
Yes	1,890	93%	572	390	478	450

decision-making. Data are the first place to begin and school counselors must acknowledge that behind the numbers are faces (Young & Kaffenberger, 2018). The power is not in the numbers or the faces, rather in the stories that represent the data. Examine the fictitious data in Table 2.1 that could simulate inequities across anywhere in the United States. The glaring gaps in ethnicity, SES, and AP and honors enrollment data suggest that discussions should occur immediately with all stakeholders, to include the students. This data can be used as an example for how to begin to examine data at your school. For the purposes of this chapter, the data will be used as part of Activity 1 located at the end of this chapter.

College Readiness Practices for School Counseling

In a study conducted by the National Association for College Admissions Counselors (NACAC) approximately half of principals surveyed selected "helping students to prepare for postsecondary schooling," as their top priority for the school counselors (Radford et al., 2016). According to NACAC's 2019 State of College Admission report, during the 2018–2019 school year, school counseling departments at public schools spend an average of only 19% of their time on postsecondary admission counseling (Clinedinst, 2019). The time dedicated to college planning decreases in low-income geographical locations and areas with a high concentration of students of color as funding for resources and school counselors is less than in affluent areas (Clinedinst, 2019). Instead, school counselors spend more of their time on academic planning and remediation, scheduling of courses, personal counseling, and academic testing, these activities take priority over college and career readiness interventions. The school counseling profession uses data to examine gaps in academic achievement and attainment in an effort to create interventions that increase students' requisite knowledge and skills to elevate the likelihood of transitioning to a postsecondary institution (ASCA, n.d.a). In order to do this work, school personnel must examine the ways in which the organizational culture affects the role of school counselors, the time they spend on tasks, and the ways in which other stakeholders collaborate with school counselors on their mission to prepare Black and Brown students for postsecondary success. Not only should school counselors ensure that all students have access to equitable college opportunities, school counselors need access to the students which can be a daunting task.

Various factors limit school counselor access to students. A major barrier is high student to counselor ratios. The ability of school counselors to assist students with college planning is also often hindered by unmanageable caseloads. The American School Counselor Association (ASCA) recommends the ratio of 250 students to one counselor (ASCA, n.d.b). Yet, a 2019 study found that the national average during this time was 430 students per counselor, almost doubling the recommended ratio (NCES, 2020). Schools with higher student-to-counselor ratios also were less likely to have a counselor whose duties were dedicated to college counseling (Clinedinst, 2019). Time limitations on public school counselors, compounded by high student caseloads, have consequences for college access, particularly for the students who are most likely to need support in making the transition to postsecondary education. These disparities highlight the need to use data driven practices as a means of intentionally serving the needs of Black and Brown children.

A study conducted by Lapan and colleagues (2019), with a diverse sample of 12th grade students, suggests that low student-counselor ratios combined with a well-designed data driven school counseling program may result in greater informed college decision-making for high school students. The implications suggest that lower student-counselor ratios allow more time for school counselors to focus on counseling specific college advising activities. Studies also suggest that school counselors should be allotted time and resources to provide underrepresented students and their families with an equitable opportunity to access the social capital necessary to make informed college decisions and increase postsecondary access to 2-year and 4-year institutions (Cholewa et al., 2015).

Research has demonstrated that high school counselor assignment practices influence college readiness, particularly for students and families who may not have the social capital to understand the college-going process

(Radford et al., 2016). When there is more than one school counselor within a school, how students are assigned to a counselor occurs in some of these approaches: assigning a counselor alphabetically by last name, assigning a counselor by grade level, assigning a counselor to specific learning communities, or a combination of these methods. The most common method in large urban school districts is to assign a counselor to students alphabetically (Radford et al., 2016). While this method of assignment allows a school counselor to get to know students and their families during the student's tenure in the high school, this places a lot of demands on school counselors to organize college readiness interventions for their students as each grade level has differing needs in the college readiness process. Conversely, alphabetical assignment allows school counselors to frequently collaborate with other school counselors. According to Radford et al. (2016), a method that occurs less often is assigning students by grade level. This approach allows the counselor to obtain the college knowledge and become well versed in specific grade level needs. For example, the 10th-grade counselor can prepare their entire caseload for the PSAT test and using longitudinal PSAT data, create systemic interventions to impact scores. Radford et al. (2016) report that high poverty public high schools were more likely to assign counselors by learning community. The small learning community model redesigns large urban high schools into smaller clusters of students and teachers who focus on career-oriented curriculum. Assigning a counselor using this method offers the opportunity for specific interventions related to specific career clusters. There is, however, the possibility that small learning communities stratify students based on grades, standardized test scores, and tracking methods and the college readiness counseling may differ and further promote inequities in terms of access and opportunity for certain groups of students (Radford et al., 2016). Schools need to consider how the counseling department is organized to best support student needs. Regardless of the assignments to students, all school counselors must be experts on college readiness interventions through the use of data driven practices.

Four iterations of the ASCA's national framework model indicate that school counselors play a critical role in college access for all students through the delivery of academic, social/emotional, and career counseling as outlined in the ASCA national framework (ASCA, 2003, 2005, 2012, 2019). The most recent model prescribes three primary sources of data types (participation, mindsets and behavior, and outcome) that are relevant to college readiness. Participation data provides information about which students and how many participated in counseling activities. The mindsets and behavior data show what progress students make toward attaining the standards. The mindset standards include beliefs school counselors hold about student achievement and success, and are measured in ways that can be used to close gaps through direct and indirect comprehensive school counseling services. Outcome data are related to achievement, attendance, and discipline that shows how students are measurably different as a result of the school counseling program. Data driven decision-making that results in improved student achievement, attendance, and discipline outcomes is the catalyst for the development of comprehensive school counseling programs. "Through implementation of a school counseling program, school counselors promote equity and access for all students and make a significant impact on creating a school culture free from racism and bias" (ASCA, n.d.a, p. 1). This statement speaks to school counselors' ethical obligation to address anti-racist actions (ASCA, n.d.b). The ASCA Position Statement and Ethical Standards are explicit; yet, there remains the need for additional emergence to be an anti-racist school counselor. For example, missing from the model are directives for how school counselors may apply interventions that specifically address social justice and racial inequities from an intersectional lens. School counselors must integrate socially just practices into the four components and the themes of the ASCA model from a transformative anti-racist leadership stance to successfully influence negatively that may impact students.

Convertino and Graboski-Bauer (2018) argue that approaches to college readiness hold that personal motivation and effort are the main determinants of success and take the responsibility away from the institutional structures and those within them that hold deficit beliefs implying that postsecondary education is only for those who are deemed worthy of it, who follow the rules established by White middle-class norms and values. They argue that this personal deficit belief system produces a discourse of college worthiness versus college readiness (Convertino & Graboski-Bauer, 2018). We believe the narrative of student deficiencies in intelligence, academic preparedness, aspiration, and motivation must be eliminated and that school counselors and educational professionals must focus actions toward examining data through the lens of institutional beliefs and access and opportunity gaps that are perpetuated by racist policies and practices. This narrative allows the onus of transformation not to be on the student to make the necessary changes in order to fit the mold of a traditional view of college readiness, but rather the impetus for change is institutional and becomes a collaborative responsibility to create the space and commitment of college readiness for all students. Convertino and Graboski-Bauer (2018) further argue that strategies must include confronting and eradicating manifestations of deficit beliefs to establish new organizational norms. In this organizational culture, all stakeholders, procedures, and policies are aligned to convey a message of active support for every student's postsecondary goals. The narrative shift from *college worthy* to *college ready* requires paradigm shifts in beliefs and actions to include data-driven practices that expose systems and not student deficiencies (Weinstein & Savitz-Romer, 2009). The chart in Figure 2.1 outlines an example in practice.

College Worthy Practices	College Ready Practices
Increasing the number of AP courses so that eligible students have more opportunities to take Advanced Placement courses.	Examine the policy in determining who can enroll in AP courses. Survey students about their experiences in these courses. Examine pedagogical practices and curriculum in these courses. Examine teacher beliefs and expectations about Black and Brown students in advanced courses.

Figure 2.1 College worthy versus college ready practices.

Leading Social Justice Policies

When the data exposes the inequities, school counselors must serve as social justice advocate leaders regardless of whether they are serving in a supervisory role and they must choose to lead where they currently serve (Young & Miller-Kneale, 2013). ASCA encourages school counselors to lead efforts that "challenge policies, procedures, traditions or customs that perpetuate intentional or unintentional racist and biased behaviors and outcomes" and "advocate for those policies and procedures that dismantle racism and bias that promote equity for all" (ASCA, n.d.a, p. 3). This shift in college and career readiness practices changes the work of school counselors to embody an anti-racist stance. Anti-racism is defined as the action of actively opposing racism and racist practices by advocating for changes in anti-racist policy including the belief that racial groups are equals and do not need remediating (Kendi, 2019). Anti-racist school counseling shifts from traditional practices to examining and correcting educational policies that produce racialized outcomes and replace them with conscious beliefs about the potential of BIPOC children (Holcomb-McCoy, 2020). This may prove difficult for some individuals that have been conditioned to not discuss race or racism. Therefore, it must begin with school counselors examining their own racialized beliefs and examining how their intersectional identity affords power and privilege. It also includes dismantling oppressive systemic practices by examining the unconscious beliefs of educators and reeducating about the history of racist practices and decolonizing curriculum and curricular practices. Furthermore, anti-racist school counselors should choose to serve as leaders through giving the power to all students, especially Black and Brown who may not feel worthy of postsecondary education opportunities, to provide meaning of their lived experience and future goals (Holcomb-McCoy, 2020).

When school counselors work from an anti-racist position, they also delve deeper into the data by examining the experiences of Black and Brown student's intersectional identities. This includes students who are first generation, receive free and reduced meals (FARMS), or live in zip codes that have been labeled problematic and excluded from equitable opportunities. Examining college and career readiness data through an anti-racist lens requires a significant commitment on behalf of the institution to examine the policies, procedures, and practices that lead to racialized outcomes.

College Readiness Accountability

The core curriculum integrates college and career readiness through academic advisement and access to rigorous courses with the support needed for successful completion. There should be ongoing formative assessment measures in addition to pre- and post-assessment. This includes collecting data that exposes inequitable outcomes such as disproportionate rates of discipline and suspension for students of color as a result of zero-tolerance policies or underrepresentation of students of color in rigorous classes such as honors, Advanced Placement and International Baccalaureate courses. Furthermore, school counselors can use data to bring unconscious beliefs about college worthiness to the surface by conducting an equity audit that examines data by race to show where the inequities persist; this allows educators to discuss the data's meaning and strategize for solutions (McKenzie & Scheurich, 2004).

Once school counselors are aware of all the determinants of college readiness, they should become aware of the data sources available to access. Table 2.1 would lead school counselors to review data sources such as attainment and achievement related. Doing so, exposes underlying contributing factors associated with discipline referrals, attendance issues, familial support, and enrollment patterns. A data-driven comprehensive school counseling program and a college-readiness school counseling program should be one in the same. The intentionality and work needed to promote an anti-racist college readiness program deepens the rudimentary necessity for beliefs and evidence-based interventions that drive policy and practices toward creating systemic change. Young and Kaffenberger (2018), pose a cyclical data and accountability model that is applicable for college readiness school counseling programs. The cyclical graphic in Figure 2.2 provides examples of how school counselors might use data and accountability strategies.

Share the Journey and Make an Impact

The impact of college readiness interventions through outcome data completes the data cycle process and has the potential to bring about more

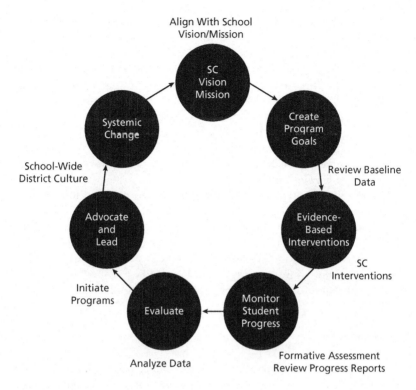

Figure 2.2 Accountability model.

questions and opportunities for "next steps" to close opportunity gaps. School counselors must consider the meaning of the results, ways in which disseminating results will have the greatest impact for advocacy purposes, such as considering who has the power within the organizational culture to directly impact college and career readiness strategies and sharing data outcomes to inform and empower students and families. Sharing outcome results allows the school counselor to gain credibility, show how school counseling interventions make a difference in closing gaps, and furthermore advocates for their role within the school (Stone, 2011; Young & Kaffenberger, 2011). School counselors, however, need to be mindful about what outcome results mean, when to share the results, and how they will be used to shape policy. Communication is imperative for the dissemination of outcome data. Consider all the opportunities for discussion and feedback with other stakeholders, including administrators. School counselors are reminded these conversations need to be based on school stakeholder needs and focused on positive student outcomes. Furthermore, dialogue around the impact of results need to be explored as school leaders may want to limit disclosure of the results in order to protect the status of the school, may use the results as evidence of a practitioner's success or failure, or results may impact funding for resources. Therefore, explicit disclosure about sharing outcome data results to general and specific audiences need to occur before the data cycle gets underway. Young and Kaffenberger (2018) suggest sharing results through the use of tables and charts within summary reports as administrators may appreciate concise visuals when seeking to improve the instructional learning environment. The chart in Figure 2.3 provides an example of how a school counselor might identify and share an issue, create and analyze the impact of interventions, and share the results. Fernandez and colleagues (2003), suggest that the offer to share results should extend to all stakeholders to include those who may benefit directly or indirectly from learning the outcome results. There is an obligation to present the results in a clear manner in which participants can comprehend. School counselors can consider sharing results with students and families through email blasts, newsletters, pamphlets, and presentations. Furthermore, informing students and families of outcome data presents opportunities for areas of growth within the school.

Collaboration

Typically, the school counseling plan for college readiness involves bombarding students and families with information on different colleges and their admissions requirements, college applications, and financial aid information. Yet do we know to what extent students, particularly Black and Brown students, absorb and take advantage of this information and its impact in their lives. While it is helpful for school counselors to offer information and various types of interventions and supports, another key factor is whether students and their families access this assistance, so it is important to explore the most effective ways to convey this information and intervene on behalf of students. For example, school counselors can collaborate with teachers within a curricular department to examine who is being taught by whom. Are the most highly qualified teachers with the most experience working only with the gifted and talented students or are they working with the students who are labeled as "less than"? Who and how are those decisions being made?

IMPLICATIONS FOR SUSTAINABILITY

The profession of school counseling has centered its training on college readiness through college advising tasks such as writing recommendation

Purpose: This urban high school has approximately 35% of the student population enrolled in an honors, AP/IB, or dual enrollment course. None of the students enrolled in the classes are students of color. The school counselors are leading efforts through collaboration with administrators and teachers to eliminate barriers that contribute to declining or sustained enrollment in honors, AP/IB, and dual enrollment classes.

SMART Goal: To implement college readiness interventions that increase student enrollment in honors, AP/IB, or dual enrollment by 10% for the current school year compared to previous year.

The following procedures will be used to increase enrollment:
- Review school-based data about enrollment patterns for all students, especially students of color.
- Lead stakeholder discussions about college worthy versus college readiness.
- Develop intentional college readiness interventions.
- Monitor student progress through formative and summative assessment.

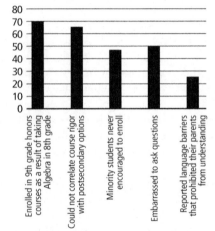

- 35% enrolled in high school courses
- Enrolled in 9th grade honors course as a result of taking Algebra in 8th grade
- 70% didn't correlate course rigor with post-secondary options
- 55% minority students never encouraged to enroll
- 50% embarrassed to ask questions
- 25% reported language barriers prohibited their parents from understanding

Recommendations:
- Promote the mission and vision of the school counseling college-readiness program.
- Implement inclusive college readiness interventions.
- Conduct ongoing program assessment.
- Share results of pre and post assessment survey.
- Create postsecondary plans for all students.
- Take a courageous stance to lead a college-readiness culture in the school and community.

Figure 2.3 Sharing results with stakeholders: An example.

letters, passing along information about college requirements, and preparing students for standardized testing (Holcomb McCoy, 2020). In order to create the systemic change needed to address inequitable policies, practices, and procedures that lead to equity particularly for Brown and Black students, school counselors in training need to be exposed early and often in their graduate program strategies such as the data cycle and see its application through field experiences in schools. Young and Kaffenberger (2011) suggest that school counseling courses help students ground their philosophical beliefs about data practices and integrate data assignments throughout the curriculum. In introductory school counseling courses students can go through the data cycle by reviewing mock school data to identify opportunity gaps related to college and career readiness and design a comprehensive school counseling program that includes the use of pre- and post-tests to measure the impact of interventions for Black and Brown students. Savitz-Romer (2012) suggests that counselor education programs embed college readiness practices into the school counselor training curriculum through a distinct college readiness course or as part of career counseling coursework. Furthermore, joint coursework with other programs such as higher education graduate training programs can nurture a collaborative relationship between school counselors and college admissions officials (Savitz-Romer, 2012). As part of field experiences, school counselors-in-training must work with site supervisors to use strategies to build a college readiness culture at the school site. This includes being intentional in collaborating with administrators, teachers, and families in order to use data to expose inequities and promote college readiness practices. Through conducting college readiness action research in partnership with their on-site supervisors, counselors in training can demonstrate their knowledge of the data cycle process and skills needed to implement data-driven programs (Young et al., 2014). Counseling students can model data practices for school counseling supervisors who were not trained to use the data cycle.

Although critical for counselors-in-training, school counselors must also create opportunities for college readiness, professional growth and development. Site supervisors can benefit from observing counselors in training as they gain professional development through observation of interns and through the relationship with the university supervisors (Young et al., 2014). Additionally, these relationships with school districts pave the way for counselor educators to conduct additional research that can impact students' college and career readiness needs far beyond the individual field experience.

SUMMARIZING SUGGESTIONS FOR IMPACTFUL COLLEGE READINESS

All students is an inclusive term that denotes every student within the scope and practice of the school counseling program. In addition to the aforementioned strategies provided in "Implications for Sustainability" section, postsecondary educational opportunities must become a practice for all students regardless of the race, ethnicity, sexual orientation, or the geographic location of their zip code. This chapter was intended to stimulate discussions about impactful college readiness practices that expand career opportunities. Counselor educators, counselor-in-training, and school counselors can use the content of this chapter to guide curriculum for professional development training. There should also be opportunities to explore individual racial identities through autobiography exercises. Most importantly, is the need to actualize advocacy through action as the greatest pivotal resource for schoolwide sustainability.

DISCUSSION QUESTIONS

1. What beliefs do you harbor that may require further reflection to increase your college readiness attitude, knowledge, and skills?
   How does the concept of college worthy versus college readiness resonate in your current school environment?
   Imagine that you are a new high school counselor recently hired in a school with a marginal college-going culture. What steps would you take to develop a data-driven college readiness comprehensive school counseling program?

ACTIVITIES

1. Imagine that you are a high school counselor in the school depicted in Table 2.1. Which stakeholders would you immediately consult? Use the graphic in Figure 2.4 to examine what resonates with you. Then, outline your next steps. What specific steps to ensure equitable college access and preparation for all students are needed?
2. Using the accountability model (Figure 2.2) review the reflective chart in Table 2.2 to brainstorm how a school counselor would implement strategies and interventions from an anti-racist lens.

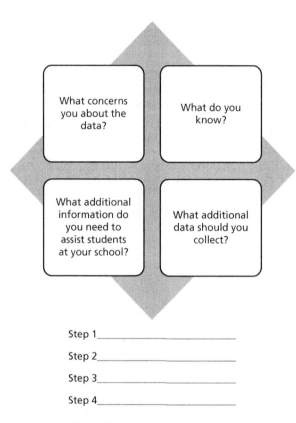

Step 1_____

Step 2_____

Step 3_____

Step 4_____

Figure 2.4 Data in practice reflective activity.

TABLE 2.3 College Ready Practices		
Cyclical Steps	**Description**	**College Ready Practice**
School Counseling Vision and Mission	Develop an aerial view that encompasses the needs of all students. Align with the instructional mission and vision. Provide the direction for the future of students' accomplishment.	
Create Program Goals	Identify program goals from baseline data. Support the school counseling vision and mission. Create goals that are Specific–Measurable–Attainable–Relevant–Timebound (SMART)	

(continued)

TABLE 2.3 College Ready Practices (continued)		
Cyclical Steps	Description	College Ready Practice
Evidence-Based Interventions	Review data to determine existing gaps. Collect and analyze data to identify achievement gaps, understand educational issues, and identify evidence-based interventions that make a difference for all students.	
Monitor Student Progress	This is an iterative process of continual data review. Review school improvement plan. Collaborate with teachers. Monitor student attendance. Review disciplinary referrals. Conduct formative assessment—survey students about how it feels to be a student in an AP or IB program. Are all students' identities reflected in the curriculum?	
Evaluate and Demonstrate Program Effectiveness	Evaluate the effectiveness interventions. Share the data that has been collected. Teach students resilience.	
Advocate and Lead	Give voice to the needs of the students. Take initiative and create programs. Use influence to chart the vision. Consult with administrators. Do students feel empowered and have a voice?	
Systemic Change	Remove the barriers to create lasting and sustainable outcomes.	

REFERENCES

American School Counselor Association. (n.d.a). *Eliminating racism and bias in schools: The school counselor's role.* https://www.schoolcounselor.org/getmedia/542b0 85a-7eda-48ba-906e-24cd3f08a03f/SIP-Racism-Bias.pdf

American School Counselor Association. (n.d.b). *The role of the school counselor.* https://www.schoolcounselor.org/getmedia/ee8b2e1b-d021-4575-982c -c84402cb2cd2/Role-Statement.pdf

American School Counselor Association. (2003). The ASCA national model: A framework for school counseling programs. *Professional School Counseling,* 165–168.

American School Counselor Association. (2005). *The ASCA national model: A framework for school counseling programs* (2nd edition).

American School Counselor Association. (2012). *The ASCA national model: A framework for school counseling programs* (3rd ed.).

American School Counselor Association. (2019). *The ASCA national model: A framework for school counseling programs* (4th edition).

Castleman, B. L., & Page, L. C. (2014). A trickle or a torrent? Understanding the extent of summer "melt" among college-intending high school graduates. *Social Science Quarterly (Wiley-Blackwell), 95*(1), 202–220. https://doi.org/10.1111/ssqu.12032

Cholewa, B., Burkhardt, C. K., & Hull, M. F. (2015). Are school counselors impacting underrepresented students' thinking about postsecondary education? A nationally representative study. *Professional School Counseling, 19*(1), 144–154. https://doi.org/10.5330/1096-2409-19.1.144

Clinedist, M., Hurley, S., & Hawkins, D. (2011). *The state of college admission.* National Association for College Admission Counseling.

Clinedinst, M. (2019). *2019: State of college admission.* National Association for College Admission Counseling. https://www.nacacnet.org/globalassets/documents/publications/research/2018_soca/soca2019_all.pdf

National Office for School Counselor Advocacy. (2011). *Own the turf.* https://secure-media.collegeboard.org/digitalServices/pdf/nosca/OTT_Webcast_10-26-2011_Forum-2011.pdf

Convertino, C., & Graboski-Bauer, A. (2018). College readiness versus college worthiness: Examining the role of principal beliefs on college readiness initiatives in an urban U.S. high school. *Urban Review, 50*(1), 45–68. https://doi.org/10.1007/s11256-017-0429-6

Dorn, E., Hancock, B., Sarakatsannis, J., & Viruleg, E. (2020). *Covid-19 and student learning in the United States: The hurt could last a lifetime.* McKinsey & Company. https://www.mckinsey.com/industries/public-and-social-sector/our-insights/covid-19-and-student-learning-in-the-united-states-the-hurt-could-last-a-lifetime#

Espinosa, L. L., Turk, J. M., Taylor, M., & Chessman, H. M. (2019). *Race and ethnicity in higher education: A status report.* American Council on Education. https://www.equityinhighered.org/resources/report-downloads/

Fernandez, C., Kodish, E., & Weijer, C. (2003). Informing study participants of research results: An ethical imperative. *IRB: Ethics & Human Research, 25*(3), 12–19. https://doi.org/10.2307/3564300

Garcia, A., & Barker, G. (1997). College begins in kindergarten. *Teacher Education Quarterly, 24.*

Haycock, K. (1999). *About the education trust.*

Holcomb-McCoy, C. (2010). Involving low-income parents and parents of Color in college readiness activities: An exploratory study. *Professional School Counseling, 14*(1), 115. https://doi.org/10.1177/2156759X1001400111

Holcomb-Mcoy, C. (2020, July). Guest blog: Well-meaning college advising is not enough. *ACT Center for Equity in Learning.* https://equityinlearning.act.org/equity-in-action/guest-blog-well-meaning-college-advising-is-not-enough/

Kendi, I. (2019). *How to be an antiracist.* Penguin Random House.

Lapan, R., Poynton, T., Balkin, R., & Jones, L. (2019). ASCA National Model implementation and appropriate school counselor ratios promote more informed college decision-making.

McDonough, P. (2006). *Overview of college going culture theory.* UCLA. Graduate School of Education and Information Studies.

McKenzie, K. B., & Scheurich, J. J. (2004). Equity traps: A useful construct for preparing principals to lead schools that are successful with racially diverse students. *Educational Administration Quarterly, 40*(5), 601–632. https://doi.org/10.1177/0013161X04268839

National Center for Education Statistics. (2020). *The condition of education.* https://nces.ed.gov/pubsearch/pubsinfo.asp?pubid=2020144

No Child Left Behind Act of 2001, P.L. 107-110, 20 U.S.C. § 6319 (2002).

Pool, R. W., & Putten, J. V. (2015). *The no child left behind generation goes to college: A longitudinal comparative analysis of the impact of NCLB on the culture of college readiness.* https://doi.org/10.2139/SSRN.2593924

Radford, A. W., Ifill, N., Lew, T. (2016). *A national look at the high school counseling office: What is it doing and what role can it play in facilitating students' paths to college?* National Association for College Admission Counseling. https://www.nacacnet.org/news—publications/Research/nationallookhscounselingoffice/

Savitz-Romer, M. (2012). The gap between influence and efficacy: College readiness training, urban school counselors, and the promotion of equity. *Counselor Education & Supervision, 51*(2), 98–111. https://doi.org/10.1002/j.1556-6978.2012.00007.x

Stone, C. B., & Dahir, C. A. (2011). *School counselor accountability: A MEASURE of student success.* Pearson Higher Ed.

Tamene, M., Hailu, A. E., Berkowitz, R. L., & Gao, X. (2020, September 15). Why Black, indigenous and other people of color experience greater harm during the pandemic. *Smithsonian Magazine.* https://www.smithsonianmag.com/smithsonian-institution/why-blacks-indigenous-and-other-people-color-experience-greater-harm-during-pandemic-180975773/

Torrez, N. (2004). Developing parent information frameworks that support college preparation for Latino students. *High School Journal, 87(3),* 54–63.

Young, A., Gonzales, I., Owen, L., & Heltzer, J. V. (2014). The journey from counselor-in-training to practitioner researcher. *Professional School Counseling, 18*(1), 217–226. https://doi.org/10.1177/2156759X0001800120

Young, A., & Kaffenberger, C. (2011). The beliefs and practices of school counselors who use data to implement comprehensive school counseling programs. *Professional School Counseling, 15*(2), 67–76. https://doi.org/10.1177/2156759X1101500204

Young, A., & Kaffenberger, C. (2018). *Making data work.* American School Counselor Association.

Young, A., & Kneale, M. M. (2013). *School counselor leadership: The essential practice.* American School Counselor Association.

Weinstein, L. A., & Savitz-Romer, M. (2009). Planning for opportunity: Applying organizational and social capital theories to promote college-going cultures. *Educational Planning, 18*(2), 1–11.

Welton, A., & Williams, M. (2015). Accountability strain, college readiness drain: Sociopolitical tensions involved in maintaining a college-going culture in a high "Minority," high poverty, Texas high school. *High School Journal, 98*(2), 181–204. https://doi.org/10.1353/hsj.2015.0001

CHAPTER 3

SCHOOL COUNSELORS AS LEADERS

Best Practices for Developing Postsecondary Readiness Programming

E. C. M. Mason
Georgia State University

Carla B. Cheatham
Governors State University

Beth H. Gilfillan
Northeastern Illinois University

Bobby B. Gueh
Gwinnett County Public Schools

H. Brent Henderson
Gwinnett County Public Schools

Adrianne Robertson
Georgia State University

Equity-Based Career Development and Postsecondary Transitions, pages 47–81
Copyright © 2022 by Information Age Publishing
www.infoagepub.com
47

ABSTRACT

The role of the school counselor as a leader has been emphasized by national groups including the American School Counselor Association (ASCA, 2019) and the National Association of College Admission Counselors (NACAC, 2000). This leadership role is vital to the development of postsecondary readiness and programming for students at all school levels. This chapter provides a clear rationale for why students need school counselor leaders who have a comprehensive, equity, and advocacy-driven approach to postsecondary options in the context of today's society. The authors also provide practical actions and recommendations for school counselors in implementing interventions that address systemic and institutional barriers, support families and communities, and result in access and opportunity for all students.

School Counselors are leaders. The authors start by exploring the topic of school counselor leadership and making a case for how school counselor leadership is vital to postsecondary readiness programming. We follow up this exploration by examining three other overarching topics that we believe are important to understanding the school counselor's role as a leader in relationships to this work: context, equity, and ethics. From there, we outline what postsecondary readiness programming looks like at each level: elementary, middle, and high school. Finally, the authors end the chapter by discussing recommendations for research, practice, and policy.

SCHOOL COUNSELING LEADERSHIP

The topic of leadership within the school setting is a never-ending discussion. The events of 2020 including the COVID-19 pandemic, the murder of George Floyd, and many other unarmed Black persons by police, followed by the insurrection at the Capitol on January 6, 2021 left the public floundering, confused, and at odds about our nation's leadership. At the time of this writing, these events have transferred onto school communities in innumerable ways and school leadership is daily in question. School districts, colleges, and universities across the country are grappling with community demands for ongoing education, racial justice, and employees' demands for safety and respect.

The question often arises, beyond the principal, who else serves as leaders? With a broad, inclusive definition of leadership, one might include teachers, assistant principals, administrative assistants, clerks, students, and counselors. School counselors work in complex settings with job requirements and expectations that involve unique training, including management of large caseloads and the ability to address the academic, career, and personal/social development of all students (ASCA, 2012). School counseling preparation programs prepare future school counselors with a host of knowledge and skills, including human growth and development, social and cultural diversity, and advocacy, that aid in their implementation of prevention and intervention strategies for the success of all students (CACREP, 2016). Despite this in-depth training and unique skill set, leadership is often intimidating to many school counselors, and counseling students (Holcomb-McCoy, 2007), and some do not consider it part of counseling. On the contrary, school counselors' training and skills are a critical part of the school system, therefore they play a vital role in leadership at the local school level, school district level, state level, and national level (Gueh, 2020). Since 2003, the ASCA has included leadership as one of the four themes in the national model.

ADVOCACY AND LEADERSHIP

The authors believe that when it comes to postsecondary readiness programming, leadership and advocacy are interconnected. One way to look at the responsibility of leadership is to consider the American Counseling Association's (ACA) advocacy competency model (Toporek & Daniels, 2018). The ACA advocacy competencies describe necessary counselor skills, knowledge, and behavior that can be implemented to address systemic barriers and issues facing students, clients, client groups, or whole populations (Toporek & Daniels, 2018). Within the ACA competencies, advocacy happens at the individual level, the community and organization level, and the public arena. For example, consider a school counselor working with a student who is first generation to provide individual empowerment to manage the postsecondary planning process. School counseling leadership can also connect to advocacy when the school counselor takes the student's needs from the individual to the school level to address the inequities they might be facing in that setting (e.g., misunderstanding of college terms, unfamiliarity with logos or events). This level of leadership and advocacy might involve training for staff or advocating to the administration to make systemic changes. Advocacy in counseling involves not only systems change but also the implementation of empowerment strategies in direct counseling with students and indirect student advocacy on a wide range of issues (Cheatham & Mason, 2021; Ratts & Hutchins, 2009; Toporek et al., 2009). Furthermore, as leaders in the systems that affect their students most directly, school counselors are encouraged to take advocacy to the macro-level of social-political involvement (McMahan et al., 2010). Such examples might include writing advocacy briefings, testifying at hearings, appearing in mass media, and getting involved with state and national campaigns for school issues of social justice and equity (Gueh, 2020). School counselors can play a paramount role in the leadership of the school building, the community, and in the public arena in many ways. As social justice advocates and supporters of systemic change, school counselors cannot afford to sit on the sidelines of the educational landscape. They must not be complicit in the oppression of students from minoritized groups who are often victims of a broken educational system (Gueh, 2020). School counselors are leaders and advocates who are highly equipped to address the academic, postsecondary, and social-emotional development of all students.

POSTSECONDARY SCHOOL COUNSELING LEADERSHIP

School counseling leadership looks different in each setting and at each level. A school counselor working at the elementary, middle, or high school level will have variations in their approach to their practice to meet the developmental stage of their students. Similarly, a school counselor working in an urban, rural, or suburban setting, may encounter unique issues within their community as students and families deal with 21st-century changes in society (Steen & Rudd, 2009). With the world of work and social changes occurring rapidly, school counselors are called to take the lead in the postsecondary education of all students (Turner & Lapan, 2013). For example, elementary level school counselors organize career awareness activities like career day, where local career professionals come to the school to talk to students about their careers. At the middle school level, school counselors coordinate field trip experiences for students to explore various companies. High school counselors dedicate months of time and energy to implementing internship experiences that will support students' postsecondary education. Career development is a lifelong process that begins in childhood and continues throughout adulthood. School counselors can use this career exploration knowledge and training to lead a robust postsecondary career development experience and begin the lifelong process of preparing them for success in the world of work (Niles & Harris-Bowlsbey, 2017).

CHALLENGES TO SCHOOL COUNSELING LEADERSHIP

School counselors are called to be leaders, yet there are challenges that they must prepare for and work to overcome. Within the specific context of postsecondary readiness programming, additional challenges arise. One of the most crucial challenges to confront is that of racist and unjust education systems. In their roles as social justice agents and advocates, school counselors need to be aware of these systems and intervene when students are unsafe, not provided, or denied opportunities and resources to succeed.

Ratts and Greenleaf (2018) provide a school counseling leadership framework for multicultural and social justice counseling competencies. Part of the rationale for this framework was a response to racist and unjust systems.

> Emboldened by divisive political rhetoric and the rise of white nationalists into central positions of power in the White House, many of those with extremist right-wing views toward immigrants; Muslims; Jews; and lesbian, gay, bisexual, and transgender (LGBTQ) individuals are openly expressing their hateful speech in a manner not seen in the United States in decades. This divisive rhetoric has stoked fears and racial tensions in America's schools. (Ratts & Greenleaf, 2018, p. 1)

School counselors work within systems that are biased against students of color and other marginalized student groups. In addition to the challenges outlined below, working within these systems presents an overarching challenge of continuously fighting against racist and unjust policies and practices.

LACK OF UNDERSTANDING OF THE SCHOOL COUNSELOR'S ROLE

A common challenge cited in school counseling leadership research is a lack of understanding of the role of the school counselor (Walsh & Gibson, 2019). Often, administrators and official leadership personnel in a district do not realize that school counselors are trained to lead and can support other leaders within the school. In their research with school counseling directors, Walsh and Gibson (2019) found that there are several factors that negatively impact these school counseling leaders' job satisfaction: role ambiguity, burnout, and lack of support for the counseling program. Other researchers have cited this role ambiguity and lack of support (e.g., Cervoni & DeLucia-Waack, 2011; Pyne, 2011) as a challenge for school counselors.

LACK OF TRAINING

Lack of training is one of the foremost challenges to school counselors' leadership potential and practice, which also applies to their work in postsecondary readiness programming. With the multitude of requirements in school counseling preparation programs, leadership training is often overlooked or glossed over. There are few resources that help school counselors in training, or their school counselor educators, to determine leadership qualities, develop leadership skills, or determine the impact of these practices (Miller Kneale et al., 2018). Among the findings of their study with school counseling directors, Walsh and Gibson (2019) found that the lack of training in school counseling-specific leadership was a hindrance to their leadership development and identity. The researchers called for graduate programs and school districts to enhance school counseling-specific leadership training opportunities.

Training and continued professional development are vital not only on school counselor leadership topics but also in postsecondary readiness programming. School counselors are typically not required to learn about their role in the postsecondary readiness process, yet they are expected to understand and facilitate this process. School counselors need training on how to support students in their postsecondary planning process, to implement postsecondary readiness programs, and to identify ways to advocate for marginalized students (Gilfillan, 2018). Currently, there is not a set of standards, skills, or competencies within postsecondary readiness counseling that is widely accepted, which leaves school counseling training programs on their own to develop training. If a training program does not incorporate these skills and knowledge sets into their courses, school counselors graduate with little preparation to support students. When this happens, marginalized students, such as first-generation college students, students of color, and students from lower socioeconomic backgrounds suffer the most (Bryan et al., 2009; Cabrera & La Nasa, 2001; Cholewa et al., 2015; Gilfillan, 2018).

CONTEXT

Equity-based career development and postsecondary transition warrant discussion and action due to systemic racism and anti-Blackness continuing to permeate American society. Systemic racism allows for dominant groups to deny their role in sustaining inequality, discrimination, and injustice toward minoritized groups, including Black, Brown, and Indigenous populations while refusing to acknowledge the history and impact of oppression. This oppression has created unequal systems of privilege and power in the United States. In addition to affecting students from marginalized races and ethnicities, those from lower socioeconomic backgrounds, with different abilities, and LGBTQ+ individuals are dehumanized by systems of oppression (Parikh, et al., 2011). Systemic racism and oppression are manifested through policies, legislation, and rules that are created to perpetuate inequity and injustice on minoritized groups (Ratts et al., 2016). Historically, Whites have benefitted from the inequities they have created by legalizing systemic racism through centuries of slavery, reconstruction, Jim Crow, lack of voting rights, redlining, lack of access to education, health care, economics and employment, the school-to-prison pipeline, and other attacks on minoritized groups in general, and Blacks in particular (Lipsitz, 2011; Love, 2020).

The time in which we are writing this chapter has awakened allies and co-conspirators on the discourse of Black Lives Matter and the unequal access to equity and basic human rights. Those who heed the calls for justice join yet another discussion about the lack of access minoritized groups have to healthcare, technology, education and employment, and the role of White privilege and systemic racism. Since schools are a reflection of society the effects of systemic racism, anti-Blackness and oppression have continued to exist in school systems (Love, 2020). The outcomes of these systems are persistently reflected in a racist ideology that has marginalized groups fighting for equality, equity, and access to rights that should be afforded to all human beings. In 2018, the unemployment rate for American Indians and Alaska Natives was 6.6%; Blacks 6.5%; Hispanics 4.7%; Native Hawaiians and other Pacific Islanders, 5.3%; Individuals of two or more races, 5.5%; Whites, 3.5%; and Asians 3.0% (Bureau of Labor Statistics, n.d.). African American and Hispanic/Latinx groups continue to experience higher unemployment and earn less income in comparison to Whites (Curry & Milsom, 2017). The work of school counselors is vital to addressing issues of inequity and access, especially as it extends to postsecondary readiness.

Public schools in the United States continue to see a decline in P–12 enrollment of White students, and an increase in students of color (Parikh et al., 2011). The policing of minoritized people is also reflected in school systems that administer unequal and disproportionate disciplinary measures against Black students who are two to three times more likely than White students to receive disciplinary actions (Yang et al., 2018). Black and Brown students, students with disabilities, and students with multiple marginalized identities are more likely to receive higher disciplinary action against them. The school-to-prison pipeline is based on discipline policies disproportionately targeting minoritized youth and funneling students from in-school instruction to the criminal justice system (McMaster, 2017). School counselors must understand how the system of racism and the educational system have created and continue to fuel the school-to-prison pipeline and be prepared to disrupt the pipeline by developing best practices for postsecondary readiness programming.

EQUITY

There are many inequities at each school level for students of color and other marginalized groups when it comes to college and career development. School counselors not only have the leadership and advocacy skills to challenge these inequities, but they also have an ethical obligation to provide services to all students. ASCA Ethical Standard A.3.b (2016) states school counselors will "provide students with a comprehensive school counseling program that ensures equitable academic, career and social/ emotional development opportunities for all students" (p. 3). For school counselors to enact leadership, they must first examine their unique worldview and cultural background and understand how they influence their narrative and space, and practice "cultural humility" when working with diverse students (Hook et al., 2013, p. 354).

"On average, African American and Latino youth have lower-status occupational expectations and larger occupational status gaps than European American and Asian American youth" (Hughes, 2011, p. 369). When it comes to representation, students of color do not see people who share the same ethnicity or gender in high-status careers. Such an experience can have an impact on their understanding of potential future occupations because of limited representations of successful individuals and potential role models (Albritton et al., 2020). Since students' beliefs about their abilities may influence their efforts in career development, school counselors can have a crucial impact on those beliefs (Yuen et al., 2010). Students may experience many different types of barriers that can affect their career development. School counselors possess the leadership skills to help students and their families identify these barriers and formulate a plan based on their needs and abilities. It is vital that school counselors provide continued support, and address equity issues with school personnel so that each student has the opportunity to be a successful learner (Coogan, 2016).

Equity, in today's society, cannot be discussed without mentioning technology. A report from ACT summarized the geographical, income, and racial/ethnic disparities regarding access to technology (Moore & Vitale, 2018). Overall most students reported access to an electronic device and internet, but the kind of device, number of devices, and what kind of internet (home or cell phone) varied by race. School counselors must recognize this as a potential barrier when working with students. Many students do not have appropriate devices, and even those that do, may not have appropriate access to the Internet. Further, those students may live in an area where they are unable to walk to a coffee shop, library, or other local businesses to access Wi-Fi. School counselors possess the leadership skills to advocate for students when delivering career development lessons or when providing resources such as FAFSA completion nights. An example is a high school counselor who advocates for computer lab access and support for students who are unable to complete college applications at home.

Technology is just one of the many inequities students face when it comes to postsecondary readiness. Language, disability, race/ethnicity, gender, sexuality, and access to resources are other common obstacles. Black boys, for example, are frequently over referred to special education, under referred to gifted education, and more likely to be disciplined at school than their White peers (Wright & Ford, 2019). Wright and Ford (2019) suggest that this is due in part to the overrepresentation of White female educators who are complicit in marginalizing Black boys. Hispanic students who speak a first language other than English and need language supports can be mistakenly identified for special education while others remain in ESOL programs over many years and are passed by for special education services (Becker & Deris, 2019). School counselors must be mindful of the range of inequities and also the intersection of inequities when integrating college and career programming into their schools.

ETHICS

School counselors face daily ethical dilemmas and must know how to appropriately handle each unique dilemma (Brown et al., 2017). The ASCA's (2016) *Ethical Standards for School Counselors* provide a thorough set of guidelines. According to Moyer and colleagues (2012), while ethical codes outline procedures to follow in handling situations (i.e., duty to warn, self-harm, confidentiality, advocacy, rights of students and parents), ethical codes do not offer specific steps to follow. School counselors must be familiar with the code of ethics as well as their state's legal statutes to determine how to handle situations (Froeschle et al., 2014) and ensure equitable decisions are made on behalf of all students (Ziomek-Daigle et al., 2019).

The *ASCA Ethical Standards for School Counselors* (ASCA, 2016) also provide a consistent and clear message of the professional beliefs school counselors hold in their work with students. Additionally, the ethical standards provide guidance on specific types of student programs. Specific language is included that students should "receive critical, timely information on college, career, and postsecondary options" (ASCA, 2016, para. 2, third bullet). Therefore, it is imperative for school counselors and students in school counseling programs to stay current on trends in postsecondary options in order to assist all students.

ASCA defines a school counselor's role as one of leadership, advocacy, collaboration, and agent of systemic change (ASCA, n.d.b). By this definition, school counselors are situated to identify the needs of all students, focus on their future goals and aspirations, and the educational preparation required to fulfill those dreams (Hines et al., 2011; Pérusse et al., 2017). School counselors are ethically bound to (a) create a culture of postsecondary readiness by advocating with school leaders; (b) provide opportunities for students in Grades preK–12 to develop college and career awareness, exploration, and postsecondary planning and decision-making; (c) identify gaps in college and career access and how intentional and unintentional biases relate postsecondary planning; (d) provide opportunities for all students to develop mindsets and behaviors necessary for life after high school (ASCA, 2016, Section A.4).

School counselors are uniquely qualified not only to work with students but also to ensure equity in postsecondary readiness for all students (Goodman-Scott et al., 2015; Hines et al., 2011; Patrikakou et al., 2016). As leaders, school counselors are ethically bound not only to work with other school leaders but to advocate for all students' preparation to make informed decisions regarding postsecondary plans (Hines et al., 2011; Pérusse et al., 2017). The *ASCA Ethical Standards for School Counselors* (ASCA, 2016) are readily available to assist school counselors when dilemmas arise and serve as a guide to establishing equitable protocols and programs for all students to explore postsecondary options.

ELEMENTARY SCHOOL

ASCA's (n.d.b) *Mindsets and Behaviors for Student Success* state that career development standards guide school counseling programs to help students (a) understand the connection between school and the world of work and (b) plan for and make a successful transition from school to postsecondary education and/or the world of work and from job to job across the lifespan" (p. 1). One of the major responsibilities of a school counselor at the elementary school level is to "identify gaps in college and career access and the implications of such data for addressing both intentional and unintentional biases related to college and career counseling" (ASCA, 2012, p. 3). This is a critical responsibility for elementary level school counselors as the planning of postsecondary aspirations of students begins at the elementary level and continues throughout the lifespan. ASCA recognizes career education begins in kindergarten and is exemplified by students who are knowledgeable about options and are prepared to enroll and succeed in any postsecondary experience without the need for remediation (Gysbers, 2013).

Students' views on postsecondary options can be a difficult task for school counselors to navigate, as every student comes with a different socioeconomic worldview and perceptions of the world of work. For example, a child growing up in an urban setting rife with poverty and drugs, a child who sees in their environment a high level of crime and social injustices, or a child in an unsupervised home with no positive role models, may easily begin to consider his or her options after high school to be limited or hopeless to the possibilities of pursuing any productive career. Although these are only examples of the realities some students in marginalized communities encounter, at an early age children begin to imitate what they see, and how they see themselves in the world (Super, 1980). The elementary school years set the foundation for developing the knowledge, attitudes, and skills of careers and future aspirations necessary for children to become healthy, competent, and confident learners. Elementary school counselors have an impact on these years by implementing postsecondary counseling programs and collaborating with school staff, parents, and the community to provide a robust career experience for their students. By providing education, experiential learning, and early exposure, elementary school counselors help their students develop an understanding of career opportunities that will give them a foundational framework of what opportunities they may have in the future, whatever their background may be.

Postsecondary counseling at the elementary level must be approached with skillful intentionality and consistent creativity. Skillful intentionality is being aware of the demographics, context, and experiences of students and their families. What are the social factors students are experiencing with regard to careers and work? What messages are being spoken and not spoken that are internalized by the students? What are their hopes, dreams, and aspirations? Students from minoritized populations may find it difficult to see themselves in certain careers because of systemic inequities and oppression cast upon them due to their race, gender, or social status (Crenshaw, 2006; Reskin & Bielby, 2005). Being intentional and creative also means being student-centered by involving students in the process of developing and implementing postsecondary planning. The elementary school counselor can provide all students, especially those who are often marginalized with a strong sense of self, empowerment, and critical career awareness.

Elementary School Student Development

Elementary school counselors need to consider their students' development in a variety of aspects: psychosocial, socio-emotional, cognitive, physical, cultural, moral, gender, and career. Gottfredson's theory of circumscription and compromise tells us that children as young as elementary school are already narrowing and limiting their career options (Curry & Milsom, 2017). School counselors should design programs and interventions based on the particular age and development of their students. For example, most students in second and third grade are likely in Erickson's (1963) industry versus inferiority stage. They are working on the development of their self-concept and trying to establish competence in school and with friends. In this stage, children are typically open to more postsecondary options, so a school counselor might focus their programs on exposure to a wide variety of careers beyond those that are most common and traditional (Curry & Milsom, 2017).

Often, postsecondary planning can be left to middle and high school levels, yet there are programs and interventions that are purposeful at the elementary level. Postsecondary readiness programming at this level should consist of activities that are fun and engaging for students, such as incorporating play into experiences. In addition to awareness and exposure, programs should aim to disrupt societal constraints that often lead to students' belief that because of their culture, gender, or background, they are only allowed to pursue certain postsecondary options. For example, there are many programs, like Girls Who Code and IGNITE Worldwide, that address the shortage of women in STEM fields. These programs work to "myth bust" the common idea that women cannot or should not work in STEM fields.

Elementary School Career Development: Awareness

There are many career development models that describe the ongoing lifelong process of career exploration and provide students with access to quality career-related education (Sharf, 2013). Most critical in the literature for elementary school-aged students' career exploration is career awareness (Auger et al., 2005). During the early years, students explore the world of work through structured, age-appropriate activity and play, primary school students gain ideas about the world of work through play and storytelling, and young children can talk about the jobs they want when they grow up and be encouraged to explore a wide range of occupations. During this phase of career development, it is paramount that students are provided opportunities to learn more about themselves, their cultural background, gender, race, direct and indirect messages they hear about the world of work. Self-awareness builds awareness of strengths (Gueh, 2020), interests, and values, and connects this information to future purpose and career through reflection and related metacognitive activities (Knight, 2015). According to Gottfredson (2005), individuals eliminate careers based on gender, academic ability, social prestige, personal interest, and their beliefs on attainability. Hence, career development at the elementary level should be more focused on fostering students' identity as it relates to careers, not pushing students to make career decisions (Akos et al., 2011b). Being more effective and reaching all students, especially traditionally underserved populations may require school counselors to work differently, and to be more intentional about providing an equitable career awareness experience for all students.

One state that has developed a career development model for schools to implement is Georgia. The "Bridge Bill," Georgia House Bill 713, mandates a minimum course of study in career education in Grades K–12. To support schools in fulfilling these requirements, the grade-specific career awareness activities are listed as an indicator on the College and Career Ready Performance Index (GaDOE, 2020). These indicators are focused on specific *career clusters* that students begin learning starting in the first grade. The elementary level career clusters are:

Grade 1 (Agriculture, Food and Natural Resources; Transportation, Distribution, and Logistics; Law, Public Safety, Corrections, and Security)

Grade 2 (Arts, A/V Technology, and Communications; Health Science; Education and Training)

Grade 3 (Hospitality and Tourism; Human Services; Energy)

Grade 4 (STEM; Manufacturing; Business Management and Administration; Architecture and Construction)

Grade 5 (Finance; Information Technology; Marketing; Government and Public Administration)

The goal of these career clusters is to aid students in developing a sense of self and areas of interest, acquiring positive attitudes, a sense of career awareness, and the relationship with academics and personal interests (GaDOE, 2020). School counselors are uniquely trained in career and human development theories, which provides a framework for school counselors to build a developmentally appropriate career program in their school buildings (Dahir et al., 2009; Holcomb-McCoy, 2007). The need for a strong and equitable postsecondary program at the elementary level is essential and can be the incubator for which students begin to dream about their futures; school counselors are the natural leaders for this work.

Inclusion of Families, Staff, and Communities

School counselors are not alone in their passion for supporting students. Furthermore, current researchers support the value of family involvement in students' career development, especially for diverse populations, as many traditional career theories are individualistic in nature and derive from a White, eurocentric worldview (Storlie et al., 2019, 2017). Parents/guardians, teachers, and other school personnel, and the community are all valuable partners to an elementary school counselor. Elementary school students are typically most influenced by their immediate family, particularly their parents/guardians. By collaborating with families, school counselors can expand their reach, leading to enhanced outcomes for their students. For example, an elementary school counselor might plan a career day to expose students to a wide variety of careers. They could invite parents/guardians to participate by being a speaker or volunteer for the program.

Often, this type of collaboration strengthens the relationship between the school counselor and the family and also exposes the family to the content being delivered, such as learning about new careers.

In their research on the importance of parent involvement in a high-poverty, high-minority serving elementary school, Bower and Griffin (2011) found that school staff may need to rethink how they engage with parents:

> For some schools, this may mean redefining parent involvement from purely academic roles toward more collaborative roles with other parents, such as parent support groups, parent teams for school events, or presenters in classroom cultural or enrichment activities. These networks could impact academic achievement not only by helping parents engage more directly with the school but also by empowering parents to serve as supports for each other. (p. 84)

Along these lines, elementary school counselors can consider running parent/guardian workshops or send home educational materials about postsecondary planning at this stage. Often, young children pick up on thoughts, language, and limitations around careers that they hear at home (Curry & Milsom, 2017). Educating parents/guardians about their influence and the importance of encouraging their children to keep their options open at this age can contribute positively to the goals of the school counseling program.

Another valuable partnership for elementary school counselors is with teachers. Elementary teachers are often willing to collaborate with school counselors on curriculum design and lesson plans, especially when the school counselor can tie their lesson to academic outcomes and standards. For example, a school counselor might work with an English language arts teacher on a career exploration unit, incorporating reflective writing about their ideas about careers, their futures, and what they learn based on the lessons. Alternatively, the school counselor might partner with a teacher on lessons related to self-concept and confidence because the links between academic outcomes and self-concept are so strong (Curry & Milsom, 2017).

Elementary school counselors can partner with community organizations and businesses to enhance their programs and postsecondary readiness curriculum. Researchers have shown that these types of partnerships increase academic outcomes for students, particularly for marginalized students (Bryan & Henry, 2012; Holcomb-McCoy, 2010). An elementary school counselor might benefit from incorporating community partners into the career day mentioned above or participate in field trips for students. Awareness of careers can be deepened by exposing students to different places of employment so that students can see various work settings and the workers in action.

MIDDLE SCHOOL

Middle school counselors must use their leadership skills to coordinate events and establish and maintain a school culture that supports an equity-focused approach to postsecondary readiness programming. Generational and personal differences of school staff may influence their communication to students about postsecondary options. Therefore, school counselors can take the lead in presenting to staff the current data on the student population, trends in the labor market, and potential policies or practices that may be barriers to students' access to all available options (Dougherty et al., 2017).

Critical to the leadership of middle school counselors in postsecondary readiness programming is understanding forces of systemic racism, White supremacy, and other forces of marginalization in schools, colleges, and in the workforce that have historically closed career paths for certain student groups such as students of color, those with disabilities, undocumented students, and those who identify with the LGBTQ community. This is particularly important at middle school because this is a heightened stage of identity development (Erikson, 1950). Research supports that students from such groups have unique needs and require unique supports (Albritton et al., 2020). Once again, traditional career theories that uphold western, White norms of success and achievement, often dismiss values held by diverse student groups. Frameworks such as relational cultural theory (RCT), social cognitive career theory (SCCT), or positive youth development (PYD; Albritton, 2020; Storlie et al., 2017, 2019a, 2019b). Such oppressive forces, which have often impacted generations in the form of policies, mean that some students have little or no knowledge of all the options that are available to them. Thus, critiquing practices (e.g., enrollment in gifted and special education programs) and challenging postsecondary-related stereotypes (e.g., all Black males are interested in sports) is essential to the school counselor's role. Highlighting, and then working to dismantle such policies with and on behalf of students is essential. Furthermore, involving students themselves in the specific tasks associated with the planning of events like college or career fairs, STEM or STEAM-related events, and career-based clubs (e.g., robotics) can increase engagement and afford the opportunity to teach valuable employability skills (e.g., marketing, oral and written communication, project management).

Middle School Student Development

The overall development of the middle school student is especially relevant to discussing postsecondary readiness programming. Middle school generally represents the age range from 11 to 14 years and can include 5th grade to 9th grade depending upon individual school configurations. Middle school is when students' cognitive development moves from concrete to formal operations so they can think more abstractly and engage in critical thinking (Piaget, 1971). Physically, middle school students are in a phase of extreme growth with the onset of puberty; the size, shape, and rate of growth of these students can range widely (Tanner, 1962). During this period, gender identity, sexual orientation, and the expression of both are explored (Orthner et al., 2013). Friends and social networks in and out of school play a critical role in identity development and relationships outside of the family (Erikson, 1950). Intersectionality (Crenshaw, 1991) becomes important developmentally at this age because identity development is so prominent. School counselors at the middle school level must be adept at considering the potential postsecondary experiences, assets, and barriers for students based on identities of privilege and oppression.

Middle School Career Development: Exploration

Focusing on programming at the middle school level with a developmental lens contributes to the increased self-efficacy, self-concept, and self-esteem of students (Coogan, 2016). School counselors can also use intersectionality as a career development framework when working with students who have multiple marginalized identities (Storlie et al., 2019a) by ensuring that there is careful attention to implicit bias in programming decisions, material selection, speaker recruitment, and accessibility. School counselors can lead appropriate postsecondary programming by emphasizing the exploration of options at the middle school level. Beyond simple exposure to careers and postsecondary opportunities, middle school students need to understand how their interests and skills can connect to career pathways. For example, STEM is a career field focused on science, technology, engineering, and math, and within each of those strands there are career pathways such as agriculture, business, family and consumer sciences, marketing, skilled trades, and technology (Wu-Rorrer, 2017). Students can connect their skills in math with interests in marketing and from there investigate major companies where employees examine consumer buying habits.

Because of students' increase in abstract thinking, middle school counselors can use activities that ask them to think about personal values, analyze the job market, consider the future, and explore self-awareness of talents (Yuen et al., 2010). Middle school students, although often here-and-now oriented, are capable of connecting the dots between school and work, imagining new realities for their adult lives, and innovating solutions to societal problems that could lead to new jobs. In a post-pandemic world, this type of innovation and creative problem-solving will be in high demand. As leaders, middle school counselors can understand this capacity and design programming that is interactive and covers a wide range of options such as traditional college, career, and technical education, military, and apprenticeships and internships.

Inclusion of Families, Staff, and Communities

Perhaps more influential than any other source on students' postsecondary development is the family. Students typically experience the careers of their parents before any other exposure to career development (Orthner et al., 2013). School counselors, as leaders in social justice in the school, must use an equity-based approach to postsecondary readiness programming, which means including families and understanding students' personal contexts. Embedded within families are significant lived experiences, cultural norms, and values that shape students' expectations around postsecondary options and success (Storlie et al., 2017). These differences mean that school counselors must pay close attention to aspects of the postsecondary planning process that may privilege or marginalize student groups. Families who have positive lived experiences with schools or their own planning for college and career may be likely to attend typical postsecondary events like information sessions on high school graduation requirements or 4-year planning. School counselors must take leadership by challenging the normal practices of the school to make sure that those families who have no experience or potentially negative lived experiences with planning for college or career have equal access to the same information. This may necessitate school counselor leadership in brokering more resources such as interpreters, college advisors that serve students with disabilities, and greater diversity in speakers with respect to race, ethnicity, gender, sexual orientation, disability status, socioeconomic and documentation status.

School counselors who are leaders in their middle schools also take opportunities to update their knowledge of the rapid changes in workforce development, job trends, college admissions requirements, and local and state employment markets. Even at the middle school level, families benefit from financial planning information for postsecondary options. Middle school counselors can use and provide families with tools like the ASCA (n.d.a) middle school career conversation starters, also available in Spanish, as a way to encourage discussion about postsecondary options at home. Working in collaboration with the local high school counselors can strengthen the postsecondary planning process by providing a smoother transition from middle to high school. Middle and high school counselors can co-host events and send out information to both sets of families, which may not only increase efficiency but also broaden reach.

School counselors cannot provide successful postsecondary readiness programming without the support of school staff and administration. Schoolwide postsecondary projects such as college or career fairs, in particular, require substantial time and resources. The classroom setting provides opportunities for school counselors and teachers to co-teach by aligning the ASCA mindsets and behaviors (ASCA, 2016) with academic standards to explore postsecondary-related issues. Research indicates that middle school teachers value integrating career-related curricula into their courses (Akos et al., 2011a). In a study by Lapan et al. (2016), a college and career readiness curriculum was incorporated into seventh grade ELA classes using writing. It is evidence that school counselors and teachers can collaborate while limiting interruptions to academic learning, and in fact, enhance learning for students. School counselors can also collaborate with administrators, librarians, media specialists, instructional coaches, psychologists, or social workers to creatively partner on postsecondary readiness activities. Many middle school students have hands-on, tactile, and social-based learning preferences so the creative use of project-based learning, maker spaces (Baker & Alexander, 2018), experiments, or artistic collaborations (Cook-Sather et al., 2018), can be used to explore school to work.

Postsecondary readiness programming benefits greatly from partnerships with the community. Students' understanding of their postsecondary options are influenced by the businesses, places of worship, rec centers, libraries, universities, and shops where they live and go to school (Miles et al., 2015; Wu-Rorrer, 2019). School counselors' natural leadership and connecting skills can be used to find local partners that value community service and thus can be key stakeholders in the school. Partners may provide financial support through donations that support postsecondary events such as food, materials, gift cards, or raffle items. However, long term partnerships with entities that can provide services are extremely valuable to a school counseling program. These types of partners may include local colleges or technical institutions that provide tours for students or families, community-based courses, or tutoring. Colleges and universities can work with school counselors to communicate the value of an education and assist in the removal of perception barriers based on race and gender (Glessner et al., 2017). School counselors can take the lead on surveying families in the school as well as the local community for business partners who may be able to provide small grants, mentors, or offer apprenticeships (Hausman et al., 2017). Other specialized programs like Junior Achievement already work with area businesses to provide schools with a curriculum on employability skills and financial literacy.

HIGH SCHOOL

Postsecondary counseling is a critically important part of a comprehensive school counseling program for students in kindergarten through 12th grade (ASCA, 2019; Gysbers, 2013; Poyton & Lapan, 2016). Students must have opportunities to explore careers and other postsecondary options throughout their school careers. While postsecondary readiness programming is part of the K–12 experience for students, in high school it takes on more urgent and all-important meaning as students need exposure to specific opportunities that are available to them after graduation. High school counselors prepare students for postsecondary careers and for college admission, retention, and success through delivering engaging comprehensive school counseling programs (Gysbers, 2013).

Research provides evidence of the vital roles school counselors play in assisting students develop career and college plans. According to Gilfillan (2018), African American and first-generation students consider their school counselors as the most beneficial person in working with them through the college readiness process. Choi and colleagues (2015) found that the more time students spent participating in career development interventions, the more certain they felt about their future career aspirations. According to Poyton and Lapan (2016), when school counselors regularly provide college and career readiness services, students acquire skills associated with more successful transitions from high school to postsecondary life. Research shows the rate of graduating seniors applying to college increases when more time is spent between students and school counselors (Bryan et al., 2011; Poyton & Lapan, 2016). Additional research found an increase in 4-year college attendance rates for students from schools that spent more time in college counseling activities (Engberg & Gilbert, 2014; Poyton & Lapan, 2016). This research is important in that it provides evidence of the important roles that school counselors play in the development of students' postsecondary plans.

Allowing substantial time for students to explore postsecondary opportunities is vital. Some state departments of education have adopted career clusters or pathways that students are required to explore. As mentioned earlier, in Georgia, students must be exposed to 17 career clusters (Georgia Department of Education [GDOE], 2020). Within the clusters are pathways that students work to complete based on courses they take. Courses that complete the pathways have been predetermined. Some pathways lead to industry certification, thus, providing students an opportunity for advanced placement in a career. The GDOE has specific career activities that must be completed at each grade level, beginning in middle school. These activities provide opportunities for students to explore the career clusters. The expected outcome for students is increased knowledge and interest in career fields.

According to Edwin and Hussman (2020), the training school counselors receive makes them highly qualified to provide career development and postsecondary interventions to students. School counselors, as leaders, use a variety of modalities to bring postsecondary options to students by building partnerships in the community including those with businesses, colleges, and families. Additionally, they engage in professional learning to secure new resources and to stay abreast of opportunities for students. As high school counselors do this work, they must be diligent to ensure that equitable access is provided to all students. School counselors must use their social justice lens when planning postsecondary readiness programming; this means being attuned to students' multiple identities, cultural and societal context, and the ever-changing workforce.

High School Student Development

High school in the United States generally encompasses Grades 9 to 12 and students range from 14–18 years of age. During high school, adolescents face a number of developmental challenges, including handling changes in their bodies, managing their sexual interests, and planning their academic and occupational futures (Perry & Pauletti, 2011). Additionally, significant cognitive changes occur during adolescence (Wang & Eccles, 2011) as the brain continues to develop. The cognitive changes allow for students to make concrete inferences about postsecondary options. For many students learning to navigate through contextual factors over which they have no control (e.g., socioeconomic status, family makeup, parental involvement, access to quality secondary education, community safety) also creates potential obstacles. School counselors help students remove all possible barriers that may impede students' success and access to postsecondary options. This is vital since having greater access to a school counselor leads to an increased number of college applications (Bryan et al., 2011; Poyton & Lapan, 2016) especially for minoritized student populations (Bryan et al., 2011).

Parents/Caregivers

Parents/caregivers provide students with their initial understanding of specific careers (Orthner et al., 2013). Many students grow up thinking they will follow in their parents' footsteps, due to the limited amount of knowledge they may have about other careers (Rogers et al., 2018). School counselors can take the lead and fill in the gaps by having local school parents/caregivers present to students about the work they do. This has the potential to broaden students' knowledge of careers that exist. Additionally, students will have someone they may feel comfortable contacting to gain further information.

Institutions of Higher Education

Establishing partnerships with local colleges and universities has the potential to provide high school students with many opportunities. When college admissions representatives are able to come to the high school campus and communicate the value of an education (Glessner et al., 2017). While visiting a college campus is important to ensure there is a "fit" for the student, being able to speak with college representatives in a safe environment allows students to get first-hand knowledge about specific institutions. For many high school students, moving away to attend college is simply cost-prohibitive. However, learning about postsecondary institutions within or near the community allows students to see attending college is possible while being able to live at home.

Community Partners

Career and college exploration are important activities for students in high school to engage in from freshman year through senior year. Due to course work in graduate programs and the availability of professional development, school counselors are able to provide career exploration activities to their students. Career and college exploration is enhanced when school counselors form partnerships within the community. In fact, it is essential that school counselors go beyond the school building to form community partnerships (Curry & Milsom, 2017; Evans et al., 2011). Community partners should reflect the racial makeup of the students. Students need to see people who look like them working in specific fields, and school counselors can ensure this occurs (Yuen et al., 2010). Additionally, breaking gender stereotypes and having broad representation (e.g., female doctors, male nurses, etc.) is important for students. School counselors may consider some of the following community partners to enhance the career and college exploration of their students.

Career, Technical, and Agricultural Educators

Collaboration with teachers is an important way for school counselors to showcase their knowledge of postsecondary career planning. Additionally, it has the added benefit of enhancing the understanding of the school counselor's role within the school and the curriculum (Henderson, 2020). Career, technical, and agricultural educators (CTAE) are invaluable resources for providing career exploration to high school students. These educators have received specific training in careers and each person has specific qualifications and training. School counselors could partner with the CTAE in the building to help facilitate career exploration activities. The collaboration could highlight the nexus between high school classroom activities and skills needed for particular career, technical, and agricultural fields. For example, school counselors could collaborate with CTAE to develop and teach lessons pertaining to the career opportunities within the electrical engineering field.

Internships and Apprenticeships

Internships and apprenticeships provide high school students with experiential career learning opportunities that provide knowledge of skills needed for particular careers (Deil-Amen & DeLuca, 2010; Hernandez-Gantes et al., 2018). These experiential learning opportunities allow high school students to immerse themselves in a selected career, thus, allowing them to make decisions of pursuing the career based on the actual work. This could save high school students time and resources if they determine the functions of a job do not match their interests. The appeal of apprenticeships for high school graduates is growing and school counselors must have knowledge of the opportunities. Typically, upon completion of an apprenticeship program, individuals are ready for certification in the industry. An added benefit of an apprenticeship program is there is no student debt for attending an institution. For both internships and apprenticeships, high school students not only earn a nominal salary, but they also gain important employability skills (i.e., soft skills) not often taught in the classroom (Hernandez-Gantes et al., 2018).

Employers

Partnering with local businesses is an important activity in which school counselors can engage (Malin & Hackman, 2017; Paolini, 2019). Some high school students are content with staying in their hometown after graduation. Having employers come in to speak with students or hold job fairs has a positive impact on both parties. For students, they learn about businesses in the community and may find particular businesses of interest for future employment. The employers are able to gain local community members to their workforce, thus keeping down the costs of recruiting and onboarding new employees.

Community Centers or Agencies

An important piece of career exploration is teaching students how to prepare for job interviews and meet prospective employers. Students have done the research on particular careers they are interested in pursuing; however, they need to know how to prepare for obtaining a job. Having individuals from local community centers and agencies (e.g., employment agencies, Goodwill) provide students with skills in writing resumes and completing job applications is a crucial step in career exploration. Resumes are not easy to understand and can be frustrating to understand especially in completing them the first time. Additionally, teaching students how to complete a job application cannot be overemphasized. Small tips like using a blue or black ink pen as opposed to a pencil, signing their names, and writing legibly are important yet often overlooked skills. Having individuals from communities come in and teach these skills opens windows of opportunities to students. For example, inviting a human resources representative from a school's local business sponsors to provide this type of training.

Career Planning and Preparation

The Every Student Succeeds Act (ESSA) is federal legislation for P–12 education, which was signed into law in 2015 by former President Barack Obama to address the preparation of all students for college, career readiness, and employability skills (Darrow, 2016). School counselors are responsible for assisting students in navigating the ESSA postsecondary readiness requirements (Henderson, 2020). In working on career development, school counselors work with students to research best-fit career areas (Fickling, 2016). Illinois has created a college and career readiness framework called the Illinois PaCE (Postsecondary and Career Expectations; Advance Illinois, n.d.) to assist students in reaching college and career readiness benchmarks. For example, school counselors administer a career interest survey to and meet with 9th grade students to discuss the relationship between coursework, attendance, and postsecondary interest areas. School counselors continue the discussion of career awareness and exploration with 10th graders by having them select a career pathway with a career cluster of interest. School counselors work with 11th and 12th grade students and parents to revisit career survey results or retake the survey to address changes in interests, skills, and knowledge. Students create a resume, attend college fairs, research the cost and realistically estimate where they can attend school and understand academic debt.

Intentional planning and attention to cultural influences, student identities, and activities that challenge White supremacist norms in career development must be prioritized. Storlie (2016) suggested hosting a career fair that includes representatives from diverse populations. School counselors working with students from collective-focused cultures as opposed to individual-focused cultures will find it helpful to recognize and incorporate techniques that may assist students. For example, small groups rather than one-on-one meetings may benefit African American males students with lessons in career development (Cheatham & Mason, 2021). Creative applications that are both relevant and youth-centered, such as hip-hop, can also be used to engage high school students in career development (Emdin et al., 2016).

RECOMMENDATIONS

Research

Intervention research in school counseling, on the whole, is greatly needed (Griffith, et al., 2019; Mason & Trezek, 2020), therefore studies of postsecondary readiness programming in schools and by school counselors would be welcome. Of particular import is research that investigates effective programming with students of color and other marginalized groups. The increasingly diversifying student population, along with the shifting landscape of the workforce, means that school counselors and other school leaders would benefit from knowing a variety of research-based practices that work to best serve a range of school student populations.

Some recommendations for leadership actions in the research area include:

- Effective postsecondary interventions with Black, indigenous, people of color (BIPOC) students; LGBTQ+; students with disabilities; and students in low-income families
- longitudinal studies of postsecondary access and decision-making from K–12
- postsecondary counseling experiences of students with multiple marginalized identities (e.g., Latina and lesbian, Asian with a disability)
- impact of workforce changes on the social and economic mobility of the Millennial and Gen Z generations
- effective educational leadership models to promote equity and access in postsecondary readiness

Practice

If school counselors are leaders in postsecondary programming, they must be fully knowledgeable of all local and state resources, initiatives, and opportunities related to college and career. It is recommended that school counselors at all levels include viable postsecondary partners in their advisory councils, gather available data from partners about the local workforce, maintain relationships with community businesses, and physically visit or invite to the school local college representatives, public officials, and other public servant groups. Often, school administrators are involved in these opportunities and initiatives, so it would be beneficial for school counselors to partner with their building and district colleagues on these efforts.

School counselors may wish to use frameworks such as the ASCA National Model (2019) or Multi-Tiered Systems of Support (Goodman-Scott et al., 2019) to organize their postsecondary interventions but there is no one-size-fits-all solution so an equity-focused approach must meet the unique needs of each school population. Given the systemic inequities that can be present in postsecondary access (e.g., lack of information in non-English languages, the unfamiliarity of the college application process for first-generation families) it is important for school counselors to take an ecological view of their schools (McMahon et al., 2014) and assess where and with whom interventions can create the most change. Through consultation and by offering workshops or other professional development, school counselors can better inform and equip the adults in students' lives (Springer et al., 2020). These professional development opportunities may be geared toward teachers, school administrators, and other school personnel to ensure everyone has a foundational knowledge of postsecondary options, processes, and equity and access issues.

Some recommendations for leadership actions in the practice area include:

- Use needs assessments to determine where to focus your postsecondary efforts and then plan a calendar of programming.
- Fall back on the tried and true activities but introduce some new ones to keep the programming innovative and centered on changing student needs.
- Involve students in planning (e.g., voting on career day speakers, contacting college reps, utilizing student clubs with a career focus).
- Coordinate postsecondary programming for students with companion programming for families (e.g., when delivering a classroom lesson, send families a short video overview and/or handout).
- Collaborate across levels (i.e., elementary, middle, high) for large-scale events to engage families.

- Ensure accessibility at events and with materials for those with disabilities or non-native English speakers.
- Partner with teachers in your building to offer workshops and learning opportunities for students (e.g., an activity researching and journaling about careers can be a collaboration between the English teachers and school counselors).

Policy

Policy is the area where school counselor leadership may be needed most when it comes to postsecondary readiness programming. In the policy space, leadership can be taken in the form of advocacy, and school counselors are positioned well for this work because of their ability to understand the needs of individual students, groups of students, and the larger school community (Cheatham & Mason, 2021). School counselors can use advocacy to challenge policies related to student tracking into programs (e.g., special education, gifted education) by finding and presenting data that demonstrates inequities.

Some recommendations for leadership actions in the policy area include:

- Share school data that illuminates postsecondary inequities in staff meetings.
- Suggest more equitable policies to school administrators at the school and district levels.
- Host community or state legislative officials at a schoolwide event.
- Present with colleagues at a school board meeting.
- Seek membership on the district, local, or state groups for career initiatives.
- Seek membership on boards at local colleges, universities, or technical schools.
- Work with others to edit or draft new policy or legislation that increases postsecondary opportunities and access.

QUESTIONS AND CHAPTER REFLECTIONS

1. Why do students need school counselor leaders who have a comprehensive, equity, and advocacy-driven approach to postsecondary options in the context of today's society?
2. Based on the chapter, what are examples of school counselors' leadership at the local, state, and national levels?

3. How can school counselors demonstrate their roles as leaders, advocates, collaborators, and agents of systemic change in postsecondary readiness at the elementary, middle school, and high school levels?

CASE STUDY AND ACTIVITIES

Karima is a 17 year old senior at Carter High School in the Southeast region of the United States. She was born in the Dominican Republic and came to the United States when she was 2 years old. Karima's family came to the United States for a better life, and to escape the social challenges they faced in their home country. When Karima entered grade school, it was quickly noticed by her teachers and parents that she was a gifted student. Throughout her school years, she was in honors and gifted classes, active in student leadership groups, and maintained a healthy social group of friends who all dreamed of going to school and starting their adult lives together. During the Fall semester of senior year, Karima and her friends started applying to colleges with hopes that they would all be attending the same one. After applying to several top Division 1 institutions in her state, she received one of the most traumatizing responses from her dream college. The message stated, "After reviewing your application, it was determined that you do not meet the requirements to matriculate to our institution, due to your resident status." Confused as to what the response meant, Karima took the letter to her counselor for answers. The counselor explained to Karima that the letter stated that she was not a legal resident of the United States because she was born in the Dominican Republic and she never received a green card or citizenship in the United States. It was also discovered that Karima did not have her social security number which meant that not only could she not apply to the college of her dreams, if she applied to any other college in her state, she must pay out of state tuition; plus, she did not qualify for any federal student financial aid or any state financial aid. With this devastating news, feeling hopeless, like an outcast, and lost, Karima quickly went into a deep depression and even contemplated suicide. The pain and disappointment of her dreams being ripped away after years of working hard, due to state law, did not make sense and was very difficult for her to handle.

ACTIVITIES

Activity #1

Discuss how school counselors can use their leadership, social justice, and advocacy training to assist Karima with postsecondary planning and social emotional support by exploring initiatives and resources at the local, state, and national level for undocumented students.

Activity #2

As the school counselor for Karima, she brings this letter to you. Considering the leadership, social justice, and advocacy implications discussed in the chapter, list the challenges you see that need to be addressed in this scenario. Then, come up with a timeline of strategies, goals, and action steps, you would take as her school counselor.

AUTHOR NOTE

Erin Mason ORCID https://orcid.org/0000-0003-2658-9733
We have no known conflicts of interest to disclose.

REFERENCES

Advance Illinois. (2021). *Postsecondary and Workforce Readiness Act.* https://pwract.org

Akos, P., Charles, P., Orthner, D., & Cooley, V. (2011a). Teacher perspectives on career-relevant curriculum in middle school. *Research in Middle-Level Education Online, 34*(5), 1–9. https://doi.org/10.1080/19404476.2011.11462078

Akos, P., Niles, S. G., Miller, E. M., & Erford, B. T. (2011b). Developmental classroom guidance. In B. T. Erford (Ed.), *Transforming the school counseling profession* (pp. 202–221). Pearson.

Albritton, K., Cureton, J. L., Byrd, J. A., & Storlie, C. A. (2020). Exploring perceptions of the path to work/life success among middle school students of color. *Journal of Career Development, 47*(4), 440–453. https://doi.org/10.1177/0894845319832667

American School Counselor Association. (n.d.a). *Middle school career conversations.* https://www.schoolcounselor.org/getmedia/a7fbb087-9d84-4697-a176-6672dcff3584/Career-Conversations-Middle-School.pdf

American School Counselor Association. (n.d.b). *Mindsets and behaviors for student success: K–12 college-, career-, and life-readiness standards for every student.* https://www.schoolcounselor.org/getmedia/7428a787-a452-4abb-afec-d78ec77870cd/Mindsets-Behaviors.pdf

American School Counselor Association. (2012). *ASCA national model: A framework for school counseling programs* (3rd ed.).

American School Counselor Association. (2016). *ASCA ethical standards for school counselors.* https://www.schoolcounselor.org/getmedia/f041cbd0-7004-47a5-ba01-3a5d657c6743/Ethical-Standards.pdf

American School Counselor Association. (2019). *ASCA national model: A framework for school counseling programs* (4th ed.).

Auger, R. W., Blackhurst, A. E., & Wahl, K. H. (2005). The development of elementary aged children's career aspirations and expectations. *Professional School Counseling, 8*(4), 322–329. https://www.jstor.org/stable/42732626

Baker, S. F., & Alexander, B. (2018). A major making undertaking: A new librarian transforms a middle school library into a makerspace aligned to high school career endorsements. *Knowledge Quest, 46*(5), 64–69. https://eric.ed.gov/?id=EJ1182647

Becker, G. I., & Deris, A. R. (2019). Identification of Hispanic English language learners in special education. *Education Research International,* 1–9. https://doi.org/10.1155/2019/2967943

Bower, H. A., & Griffin, D. (2011). Can the Epstein model of parental involvement work in a high-minority, high-poverty elementary school? A case study. *Professional School Counseling, 15*(2), 77–78. https://doi.org/10.1177/2156759X1101500201

Brown, T., Armstrong, S. A., Bore, A., & Simpson, C. (2017). Using an ethical decision-making model to address ethical dilemmas in school counseling. *Journal of School Counseling, 15*(13), 1–30. https://files.eric.ed.gov/fulltext/EJ1158281.pdf

Bryan, J., & Henry, L. (2012). A model for building school-family-community partnerships: Principles and process. *Journal of Counseling and Development, 90,* 408–420. https://doi.org/10.1002/j.1556-6676.2012.00052.x

Bryan, J., Holcomb-McCoy, C., Moore-Thomas, C., & Day-Vines, N. L. (2009). Who sees the school counselor for college information? A national study. *Professional School Counseling, 12,* 280–291. https://doi.org/10.1177/2156759X0901200401

Bryan, J., Moore-Thomas, C., Day-Vines, N. L., & Holcomb-McCoy, C. (2011). School counselors as social capital: The effect of high school college counseling on college application rates. *Journal of Counseling & Development, 89,* 190–199. https://doi.org/10.1002/j.1556-6678.2011.tb00077.x

Bureau of Labor Statistics. (2020). *Labor force statistics from the current population survey.* https://www.bls.gov/web/empsit/cpsee_e16.htm

Cabrera, A. F., & La Nasa, S. M. (2001). On the path to college: Three critical tasks facing America's disadvantaged. *Research in Higher Education, 42,* 119–149. https://doi.org/10.1023/A:1026520002362

Cervoni, A., & DeLucia-Waack, J. (2011). Role conflict and ambiguity as predictors of job satisfaction in high school counselors. *Journal of School Counseling, 9*(1). http://jsc.montana.edu/articles/v9n1.pdf

Cheatham, C., & Mason, E. C. M. (2021). Using the ACA Advocacy Competencies as a guide to group work for supporting the career development of school-aged African American males. *Journal of Specialists in Group Work, 46*(1) 62–74. https://doi.org/10.1080/01933922.2020.1856253

Choi, Y., Kim, J., & Kim, S. (2015). Career development and school success in adolescents: The role of career interventions. *The Career Development Quarterly, 63*(2), 171–186. https://doi.org/10.1002/cdq.12012

Cholewa, B., Burkhardt, C. K., & Hull, M. F. (2015). Are school counselors impacting underrepresented students' thinking about postsecondary education? A nationally representative study. *Professional School Counseling, 19*, 144–154. https://doi.org/10.5330/1096-2409-19.1.144

Council for Accreditation of Counseling and Related Educational Programs. (2016). *CACREP policy document.* http://www.cacrep.org/wp-content/uploads/2017/07/2016-Policy-Document-July-2017.pdf

Coogan, T. A. (2016). Supporting school counseling in Belize: Establishing a middle school career development program. *International Electronic Journal of Elementary Education, 8*(3), 379–390. https://eric.ed.gov/contentdelivery/servlet/ERICServlet?accno=EJ1096526

Cook-Sather, A., Kenealy, A., Rippel, M., & Beyer, J. (2018). Discovering voices: College students and middle schoolers explore identities, differences, and connections through the structure of a poem. *International Journal of Multicultural Education, 20*(2), 133–149. https://doi.org/10.18251/ijme.v20i2.1564

Crenshaw, K. (1991). Mapping the margins: Intersectionality, identity politics, and violence against women of color. *Stanford Law Review, 43*(6), 1241–1299. https://doi.org/10.2307/1229039

Cressey, J. M., Whitcomb, S. A., McGilvray-Rivet, S. J., Morrison, R. J., & Shander-Reynolds, K. J. (2015). Handling PBIS with care: Scaling up to school-wide implementation. *Professional School Counseling, 18*(1), 90–99. https://doi.org/10.1177/2156759X0001800104

Curry, J. R., & Milsom, A. (2017). *Career and college readiness counseling in P–12 schools* (2nd ed.). Springer Publishing Company.

Dahir, C. A., Burnham, J. J., & Stone, C. (2009). Listen to the voices: School counselors and comprehensive school counseling programs. *Professional School Counseling, 12*(3), 182–192. https://doi.org/10.1177/2156759X0901200304

Darrow, A. (2016). The Every Student Succeeds Act (ESSA). *General Music Today, 30*, 41–44. https://doi.org/10.1177/1048371316658327

Deil-Amen, R., & DeLuca, S. (2010). The underserved third: How our educational structures populate an educational underclass. *Journal of Education for Students Placed at Risk, 15*(2), 27–50. https://doi.org/10.1080/10824661003634948

Dougherty, S. M., Goodman, J. S., Hill, D. V., Litke, E. G., & Page, L. C. (2017). Objective course placement and college readiness: Evidence from targeted middle school math acceleration. *Economics of Education Review, 58*, 141–161. https://doi.org/10.1016/j.econedurev.2017.04.002

Edwin, M., & Hussman, M. D. (2020). Factors influencing school counselors' time spent on career planning with high school students. *Professional School Counseling, 23*(1), 1–11. https://doi.org/10.1177/2156759X20947724

Emdin, C., Adjapong, E., & Levy, I. (2016). Hip-hop based interventions as pedagogy/therapy in STEM. *Journal for Multicultural Education, 10*(3), 307–321. https://doi.org/10.1108/JME-03-2016-0023

Erikson, E. H. (1950). *Childhood and society.* Norton.

Evans, M. P., Zambrano, E., Cook, K., Moyers, M., & Duffey, T. (2011). Enhancing school counselor leadership in multicultural advocacy. *Journal of Professional Counseling: Practice, Theory, and Research, 38*, 52–67. https://doi.org/10.1080/15566382.2011.12033871

Fickling, M. J. (2016). An exploration of career counselors' perspectives on advocacy. *The Professional Counselor, 6,* 174–188. https://doi.org/10.15241/mf .6.2.174

Georgia Department of Education. (2020). *Career clusters/pathway.* https://www.gadoe.org/Curriculum-Instruction-and-Assessment/CTAE/Pages/CTAE-Georgia-Career-Clusters.aspx

Gilfillan, B. H. (2018). School counselors and college readiness counseling. *Professional School Counseling, 21*(1), 1–10. https://doi.org/10.1177%2F2156759 X18784297

Glessner, K., Rockinson-Szapkiw, A. J., & Lopez, M. L. (2017). "Yes, I can": Testing an intervention to increase middle school students' college and career self-efficacy. *Career Development Quarterly, 65*(4), 315–325. https://doi.org/10.1002/ cdq.12110

Goodman-Scott, E., Betters-Bubon, J., & Donohue, P. (2019). *The school counselors' guide to multi-tiered systems of support.* Routledge.

Goodman-Scott, E., Betters-Bubon, J., & Donohue, P. (2015). Aligning comprehensive school counseling programs and positive behavioral interventions and supports to maximize school counselors' efforts. *Professional School Counseling, 19*(1), 57–67. https://doi.org/10.5330/1096-2409-19.1.57

Gottfredson, L. S. (2005). Using Gottfredson's theory of circumscription and compromise in career guidance and counseling. In S. D. Brown & R. W. Lent (Eds.), *Career development and counseling: Putting theory and research to work* (pp. 71–100). Wiley.

Griffith, C., Mariani, M., McMahon, H. G., Zyromski, B., & Greenspan, S. B. (2019). School counseling intervention research: A 10-year content analysis of ASCA- and ACA-affiliated journals. *Professional School Counseling, 23*(1). https://doi .org/10.1177/2156759X19878700

Gueh, B. B. (2020). *And still we rise: A critical narrative of the experiences of Black male school counselors* [Doctoral dissertation, University of Georgia]. ProQuest Dissertations & Theses Global. (Publication No. 27831000)

Gysbers, N. C. (2013). Career-ready students: A goal of comprehensive school counseling programs. *Career Development Quarterly, 61*(3), 283–288. https://doi. org/10.1002/j.2161-0045.2013.00057.x

Henderson, H. B. (2020). *A framework for success: Principals' perspectives about comprehensive school counseling programs* [Doctoral dissertation, University of Georgia]. ProQuest Dissertations & Theses Global. (Publication No. 27959778)

Hicks, J. G. F., Noble, N., Berry, S., Talbert, S., Crews, C., Jiaqi, L., & Castillo, Y. (2014). An ethics challenge for school counselors: Part 2. *Journal of School Counseling, 12*(1), 1–23. https://eric.ed.gov/?id=EJ1034758

Holcomb-McCoy, C. (2010). Involving low-income parents and parents of color in college readiness activities: An exploratory study. *Professional School Counseling, 14,* 115–124. https://doi.org/10.1177/2156759X1001400111

Holcomb-McCoy, C. (2007). *School counseling to close the achievement gap: A social justice framework for success.* Corwin.

Hernandez-Gantes, V. M., Deighobadi, S., & Fletcher, E. C., Jr. (2018). Building community bonds, bridges, and linkages to promote the career readiness of high school students in the United States. *Journal of Education and Work, 31*(2), 190–203. https://doi.org/10.1080/13639080.2018.1434871

Hines, P. L., Lemons, R., & Crews, K. (2011). *Poised to lead: How school counselors can drive college and career readiness.* The Education Trust.

Knight, J. L. (2015). Preparing elementary school counselors to promote career development: Recommendations for school counselor education programs. *Journal of Career Development, 42*(2), 7585. https://doi.org/10.1177/0894845314533745

Lapan, R. T., Marcotte, A. M., Storey, R., Carbone, P., Loehr-Lapan, S., Guerin, D., Thomas, T., Cuffee-Grey, D., Coburn, A., Pfeiffer, T., Wilson, L., & Mahoney, S. (2016). Infusing career development to strengthen middle school English language arts curricula. *Career Development Quarterly, 64*(2), 126–139. https://doi.org/10.1002/cdq.12046

Lipsitz, G. (2011). *How racism takes place.* Temple University Press.

Love, B. L. (2020). *We want to do more than survive: Abolitionist teaching and the pursuit of educational freedom.* Beacon Press.

Malin, J. R., & Hackman, D. (2017). Urban high school principals' promotion of college-and-career readiness. *Journal of Educational Administration, 55*(6), 606–619. https://doi.org/10.1108/JEA-05-2016-0054

Mason, E. C. M., & Trezek, B. J. (2020). Using the CSCORE protocol to identify evidence-based practices in school counseling intervention research. *Counseling Outcome Research and Evaluation, 12*(2), 91–104. https://doi.org/10.1080/21501378.2020.1796480

McMahan, E. H., Singh, A. A., Urbano, A., & Haston, M. (2010). The personal is political: School counselors' use of self in social justice advocacy work. *Journal of School Counseling, 8*(18), 1–29. https://files.eric.ed.gov/fulltext/EJ885221.pdf

Miles, R., Slagter van Tryon, P. J., & Mensah, F. M. (2015). Mathematics and science teachers professional development with local businesses to introduce middle and high school students to opportunities in STEM careers. *Science Educator, 24*(1), 1–11. https://eric.ed.gov/?id=EJ1069973

Moore, R., Vitale, D., & ACT Center for Equity in Learning. (2018). High school students' access to and use of technology at home and in school. *Insights in Education and Work.* https://eric.ed.gov/contentdelivery/servlet/ERICServlet?accno=ED593126

Moyer, M. S., Sullivan, J. R., & Growcock, D. (2012). When is it ethical to inform administrators about student risk-taking behaviors? Perceptions of school counselors. *Professional School Counseling, 15*(3), 98–109. https://doi.org/10.1177/2156759X1201500303

Miller Kneale, M. G., Young, A. A., & Dollarhide, C. T. (2018). Cultivating school counseling leaders through district leadership cohorts. *Professional School Counseling, 21*(1b), 1–9. https://doi.org/10.1177/2156759X18773275

Niles, S. G., & Harris-Bowlsbey, J. E. (2017). *Career development interventions in the 21st century* (5th ed.). Pearson.

Orthner, D. K., Jones-Sanpei, H., Akos, P., & Rose, R. A. (2013). Improving middle school student engagement through career-relevant instruction in the core curriculum. *Journal of Educational Research, 106*(1), 27–38. https://doi.org/ 10.1080/00220671.2012.658454

Paolini, A. C. (2019). School counselors promoting college and career readiness for high school students. *Journal of School Counseling, 17*(2), 1–21. https://eric .ed.gov/contentdelivery/servlet/ERICServlet?accno=EJ1203651

Parikh, S. B., Post, P., & Flowers, C. (2011). Relationship between a belief in a just world and social justice advocacy attitudes of school counselors. *Counseling and Values, 56*, 57–72. https://doi.org/10.1002/j.2161-007X.2011.tb01031.x

Patrikakou, E., Ockerman, M. S., & Hollenbeck, A. F. (2016). Needs and contradictions of a changing field: Evidence from a national response to intervention implementation study. *The Professional Counselor, 6*(3), 233–250. https://doi .org/10.15241/ep.6.3.233

Piaget, J. (1971). The theory of stages in cognitive development. In D. R. Green, M. P. Ford, & G. B. Flamer (Eds.), *Measurement and Piaget* (pp. 1–11). McGraw-Hill.

Perry, D. G., & Pauletti, R. E. (2011). Gender and adolescent development. *Journal of research on adolescence, 21*(1), 61–74. https://doi.org/10.1111/j.1532 -7795.2010.00715.x

Pérusse, R., DeRonck, N., & Parzych, J. (2017). School counseling: Partnering with a school district to provide postsecondary opportunities for first generation, low income, and students of color. *Psychology in the Schools, 54*, 1222–1228. https://doi.org/10.1002/pits.22084

Pyne, J. R. (2011). Comprehensive school counseling programs, job satisfaction, and the ASCA national model. *Professional School Counseling, 15*, 88–97. https:// doi.org/10.1177/2156759X1101500202

Ratts, J. M., & Greenleaf, A. T. (2018). Multicultural and social justice counseling competencies: A leadership framework for professional school counselors. *Professional School Counseling, 21*(1b), 1–9. https://doi.org/10.1177/ 2156759X18773582

Ratts, M. J., & Hutchins, A. M. (2009). ACA advocacy competencies: Social justice advocacy at the client/student level. *Journal of Counseling and Development, 87*, 269–275. https://doi.org/10.1002/j.1556-6678.2009.tb00106.x

Ratts, M. J., Singh, A. A., Nassar-McMillan, S., Butler, S. K., & McCullough, J. R. (2016). Multicultural and social justice counseling competencies: Guidelines for the counseling profession. *Journal of Multicultural Counseling and Development, 44*, 28–48. https://doi.org/10.1002/jmcd.12035

Reskin, B. F., & Bielby, D. D. (2005). A sociological perspective on gender and career outcomes. *Journal of Economics Perspectives, 19*(1), 71–86. https://doi .org/10.1257/0895330053148010

Rogers, M. E., Creed, P. A., & Praskova, A. (2018). Parent and adolescent perceptions of adolescent career development tasks and vocational identity. *Journal of Career Development, 45*(1), 34–49. https://doi.org/10.1177/0894845316667483

Sharf, R. S. (2013). Advances in theories of career development. In W. B. Walsh, M. L. Savickas, & P. J. Hartung (Eds.), *Handbook of vocational psychology* (4th ed., pp. 3–32). Routledge.

Springer, S. I., Mason, E. C. M., Moss, L. J., Pugliese, A., & Colucci, J. (2020). An intervention to support elementary school faculty in meeting the needs of transgender and gender non-conforming students. *Journal of Child and Adolescent Counseling, 6*(3), 1–19. https://doi.org/10.1080/23727810.2019.1689765

Steen, S., & Rudd, T. (2009). Preparing the 21st century school counselor: Alternatives and implications for counselor educators. *Counseling & Human Development, 42*(2), 1–12. https://search.proquest.com/openview/a14682f8d23192 b6341fc419b7aec12a/1?pq-origsite=gscholar&cbl=48224

Storlie, C. A., Albritton, K., Cureton, J. L., & Byrd, J. A. (2019a). African American and Latino male youth: Perceived strengths in career exploration. *Journal of Counselor Practice, 10*(2), 22–50. https://doi.org/10.22229/aal1022019

Storlie, C. A., Chan, C. D, & Vess, L. (2019b). Examining positive youth development in diverse youth through the future career autobiography. *Journal of Child and Adolescent Counseling 5*(2), 189–203. https://doi.org/10.1080/2372 7810.2019.1609837

Storlie, C. A., Albritton, K., & Cureton, J. L. (2017). Familial and social influences in career exploration for female youth of color: A study of relational cultural theory. *The Family Journal, 25*(4), 351–358. https://doi.org/10 .1177/1066480717732142

Storlie, C. A. (2016). Exploring school counselor advocacy in the career development of undocumented Latino youth. *Journal for Social Action in Counseling & Psychology, 8*(1), 70–88. https://doi.org/10.33043/jsacp.8.1.70-88

Super, D. E. (1980). A life-span, life-space approach to career development. *Journal of Vocational Behavior, 16*(3), 282–298. https://doi.org/10.1016/0001 -8791(80)90056-1

Tanner, J. M. (1962). *Growth at adolescence* (2nd ed.). Blackwell Scientific.

Toporek, R. L., & Daniels, J. (2018). *2018 update and expansion of the 2003 ACA Advocacy Competencies: Honoring the work of the past and contextualizing the present.* https://www.counseling.org/docs/default-source/competencies/aca -advocacy-competencies-updated-may-2020.pdf?sfvrsn=f410212c_4

Toporek, R. L., Lewis, J., & Crethar, H. C. (2009). Promoting systemic change through the Advocacy Competencies. In the special section on advocacy competencies. *Journal of Counseling and Development, 87,* 260–268. https://doi .org/10.1002/j.1556-6678.2009.tb00105.x

Turner, S. L., & Lapan, R. T. (2013). Promotion of career awareness, development, and school success in children and adolescents. In S. D. Brown & R. W. Lent (Eds.), *27 career development and counseling: Putting theory and research to work* (2nd ed., pp. 539–564). Wiley.

Walsh, R., & Gibson, D. M. (2019). "What don't we do?": The experiences of school counseling directors in relation to leadership and job satisfaction. *Professional School Counseling, 23*(1), 1–11. https://doi.org/10.1177/2156759X19886823

Wang, M.-T., & Eccles, J. S. (2011). Adolescent behavioral, emotional, and cognitive engagement trajectories in school and their differential relations to educational success. *Journal of Research on Adolescence, 22*(1), 31–39. https://doi. org/10.1111/j.1532-7795.2011.00753.x

Wright, B. L., & Ford, D. Y. (2019). Remixing and reimagining the early childhood school experiences of brilliant Black boys. *Boyhood Studies: An Interdisciplinary Journal, 12*(1), 17. https://doi.org/10.3167/bhs.2019.120103

Wu-Rorrer, R. (2017). Filling the gap: Integrating STEM into career and technical education middle school programs: There is no single strategy for approaching STEM integration. *Technology & Engineering Teacher, 77*(2), 8–15. https://eric.ed.gov/?id=EJ1156370

Wu-Rorrer, R. (2019). Developing STEAM programs for middle school girls through community collaborations. *Technology and Engineering Teacher, 79*(3), 8–13. https://eric.ed.gov/?id=EJ1232282

Yang, J. L., Anyon, Y., Pauline, M., Wiley, K. E., Cash, D., Downing, B. J., Greer, E., Kelty, E., Morgan, T. L., & Pisciotta, L. (2018). "We have to educate every single student, not just the ones that look like us": Support service providers' beliefs about the root causes of the school-to-prison pipeline for youth of color. *Equity & Excellence in Education, 51*(3–4), 316–331. https://doi.org/10.1080/10665684.2018.1539358

Yuen, M., Gysbers, N., Chan, R. C., Lau, P. Y., & Shea, P. K. (2010). Talent development, work habits, and career exploration of Chinese middle-school adolescents: Development of the Career and Talent Development Self-Efficacy Scale. *High Ability Studies, 21*(1), 47–62. https://doi.org/10.1080/13598139.2010.488089

Ziomek-Daigle, J., Cavin, J., Diaz, J., Henderson, B., & Huguelet, A. (2019). Specialized services for students with intensive needs. In E. Goodman-Scott, J. Betters-Bubon, & P. Donohue (Eds.), *The school counselors' guide to multi-tiered systems of support* (pp. 163–188). Routledge.

CHAPTER 4

PREPARING STUDENTS FOR UNCERTAIN FUTURES

The Role of College Knowledge and Student Preferences for Receiving College and Career Information

Timothy A. Poynton
University of Massachusetts–Boston

Laura Owen
San Diego State University

ABSTRACT

The knowledge needed to successfully aspire to, plan for, and enroll in college is lacking for many high school students. While schools claim to address postsecondary opportunity gaps, evidence reveals increasing variability in how this occurs, exacerbating a widening chasm—with already-advantaged, mostly White and Asian, students gaining more college knowledge during their time in high school than first-generation, low income, and marginalized student groups. School counselors play a critical role in the dissemination of college and career information, especially for historically marginalized stu-

Equity-Based Career Development and Postsecondary Transitions, pages 83–107

dent groups. Students prefer to receive postsecondary information through one-on-one advising, yet high counselor to student ratios and competing demands for school counselor time often limit availability and access to these desired individualized student meetings, funneling students to the less preferred sources like the Internet, to inform their postsecondary decisions. We provide tangible, actionable direction for equity minded educators, college access, and higher education professionals.

Prior to the pandemic approximately 69% of high school graduates enrolled in college the Fall immediately following high school graduation, totaling approximately 2.2 million students (Hussar et al., 2020). Although high school graduation rates remained steady for the class of 2019–2020, direct high school to college enrollment fell 6.8% percent (National Student Clearinghouse Research Center, 2020). The disproportionate impact of COVID19 in communities of color revealed what many educators already knew—educational opportunity is interwoven with wealth and privilege (Hines et al., 2021). Disparities in access led to a 10.7% college enrollment decrease for students attending low-income high schools, compared to 4.6% for students enrolled in higher income schools (National Student Clearinghouse Research Center, 2020). Enrollment for students transitioning from high poverty schools fell by 11.4% versus 2.9% for low-poverty schools (National Student Clearinghouse Research Center, 2020). High minority schools saw an overall enrollment decline of 9.4%, while enrollment from low minority schools decreased by 4.8% (National Student Clearinghouse Research Center, 2020). High school graduates in 2020 who attended low income and high minority high schools submitted fewer college and FAFSA applications and early indicators warn these dramatic losses may be even greater for the high school class of 2021 (Goldman & Korn, 2020; Hines et al., 2021; Watson & Pananjady, 2020).

Racial disparities in college attendance have long been noted—fewer Black and Hispanic high school graduates attend college than their White and Asian classmates (Hussar et al., 2020). Further, approximately 56% of all college students are from families with parents or guardians who have not earned a bachelor's or higher degree (U.S. Department of Education, 2014), commonly referred to as first generation college students. Students who are not first generation college students are commonly referred to as continuing generation college students. First generation college students are more likely to come from families with lower socioeconomic status and identify as racial minorities—in fact, nearly 1 in 3 college students possess the intersecting identities of being both first generation college students and racial minorities (U.S. Department of Education, 2014). If you believe that education is a tool that can provide access to opportunities for lifelong social and financial success and stability, then you know how important access to information and college knowledge are (Arnold et al., 2020).

School counselors play a pivotal role in establishing a college going culture and preparing all students for postsecondary success by collaborating with stakeholders to combat racism and biases in the postsecondary readiness process (Bryan et al., 2009; Hines et al., 2021). We expect this chapter to provide helpful, actionable information you can use in your practice.

One way to improve equitable access to the opportunities a college education affords comes from providing information to support students and their families to aspire and get to college. This information is sometimes referred to as *college knowledge*. Conley (2007, 2010) introduced college knowledge as a critical construct in the college search, application, entry, retention, and graduation process, and research findings support the role college knowledge plays in successful transitions from high school to college (e.g., Roderick et al., 2009). Poynton et al. (2019) developed an instrument to measure college knowledge, dubbed the College Admissions Knowledge Evaluation (CAKE), and define college knowledge as "the discrete, factual knowledge students need to effectively aspire to, plan for, and enroll in college" (p. 98).

Researchers consistently find that students from disadvantaged high schools lack access to the information needed to adequately navigate important college and career decisions, leaving those searching for college information on their own to navigate their college path (Hoxby & Turner, 2013, 2015: Poynton et al., 2019). Providing college information and guidance does not require a lot of money, but it does demand human and social capital to ensure that all students have the resources needed to make informed college decisions (Owen et al., 2020; Owen & Westlund, 2016). Social and human capital play important roles in both access to information and connection to valuable sources of support (Mulhern, 2021; Owen et al., 2020; Robinson & Roksa, 2016).

College knowledge has been recognized as a form of both social and cultural capital. Origins of the terms social capital and cultural capital are generally attributed to Bourdieu (1986), who defined cultural capital as "a person's education (knowledge and intellectual skills) that provides advantage in achieving a higher status in society" (p. 55) and social capital as "actual and potential resources linked to the possession of a durable network of institutionalized relationships of mutual acquaintance and recognition" (p. 56). Similarly, Burton and Welsh (2015) defined social capital as the "resources that are accessible through social interactions and extended networks of social ties" (p. 3). Members of disadvantaged groups tend to have few of these "valuable bridging ties" (Burton & Welsh, 2015, p. 3) due to social isolation and multiple other forms of exclusion (Krivo et al., 2013; Tigges et al., 1998; Wilson, 1987). While social and cultural capital are related, the slight change in emphasis among the terms is a useful and important distinction. St. John et al. (2015) placed their definition of college knowledge explicitly within the realm of cultural capital, defining college knowledge as "a form of cultural capital students develop as they learn about and gain experience with navigating educational pathways" (p. 100).

COLLEGE KNOWLEDGE RESEARCH AND IMPLICATIONS FOR EQUITY-FOCUSED PRACTICE

The CAKE is the only known measure of college knowledge in the peer-reviewed literature and demonstrates good initial reliability and validity characteristics. As described in Poynton et al. (2019), the CAKE was developed as a knowledge-based assessment with input from a variety of experts in the college-going process—public and private high school counselors, a TRIO program administrator, an admissions counselor, and an administrator of enrollment management at a higher education institution. This diverse group of experts reviewed all of the potential CAKE items—essentially multiple choice and true/false test items—to assess the relevance and importance of each item and identify any areas that were missing. This expert review process yielded a total of 76 items, which were then administered to more than 500 graduating high school seniors late in the year (Poynton et al., 2019). Overall, the findings of this research were frankly shocking. The average score on the full version of the CAKE was 42% correct—clearly, a failing grade in any classroom. The data from these 500+ students was used to run several analyses to assess the psychometric properties of the CAKE. You can read the details of the factor analyses (exploratory and confirmatory), item response theory (IRT), and differential item functioning (DIF) analyses in Poynton et al. (2019), but I'll summarize briefly. Of the 76 original items on the CAKE, 42 were supported by all of the psychometric analyses and judged to be "good" items. A good item, in this context, is an item that can discriminate between people who know the answer and people who do not. For example, items that are too easy, too hard, and not correlated with the total CAKE scores were dropped from the 42 item, psychometrically sound version of the CAKE. Several of the items dropped from the full CAKE assessment were too hard for the high school seniors. In other words, the majority of the seniors did not have basic information and facts that the expert reviewers deemed to be important when transitioning from high school to college. To assess the fairness of the 42 psychometrically supported CAKE, differential item functioning analyses were conducted to compare students who identified as White and all other ethnicities, and indicated one item functioned differently (Poynton et al., 2019). Additional, unpublished analyses of CAKE data by race indicates that Asian or Pacific Islander students scored highest, followed by Latino/a students, then White students, then African American students.

However, CAKE scores varied tremendously by school as well—and without a randomized control trial, attributing any observed differences in college knowledge to a single variable (i.e., race, ethnicity, socioeconomic status, gender) is not warranted.

Factor analyses of the CAKE revealed and supported two factors—the knowledge of college life (KCL) factor, and the admissions procedures and financial aid (APFA) factor. The KCL factor consists of 15 items related to how colleges are structured and operate, with an emphasis on things that are different in high school and college such as how syllabi are used, where to get help with academics in college, class attendance, and how the curriculum is structured. The APFA factor consists of 27 items related to how colleges make admissions decisions, typical admission-related processes, and financial aid terms and concepts. The graduating high school seniors in our sample evidenced more KCL than APFA knowledge, getting approximately 65% of the KCL items correct and 43% of the APFA items correct.

If you want to use the CAKE in your own work, please keep this in mind—just because an item was not deemed to be "good" by the psychometric analyses does not mean it is not useful or related to important information. For example, one of the items dropped from the psychometrically supported version of the cake was a true/false question, "Community colleges always cost less to attend than 4 year colleges." The correct answer is false, but only 15% of students recognized this. Fact is that, after including scholarships from 4-year colleges, community college can be more expensive for some students—particularly those who have academic achievement levels above the average for the 4-year college they applied to. For first generation students, not knowing this may lead to undermatching (Nagaoka et al., 2016), as they may not even consider more selective colleges because they feel like the cost is prohibitive. We would therefore encourage you to review all of the CAKE items if you are interested in explicitly assessing college knowledge in your own practice and/or research.

While the Poynton et al. (2019) study focused on describing the development and initial validation of the CAKE using data from high school seniors, schools that participated in the study were also asked to collect data from younger students who had not yet participated in the school's formal college-going programs and services. These younger students were 9th or 10th grade students, and the grade level selected for participation in the study was selected by a school counselor at the school. The initial goal of collecting this data was to help with establishing the incremental validity of the CAKE, as students not yet exposed to a school's college-going programs and services should evidence less college knowledge than the graduating high school seniors who had accumulated all of the college knowledge they were likely to gain from their high school experience. However, in looking at the data, what struck us most was the inequality in students' measured

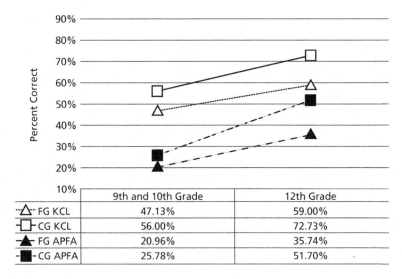

	9th and 10th Grade	12th Grade
··△·· FG KCL	47.13%	59.00%
─□─ CG KCL	56.00%	72.73%
─▲─ FG APFA	20.96%	35.74%
─■─ CG APFA	25.78%	51.70%

Figure 4.1 Percent of KCL and APFA items correctly answered by generation status across grade levels, from Poynton et al. (2021). *Note:* FG = first generation, CG = continuing generation.

college knowledge—first generation students not only evidenced less college knowledge than continuing generation students, but the gap actually widens as students approach high school graduation, as depicted in Figure 4.1. If we believe that public schools are places that can "level the playing field" for disadvantaged young people by addressing the many inequities and inequalities we know exist, this leveling function does not appear to be happening in the college knowledge domain. The data represented in Figure 4.1 indicate that, at least for the schools in our sample, the college-going programs and services further advantage the already-advantaged students and are not being provided in an equitable fashion, leading to inequality in students' measured college knowledge (Poynton et al., 2021).

Areas of Focus to Address the College Knowledge Gap

To provide clarity and detail from our research findings to promote equity-focused school counseling practice, the specific items from the CAKE evidencing the largest gaps between first and continuing generation students will be elaborated below. Remember, we administered the CAKE to graduating high school seniors near the end of their senior year—after the college application process was completed for the vast majority of students and all of the college knowledge they were going to have in making college-related decisions had already been acquired. Disconcertingly, of all 76 CAKE items, only two were answered correctly by first generation students more frequently than continuing generation students (3% and 1%). First generation students answered *every single* psychometrically supported item correct less often than continuing generation students. We hope that detailing the CAKE items here with the largest discrepancy between first and continuing generation students can help you promote equity in the provision of your college-going programs and services, and ultimately col lege knowledge equality.

Knowledge of College Life

The items below are from the KCL subscale of the CAKE, and therefore are among the 42 psychometrically supported CAKE items. The items in this subscale with the largest discrepancy between first and continuing generation students are described below.

High school transcript.   Two items assessed student knowledge related to the importance of the high school transcript as a piece of the college application. The first item asked of students is: "When reviewing your high school transcript, college admission offices are . . ."; with the correct answer being "all of the above." The response options were: "looking to see if you took the most challenging courses available," "assessing your performance in high school over time," and "ensuring you have taken the required courses to satisfy their admission requirements." Seventy three percent of continuing generation students answered "all of the above" correctly, while 53% of first generation students did so. While this item might conceptually fit better under the APFA subscale, the factor analyses indicated it fit better in the KCL subscale—one of the few items to not fit well both conceptually and statistically. However, it is the item on the KCL subscale with the largest discrepancy between first and continuing generation students. The observed 20% gap in knowledge of this item was just under a 16% gap earlier in high school (9th or 10th grade).

The second item assessing knowledge related to the transcript asked students to identify "the piece of your college application that has the most impact for admission counselors when deciding whether or not to admit you is." Half of the continuing generation students correctly answered "high school transcript," compared to 33% of first generation students. Among freshmen and sophomores, 31% of continuing generation students correctly answered, while 23% of first generation students did so. Why is this kind of knowledge about high school transcripts important in equity-focused school counseling practice? Because knowing what college admissions offices look for might help young people choose courses in high school that challenge them to the best of their ability, and perhaps help them realize that grades in all of their classes across their high school career matter to colleges when they make admissions decisions. These data demonstrate continuing generation students are more likely to have this knowledge than first generation students.

Calendar system. Three items assessed students' knowledge of the most common calendar systems used by colleges—semester, trimester, or quarter. While the item assessing the semester system was not psychometrically supported, the items related to the quarter and trimester systems evidenced large gaps between first and continuing generation students—18% and 17% respectively. Earlier in students' high school career, the gaps were 12% to 15%—indicating that the gap not only persists but widens a little. Why is knowing the varied calendar systems colleges employ important in equity-focused school counseling practice? Because the calendar system a college uses dictates when classes are in and out of session and can have a substantial impact on when breaks occur. For example, if a student plans on working over breaks, they may not realize how the different calendar systems impact when breaks actually occur, and they can differ substantially from the "traditional" times. Most colleges follow the semester system but knowing that other options exist at some colleges enhances overall knowledge of the options that exist.

Changing majors. A true/false item assessed students' knowledge of how changing majors works at most colleges. "Once you decide on a major in college, it is unlikely you will be able to change it" was the original item. Eighty four percent of continuing generation students selected the correct answer, compared to 67% of first generation students. The gap between first and continuing generation students was only 8% early in students' high school experience but grows to 17% as they approach graduation. Nearly 1 in 3 first generation students failed to recognize that changing majors is actually a fairly common occurrence. While the act of changing majors may be easy, the consequences can be challenging—changing majors can lead to delays in on-time graduation, costing both time and money first generation students so often do not have. Coincidentally, approximately 1 in 3 college students with a declared major change their major at least once, with 10% of all college students changing their major more than once (U.S. Department of Education, 2017). How many 18 year old college freshmen really have enough information about themselves and various occupations to make a truly informed decision about which major is best for them? We would argue not many. From a career development perspective, we view a student changing their major as a form of career exploration. Unfortunately, most colleges are not structured to facilitate very much exploration before it has the potential to impact on-time graduation—particularly in STEM fields, where majors typically require more credits than those in liberal arts or social sciences. With that said, knowing that changing majors is fairly common can potentially help students consider making such a change sooner in their college career, minimizing the potential for negative effects.

Core and major requirements.   One item assessed student knowledge of college core curriculum requirements by asking the following true/false question: "Typically, colleges have a set of course requirements everyone takes regardless of your major." Eighty percent of continuing generation students answered this correctly, compared to 67% of first generation students. The gap between first and continuing generation students was just under 10% for freshmen/sophomores, widening slightly as students neared the end of high school. Relatedly, a second item was asked to see if students knew how many of their classes would be in their major. While the majority of students taking the CAKE did recognize that some classes would be core curriculum classes, only 7% of students realized that most college majors consume less than half of the credits required to graduate (first and continuing generation students scored equally on this item). While it is true that STEM majors often require more credits in the major than other majors, they still consume only about half of the credits required to earn a bachelor's degree—leaving at least half of the classes a student takes counting towards a minor, core curriculum requirements, and/or free electives. Understanding that many of the classes a student takes in college are not in their major is important to helping them frame their studies and expectations appropriately.

Class size.   To assess if students recognize how class sizes can be very different from what they experienced in high school, students were asked the following question: "While most high school classes have less than 30 students, college classes can have . . ."; with response options ranging from less than 10 to more than a hundred and an "all of the above" option. Sixty eight percent of continuing generation students correctly answered "all of the above," while 56% of first generation students correctly answered. Freshmen and sophomore first generation students answered this correctly 44% of the time, compared to 55% of continuing generation freshman and sophomores, indicating the gap remains consistent over time. Of course, how a college structures its offerings in terms of class size can be one of its defining features for prospective students—there are some colleges with no classes larger than 30, for example—but generally speaking, class sizes in college are much more variable than they are in high school. Knowing this can be helpful as students consider which colleges to apply to and attend. For example, if the thought of taking a 300 student lecture is not appealing, the student should consider looking at class size and the structure of a college's offerings when deciding whether or not to submit an application there.

Admissions Procedures and Financial Aid

The items below are from the APFA subscale of the CAKE. Twelve of the 27 APFA items will be reviewed here, as differences among these items between first and continuing generation students ranged from a 17% difference to a whopping 27% difference. While one could argue that admissions and financial aid policies and procedures vary over time—making what a parent knows about them inconsequential to their children—the data we obtained does not support such an argument, given the magnitude of the observed differences between continuing and first generation students.

Early action/early decision. Two similarly structured CAKE items assessed knowledge of early action and early decision admission policies, with continuing generation students answering the items correctly 27% and 22% more often than first generation students. Most freshmen and sophomores did not know the correct answers to these items, but the gap between first and continuing generation students was only about 10%. Further examination of the graduating seniors' data indicates that most of the students who got one of the items correct got both incorrect (71%, to be precise), suggesting that most of them did not understand both policies, or the important difference between them. Part of the reason for such a large gap between first and continuing generation students in knowledge of these policies may be that applying early decision is a privilege afforded to students and families for whom cost is not an issue. The key difference between early action and early decision is in the binding nature of the early decision agreement—if you apply to a school as an early decision applicant and are accepted, you are agreeing to attend that school and decline any offers from other schools (early action is not binding, but you still get an answer from the admissions office sooner). The CAKE contained an item assessing knowledge of the only reason students can be released from an early decision agreement—ability to pay the offered price. Unsurprisingly, there was a 23% gap between first and continuing generation students who correctly answered this item. With more and more colleges opting to offer early decision admission policies, students and families need to know the implications, benefits, and problems. From an equity-based counseling perspective, it is hard to advocate for having students apply early decision, given the possible financial implications. On the other hand, there is no stronger way to demonstrate interest than to apply early decision, as in effect you are telling the college "I want to attend your college, and no other college."

Demonstrated interest. One item asked students, "What is demonstrated interest?" Fifty three percent of continuing generation students correctly answered, "When you contact a college or university to gain more information about them," while 33% of first generation students answered correctly. In other words, not only do 1 in 3 first generation students not know what demonstrated interest is or how they might show a college they are truly interested in them and that they are not just a "safety school" on their list, these students also do not know that demonstrated interest is a non-academic factor some colleges use when making admissions decisions. Let me reiterate that last point . . . demonstrating interest can be the difference between getting admitted or denied at a college. For students who are not aware of this, they may not realize that not being able to afford to go visit campus, for example, might weigh against them in the college's decision-making about whether or not to admit them. We have heard several stories over the years of admission decisions that do not seem to make sense, where ultra-qualified applicants are rejected for seemingly no good reason. There is a good chance at least part of the reason may be that the applicant did not demonstrate interest. For example, we heard of one student who was not admitted to a good but not overly selective college but was accepted at the Massachusetts Institute of Technology—one of the most selective colleges in the country. His sister attended a less selective college than MIT, and he visited her several times, so he did not feel like he needed to participate in an admission-oriented campus tour or exert much effort in learning about the college because he felt he had a good idea from his own experience on the campus, and from his sister. Had he known that demonstrated interest was a factor they considered when making admission decisions, maybe he would have reconsidered not doing that campus tour.

If you are working with a student who is very interested in a college they cannot afford to visit before submitting an application, be sure to find out if the college uses demonstrated interest as a factor in their decision-making process. You can always ask an admissions counselor, or you can see if the college participates in the voluntary Common Data Set (CDS) initiative (www.commondataset.org). The easiest way to see if a college participates in the CDS initiative is to conduct a web search for "common data set" with the college's name (e.g., "common data set Northeastern University," without quotes). You will find information about how important various academic and nonacademic factors are to the college when they make admissions decisions in Section C7 of the report, with "level of applicant's interest" listed at the very bottom of the table. You might be surprised to find that quite a few colleges consider demonstrated interest to be just as important as some of the academic factors.

Admission rate/selectivity. One item assessed students' knowledge of the definition of the admission rate, which is the percentage of students who are admitted to a college of all those who applied. Continuing generation students correctly answered this item 66% of the time, while first generation students were correct 44% of the time. The gap between first and continuing 9th and 10th grade students on this item was 19%, with 36% of first generation students answering correctly compared to 55% of continuing generation students. The admission rate describes a college's selectivity and is an important (albeit obtuse) metric students and families can use to gauge how successful they might be in gaining admission to a college. Given all the hype around college admissions, some students and families may find it surprising that most colleges accept the vast majority of the students who apply. According to the IPEDS Data Center (National Center for Education Statistics, 2020), colleges that primarily offer bachelor's or higher degrees admit, on average, 67% of their first-time, full-time freshmen. Further, 3 out of 4 colleges admit more than half (56%) of their applicants. Knowing what the admission rate for a school can help students and families "ballpark" their chances of admission, but it is not as helpful as speaking with a school counselor or one of the college's admission counselors to get a better sense of each individual's chances for success in the admission process. While there are highly selective colleges (e.g., Harvard, Yale, MIT, Stanford) where very few of the students who apply are admitted, the vast majority of colleges in the United States have odds weighted more in the applicant's favor—and we believe knowing this can provide a measure of comfort during what can be a stressful and anxiety-provoking time for students and families. While all students benefit from knowing this, communicating these kinds of facts to first generation students is particularly important.

Major specific admissions.   While admission policies vary tremendously from college to college, some have specific and more stringent requirements for competitive majors such as nursing. Relatedly, some colleges have you apply to a particular school or division within the college (e.g., engineering, health sciences, liberal arts, social science) where applications are reviewed in such a way that an applicant might qualify for admission in one school/division but not another—at the same college. To get a sense of students' knowledge of this, the following true/false item was posed: "Some universities may have different admission requirements based on a student's choice of intended major." While 73% of continuing generation students recognized this was true, only 51% of first generation students did. Among 9th and 10th grade students, first generation students correctly answered this item 40% of the time and continuing generation students answered correctly 56% of the time. While a college's admission counselors can be very helpful to students and families in learning about the requirements for competitive majors, schools, and divisions, the public-facing data available from IPEDS/College Navigator and tools like Naviance will not reflect such nuances. Students and families may need to work harder to gather the information needed at such colleges on their list.

Lifetime earnings.   While there are no guarantees that going to college will lead to higher-wage jobs than one might be able to obtain without a college degree, the available evidence suggests that going to college makes earning more money likely (Carnevale et al., 2011; Tamborini et al., 2015). To assess knowledge of this, one true/false item asserted "The amount of money people who have a college education earn across their lifetime is not enough to justify the expense of attending college." First generation students correctly answered false 30% of the time, while continuing generation students did so 51% of the time. The gap between 9th and 10th grade first and continuing generation students was half what it was among the graduating high school seniors, with 28% of first generation students answering this item correctly and 39% of continuing generation students did so. While estimates vary depending on the source, Carnevale et al. (2011) calculated the difference in earnings over a lifetime between people with a high school diploma and those with a bachelor's degree to be $964,000 (in 2007 to 2009). Tamborini et al. (2015) found more conservative but still substantial earnings differences based on education attainment. Their analyses also included gender, which unfortunately showed that women have lower lifetime earnings than men. Men with bachelor's degrees earn about $900,000 more than men with high school diplomas, but women with bachelor's degrees earn about $630,000 more than women with high school diplomas. So, to the original question asking if the cost of college is worth the time and money investment, the answer is yes—at least from a purely financial perspective. We would further argue that going to college also opens more employment opportunities, increasing the likelihood of finding not only better paying work, but satisfying, meaningful work as well.

Test optional admissions policy.   As we write, the world is currently in the midst of the COVID-19 pandemic. This has led many colleges to adopt a test optional admissions policy, given the dangers associated with in person administration of college admission tests such as the SAT and ACT. One item assessed knowledge of test optional admissions policies, which allow applicants to choose whether or not they submit college admission test scores—regardless of whether or not a student actually took one of the exams. While 66% of continuing generation students identified the correct answer, only 46% of first generation students did so. The observed gap between first generation and continuing generation students in the 9th and 10th grades doubled, with 34% and 44% (respectively) of the students answering this item correctly. It is important for all students, but first generation students in particular, to understand the implications of choosing whether or not to submit test scores. For example, some colleges will not require admission test scores to consider an applicant for admission, but the scores are required to qualify for institutional grants and scholarships—financial aid that often constitutes the majority of financial assistance students at private colleges receive.

CSS profile.   The College Scholarship Service (CSS) Profile is run by the College Board (same company that administers the SAT) to provide colleges with additional financial information beyond what the FAFSA requires about an applicant and their family to help determine how much institutional aid they may be eligible for. Two items assessed knowledge of the CSS Profile. One item assessed whether or not students knew what the CSS acronym represented; 42% of continuing generation students knew this, while 22% of first generation students did. The second item assessed if students knew what the CSS Profile was used for, and 33% of continuing generation students answered correctly compared to 24% of first generation students. A similar trend was observed among freshmen and sophomores; more continuing generation students knew the correct answer than first generation students for both the acronym (24% and 16% respectively) and the function (19% and 15% respectively) of the CSS Profile. About 200 mostly private colleges use the CSS Profile for students from the United States (see https://profile .collegeboard.org/profile/ppi/participatingInstitutions.aspx). Students applying to one of these colleges need to prepare for and anticipate that the CSS Profile is required. First generation students may need additional support completing both the FAFSA and the CSS Profile.

Superscoring. Superscoring of the SAT or ACT simply means that the college will accept the highest scores a student attained across all the times they took the SAT or the ACT. For example, if a student scores 500 in math and 550 in reading and writing when they took the SAT in the spring of their junior year, and a 550 in math and 500 in reading and writing when they took the test again in the fall of their senior year, the college would use the highest scores (550 in this case) for both the math, and the reading and writing sections. For the item assessing knowledge of the superscoring admissions policy, 45% of continuing generation students identified the correct answer, compared to 25% of first generation students. There was only a 5% gap between freshman and sophomores on this item (24% continuing generation and 19% first generation). While superscoring only applies to students who take a college entrance exam more than once, it is also important for equity-focused school counselors to understand how students qualify for fee waivers for both the SAT and ACT, and what the waivers include. For example, the College Board currently allows students who qualify for a fee waiver to take the SAT twice, unlimited sending of score reports to colleges, a free CSS Profile application, and an application fee waiver at participating colleges. The ACT offers similar benefits to those who qualify for the waiver, and the school counselor plays a critically important role in helping students and families access the fee waiver programs.

Items Not in a Factor

The items below did not meet all the statistical criteria for inclusion on the psychometrically supported 42 item version of the CAKE. Specifically, for these 4 particular items, they were each not included in the psychometrically supported version of the CAKE because the item performed poorly in the IRT analysis. As noted previously, just because an item was not supported by the psychometric analyses does not mean the knowledge assessed by the item is not relevant or important. The items below evidence large gaps (17% to 24%) between first and continuing generation students and are therefore important to consider from an equity-focused counseling perspective.

Retention rate.   The retention rate of a college describes the percentage of students who start in the fall as first-time, full-time freshmen and return to the college the following fall. We like to refer to this readily available statistic as the "freshmen satisfaction score" because it describes the number of freshmen who were satisfied with and supported by the college enough for them to return as sophomores. We believe the retention rate is under-utilized by most students and families when choosing where to apply and attend, and that considering the retention rate as part of the college search and selection process is critically important to making truly informed decisions. Continuing generation high school seniors identified the correct response to this item 41% of the time, compared to only 17% of first generation students. Continuing generation freshmen and sophomores correctly answered 21% of the time (20% increase), compared to 12% of first generation students (5% increase), suggesting that first generation students are much less likely to acquire knowledge of what the retention rate is than continuing generation students.

Thinking about the retention rate in context is important in equity-focused college counseling. Generally speaking, as selectivity increases, so too does a college's retention rate. The so-called highly selective ivy league colleges like Harvard and Yale have retention rates approaching 100%. For students who are applying to less selective colleges, however, the retention rate can be highly variable—and therefore an important piece of fact-based information to consider in the college choice process. We recommend students use the retention rate as a data point (along with 4 and 6 year graduation rates) to assess how well the college supports its students through the first year and ultimately to graduation. We do not recommend students base their decisions entirely on retention (or graduation) rates, but we do recommend students and families gather more information about colleges they are interested in that have lower retention rates than other colleges on your list. In our experience, admissions counselors are aware of their retention rates and can provide insight into why students choose to leave and perhaps even how to prevent such an outcome, but they are not likely to bring up their college's retention rate unless asked.

Deferred decisions.   Colleges "defer" making an admission decision on an application when they feel like they need more information. Sometimes students who apply early action or early decision will be deferred to the regular admission pool, and other times the college may want to wait for more grades from senior year classes before making a decision, for example. Half of the continuing generation seniors (50%) answered this item correctly, compared to 26% of first generation students. Among freshmen and sophomores, continuing generation students answered correctly 30% of the time, compared to 22% of the time for first generation students. When preparing students and families to receive admission decisions from the colleges they applied to, we believe it is important to also include deferred admission decisions as one of the possible outcomes in addition to acceptance, rejection, or being placed on a waitlist.

AP course credit in college. One item assessed student knowledge of the way colleges award credit for AP classes, and asked students to respond with true or false to the following statement: "Colleges are required to give you academic credits for Advanced Placement (AP) classes if you scored higher than 3 on the AP exam." Continuing generation seniors correctly responded with "false" 48% of the time, while only 26% of first generation seniors did so. Among freshmen and sophomores, 26% of continuing generation students answered correctly, compared to 17% of first generation students. While knowing how colleges award credit for AP classes only applies to those students who actually take an AP class, knowing that individual colleges determine what level of AP exam performance is required when deciding whether or not to award credit for AP classes can help students appropriately plan for taking AP classes, and exploring the policies for earning credit during the college search and selection. While it is true that many colleges require a minimum score of 3 on an AP exam to qualify for college credit, the required minimum score can vary for different subjects. For example, a score of 3 on the Spanish Language AP exam may qualify a student for credit for the first-level Spanish course at the college, while a score of 4 qualifies for the second level Spanish course.

High school profile. A high school's profile is a part of most college applications, and most often provided to a college by the school and not by the applicant. One item assessed whether or not students understood what information the high school profile provided to admissions reviewers at colleges. The item asked, "Colleges may request your high school's profile to help them...": with "understand the course offerings in the student's high school," "assess how rigorous the student's high school course of study was," "understand how grades are calculated in the school," and "all of the above" as response options. Graduating high school seniors answered this item correctly 67% of the time, compared to 50% of first generation students. Among freshmen and sophomores, 57% of continuing generation students answered correctly, compared to 42% of first generation students. While we are certain equity-focused school counselors strive to ensure all of their students are taking the most rigorous courses available to them, this is particularly important for first generation students early in their high school career who, according to our findings, are not likely to recognize the impact the courses they choose have on their college applications years down the road.

Once you have identified the college knowledge gaps for your students, you must plan to intentionally address these gaps and lack of knowledge. To do this well, it will require a solid understanding of your student's preferences for receiving college and career information.

IMPLICATIONS FOR EQUITY-FOCUSED PRACTICE

The Gallup-Strada Education Network conducted one of the largest studies to date on preferences for college and career information and advice (Gallup Inc., 2017). To gain a better understanding of information sources, Gallup and Strada's Education Consumer Pulse surveyed more than 22,000 18 to 65 year-old U.S. residents to identify where they received advice about choosing a college major and the perceived helpfulness of the advice given. The researchers broke the responses down into four broad categories of sources:

- formal sources (*high school and college counselors, media, Internet and print*),
- informal social networks (*family, friends and community leaders*),
- informal school-based networks (*high school teachers, high school coaches, college faculty, or miscellaneous staff*), and
- informal work-based sources (*employers, coworkers, people with experience in the field, and military.* (Gallup Inc., 2017, p. 4)

Key findings from the Gallup Strada Survey (Gallup Inc., 2017) included:

1. Most people receive advice about their major from informal social network sources like family members and friends.
2. First generation college students and students pursuing a 2-year degree are less likely than others to get advice about their major from their informal social network.
3. Older enrollees are more likely than younger enrollees to consult work-based sources of advice about their college major.
4. Informal work-based sources of advice are rated as the most helpful, and the consumers mentioning them would be less likely to choose another major if they had to start over.
5. First generation students, Blacks and Hispanics, rate all sources of advice highly and most regard formal sources of advice as helpful. But, like other groups, they give the highest ratings to informal work-based sources. (p. 5)

Researchers concluded that "access to work-based experiences could be particularly beneficial for first-generation, Black and Hispanic students, who may have less access to professional guidance and expertise in their social networks, but regard advice from work-based sources as especially helpful" (Gallup Inc., 2017, p. 5). High school students under the age of 18 were not included in the Gallup Strada survey sample and many of the adults surveyed were forced to rely on memories of how they felt about advice received many years previously (Owen et al., 2020), yet after the release of the Gallup/Strada survey results, researchers concluded that the "traditional model of advising" should be refined for first-generation, Black and Hispanic students and this could be accomplished by increasing students' exposure to informal work-related experiences (Gallup Inc., 2017).

The Gallup Strada survey did not seek to understand, from a high school student's perspective, how they prefer to receive college information and from whom they prefer to receive advice (Owen et al., 2020). Building on the findings from the Gallup-Strada survey, we asked high school aged students similar questions to understand who they prefer to receive college information from, and how they prefer to receive it. An online survey was administered to a random sample of 64,717 students from the 107,868 12th-grade students who had registered to take the ACT in February 2018. Sixty percent of 12th graders were randomly selected to participate in the survey, and we had a 4.5% response rate. A total of 2,901 high school seniors (70% female; 30% male) who took the ACT test in February of 2018 participated (Owen et al., 2020). We wanted to understand:

1. How helpful have various people and resources been in helping high school students think about a major/field of study?
2. Who do high school students prefer to receive college and career information from?
3. How do high school students prefer to receive college and career information?

The findings of our study both confirmed and challenged some of the research investigating sources of and preferences for receiving college and career information and provided insight into where and how high school seniors acquire such information and how helpful it was perceived to be (Owen et al., 2020). Our first research question assessed how helpful various interpersonal and media-based sources of information were in helping students decide on a field of study to pursue in college and revealed that parents and friends were the most helpful and employers were among the least helpful (Owen et al., 2020). The perceived helpfulness of parents increased in lock-step fashion with their education levels, while the helpfulness of high school counselors decreased in a similar, lock-step manner.

Similarly, the perceived helpfulness of high school counselors increased as parent income levels decreased. These findings point to school counselors serving as a "leveling agent" for first generation and low-income students (Owen et al., 2020).

The second research question examined the interpersonal information sources students would prefer to receive college and career information from and indicates that formal networks—high school and admission counselors in particular—are the most preferred sources. This finding was even more pronounced for first- generation students and low-income students, confirming the important role and function counselors serve for those students (Bryan et al., 2011). Other major findings included:

- Parents with bachelor's and graduate degrees were perceived by students to be significantly more helpful than parents with some college or less, with perceived helpfulness ratings increasing in a linear fashion with parent education level.
- Admission counselors and high school counselors were more helpful to first-generation students than continuing generation students.
- Black students rated the helpfulness of each of the five sources higher than all other ethnicities, and these information sources were significantly more helpful to Black students than White students' college major decision-making.
- Hispanic and Asian students rated parents as significantly less helpful than Black and White students; and White students rated high school counselors as significantly less helpful than all other ethnicities.
- Black students most preferred to receive information from high school counselors more frequently than White students, and White students selected parents more frequently than ethnic minority students.
- Black students selected admission counselors as the most-preferred source more frequently than all other ethnicities.
- Students from the highest income bracket selected parents as the most helpful more frequently than students from lower income brackets.
- As parent education increased, students selected the high school counselor less often and parents more often as the most-preferred information source, and students with parents holding bachelor's or graduate degrees selected the admission counselor as their most-preferred source less often than students with parents who did not complete a bachelor's or graduate degree (Owen et al., 2020).

Finally, our third question found that students see the Internet as their most helpful source of college and career information and email and one on one conversations are the most preferred means of communicating college and career information (69% prefer email and 48% prefer one on one).

Although information is readily available on the Internet, it does not mean students have knowledge, access, or understanding of what is available or how to discriminate between accurate, helpful information versus harmful guidance on the Internet (Owen et al., 2020). While the Internet was rated to be a helpful source of information, it was among the least-preferred information sources, with interpersonal communication methods (email and one-on-one) being the most preferred.

Students need help determining which Internet resources are useful, accurate, and meet their needs. This finding was replicated in another study and upon further conversation with the students, they were utilizing email as a protective shield to help them sort out communication that they did not want to engage in (Owen, 2021). As a college and career counselor, this was somewhat alarming given the high rate of communication that higher ed institutions send out through email. Many students have missed key pieces of information because they were not opening their inbox. Understanding the ways in which students are engaging with technology is an important piece of the advising puzzle. We can educate college and career advising professionals on this common practice so that they can begin to help students understand how email is used by higher ed institutions. Also, we may be seeing another manifestation of relationships. Students prefer one on one contact, which makes complete sense given the complex yet personal nature of navigating the postsecondary pipeline. Students open email from someone they trust, just as they engage in conversations with someone who they find as knowledgeable, trustworthy, and accurate (Owen et al., 2020).

RECOMMENDATIONS

Having a trusted adult to rely on for postsecondary guidance is essential. However, assuming that anyone can provide this support or that all college and career advice is equal is not only misguided, but also dangerous. Researchers, practitioners, parents, and students have long noted that the postsecondary counseling and advising system was never designed to serve all students (Brown et al., 2017). We need not only call this out, but we must also review school policies and procedures and dismantle practices that lead to inequity and decreased opportunity (Owen, 2021).

- We need to guarantee a baseline set of skills, college knowledge and competency for any person who will be positioned as a postsecondary guide during these critical decision points.

- Standardizing the preparation of all professionals who provide college and career guidance is needed. From preservice training to ongoing professional development, the requisite college knowledge, skills, and aptitudes needed to support students as they navigate their college options should be central tenants of all training programs.
- COVID-19 has disproportionately impacted Black, Brown, and Indigenous students, exposing long-standing systemic, structural and institutional educational inequities. We must be intentional in our pandemic recovery to support the postsecondary journey of Black, Brown, and Indigenous students.
- New postsecondary advising and counseling models should embrace diverse perspectives, call out racist policies and practices and ensure substantive counseling and advising support is provided to students who have been marginalized, especially those who are attending high minority, low-income schools.
- Use intersectional understandings of college readiness to increase traditionally marginalized student's opportunities to finish high school and pursue a postsecondary education (Gray-Nicolas & Miranda, 2020)
- Given the especially critical role school counselors play in helping students attending high minority, high poverty schools, professional development is needed to empower school counselors to challenge the inequities built into the educational system, to call out the policies and practices that perpetuate inequality and the deficit lens that educators often see Black, Brown, and Indigenous children and families through (Owen, 2021).
- We should be explicit in providing college knowledge to students and their parents, particularly for first generation students to close the college knowledge gap that exists between first and continuing generation students. Explicitly providing college knowledge can happen formally with inclusion in college-going programming, and more informally as opportunities present themselves through natural interactions with students and families.

CONCLUSION

Schools are in the business of helping young people acquire the knowledge and skills they need for success later in life. College knowledge, we believe, provides a foundation upon which to make informed decisions about life after high school—and is a topic that has received little meaningful attention from the K–12 education community. The research described in this chapter provides tangible ideas and techniques that can help all educators working with high school students—teachers, counselors, administrators, college access professionals, and college and career advisors—equitably provide college and career related information, including but not limited to college knowledge. The research described in this chapter also demonstrates that if schools are to be places to correct systemic inequalities, there is still much work to be done in the realm of college knowledge and career information. If you would like to obtain a copy of the CAKE instrument, you can email the first author or fill out a form at http://www.collegesanity.com/request/

DISCUSSION QUESTIONS

1. Marginalized student groups rely heavily on school counselors for college and career advice, yet many schools do not provide sufficient access to postsecondary counseling activities. How will you ensure that Black, Brown, Indigenous, and other marginalized student groups are prioritized in the delivery of information and access to their school counselor?
2. John is a practicing school counselor dedicated to serving all students on his caseload. Frequently John skips professional development opportunities to meet with his students. While prioritizing their needs, John has shortchanged his own college and career knowledge growth and his advising methods are now outdated, and John lacks an understanding of equity centered practice. What recommendations would you give John to strengthen his own college and career knowledge?

ACTIVITIES

1. Take the College Admissions Knowledge Evaluation (CAKE) at http://www.collegesanity.com/college-knowledge/
   a. Note your score, and reflect on your experience taking this interactive version of the CAKE.
   b. Thinking about your current or intended place of work, how do you think students and/or families might respond to taking the CAKE?
   c. How will you seek out professional development opportunities centered in equity based college and career advising?
2. Administer a school wide CAKE assessment. You can get the CAKE by emailing Tim.Poynton@umb.edu or filling out a short form at http://www.collegesanity.com/request/
   a. Outline the steps you will take to administer the assessment.

    b. How will you share CAKE results with administrators, teachers, students, and parents?

    c. Describe the steps you will build in to ensure that the CAKE informs your comprehensive school counseling program.

AUTHOR NOTE

Poynton ORCID https://orcid.org/0000-0003-1951-0054
Laura Owen ORCID https://orcid.org/0000-0002-2329-860X

We have no known conflict of interest to disclose. Correspondence concerning this article should be addressed to Timothy Poynton, Department of Counseling and School Psychology, College of Education and Human Development, University of Massachusetts-Boston, Boston, MA 02125.

REFERENCES

Arnold, K., Lewis, J., & Owen, L. (2020). Inside the black box of text-message college advising. *Journal of College Access 5*(2), 52–80.

Bourdieu, P. (1986). The forms of capital. In J. Richardson (Ed.), *Handbook of theory and research for the sociology of education* (pp. 46–58). Greenwood.

Brown, J., Hatch, T., Holcomb-McCoy, C., Martin, P., Mcleod, J., Owen, L., & Savitz-Romer, M. (2017). *The state of school counseling: Revisiting the path forward.* The National Consortium for School Counseling and Postsecondary Success.

Bryan, J., Holcomb-McCoy, C., Moore-Thomas, C., & Day-Vines, N. (2009). Who sees the school counselor for college information? A national study. *Professional School Counseling, 12*(4), 280–291. https://doi.org/10.1177/2156759X0901200401

Bryan, J., Moore-Thomas, C., Day-Vines, N. L., & Holcomb-McCoy, C. (2011). School counselors as social capital: The effects of high school college counseling on college application rates [Research report]. *Journal of Counseling and Development, 89*(2), 190–199. http://aca.metapress.com/link.asp?id=ck4h078 737t137t5

Burton, L. M., & Welsh, W. (2015). *Inequality and opportunity: The role of exclusion, social capital, and generic social processes in upward mobility.* https://wtgrantfoundation .org/library/uploads/2016/01/Inequality-and-Opportunity-Burton-and-Welsh -William-T.-Grant-Foundation.pdf

Carnevale, A. P., Rose, S. J., & Cheah, B. (2011). *The college payoff: Education, occupations, and lifetime earnings.* https://www2.ed.gov/policy/highered/reg/ hearulemaking/2011/collegepayoff.pdf

Castleman, B., Owen, L., & Page, L. (2015). Stay late or start early? Experimental evidence on the benefits of college matriculation support from high schools versus colleges. *Economics of Education Review, 47,* 168–179. https://doi.org/10 .1016/j.econedurev.2015.05.010

Conley, D. T. (2007). *Redefining college readiness, Volume 3*. Educational Policy Improvement Center.

Conley, D. T. (2010). *College and career ready: Helping all students succeed beyond high school*. Jossey-Bass.

Gallup, Inc. (2017). *Major influence: Where students get valued advice on what to study in college*. https://news.gallup.com/reports/219236/major-influence-students-advice-study.aspx

Goldman, M., & Korn, M. (2020, November 9). College-admissions season was already stressful: Pandemic made it chaotic. *Wall Street Journal*. https://www.wsj.com/articles/college-admissions-season-was-already-stressful-pandemic-made-it-chaotic-11604917801

Gray-Nicolas, N. M., & Miranda, C. P. (2020). Intersectional understandings of on-time high school graduation and college readiness for traditionally marginalized high school students. *Journal of School Leadership*, *30*(5), 424–443. https://doi.org/10.1177/1052684619884252

Hines, E., Harris, P., Mayes, R., & Owen, L. (2021). College and career readiness for students of color: Using an antiracist ecological framework. In C. Holcomb-McCoy (Ed), *Antiracist counseling in schools and communities* (pp. 81–101). American Counseling Association.

Hoxby, C., & Turner, S. (2013). Expanding college opportunities: Intervention yields strong returns for low-income high-achievers. *Education Next*, *13*(4), 66–73.

Hoxby, C., & Turner, S. (2015). What high-achieving low-income students know about college. *American Economic Review*, *105*(5), 514–517. https://doi.org/10.1257/aer.p20151027

Hussar, B., Zhang, J., Hein, S., Wang, K., Roberts, A., Cui, J., Smith, M., Bullock Mann, F., Barmer, A., & Dilig, R. (2020). *The condition of education 2020* (NCES 2020-144). National Center for Education Statistics. https://nces.ed.gov/pubsearch/pubsinfo.asp?pubid=2020144

Krivo, L., Washington, H., Peterson, R., Browning, C., Calder, C., & Kwan, M. (2013). Social isolation of disadvantage and advantage: The reproduction of inequality in urban space. *Social Forces*, *92*(1), 141–164. https://doi.org/10.1093/sf/sot043

Mulhern, C. (2021). Changing college choices with personalized admissions information at scale: Evidence on naviance. *Journal of Labor Economics*, *39*(1), 219–262. https://doi.org/10.1086/708839

Nagaoka, J., Holsapple, M. A., & Roderick, M. (2016). The college match indicator: Linking research to practice. In A. Kelly, J. Howell, C. Sattin-Bajaj, (Eds), *Matching students to opportunity: Expanding college choice, access, and quality* (pp. 15–32). Harvard Education Press

National Center for Education Statistics. (2020). *Integrated postsecondary education data system (IPEDS)*. https://nces.ed.gov/ipeds/datacenter

National Student Clearinghouse Research Center. (2020). *2020 high school benchmarks with covid-19 special analysis: National college progression rates*. https://nscresearchcenter.org/wp-content/uploads/2020_HSBenchmarksReport.pdf

Owen, L. (2021). *Got college and career information? It's complicated*. https://leadershipblog.act.org/2021/03/college-and-career-information-laura-owen.html

Owen, L., Poynton, T., & Moore, R. (2020). Student preferences for college and career information. *Journal of College Access 5*(1), 67–100. https://scholarworks.wmich.edu/jca/vol5/iss1/7

Owen, L., & Westlund, E. (2016). Increasing college opportunity: School counselors and FAFSA completion. *Journal of College Access 2*(1), 7–26. https://scholarworks.wmich.edu/jca/vol2/iss1/3/

Poynton, T. A., Ruiz, B., & Lapan, R. T. (2019). Development and validation of the college admissions knowledge evaluation. *Professional School Counseling, 22*(1a), 98–103. https://doi.org/10.1177/2156759X19834441

Poynton, T. A., Lapan, R. T., & Schuyler, S. W. (2021). Reducing inequality in high school students' college knowledge: The role of school counselors. *Professional School Counseling, 24*(1b), 1–9. https://doi.org/10.1177/2156759X211011894

Robinson, K., & Roksa, J. (2016). Counselors, information, and high school college-going culture: Inequalities in the college application process. *Research in Higher Education, 57*(7), 845–868. https://doi.org/10.1007/s11162-016-9406-2

Roderick, M., Nagaoka, J., & Coca, V. (2009). Potholes on the road to college: High school effects in shaping urban students' participation in college application, four-year college enrollment, and college match. *Sociology of Education, 84*(3), 178–211. https://doi.org/10.1177/0038040711411280

St. John, E. P., Masse, J. C., Lijana, K. C., & Bigelow, V. M. (2015). *Left behind: Urban high schools and the failure of market reform.* Johns Hopkins University Press.

Tamborini, C. R., ChangHwan, K., & Sakamoto, A. (2015). Education and lifetime earnings in the United States. *Demography, 52*(4), 1383–1407. https://dx.doi.org/10.1007/s13524-015-0407-0

Tigges, L. M., Browne, I., & Green, G. P. (1998). Social isolation of the urban poor: Race, class, and neighborhood effects on social resources. *The Sociological Quarterly 39*, 53–77. https://doi.org/10.1111/j.1533-8525.1998.tb02349.x

U.S. Department of Education. (2014). *Web tables: Profile of undergraduate students: 2011–12* (Report No. NCES 2015-167). https://nces.ed.gov/pubs2015/2015167.pdf

U.S. Department of Education. (2017). *Beginning college students who change their majors within 3 years of college enrollment.* https://nces.ed.gov/pubs2018/2018434.pdf

Watson, A., & Pananjady, K. (2020). College financial aid applications down 16% this school year. *CT Mirror.* https://ctmirror.org/2020/12/11/college-financial-aid-applications-down-16-this-school-year/

Wilson, W. J. (1987). *The truly disadvantaged: The inner city, the underclass, and public policy.* University of Chicago Press.

CHAPTER 5

USING EQUITY-FOCUSED SCHOOL–FAMILY–COMMUNITY PARTNERSHIPS TO ENHANCE CAREER DEVELOPMENT AND POSTSECONDARY TRANSITIONS FOR STUDENTS OF COLOR

Mary Edwin
University of Missouri–St. Louis

Latoya Haynes-Thoby
University of Florida

Julia Bryan
The Pennsylvania State University

Equity-Based Career Development and Postsecondary Transitions, pages 109–135
Copyright © 2022 by Information Age Publishing
www.infoagepub.com
109

ABSTRACT

School–family–community partnerships are collaborative initiatives between various school, family, and community stakeholders that are focused on creating access and equity for PK–12 students, especially students from marginalized backgrounds, like students of color or students from low-income homes. Equity-focused partnerships build strength and resilience in students; support their college-career, academic, and social-emotional outcomes; and close opportunity gaps that hinder their college and career access (Bryan & Henry, 2012). Partnerships between school counselors and school administrators, teachers, parents, colleges, businesses, community members, and other school stakeholders are important for supporting the career development and postsecondary transitions of all students, especially students of color and low-income students. Such partnerships allow stakeholders to provide the support, resources, and opportunities necessary to holistically meet students' career development and college readiness needs. Counselors are leaders in building partnerships with school stakeholders to promote the career development and postsecondary transitions of students of color (American School Counselor Association, 2016; Bryan, 2005). This chapter describes the role of school counselors in PK–12 schools in establishing equity-focused school–family–community partnerships that enhance the career development and postsecondary transitions and opportunities of students of color. We highlight the career development and postsecondary transition needs of students of color, discuss an equity-focused partnership process model for building school–family–community partnerships focused on students' career development and postsecondary transitions, and offer strategies for collaborating with Black, Latinx, and Indigenous families to support students' career development, postsecondary transitions, and access.

School–family–community partnerships are collaborative initiatives between various school, family, and community stakeholders that are focused on building strength and resilience in PK–12 students; supporting students' college-career, academic, and personal/social outcomes; and closing opportunity gaps that hinder students' college and career access (Bryan & Henry, 2012). Through partnerships, the responsibilities of the school, home, and community in children's career outcomes are recognized and championed. Partnerships between school counselors and school administrators, teachers, parents, colleges, businesses, community members, and other school stakeholders are important for supporting the career development and postsecondary transitions of all students, especially students of color.

In this chapter, we maintain that a key goal of PK–12 career development is preparing students to have successful postsecondary transitions including but not limited to developing career aspirations, college-career knowledge, college access and application, and career decision-making skills. We assert that some form of postsecondary education or training is required for success in high skill, high wage jobs in the United States. In discussing post-secondary transitions, we use the term "college" to refer to a wide range of postsecondary institutions, including community colleges and 4-year colleges, as well as technical and vocational institutions. Effective career development that leads to successful postsecondary transitions for students of color requires community, college/university, and especially, family partnerships and collaboration (Turner et al., 2003; Turner & Lapan, 2002; Whiston & Keller, 2004).

The influence of parental/family support on the career development and postsecondary outcomes of students, especially students of color, has been well documented (Amundson & Penner, 1998; Constantine et al., 2005; Turner et al., 2003; Turner & Lapan, 2002; Whiston & Keller, 2004). Parental/family support has been shown to be a key factor in the development of adolescents' career self-efficacy, students' perceptions of educational and career related barriers, and students' perceived ability to cope with potential barriers (Alliman-Brissett et al., 2004; Turner et al., 2003). Indeed, Turner and Lapan (2002) reported, in a study of middle school students, that perceived parental/family support accounted for 29% to 43% of the unique variance in students' career self-efficacy, that is, beliefs in their ability to obtain desired career outcomes. In another national study, Militello et al. (2011) found that collaborative partnerships, parental outreach, teamwork, and multilevel systemic interventions are critical in successfully supporting the postsecondary transitions of students in high-poverty, high-minority schools.

Furthermore, studies have found that parental or family support and educational expectations can increase the career certainty of students from low-socioeconomic (SES) families. Constantine et al. (2005) found that perceived parental support significantly increased students' certainty in their career aspirations. In another study, students from low-SES families whose parents had higher educational expectations for them also had higher levels of certainty in their career aspirations (Gutman et al., 2012). Moreover, Galliott et al. (2015) found a significant relationship between the career uncertainty of students from low-SES families and their perceptions of their parents and family having low expectations for them, emphasizing the importance of including parents and guardians in the career development of their children. Parents or family members of color often have high academic and career expectations for their children—which includes attending college—and a desire to support them in college going, but often lack the necessary knowledge and experience to support their students' college application and career readiness process (Auerbach, 2004; Bryan et al., 2020). Additionally, parents in under-resourced neighborhoods are less likely to be involved in school activities due to work responsibilities and persistent feelings of not being accepted in schools which can present as a barrier for these parents (Amatea & West-Olatunji, 2007). School counselors are leaders in building partnerships to promote the career development and college readiness of all students and can be important sources of social capital for parents/families of colors in supporting their children's career development and postsecondary transitions (American School Counselor Association [ASCA] 2016; Bryan et al., 2018; Cholewa et al., 2015; Engberg & Gilbert, 2014).

SCHOOL COUNSELORS' ROLE

Social capital refers to the norms, resources, and information channels available to parents and students through their social networks. McKillip et al. (2012) maintain that access to social capital during the PK–12 years is important for students' postsecondary success. Students of color often have limited access to social capital because of poverty and living in segregated and homogeneous communities. Limited access to information like academic benchmarks, application and admissions processes, and financial aid resources create barriers to parents of color abilities to support their children's college access and successful postsecondary transitions (Farmer-Hinton & Adams, 2006; McKillip et al., 2012; Vela-Gude et al., 2009). School counselors provide access to and serve as social capital by building equity-focused partnerships that help parents and families of color navigate the college application process and serve as a source of information and resources that support school success, college access, and increase social mobility (Holland, 2015). When school counselors develop partnerships that result in networks of support, information sources, postsecondary transition strategies and resources for students and their families, they help build social capital that can improve parents/families of color's ability to support their children's career development and postsecondary transitions. As research shows, students of color and students from low-income backgrounds often need the most support in navigating their career development and postsecondary transitions.

Through intentional equity-focused, school–family–community partnerships, school counselors can develop a comprehensive career development program that targets students' needs at multiple levels and intervene in ways that change the culture and environment of their schools (McDonough, 2005). To develop equity-focused partnerships, school counselors must also adopt an antiracist lens. According to Bryan et al. (2021), for anti-racist partnerships to be developed, counselors must interrogate four main areas for themselves and their partners: their beliefs and narratives about students of color and their postsecondary optionals and attainment ability, the interactions and relationships that counselors and partners have with students and families of color, the postsecondary goals and outcomes counselors focus on for students of color, and the policies and practices that guide postsecondary programs. Knowing that students of color often lack opportunities and access to adequate career development and college readiness programs, school counselors can leverage partnerships to develop interventions and programs that support the unique career development needs and postsecondary transitions of students of color. However, the programs that partnerships create must consider that college and career readiness frameworks often adopt colorblind approaches that perpetuate racism and invalidate the structural inequities that present barriers to the career development and postsecondary transitions of students of color (Bryan et al., 2021). Equity-focused partnerships must aim to address structural barriers, decenter whiteness and White norms and beliefs when establishing goals, and avoid focusing on individual-level solutions and focus on dismantling racist policies and practices that keep students of color from successful postsecondary outcomes. It is important to note that partnerships should be established with all parents/family members regardless of their race or SES, however, partnerships that aim to serve students of color must consider the systemic and structural inequities that students of color must navigate in their postsecondary transitions. Table 5.1 highlights some examples of programs across several partnership types.

CAREER DEVELOPMENT AND POSTSECONDARY TRANSITION NEEDS OF STUDENTS OF COLOR

As students prepare for the transition to postsecondary education, they are challenged to navigate testing, seeking appropriate letters of support, college application processes, college selection, funding, and general career planning. School counselors are essential in aiding students to prepare for these transitions. Due to the history of stratified opportunities, many students of color, and low-income students, may lack the social capital necessary to seamlessly navigate this transition. It is important for school counselors to understand the student body that they serve, as well as the historically rooted barriers that may currently impede student success during this transition.

Historical and Current Political Barriers

The United States has a long and storied history of racial and economic segregation that has limited access to a variety of resources, including education funding for communities of color (Baker, 2014; Ladson-Billings, 2017; Massey, 2016; McGrew, 2018; Monarrez et al., 2019). In spite of governmental spending formulas utilized today that are intended to address the

TABLE 5.1   Examples of Partnership Programs That Facilitate Career Development and Postsecondary Transitions
School–Family Partnership Programs
Parent/family education workshops in school and community locations. Potential topics include course selection, benefits of rigorous curriculum, and financial aid.
Parent/family career spotlights—Invite parents into the classroom to talk about their careers.
Parent/family newsletters—Send a monthly newsletter home to parents sharing relevant, developmental career tasks for their child with suggestions for how to have career conversations at home.
Parent/Family nights where volunteers lead parents and students in interactive career awareness and assessment activities.
School–College Partnership Programs
Mentorship programs—connecting high school students with college mentors to expose them to the college experience early on.
Summer camps, pre-college, and enrichment programs—to foster students' ability to take rigorous courses and earn college credits before graduation.
College visits and tours—to build a college going culture in schools from the elementary level.
Collaborating with STEM college programs and college representatives to provide classroom-based STEM career information.
School–Family–Community Partnership Programs
Partnering with employers to provide career development information to parents during lunch breaks for parents with less flexible work schedules.
Community work site visits and tours to expose students to diverse career opportunities.
Work-based learning and opportunities for students to earn industry recognized credentials.
Collaborating with employers to provide internships, apprenticeships, job shadowing, and job training for students.
Partnering with business and family members to provide classroom career presentations, career fairs, and mock interview days.

inequitable distribution of funding of schools across states, school spending continues to be unequal, especially within districts that predominantly serve students of color (Baker, 2014; Baker et al., 2020; EdBuild, 2019). Majority Black and Latinx schools are often underfunded, and this phenomenon has not been completely explained by poverty alone. In a comparison of low resourced schools, EdBuild (2019) found that while majority White school districts that are low-income receive less funding than the national average, school districts that are majority students of color receive even less funding than their White economic counterparts. School districts that serve majority students of color are challenged to navigate disparities that are rooted in enduring racial, economic, and social barriers that trace the history of segregation and redlining in the United States (Ladson-Billings, 2017; Massey, 2020). Furthermore, economic and health crises such as the

COVID-19 pandemic of 2020 tend to result in increased joblessness, food insecurity, and domestic violence, all of which impact families of color at disproportionately higher rates (Kuhfeld et al., 2020; Schneider et al., 2016; Wolf & Morrisey, 2017). Additionally, the high profile police shootings of Black people such as George Floyd in Minneapolis and Breonna Taylor in Louisville, led to civil unrest and protests that resulted in even more violence against the Black community. Police killings can result in racial trauma that negatively impacts students' academic achievement, emotional regulation, attendance, high school graduation, and college enrollment rates (Ang, 2020; Gershenson & Hayes, 2018; Kuhfeld et al., 2020).

Economic Barriers

More than 50 years since the *Brown v. Board of Education* ruling by the U.S. Supreme Court, many schools continue to be segregated (Monarrez et al., 2019) by race and SES status. Segregation set into motion in the 1930s, and the related community-level choice-driven segregation of today have been described as contributors to the wealth gap in school funding (Ladson-Billings, 2017; García, 2020). Children of color now account for 49% of the population of Americans under the age of 18, and 46% of those who are college-aged (de Brey et al., 2019). With the growing numbers of diverse students, there is evidence that funding continues to be disparate across racial and economic lines (EdBuild, 2019; Morgan & Amerikaner, 2018). Schools that serve majority students of color receive about $1,800 less per student than White schools, and students of color receive nearly $1,000 less per student than high poverty White schools (Morgan & Amerikaner, 2018). In 2016, the U.S. Department of Education decried structural barriers as a hindrance to the potential success of schools and our students. Education funding disparities serve as a hurdle to equal education for all children, and this disparity has been ongoing across generations for many communities of color, despite the U.S. Supreme Court's ruling making racial segregation in public schools unconstitutional (Monarrez et al., 2019; Morgan & Amerikaner, 2018). Funding disparities in PK–12 schools impacts educational outcomes, career, and wealth potential for students and their entire communities (Jackson et al., 2015; Owens, 2020).

Familial Barriers

Researchers (e.g., Ladson-Billings, 2017; Massey; 2016) have made clear the ongoing relationship between the opportunity stratification for PK–12 students and the U.S. history of segregation and redlining. In a study examining school and community level segregation patterns, Owens (2020) described the interlocking relationship between segregation at the community level and segregated schools. Many families' neighborhood choices are informed by the quality of available schools, and the perceived quality of neighborhoods might also impact the quality of schools (Owens, 2020). These choices that families make also follow and inform funding and performance patterns, as higher resourced communities have been shown to positively impact student outcomes (Jackson et al., 2015). These patterns harken back to the intentional investment lockouts that communities of color were subjected to during early redlining (Ladson-Billings, 2017). The impact of segregation has continued across generations for many students of color and their families (Owens, 2020), resulting in present day disparities in educational attainment and career opportunity. In 2016, 14–29% of Black and Latinx adults held a college degree, in comparison to 45% of White adults (Hussar et al., 2020). In 2012, 20% of Black parents, 16% of Hispanic or Latinx parents, and 17–20% of Native American parents held a college degree, in comparison to 44% of White parents and 59% of Asian parents—not accounting for underrepresented Asian communities such as Cambodian families (Ross et al., 2012). Though this educational disparity puts families of color at a disadvantage, a PEW Research Center (2015) report showed that 79% of Black and 86% of Hispanic parents described postsecondary education as important. Hope for the potential success related to postsecondary educational attainment adds to the opportunities for school counselors to partner with parents and families as they negotiate postsecondary education planning.

APPLYING THE EQUITY-FOCUSED SEVEN-STAGE PARTNERSHIP MODEL TO THE CAREER DEVELOPMENT AND POSTSECONDARY TRANSITION NEEDS OF STUDENTS OF COLOR

Given the historical, economic, and sociopolitical barriers that students face in career and postsecondary transitions, counselors must be intentional in collaborating with family and community partners to alleviate the barriers students face. To this end, we outline an equity-focused partnership process model (Bryan & Henry, 2012; Bryan et al., 2019; Bryan, Williams et al., 2020) that counselors may use to plan, implement, and evaluate partnership programs that increase students' of color career development and postsecondary transitions. The most effective partnerships are built on equity-focused principles, that is democratic collaboration, empowerment, social justice, and strengths-focused.

By *democratic collaboration,* we mean that counselors should involve parents and family members, community members, and school staff, making sure that they share in the decision-making and designing of the program. Parents and family members are "experts" in their children's lives and their perspectives, and input in developing programs are valuable. *Empowerment* is linked to democratic collaboration and is central to equity-focused partnerships because power dynamics in schools often disempower parents of color and other marginalized parents. Counselors who collaborate with an empowerment lens make sure that parents of color come to the table as equal and mutual partners and that their voices are heard. Partnerships focused on *social justice* aim to reduce and eliminate the barriers that students face and create access to opportunities, information, networks of adults, and programs that students need to succeed. Counselors should use data to identify the career and college needs of students of color and connect them to opportunities and programs that support successful careers and postsecondary transitions. Partnerships that enhance equity and access to college and careers after high school, must be strengths-focused rather than deficit focused. Deficit views of marginalized students by school staff and counselors create barriers that further limit access for students who typically have limited access to adequate college and career readiness. When counselors and partners build strengths-focused partnerships they intentionally build the developmental assets and protective factors for students.

Navigating College and Career Readiness Partnerships

Building school–family–community partnerships is a seven-stage partnership process: (a) preparing to partner, (b) assessing needs and strengths, (c) coming together, (d) creating shared vision and plan, (e) taking action, (f) evaluating and celebrating progress, and (g) maintaining momentum (Bryan & Henry, 2012; Bryan et al., 2019; Bryan, Griffin et al., 2020). See Table 5.2 for an overview of the main tasks and questions to ask for each stage.

Preparing to Partner: Where Do I Begin?
Prior to building partnerships counselors should become familiar with students who typically have less access to career development and college readiness opportunities, programs, and information. Additionally, counselors should explore research on college and career readiness and access and career development, especially of marginalized students. This gives them an opportunity to begin to understand the barriers to successful postsecondary transitions that students and their families face. Furthermore, getting to know families and students of color and low-income students provides an opportunity to build cross-cultural trust, which is crucial for

TABLE 5.2   An Equity-Focused School–Family–Community Partnerships Process Model for Promoting College and Career Readiness

Stage	Main Tasks	Questions
1. Preparing to Partner *Where do I begin?*	1. Become familiar with students and families of color (SOC) and other cultural groups in the school. 2. Examine and challenge own personal beliefs, stereotypes, & biases about SOC and low-income students. 3. Examine research on college and career access and disparities/inequities faced by SOC. 4. Align your vision with the school's vision and improvement plan to get administration and faculty buy-in. 5. Use rationale based on research-based evidence about the benefits of partnerships for fostering college and career access for SOC.	1. What are your college expectations for SOC? What are your assumptions about the student groups who are less represented in college going? What do you believe about parents' college knowledge and role in the college search process? 2. What is your vision for college and career readiness and access in the school? 3. What is the school's vision for students to be college and career ready? 4. Why should administration support your efforts to build college and career readiness partnerships?
2. Assessing Needs and Strengths *How do I identify the goals of the partnership?*	1. Conduct needs and strengths assessment about SOC college and career readiness (surveys and interview students, school personnel, parents/families, and community members). 2. Examine college and career related data. Identify students who are less represented in college going. 3. Attend college and community events, meet cultural brokers and persons of influence who are potential partners. 4. Identify potential partners and allies (in the school and community) including existing college and career programs. 5. Create a community asset map (of people, services, resources, organizations, spaces), for college and career development.	1. What are the needs and strengths of students, parents, and guardians? Which students are not ready for career or college transitions? Why are some groups of students not going to college? 2. What are the needs and strengths of community members and organizations? 3. What college and career readiness partnerships already exist? What are they doing that works? 4. Who are your potential partners/stakeholders in the school's local and wider community?

(continued)

TABLE 5.2 An Equity-Focused School–Family–Community Partnerships Process Model for Promoting College and Career Readiness (continued)

Stage	Main Tasks	Questions
3. Coming Together *How do I bring partners together?*	1. Use identified strengths to create a partnership leadership team (PLT) with a focus on career development and college readiness; include family and community members of color. 2. Examine and share identified career and college-readiness needs and strengths as a team. 3. Keep inequities, disparities, and institutional barriers & policies as a focus. 4. Discuss partners' potential contributions, commitments, and partnership roles. 5. Get partners' feedback and ideas on addressing inequities, paying attention to parent and community members' voices about increasing career development and college readiness.	1. Who are potential PLT members (who has high college expectations and care passionately for students)? 2. Who are your potential partners and what roles are they willing to play? What are the strengths of the PLT members? 3. Who are your identified community partners? Who are the identified cultural brokers and persons of influence? 4. What is the role of the school counselor on the PLT?
4. Creating a Shared Vision and Plan *How do I get everyone on board and on the same page?*	1. Use identified needs to create a partnership plan for college readiness: 2. Build on existing partnerships. 3. Consider starting at least one new partnership. 4. Determine the goals and expected outcomes of your partnership(s). 5. Share the proposed plan with school administrators and parents and get their feedback and ideas. 6. Create 1-year and 3- to 5-year plans to build a college culture using a logic model. 7. Create a timeline for the year's college-readiness partnership activities.	1. What strategies would you use to create a shared vision and plan for college readiness? 2. What existing partnerships are already meeting identified needs? 3. What new partnership programs would be beneficial in meeting identified college and career needs? 4. How will you get buy-in from staff? 5. How will you reach parents? 6. What are your goals and expected outcomes? What career development and college access outcomes are you targeting?

(continued)

TABLE 5.2 An Equity-Focused School–Family–Community Partnerships Process Model for Promoting College and Career Readiness (continued)

Stage	Main Tasks	Questions
5. Taking Action *What will we do and how?*	1. Recruit volunteers (e.g., parents, mentors, tutors, etc.) including from communities of color. 2. Delegate responsibilities for each team member (based on the PLT's and your partners' strengths) making sure that partners of color (e.g., parents) have leadership roles and responsibility. 3. Build alliances with teachers, family, and community members who will help advocate for students of color and for college and career readiness programs. 4. Plan for challenges you expect but implement anyway. 5. Implement partnership activities according to the timeline.	1. What strategies/partnerships would you and the team use to implement the plan? 2. What is the timeline and implementation plan? 3. When will you have progress meetings? 4. How will you overcome any expected barriers and challenges in implementing your plan? 5. What are the benefits of involving the media (if any)?
6. Evaluating and Celebrating Progress *How will I measure our success?*	1. Conduct evaluations (before & after events & at identified points in school year). 2. Include family and community partners of color in the evaluation process. 3. Analyze outcomes (e.g., career awareness and knowledge, college knowledge, college & career readiness skills, college application and enrollment rates, etc.), disaggregate outcomes, & create user-friendly presentation of data. 4. Examine whether the program is helping to reduce inequities, disparities, and institutional barriers & policies in career knowledge and awareness, college and career readiness, college application, and enrollment rates. 5. Share partnership outcomes & accomplishments with all stakeholders (administration, teachers, other staff, students, families, and the community members). 6. Celebrate all partners including volunteers & students & partnership accomplishments.	1. How will you measure and evaluate each partnership to show the results/outcomes? 2. What impact did the partnership have on career and college readiness and access? 3. What worked? What did not work? What can be done to improve and strengthen the partnerships and programs? 4. How will you share accomplishments? 5. How will you celebrate your partners', students', and parent accomplishments?

(continued)

TABLE 5.2   An Equity-Focused School–Family–Community Partnerships Process Model for Promoting College and Career Readiness (continued)

Stage	Main Tasks	Questions
7. Maintaining Momentum *How will I sustain this partnership?*	1. Revisit your plan for enhancing college readiness and access. 2. PLT should use evaluation results to improve & make revisions to the plan. 3. Contact partners and cultural brokers at end of school year and prior to the start of the new school year (e.g., retreat) to plan. 4. Continually seek new partners and cultural brokers including from communities of color throughout the year. 5. Identify possible new team members and new partners as new teachers and parents come to the school every year. 6. Build alliances with other partnerships or community organizations who can provide support for the PLT's agenda & help advocate for Black youth. 7. Share the new plan with your students, teachers, families, and community partners.	1. What strategies will you use to improve or build on the partnerships? 2. How will you sustain the partnerships? 3. Who are the new team members and partners? 4. Who can you build alliances with to better meet your goals?

Source: Adapted from Bryan & Henry, 2012.

effective partnerships between counselors and marginalized families and communities. Counselors who are committed to creating access and equity must also question their own beliefs and stereotypes about who is going to college and who is not. They must also examine policies and practices in the school that limit students' exposure to college and career awareness and planning and how partnerships can enhance students' exposure to such activities. This knowledge will help counselors develop a mission and vision for their program that encompasses college and career readiness and provides a rationale for college and career readiness partnerships with teachers, families, and community members.

Assessing Needs and Strengths: How Do I Identify the Goals of the Partnership?

School counselors should use data to guide the development of partnership programs. They should examine and disaggregate the data related to career and college readiness (e.g., postsecondary aspirations, access to career and technical education, work experience programs, and college application and enrollment rates). These data should be disaggregated by race, gender, disability status, and free-and-reduced lunch status (if allowed) to identify inequities and disparities. School counselors should also be guided by needs and strengths assessments that provide a clear picture of the needs of students who face disparities in college and career access, types of partnership programs that would best meet these needs, and school and community strengths and resources (Bryan & Henry, 2012; Bryan, Griffin et al., 2020). Counselors can collaborate with teachers and parents to develop a community assets map that identifies strengths such as potential partners and cultural brokers that can support college and career enrichment and readiness associations (Griffin & Farris, 2010). Cultural brokers are individuals who understand and are connected to the community, and therefore, can help counselors and partners connect to the community (Bryan et al., 2019; Bryan & Henry, 2008, 2012).

Coming Together: How Do I Bring Partners Together?

Once school counselors identify needs and potential partners, it is time to bring together potential partners to develop a partnership leadership team (PLT). The PLT may comprise teachers, school administration, student services personnel, as well as parent and family and community members, including family members from student groups who typically face disparities in the career and college readiness process. Engaging diverse families in the process ensures that diverse perspectives are heard and inform the partnership work. The PLT (also called an action team in Epstein's model; Epstein & Van Voorhis, 2010) is responsible for the development, implementation, evaluation, and maintenance of the school's partnership plan and program. In addition, the PLT is responsible for recruiting other partners and leaders, creating and spreading the partnership vision, and sustaining partnership programs. The team examines the needs and strengths assessments data and the school's college and career readiness outcome data and discusses strategies that would work to enhance disparities in college and career outcomes. These data will help the PLT to determine its goals and outcomes focused on students' needs and creating equity and access for students less likely to have the skills necessary for successful postsecondary transitions to college and careers (Bryan, Griffin et al., 2020; Bryan et al., 2019).

Creating Shared Vision and Plan. How Do I Get Everyone on Board and On the Same Page?

Once the PLT is formed, they need to collaborate to build consensus and begin planning, developing, implementing, and evaluating the partnership program and activities. This involves creating a short- and long-term plan using a logic model to help determine the program inputs, activities, outputs, and outcomes, and how these outcomes will be measured (Bryan & Henry, 2012). Integral to this stage is the PLT creating a common vision and plan with buy-in from the members of the team. As they plan the partnership work, it is important that counselors keep equity and access for marginalized students at the forefront of the partnership agenda. In addition, counselors should practice empowerment, including challenging and reframing deficit narratives, and focus on the strengths of students, families, and communities.

Taking Action: What Will We Do and How Will We Do It?

Once the PLT has a plan and a timeline, has decided on their goals and how they will measure outcomes, and has assigned responsibilities to every team member, it is time to implement the program (Bryan & Henry, 2012; Bryan, Griffin et al., 2020). Counselors and PLTs should seek to implement culturally sensitive, evidence-based programs (Bryan et al., 2019). For example, in implementing career interventions for children, if research indicates that job shadowing and internships increase career certainty and aspirations (Edwin, 2018), then these programs should be included as part of the partnership program. In addition to career awareness and college and career readiness skills, partnership programs should seek to foster the protective factors, and noncognitive skills that students need to be ready for postsecondary transitions to careers and college. Further, the PLT should find a variety of traditional and nontraditional ways—such as text messages and phone calls, home visits, visits to places of worship or community groups—to reach out to and engage parents and family members in the partnership activity (Bryan, Griffin et al., 2020; Bryan et al., 2019). In addition to helping students develop skills, the partnership program should include advocacy to school personnel and school administration to remove structural barriers that hinder students' access to college and careers.

Evaluating and Celebrating Progress. How Will We Measure Our Progress?

School counselors should collaborate with the PLT to develop an evaluation plan while planning the partnership program and activities. An evaluation team comprising PLT members and including parent/family members should collect data via surveys, other assessments, and interviews prior to, during, and post implementation of the partnership program (Bryan, Griffin et al., 2020). The PLT should analyze the data to share the results and accomplishments of the program, presenting the data in a user-friendly way to school staff, parents and family members, and community stakeholders. Further, counselors should focus on whether the partnership has helped to alleviate any disparities in college and career outcomes (Griffin et al., 2021).

Maintaining Momentum: How Will We Sustain the Partnership?

Partnership programs are often successful in schools, but quickly die out after a year or two. For partnerships to be sustainable, PLTs should be intentional about taking steps to maintain the partnership such as

> sharing partnership results; celebrating and focusing on small successes; recruiting new partners throughout the school year; recognizing partners' and volunteers' contributions; and inviting the PLT and new team members to a retreat at the beginning of the school year to plan partnership activities for the year. (Bryan, Griffin et al., 2020, p. 10)

Celebrating accomplishments, revising the partnership plan, and planning the partnership prior to or early at the beginning of the academic year are important steps in maintaining momentum. Even more important is continually recruiting partners and volunteers, especially those from minority communities, throughout the year.

RECOMMENDATIONS FOR PRACTICE AND RESEARCH

Communities of color have historically faced systematic disenfranchisement and exclusion within the American school system and within American society (Ladson-Billings, 2017; Massey, 2016; Owens, 2020). While efforts to provide inclusive and equity-focused services are imperative, community engagement that communicates a respect for the resilience necessary for families to prepare their students for the next steps may aid in building trust. Similarly, continued engagement with parents and community brokers will position school counselors to remain connected through partnerships built on trust. These efforts might also aid in countering narrative deficits and contribute to transitioning students' self-concept. Utilizing school–family–community partnerships in ways that honor key features that will aid in postsecondary success may support students of color as they embark upon new terrain, often at predominately White postsecondary institutions. Additionally, school counselors' operationalization of trauma-informed and culturally relevant approaches to student and family engagement can aid in building trust.

Recommendations for Practice

Research has shown that families of color often have high academic and career expectations for their children but lack the resources and information necessary to support their children's endeavors. It is imperative that partnerships that educate, empower, and include parents and families in their children's career development and postsecondary transitions are developed. Additionally, studies have demonstrated that family, friends, religious leaders, and more play important roles in the lives of students of color, especially Asian, Black, and Latinx students (Moore-Thomas & Day-Vines, 2010; Suro et al., 2007). Further, research has shown that students' main source of college and career information are their parents (Griffin et al., 2011) and that parental involvement relates to academic and career success (e.g., Bryan et al., 2016; Henry et al., 2017). However, parents and families of color have historically been wary of the school environment due to anxiety, and distrust, and lack of knowledge about the school culture, norms, and expectations (Bryan et al., 2013). To develop effective partnerships, school counselors must work to build trust with families of color.

Building Trust With Families of Color

Families of color might have an inherent wariness of the school and school staff that might make developing partnerships with them challenging (Auerbach, 2004; Gandara, 2002). The deficit lens through which schools tend to view students and parents of color in addition to parents' own previous negative experiences in schools can lead to a mistrust of school staff by parents (Bryan & Henry, 2008; Bryan et al., 2019). According to Bryan et al. (2013), "True partnerships can only begin on a foundation of trust" (p. 473). To build trust with parents and families of color, school counselors, teachers, and other school staff must demonstrate an explicit appreciation and respect for the attitudes, beliefs, and values of families of color. Schools can work on building rapport and relationships with families and parents of color—relationships that are not established on sharing students' problem behaviors but rather on connecting with the families. School counselors, PK–12 teachers, and school staff can use active listening skills to build empathy and compassion for parents and families of color, hear parents' concerns about their children's experiences in schools, validate those concerns, and work collaboratively to develop solutions. Moreover, school counselors can build trust specifically around career development by seeking to learn more about families' beliefs about and attitudes towards college, careers, and postsecondary options in general. The work of engaging with families can be strengthened and maintained, especially within partnerships that include both counselors and teachers partnering to support families (Trauma and Learning Policy Initiative, 2013). Sharing regular updates with parents in the form of phone calls, newsletters, and handwritten letters is another way to keep parents in the loop about happenings in school and build trust.

For parents for whom English is not their first language, schools must be intentional about sending translated versions of all materials home with students—to do this, schools would have to be in the know about which parents speak English as a second language or do not speak English at all. This requires intentional conversations with each parent. School counselors and school staff can make a concerted effort to be a part of the community by going to community events, learning about the neighborhood, and advocating for the community to build trust with parents and families. In learning about the communities, schools should identify a culture broker(s) that can educate schools about effective ways to communicate and share information with parents and families of color. Schools must be intentional about identifying culture brokers that are a part of the community, and not outsiders who happen to live in the community. Embracing cultural humility—maintaining an interpersonal, other-oriented stance when learning about other cultures—is critical in building trust with families of color. Once trust and a relationship has been established, schools can share information and plan career development and postsecondary transition events that cater to the needs of various populations.

Including Families of Color in Career Development Interventions

To collaborate with parents and families of color in supporting the career development and postsecondary transitions of their students, schools can share (a) information about the career development process; (b) information about college, the college application process, and postsecondary options; and (c) strategies for engaging in career talk with parents. School counselors can send home newsletters or written notes detailing the career development goals they have for students at the start of each semester or quarter. School counselors can share information about the impact of environment, exposure, and representation or role models on students' career aspirations. Sharing this information with parents of color is especially important as students of color may not have the same opportunities for exposure to various careers when compared to their colleagues who are White, in higher income neighborhoods, or have access to more social capital. To serve as effective sources of social capital for students and their parents, school counselors can share information about postsecondary options with children and their parents including application deadlines, application requirements, sources of funding, information about the college experience, and more. Studies have found that parental involvement is a significant predictor of college application and enrollment (Bryan et al., 2011; Cabrera & La Nasa, 2001). As such, including parents in postsecondary planning, especially parents of color who often have high expectations for their children, is crucial. Schools can host evening or weekend workshops—that working parents might be more likely to attend—where they invite local experts to lead parents and their children through various aspects of the postsecondary transition process. During these workshops, schools can teach parents how to fill out FAFSA forms, how to use the internet to search for scholarship options, and how to find admission criteria, that way, parents can support their children outside of school and the workshops. Schools can also work to have webinars or on-demand trainings about postsecondary transitions available for all parents to review at a time that is convenient for them, while ensuring the videos are available in multiple languages for non-English speaking parents and families.

Finally, school counselors can educate and help parents identify specific strategies for facilitating career development and fostering career talk with their children. Some of these strategies may include parents discussing the importance of work values with their children and providing children with opportunities to practice decision-making skills. Schools can share career-related events happening in the community such as exhibitions at museums or libraries and so on, that parents can take their children to and expose them to various industries and professionals both within and outside their communities. Schools should remember to ensure that all such resources are available in multiple languages and accessible to parents who may have disabilities.

Recommendations for Research

While students of color are underrepresented in higher education, and in educational attainment, there continues to be a scarcity of research that delineates educational attainment status across racial/ethnic groups. Collectively, Asian students' educational attainment appears higher than that of White students (Espinosa et al., 2019), but many students from Southeast

Asian communities achieve much lower degree attainment than other groups (de Brey et al., 2019). Similarly, variations in educational attainment exist across and within communities of color and marginalized groups. Research that explores the array of experiences, sources of resilience, and the barriers faced by groups within communities of color, such as Black families across the diaspora, Hispanic and Latinx communities, Indigenous populations, and students with disabilities will aid school counselors to better position students for successful navigation of postsecondary transitions. This area of research might also strengthen school counseling engagement initiatives that build trust that fosters family and community resilience.

Recommendations for Policy

Education policy-makers and district and school leaders recognize the importance of building school–family–community partnerships and their role in promoting student outcomes, including academic achievement, college and career readiness, and college going. Indeed, family engagement and community partnerships are embedded in every education law during the past 50 years, including in the recent Every Student Succeeds Act (ESSA; U.S. Department of Education, n.d.). School counselors are convinced of the importance of partnerships and are willing to utilize them. However, they are often hindered in building these partnerships due to large caseloads and lack of time to allow them to invest in building partnerships. Therefore, policy-makers and leaders must take the necessary steps to increase the number of counselors in schools and to ensure that school counselor caseloads are the recommended 250 students per counselor as recommended by ASCA, especially given the positive benefits of reduced caseload to increasing college application and college enrollment rates (Bryan et al., 2011). The onus is on federal, state, and district policy-makers to consider and incorporate research findings on the causal impacts of the number of counselors, and student-counselor ratios, counselor caseloads on student outcomes into education policy. Further, they must implement mandates to reduce the non-counseling duties such as enormous administrative paperwork that draw school counselors away from implementing interventions focused on facilitating college and career development and postsecondary transitions.

CONCLUSION

School–family–community partnerships are collaborative initiatives between various school, family, and community stakeholders that are focused on creating access and equity for PK–12 students, especially students from marginalized backgrounds, like students of color or students from low-income homes. Equity-focused partnerships build strength and resilience in students; support their college-career, academic, and social-emotional outcomes; and close opportunity gaps that hinder their college and career access (Bryan & Henry, 2012). Partnerships between school counselors and school administrators, teachers, parents, colleges, businesses, community members, and other school stakeholders are important for supporting the career development and postsecondary transitions of all students, especially students of color and low-income students. Such partnerships allow stakeholders to provide the support, resources, and opportunities necessary to holistically meet students' career development and college readiness needs.

DISCUSSION QUESTIONS

1. In what ways might implementing partnerships at each of the seven stages look different during and post a global health crisis like a pandemic (e.g., COVID-19)? How might you engage cultural brokers in the community during a global pandemic to access community assets that may aid students in your students' postsecondary transitions?
2. Your disaggregated school data shows that 40% of Hispanic female students in your school are dealing with challenges such as economic distress, losing family members, being cut off from resources, and so on. How would you develop a partnership that provides systemic support and services that the students need for successful postsecondary transitions? How would your partnership build in support for the different types of trauma and grief that students are experiencing?
3. How might postsecondary transition resources (e.g., professionals to write strong letters of recommendations, career readiness interventions, and knowledge about financial aid requirements and processes) and access to those resources differ in urban, suburban, and rural communities in your region?

ACTIVITIES

1. Gerard is a 17-year-old Black male identifying student who is trying to narrow down his postsecondary options. Gerard's family is currently facing economic distress while also navigating the grief of losing family members during a global pandemic. What considerations

might be necessary as you consider supporting Gerard in his post-secondary transition? Using the seven-stage model presented in this chapter, develop a partnership strategy to support Gerard and his family as they navigate postsecondary transitions in a virtual world.

2. Visit a district website in your region and find a school of your choice. Review their data to better understand the school population and their postsecondary gaps. Based on this data, build a community asset map that helps you connect to key stakeholders and uncover important cultural brokers and assets in the community that you can partner with to better serve students and connect them and their family to resources.

AUTHOR NOTE

Mary Edwin https://orcid.org/0000-0002-3542-5856
Latoya Haynes-Thoby https://orcid.org/0000-0002-3308-7400
Julia Bryan https://orcid.org/0000-0002-1471-1677

Correspondence concerning this article should be addressed to Mary Edwin, University of Missouri–St. Louis, 1 University Blvd, 457 Marillac Hall, St. Louis, MO, 63103. Email: edwinmo@umsl.edu

REFERENCES

Alliman-Brissett, A. E., Turner, S. L., & Skovholt, T. M. (2004). Parent support and African American adolescents' career self-efficacy. *Professional School Counseling, 124–132.* https://doi.org/10.1037/e345542004-001

Amatea, E. S., & West-Olatunji, C. A. (2007). Joining the conversation about educating our poorest children: Emerging leadership roles for school counselors in high-poverty schools. *Professional School Counseling, 11*(2). https://doi.org/10.1177/2156759X0701100202

American School Counselor Association. (2016). *The school counselor and school–family–community partnerships* [Position statement]. Retrieved from https://school-counselor.org/Standards-Positions/Position-Statements/ASCA-Position-Statements/The-School-Counselor-and-School-Family-Community-P

Amundson, N. E., & Penner, K. (1998). Parent involved career exploration. *The Career Development Quarterly, 47*(2), 135–144.

Ang, D. (2020). The effects of police violence on inner-city students. *Quarterly Journal of Economics.* https://doi.org/10.1093/qje/qjaa027

Auerbach, S. (2004). Engaging Latino parents in supporting college pathways: Lessons from a college access program. *Journal of Hispanic Higher Education, 3*(2), 125–145.

Baker, B. D. (2014). *America's most financially disadvantaged school districts and how they got that way: How state and local governance causes school funding disparities.* Center for American Progress. https://files.eric.ed.gov/fulltext/ED561094.pdf

Baker, B. D., Srikanth, A., Cotto, R., & Green, P. C., III. (2020). School funding disparities and the plight of Latinx children. *Education Policy Analysis Archives, 28*(135). https://doi.org/10.14507/epaa.28.5282

Bryan, J. (2005). Fostering educational resilience and achievement in urban schools through school-family-community partnerships: School counselors' roles. *Professional School Counseling, 8,* 219–227.

Bryan, J., & Henry, L. (2008). Strengths-based partnerships: A school–family–community partnership approach to empowering students. *Professional School Counseling, 12,* 149–156.

Bryan, J., & Henry, L. (2012). A model for building school-family-community partnerships: Principles and process. *Journal of Counseling and Development, 90,* 408–420.

Bryan, J., Farmer-Hinton, R., Rawls, A., & Woods, C. S. (2018). Social capital and college-going culture in high schools: The effects of college expectations and college talk on students' postsecondary attendance. *Professional School Counseling, 21,* 95–107. https://doi.org/10.5330/1096-2409-21.1.95

Bryan, J., Griffin, D., & Henry, L. (2013). School–family–community partnership strategies for promoting college readiness and access. *National Association for College Admission Counseling, 3,* 42–58.

Bryan, J., Griffin, D., Henry, L., & Gilfillan, B. (2020). Building culturally relevant school–family–community partnerships that promote college readiness and access. In *Fundamentals of college admission counseling* (5th ed., Chapter 26). NACAC.

Bryan, J., Griffin, D., Kim, J., Griffin, D. M., & Young, A. (2019). School counselor leadership in school–family–community partnerships: An equity-focused partnership process model for moving the field forward. In S. Sheldon & T. Turner-Vorbeck (Eds.), *The Wiley handbook on family, school, and community relationships in education* (pp. 265–287). Wiley. https://doi.org/10.1002/9781119083054.ch13

Bryan, J., Henry, L. M., Daniels, A. D., Edwin, M., & Griffin, D. M. (2021). Infusing an antiracist framework into school–family–community partnerships. In C. Holcomb-McCoy (Ed.), *Antiracist counseling in schools and communities* (pp. 129–149). American Counseling Association Press.

Bryan, J., Kim, J., & Liu, C. (2021). School counseling college-going culture: Counselors' influence on students' college-going decisions. *Journal of Counseling & Development.* https://doi.org/10.1002/jcad.12408

Bryan, J., Moore-Thomas, C., Day-Vines, N., & Holcomb-McCoy, C. (2011). School counselors as social capital: The effects of high school college counseling on college application rates. *Journal of Counseling & Development, 89,* 190–199.

Bryan, J., Williams, J. M., & Griffin, D. (2020). Fostering educational resilience and opportunities in urban schools through equity-focused school–family–community partnerships. *Professional School Counseling, 23,* 1–14. https://doi.org/10.1177/2156759X19899179

Bryan, J., Young, A., Griffin, D. C., & Henry, L. (2016). Preparing students for higher education: How school counselors can foster college readiness and access.

In J. L. DeVitis & P. Sasso (Eds.), *Higher education and society* (pp. 149–171). Peter Lang.

Cabrera, A. F., & La Nasa, S. M. (2001). On the path to college: Three critical tasks facing America's disadvantaged. *Research in Higher Education, 42,* 119–150.

Cholewa, B., Burkhardt, C. K., & Hull, M. F. (2015). Are school counselors impacting underrepresented students' thinking about postsecondary education? A nationally representative study. *Professional School Counseling, 19,* 144–154. https://doi.org/10.5330/1096-2409-19.1.144

de Brey, C., Musu, L., McFarland, J., Wilkinson-Flicker, S., Diliberti, M., Zhang, A., Branstetter, C., & Wang, X. (2019). *Status and trends in the education of racial and ethnic groups 2018* (NCES 2019-038). National Center for Education Statistics. Retrieved from https://nces.ed.gov/pubs2019/2019038.pdf

EdBuild. (2019). *Nonwhite school districts get $23 billion less than white school districts despite serving the same number of students.* https://edbuild.org/content/23-billion/full-report.pdf

Edwin, M. (2018). Understanding relations between school counseling career development interventions, sociodemographic factors and high school students' career aspirations and career certainty [Doctoral dissertation, Pennsylvania]. ETDA. https://etda.libraries.psu.edu/catalog/15434mqe5145

Engberg, M. E., & Gilbert, A. J. (2014). The counseling opportunity structure: Examining correlates of four-year college-going rates. *Research in Higher Education, 55,* 219–244. https://doi.org/10.1007/s11162-013-9309-4

Epstein, J. L., & Van Voorhis, F. L. (2010). School counselors' roles in developing partnerships with families and communities for student success. *Professional School Counseling, 14,* 1–14.

Espinosa, L. L., Turk, J. M., Taylor, M., & Chessman, H. M. (2019). *Race and ethnicity in higher education: A status report.* American Council on Education. https://1xfsu31b52d33idlp13twtos-wpengine.netdna-ssl.com/wp-content/uploads/2019/02/Race-and-Ethnicity-in-Higher-Education.pdf

Farmer-Hinton, R. L., & Adams, T. L. (2006). Social capital and college preparation: Exploring the role of counselors in a college prep school for black students. *Negro Educational Review, 57*(1–2), 101–116.

Galliott, N., Graham, L. J., & Sweller, N. (2015). Who struggles most in making a career choice and why? Findings from a cross-sectional survey of Australian high-school students. *Journal of Psychologists and Counsellors in Schools, 25*(2), 133–151. http://doi.org/10.1017/jgc.2015.7

Gándara, P. (2002). A study of high school puente: What we have learned about preparinglatino youth for postsecondary education. *Educational Policy, 16*(4), 474–495.

García, E. (2020, February 12). *Schools are still segregated, and Black children are paying a price.* Economic Policy Institute. https://www.epi.org/publication/schools-are-still-segregated-and-black-children-are-paying-a-price/

Gershenson, S., & Hayes, M. S. (2018). Police shootings, civic unrest and student achievement: Evidence from Ferguson. *Journal of Economic Geography, 18*(3), 663–685. https://doi.org/10.1093/jeg/lbx014

Griffin, D., & Farris, A. (2010). School counselors and collaboration: Finding resources through community asset mapping. *Professional School Counseling, 13*(5), https://doi.org/10.1177/2156759X1001300501

Griffin, D., Hutchins, B. C., & Meece, J. L. (2011). Where do rural high school students go to find information about their futures? *Journal of Counseling & Development, 89,* 172–181.

Griffin, D., Williams, J. M., & Bryan, J. (2021). School–family–community partnerships for educational success and equity for Black male students. *Professional School Counseling, 25*(1_part_4), https://doi.org/10.1177/2156759X211040036.

Gutman, L. M., Schoon, I., & Sabates, R. (2012). Uncertain aspirations for continuing in education: Antecedents and associated outcomes. *Developmental Psychology, 48*(6), 1707–18. https://doi.org/10.1037/a0026547

Henry, L. M., Bryan, J., & Zalaquett, C. P. (2017). The effects of a counselor-led, faith-based, school–family–community partnership on student achievement in a high-poverty urban elementary school. *Journal of Multicultural Counseling and Development, 45*(3), 162–182.

Holland, M. M. (2015). Trusting each other: Student-counselor relationships in diverse high schools. *Sociology of Education 88*(3), 244–262.

Hussar, B., Zhang, J., Hein, S., Wang, K., Roberts, A., Cui, J., Smith, M., Bullock Mann, F., Barmer, A., & Dilig, R. (2020). The condition of education 2020 (NCES 2020-144). National Center for Education Statistics. https://nces.ed.gov/pubsearch/pubsinfo.asp?pubid=2020144

Jackson, C. K., Johnson, R., & Persico, C. (2015). Boosting educational attainment and adult earnings: Does school spending matter after all? *Education Next, 15*(4). https://www.educationnext.org/boosting-education-attainment-adult-earnings-school-spending/

Kuhfeld, M., Soland, J., Tarasawa, B., Johnson, A., Ruzek, E., & Liu, J. (2020). Projecting the potential impact of COVID-19 school closures on academic achievement. *Educational Researcher, 49*(8), 549–565. https://doi.org/10.3102/0013189X20965918

Ladson-Billings, G. (2017). "Makes me wanna holler": Refuting the "culture of poverty" discourse in urban schooling. *Annals of the American Academy of Political and Social Science, 673*(1), 80–90. https://doi.org/10.1177/0002716217718793

Massey, D. S. (2016). Residential segregation is the linchpin of racial stratification. *City Community, 5*(1), 4–7. https://doi.org/10.1111/cico.12145

Massey, D. S. (2020) Still the linchpin: Segregation and stratification in the USA. *Race Social Problems, 12*(1), 1–12. https://doi.org/10.1007/s12552-019-09280-1

McDonough, P. M. (2005). Counseling matters: Knowledge, assistance, and organizational commitment in college preparation. In W. G. Tierney, Z. Corwin, & J. E. Colyar (Eds.), *Preparing for college: Nine elements of effective outreach* (pp. 69–87). State University of New York Press.

McGrew, T. (2018). The history of residential segregation in the United States, title VIII, and the homeownership remedy. *American Journal of Economics and Sociology, 77*(3–4), 1013–1048. https://doi.org/10.1111/ajes.12243

McKillip, M. E., Rawls, A., & Barry, C. (2012). Improving college access: A review of research on the role of high school counselors. *Professional School Counseling, 16*(1). https://doi.org/10.1177/2156759X1201600106.

Militello, M., Schweid, J., & Carey, J. (2011). Si se Puede Colaboracion! Increasing college placement rates of low-income students. *Teachers College Record, 113*(7), 1435–1476.

Monarrez, T., Kisida, B., & Chingos, M. (2019). *When is a school segregated? Making sense of segregation 65 years after* "Brown v. Board of Education" [Research report]. Urban Institute. https://files.eric.ed.gov/fulltext/ED601785.pdf

Moore-Thomas, C., & Day-Vines, N. L. (2010). Culturally competent collaboration: School counselor collaboration with African American families. *Professional School Counseling, 14,* 53–63.

Morgan, I., & Amerikaner, A. (2018). *Funding gaps: An analysis of school funding equity across the U.S. and within each state.* The Education Trust. https://edtrust.org/wp-content/uploads/2014/09/FundingGapReport_2018_FINAL.pdf

Owens, A. (2020). Unequal opportunity: School and neighborhood segregation in the USA. *Race Social Problems, 12*(1), 29–4. https://doi.org/10.1007/s12552-019-09274-z

PEW Research Center. (2015). *Parenting in America: Outlook, worries, aspirations are strongly linked to financial situation.* https://www.pewresearch.org/wp-content/uploads/sites/3/2015/12/2015-12-17_parenting-in-america_FINAL.pdf

Ross, T., Kena, G., Rathbun, A., KewalRamani, A., Zhang, J., Kristapovich, P., & Manning, E. (2012). Higher education: Gaps in access and persistence study (NCES 2012-046). National Center for Education Statistics. https://nces.ed.gov/pubs2012/2012046.pdf

Schneider, D., Harknett, K., & McLanahan, S. (2016). Intimate partner violence in the Great Recession. *Demography, 53*(2), 471–505. https://doi.org/10.1007/s13524-016-0462-1

Suro, R., Escobar, G., Livingston, G., Hakimzadeh, S., Lugo, L., Stencel, S., Green, J. C., Smith, G. A., Cox, D., & Chaudhry, S. (2007). *Changing faiths: Latinos and the transformation of American religion.* Pew Research Center. http://www.u.arizona.edu/~jag/POL596A/pewrligion.pdf

Trauma and Learning Policy Initiative. (2013). *Helping traumatized children learn: Creating and advocating for trauma-sensitive schools (Vol. 2).* Massachusetts Advocates for Children and Harvard Law School. https://traumasensitiveschools.org/wp-content/uploads/2013/11/HTCL-Vol-2-Creating-and-Advocating-for-TSS.pdf

Turner, S., & Lapan, R. T. (2002). Career self-efficacy and perceptions of parent support in adolescent career development. *The Career Development Quarterly, 51*(1), 44–55.

Turner, S. L., Alliman-Brissett, A., Lapan, R. T., Udipi, S., & Ergun, D. (2003). The career-related parent support scale. *Measurement and Evaluation in Counseling and Development, 36*(2), 83–94.

U.S. Department of Education. (n.d.). *Every Student Succeeds Act* (ESSA). http://www.ed.gov/essa

Vela-Gude, L., Cavazos, J., Jr., Johnson, M. B., Cheryl, F., Cavazos, A. G., Leslie, C., & Iliana, R. (2009). "My counselors were never there": Perceptions from Latino college students. *Professional School Counseling, 12*(4). https://doi.org/10.1177/2156759X0901200407

Whiston, S. C., & Keller, B. K. (2004). The influences of the family of origin on career development: A review and analysis. *Counseling Psychologist, 32,* 493–568.

Wolf, S., & Morrissey, T. (2017). Economic instability, food insecurity, and child health in the wake of the Great Recession. *Social Service Review, 91*(3), 534–570. https://doi.org/10.1086/694111

CHAPTER 6

SERVING NATIVE AMERICAN CHILDREN AND FAMILIES

Considering Cultural Variables

Carol Robinson-Zañartu
San Diego State University

ABSTRACT

As a group, Native American people are perhaps the least understood and most underserved populations in schools. Native American is a collective term representing a large variety of cultures, language groups, customs, traditions, levels of acculturation, and levels of traditional language use. In the context of this variation, I raise and discuss a number of common patterns in their traditions and histories: worldview and belief systems, acculturation stress, school–home discontinuity, learning styles, and communication patterns, which are useful reference points from which to develop more culturally compatible evaluation approaches. The ecosystems and dynamic/mediational approaches are suggested as promising.

Historically and currently, children of Native American nations have been so underserved and misunderstood that they stand at the forefront of our

Equity-Based Career Development and Postsecondary Transitions, pages 137–161
Copyright © 2022 by Information Age Publishing
www.infoagepub.com
137

populations "at risk" for low achievement, overrepresentation in special education, and dropping out. Historically, schools have participated in devaluing Native American languages, cultures, and traditional ways of learning and knowing. Currently, the rates at which children of Indian nations leave or are "pushed out" of the school system—frustrated, alienated, and underserved—are staggering.

Historical government grouping has made "Native American" a term of convenience, although some prefer the terms American Indian, First Americans, First Nations People, or Native. For the purpose of this article, I use the term Native American to refer to those persons having origins in any of the indigenous peoples of North America and who maintain cultural identification through tribal affiliation or community recognition (Chinn & Hughes, 1987). Within these groupings, tremendous linguistic and cultural diversity must be recognized. Each Native American person needs to be understood within the context of the tribe or nation (e.g., Choctaw, Sioux, or Navajo) with which he or she identifies. Currently, over 450 such groups are self-identified in the continental United States; of those, the U.S. government recognizes 319 tribes (also known as nations); 120 more are in various stages of petition for federal recognition, and 30 are recognized by their states. Approximately 1.9 million people self-identify as American Indian in the United States, with 1.2 million of those tribally enrolled (Russell, 1994).

Tribal populations vary greatly in size, with Cherokee the largest at 308,000, four tribes or nations over 100,000, and a few with only a handful of enrolled members. Approximately 200 Native American languages are spoken (Leap, 1993). The Native American population is young and growing, with 39% under 20 years of age, and the median age (26) considerably younger than the U.S. median of 33 years (U.S. Bureau of the Census, 1993).

Undergirding this tribal diversity, many commonalities and cultural themes are found across these groups, which I discuss here as Native American issues. Hopefully, they will serve as a springboard from which speech-language pathologists and other school personnel may examine the issues that face the particular tribal communities or urban Indian populations they serve.

Seventy-eight percent of Native Americans live in urban areas. Percentages of Native American students enrolled in individual public schools vary widely, and proportional enrollments reported by districts minimize a significant group, creating a false invisibility. For instance, although Native American students in California public schools account for only 0.7% of the state's overall enrollment (U.S. Department of Education, 1989), more Native Americans live in California than in any other state except Oklahoma (Russell, 1994). Most of this population is urban.

Although small percentages may hold true within school districts, Native American student enrollment in *individual* schools may account for as much as 27% of a school's population (San Diego County Office of Education, 1988). Furthermore, because Native American people often have Spanish, French, or English surnames (based on who conquered their tribal territories; Tafoya, 1994), they are often not counted as Native Americans.

The much publicized "cycle of failure" experienced by Native American children in schools has been perpetuated by public school personnel who lack training in models and methods that reflect cultural heritage and are adapted to culturally or linguistically diverse students. Havighurst (1970), for example, reported that 66% of teachers nationwide did not appear to know, understand, or appreciate cultural differences between themselves and Native American students. The depth of this difference can be profound.

Even with an increasing emphasis on multicultural competence in training, unless a student takes a *special* interest in Native Americans, their exposure generally will be minimal. Thus, we must begin to remedy a situation in which school personnel have not been exposed to: (a) the cultural heritage and history impacting Native American relationships with schools, (b) the cultural differences that make most mainstream educational procedures and curricula inadequate, and (c) the intertwining causative factors behind the cycle of failure for Native American children.

Ideally, this situation should be addressed by increasing the number of Native American educational support professionals (e.g., speech-language pathologists) who bring a knowledge of cultural, linguistic, behavioral, and norm characteristics of a nation or tribe, while simultaneously providing much needed role models and advocacy for Native American youth (Johnson, 1989; Ramirez & Tippeconnic, 1979; U.S. Senate, 1969). However, recruitment is problematic: some 70% of the small number of Native American students who enter higher education drop out (Yates, 1987). Further, only a very few training programs provide focused studies of Native American issues or supervised field experiences in Native American communities (Robinson, 1990). Thus, it remains incumbent on the education professional to engage in systematic, continuing education with respect to these issues and the development of such competencies.

To attend to ecologically relevant or culturally compatible service delivery issues for Native American students and communities, we must gain a better understanding of the relationships between those cultures and the educational experience. In this context, this article has several purposes: (a) to introduce speech-language pathologists to Native American issues, (b) to examine some current practices in relation to Native American children, (c) to provide a frame for thinking about Native American children and their families, and (d) to explore culturally compatible service delivery models. Thus, the implications of demographics, the concept of worldview, the impact of acculturation stress, and discontinuity between school and the Native American home are addressed. Cultural characteristics are offered as a base from which to raise hypotheses in service delivery and to learn about the characteristics of local Native American communities.

DEMOGRAPHICS AND THEIR IMPLICATIONS

Because the Native American school-aged population is young and growing, and a high percentage live in urban areas, widely spread across school systems, today's speech-language pathologists are likely to encounter Native American children and their families. The Native American dropout rate of 50% nationally is the highest of any ethnic group (McShane, 1983; Yates, 1987). Some areas have far more dismal statistics, with rates as high as 96%! The lack of success in the system as early as Grade 4 contributes directly to this phenomenon. Poverty, health, and unemployment compound education issues. Nationally, 51% of Native American families were living below the poverty level in 1989 (U.S. Bureau of the Census, 1993).

Although economic disparity and disadvantage exist, and must not be overlooked, it is also important to understand that poverty by traditional Native American standards is defined differently from the economic sense of the mainstream. Red Horse (1988) described a gifted Native American (Ogewabenais) who knew ritual custom, passed it on to his namesake, and served as a role model and mentor. By his tribe's standards, he was a wealthy man. In contrast, Red Horse tells of Behmahseis, who was an honor student, a 4-year letterman, schooled in formal science and profit margins who was about to matriculate at Harvard, yet was described by tribal traditions as likely to die in poverty because he had given up his natural gifts, his traditional language and tradition, and had not planted their seeds and served as a role model or mentor.

Often, educators and Native American youth confuse so-called low economic status and lifestyle with the Indian way of life (Emerson, 1986). Faced with the views and attitudes of the dominant culture, heavily emphasized in the media, and with school situations that have neither valued nor reflected Native American ways and worldviews, individuals who have not had the opportunity to invest the necessary time and thought to clarify their Native American identity are likely to be confused, and experience resultant stress. Emerson (1986) suggested that misconceptions equating the Native way of life and poverty must be diffused and reframed, thus separating difference from deficit.

Rather than tracking child failure, we have been tracking system failure, which will require different remedial approaches (Dronek, as cited in Winget, 1989), or a shift away from the closed-system, psychometrically driven approaches that have led to wrong assumptions and often misguided service delivery. At the heart of the problem has been limited information, *especially* concerning cultural variables, and a limited perspective on learning and communication. These misunderstandings have fueled deficit model thinking, which views many of the above issues as intrinsic problems for large numbers of Native American children. On this note, McDermott (as cited in Moll, 1991) commented:

> By making believe that failure is something that kids do, as different from how it is done to them, and then by explaining their failure in terms of other things they do, we likely contribute to the maintenance of school failure. (p. 363)

We must examine the needs of this population from a system-wide perspective, and then reframe our own roles in response.

DIFFERENT WORLDVIEWS AND BELIEF SYSTEMS

The lack of attention to and respect for worldview differences is often raised by Native Americans as a primary issue in educational discrimination (Deloria, 1991; Locust, 1988). Worldview refers to a set of belief systems and principles by which individuals understand and make sense of the world and their place in it. Understanding the Native American child necessitates, first and foremost, understanding that their belief systems are fundamentally different from those of non-Native Americans.

Deloria (1991) described the historic White worldview (which drives the culture of the schools) as characterized by reductionism and enhanced by the success of modern technology. He proposed that this view emerged from "a complex mixture of folklore, religious doctrine, and Greek natural sciences" (p. 9) and has since been held as the highest intellectual achievement of our species. In contrast, he described the Indian worldview in terms of Indian metaphysics: "Indian knowledge of the natural world, of the human world, and of whatever realities exist beyond our senses has a consistency which far surpasses anything devised by western civilization" (p. 9).

One outcome of worldview differences is reflected in differential emphases in Native American versus non-Native values. For example, Native Americans typically value present time, patience, extended family, "we" thinking, few material possessions, being in balance with nature, holistic thinking, and the spiritual (Philips, 1983; M. Robinson, personal communication, February 17, 1992). Each of these values must be seen as part of a mosaic that only has meaning as a whole. At the heart of the Native American worldview is the belief that all aspects of life are integrated or related. Even the secular and sacred aspects of life are inseparable.

Belief systems go beyond cognitive systems of thinking to integrate traditional knowledge, which derives from centuries of tribal tradition and incorporates ways of gaining knowledge from natural sources. For instance, traditional songs and stories are teaching methods. At one level, they teach such building blocks of learning and thinking as sequence, cause/effect, and temporal orientation; at a deeper level, they have a holistic transcendence meant to teach deeper lessons concerning life. Using Native American student interpretations as authentic assessment measures might then involve (a) incorporating their current levels of insight and (b) using that level of interpretation to guide the teacher in providing the next set of learning experiences (Tafoya, 1994).

Those steeped in Western thinking may misinterpret Native American worldview as lacking precision due to a de-emphasis on or a rejection of mathematical descriptions of nature (Deloria, 1991). However, although precise attention to detail clearly is found in many Native American practices (e.g., oral history requires tremendous precision), accuracy within this worldview necessitates attention to a greater reality.

For concepts, cause–effect relationships, or actions to have meaning, consistency with cultural wisdom is required. Without that cultural wisdom and consistency, meanings and concepts such as those typically discussed in schools will appear culturally deficient, or incomplete, and thus hard to understand or accept. As an example of this dilemma, a student raised in a traditional environment when asked the meaning of a story based on immediate recall of surface content, may produce (a) a response that appears to be somewhat roundabout or irrelevant or (b) a paucity of content because the request may seem inappropriate. In contrast, traditional interpretation comes over time and with experience: It is implicit, and often not voiced. Allegory and metaphor are the mechanisms by which life lessons are passed on.

ACCULTURATION AND ACCULTURATION STRESS

Historically, Native Americans have been expected by the U.S. government, schools, institutions, and religious groups to give up virtually all that was sacred and unique in their traditional lifestyles. The removal of children from their cultures via government-sanctioned and -supported boarding schools has for generations had profound effects. As early as 1865, President Grant recommended that Indian children be removed from their homes and tribes for the purpose of "civilization" and the elimination of Indian identity (Fuchs & Havighurst, 1973). Between 1889 and 1892, 12 boarding schools were opened to force this assimilation.

During this time, children were removed, sometimes forcibly, from their homes and sent long distances. By 1890, attendance in government-run Bureau of Indian Affairs (BIA) schools was supported as official policy. This practice accelerated in the 1950s and 1960s: close to 70% of the children for whom the BIA had direct responsibility were in boarding schools (Fuchs & Havighurst, 1973). Unfortunately, curriculum in these schools was often questionable and home language and cultural practices were forbidden. Supervision by aides charged with creating a family atmosphere was available at an average ratio of 1 aide to 120 children.

Although official policy in the 1950s supposedly encouraged the education of elementary school-aged children in their home environments, in reality, sufficient day schools were unavailable. When they were "available," children had to live in such restricted proximity to attend that those living on expansive reservations were ineligible.

The boarding school experience systematically removed generations of Native American children from their homes and cultures, devalued those cultures and families, dealt a severe blow to traditional family and community bonding, and left deeply rooted, traumatic emotional scars (Locust, 1988). Current practices protract the problem. Very large numbers of Native American children are still in out-of-home placements, with 85% of those placements being with non-Native American families (Yates, 1987).

When levels of acculturation vary significantly between parent/community and children, acculturation stress develops. This results in disharmony and the diffusion of identity and sense of belonging in the world (Yates, 1987). Without that base in cultural validation, the imposition of another culture through schooling results in what Dupris (1979) termed coercive assimilation. Coercive assimilation leads to alienation, making integration into either culture difficult, at best.

Acculturation stress and its subsequent alienation disrupts the natural intergenerational transmission of culture and the mediation of learning. When this occurs, a repertoire of information and experience is lost, as is the unique human characteristic of learning engendered in that transmission process (Jensen et al., 1988). It is that bonded interaction that promotes early learning and communication of that learning in the context of one's culture, which is so important for crossing cultures (as in home to school), especially when these cultures vary significantly. Yates (1987) posited that acculturation-related stressors contribute to the high numbers of symptomatic behaviors seen in schools, as well as community-based symptoms still lingering from the profound stresses of the boarding school experience.

The range of levels of cultural maintenance or acculturation is extremely wide among Native Americans. Although some choice clearly exists in current levels of acculturation for any Native American individual or family, it must be contextualized in these broad historical realities. The variation is influenced by location, marriage patterns, and language retention or loss. Red Horse (1988) discussed this variability as a spectrum of family systems including the traditional, neotraditional, transitional, bicultural, and acculturated. This variability is based on changes in modal behaviors, such as language, kin structure, religion, land, and health practices. Movement along the spectrum is not necessarily linear or unidirectional. The last category is pan renaissance, in which renewal and revitalization of tradition is key. Change in any one of the modal behaviors (e.g., adoption of a second language or new ritual procedures) will move the unit to a different level of acculturation.

In the acculturated family, English is the preferred language, primary social relationships are with non-Indians, religion is non-Native, land is viewed as utilitarian, and American institutional care is preferred. Movement from acculturation to pan renaissance, in Red Horse's schema, includes the unit readopting traditional language, reorganizing natural extended kinship arrangements, and revitalizing aspects of historic ritual customs, sacred views of the land, and historic beliefs around the etiology of disease. Because full acculturation never brought the promised rewards, pan renaissance is seen as a movement forward in consciousness, an appropriate and renewing response to the accumulated negative effects of wholesale coerced acculturation.

Cultural and linguistic preservation and enrichment are seen by many Native American people as "hinges upon which Native American survival and integrity exist" (Emerson, 1986, p. 2). Within the linguistic traditions reside many important elements of culture that bring meaning to existence and communication. For instance, the use of certain words, phrases, songs, and sequences in specific culturally mandated circumstances link the person with a larger spiritual belief system, which may extend far back in time. If those linguistically linked traditions are lost, the deep meaning of existence is potentially lost to that individual as well.

Language is a socially acquired, culturally constructed phenomenon (Leap, 1993). Linguistic tradition cues such things as humor, appropriateness, nature of relationships, bonding, wisdom, and timing. For instance, direct and timed question and answer sequences common in psychometric testing and in classroom discourse are experienced as culturally inappropriate in many Native American groups. Such questioning may elicit silence, an "I don't know" response, or a reply that may seem unrelated. The (cultural-) linguistic tradition of the Native child established the given response as the best way to indicate that the question was inappropriate. All too often, the school-based interpretation labels students as unable, unskilled, or resistant (Leap, 1993).

The use (in schools) of what Leap (1993) called American Indian English (Native American versions of English tied specifically to an ancestral language base) is another outgrowth of acculturation. American Indian English is a mechanism of cultural maintenance. Leap (1993) detailed the example of the Colorado River Reservation, where four distinct and traditionally unrelated tribal groups (Mohave, Chemehevi, Hopi, and Navajo) reside. Here, he found distinct dialects linked to each ancestral language, which serve an important function for each community and its members. To speak English in a Mohave way, for instance, is to maintain cultural distinction, heritage, and connectedness to the tribe.

SCHOOL-HOME DISCONTINUITY

Secada (1991) proposed the construct of cultural discontinuity. Children enter school with a wide range of experiences tied to home socialization patterns, which, hopefully, will be continuous with the experiences they will encounter in school. However, most schools convey content in a manner that is closely aligned to the specific norms of the majority culture. Children must translate behaviors and values across cultures and then assimilate the school culture, which may be at odds with the home culture. Thus, potentially, schools become highly decontextualized, discontinuous learning experiences for Native American children, resulting, at times, in opposition or resistance to learning.

The following examples are illustrative: Many Native American children are expected to engage in meaning-centered tasks at home under adult supervision, and never display knowledge before the child determines it is ready for display (Deyhle, 1987). Yet, in most public school classrooms, Native American children are expected to work out of cultural context and to display their work while it is in progress. Traditionally, sharing and generosity are expected, competition is discouraged, and the Native American student will not compete if it would shame another person. However, non-Indians may misinterpret helping each other or not competing as being poorly motivated or lazy. Traditionally, respect for elders and teachers is shown by humble acceptance, (e.g., not looking directly at the person and not questioning). However, the Native American child demonstrating such respect for a teacher may be described as withdrawn, shy, or having low self-esteem. Traditionally, orientation to present time and to the needs of the whole community are the norm; orientation to future time (e.g., deadlines) are a secondary priority. However, lack of timeliness with school work may be misinterpreted as laziness or irresponsibility, while within a cultural context, the Native American student may be engaged in alternative activities considered to be *more* responsible by the community (Yates, 1987).

Similarly, Fuchs and Havighurst (1973) referred to a study by Robert Bergman where many (Navajo) Indian children reportedly learned "nothing" (academic) in school, but actually performed non-scholastic (Navajo) tasks extremely well. Wolcott (1987) relayed another striking example of home-school discontinuity during his years of teaching in the Blackfish Village in British Columbia. He interpreted his students' behaviors from an ethnocentric perspective, characterizing their interactions with him as "a firmly entrenched pattern of pupil hostility" (p. 137). Although on the one hand, Wolcott recognized that governmental efforts to force acculturation had been highly detrimental, he wrote: "I was not assigned to the village to teach villagers their way of life; I was assigned to teach them something about mine" (p. 145). It seems difficult to shake this kind of ethnocentric myopia, which implies that the only responsibility for crossing cultures belongs to the students, and the only culture to be used as a learning base is the dominant or Euro-American culture.

The stereotypes that emerge from ethnocentric interpretations of culture-based behaviors must be recast and rethought from a culturally affirmative knowledge base. A key issue for educators is to provide or facilitate classroom-based learning experiences that validate both cultures "with minimum disruption in [students'] lives and without suffering the loss of Native identity or heritage" (Emerson, 1986, p. 9). Smolkin related an example of such harmony in the classroom of a master teacher (Katherine). This teacher successfully reframed the cultural norm of cooperation on tasks and practice before sharing with the elder into a school norm of group time for "private practice":

> The warp that Katherine stretches on her students' mental looms boasts more than a simple threading of standard English forms. What glistens in the fabric of her teaching is the access she provides beyond the syntactic to the discourse level structures of the dominant world. "At the end of presentations," she quizzes her pupils, "what is it good to do?" That her students are internalizing this dominant world discourse structure is evident in the child's smile and immediate response. (Suina & Smolkin, 1994, p. 129)

BROADER ISSUES OF LEARNING STYLE AND COMMUNICATION

Deloria (1991) explained that a key to understanding Native American ways of knowing is to remember that the emphasis is on the particular, not on general laws and explanations of how things work: "Indians as a rule do not try to bring existing bits of knowledge into categories and rubrics which can be used to do further investigation and experimentation with nature. The Indian system requires a prodigious memory" (p. 14). Relational thinking styles, often associated with traditional Native American students, must be understood for their inherent value and meaning. Traditional information gathering may be characterized as correlational or relational rather than by cause-effect sequences. Deloria (1991) illustrated:

Being interested in the psychological behavior of things in the world and attributing personality to all things. Indians began to observe and remember how and when things happened together. Thus, they made connections between things that had no sequential relationships, and no firm belief in cause and effect (which plays such an important role in western science and thinking) resulted. But Indians were well aware that when certain sequence of things began, certain other elements or events would also occur. (p. 18)

Analyses of oral and written discourse will often reveal these patterns. To the non-Native American thinker, ideas may appear unconnected *because* they are nonlinear, and often that nonlinear path is a long trail. In my experience and that of others (e.g., Suina & Smolkin, 1994; Tharp, 1994), the connectedness may be unspoken, although available in the broader context. Suina told a story of asking his (Pueblo) father what he needed to do to participate in a certain ceremony. The scope of the context extended back to the history of when the ceremony was last performed (some 40 years before), Suina's memory of his grandfather, who had been present, and the social conditions that had precipitated the need for the ceremony. He described the effect the speech (the contextualizing of his part) had on him:

> ... the same sense that I get when I look at mountains and boulders, a sense of eternity, a sense of connection between generations, events. I felt connected with people, with long chains of events, and intensely felt that I was just a small piece in all of this. And I knew that the small piece was not what was important, but rather, what was absolutely crucial was the whole picture. (Suina & Smolkin, 1994, p. 119)

Similarly, Tharp (1994) described Native American cognition as the "anchor example" for holistic thought, in which the pieces derive their meaning from the pattern of the whole, rather than the whole being revealed through the analysis of each of its sections. One of Tharp's (1994) examples described a lesson plan devised by Yukon elders to learn a traditional craft, making moccasins of Caribou skin:

> The 16 week unit began with preparations for the hunt; moccasins per se did not appear until the 15th week. To the elders' way of thinking, it is not possible to understand the moccasin outside the context of the leather, which is not understandable outside the spiritual relationship of the caribou to the land. Contrast this with the analytic way of proceeding, in which we probably would have given the children the pattern to start cutting out the leather in the first 15 minutes. (p. 90)

For the speech-language pathologist, written text analysis should consider the influences of holism, by consideration of the entire text. This consideration allows representation of the story's structural form (Tharp, 1994).

Leap (1993) cautioned that whatever the topic, studies of Indian English codes must explore the study of discourse without isolating knowledge of language from language use.

To complete the circle, then, Native American thinking is neither linear or hierarchical. Rather, it is concerned with life and all its interrelationships; sensory, cognitive, emotional, intuitive, and spiritual aspects are all drawn into relationships in order to affect perception. Prayers, songs, and symbology all have a structure, content, context, and process behind them (Emerson, personal communication, October, 1992).

PARENT INTEREST AND INVOLVEMENT

Extremely low Native American parent involvement (Cleary & Peacock, 1998) is a reality and a complex issue, which also must be addressed with new understanding. Historically, educators have viewed the culture and language of the Native American as detrimental to the child's future. The person inside the trappings of a "useless" Native culture and language needed to be salvaged. Parent involvement, in that context, was seen as detrimental because parents embodied Native American cultures and languages (Emerson, 1986). Thus, the relationship of school personnel and Native American parents has been adversarial. "Conditioned by years of the federal government's policy of preventing parental or community involvement with education," relates Joe (1994), "many Navajo families are still reluctant to question and/or visit their children's schools."

All too often, system failures with Native American children are wrongly attributed to the apathy of Indian parents. For example, when a Native American child does not show up at school, educators have assumed that the parent does not value education enough to send the child to school. Rather, we must look beyond the possibility of "hooky" to the probability of tribal responsibilities, ceremonial mandates, the school's role in unawarely creating a hostile environment, or other equally compelling reasons for nonattendance.

Historically, many Native American leaders placed emphasis on education above political or economic development (Emerson, 1986). Children were greatly loved in most tribes and their education was viewed as important to the future of the communities (Deloria, 1991). Currently, many Native American tribes and organizations are contributing responsible leadership to overcome the gaps in education at all levels. Surveys have documented education as among the top reported priorities of concern in some urban Native American communities, second only to "how to deal with the dominant society" (San Diego State University, 1988). Non-Native groups typically underestimate the importance of education in the Native American experience.

Within some Native American nations, two cultural principles may lend additional hypotheses and insights into why the parent may not come to the school. The principle of noninterference assumes that children are not the property of the parents and are responsible for their own choices. Thus, parents do not interfere in natural development and consequences, but expect children to learn from them (Yates, 1987). Because parents may not overtly teach or punish, their attitudes may be misinterpreted as non-involvement. To these Native American parents, school personnel often appear prying, giving unwanted advice or involving themselves in Native American business (Pepper & Henry, 1989).

A second principle common among Native American cultures is avoiding disharmony. Because life is seen as an integrated whole, refusal to come to school may be a result of perceived or predicted disharmony and its possible consequences. If coming to school leads to the depletion of spiritual energy, for example, illness could result and affect the entire community. Thus, the parent may choose to avoid disharmony with the schools and deal with the child at home (Locust, 1988).

Disharmony must be framed in a larger context as well. U.S. schools seem to have, at their core, values that are antithetical to those of traditional Native American cultures. In a national survey of Native American parents' attitudes toward education, lack of understanding and attention to and valuing Native American cultures was cited as a major contributor to dissatisfaction with schools (Robinson-Zañartu & Majel-Dixon, 1993). Social and behavioral problems among Native American children are often blamed, as well, on the failure of the school to teach them to respect their culture (Joe, 1994).

The U.S. educational system is seen as an (American-style) opportunity for economic and social gain for non-Indians—an economic venture and preparation ground based on rugged individualism, private ownership, and profit linked with success. For traditional Native Americans, this represents neither their cultural and linguistic heritage nor a view of education that would attend to the collective consciousness and to the worldview discussed earlier. The behaviors of non-Native teachers, students, and parents are foreign, even though most Native Americans have received some schooling in the system. Because they have no alternative in which they could be valued and truly involved, and because of legal mandates and economic realities. Native American parents may passively accept this system (Emerson, personal communication, October, 1992). Whatever the conglomerate of issues behind a particular Native American parent's "noninvolvement," we must keep in mind that large systemic issues are central, cultural difference is a given, and that the nonvaluing of education by Native American parents is usually the wrong hypothesis.

ASSESSMENT AND EVALUATION

Given the complexity of cultural difference, one might logically assume that assessment across cultures would extend the range of procedures, expand the recommendations, and build culture into the forefront of the evaluation. In contrast, McShane (1979, 1983) found a *narrower* range of evaluation procedures, a *restricted* number of recommendations, and that culture was not taken into account as an important variable in the evaluation reports of Native American children referred for special education.

The speech-language assessment of culturally and linguistically diverse children requires alternative models that acknowledge the differences in narrative socialization experiences and explore assumptions concerning audience involvement (Gutierrez-Clellen & Quinn, 1993). More globally, the assessment of communication must reflect its holistic functions within naturalistic contexts (Crystal, 1987; Damico, 1993; Oiler, 1979; Tharp, 1994).

As speech-language pathologists have begun to explore information and cross-cultural research, systemic issues are emerging as primary in language assessment and intervention, rather than the traditional intrinsic factors believed to be at the root of apparent dysfunction or disfluency. Damico (1991, 1993), for instance, posed specific questions to determine whether "extrinsic explanatory factors" may be ruled out before considering factors intrinsic to the individual. Thus, the examiner asks a series of questions that probe for evidence that "problem behaviors" can be explained according to, for example: normal second language acquisition or dialectal phenomena; cross-cultural interference or related cultural phenomena; differences in the student's past history or experience; or any bias effect that was in operation before, during, or after the assessment (such as language learning environment, disempowered community or lowered expectations, or bias in referral). Gutierrez-Clellen and Quinn (1993) contributed a complementary and equally important set of issues to explore when assessing narratives across cultures, including world knowledge, interaction styles, and paralinguistic conventions.

Assessment of the Native American child is particularly challenging. We must question the core validity of virtually all existing tools and instruments. The traditional Native bookless learning, tied to ecological principles and to spirit, certainly has no corollaries in such standardized measures as the Goldman-Fristoe Test of Articulation (Goldman & Fristoe, 1986), the Boehm Test of Basic Concepts (Boehm, 1986), the Illinois Test of Psycholinguistic Abilities (Kirk et al., 1968), or the Woodcock-Johnson Psychoeducational Battery-Revised (Woodcock & Johnson, 1989), or even most conventional observation procedures. It is possible that the cultural assumptions in these tests and evaluation tools are so divergent from Native

American learning as to make the current repertoire irrelevant as valid indicators of Native American learning.

Two recent examples of responses to the social studies subtest of the Woodcock-Johnson illustrate what Majel-Dixon (personal communication, October 19, 1994) calls tribal influences on the responses of a Luiseño boy. In response to a question about what type of boat is in the picture (a canoe), the child looked hard and then replied, "looks Chippewa to me!" He lives on a rural Indian reservation in California, surrounded by extended kinship relationships. In reply to the question, "What is a neighbor?" he responded, "Family or close friend." When prompted, "Tell me more," he replied, "Aunt Lorena, Uncle Andy, Temet." These answers reflect his cultural reality and attention to detail. Yet, by using standardized scoring, he would have missed both questions.

TEST INTERPRETATION OF LINGUISTIC AND VERBAL SKILLS

Many verbal skills common in mainstream school culture and expected on standardized measures, are not a part of traditional Native American upbringing. Frequently, silence is culturally appropriate, although it is often misinterpreted in school as inappropriate or a sign of difficulty. Although several writers have posited that Native American children are taught not to question at home (Lee, 1937; Pepper & Henry, 1989; Yates, 1987), Emerson (personal communication, October, 1992) suggested that, in part, Native American children may have been "taught" not to question in school as an outgrowth of the historical and ongoing assault on Native ways. Questioning, he says, is part of the spiritual and learning process. Among Native American communities, children's questions may, at times, be overlooked because they may be deemed inappropriate. Certain assumptions of Native spirituality rest on their not being questioned, or children may have been deemed not ready for answers to their questions.

Philips (1983) pointed out that Native American children are not "nonverbal," but that interaction systems in different cultures allocate verbal-visual cues differently. The type of questioning typically found in schools is generally not an interactive strategy employed by Native American people (Pepper & Henry, 1989). Nonetheless, the question-asking style, in its most exaggerated form, is imposed by standardized assessment procedures (e.g., using direct and often abrupt question and answer sequences and timed responses; Brandt, 1984; Philips, 1983; Sattler, 1982). Thus, cultural difference, linguistic difference, and systems variables must be considered in the interpretation of verbal measures for Native American children.

In addition, standard English forms pose difficulty for large percentages of Native Americans, even when their first language is English. A national survey by Brod and McQuiston (1983) found that 75% of Native American adults speak some form of English, and that most experience some level of difficulty when they speak it. Approximately 44% learned English as a second language in a setting away from the home. Leap (1993) reported that 31% of the Native American adult population has been exclusive speakers of some form of English, and that a large percentage of those exclusive English speakers report having difficulty with the language.

Even when English is the first language of the home, Native languages have been found to influence the acquisition of English significantly, especially in deep structure (Tafoya, 1994). Ancestral language tradition provides the basis and the most powerful explanation for knowledge of Indian English grammar, and the use of that knowledge in specific discourse settings (Leap, 1993). Because some 200 Native American languages are in use, representing over 20 language families, no one characterization of Indian English is possible. In some speech communities, "Indian English rules of pronunciation draw heavily on ancestral language sound contrasts; in others, pronunciation closely parallels sound inventories found in local or regional vernacular English, combines principles from both sources, or approximates standard English models" (Leap, 1993, p. 93). In addition, the phenomenon of American Indian English must be viewed as a culture carrier of sorts. Facility in the heavily influenced language is seen as a cultural asset (Leap, 1993), adding yet another dimension to the language issue. Some speakers of Indian English are also speakers of Standard English, with their choice of code clearly dependent on political rather than grammatical factors. Thus, questions of power, politics, and inequality are more likely sources of barriers and resistance than language (Leap, 1993, p. 3).

When English is the second language of the Native American child, the many differences between English and most Native American languages further complicate the situation. Bilingualism or multilingualism is not a recent phenomenon for Native Americans. When Europeans first arrived in North America, more than 500 American Indian and Alaskan Native languages were spoken, "Some as different in grammatical form and rules of discourse as Russian and Chinese, Burmese and Bantu, or English and Arabic" (Leap, 1993, p. 148). Dupris (1979) reported that in the 19th century, when the Cherokee had control over their own bilingual schools, they were 95% literate in their language, and the Oklahoma Cherokees had a higher English literacy level than native English speakers in either Texas or Arkansas.

Mastery of Standard English is extremely challenging, because of cross-linguistic variations. For instance, in the Navajo language, the verb form may depend on the shape of the object of reference. Most Native American languages do not have the same syntactical structure as European languages.

Word order may change within the same language, depending on the intended meaning, with the sequence guided by the first word (which indicates the speaker's intended emphasis; Tafoya, 1994). For example, "In Arapaho English and Yavapai English, the entire Standard English-based word order is regularly reversed, with supporting/modifying materials preceding, instead of following, the subject-verb sequence: From the family is where we learn to be good (Arapaho)" (Leap, 1993, p. 77). Further, pronoun deletion "shows up in every variety of Indian English ... (however, it does) not occur in all sentence environments, and the conditions which specify the locations favoring deletion are not the same in all codes" (Leap, 1993,p. 58).

The amount of pause time between sentences varies significantly between English and most native languages, and may become another source of misinterpretation (with long pauses often misinterpreted as resistance or not knowing). Tafoya (1994) reported that in contrast to the .9 second pause time typical in English, many reservation communities' pause times were double that amount, with some averaging between 4–5 seconds.

SPECIAL EDUCATION

Special education may be an unknown concept to many Native Americans. Although most non-Native parents have some knowledge of the legislation supporting special education services, Native American parents tend to have very little knowledge of the specific services (Connery, cited in Johnson, 1989). Further, most traditional Native American languages do not have words for retardation, disability, or handicapping conditions (Locust, 1988). Thus, children classified as having disabilities in schools may not be labeled in their home communities "and in fact function as (fully) contributing members of their society" (Locust, 1988, p. 326).

Native American parents' views of special education generally fall in the range of negativity. Robinson-Zañartu and Majel-Dixon's (1993) survey of Native American parents encompassed 55 bands or tribal groups and found the vast majority reporting that when a child had been referred for special education services, parents neither understood nor agreed with the idea of placement. In addition, culture had almost never been considered in the placement evaluation. Some parents reported that they had removed children from school rather than agree to special education services.

CULTURALLY COMPATIBLE SERVICE DELIVERY MODELS

A model of service delivery is needed that targets the system's issues impacting education, with culture being a central system in that process. The assessment/intervention component must validate culture, individual potential, and the modifiability of students in relation to those systems (Jensen et al., 1992). This model must be comprehensive, attending to the ecologies (i.e., home, school, community) and transactions surrounding the child. It must focus on the learning processes of the child (McShane, 1983; Tafoya, 1982) as well as content, and must be sensitive to the potential for change for that child.

Two theoretical models, ecosystemic (Damico, 1993; Larry P. Task Force, 1989), and modifiability enhancement (dynamic; Gutierrez-Clellen & Quinn, 1993; Jensen, 1992; Jensen et al., 1992), may contribute to appropriate service delivery for American Indian children. These models are compatible and responsive to the need to design interventions, and focus on outcomes of significance. Both view the culture of the student as central in the learning process.

Ecosystems Contributions

The ecosystems approach (Damico, 1993; Plas, 1986; Robinson & Cook, 1990) views culture as a permeating influence on the child's behavior and learning, rather than a separate component to be evaluated. The ecosystems assessor brings culture to the forefront, uses it as a basis for hypothesis generation, and seeks to identify the strengths of the culture that may be used for systems change (Larry P. Task Force, 1989). Within this approach, both internal and external forces operate together and the interaction between them accounts for behavior.

Ecology is the grouping of behavioral settings with a significant number of common elements (such as home, school, and community). Native American children usually have more ecologies to navigate because they must transact within and across Native and mainstream cultural communities. From this perspective, the child's culture, ethnicity, socioeconomic status, attitudes, self-concept, learning style, and motivation transact simultaneously with teacher attitudes and behavior, culture, ethnicity, learning/teaching style, self-concept, and motivations, in a setting that has physical, social, cultural, cognitive, and affective elements (Larry P. Task Force, 1989).

Ecosystemic assessment looks, first, at broad patterns within the larger interacting systems, without necessitating a level of intrusive evaluation of the child (Cook & Robinson, 1990). For instance, at the school site, we examine the pattern of referrals for various cultures across the variables of behavior, special education referral, or speech and language evaluation. If there is a definite pattern by culture, then a total systems intervention should be the first order of business. For instance, information regarding American Indian English or cultural stereotypes of behavior might be reframed in a cultural context in order to change interactions between teachers and students from that culture.

The next level of ecosystemic analysis involves examining patterns over time of (a) achievement at a given school, grade, home situation, and school expectations; (b) achievement or involvement within a given cultural context, grade, home situation, and school expectations; and (c) home/school interactions and expectations. In one such analysis, I found that within the home/cultural milieu, one Luiseño child was active with his community and family (a dancer, a caretaker for his younger siblings, and involved with his parents in the art community), was articulate at the tribal education center, and read within average limits from a book at his grade level by a Native American author. In contrast, school personnel had characterized him as withdrawn, possibly depressed, weak in reading, and from a "deprived" home that lacked certain physical amenities (implying a level of causation of the "problem"). The differences were striking and were used to help reframe the school situation to become more culturally compatible.

DYNAMIC ASSESSMENT TO MEDIATE LEARNING AND COMMUNICATION

The literature on mediated learning (see, e.g., Gutierrez-Clellen & Quinn, 1993 and Lidz & Peña, this volume, for applications to speech and language) has evolved from the work of Vygotsky (1934/1962, 1978), Piaget (1952), and Feuerstein (1970; Feuerstein & Jensen, 1980; Feuerstein & Rand, 1974; Feuerstein et al., 1979; Jensen & Feuerstein, 1987). It is based on a paradigm that assumes change rather than stability of potential, and that posits that human nature is cultural. Accordingly, learning involves the processing of contextually (e.g., culturally) meaningful symbols, and is a dynamic and open process in which active mediation by an adult can enhance functioning. Among the most current work in this area is Jensen's (1990, 1992) modifiability enhancement theory (MET). MET holds that learning begins with the primary caregiver whose context is the shared primary culture and language.

Applications of dynamic assessment use a series of tools, ranging from decontextualized materials such as Ravens Progressive Matrices, to academically or culturally contextualized tools such as reading materials or skill-based observations of cultural events. Within the various contexts, the evaluator seeks to observe and intervene in the learning process, determining how best to modify the child's learning behavior based on trial learning experiences. The interaction between the child and examiner is characterized by the mediation (five methods are detailed) of a variety of cognitive functions. Modification of the most salient inefficient functions builds on current levels of efficiency in others in order to develop recommendations that can be reinforced both at home and at school. Assessment can be done in the presence of other people and in an authentic environment, such as the reservation community.

The following is an example from a dynamic assessment of the Luiseno child described earlier. Following an examination of school records, observations in a cultural context, and visiting time with the family, we began the dynamic assessment by using three of Feuerstein's decontextualized tools. In nonculturally based materials, I found patterns of blocking linked with feeling incompetent, coupled with a tendency to respond impulsively (rather than to using hypothesis testing, categorizing, and organizing behaviors). We worked to mediate those new functions, and then to "bridge" those skills found efficient in the contexts of his dance and art, to his school work. Next, we mediated bridging the use of the same skills to academic reading. During this task, his affect evolved from initial apprehension to almost delight.

Schools, families, and communities, in partnership, can target mediated learning experiences simultaneously. Native American tribal leaders, educators, and parents should be critical players in the design of culturally appropriate mediational interventions and can lend insight to school practices that will better mediate high levels of academic learning by Native American children.

CONCLUSIONS

Our school system has, at best, underserved Native American children and communities; at worst, it has engendered suffering and disharmony. Many historical wrongs were intentional. Most current ones are caused by ignorance. Fortunately, ignorance has an antidote: learning. Therefore, we must learn, and in doing so, heal the wounds of isolation, rejection, and disservice, and begin to regain harmony through culturally affirmative action. This learning, which involves differing worldviews, will only occur over time. Furthermore, it must be done with the knowledge that each tribal nation must be considered uniquely, with the broad considerations presented here used for hypothesis generation.

New competencies must be mastered by speech-language pathologists who serve Native American children, including: (a) a broad role that includes situationally based assessment and intervention within the context of transactions between the Native American child's culture and the school culture; (b) familiarity with the literature and research, and technical competence with alternative means of evaluation that consider cultural variables; (c) a growing knowledge and respect for the history and legal issues that compel unique service delivery to Native American children and communities; (d) knowledge of and experience with local Native American cultures; and (e) a proactive interpretation of their relationships to learning, language, and communication. The ecosystemic and dynamic assessment methods lend themselves to culturally compatible interventions that show promise in this venture.

ACKNOWLEDGMENTS

I would like to express my deep gratitude for the continuing guidance and teachings of Larry W. Emerson (Navajo) of Niha'alchiniba Educational Programs, from whom I have begun to learn new ways of accessing both what and how to learn in a more deeply and richly contextualized manner, and to my many other teachers on this path, especially to Marilyn Robinson (Cayuga), Juanita Majel (Luiseño), Shirley Murphy (Oglala Lakota), and Flora Howe (Absentee Shawnee).

NOTE

Reprinted with permission.

Robinson-Zañartu, C. (1996). Serving Native American children and families: Considering cultural variables. *Language, Speech & Hearing Services in Schools,* 27(4), 373–384. https://doi.org/10.1044/0161-1461.2704.373

Contact author: Carol Robinson-Zañartu, Department of Counseling & School Psychology, San Diego State University, San Diego, CA 92182-0162.

REFERENCES

Boehm, A. E. (1986). *Boehm test of basic concepts manual.* Pyschological Corp.

Brandt, E. A. (1984). The cognitive functioning of American Indian children: A critique of McShane & Plas. *School Psychology Review, 13,* 74–82.

Brod, R., & McQuiston, J. M. (1983). American Indian adult education and literacy: The first national survey. *Journal of American Indian Education, 22*(2), 1–16.

Chinn, P. C., & Hughes, S. (1987). Representation of minority students in special education classes. *Remedial and Special Education, 8*(4), 11–46.

Cleary, L. M., & Peacock, T. D. (1998). *Collected wisdom: American Indian education.* Allyn & Bacon.

Cook, V. J., & Robinson, C. A. (1990, April 20). *Alternative assessment: Ecological and dynamic.* An invited preconvention workshop for the annual meeting of the National Association of School Psychologists, San Francisco, CA.

158 ■ C. ROBINSON-ZAÑARTU

Crystal, D. (1987). Towards a "bucket" theory of language disability: Taking account of interaction between linguistic levels. *Clinical Linguistics and Phonetics, 1*, 7–22.

Damico, J. S. (1991). Descriptive assessment of communicative ability in LEP students. In E. V. Hamayan & J. S Damico (Eds.), *Limiting bias in the assessment of bilingual students* (pp. 157–218). Pro-Ed.

Damico, J. S. (1993). Language assessment in adolescents: Addressing critical issues. *Language, Speech, and Hearing Services in Schools, 24*(1), 29–35. https://doi.org/10.1044/0161-1461.2401.29

Deloria, V. (1991). *Indian education in America.* American Indian Science and Engineering Society.

Deyhle, D. (1987). Learning failure: Tests as gatekeepers and the culturally different child-Success or failure? In H. Trueba (Ed.), *Learning and the language minority child* (pp. 85–108). Newbury House.

Dupris, J. C. (1979). The national impact of multicultural education: A renaissance of Native American culture through tribal self-determination and Indian control of education. In *Multicultural education and the American Indian* (pp. 43–54). University of California, American Indian Studies Center.

Emerson, L. W. (1986, July). *Feuerstein cognitive education theory and American Indian education* [Paper presentation]. Mediated Learning Experience International Workshop, Jerusalem, Israel.

Feuerstein, R. (1970). A dynamic approach to causation, prevention and alleviation of retarded performance. In H. C Haywood (Ed.), *Social-cultural aspects of mental retardation* (pp. 341–377). Appleton-Century-Crofts.

Feuerstein, R., & Jensen, M. R. (1980). Instrumental enrichment: Theoretical basis, goals and instruments. *The Educational Forum, 44*(4), 401–423.

Feuerstein, R., & Rand, Y. (1974). Mediated learning experience: An outline of the proximal etiology for differential development of cognitive functions. In L. Gold Fein (Ed.), *International understanding: Cultural differences in the development of cognitive processes* (pp. 7–37). International Council of Psychologists.

Feuerstein, R., Rand, Y., & Hoffman, M. B. (1979). *The dynamic assessment of retarded performers: The learning potential assessment device, theory, instruments and techniques.* Scott Foresman & Co.

Fuchs, E., & Havighurst, R. J. (1973). *To live on this earth American Indian education.* Doubleday.

Goldman, R., & Fristoe, M. (1986). *Goldman-Fristoe test of articulation.* American Guidance Service.

Gutierrez-Clellen, V. F., & Quinn, R. (1993). Assessing narratives of children from diverse cultural/linguistic groups. *Language, Speech, and Hearing Services in Schools, 24*, 2–9.

Havighurst, R. J. (1978). The education of American Indian children and youth. *Summary Report and Recommendations: National Study of American Indians Education, Series No. 4. No. 6).* University of Minnesota.

Jensen, M. R. (1990). Change models and some evidence for phases and their plasticity in cognitive structures. *International Journal of Cognitive Education and Mediated Learning, 1*(1), 5–16.

Jensen, M. R. (1992). Principles of change models in school psychology and education. *Advances in Cognition and Educational Practice, 1B*, 47–72.

Jensen, M. R., & Feuerstein, R. (1987). The learning potential assessment device: From philosophy to practice. In C. S. Ldz (Ed.), *Dynamic assessment: An interactional approach to evaluating learning potential* (pp. 379–402). Guilford.

Jensen, M. R., Feuerstein, R., Rand, Y., Kaniel, S., & Tzuriel, D. (1988). Cultural difference and cultural deprivation: A theoretical framework for differential intervention. In R. M. Grupta & P. Coxhead (Eds.), *Cultural diversity and learning efficiency* (pp. 64–88). Macmillan.

Jensen, M. R., Robinson-Zafiartu, C., & Jensen, M. L. (1992). *Dynamic assessment and mediated learning: Assessment and intervention for developing cognitive and knowledge structures: An alternative in the era of reform* [Monograph]. The California Department of Education.

Joe, J. R. (1994). Revaluing Native-American concepts of development and education. In P. M. Greenfield & R. R. Cocking (Eds.), *Cross-cultural roots of minority child development,* (pp. 107–113). Lawrence Erlbaum Associates.

Johnson, M. J. (1989, March). *Statement to U.S. House of Representatives Subcommittee on Select Education: Hearings on Discretionary Programs of EHA.* ttps://archive .org/stream/ERIC_ED312852/ERIC_ED312852_djvu.txt

Kirk, S., McCarthy, J., & Kirk, W. (1968). *Illinois test of psycholinguistic abilities.* University of Illinois Press.

Larry P. Task Force. (1989). Ecological assessment. In *Larry P. task force report: Policy and alternative assessment guideline recommendations* (pp. 75). California State Department of Education.

Leap, W. L. (1993). *American Indian English.* University of Utah Press.

Lee, M. (1937). *Indians of the Oaks.* Ginn & Co.

Locust, C. (1988). Wounding the spirit: Discrimination and traditional American Indian belief systems. *Harvard Educational Review, 58*(3), 315–330.

McShane, D. (1983). Explaining achievement patterns of American Indian children: A transcultural and developmental model. *Peabody Journal of Education, 61,* 34–48.

Moll, L. C. (1991). Social and instructional issues in literacy instruction for "disadvantaged" students. In M. S. Knapp & P. M. Shields (Eds.), *Better schooling for children of poverty: Alternatives to conventional wisdom,* (pp. 61–84). McCutchan.

Oiler, J. W., Jr. (1979). *Language tests at school.* Longman.

Pepper, F. C., & Henry, S. (1989). Social and cultural effects on Indian learning style: Classroom implications. In B. J. Robinson Shade (Ed.), *Culture, style, and the educative process: Making schools work for racially diverse students.* Charles C. Thomas.

Philips, S. U. (1983). *The invisible culture: Communication in classroom and community on the Warm Springs Indian reservation.* Longman.

Piaget, J. (1952). *The origins of intelligence in children* (M. Cook, Trans.). International University Press.

Plas, J. M. (1986). *Systems psychology in the schools.* Pergamon Press.

Ramirez, B. R., & Tippeconnic, J. W. (1979). Preparing teachers of American Indian handicapped children. *Teacher Education and Special Education, 2*(4), 27–33.

Red Horse, J. (1988). Cultural evolution of American Indian families. In C. Jacobs & D. D. Bowles (Eds), *Ethnicity and race: Critical concepts in social work,* (pp. 86–102). National Association of Social Workers.

Robinson, C. A. (1990) *Collaboration across communities: American Indian specialty in school psychology project* (Federal Project # H029E00051). U.S. Department of Education, Office of Special Education Projects.

Robinson, C. A., & Cook, V. J. (1990) . Alternative assessment: Ecological and dynamic. *NASP Communique, 18*(5), 28–29.

Robinson-Zañartu, C., & Majel-Dixon, J. (1993, April). *American Indian parent attitudes toward education: A national survey* [Paper presentation]. National Association of School Psychologists Annual Meeting, Washington, DC.

Russell, G. (1994). *American Indian digest. 1995 edition: Contemporary demographics of the American Indian.* Thunderbird Enterprises.

San Diego County Office of Education. (1988). *Demographic characteristics of schools.*

San Diego State University. (1988, February). *Proceedings of the symposium on American Indian studies and community applications.*

Sattler, J. M. (1982). *Assessment of children's intelligence and special abilities.* Allyn and Bacon.

Secada, W. G. (1991). Selected conceptual and methodological issues for studying the mathematics education of the disadvantaged. In M. S. Knapp & P. M. Shields (Eds.), *Better schooling for the children of poverty: Alternatives to conventional wisdom* (pp. 149–168). McCutchan.

Suina, J. H., & Smolkin, L. B. (1994). From natal culture to school culture to dominant society culture: Supporting transitions for Pueblo Indian students. In P. M. Greenfield & R. R. Cocking (Eds.), *Cross-cultural roots of minority child development* (pp. 115–130). Lawrence Erlbaum Associates.

Tafoya, T. (1982). Coyote's eyes: Native cognition styles. *Journal of American Indian Education, 2*(2), 21–33.

Tafoya, T. (1994, June). *Understanding and infusing American Indian issues in college curricula* [Paper presentation]. Multicultural Educational Infusion Collective, San Diego State University, San Diego, CA.

Tharp, R. G. (1994). Intergroup differences among Native Americans in socialization and child cognition: An ethnogenetic analysis. In P. M. Greenfield & R. R. Cocking (Eds.), *Crosscultural roots of minority child development* (pp. 87–105). Lawrence Erlbaum Associates.

U.S. Bureau of the Census. (1993). *We the first Americans.* U.S. Department of Commerce.

U.S. Department of Education. (1989). *Digest of education statistics* (25th ed.). National Center for Education Statistics.

U.S. Senate. (1969). *Indian education: A national tragedy-A national challenge.* Committee on Labor and Public Welfare, Special Subcommittee on Indian Education.

Vygotsky, L. S. (1962). *Thought and language* (E. Hanfman & G. Vakar, Trans.). MIT Press. (Original work published 1934)

Vygotsky, L. S. (1978). *Mind in society: The development of higher psychological processes* (M. Cole, V. John-Steiner, S. Scribner, & E. Souberman, Eds., & Trans.). Harvard University Press.

Winget, P. (1989). Exploding cross-cultural populations: Prompt reform of special education. *The Special Edge, 5,* 3.

Woodcock, R. W., & Johnson, M. B. (1989). *Woodcock-Johnson psychoeducational battery—Revised.* DLM Teaching Resources.

Wolcott, H. F. (1987). The teacher as an enemy. In G. D. Spindler (Ed.), *Education and cultural process: Anthropological approaches* (2nd ed., pp. 136–150). Waveland Press.

Yates, A. (1987). Current status and future directions of research on the American Indian child. *American Journal of Psychiatry, 144,* 1135–1142.

CHAPTER 7

FACTORS IMPACTING POSTSECONDARY TRANSITIONS FOR BLACK STUDENTS

Erik M. Hines
Florida State University

Paul Singleton II
University of Connecticut

Mia R. Hines
Florida State University

Sophia L. Ángeles
University of California, Los Angeles

Bobbi-Jo Wathen
University of Connecticut

Tyron Slack
Florida State University

Damian Brown Jr.
Florida Agricultural and Mechanical University

ABSTRACT

Attaining postsecondary credentials gives an individual access to a career, higher salaries, and other benefits such as health insurance. Unfortunately,

Equity-Based Career Development and Postsecondary Transitions, pages 163–183
Copyright © 2022 by Information Age Publishing
www.infoagepub.com

everyone in the United States does not get the opportunity to pursue post-secondary options. Specifically, Black students in K–12 have experienced bar-riers to postsecondary pathways. In this chapter, we discuss the factors that impact the postsecondary transitions of Black students. Last, we discuss the practice, policy, and research recommendations for improving postsecondary transitions for Black students.

Getting an education beyond high school can be advantageous to increas-ing one's quality of life. According to Carnevale et al. (2011) an individual can make over one million dollars more in compensation over a lifetime than a person with a high school diploma. It is important that ALL indi-viduals have the opportunity to pursue a postsecondary education. Unfor-tunately, the United States has inequities in the education system that pre-vent all students from having the chance to be prepared for postsecondary attainment (Lee & Goodnough, 2019). Given the racial issues we have seen from Trayvon Martin to George Floyd and the COVID-19 pandemic, it is clear that Black students need more support academically, with their men-tal health, and postsecondary readiness. For example, when Black males graduate from high school, their choices are often to continue their ed-ucation by seeking postsecondary opportunities (e.g, college, vocational, workforce, military; Hines et al., 2020). Yet they are often less prepared for their college and career (Scott et al., 2013). Also, Black girls tend to experi-ence adultification (treated as if they were adults and not children) and do not get the resources or support needed to postsecondary readiness (Neal-Jackson, 2018). For many of these students, their preparation for college and career is woefully inadequate in comparison to their White counter-parts (Dulabaum, 2016). To ensure a successful postsecondary transition, students must have access to rigorous courses or career preparatory classes, culturally responsive teachers, familial support, and develop personal char-acteristics, such as leadership, a willingness to take risks, initiative, a sense of social responsibility, and so forth (Hudley et al., 2009; Sommerfeld & Bowen, 2013; Sandoval-Lucero et al., 2014; Wilkins, 2014).

Participation in postsecondary access programs can help Black students prepare for their postsecondary opportunities. There are a myriad of ben-efits for Black students who participate in postsecondary programs. Having the proper supports (i.e., prior knowledge, experiences, and postsecond-ary preparation) increases the likelihood of postsecondary success, belief in being college and career ready, awareness to distinguish between high school and postsecondary education, and the ability to use skills related to self-advocacy and self-determination (Erford, 2019).

In many Black communities, college degree attainment is regarded as one of the primary solutions to reduce poverty and close wealth gaps between Blacks and Whites in the United States (Bryant, 2015). With the changing labor market and a more globalized economy, a far greater number of careers require a postsecondary credential. Currently, it is estimated that two-thirds of jobs will require college experience, with 30% of those careers requiring at least a bachelor's degree and 36% of jobs requiring at least some college or an associate degree (Carnevale et al., 2013). This creates a barrier and can be challenging for Black students, many of whom are unprepared for the rigors of college.

As the demographics of the United States shift and a majority of our nation's students are children of color, their lack of preparation for postsecondary opportunities has significant implications for their communities, generational capital, American labor market, and economy (Kozleski & Proffitt, 2020; Pavlakis & Pryor, 2020; Wolf, 2017). Thus, having prior knowledge, experiences, and proper postsecondary preparation provides Black students a solution to overcome barriers like low teacher expectations, underprepared school counselors, and lack of academic rigor that may hinder postsecondary outcomes for many Black students. Nationally, most public school students believe that they will earn a bachelor's degree or more as they head towards graduation (Roderick et al., 2009; Rooney et al., 2006).

Given the individual benefits (e.g., intellectual development, better employment opportunities/compensation, etc.) and societal benefits (e.g., more civic involvement, greater tax contributions, etc.), the pursuit of higher education is an achievable and beneficial goal. Once students are exposed to a new career and educational opportunities and the potential social and economic benefits that accompany them, Black students are now provided an even greater incentive to enroll in postsecondary preparation and postsecondary education (Alleman & Holly, 2013). Typically, community organizations like the YMCA, Black Achievers, and the National Boys and Girls clubs foster relationships among students and within the schools in order to provide exploratory trips to nearby businesses, cities, state and national parks, historical sites, and other sorts of guided cultural experiences. However, postsecondary preparatory programs, civic organizations, higher education institutions, and public agencies also sponsor trips to leadership seminars, regional or national writing or speech contests, or on-campus college introduction weekends for individuals or small groups (Holland, 2017). This range of supports provides assistance to the work done by schools through reinforcing educational goals and programs, building students' self-efficacy and vocational imagination through connections to cultural, historical, natural, and other types of area resources, and by providing a safety net for Black students in need of additional assistance or encouragement (Holland, 2017).

For many, becoming properly prepared for postsecondary opportunities remains unattainable until barriers, policies, and laws that limit Black students from having access to post secondary preparation are modified. Dulabaum (2016) furthered this thought by including barriers such as poor writing skills, inconsistent time management skills, lack of technology in the home, anxiety, and not being prepared for placement tests. This is common for Black students especially those in urban communities, where students tend to receive little to no support/guidance from their families in their postsecondary preparation (Roderick et al., 2009). Therefore, Black students are less prepared to pursue college and achieve academic success compared to their White counterparts (Dulabaum, 2016). The purpose of this chapter is to discuss the factors impacting Black students to successfully transition to postsecondary institutions as well as policy, practice, and research recommendations to improve college and career readiness outcomes.

LITERATURE REVIEW

High School Graduation and College Enrollment

There is a need to increase high school retention and graduation rates for Black students, decrease dropout rates, and narrow the college enrollment gap between Black students and their White counterparts. Although the average U.S. high school graduation rate was 85% in 2017, the graduation rate for Black students was lower at 78% (McFarland et al., 2017). Black students have ranked fourth behind Asian-Pacific Islander students whose graduation rates were 91%, whereas White students had a graduation rate of 89%, and Hispanic students had a graduation rate of 80% (McFarland et al., 2017).

College Enrollment Rate for Black Students

Data captured by The National Center for Education Statistics ([NCES]; 2020) shows an increase in college enrollment rates for 18 to 24 year old Black students from 2000 to 2018 (31% to 37%). However, these numbers are still lower than their White counterparts in which there were 42% of 18 to 24 year olds enrolled in college in 2018 (NCES, 2020). This data represents college enrollment in all higher education institutions, including community college and nondegree institutions, such as technical and trade schools. In 2018–2019, the percentage of Black students that were pursuing associates degrees or were nondegree seeking made up almost 40% of the total population of Black students enrolled in higher education. For White students, only approximately 10% of students pursuing higher education were pursuing associates degrees or were nondegree seeking. As we can see, Black students are disproportionately represented in the community colleges, technical schools, and trade schools (Monarrez & Washington, 2020). It is also important to note that for years the majority of Black that did attend college enrolled and completed their degrees at historically Black colleges and universities ([HBCU]; Allen et al., 2018, p. 45). HBCUs served as an institution to educate Black, particularly when Blacks were denied admission to historically White institutions during segregation. Moreover, HBCUs tend to graduate more Black students with degrees in the area of science, technology, engineering, and mathematics (Owens et al., 2012). Since the mid 1970s, there has been a slight diversification in what types of schools Black students have enrolled and completed their degrees in, however there is still a disproportionate amount of young people absent on college campuses:

> College enrollments for both African American women and men have been persistently disadvantaged. Regarding the Public Ivies and flagships, African American enrollments have mostly remained stagnant, hovering near the same, very low levels apparent in 1976. African American enrollments on these prestigious campuses dropped precipitously after affirmative action programs were attacked and rolled back. (Allen et al., 2018, p. 68)

Black students are being left out of higher education and therefore the opportunity to participate in some of the country's most innovative and well paid industries. The aforementioned has been happening for decades and to understand why, the authors have explained the historical context in the next section.

Historical Context to Postsecondary Readiness Gap

Black students have not been given equitable access to education since the induction of formal K–12 schooling in the United States. At the beginning of slavery in the United States in 1619, many children were not being formally educated. However, White children still had access to tutors and were taught literacy and math skills (McClellan, 1988) while enslaved men, women, and children were forbidden from learning to read and write. When public schools were formed, also known as "common schools" during the Antebellum Era (1830–1860), Blacks were still enslaved. This means while White children were beginning to receive formal and standardized training in English, math, science, and other areas, Black children were already behind.

The abolishment of slavery in 1865, is the first time Black people were given the opportunity to be formally educated. In South Carolina this was known as the Port Royal Experiment (Goldstein, 2014, p. 48). This was the government's plan to teach the former slaves how to run their former slave master's property so that resources that came from their plantations would be sustained in society. Free Blacks were brought from the North to take on the role as teachers. Their goal was to provide intellectual, moral, and religious instruction (Goldstein, 2014, p. 48). Teachers were subjected to teach large numbers of people in one class, ranging from toddlers to the elderly.

Laws were eventually put into place which prohibited states from not educating Black students, but their schools were left separate from their White peers. "In 1896 the Supreme Court permitted states and school districts to designate some schools whites-only and others Negros-only" (Strauss, 2014, p. 1), which led to reinforced school segregation. According to Maruca (2004), Black students often "learned in schools that were no more than one-room shacks with tar paper roofs and not enough textbooks to go around" (p. 7). The lack of access to academic resources fueled Black families to join forces with the National Association for the Advancement of Colored People (NAACP) to petition the Supreme Court to investigate the "separate but equal" doctrine (Maruca, 2004). This case became known as *Brown v. Board of Education* and on May 17, 1954 the Supreme Court ruled to overturn the 1896 case *Plessy v. Ferguson* that institutionalized "separate but equal" (Maruca, 2004). This meant schools were prohibited from segregating based on race and the Black community believed this would be the beginning of equitable access to academic resources for Black students (Goldstien, 2014). Nevertheless, funding disparities within predominantly Black school districts still exist today. School districts/counties that have predominantly students of color are spending far less on resources for their students per year than school districts/counties that are predominately White (Ladson-Billings, 2006).

Furthermore, educational researchers purposefully left people of color out of early education reform initiatives in the beginning of the 20th century through eugenic ideology, which explicitly states "Jews, Africans, and Latinos were predisposed to carry a disproportionate number of defective traits, which they termed as feebleminded" (Stoskopf, 2002, p. 127). All of these practices, laws, and ideologies contribute to the foundations of systemic racism and why inequities between Black and White students exist within college readiness.

Systemic Barriers and Interventions

Systemic barriers to Black students' timely graduation and postsecondary attainment continue to negatively impact their educational and life success even though several programs have been implemented to address this problem (Kena et al., 2014; Morgan, 2014). Several factors impede Black students' high school completion (not exhaustive). These include their overrepresentation in special education, underrepresentation in gifted and talented programs, and lack of access to college-preparatory courses

(Ford & Moore, 2013; Scott et al., 2013). High school interventions have attempted to address their early departure from high school and stagnation of their college enrollment. Systemic interventions focused on improving Black high school graduation rates include extended school days, pre-college programs, Saturday school, rigorous instructional strategies, culturally sustaining pedagogies, mentor programs, and networks that connect home, school, and community (Alim & Paris, 2017; American Psychological Association, 2012; Morgan, 2014; Scott et al., 2013).

The barriers to college and career readiness are discussed with reference to the three dimensions of the definition: academic preparedness, lack of resources, and college and career knowledge. Black students often lack the rigorous academic preparation of their peers with college-educated parents because their parents do not understand the importance of taking challenging courses (Martinez & Klopott, 2005; Warburton et al., 2001). In addition, Black students are often not encouraged by teachers and school counselors to take college ready courses, such as Advanced Placement and dual enrollment. The disparity between secondary and postsecondary views of academic preparedness for college may result in high school college preparatory courses that are less rigorous than needed to meet expectations of higher education institutions (Mueller & Gozali-Lee, 2013).

Moreover, this tends to be especially the case at high schools attended by low-income students and students of color where the rigor of courses and the quality of instruction is often lower as well (Schultz & Mueller, 2006; The Postsecondary and Workforce Readiness Working Group, 2009). Even students who have completed a college preparatory curriculum are often not prepared for college, emphasizing the importance of rethinking how students should become college and career ready (National Center for Public Policy and Higher Education, 2010). The effects of a lack of financial resources lead to the perceived lack of importance around college and career readiness for Black students.

An additional barrier to college and career readiness is time spent out of the classroom learning environment (Falcon, 2015). Regardless of the class setting, Black students are often met with deficit perspectives and microaggressions from educators (Ford et al., 2013; Mayes et al., 2014; Mayes & Moore, 2016; Stambaugh & Ford, 2015).

Other factors impacting students' high school graduation rates also involve the school culture created and sustained by school leaders and stakeholders (Scott et al., 2013) and how they carry out their roles and utilize leadership strategies can influence students' high school graduation rates (Coelli & Green, 2012; Hays, 2013; Romero, 2015). At the heart of transforming K–12 schools, there is a need to understand why educational institutions sabotage them by "exposing environmental toxins that persistently undermine [their] success" (Harper & Kuykendall, 2012, p. 25).

Specifically, institutions must reflect on their "institutional activities, measure institutional commitment, and systematically assess institutional effectiveness" (Harper & Kuykendall, 2012, p. 25). By working to implement cradle-to-college-and-career strategies (My Brother's Keeper Task Force, 2014) that bring together (a) leadership in the public, private, and community sectors; (b) the expertise of education, workplace, and youth development professionals; and (c) an engaged and supportive community in order to increase graduation rates while properly preparing students for their postsecondary opportunities (Addis & Withington, 2016). Improving high school graduation rates is one key step to building pathways to economic self-sufficiency for Black students.

Access to Academic Rigor and Postsecondary Transitions

There is a strong link between rigorous high school coursework and completing college specifically for Black students (Dervacris, 2005). "75 percent of Black with a rigorous high school curriculum ultimately finish college, but the college success rate for Black without that curriculum is much lower at 46 percent" (Dervarics, 2005, p. 6). Furthermore, students who participated in Advanced Placement, early college experience, and career and technical education courses in high school had higher persistent rates in higher education and college graduation rates (Morgan et al., 2018). Morgan et al. (2018) indicated that participation in college level coursework will also teach students important soft skills for college, such as time management, stress management, and self-care.

Only 9.2% of Black students are taking college level courses, such as Advanced Placement in comparison to 55.9% of their White peers (College Board, 2014). In addition they.are also taking fewer rigorous math and science courses than their White peers. Bryant (2015), found that only 57% of Black students took courses such as Algebra I, Algebra II, geometry, biology, chemistry, and physics, while 71% of White students and 81% of Asian students took these courses while enrolled in high school (Bryant, 2015, p. 6). This may be due to low expectations of teachers and school counselors as well as the lack of resources schools may have to offer a variety of courses outside of graduation requirements.

Regardless of the reason, one of the most prominent factors of college enrollment for students is their grade point average ([GPA]; Cartledge et al., 2015) and in order to obtain a competitive GPA one must take rigorous coursework. College level courses such as Advanced Placement and International Baccalaureate often allow students to earn more quality points (up to 5 or 6) towards their GPA than quality points (up to 4) of a regular high school course. Without access to these courses, even a student with good grades might not be deemed a competitive candidate by college admission officers. School counselors must work with families and students to advocate for enrollment in rigorous coursework that will prepare students for success in college. School counselors have a major role in ensuring that students enroll in a college ready coursework, and should work hard to push students beyond the minimum requirements for graduation (Bryant, 2015).

Partnering with local colleges to bring students to campuses often is highly recommended. The campus visit is still considered the most important factor in determining enrollment. Secore (2018) argues, "The visit is a brief trial run at what life might look like at that institution" (p. 151). His study found that 74% of students at Ramapo College in New Jersey who attended an admitted student's campus event enrolled (Secore, 2018, p. 152). Studies like this have been duplicated at colleges across the country affirming a positive correlation between campus visit and enrollment.

Black students who participate in college visits while in high school begin to familiarize themselves with this type of environment and start to envision themselves on a college campus. Some colleges and universities may be able to offer a themed college visit for Black students. Reaching out to the schools' cultural centers, greek life, or academic clubs (i.e., National Society of Black Engineers, NAACP campus chapters, etc.) to partner in a campus visit would be fruitful as well. This is particularly helpful for Black students as they will see spaces and groups where they may share the same lived experiences, feeling a sense of belonging and support.

In addition to on campus tours, colleges are embracing many ways to connect with prospective students through school media and virtual tours, open houses, and interviews (Jaschik, 2020; Secore, 2018). Jaschik (2020), reported that in 2020 more high school seniors engaged in virtual tours more than any other year before. The rise of virtual college tours removes a barrier for Black students and their families who may not have access or time to go to the physical campus. School counselors can create materials for their students and families with ways in which they can access in-person and virtual college tours throughout the school year.

Teacher Expectations

Teacher expectations of student achievement can be too high or too low when compared with the actual student's achievement level. While high teacher expectations have positive effects on student achievement, low teacher expectations are acknowledged as one factor that contributes to student failure (Good & Nichols, 2001). The effect of teacher expectations on Black student performance has been well documented (Egalite et al., 2015; Jussim & Harber, 2005; Rosenthal & Jacobson, 1968). This phenomenon is called biased expectations (de Boer et al., 2010; Timmermans et al., 2015). Biased teacher expectations tend to be the product of the student characteristics, such as students' gender, ethnicity, and socioeconomic status ([SES]; e.g., De Boer et al., 2010; Timmermans et al., 2015). Currently, teachers tend to have negatively biased expectations for the future academic performance of Black students and students from low-income families (e.g., Glock et al., 2013; Speybroeck et al., 2012).

School Counselor Preparation

In secondary education, school counselors (SC) play a significant role in assisting Black students' postsecondary preparation and planning (American School Counselor Association [ASCA], 2012, 2019; College Board, 2010). One of the primary roles of SC's is to use evidence-based practices for improving student outcomes, by identifying gaps in achievement, opportunity, and attainment (ASCA, 2012). They also are responsible for developing and implementing data-driven comprehensive school counseling programs that are tailored to address students' academic performance, college and career readiness, and social-emotional needs (Dahir, 2004; Johnson & Johnson, 2003).

However, depending on the school and/or school district, the SC working with Black students may encounter challenges like a lack of proper resources, preparation, and clarity on their role to properly support these students. Specifically, counseling in urban schools differs significantly from school counseling in other contexts (Lee, 2005); unfortunately, in many cases, SCs are burdened with clerical and noncounseling duties (Martin, 2002). This concept was explored in a study conducted by Vega et al. (2015) where participants reported that their SCs provided them with minimal assistance in postsecondary preparation, negatively impacting their high school careers and their preparation for postsecondary success. Conversely, students from that same district who participated in postsecondary preparatory programs (Upward Bound) to supplement the preparation they did not receive in their schools were at an advantage as they attended classes on weekends, received individualized support (e.g., academic advising, college preparation) throughout the school year and summer, college visits, and participated in the Summer Institute (Vega et al., 2015).

Although there's an emphasis on immersing preservice SCs in field experiences, there is still a lack of college and career readiness preparation in SC training programs (Hines et al., 2011). In fact, many counselor training programs do not prioritize college readiness counseling which has been highlighted as a major barrier when working with Black students (DeSimone & Roberts, 2016). Occasionally, counselor education programs will state this material is covered in their career counseling courses (Council of National School Counseling & College Access Organizations, 2016), but practicing SCs state they felt largely unprepared by their graduate programs to engage in this work (Brown et al., 2016). Savitz-Romer (2012) provided an example of this in an article where she discussed how low resourced and underprepared SCs typically do not have knowledge or training in financial aid, so they cannot help students and families understand the costs of college.

RECOMMENDATIONS

Practice

School counselors are uniquely positioned to assist students "in making the transition to postsecondary education" (Patel & Clinedinst, 2019, p. 2). While students' access to SCs varies across the United States, SCs continue to play an important role in improving college readiness levels. By engaging in individual counseling, small groups, and larger classroom activities, SCs can increase access to critical information that can support students' attainment of future goals (Dunlop Velez, 2016; Hurwitz & Howell, 2013). For example, Reid and Moore (2008) share the positive impacts SCs' active encouragement and sharing of information regarding the college admissions and financial aid process has on Black students' college readiness levels. This coupled with the creation of academic plans that suit each students' college and career goals is essential to ensuring they are accessing required coursework to meet their long-term goals (Reid & Moore, 2008). Considering that Black are "underrepresented at more public institutions, regardless of selectivity" (Monarrez & Washington, 2020, p. 3), SCs must actively engage in conversations and presentations that distinguish between the "various types of postsecondary institutions and which college could be the best 'fit' for them" (Hines et al., 2020, p. 135). The process of preparing students to be college and career ready begins from the moment students arrive on campus (Dunlop Velez, 2016; Hines et al., 2020).

School counselors play an essential role in working with students' families (ASCA, 2016). This is especially true when working with Black students. Many Black students are first-generation college students which means partnering with families is of utmost importance in efforts to prepare Black students to be college ready. As Smith (2001) finds, Black parents desire to be more informed about the college admissions process. Collaborating with family members has been found to enhance students' career readiness given that they can help improve students' attitudes toward school and motivation to succeed (Paolini, 2015). Creating a system that facilitates this open-communication and transmits important information about academics, colleges, and careers is one way SCs can be sure to include families (Reid & Moore, 2008). Hosting workshops with students and parents is also another way to address any questions and concerns and dispel any myths concerning the college admissions and financial aid process (Hines et al., 2020). Because family members play such a key role in the formation of postsecondary aspirations and success, SCs must view their work with Black students as inclusive of family members as they help the family unit navigate postsecondary institutions (Hines et al., 2015).

School counselors continue to have an impact in college and career readiness and postsecondary planning. Because Black students are relying on SCs, it is imperative that these counselors are prepared to address the specific needs of Black students. School counselors have to look at traditional practices and traditional systems and evaluate if these are working for Black students. Below we will discuss ways in which SCs can reimagine how they support students through empowerment and social and cultural capital.

Several studies from the 1960s through early 2000s show a progression in the way that SCs worked to advance their Black students. Three models that emerged were a "culturally deprived approach," a multicultural training approach, and an empowerment approach (Dye, 2012, pp. 48–50). When students received interventions that came from the culturally deprived approach the counselors approached their service to Black students as though the child were problematic, inadequate, or difficult. These interventions fell short (Dye, 2012, p. 49). However, when SCs used an empowerment approach, they found that not only did students experience higher self-esteem, they also increased the students' academic performance (Dye, 2012, p. 50). This review of historical approaches to serving Black students clearly shows that working with students' strengths and building self-esteem will have longer lasting effects than the deficit approaches. We highly recommend that SCs take this empowerment approach when working with Black students.

"Social capital refers to a student's access to knowledge and resources about postsecondary education relayed through relationships that comprise" (Cholewa et al., 2018, p. 145). It is known that students who have families who have accessed college do not seek out the same amount of support in the college application process. Where students lack social and cultural capital, SCs are charged to fill in those gaps in access with their extensive knowledge and training in college and career readiness.

Use of cultural and social capital will come in many forms. One is the use of relationships with outside people and institutions to advance our students (Mellin et al., 2015, p. 3). School counselors often make great relationships with admissions counselors, military recruiters, and local businesses. These relationships should be leveraged for our students' best interest by making personal introductions, making additional phone calls for references, and working collaboratively on college readiness programs.

Earlier we discussed the importance of relationships in working with Black students. When linking SCs' social and cultural capital with students it requires trust and careful planning (Mellin et al., 2015, p. 11). School counselors should not assume that students will automatically trust their colleagues. Thoughtful introductions and continued support from the counselor will be important.

Policy

Schools should implement policy that intentionally improves the postsecondary outcomes of Black students. Specifically, policy around meeting with students and parents to discuss options should be mandated. Moreover, making career and college fairs a mandate within the school can impact the trajectory of Black students. Moreover, SCs can work with their state and local school counseling association to advocate for policy that mandates equitable outcomes for Black students when it comes to postsecondary readiness and transition from high school. Further, school counseling district leaders can collaborate with their SCs across the district to create policies and procedures to ensure Black students are properly prepared for postsecondary opportunities and into classes that have academic rigor. Last, SCs can advocate for culturally responsive training for educators to ensure they are engaging Black students free of bias and low expectations.

Research

More research is needed in understanding successful transitions to postsecondary institutions for Black students. Specifically, quantitative studies can contribute to providing more evidence around this topic. Researchers can use secondary data and look at variables such as involvement in enrichment activities (e.g., Trio, AVID, Gear up) rigorous coursework taken (i.e., honors, and gifted courses), and the type of coursework taken (e.g., level of math and science). Another research study can examine the relationship between school counselors' postsecondary knowledge and college-going activities and their number of meetings (or interactions) with their Black students.

Qualitative studies are needed on understanding the factors impacting postsecondary transition for Black students. For example, researchers can interview high school seniors about their school process and how it prepared them for transitioning out of high school. Another research study can be a case study of a school with a record of successfully transitioning students to postsecondary opportunities. Observations of the college going process in the school, interviews with SCs, administrators, and teachers, and interviews with parents can inform research when it comes to understanding postsecondary transitions.

CONCLUSION

Assisting Black students successful transition to postsecondary opportunities needs to be an American imperative as stated in the title of the edited volume. A diverse workforce is crucial for a thriving United States as the uniqueness of different racial and ethinic populations is our strength. Educators, specifically SCs, play a very important role in eliminating barriers and serving as gate openers rather than gatekeepers to provide access to all resources that will help Black students maximize their potential in K–12 to successfully enroll in a postsecondary institution.

DISCUSSION QUESTIONS

1. Discuss how the dual pandemic (racism and COVID-19) has impacted the postsecondary readiness and attainment of Black students. How can educators (school counselors, administrators, teachers, school psychologists, etc.) assist Black students with postsecondary transitions. What would assistance look like post-pandemic?
2. What types of resources are needed to train preservice and in-service educators knowledgeable in working with Black students around postsecondary transitions?

ACTIVITY

1. Interview an educator and ask them about the initiatives in their school to help Black students successfully transition to postsecondary institutions.
2. Interview an admissions counselor or a staff member of a Black infinity group (Black cultural center or Black learning center) at a postsecondary institution. Ask them how they integrate Black students into their institution during their first year to help them be successful.

AUTHOR NOTE

Erik M. Hines ORCID https://orcid.org/0000-0002-6025-0779

We have no known conflict of interest to disclose.

Correspondence concerning this article should be addressed to Erik M. Hines, Dept of Educational Psychology and Learning Systems, 1114 W. Call St., Tallahassee, FL 32306

REFERENCES

Addis, S., & Withington, M. C. (2016). *Improving high school graduation rates among males of color.* National Dropout Prevention Center/Network. https://dropout prevention.org/wp-content/uploads/2017/11/rwjf-ndpscn-moriah-Improving GradRatesMalesofColor-2016.pdf

Alim, H. S., & Paris, D. (Eds). (2017). *Culturally sustaining pedagogies: Teaching and learning for justice in a changing world.* Teachers College Press.

Alleman, N. F., & Holly, N. L. (2013). Multiple points of contact: Promoting rural postsecondary preparation through school–community partnerships. *The Rural Educator, 34*(2). https://doi.org/10.35608/ruraled.v34i2.398

Allen, W. R., McLewis, C., Jones, C., & Harris, D. (2018). From Bakke to Fisher: African American students in U.S. higher education over forty years. *RSF: The Russell Sage Foundation Journal of the Social Sciences, 4*(6), 41–72. https://doi.org/10.7758/rsf.2018.4.6.03

American Psychological Association. (2012). *Facing the school dropout dilemma.* http://www.apa.org/pi/families/resources/school-dropout-prevention.aspx

American School Counselor Association. (2012). *The ASCA national model: A framework for school counseling programs* (3rd ed.).

American School Counselor Association. (2016). *The school counselor and school–family–community partnerships.* https://schoolcounselor.org/Standards-Positions/Position-Statements/ASCA-Position-Statements/The-School-Counselor-and-School-Family-Community-P#:~:text=School%2Dfamily%2Dcommunity%20partnerships%20have,to%20these%20helpful%20collaborative%20relationships

American School Counselor Association. (2019). *The ASCA national model: A framework for school counseling programs* (4th ed.).

Brown, J., Hatch, T., Holcomb-McCoy, C., Martin, P., Mcleod, J., Owen, L., & Savitz-Romer, M. (2016). *The state of school counseling: Revisiting the path forward.* National Consortium for School Counseling and Postsecondary Success. https://www.american.edu/centers/cprs/upload/revisiting-the-path-forward-report-full-report.pdf

Bryant, R. T. (2015). *College preparation for African American students: Gaps in the high school educational experience.* Center for Law and Social Policy, Inc. https://www.clasp.org/sites/default/files/public/resources-and-publications/publication-1/College-readiness2-2.pdf

Carnevale, A. P., Rose, S. J., & Cheah, B. (2011). *The college payoff: Education, occupations, lifetime earnings.* The Georgetown University Center on Education and the Workforce. https://cew.georgetown.edu/cew-reports/the-college-payoff/

Carnevale, A. P., Smith, N., & Strohl, J. (2013). *Recovery: Job growth and education requirements through 2020.* The Georgetown University Center on Education and the Workforce. https://cew.georgetown.edu/wp-content/uploads/2014/11/Recovery2020.FR_.Web_.pdf

Cartledge, B. H., Baldwin, M. S., Persall, J. M, & Woolley, T. M. (2015). College choice determinants of African-American enrollment at a private college. *Journal of Academic Administration in Higher Education, 11*(1), 1–8. https://files.eric.ed.gov/fulltext/EJ1139332.pdf

Cholewa, B., Burkhardt, C. K., & Hull, M. F. (2018). Are school counselors impacting underrepresented students' thinking about postsecondary education? A nationally representative study. *Professional School Counseling, 19*(1). https://doi.org/10.5330/1096-2409-19.1.144

Coelli, M., & Green. D. A. (2012). Leadership effects: School principals and student outcomes. *Economics of Education Review, 31*(1), 92–109. https://doi.org/10.1016/j.econedurev.2011.09.001

College Board. (2010). *Eight components of college and career readiness counseling.* https://secure-media.collegeboard.org/digitalServices/pdf/nosca/11b_4416_8_Components_WEB_111107.pdf

College Board. (2014, February 11). *The 10th annual AP report to the nation.* https://secure-media.collegeboard.org/digitalServices/pdf/ap/rtn/10th-annual/10th-annual-ap-report-to-the-nation-single-page.pdf

Council of National School Counseling & College Access Organizations. (2016). *Building college access/admission counseling competencies: Review of the coursework.* http://schoolcounselingcollegeaccess.org/wp-content/uploads/2016/03/CouncilReport.pdf

Dahir, C. A. (2004), Supporting a nation of learners: The role of school counseling in educational reform. *Journal of Counseling & Development, 82,* 344–353. https://doi.org/10.1002/j.1556-6678.2004.tb00320.x

de Boer, H., Bosker, R. J., & van der Werf, M. P. C. (2010). Sustainability of teacher expectation bias effects on long-term student performance. *Journal of Educational Psychology, 102*(1), 168–179. https://doi.org/10.1037/a0017289

Dervarics, C. (2005). Report: High school rigor essential for students of color. *Black Issues in Higher Education, 21*(24), 6–7.

DeSimone, J. R., & Roberts, L. A. (2016). Fostering collaboration between pre-service educational leadership and school counseling graduate candidates. *The Journal of Counselor Preparation and Supervision, 8*(2). http://dx.doi.org/10.7729/82.1081

Dulabaum, N. L. (2016). Barriers to academic success: A qualitative study of African American and Latino male students. *Innovation Showcase, 11*(6). https://www.league.org/innovation-showcase/barriers-academic-success-qualitative-study-african-american-and-latino-male

Dunlop Velez, E. (2016). *How can high school counseling shape students' postsecondary attendance.* National Association for College Admission Counseling.

Dye, L. T. (2012). *School counselors' activities in predominantly African American urban schools* (no. 55). [Doctoral Dissertation, Western Michigan University]. https://scholarworks.wmich.edu/dissertations/55

Egalite, A. J., Kisida, B., & Winters, M. A. (2015). Representation in the classroom: The effect of own-race teachers on student achievement. *Economics of Education Review, 45*, 44–52. https://doi.org/10.1016/j.econedurev.2015.01.007

Erford, B. T. (2019). *Transforming the school counseling profession* (5th ed.). Pearson.

Falcon, L. (2015). Breaking down barriers: First-generation college students and college success. *Innovation Showcase, 10*(6). https://www.league.org/innovation-showcase/breaking-down-barriers-first-generation-college-students-and-college-success

Ford, D. Y., & Moore, J. L., III. (2013). Understanding and reversing underachievement, low achievement, and achievement gaps among high-ability African American males in urban school contexts. *Urban Review, 45*(4), 399–415. https://doi.org/10.1007/s11256-013-0256-3

Ford, D. Y., Trotman Scott, M., Moore, J. L., & Amos, S. O. (2013). Gifted education and culturally different students: Examining prejudice and discrimination via microaggressions. *Gifted Child Today, 36*, 205–208. https://doi.org/10.1177/1076217513487069

Glock, S., Krolak-Schwerdt, S., Klapproth, F., & Böhmer, M. (2013). Beyond judgment bias: How students' ethnicity and academic profile consistency influence teachers' tracking judgments. *Social Psychology of Education: An International Journal, 16*(4), 555–573. https://doi.org/10.1007/s11218-013-9227-5

Goldstein, D. (2014). *The teacher wars: A history of America's most embattled profession*. Doubleday.

Good, T. L., & Nichols, S. L. (2001). Expectancy effects in the classroom: A special focus on improving the reading performance of minority students in first-grade classrooms. *Educational Psychologist, 36*(2), 113–126. https://doi.org/10.1207/S15326985EP3602_6

Harper, S. R., & Kuykendall, J. A. (2012). Institutional efforts to improve Black male student achievement: A standards-based approach. *Change, 44*(2), 23–29. https://doi.org/10.1080/00091383.2012.655234

Hays, P. S. (2013). Narrowing the gap: Three key dimensions of site-based leadership in four Boston charter public schools. *Education and Urban Society, 45*(1), 37–87. https://doi.org/10.1177/0013124511404065

Hines, E. M., Borders, L. D., & Gonzalez, L. M. (2015). "It takes fire to make steel": Stories of two African American males finding purpose through their college experiences. *Journal for Multicultural Education, 9*(4), 225–247.

Hines, E. M., Hines, M. R., Moore III, J. L., Steen, S., Singleton, P., Cintron, D., Golden, M. N., Traverso, K., Wathen, B., & Henderson, J. (2020). Preparing African American males for college: A group counseling approach. *The Journal for Specialists in Group Work, 45*(2), 129–145. https://doi.org/10.1080/01933922.2020.1740846

Hines, P. L., Lemons, R. W., & Crews, K. D. (2011). *Poised to lead: How school counselors can drive college and career readiness*. Education Trust. https://edtrust.org/wp-content/uploads/2013/10/Poised_To_Lead_0.pdf

Holland, N. E. (2017). Beyond conventional wisdom: Community cultural wealth and the college knowledge of African American youth in the United States. *Race Ethnicity and Education, 20*(6), 796–810. https://doi.org/10.1080/1361 3324.2016.1150823

Hudley, C., Moschetti, R., Gonzalez, A., Cho, S.-J., Barry, L., & Kelly, M. (2009). College freshmen's perceptions of their high school experiences. *Journal of Advanced Academics, 20*(3), 438–471. https://doi.org/10.1177/1932202X0902000304

Hurwitz, M., & Howell, J. (2013). *Measuring the impact of high school counselors on college enrollment.* College Board Advocacy & Policy Center. http://secure-media .collegeboard.org/digitalServices/pdf/advocacy/policycenter/research -brief-measuring-impact-high-school-counselors-college-enrollment.pdf

Jaschik, S. (2020, April 20). *Virtual tours grow, but will they have same impact?* Inside Higher Education. https://www.insidehighered.com/admissions/article/2020/ 04/20/virtual-tours-boom-will-they-have-same-impact

Johnson, S., & Johnson, C. (2003). Results-based guidance: A systems approach to student support programs. *Professional School Counseling, 6*(3), 180–184. http://www.jstor.org/stable/42732427

Jussim, L., & Harber, K. D. (2005). Teacher expectations and self-fulfilling prophecies: Knowns and unknowns, resolved and unresolved controversies. *Personality and Social Psychology Review, 9*(2), 131–155. https://doi.org/10.1207/ s15327957pspr0902_3

Kena, G., Aud, S., Johnson, F., Wang, X., Zhang, J., Rathbun, A., Wilkinson-Flicker, S., Kristapovich, P., Notter, L., Robles-Villalba, V., Nachazel., T., & Dziuba, A. (2014). *The condition of education 2014.* National Center for Education Statistics, U.S. Department of Education. https://nces.ed.gov/pubs2014/2014083.pdf

Kozleski, E. B., & Proffitt, W. A. (2020). A journey towards equity and diversity in the educator workforce. *Teacher Education and Special Education, 43*(1), 63–84. https://doi.org/10.1177/0888406419882671

Ladson-Billings, G. (2006). From the achievement gap to the education debt: Understanding achievement in U.S. Schools. *Educational Researcher, 35*(7), 3–12.

Lee, C. (2005). Urban school counseling: Context, characteristics, and competencies. *Professional School Counseling, 8*(3), 184–188. http://www.jstor.org/stable/ 42732457

Lee, V. L., & Goodnough, G. E. (2019). Systemic, data-driven school counseling practice and programming for equity. In B. T. Erford, *Transforming the school counseling profession* (5th ed. pp. 67–93). Pearson.

Martin, P. (2002). Transforming school counseling: A national perspective. *Theory Into Practice, 41*(3), 148–153. http://www.jstor.org/stable/1477235

Martinez, M., & Klopott, S. (2005). *The link between high school reform and college access and success for low-income and minority youth.* American Youth Policy Forum and Pathways to College Network. http://www.aypf.org/wp-content/ uploads/2014/07/HSReformCollegeAccessandSuccess.pdf

Maruca, M. (2004). *Brown v. board of education: Historical handbook.* National Parks Association.

Mayes, R. D., Hines, E. M., & Harris, P. C. (2014). Working with twice-exceptional African American students: Information for school counselors. *Interdisciplinary*

Journal of Teaching and Learning, 4(2), 125–139. https://files.eric.ed.gov/fulltext/EJ1063067.pdf

Mayes, R. D., & Moore, J. L. (2016). The intersection of race, disability, and giftedness: Understanding the education needs of twice-exceptional, African American Students. *Gifted Child Today, 39*(2), 98–104. https://doi.org/10.1177/1076217516628570

McClellan, B. E., & Reece, W. J. (1988). *The social history of American education.* University of Illinois Press.

McFarland, J., Hussar, B., de Brey, C., Snyder, T., Wang, X., Wilkinson-Flicker, S., Gebrekristos, S., Zhang, J., Rathbun, A., Barmer, A., Bullock Mann, F., & Hinz, S. (2017). *The condition of education 2017* (NCES 2017-144). National Center for Education Statistics, U.S. Department of Education. https://nces.ed.gov/pubs2017/2017144.pdf

Mellin, E. A., Belknap, E. E., Brodie, I. L., & Sholes, K. (2015). Opening school doors to communities and families: A social capital perspective for multiparty collaboration. *Journal for Social Action in Counseling and Psychology, 7*(1), 1–18. https://doi.org/10.33043/JSACP.7.1.1-18

Monarrez, T., & Washington, K. (2020). *Racial and ethnic representation in postsecondary education.* Center on Education Data and Policy, Urban Institute. https://www.urban.org/sites/default/files/publication/102375/racial-and-ethnic-representation-in-postsecondary-education_1.pdf

Morgan, L. M. (2014). *Review of the literature in dropout prevention.* Colorado Department of Education. https://www.academia.edu/34585313/Review_of_the_Literature_in_Dropout_Prevention

Morgan, T. L., Zakem, D., & Cooper, W. (2018). From high school access to postsecondary success: An exploratory study of the impact of high-rigor coursework. *Education Sciences, 8*(191). https://doi.org/10.3390/educsci8040191

My Brother's Keeper Task Force. (2014, May). *Report to the president.* https://obamawhitehouse.archives.gov/sites/default/files/docs/053014_mbk_report.pdf

Mueller, D., & Gozali-Lee, E. (2013). *College and career readiness: A review and analysis conducted for Generation Next.* Wilder Research. https://www.wilder.org/sites/default/files/imports/GenerationNext_CollegeCareerReadiness_4-13.pdf

National Center for Educational Statistics. (2020). *College enrollment rates* [Data set]. https://nces.ed.gov/programs/coe/indicator_cpb.asp

National Center for Public Policy and Higher Education. (2010). *Beyond the rhetoric: Improving college readiness through coherent state policy.* https://www.highereducation.org/reports/college_readiness/CollegeReadiness.pdf

Neal-Jackson, A. (2018). A meta-ethnographic review of the experiences of African American girls and young women in K–12 education. *Review of Educational Research, 88*(4), 508–546. https://doi.org/10.3102/0034654318760785

Owens, E. W., Shelton, A. J., Collette, M., Bloom, C. M., & Cavil, J. K. (2012). The significance of HBCU's to the production of STEM graduates: Answering the call. *Educational Foundations, 26*(3–4), 33–47.

Patel, P., & Clinedinst, M. (2019). *State-by-state student-to-counselor ratio maps by school district.* National Association for College Admission Counseling. https://www.nacacnet.org/globalassets/documents/publications/research/researchstateratiosreport.pdf

Pavlakis, A. E., & Pryor, K. N. (2020). Planning the future in an uncertain present: Postsecondary possibilities for accompanied youth of color experiencing homelessness. *The Urban Review 53*, 354–382. https://doi.org/10.1007/s11256-020-00572-0

Paolini, A. C. (2015). School counselors: Key stakeholders helping underserved students to be career ready. *Journal of Curriculum and Teaching, 4*(1), 133–144. https://doi.org/10.5430/jct.v4n1p133

Reid, M. J., & Moore, J. L. (2008). College readiness and academic preparation for postsecondary education: Oral histories of first-generation urban college students. *Urban Education, 43*(2), 240–261. https://doi.org/10.1177/0042085907312346

Roderick, M., Nagaoka, J., & Coca, V. (2009). College readiness for all: The challenge for urban high schools. *The Future of children, 19*(1), 185–210. https://doi.org/10.1353/foc.0.0024

Romero, L. S. (2015), Trust, behavior, and high school outcomes. *Journal of Educational Administration, 53*(2), 215–236. https://doi.org/10.1108/JEA-07-2013-0079

Rooney, P., Hussar, W., Planty, M., Choy, S., Hampden-Thompson, G., Provasnik, S., Fox, M. A., Kridl, B., Livingston, A., & Synder, T. (2006). *The condition of education 2006* (NCES 2006-071). National Center for Education Statistics, U.S. Department of Education. https://nces.ed.gov/pubs2006/2006071.pdf

Rosenthal, R., & Jacobson, L. (1968). *Pygmalion in the classroom: Teacher expectation and pupils' intellectual development.* Holt, Rinehart & Winston.

Sandoval-Lucero, E., Maes, J. B., & Klingsmith, L. (2014). African American and Latina(o) community college students' social capital and student success. *College Student Journal, 48*, 522–533. https://www.hartnell.edu/sites/default/files/u714/peer_reviewed_journal_article_2.pdf

Savitz-Romer, M. (2012). The gap between influence and efficacy: College readiness training, urban school counselors, and the promotion of equity. *Counselor Education and Supervision, 51*(2), 98–111. https://doi.org/10.1002/j.1556-6978.2012.00007.x

Scott, J. A., Taylor, K. J., & Palmer, R. T. (2013). Challenges to success in higher education: An examination of educational challenges from the voices of college-bound Black males. *The Journal of Negro Education, 82*(3), 288–299. https://www.jstor.org/stable/10.7709/jnegroeducation.82.3.0288

Secore, S. (2018). The significance of campus visitations to college choice and strategic enrollment management. *Strategic Enrollment Management Quarterly, 5*(4), 150–158. https://doi.org/10.1002/sem3.20114

Schultz, J. L., & Mueller, D. (2006). *Effectiveness of programs to improve postsecondary education enrollment and success of underrepresented youth: A literature review.* Wilder Research. https://www.wilder.org/sites/default/files/imports/Northstar LitReviewWithoutRICF_11-06.pdf

Smith, M. J. (2001). Low SES Black college choice: Playing on an unlevel playing field. *Journal of College Admission,* (171), 16–21. https://pdxscholar.library.pdx.edu/cgi/viewcontent.cgi?article=1075&context=edu_fac

Sommerfeld, A. K., & Bowen, P. (2013). Fostering social and cultural capital in urban youth: A programmatic approach to promoting college success. *Journal of Education, 193*(1), 47–55. https://doi.org/10.1177/002205741319300106

Stambaugh, T., & Ford, D. Y. (2015). Microaggressions, multiculturalism, and gifted individuals who are Black, Hispanic, or low income. *Journal of Counseling & Development, 93*, 192–201. https://doi.org/10.1002/j.1556-6676.2015.00195.x

Stoskopf, A. (2002). Echoes of a forgotten past: Eugenics, testing, and education reform. *The Educational Reform,* 66(2), 126–133.

Strauss, V. (2014, April 24). How after 60 years *Brown v. Board of Education* succeeded and didn't. *The Washington Post.* https://www.washingtonpost.com/news/answer-sheet/wp/2014/04/24/how-after-60-years-brown-v-board-of-education-succeeded-and-didnt/

Speybroeck, S., Kuppens, S. P. E., Van Damme, J., Van Petegem, P., Lamote, C., Boonen, T., & de Bilde, J. (2012). The role of teachers' expectations in the association between children's SES and performance in kindergarten: A moderated mediation analysis. *PLoS ONE,* 7(4). https://doi.org/10.1371/journal.pone.0034502

The Postsecondary and Workforce Readiness Working Group. (2009). *The road map to college and career readiness for Minnesota students.* https://www.lcsc.org/cms/lib/MN01001004/Centricity/Domain/18/College_and_Career_Readiness_Paper-FINAL.pdf

Timmermans, A. C., Kuyper, H., & Van der Werf, G. (2015). Accurate, inaccurate or biased teacher expectations: Do Dutch teachers differ in their expectations at the end of primary education? *British Journal of Educational Psychology, 85*, 459–478. https://doi.org/10.1111/bjep.12087

Vega, D., Moore, J. L., III., & Miranda, A. H. (2015). In their own words: Perceived barriers to achievement by African American and Latino high school students. *American Secondary Education, 43*(3), 36–59.

Warburton, E. C., Bugarin, R., Nunez, A. M., & Carrol, C. D. (2001). *Bridging the gap: Academic preparation and postsecondary success of first-generation students.* National Center for Education Statistics, U.S. Department of Education. https://nces.ed.gov/pubs2001/2001153.pdf

Wilkins, A. C. (2014). Race, age, and identity transformations in the transition from high school to college for Black and first-generation White men. *Sociology of Education, 87*(3), 171–187. https://doi.org/10.1177/0038040714537901

Wolf, L. (2017). *Hear my voice: Strengthening the college pipeline for young men of color in California.* Education Trust-West. https://west.edtrust.org/wp-content/uploads/2015/11/Ed-Trust-West-Hear-My-Voice-Report-FINAL-June-2017.pdf

CHAPTER 8

CULTURALLY RESPONSIVE POSTSECONDARY ADVISING FOR LATINX STUDENTS

Diana Camilo
California State University, San Bernardino

Robert Martinez
University of North Carolina at Chapel Hill

ABSTRACT

According to the 2020 U.S Census, Latinx origin accounts for 60.6 million people, or 18.5% of the U.S. population (U.S. Census Bureau, 2020), a 2.5% increase from the 2010 Census figures. Today, 1 in 5 children under the age of 18 is Latinx. It is suggested that by 2050, 2 in 5 children under the age of 18 will be Latinx (Cárdenas & Kerby, 2012). This positions Latinx students as the future of this nation; calling for the promotion of the college readiness of Latinx students as one of the most useful contributions by K–12 schools (Martinez et al., 2020). As of 2016, postsecondary enrollment for Latinx students (85%) tends to be public institutions; an overrepresentation in open-access and community colleges, and underrepresented in 4-year institutions. Latinx students also maintain the lowest college graduation rate

Equity-Based Career Development and Postsecondary Transitions, pages 185–218
Copyright © 2022 by Information Age Publishing
www.infoagepub.com
185

when compared to other racial groups (Perez Huber et al., 2015). Factors influencing postsecondary enrollment include content knowledge, postsecondary academic preparation, possible student status as first-generation and/or undocumented immigrant, schoolcentric epistemologies, and patterns of existing disparities among Black, Brown, and Indigenous undergraduate students with regards to college enrollment rates (Acevedo-Gil, 2017; Lukes, 2015; Martinez et al., 2020; Perez Huber et al., 2015). The chapter provides an overview of the unique advising needs of Latinx students and introduces a culturally responsive advising (CRA) framework, as part of the college application completion process.

Although considered the largest ethnic minority in the United States, it is predicted that 1 out of every 4 Americans will be Hispanic or Latino/a/x by 2060 (Colby & Ortman, 2015). Adopted in the 1970s by the U.S. government, the term *Hispanic* was introduced to describe individuals whose heritage traced back to Mexico, Cuba, and other Spanish-speaking nations in Central and South America as well as Spain (Jones-Smith, 2019). Hispanic was added to the U.S. Census in 1980 to indicate the heritage, nationality, group, lineage, or country of birth of the person or person's ancestors before their arrival in the United States. People who identify their origins as Hispanic, Latino, or Spanish may be of any race (U.S. Census Bureau, 2012). The peoples of countries considered as Hispanic or Latino American groups by the Census Bureau were the following: Spain, Argentina, Mexico, Puerto Rico, Cuba, Dominican Republic, Costa Rica, Guatemala, Honduras, Nicaragua, Panama, El Salvador, Bolivia, Chile, Colombia, Ecuador, Paraguay, Peru, Uruguay, and Venezuela. The term *Latino/a* was later adopted to reference "Latin Americans" from Mexico and other Spanish-speaking countries in Central and South America and the Caribbean Islands (Cuba, Dominican Republic, Puerto Rico). Important to note, Latino/a are individuals of Latin American descent and Hispanic refers to the Spanish language. For example, individuals of Brazilian and/or Portuguese heritage are considered Latino/a, but not Hispanic (Jones-Smith, 2019).

Initially adopted in most academic and activist spaces, the use of the "x" in Latinx (pronounced "La-teen-ex") was first introduced in a Puerto Rican psychological periodical to challenge traditional gender binaries that are a part of the Spanish language (Salinas, 2020). Because the Spanish language consists of the nouns ending in "o" to refer to the masculine and the "a" as feminine, the use of the "x" has allowed the ungendering of Spanish and the "relationship among language, subjectivity, and inclusion" (Milian, 2017, p. 122). According to Salina and Lozano (2019), the term *Latinx*, as an inclusive term, recognizes the intersectionality of sexuality, language, immigration, ethnicity, culture, and phenotype. Salinas (2020) also states that Latinx as an inclusive term "attempts to not to ignore but amplify race-gendered terminologies as a form of decolonizing an intersectional linguistic, racial, and gender reality" (p. 163). Because of the continued (mis)understandings and (mis)using of the term Latinx, Salinas suggests the academic community consider adopting the term Latin* (pronounced Latin). According to Baez et al. (as cited in Chang et al., 2017),

> The gender bending in "x" aims to critically contrast the hegemonic protocol in the male construction of the universal subject. It is not the mere inclusion—politically correct—of they (him) (male) and they (her) (female) but a critique of the distributive and prescriptive sense of the male and the female in the hegemonic and habitual use of the Spanish Grammar in reference to the subjects. The uncomfortable feeling that the "x" creates in the reading and the pronunciation can be compared with the uncomfortable feeling of those who do not feel—partially or totally—represented neither like they (male) or they (female). (p. 190)

Throughout this chapter, Latinx will be used to refer to students who identify as Hispanic or Latino/a/x that may be Black/African, White Caucasian, Asian, American Indian, some other race, or mixed race. It is suggested that individuals working with Hispanic and/or Latino/a/x students consider the term they identify with.

LATINX DIASPORA IN THE UNITED STATES

Latinx Americans are heterogeneous in terms of immigration, acculturation experiences, and other cultural perspectives. While commonalities in various experiences may exist for students from very different countries, it is important to recognize not all Latinx students have shared experiences as a whole. In other words, Latinxs aren't monolithic, but individuals who share many common cultural and linguistic qualities. Today, *Latinx diaspora* refers to a concept that explains how people with origins in Latin American countries live in countries outside of Latin America while maintaining connections to that region and/or their specific country or countries of origin, and to people who are similarly tied to those places in Latin America. The United States has the largest number of Latinxs or people who might be considered part of the Latinx diaspora (Ortiz, n.d). Thus, while understanding the use of Latinx within the United States and academic settings, students may also identify as Afro-Latinx, Asian-Latinx, and/or Afro-Caribbean. The diaspora also considers identities such as immigrant, undocumented-immigrant, as well as other historical experiences related to identity, immigration reform, labor conditions, education, and civil rights.

LATINX AMERICAN POPULATION IN THE UNITED STATES

According to the 2020 U.S Census, Latinx origin accounts for 60.6 million people, or 18.5% of the U.S. population (U.S. Census Bureau, 2020). This is a 2.5% increase from the 2010 Census figures. A gradual increase of the Latinx population has taken place since the 1960s, including both foreign and U.S. born Latinx. Today, there are approximately 30 million more U.S.-born Latinx in the United States than in 1960 (Colby & Ortman, 2015). Overall, immigration is considered the primary source of growth for the Latinx population (Jones-Smith, 2019). Today, 1 in 5 children under the age of 18 is Latinx. It is suggested that by 2050, 2 in 5 children under the age of 18 will be Latinx (Cárdenas & Kerby, 2012). About 75% of the Latinx population in the United States is noted to live in either the West or South. The Northeast account for 14% of the Latinx population and the Midwest account for 9%. Over half of the Latinx population lives in California, Texas, Florida, and New York (Jones-Smith, 2019). Today, the Latinx school-age population is approaching one-half of all students—positioning Latinx students as the future of this nation. Therefore, promoting the college readiness of Latinx students is one of the most useful contributions a school can provide (Martinez et al., 2020).

While the socioeconomic status of the Latinx population has improved in the last decade, the median household income for all Latinx families was $51,404, which is below the national median income of $62,843 for all families (U.S. Census Bureau, 2020; Jones-Smith, 2019). It has been noted that the high poverty rates of the Latinx population can be attributed to both access to educational opportunities and because of the disadvantage by which many face once they arrive in the United States (Jones-Smith, 2019; Short, 2011).

POSTSECONDARY ENROLLMENT TRENDS

While Latinx represent the largest minoritized group in the United States, as a collective, their educational attainment rates fall below all racial and ethnic groups. According to the *Condition of Education 2020* report (Hussar et al., 2020), the immediate college enrollment rate of high school completers for White students was higher in 2018 (70%) than in 2000 (65%). The immediate college enrollment rate for Latinx students was 63% in 2018 versus 49% in 2000. The immediate college enrollment rate for Black students (62%) and Asian students (78%) was not measurably different from 2000–2018 enrollment rates. Additionally, in 2018, the college enrollment rate was higher for 18- to 24-year-olds who were Asian (59%) than for those who were White (42%), Black (37%), and Hispanic (36%).

As of 2016, postsecondary enrollment for Latinx students (85%) tends to be in public institutions, a higher percentage than any other race/ethnicity group (Postsecondary National Policy Institute [PNPI], 2020). Thus, Latinx students are overrepresented in open-access and community colleges and underrepresented in 4-year institutions. A review by the PNPI (2020) showed that in 2018, 20% of Latino students were enrolled in public 4-year institutions and 27% were enrolled in public 2-year institutions. The PNPI also notes that completion rates are increasing among Latinx students; thus Latinx individuals aged 25–29 with at least an associate's degree increased from 15% to 31% from 2000 to 2019. However, PNPI states that the increase among White students of the same age who had earned at least an associate's degree increased from 44% to 56% over the same time period, leaving the current attainment gap intact. As can be noted, postsecondary enrollment for Latinx students has consistently been in community college (Ma & Baum, 2016). This is attributed to Latinx students' unwillingness to take on student debt to foot college's rising costs (Dennon, 2021). Because of available career training and an affordable bridge to a bachelor's degree, community colleges enroll the greatest proportion of Latinx and Black students (Carnevale & Strohl, 2013; Clark-Ibañez; 2015).

Because Latinx students generally begin in community colleges and/or open access institutions with dismal completion rates (Carnevale & Strohl, 2013), worth noting is the difference between enrollment and graduation rates. Latinx students also maintain the lowest college graduation rate when compared to other racial groups (Pérez Huber et al., 2015). Currently, 14% of 25 years and older Latinx adults have a bachelor's degree (Stepler & Brown, 2016). Currently, the degree attainment rate for Latinx enrolled at a 4-year public institution is 51% and 31% for 2-year public institutions. Thus, Latinxs' graduation rate was 12% lower at 4-yr institutions and 2% lower at 2-year institutions than that of their White non-Hispanic peers in the United States (Excelencia in Education, 2020). The educational attainment of Latinx who ages 25 and older in 2017 varied significantly by level of education. For Latinx males, 30.5% did not complete high school, and for the 69.5% that graduated high school, 13.9% had some college, but no degree, 6.9% had an associates degree, 11.4% had a bachelor's degree, 3.3% earned a master's degree, 0.5% earned a professional degree, and 0.7% earned a doctoral degree. For Latinx females, 28.4% did not complete high school, and for the 71.6% that graduated high school, 14.9% had some college, but no degree, 9% had an associates degree, 12.9% had a bachelor's degree, 4.5% earned a master's degree, 0.4% earned a professional degree, and 0.7% earned a doctoral degree (Espinosa et al., 2019). Despite the noted enrollment and graduation rates, Latinx students maintain high educational aspirations with 84% of male and 95% of female students seeking to earn a college degree (Taylor et al., 2009).

An enrollment review by Acevedo-Gil (2019) showed that although Latinx students as a group maintain the lowest college enrollment, persistence, and completion rates, they are not a homogenous group. According to the author, students who identify as Chicanx or Central American have significantly lower educational outcomes than those who are of Puerto Rican and Cuban descent. This disparity is in part due to Chicanx students experiencing issues related to immigration status and income and funding needs.

Key Content Knowledge

According to Conley (2010), the concept of *key content knowledge* highlights a primary factor influencing postsecondary enrollment for low-income or underrepresented Latinx students whose families have not attended college. This knowledge is defined as "an understanding of the complex college admission and selection processes, the options available to help pay for postsecondary education, the academic requirements for college-level work, and the cultural differences between secondary and postsecondary education" (p. 35). For school counselors and college access partners, it is important to note that successful enrollment in postsecondary education is more than the academic preparation of Latinx students.

Consistently, it is noted that Latinx students, specifically first-generation and/or undocumented immigrant students, are more likely than their peers to not know how to pick, apply for, enroll in, and pay for college (Clark-Ibañez, 2015; Hooker & Brand, 2010; Karp, 2012; Perna, 2006; Perna & Kurban, 2013; Valadez, 2008). According to Valadez (2008), first- generation Latinx immigrant students were less likely to enroll in college even when they were academically prepared because neither they nor their family understood the steps required to complete financial aid paperwork, college entrance exams, or college applications. Karp (2012) further found when interviewing students at the beginning of a dual-enrollment college in high school program that students could not explain what it meant to be a college student. Hooker and Brand also (2010) state that because the communities that first-generation students live in are less likely to possess knowledge of the college enrollment process, these students often lack access to social networks that can help them to understand the process. In addition, the schools these students attend often lack financial resources to provide students with access to technological and human support that would help them to attend college (Lukes, 2015).

Postsecondary Academic Preparation

Academic preparation has consistently been shown to predict enrollment and retention in college (Perna & Kurban, 2013). Studies show that

Latinx students who attended less rigorous high schools were significantly less likely to earn a college degree than those who enrolled in the most rigorous high schools (Bowen et al., 2009). Bowen et al. (2009) also found that the less rigorous schools had significantly higher numbers of Latinx students, low-income students, and students whose parents had not attended postsecondary institutions. One of the reasons for this lack of postsecondary completion could be that less rigorous schools often do not offer postsecondary education preparatory courses starting in ninth grade whereas the more rigorous schools do (Engle, 2007). Even when schools do offer rigorous courses, there is a clear tracking that occurs in schools that pushes students who have not traditionally been considered "college material" into less rigorous courses than those taken by their peers who have more social and economic capital (Bonous-Hammarth & Allen, 2005; Conley, 2010). Tierney et al. (2005) noted how, throughout U.S. history, these populations have been considered inferior or unmotivated in their learning processes. These ideas regarding the educational potential of Latinx students have been used, and still are used today, to explain why these populations are not attaining higher education at the same rates as their White peers (Bonilla-Silva, 2010). In addition, the continued belief in the inferiority of some populations provides schools with a rationale to continue to track these groups into noncollege preparatory pathways in elementary and secondary education (Tierney et al., 2005).

Hispanic Serving Institutions

Hispanic serving institutions (HSI) "are federally funded nonprofit, degree-granting postsecondary institutions whose enrollment is at least 25% Latinx undergraduate students" (Garcia & Guzman-Alvarez, 2021, p. 1). Critical to note is that HSI designation has been increasing with 65% of Latinx undergraduates enrolling in HSIs (Excelencia in Education, 2018). While the growth in Latinx enrollment in HSIs has consistently increased, Garcia and Guzman-Alvarez (2021) state that disparities between enrollment of Latinx undergraduates and the employment of Latinx faculty teaching in HSIs exist. Thus, for students, the disparity can further compound their experiences of systemic injustices similar to those faced in K–12 settings. Garcia and Guzman-Alvarez further emphasize that cultural affinity, including the representation of faculty and staff on campus, significantly impacts students' persistence and postsecondary success. According to the authors, Latinx faculty often advocate for students while "disrupting the institutional systems that prevent students from succeeding" (p. 198). Latinx faculty representation also provides in-class and out-of-class validating experiences and helps to develop their identities as knowers, thinking, and producers of expertise in their selected fields (Alcantar & Hernandez, 2018; Gonzales, 2015).

First-Generation Latinx Students

First-generation Latinx students are students whose parents do not have a postsecondary (2-year or 4-year) degree. In some cases, the parents of first-generation Latinx students may have completed some coursework, but these students will be the first in their immediate family to graduate with a postsecondary degree/credential. Postsecondary scholars have found that first-generation students are at a significant disadvantage for attending and completing postsecondary education (Choy, 2001; Engle, 2007; Martinez, Baker, & Young, 2017; Martinez, Dye, & Gonzalez, 2017). First-generation students are more likely to be Latinx, as well as to come from lower socioeconomic groups than their counterparts, which previous researchers have found decreases in the probability of these students attending and completing postsecondary education (Choy, 2001; Engle, 2007).

Undocumented Immigrant Students College Enrollment

The term *undocumented immigrant student* refers to immigrant children and youth who, without the benefit of legal documents, entered the United States with family members who decided to move for better jobs or educational opportunities, or with the intent to reunite with family members (Fong, 2007). Currently, approximately 100,000 undocumented students graduate from high school every year (Zong & Batalova, 2019) and less than 10% enroll in an institution of higher education (Arbeit et al., 2016). Estimates by the New American Economy show that undocumented students account for 2% of students enrolled in higher education (Presidents' Alliance on Higher Education and Immigration [PAHEI], 2020). Of those enrolled, 47% arrived as children (ages 0–12), 39% as adolescents (ages 10–16), and 14% as adults (ages 22 and above). Today, there are 216,000 DACA-eligible students enrolled in higher education. Additionally, 46% are Hispanic/Latinx, 25% are Asian American and Pacific Islander (AAPI), 15% are Black, 12% are White, and 2% account for biracial and multicultural students. The majority of undocumented students reside in California, Texas, Florida, New York, Illinois, New Jersey, Maryland, Georgia, Washington, Virginia, and North Carolina (PAHEI, 2020).

Currently, 82% of undocumented students in higher education are enrolled in 2- and 4-year public institutions with the majority enrolled in community colleges. 18% are enrolled in private institutions. Among all undocumented students, 10% are enrolled in graduate and professional degree programs. Additionally, 39% of all undocumented students completing graduate degrees have earned undergraduate degrees in science, technology, engineering, or mathematics. Although persistence and completion data is limited, available literature highlights barriers to degree completion to include financial hardships and limited access to resources and social supports (PAHEI, 2020).

Although federal law does not prohibit undocumented students from attending U.S. colleges or universities, they are not eligible for most federal loans, financial aid, and scholarships (Zong & Batalova, 2019). The U.S. Immigration and Customs Enforcement has stated that the charge is for "individual states to decide for themselves whether or not to admit [undocumented students] into their public postsecondary institutions" (National Conference for State Legislatures, 2019, para. 8). Although the Title IV of the Higher Education Act does not prohibit undocumented students from enrolling in higher education, it does forbid them from accessing federal financial aid to cover tuition, fees, housing, and books (Enyioha, 2019). Similarly, the Personal Responsibility and Work Opportunity Responsibility Act prohibits undocumented students from accessing government assistance, including financial aid. The Illegal Immigration Reform and Immigrant Responsibility Act (1996) permits states to establish eligibility criteria for undocumented students to access postsecondary benefits. Many of the eligibility criteria require that students have attended a public high school in the state for 3 years leading to high school graduation, have earned a high school diploma or a General Educational Development (GED) certificate in the state, and have lived in the state 12 months before the date of the student's enrollment in his/her first semester at the postsecondary institution (Gildersleeve, 2012). At the state level, funding support options include in-state college tuition (Perez et al., 2010) and access to state-level financial aid (National Conference for State Legislatures [NCSL], 2019). To date, there are 19 states with provisions that allow in-state tuition rates for undocumented students. Available scholarships are often referred to as Dream Funds.

The Development, Relief, and Education for Alien Minors (DREAM) Act was first introduced in 2001 to provide eligible undocumented young adults with a path to legal permanent residency. However, the DREAM Act has failed to pass on numerous occasions. Following immigrant youth-led organizing efforts across the country, former President Barack Obama signed the Deferred Action for Childhood Arrivals (DACA) into action on June 15, 2012. On June 3, 2019, the House passed the American Dream and Promise Act. If it becomes law, eligible undocumented young adults would be granted 10 years of legal permanent status. On September 5, 2017, the Trump administration's decision to rescind DACA resulted in roughly 196,000 undocumented high school students that graduated in 2018 and

2019 unable to apply for DACA. On June 18, 2020, the Supreme Court ruled to uphold DACA reinstating the 2012 Obama policy. On June 15, 2021, nine years since undocumented youth advocated and mobilized for DACA, a result decision has yet to be made.

COVID-19 Pandemic

According to the National Student Clearinghouse Research Center ([NSCRC]; Causey et al., 2021), the COVID-19 pandemic further highlighted the patterns of existing disparities among Black, Brown, and Indigenous undergraduate students with regards to college enrollment rates. Most disproportionately impacted were 2020 high school graduates of low-income, high poverty, and high minority schools. In the *COVID-19 Special Analysis High School Benchmarks* report, NSCRC reports that while high school graduation rates were unaffected by COVID-19, undergraduate enrollments declined by 6.8%, or 4.5 times greater than previous undergraduate enrollment. Undergraduate enrollment by race/ethnicity and gender unveiled great disparities for Latinx students. While a 2.1% enrollment increase has been noted year-over-year for Latinx students, post pandemic, they had a total of 8.2% decline in undergraduate enrollment for Spring 2021. Males experienced a 12.6% decline and females a 5.1% decline. Disparities were also noted between types of postsecondary institutions. At public 4-year institutions, a 1.9% decrease was noted, however, a decrease of 13.7% was noted at community colleges (Causey et al., 2021). Data shared by NSCRC highlights how a national crisis such as the pandemic can undo years of gains established by policies, national efforts, and best practices at the institutional level. In other words, the international crisis serves as a reminder of how fragile the systems of support remain and the efforts that must be continued to ensure minoritized communities have access to postsecondary opportunities. School disruptions, health risks, and income loss experienced during the pandemic have significantly widened historical racial gaps that exist in education.

POSTSECONDARY ADVISING AND ENROLLMENT BARRIERS

While several support structures and policies aim to close the enrollment gap for Latinx students, barriers continue to deter this group from matriculating into higher education. *Schoolcentric* epistemologies, or the normalization that educators are experts regarding how students are characterized and serviced (Khalifa, 2018), are exhibited through discriminatory practices. These include poorly implemented laws, policies, and practices that cause Latinx students to experience discrimination and prejudice from high school staff (Pérez et al., 2010; Lukes, 2015). For example, despite enrolling in high school with strong academic records, undocumented students are more likely to be placed in English language development (ELD) classes (Clark-Ibañez, 2015) or remediation courses (Suárez-Orozco & Yoshikawa, 2013). Thus, students are tasked with having to convince school counselors to place them in rigorous or college preparatory classes. Systemic barriers include expressed low expectations from staff and the K–12 system as a whole (Nienhusser, 2013; Vega et al., 2015); poor school climate (Martinez et al., 2004); lack of access to rigorous, advanced, and/ or college-prep classes; and limited access to college opportunities and/or advising (Clark-Ibañez, 2015; Patrick et al., 2020).

Current literature suggests poorly trained school staff (U.S. Department of Education, 2015), continued systemic oppression, educators' limited knowledge of immigration rights and laws, funding issues, and the limited use of culturally appropriate advising practices continue to impede college access partners from supporting and including such students in the college application process (NCSL, 2019). Additionally, when scholarship opportunities are merit-based, low achievers tend to be excluded from educational opportunities (Flores, 2016).

Regardless of advances toward supporting Latinx students to gain access to postsecondary opportunities, student testimonials show they continue to face racism and invalidating experiences when interacting with school personnel (Martinez et al., 2019). Many minoritized students, including Latinxs, share postsecondary advising often focused on selecting undermatched colleges. An analysis by Patrick et al. (2020) highlights that minoritized students living in poverty are overwhelmingly concentrated in the lowest-achieving schools. Also depicted is that when educators share a belief that minoritized students lack readiness, can't handle the rigor of higher education, or perceive students who do not visit the counseling office as unmotivated, students may be excluded from receiving information or access to other opportunities. For example, undocumented students continue to not be enrolled in advanced and/or college preparatory classes and are often excluded from guidance lessons regarding the college application process (Nienhusser, 2013). According to Clark-Ibañez (2015), this results in students feeling dismissed and unwanted in the general high school climate; often seeking community and support from English second language (ESL) or Advancement Via Individual Determination (AVID) teachers, or peers perceived as "knowledgeable" (Lad & Braganza, 2013).

Although college enrollment has increased for minoritized groups, specifically Latinx students, significant to consider is the high school dropout rate that contributes to low college enrollment rates among this student group. In 2018, 16- to 24-year-olds who were not enrolled in school and did not have a high school diploma or its equivalent, was 5.3% (Hussar et al., 2020). White students made up 4.2%, Blacks 6.4%, and Latinx (8%), Pacific Islander (8.1%), and Native American Indian/Alaska Native (9.5%) made up the largest group. According to Martinez et al. (2019), the dropout rate of Latinx students is a significant challenge that impacts their ability to successfully enroll and obtain a postsecondary degree.

UNIQUE NEEDS WHEN ADVISING LATINX STUDENTS

Because school counselors prepare students for postsecondary success, they must understand the unique needs of Latinx students; recognizing how coloniality, immigration status, funding limitations, experienced trauma, and their bicultural experience inform postsecondary choice. According to the American School Counseling Association's (ASCA) position statements in *The School Counselor and Individual Student Planning for Postsecondary Preparation* (American School Counselor Association [ASCA], 2017), *The School Counselor and Student Postsecondary Recruitment* (ASCA, 2015), and *The School Counselor and Working With Students Experiencing Issues Surrounding Undocumented Status* (ASCA, 2019a), school counselors are critical in supporting students by helping them gain access to an equitable education that meets their needs and prepares them for postsecondary access. While educators agree minoritized students face unique challenges, those challenges are often not addressed during the college application process. As such, the disconnect leads to missed opportunities to understand how these challenges and fears influence postsecondary choice. Ensuring Latinx youth receive equitable education and advising, it is important to consider the unique needs of Latinx students when providing culturally responsive advising (CRA) within postsecondary advising practices.

Parent Role and Engagement

According to available literature, Latinx parents are central in reinforcing the urgency of earning a college degree (Acevedo-Gil, 2017). For example, Latinx parents reinforce the value of higher education (Clark-Ibañez, 2015; Gonzalez et al., 2003) while being key in providing the needed support to establish the mindset of pursuing college (Pérez Huber et al., 2015). For many Latinx students, the pursuit of a college degree begins with parental influence (Carolan-Silva & Reyes, 2013). As Martinez et al. (2019) noted in their study, Latinx students whose parents were immigrants and/

or did not attend college particularly stressed the value and importance of postsecondary education.

Irrespective of the challenges, students thrive academically and attain economic success; often for themselves and their families (Baum & Flores, 2011). For example, for many undocumented students, attending college has been cultivated from an early age, and achieving the "American Dream" would help achieve socioeconomic mobility (Salinas et al., 2019). Important to consider is *familialism*; the ideology that presumes a family is responsible for the care of its members rather than leaving that responsibility to the government (Torres, 2004). Because students are positioned to prioritize the needs of the family rather than each individual, their goals for higher education are strongly influenced by a responsibility to honor the sacrifices made by parents (Méndez-Pounds et al., 2018).

Bicultural Experience

Biculturalism is defined as a "comfort and proficiency with both one's heritage culture and the culture of the country or region in which one has settled" (Schwartz & Unger, 2010, p. 26). According to Toppelberg and Collins (2010), bicultural competence is, therefore, an outcome of the acculturation process and outline six components of bicultural competence to include: language competence, knowledge of cultural beliefs and values, positive attitudes toward both majority and minority groups, bicultural efficacy, role repertoire, and a sense of being grounded and/or establishing support networks in both cultures. Ellis and Chen (2013) state that although students embrace American values such as independence and meritocracy, they often reported a simultaneous need to stay connected to their immigrant communities. In their study, students also "reported an ability to understand different points of view and expressed a sense of connection between themselves and other marginalized individuals" (p. 256). Thus, it is critically important to recognize the responsibility Latinx students often carry to preserve their heritage and culture while incorporating Westernized values into future goals.

Kangala et al. (2016) discuss the challenges that Latinx students face when transitioning and adapting to college noting their transition is not linear, but what the authors identify as students operating *entre mundos*, or the moving back and forth among multiple contexts. These contexts include the family, *barrio*/community, native country, work, peers, and spiritual worlds. Anzaldúa (1999) further explains the challenges of entre mundos as *choque* which is when Latinx students experience liminality, separation anxiety, racial and gender microaggressions, and having to negotiate dislocation and relocation.

Funding Needs

Although Latinx students highly value education and are more likely than Black or White individuals to consider college a gateway to the middle class and that a degree will eventually pay off, they're less likely than other racial and ethnic groups to access student loans for educational purposes (Dennon, 2021). As previously noted, Latinx students tend to be first-generation college students, resulting in limited knowledge about the college application process, including funding options. According to Nienhusser (2013), the financial concern is a significant factor of low college enrollment rates among Latinx students. Compounding the stresses students face is the lack of guidance in the college application process received by high school personnel (Farmer-Hinton & McCullough, 2008).

For undocumented Latinx students, navigating postsecondary funding is also difficult, if not traumatizing. Pérez and Cortes (2011) found that even though some students receive funding through current options (i.e., DACA, scholarships, or state-level funding), they work an average of 20 to 30 hours per week to supplement their income and/or school funding needs. Within *mixed-status families,* or families that include a range of documentation patterns, students eligible to work are also the sole provider for their families (Diaz-Strong et al., 2011) impacting course load. More so, students tend to work low-wage or demanding jobs such as cleaning houses or taking care of children. Also highlighted in the literature is the responsibility many undocumented students carry to support their families upon graduating from high school (Clark-Ibanez, 2015; Williams, 2016). Undocumented immigrant and mixed-household citizen-children are often left with limited choices of schools for college (Abrego & Gonzalez, 2010) and/ or having to decide if leaving their state of residency is a viable option.

Access to Social and Cultural Capital

Social capital is the culmination of an individual's network of people and community resources used to navigate through society's institutions for the attainment of things such as education, work, or health care (Lad & Braganza, 2013; Yosso, 2005). For Latinx students, the development of strong support networks via access to social capital expands their contextual knowledge of educational pathways and often attributes to academic success (Lukes, 2015). The types of social capital students access include teachers, mentors, advisors, friends, community leaders, and knowledgeable allies or legal experts. Additionally, students access nontraditional forms of social capital that include aspirational capital, navigational capital, linguistic capital, familial capital, resistance capital, reflective capital (Clark-Ibañez, 2015), and spiritual capital (Wyttenbach, 2015).

As U.S. immigration laws and policies fluctuate between being open to immigrants and highly restrictive, Latinx undocumented students depend on social networks such as allies, activist groups, or community organizations to navigate these laws and policies. Because being undocumented is a stigmatized social identity (Yasuike, 2019), students are faced with messages they are in violation of American immigration laws and are undeserving of financial assistance or access to higher education (Gomez & Pérez Huber, 2019). Students living in communities with a high presence of Immigration Customs Enforcement (ICE) exhibit higher levels of social barriers, often choosing to keep private out of fear of deportation (Méndez-Pounds et al., 2018). For students, navigating daily activities such as going to school, attending events, or connecting with school support staff can be fearful experiences (Muñoz, 2016; Valdivia 2019).

Cultural capital is the knowledge, skills, and language that allow individuals to navigate social institutions, including K–12 and college (Bourdieu & Passeron, 1977). According to Ayala and Ramirez (2019) simply relying on the Eurocentric application of cultural capital fails to acknowledge the role of coloniality and its influence on higher education. In other words, because the foundation of education stems from White Eurocentric influence, the knowledge, skills, and experiences from a White perspective are repeatedly centralized and thus, failing minoritized students. The authors argue that those working with Latinx students must hold an awareness of how coloniality reinforces messages that students do not belong or that they are the exception whenever they excel. Furthermore, recognizing *Latinx cultural wealth*, both *ventajas* (assets or personal resources) and what Gloria Anzaldúa calls *conocimientos* (knowledge or awareness that evolves through specific life experiences; Kangala et al., 2016), should be central when providing postsecondary advising.

Community Cultural Wealth

According to Martinez et al. (2020), "A key factor for improving Latinx students' postsecondary education—going rates is school counselors' awareness, knowledge, and application of acknowledging Latinx students' community cultural wealth before entering a school and counseling space with students" (p. 216). *Community cultural wealth* describes the multiple forms of capital that communities of color possess (Yosso, 2005). Because Latinx students' cultural knowledge, skills, and abilities often go unrecognized or reflected within a school's culture, Latinx cultural wealth is used by these students as a means to navigate and survive experienced K–12 institutional neglect (Martinez et al., 2020). The author states that school counselors must establish a college-going culture inclusive of Latinx students' strengths, cultural assets, and cultural wealth. The eight different Latinx cultural wealth categories include aspirational, linguistic, social, navigational, familial, resistant, perseverant, and spiritual/faith wealth. Through the inclusion of the various cultural wealth, students develop certain knowledge or *conocimientos* (see Table 8.1) inclusive of their culture and identities.

Education as an Empowerment Tool

The literature also highlights that despite the challenges Latinx students face, access to higher education is perceived as an empowerment tool. In their study, Méndez-Pounds et al. (2018) discuss how education helped

TABLE 8.1 Forms of Latinx Cultural Capital, Resources, and Assets

Latinx Cultural Wealth	*Conocimientos*/Knowledge (Ability to)
Aspirational	• Set high aspirations • Recognize the value of education • Remain hopeful about the future regardless of obstacles and barriers
Linguistic Social Navigational	• Code blend two or more languages • Engage with formal and informal modes of expression • Create strong social networks • Make new friends and form new relationships • Operate in liminal spaces • Traverse multiple, distinct social contexts
Familial	• Dislocate and relocate • Adapt to new culture • Model the strength and determination of the family • Use knowledge gained through the value of family advice (*consejos*), sayings (*dichos*), respect (*respeto*), testimonials, and education
Resistant Perseverant	• Resist stereotypes; combat and overcome macroaggressions • Overcome hardships, such as poverty and lack of guidance and resources • Develop inner strength; become self-reliant and determined to succeed • Recognize and embrace sacrifices that must be made to attend postsecondary institutions
Spiritual/faith	• Use faith in God/higher power to overcome struggles • Develop sense of meaning and purpose • Embrace concepts such as gratitude, goodness, and compassion

Source: Martinez et al., 2020

define student narratives and was "discussed as a value in their lives and a way to acknowledge and honor their families' sacrifices" (p. 447). Latinx students' thirst for knowledge and capacity to overcome hurdles and succeed academically clearly became a part of their identity. Education as a source of empowerment is most important to Latinx undocumented students because, for them, education would "remain within them, even if deported" (Méndez-Pounds et al., 2018). Undocumented youth also learn higher education has the transformative potential to help them become productive members of society, mostly through civic engagement (Pérez et al., 2010). Higher education also provides access to social networks (Clark-Ibañez, 2015; Lukes, 2015) and other resources. Within educational spaces, students also connect with documented peers, who often serve as sources of support and identity formation (Gonzales, 2011).

Immigration Status of Latinx Undocumented Students

Although most undocumented students have been educated in the United States, the termination of legal inclusion during their K–12 years compels them to now navigate the transition to higher education with a sense of being "outsiders." The exclusion from developmental activities like applying for a work permit or driver's license is described as the start of "being undocumented." Students are also faced with the hurdles of securing financial aid and employment, which may put their dreams on hold (Pérez et al., 2010).

It's important that school counselors also recognize that many Latinx undocumented youths learn of their immigration status during the college planning process (Clark-Ibañez, 2015; Méndez-Pounds et al., 2018), and develop a *legal consciousness*, or the process of meaning making of their legal status (Muñoz, 2016). This initial realization of their unauthorized status invokes experiences of vulnerability and isolation (Gonzalez et al., 2020) and feelings of betrayal and worry (National Council of La Raza, 2015). This results in students maintaining their identity a secret for fear of being deported or discriminated against (Pérez & Cortes, 2011). Living in the "shadows" can impact students' ability to develop close relationships with peers, school counselors, or significant others. For school counselors, it is important to understand how a student's new awareness of his/her immigration status can influence how they live and manage how and to whom they may disclose their legal status. School counselors must also recognize and address how experienced or possible deportation may impact postsecondary choices. This includes whether the student will attend a school away from home or opt to remain within their communities.

CULTURALLY RESPONSIVE ADVISING

Culturally responsive [practices] is a framework to integrate relatable aspects of students' daily lives into the classroom and curriculum. Ladson-Billings (1994), defines culturally responsive [practices] as a pedagogy that empowers students intellectually, socially, emotionally, and politically by using their cultural references to impart knowledge, skills, and attitudes. Thus, a *culturally responsive pedagogy* allows for a fluid understanding of culture and the use of practices that explicitly engages questions of equity and justice (Ladson-Billings, 2014). Gay (2018) also defines culturally responsive [practices] as the "cultural knowledge, prior experiences, frames of reference, and performance styles of ethnically diverse students to make learning encounters more relevant to and effective for them" (p. 31). Lynch (2016) defines a culturally responsive pedagogy to be "a student-centered approach in which students' unique cultural strengths are identified and nurtured to promote student achievement and a sense of well-being about the student's cultural place in the world" (para. 2).

Although ASCA standards and position statements establish that school counselors support student development through the appreciation and inclusion of multiculturalism and diversity, the reality remains that school counseling practices are firmly rooted in the values of European American middle-class culture (Lee, 2001). According to Lee (2001), "School counselors need a different perspective from which to operate if they are going to ensure students from culturally diverse backgrounds have access to services that promote optimal academic, career, and personal-social development" (p. 258). In his model, Lee defines a *culturally responsive school counseling program* as one that functions within a culturally responsive school and where key school counselor roles and functions enhance the quality of instruction for all students. First, culturally responsive counselors facilitate student development through two premises: All students can and want to learn and those cultural differences must not be ignored. As such, school counselors seek to understand the cultural realities of students and how they apply to academic, career, and personal-social development. Second, school counselors advocate for students. Because most often students from diverse backgrounds are often perceived from a deficit model and limited consideration is given to the inequalities they face as a result of systemic racism, school counselors must develop a heightened awareness of the systemic barrier to education students face. They must also effectively challenge policies and initiatives that reinforce systemic barriers. Lastly, school counselors work to bridge the home and family lives of diverse students and the school. By inviting community members and/or individuals from diverse communities to provide professional development or participate in an advisory board, school counselors mitigate the outcomes of educational practices that do not validate the experiences and customs of culturally diverse home and family life.

Culturally responsive school counselors develop an understanding of how prejudice, privilege, and various forms of oppression affect students and help establish a supportive school climate where cultural differences are appreciated (Foxx et al., 2020). In their study, Smith-Adcock et al. (2006) found that although participating schools provided programs and services that addressed language barriers, additional culturally responsive counseling services were needed. The authors also discuss the need for school counselors to advocate for systemic change, outreach into communities, and involve families in the students' education. Holcomb-McCoy (2007) defines multi-cultural [school] counseling as a process where the counselor and student consider their personal and cultural experiences. To highlight the effective use of multicultural counseling, school counseling programs have regularly been referred to as *culturally proficient* and/or *culturally competent*. The term *culturally sustaining program* is used to define programs that seek to "perpetuate and foster—to sustain—linguistic, literate, and cultural pluralism as part of the democratic project of schooling" (Paris, 2012, p. 93).

CULTURALLY RESPONSIVE ADVISING FRAMEWORK

In addition to the ASCA standards, the often referenced Eight Components of College and Career Readiness Counseling (College Board, n.d.) include college aspirations, academic planning for college and career readiness, enrichment and extracurricular engagement, college and career exploration and selection processes, college and career assessments, college affordability planning, college and career admission processes, and transition from high school graduation to college enrollment. The model positions that school counselors must consider the context of the diverse student population and interventions should involve students, parents, and the community. The model encourages the use of culturally sensitive interventions with knowledge of how programs, policies, and practices impact the perspectives and experiences of diverse student groups.

To date, the college application process for high school seniors continues to adhere to school counselors supporting students to complete an application, turn in supplemental requirements (College Board, n.d.), and meet deadlines. While important, such practices do not address the cultural needs of unique student groups, specifically, undocumented students (Yasuike, 2019). The implementation of a *culturally responsive advising* (CRA) framework supports students' transition into postsecondary education while addressing the barriers and unique needs that students face. The proposed culturally responsive advising framework within the college application process adopts key principles of culturally relevant pedagogy (Ladson-Billings, 2014; Lee, 2001). CRA positions school counselors as advocates, leaders, and systems change agents while adopting practices critical to school counselors recognizing their role in the oppression of students and communities (Khalifa, 2018). The following section outlines the CRA principles and concludes with an overview of how an ecological approach can be used to implement CRA.

Culturally Advising Principles

School Counselors Seek to Empower ALL Students

Culturally responsive practices require that school counselors communicate high expectations for all students, thus, they must recognize how personal biases influence the lowering of expectations for students or the types of services and/or resources offered. Through a culturally responsive lens, the determinants of success are defined by the cultural context of students, their families, and communities instead of Euro-Western standards. School counselors seek to understand ways that all students can be empowered while recognizing their cultural realities and their importance to postsecondary goals.

School Counselors Function as Facilitators

School counselors that function as facilitators ensure counseling programs, guidance lessons, and services provided are relevant to and reflect the social, cultural, and linguistic experiences of students. Because social capital is central to Latinx students successfully navigating their path to higher education, school counselors should facilitate the inclusion of established support networks; mentors, community organizations and leaders, and allies in the college application process to inform about laws and/or resources. Important to recognize for Latinx undocumented students is the influential power of *resistance capital*, or the knowledge and skills fostered through oppositional behavior that challenges inequality (Yosso, 2005), as a form of self-empowerment for students (Clark-Ibañez, 2015) school counselors advocate for students and effectively challenge policies and initiatives that reinforce systemic barriers (Lee, 2001).

School Counselors Encourage the Inclusion of Culturally and Linguistically Diverse Students

Recognizing Latinx students face a myriad of barriers concerning college enrollment and persistence, school counselors are called to understand the barriers these students face when accessing higher education to best identify college advising strategies. Important to consider is the students' culture and language when planning college advising activities. Cultural considerations to consider include acculturation phases, external (i.e., food and arts) and internal elements of culture (i.e., values, customs, expectations, social roles, family structure); and pull factors (i.e., opportunity, freedom, educational opportunities) or push factors (i.e., poverty, oppression). Within CRA, it is equally important for school counselors to invite parents, guardians, and/ or mentors to share about the students' lives and incorporate the shared wisdom within advising practices (Witcht, 2017).

School Counselors Practice Cultural Sensitivity

Latinx students hold values and identities deeply rooted in their cultures and communities; values often not included in the college advising process. Cultural sensitivity requires school counselors to understand how prejudice, privilege, and various forms of oppression affect students (Foxx et al., 2020) and how they relate to various dimensions of students' cultural identity. Through the use of anti-biased language, school counselors help to create an anti-oppressive school environment (Khalifa, 2018), thus fostering a space where students can discuss issues such as funding needs, mixed-status households, and experienced trauma into the college application process.

School Counselors Reshape the Delivery of Services

Reshaping practices requires school counselors to analyze how current practices support or exclude Latinx students. For example, ensuring college-related presentations or guidance lessons are accessed by all students and are inclusive of information related to students' unique situation; specifically language and family needs, and/or immigration status. School counselors must also explore the role of race and racism in perpetuating social disparities between dominant and marginalized racial student groups, and consider how to address them within the college application process. School counselors should also challenge the notion of meritocracy or the "American Dream" as the norm and explore how it may/may not align with students' goals toward higher education.

School Counselors Encourage Student-Controlled Discourse

Genuine care-based counseling calls for school counselors to ask students to share personal feedback (Gay, 2018) regarding interventions, resources, and guidance lessons delivered. School counselors should establish a college application process based on shared inquiry and dialogue where Latinx students can disclose personal experiences; specifically, those that may influence their path to college. Student-controlled discourse also minimizes deficit images about students and families and validates their unique experiences and needs. For example, understanding how education and activism are empowerment tools for students and their families.

School Counselors Intentionally Engage Students' Social Capital

CRA requires school counselors to use students' social capital as informative spaces from which to develop a positive understanding of students and families. Because the ultimate goal is to strengthen the position between individuals and their environment and that they navigate systems successfully, school counselors must collaborate with students at an individual level (McMahon et al., 2014) while including the students' networks, families, and community resources into the process. While stakeholders and other identified advocates have the intention to support student achievement, school counselors must intentionally engage and include the individuals and networks students turn to as they are often best informed about policies and laws, and how to best navigate the challenges to higher education (Clark-Ibañez, 2015). Established partnerships seek to advocate for student achievement and educational equity and opportunities (ASCA, 2019b).

School Counselors Engage in Self-Reflection

Critical self-reflection, central to CRA, calls for school counselors to examine how oppression and marginalization are manifested within the school environment (Khalifa, 2018). School counselors who engaged in CRA understand how current college advising practices reinforce the oppression and/or exclusion of Latinx students. By reflecting on how they have contributed to the oppression of Latinx students, school counselors can recognize the use of microinvalidations, biases held, and/or how advising practices reinforce school-centric or meritocratic perspectives. School counselors also identify professional development needs as it relates to supporting Latinx students.

IMPLEMENTING CULTURALLY RESPONSIVE ADVISING PRACTICES THROUGH AN ECOLOGICAL FRAMEWORK

Implementing CRA through an ecological framework allows school counselors to recognize the inherent qualities of students and how the systems interact to influence the development and postsecondary decisions. Within CRA, an ecological framework departs from school-centric practices, ultimately avoiding a one-size-fits-all approach and the use of deficit perspectives. As collaborators, school counselors explore students' influencing factors toward college choice; factors aligned with the unique needs previously discussed. The systems of the ecological framework include the microsystem, mesosystem, exosystem, macrosystem, and chronosystem (Bronfenbrenner, 1979, 1986). Aligning with the focus of this chapter the systems will be explored in the context of Latinx students.

Microsystem

At the innermost level, the microsystem is the relationship between Latinx students and their immediate surroundings (Paat, 2013). For Latinx students, parenting practices, family dynamics, and relationships with peers influence their pathways to assimilation and commitment to academic success within the American school system. School counselors can consider the inclusion of the students' culture (CRA Principle 3), practicing cultural humility (CRA Principle 4), and student-controlled discourse (CRA Principle 6). For example, school counselors can discuss student concerns regarding postsecondary planning such as being first-generation or undocumented, the need to support family postgraduation, leaving their community, being *entre mundos*, or anticipating the need to navigate predominantly White institutions (PWI).

Mesosystem

The mesosystem consists of the interactions among two or more microsystems; primarily family, peers, and school. By reshaping the delivery of services (CRA Principle 5), school counselors position themselves continuously to explore existing social disparities and consider how to address them within the college application process. More so, when school counselors intentionally engage Latinx students' social capital (CRA Principle 7) and their community cultural wealth, they allow for the influences within the mesosystem to be considered. School counselors can encourage students to consider ways their social capitals can serve as resources while enrolled in college.

Exosystem

The exosystem refers to the external systems such as the neighborhood or community where school and socialization happen (Patt, 2013). The limited engagement of Latinx students with public institutions can decrease the likelihood students will access programs beneficial to their development and academic advancement. According to Suárez-Orozco and Yoshikawa

(2013), the range of negative experiences, poor work conditions, and the quality of social networks parents also experience significantly, impact the development of Latinx undocumented children. As facilitators (CRA Principle 2), the college-going practices and services school counselors provide should reflect the social, cultural, and linguistic experiences of students. Additionally, school counselors should intentionally plan for and include HSIs when hosting college fairs.

Macrosystem

The macrosystem refers to factors like the global economy, and social and cultural conditions of the countries of origin. For many Latinx students, the macrosystem is influenced by experienced prejudice, racism, and limited access to essential resources and services (Gomez & Pérez Huber, 2019). Engaging in self-reflection (CRA Principle 8) allows for school counselors to explore how the school's college-going practices reinforce the oppression and/or exclusion of Latinx students. School counselors further examine how they as individuals and/or school staff contribute to the oppression of the Latinx students by perpetuating racial injustices, setting low expectations for students, and/or using microaggression when providing postsecondary advising. Additionally, they explore the use of *exclusionary practices* or actions that contribute to students not being present, or participants in their education (Khalifa, 2018). These include schools not welcoming parents and/or community leaders and experts, hostile treatment toward students (i.e., microaggressions, color-blindness, denial of services), not valuing students' cultural contributions, and accepting student disengagement.

Chronosystem

The chronosystem focuses on normative and nonnormative life transitions which are catalysts for impetus developmental change. Normative transitions include transitions such as school entry, puberty, and entering early adulthood. Nonnormative transitions include experiences such as deportation, moving, or the loss of a job. By empowering all students (CRA Principle 1) and encouraging a student-controlled discourse, school counselors minimize the cumulative negative experiences students face as they transition to college. Most importantly, this provides the opportunity for students to deconstruct the messages of the dominant culture and identify ways to tackle obstacles as they navigate the college application process; especially through the use of solutions not traditional to the college-advising practices.

RECOMMENDATIONS

Beyond implementing culturally responsive practices, school counselors must understand that White privilege is pervasive and embedded into every aspect of who we are, and taking a "color-blind" approach denies school counselors the opportunity to be advocates and leaders (Atkins & Oglesby, 2018). While it can be difficult for school staff to talk about racism and recognize how they can be racist or maintain racist practices, not courageously doing so perpetuates racial disparities. School counselors implementing CRA are encouraged to engage in honest and real conversations about the destructive ways they may reinforce a one-size-fits-all approach or exclude Latinx students by assuming all students share similar beliefs about higher education. As noted throughout the chapter, Latinx students, while representing the largest minoritized group in the United States, aren't monolithic, but individuals who share many common cultural and linguistic qualities. Because colonial practices are deeply rooted in our education system (Atkins & Oglesby, 2018), it can be challenging to adopt new philosophies and practices. By examining how the economic, political, and legal systems influence the lives of Latinx students, school counselors can rely less on mainstream society's standard of achievement or limited data metrics to determine support and services offered.

Lastly, the nature of the day-to-day work culture of school counseling can influence counselors to remain neutral about systemic issues that ultimately cause harm or trauma to minoritized students. To fundamentally implement CRA, school counselors must critically reflect on the interventions and practices used within counseling programs, daily interactions, and personal reactions they have with students, parents/guardians, and their networks. Engaging in self-reflection allows school counselors to gain insight and develop a deeper understanding of social justice perspectives (Atkins & Oglesby, 2018). While simple in concept, recognizing "flaws" in one's professional work can be difficult and often an emotional process. Ways to practice self-reflection include seeking feedback from community leaders and partners regarding supports and interventions to embed into the college-going culture; practicing cultural humility, and connecting with trusting supervisors and/or colleagues.

CONCLUSION

Addressing access to higher education within a system where racism is discounted to the detriment of Latinx students, and where the benefit of White privilege is the ultimate goal, implementing CRA at schools with poorly prepared and knowledgeable school staff can be challenging. Given the complexities of issues Latinx students face, it can be difficult to grasp how the myriad of systems involved can operate collectively to solve educational disparities for them. However, despite the challenges Latinx students face, many achieve academic success and empower youth through mentorship, volunteering, and civic engagement (Clark-Ibañez, 2015). This is specifically true for Latinx undocumented students. To ensure Latinx students receive an equitable education that prepares them for college and career, it is imperative educators and other school staff understand the unique needs of these students. Adopting culturally responsive advising will allow school counselors to support Latinx students through an equitable and social justice lens.

DISCUSSION QUESTIONS

1. In what ways might your school's postsecondary advising include one or more of the *culturally responsive advising principles*? How would the selected principle(s) support Latinx students?
2. How do the current economic, political, and legal systems influence the lives of Latinx students and their postsecondary planning? In what ways can school counselors address possible negative influences when establishing a college-going culture?
3. In what ways can school counselors rely less on mainstream society's standard of achievement or limited data metrics to determine the supports and services offered to Latinx students?

ACTIVITIES

1. Select a Hispanic serving institution (https://www.hacu.net/hacu/HSIs.asp) and explore the ways that it may differ from predominantly White institutions (PWIs). In what ways are the services, resources, and other opportunities offered similar and/or different?
2. Assess the various social and cultural capitals, and community cultural wealth Latinx students in your school access. In what ways can their cultural knowledge, skills, and abilities be reflected within your school's culture and postsecondary advising practices. Social capitals to consider include unique networks (i.e., community leaders and organizations), advocates, mentors, and other significant allies. Cultural capitals include the knowledge and skills from Latinx students' perspectives. Community cultural wealth includes the specific ways students have learned to navigate systemic injustices and inequalities.

3. This chapter outlines various postsecondary advising and enrollment barriers that Latinx students face. Take some time to engage
in *critical self-reflection* to consider the ways that K–12 postsecondary
practices have contributed to the oppression of Latinx students in
your school. Consider your responses to the following questions:
   a. Are there practices that you have engaged in that perpetuate
the oppression and/or marginalization of Latinx students? If so,
what culturally responsive and/or strength-based practices can
you adopt?
   b. What professional development opportunities can support your
ability to provide culturally responsive advising to Latinx students?

AUTHOR NOTE

Diana Camilo https://orcid.org/0000-0002-2950-1621
Roberto Martinez https://orcid.org/0000-0001-7346-7400

Correspondence concerning this chapter should be addressed to Diana
Camilo, California State University, San Bernardino, 5500 University Pkwy,
College of Education, San Bernardino, CA 92407.
Email: diana.camilo@csusb.edu

REFERENCES

Abrego, L., & Gonzales, R. (2010). Blocked paths, uncertain futures: The postsecondary education and labor market prospects of undocumented Latino
youth. *Journal of Education for Students Placed at Risk, 15,* 144–157.

Acevedo-Gil, N. (2017). College-conocimiento: Toward an interdisciplinary college
choice framework for Latinx students. *Race Ethnicity and Education, 20*(6),
829–850.

Acevedo-Gil, N. (2019). College-going facultad: Latinx students anticipating postsecondary institutional obstacles. *Journal of Latinos and Education, 18*(2), 107–
125. https://doi.org/10.1080/15348431.2017.1371019

Alcantar, C. M., & Hernandez, E. (2018). "Here the professors are your guide, tus
guías": Latina/o student validating experiences with faculty at a Hispanic-serving community college. *Journal of Hispanic Higher Education.* https://doi.org/
10.1177/1538192718766234

American School Counselor Association (2015). *The school counselor and student
postsecondary recruitment.* https://schoolcounselor.org/Standards-Positions/
Position-Statements/ASCA-Position-Statements/The-School-Counselor-and
-Student-Postsecondary-Rec

American School Counselor Association (2017). *The school counselor and individual student planning for postsecondary preparation.* https://schoolcounselor

.org/Standards-Positions/Position-Statements/ASCA-Position-Statements/ The-School-Counselor-and-Individual-Student-Planni

American School Counselor Association (2019a). *The school counselor and working with students experiencing issues surrounding undocumented status.* https://schoolcounselor .org/Standards-Positions/Position-Statements/ASCA-Position-Statements/ The-School-Counselor-and-Working-with-Students-Exp

American School Counselor Association. (2019b). *ASCA school counselor professional standards & competencies.* https://www.schoolcounselor.org/getmedia/a8d59c2c -51de-4ec3-a565-a3235f3b93c3/SC-Competencies.pdf

Anzaldúa, G. (1999). *Borderlands: La Frontera: The New Mestiza* (2nd ed). Aunt Lute Books.

Arbeit, C. A., Staklis, S., & Horn, L. (2016). *New American undergraduates: Enrollment trends and age at the arrival of immigrant and second-generation students* (NCES 2017-414). U.S. Department of Education, National Center for Education Statistics.

Atkins, R., & Oglesby, A. (2018). *Interrupting racism: Equity and social justice in school counseling.* Routledge.

Ayala, M. I., & Ramirez, C. (2019). Coloniality and Latinx college students' experiences. *Equity & Excellence in Education, 52*(1), 129–144. https://doi.org/10.1080/ 10665684.2019.1635542

Baum, S., & Flores, S. M. (2011). Higher education and children in immigrant families. *The Future of Children, 21*(1), 171–193. https://doi.org/10.1353/foc.2011 .0000

Bonilla-Silva, E. (2010). *Racism without racists: Color-blind racism and the persistence of racial inequality in America* (3rd ed.). Rowman & Littlefield.

Bonous-Hammarth, M., & Allen, W. R. (2005). A dream deferred: The critical factor of timing in college preparation and outreach. In W. G. Tierney, Z. B. Corwin, & J. E. Colyar (Eds.), *Preparing for college: Nine elements of effective outreach* (pp. 155–172). State University of New York Press.

Bourdieu, P., & Passeron, J. C. (1977). *Reproduction in education, society, and culture.* Sage Publications.

Bowen, W. G., Chingos, M. M., & McPherson, M. S. (2009). *Crossing the finish line: Completing college at America's public universities.* Princeton University Press.

Bronfenbrenner, U. (1979). *The ecology of human development: Experiments by nature and design.* Harvard University Press.

Bronfenbrenner, U. (1986). Ecology of the family as a context for human development: Research perspectives. *Developmental Psychology, 22*(6), 723–742. https:// doi.org/10.1037/0012-1649.22.6.723

Cárdenas, V., & Kerby, S. (2012, August 8). *The state of Latinos in the United States.* Center for American Progress. https://www.americanprogress.org/issues/ race/report/2012/08/08/11984/the-state-of-latinos-in-the-united-states/

Carolan-Silva, A., & Reyes, R. J. (2013). Navigating the path to college: Latino students' social networks and access to college. *Educational Studies, 49*(4), 334–359.

Carnevale, A. P., & Strohl, J. (2013). *Separate and unequal: How higher education reinforces the intergenerational reproduction of white racial privilege.* Georgetown Public Policy Institute and the Center on Education and the Workforce. http://www .voced.edu.au/content/ngv:57695

Causey, J., Harnack-Eber, A., Ryu, M., & Shapiro, D. (2021). *A COVID-19 special analysis update for high school benchmarks*. National Student.

Chang, A., Torrez, M. A., Ferguson, K. N., & Sagar, A. (2017). Figured worlds and American dreams: An exploration of agency and identity among Latinx undocumented students. *The Urban Review, 49*, 189–216. https://doi.org/10.1007/s11256-017-0397-x

Choy, S. P. (2001). Students whose parents did not go to college: Postsecondary access, persistence, and attainment. In J. Wirt, S. Choy, D. Gerald, S. Provasnik, P. Rooney, S. Watanabe, R. Tobin, & M. Glander (Eds.), *The condition of education 2001* (pp. xviii–xliii). National Center for Educational Statistics. https://nces.ed.gov/pubs2001/2001072_Essay.pdf

Clark-Ibañez, M. (2015). *Undocumented Latino youth: Navigating their worlds.* Lynne Rienner.

Colby, S., & Ortman, J. M. (2015). *Projections of the size and composition of the U.S. population: 2014 to 2060. Population estimates and projects: Current population reports.* U.S. Department of Commerce, Economics & Statistics Administration, U.S. Census Bureau. https://www.census.gov/library/publications/2015/demo/p25-1143.html

College Board (n.d.). *Eight components of college and career readiness.* https://bigfuture.collegeboard.org/get-started/educator-resource-center/college-lesson-plans-case-studies

Conley, D. T. (2010). *College and career ready: Helping all students succeed beyond high school.* Jossey-Bass.

Dennon, A. (2021). *Latino/a student enrollment declines amid COVID-19.* Best Colleges. https://www.bestcolleges.com/blog/latino-latina-college-enrollment-decline/

Diaz-Strong, D., Gómez, C., Luna-Duarte, M. E., & Meiners, E. R. (2011). Purged: Undocumented students, financial aid policies, and access to higher education. *Journal of Hispanic Higher Education, 10*, 107–119. https://doi.org/10.1177/1538192711401917

Ellis, L. M., & Chen, E. C. (2013). Negotiating identity development among undocumented immigrant college students: A grounded theory study. *Journal of Counseling Psychology, 60*(2), 251–264. https://doi.org/10.1037/a0031350

Engle, J. (2007). Postsecondary access and success for first-generation college students. *American Academic, 3*, 25–48.

Enyioha, J. C. (2019). College access for undocumented students and law. *Educational Considerations, 45*(1). https://doi.org/10.4148/0146-9282.2168

Espinosa, L. L., Turk, J. M., Taylor, M., & Chessman, H. M. (2019). *Race and ethnicity in higher education: A status report.* American Council on Education. https://www.equityinhighered.org/resources/report-downloads/

Excelencia in Education. (2018). *Hispanic-serving institutions (HSIs): 2016–2017.* https://www.edexcelencia.org/research/data/hispanic-serving-institutions-hsis-2016-2017

Excelencia in Education. (2020). *Ensuring America's future: Benchmarking Latino college completion to 2030.* https://www.edexcelencia.org/research/latino-college-completion

Farmer-Hinton, R. L., & McCullough, R. G. (2008). College counseling in charter high schools: Examining the opportunities and challenges. *The High School Journal, 91*(4), 77–90.

Flores, A. (2016). Forms of exclusion: Undocumented students navigating financial aid and inclusion in the United States. *American Ethnologist, 43*(3). https://doi.org/10.1111/amet.12345

Fong, R (2007). Immigrant and refugee youth: Migration journeys and cultural values. *The Prevention Researcher, 14*(4).

Foxx, S. P., Saunders, R., & Lewis, C. W. (2020). Race, gender, class and achievement: A culturally responsive approach to urban school counseling. *Professional School Counseling.* https://doi.org/10.1177/2156759X19899184

Gay, G. (2018). *Culturally responsive teaching: Theory, research, and practice.* Teachers College Press.

Gomez, V., & Perez-Huber, L. (2019). Examining racist nativist microaggressions on DACAmented college students in the Trump era. *California Journal of Politics and Policy, 11*(2). https://doi.org/10.5070/P2cjpp11243089

Gonzales, R. G. (2011). Learning to be illegal: Undocumented youth and shifting legal contexts in the transition to adulthood. *American Sociological Review, 76,* 602–619.

Gonzalez, K. P., Stoner, C., & Jovel, J. E. (2003). Examining the role of social capital in access to college for Latinas: Toward a college opportunity framework. *Journal of Hispanic Higher Education, 2*(2), 146–170.

Gonzales, L. D. (2015). The horizon of possibilities: How HSI faculty can reshape the production and legitimization of knowledge within academia. In A. M. Núñez, S. Hurtado, E. Calderón (Eds.), *Hispanic-serving institutions: Advancing research and transformative practice* (pp. 82–100). Routledge.

Gonzalez, R. G., Brant, K., & Roth, B. (2020). DACAmented in the age of deportation: Navigating spaces of belonging and vulnerability in social and personal lives. *Ethnic and Racial Studies, 43*(1), 60–79. https://doi.org/10.1080/01419 870.2019.1667506

Holcomb-McCoy, C. (2007). *School counseling to close the achievement gap: A social justice framework for success.* Corwin Press.

Hooker, S., & Brand, B. (2010). College knowledge: A critical component of college and career readiness. *New Directions for Youth Development, 2010*(127), 75–85. https://doi.org/10.1002/yd.364

Hussar, B., Zhang, J., Hein, S., Wang, K., Roberts, A., Cui, J., Smith, M., Bullock Mann, F., Barmer, A., & Dilig, R., (2020). *The condition of education, 2020* (NCES 2020144). U.S. Department of Education, National Center for Education Statistics. https://nces.ed.gov/pubsearch/pubsinfo.asp?pubid=2020144

Jones-Smith, E. (2019). *Culturally diverse counseling: Theory and practice.* Sage Publications.

Kangala, V., Rendón, L., & Nora, A., (2016). *A framework for understanding Latino/a cultural wealth.* Association of American Colleges & Universities.

Karp, M. M. (2012). "I don't know, I've never been to college!" Dual enrollment as a college readiness strategy. *New Directions for Higher Education, 2012*(158), 21–28. https://doi.org/10.1002/he.20011

Khalifa, M. (2018). *Culturally responsive school leadership*. Harvard Education Press. https://www.aacu.org/diversitydemocracy/2016/winter/kanagala

Lad, K., & Braganza, D. (2013). Increasing knowledge related to the experiences of undocumented immigrants in public schools. *Educational Leadership and Administration: Teaching and Program Development, 24*. https://files.eric.ed.gov/fulltext/EJ1013134.pdf

Ladson-Billings, G. (1994). *The dreamkeepers: Successful teachers of African American children*. Jossey-Bass Publishers.

Ladson-Billings, G. (2014). Culturally Relevant Pedagogy 2.0: A.k.a. the Remix. *Harvard Educational Review, 84*(1), 74–84. https://doi.org/10.17763/haer.84.1.p2rj131485484751

Lee, C. C. (2001). Culturally responsive school counselors and programs: Addressing the needs of all students. *Professional School Counseling, 4*(4), 257–261. https://www.jstor.org/stable/42732264

Lukes, M. (2015). *Latino immigrant youth and interrupted schooling: Dropouts, dreamers, and alternative pathways to college*. Channel View Publications.

Lynch, M. (2016, April 21). *What is culturally responsive pedagogy?* The Edvocate. https://www.theedadvocate.org/what-is-culturally-responsive-pedagogy/

Ma, J., & Baum, S. (2016). *Trends in community colleges: Enrollment, prices, student debt, and completion*. College Board Research Brief. http://trends.collegeboard.org/sites/default/files/trends-in-community-colleges-research-brief.pdf

Martinez, C. R., DeGarmo, D. S., & Eddy, J. M. (2004). Promoting academic success among Latino youths. *Hispanic Journal of Behavioral Sciences, 26*(2), 128–151. https://doi.org/10.1177/0739986304264573

Martinez, M. A., Vega, D., & Marquez, J. (2019). Latinx students' experiences with college access and preparation at college preparatory charter schools. *Journal of Latinos and Education, 18*(1), 28–41. https://doi.org/10.1080/15348431.2017.1418353

Martinez, R. R., Baker, S. B., & Young, T. (2017). Promoting career and college readiness, aspirations, and self-efficacy: Curriculum field test. *The Career Development Quarterly, 65*(2), 173–188. https://doi.org/10.1002/cdq.12090

Martinez, R. R., Dye, L., & Gonzalez, L. M. (2017). A social constructivist approach to preparing school counselors to work effectively in urban schools. *The Urban Review, 49*(4), 511–528. https://doi.org/10.1007/s11256-017-0406-0

Martinez, R. R., Akos, P., & Kurz, M. (2020). Utilizing Latinx cultural wealth to create a college-going culture in high school. *Journal of Multicultural Counseling and Development, 48*(4), 210–230. https://doi.org/10.1002/jmcd.12195

McMahon, H. G., Mason, E. C. M., Daluga-Guenther, N., & Ruiz, A. (2014). An ecological model of professional school counseling. *Journal of Counseling & Development, 92*(4), 459–471. https://doi.org/10.1002/j.1556-6676.2014.00172.x

Méndez-Pounds, J., Nicholas, D. A., Gonzalez, N., & Whiting, J. B. (2018). "I am just like everyone else, except for a nine-digit number": A thematic analysis of the experiences of DREAMers. *The Qualitative Report, 23*(2), 442–455. https://nsuworks.nova.edu/tqr/vol23/iss2/12

Milian, C. (2017). Extremely Latin, XOXO: Notes on Latinx. *Cultural Dynamics, 29*(3), 121–140.

Muñoz, S. M. (2016). Undocumented and unafraid: Understanding the disclosure management process for undocumented college students and graduates. *Journal of College Student Development, 57*(6), 715–729. https://doi.org/10.1353/csd.2016.0070

National Conference for State Legislatures. (2019, June 9). *Undocumented Student Tuition: Overview.* https://www.ncsl.org/research/education/undocumented-student-tuition-overview.aspx

National Council of La Raza. (2015, January 21). *State of Hispanic America: Striving for equitable opportunity.* https://www.unidosus.org/wp-content/uploads/2021/07/SOTUSupplemental012115.pdf

Nienhusser, H. K. (2013). Role of high schools in undocumented students' college choice. *Education Policy Analysis Archives, 21*(85). http://epaa.asu.edu/ojs/article/view/1398

Ortiz, W. F. (n.d.). *What is the Latinx diaspora? Scholars and society break it down.* Culture Hub. https://boldculturehub.com/2020/10/what-is-the-latinx-diaspora-scholars-and-society-break-it-down/

Paat, Y. F. (2013). Working with immigrant children and their families: An application of Bronfenbrenner's ecological systems theory. *Journal of Human Behavior in the Social Environment, 23*(8), 954–966. https://doi.org/10.1080/10911359.2013.800007

Paris, D. (2012). Culturally sustaining pedagogy: A needed change in stance, terminology, and practice. *Educational Researcher, 41*(3), 93–97.

Patrick, K., Socol, A. R, & Morgan, I. (2020, January 9). *Inequities in advanced coursework.* The Education Trust. https://edtrust.org/resource/inequities-in-advanced-coursework/

Pérez, W., Cortez, R. D., Ramos, K., & Coronado, H. (2010). "Cursed and blessed": Examining the socioemotional and academic experiences of undocumented Latina and Latino college students. *New Directions for Student Services, 2010*(131), 35–51. https://doi.org/10.1002/ss.366

Pérez, W., & Cortes, R. D. (2011). *Undocumented Latino college students: Their socioemotional and academic experiences.* LFB Scholarly Pub. LLC.

Pérez Huber, L., Malagón, M., Ramirez, B. R., Camargo Gonzalez, L., Jimenez, A., & Velez, V. N. (2015). *Still falling through the cracks: Revisiting the Latina/o education pipeline.* Chicano Studies Research Center. https://www.chicano.ucla.edu/files/RR19.pdf

Perna, L. W. (2006). Understanding the relationship between information about college prices and financial aid and students' college-related behaviors. *American Behavioral Scientist, 49*(12), 1620–1635. https://doi.org/10.1177/0002764206289144

Perna, L. W., & Kurban, E. R. (2013). Improving college access and choice. In L. W. Perna & A. P. Jones (Eds.), *The state of college access and completion: Improving college success for students from underrepresented groups* (pp. 10–33). Routledge.

Postsecondary National Policy Institute (2020, June 19). *Fact sheet: Latino students.* https://pnpi.org/latino-students/

Presidents' Alliance on Higher Education and Immigration. (2020, April 15). *Report: Undocumented students in higher education: How many students are in U.S. colleges and universities, and who are they?* https://www.presidentsimmigrationalliance

.org/2020/04/15/report-undocumented-students-in-higher-education-how
-many-students-are-in-u-s-colleges-and-universities-and-who-are-they/

Salinas, C. (2020). The complexity of the "x" in Latinx: How Latinx/a/o students relate to, identify with, and understand the term Latinx. *Journal of Hispanic Higher Education, 19*(2), 149–168. https://doi.org/10.1177/1538192719900382

Salinas, C., Malavé, R., Torrens, O. D., & Swingle, E. C. (2019). "It is who we are.
We are undocumented": The narrative of two undocumented latino male students attending a community college. *Community College Review, 47*(3), 295–
317. https://doi.org/10.1177/0091552119850888

Schwartz, S. J., & Unger, J. B. (2010). Biculturalism and context: What is biculturalism,
and when is it adaptive? *Human development, 53*(1), 26–32. https://doi.org/
10.1159/000268137

Short, K. (2011). *The research supplemental poverty measure: 2010.* U.S. Department of Commerce, U.S. Census Bureau. https://www2.census.gov/library/publications/
2011/demo/p60-241.pdf

Smith-Adcock, S., Daniels, M. H., Min Lee, S., Arley Villalba, J., & Indelicato, N. A.
(2006). Culturally responsive school counseling for Hispanic/Latino students
and families: The need for bilingual school counselors. *Professional School
Counseling, 10*(1), 92–101. https://doi.org/10.1177/2156759X0601000104

Stepler, R., & Brown, A. (2016). *Statistical portrait of Hispanics in the United States.*
Pew Hispanic Center. http://www.pewhispanic.org/2016/04/19/statistical
-portrait-of-hispanics-in-the-united- states-key-charts/

Suárez-Orozco, C., & Yoshikawa, H. (2013). Undocumented status: Implications
for child development, policy, and ethical research. In M. G. Hernández, J.
Nguyen, C. L. Saetermoe, & C. Suárez-Orozco (Eds.), *Frameworks and ethics for
research with immigrants* (Vol. 141, pp. 61–78). Jossey-Bass.

Taylor, P., Kochhar, R., Livingston, G., Lopez, M. H., & Morin, R. (2009). *Between two
worlds: How young Latinos come of age in America.* Pew Hispanic Center. https://www
.pewresearch.org/hispanic/2009/12/11/between-two-worlds-how-young
-latinos-come-of-age-in-america

Tierney, W. G., Corwin, Z. B., & Colyar, J. E. (2005). *Preparing for college: Nine elements
of effective outreach.* State University of New York Press.

Torres, V. (2004). Familial influences on the identity development of Latino first-
year students. *Journal of College Student Development, 45*, 457–469.

Toppelberg, C. O., & Collins, B. A. (2010). Language, culture, and adaptation in
immigrant children. *Child and Adolescent Psychiatric Clinics of North America,
19*(4), 697–717. https://doi.org/10.1016/j.chc.2010.07.003

U.S. Census Bureau (2020). *Hispanic heritage month* (Release Number CB20-FF.07).
https://www.census.gov/newsroom/facts-for-features/2020/hispanic-heritage
-month.html

U.S. Department of Education. (2015, October). *Resource guide: Supporting undocumented youth. A guide for success in secondary and postsecondary settings.* https://
www2.ed.gov/about/overview/focus/supporting-undocumented-youth.pdf

Valadez, J. R. (2008). Shaping the educational decisions of Mexican immigrant
high school students. *American Educational Research Journal, 45*(4), 834–860.
https://doi.org/10.3102/0002831208320244

Valdivia, C. (2019). Expanding geographies of deportability: How immigration enforcement at the local level affects undocumented and mixed-status families: Expanding geographies of deportability. *Law & Policy, 41*(1), 103–119. https://doi.org/10.1111/lapo.12119

Vega, D., Moore, J. L., & Miranda, A. H. (2015). In their own words: Perceived barriers to achievement by African American and Latino high school students. *American Secondary Education, 43*(3), 36–59.

Williams, J. C. (2016). "It's always with you, that you're different": Undocumented students and social exclusion. *Journal of Poverty, 26*(2), 168–193. https://doi.org/10.1080/10875549.2015.1094766

Witcht, S. (2017). Culturally responsive pedagogy [Webinar]. *American School Counseling Association.* https://videos.schoolcounselor.org/culturally-responsive-pedagogy

Wyttenbach, M. M. (2015). *The educational experience of DACAmented students: Utilizing capitals to confront barriers and navigate the American educational experience* [Doctoral dissertation, University of Wisconsin-Madison]. ProQuest Dissertations & Theses Global. (Publication No. 3723200)

Yasuike, A (2019). Stigma management and resistance among high-achieving undocumented students. *Sociological Inquiry, 89*(2), 191–213. https://doi.org/10.1111/soin.12264

Yosso, T. (2005). Whose culture has capital? A critical race theory discussion of Community cultural wealth. *Race Ethnicity and Education, 8*(1), 69–91.

Zong, J., & Batalova, J. (2019, April). *How many unauthorized immigrants graduate from U.S. high schools annually?* Migration Policy Institute. https://www.migrationpolicy.org/research/unauthorized-immigrants-graduate-us-high-schools

CHAPTER 9

SCHOOL PSYCHOLOGIST AND SCHOOL COUNSELOR COLLABORATION TO SUPPORT THE COLLEGE AND CAREER READINESS OF IMMIGRANT AND REFUGEE YOUTH

Desireé Vega
University of Arizona

Jaclyn N. Wolf
University of Arizona

Marie L. Tanaka
University of Arizona

César D. Villalobos
University of Arizona

Ayanna C. Troutman
University of Florida

Equity-Based Career Development and Postsecondary Transitions, pages 219–246
Copyright © 2022 by Information Age Publishing
www.infoagepub.com

ABSTRACT

Immigrant and refugee students, including those who are undocumented immigrants, face significant barriers to college access and entry into the workforce. The cost of college alone, combined with the lack of access to financial aid for undocumented students, may discourage immigrant and refugee students from applying to college. Additionally, barriers such as lack of educator knowledge and support, low expectations, and placement in remedial tracks may prevent immigrant and refugee students from successfully gaining entry to desired postsecondary opportunities. Despite these challenges, immigrant and refugee students demonstrate strengths and perseverance and attribute support from educators, family members, and community organizations in achieving success. Moreover, school psychologists and school counselors can play a significant role in the college and career readiness (CCR) of immigrant and refugee students. CCR involves understanding available opportunities beyond the secondary level, which, for these students, involves navigating unique issues (e.g., legal issues, tuition policies, state laws, college/university climate, career opportunities). This chapter will examine the challenges immigrant and refugee students face in accessing postsecondary opportunities and supports that facilitate CCR. Additionally, this chapter will discuss the critical role school psychologists and school counselors play in preparing these students for college and the workforce. Recommendations for research, practice, and policy will also be provided.

More than 40 million immigrants live in the United States and approximately three million refugees have resettled in the United States since the establishment of the Refugee Resettlement Program under the Refugee Act of 1980 (Budiman, 2020). The Immigration and Nationality Act enacted in 1952 broadly defines immigrants as persons in the United States lawfully (e.g., permanent residents, naturalized citizens) and unlawfully (e.g., without documentation). Data from 2017 indicates that 77% of immigrants are in the United States lawfully, which includes naturalized citizens and permanent residents, and 23% are undocumented immigrants (Budiman, 2020). Additionally, while refugees are immigrants in that they have migrated to the United States (or other countries), the United States designates this status based on certain criteria (e.g., special humanitarian concern to United States, experienced or feared persecution due to race, religion, nationality, political opinion, or membership in a particular social group; for more information see https://www.uscis.gov/humanitarian/refugees-and-asylum/refugees). Experiences prior to migrating, while migrating, and in transitioning to the United States may be distinct based on one's immigration pathway and therefore, require differential support.

Compounding the challenges immigrant and refugee populations may face in their home countries that drive their decisions to migrate to the United States, the Trump administration issued various executive orders and proclamations to restrict immigration of persons from specific countries and increase immigration enforcement along the U.S.–Mexico border (Waslin, 2020). During his time in office, Trump allotted funds to construct the border wall and canceled the Deferred Action for Childhood Arrivals (DACA) program (Pierce & Selee, 2017). In 2017, under Executive Order 13780, he restricted entry of persons from primarily Muslim countries to purportedly protect the United States from terrorism; subsequent proclamations (9645, 9723, 9983) expanded the travel ban to include additional countries. Trump's policies had a significant impact on refugees; in 2017, Trump suspended the U.S. Refugee Admissions Program for 120 days to review screening policies and procedures for refugees (Waslin, 2020). He also significantly limited the number of refugees allowed in the United States. For example, during the Obama administration, the cap was set at permitting 110,000 refugees into the United States annually (Wickham Schmidt, 2019); Trump reduced the cap to a historic low of 15,000 for the 2021 fiscal year (National Immigration Forum, 2020). In his very short time in office, President Joseph R. Biden has sought to undo some of these restrictions. Through executive orders and proclamations, he has suspended deportations for the first 100 days of his term, revoked the aforementioned travel ban, and halted construction of the border wall (Federal Register, n.d.). President Biden has also vowed to work with congress to create a pathway for immigration (The White House, 2021).

The COVID-19 global pandemic has also impacted immigrant and refugee populations nationally and internationally. To prevent spreading of the virus, many countries, including the United States, have suspended incoming travel of noncitizens and closed borders blocking migration (Loweree et al., 2020). Additionally, embassies and consulates temporarily suspended operations during the first few months of the pandemic, thereby canceling visa appointments for immigrants waiting to receive approval to migrate to the United States (Loweree et al., 2020). The temporary suspension of the U.S. Refugee Resettlement Program greatly impacted the immigration processes for refugees (United Nations High Commissioner for Refugees [UNHCR], 2020b). Moreover, within the United States, the virus has not been well contained and immigrant and refugee populations have been disproportionately impacted as many are employed in positions deemed essential (e.g., food processing, grocery stores, restaurants, facilities; Grant, 2020). The pandemic is exposing long-standing disparities faced by these communities that are disproportionately affected by poverty (Cholera et al., 2020). In addition, undocumented immigrants are not eligible for government relief packages (e.g., CARES Act, 2020) or health insurance making them even more vulnerable for inadequate care (Wilson & Stimpson, 2020). COVID-19 has also led to school building closures and a transition to remote learning where socioeconomic factors such as limited or no access to internet to participate in virtual learning, housing instability, lack of childcare due to inflexible work schedules, and loss of employment impact immigrant and refugee students' ability to participate in schooling (Van Lancker & Parolin, 2020). These factors may have long-lasting effects on their educational outcomes including their college and career readiness (CCR).

Broadly, data on immigrant youth in public schools are not systematically collected given the sensitive nature of these data; however, 2014 data estimates show that 1.3% of all students were undocumented and 5.9% of all students had at least one undocumented parent (Passel & Cohn, 2016). Migration to a new country can create challenges for immigrant students such as acculturative stress, language development, and racism all while trying to succeed in a new academic setting. In response, schools must create a welcoming atmosphere that shows an appreciation and understanding for cultural and linguistic differences (Suárez-Orozco et al., 2010; Wambu & Nkabinde, 2019) while also meeting immigrant and refugee students' unique needs. In conceptualizing implementation of supports, schools must recognize that immigrant and refugee students are not a monolith. For example, refugee students' needs may often be overlooked or aggregated into populations of immigrant students whose families did not have to seek asylum (Mendenhall et al., 2017).

One area of need particularly important for immigrant and refugee youth is educational equity. Access to optimal educational opportunities for these youth, including CCR, remain disparate in K–12 settings and beyond. Long-term consequences of inequities include high dropout rates (Child Trends, 2018; Hussar et al., 2020; Zong & Balatova, 2019), low college enrollment and completion rates (Hussar et al., 2020; National Immigration Law Center [NILC], 2020), and underemployment (Gellat & Zong, 2018; U.S. Bureau of Labor Statistics, 2020). In attempting to address this disparity to advance postsecondary outcomes, educators need to be aware of the unique strengths and barriers associated with the CCR of immigrant and refugee students. This chapter will focus on these while also discussing the important role school psychologists and school counselors can play in preparing these students for college and the workforce.

LITERATURE REVIEW

Immigrant Students

Upon arrival in the United States, immigrant students may encounter myriad barriers making them more likely to experience educational difficulties when compared to their U.S.-born peers. These students may experience sociopolitical, familial, and environmental stressors related to the instability and immense change that comes with migrating to a new country; which may make them less likely to be fully engaged in the classroom setting (Suárez-Orozco et al., 2010). Moreover, we must consider the school's role in meeting immigrant students' needs. For example, some students may be learning English as a second language so schools must utilize appropriate instructional strategies to make the curriculum more accessible. Caregivers may also be unable to fully participate in their child's education as schools expect due to various factors including language differences, immigration status and fear of deportation, and differential perspectives on involvement (Cross et al., 2019; Soutullo et al., 2016; Wambu & Nkabinde, 2019). Therefore, schools must tackle these barriers to full engagement for immigrant families. In addition, some immigrant families may be migrating to the United States because of persecution or violence experienced in their native country, which may add to the changes and disruption in an immigrant student's education (Vega et al., 2015).

Of note is a phenomenon known as the *immigrant paradox*. Historically, studies have found that acculturation is associated with the attenuation of negative social-emotional outcomes (e.g., Alba & Nee, 1997). This narrative has largely shaped acculturation as a makeshift intervention that can ameliorate much of the deleterious outcomes outlined above. However, there is substantial research that supports the opposite. As immigrants acculturate to the United States (both over time and generations), their social-emotional outcomes often become worse than they were at the time of migration (i.e., immigrant paradox; Crosnoe, 2012). Poor outcomes persist even when other possible explanatory socioeconomic indicators (e.g., low income, parent education level) are controlled for (Marks et al., 2014).

A possible explanation for the paradox is immigration's effect on the family. Many immigrant youth report a greater sense of familial obligation (Van Geel & Vedder, 2009), and recent immigrant youth are more likely to report cohesive parental relationships that may act as an important protective factor in the face of discrimination and other forms of hardship at school (Salas-Wright et al., 2015). Compared to later immigrants and U.S.-born peers, they are also more likely to be engaged in school, and less likely to use substances (Salas-Wright et al., 2015). Conversely, as children acculturate, which may lead to an assimilation into U.S. culture, they may experience changes in their family dynamic (Bacallao & Smokowski, 2013). Additionally, immigrant youth who are also classified as English language learners are expected to develop English proficiency to be successful in U.S. schools. This acquisition process may inadvertently lead to language loss in their native language, particularly if opportunities to use their native language are less than those to use English (Fillmore, 2000; Stoehr et al., 2017), and may eventually impact their ability to communicate with family members. This may disrupt this protective factor and thus contribute to poorer long-term outcomes. As such, educators should not focus on acculturating immigrant youth to U.S. culture but rather find ways to infuse their existing strengths and sources of resiliency into their school environment.

Gonzalez et al. (2013) examined the influence of cultural identity variables (i.e., ethnic identity, acculturation) and perceptions of barriers on the aspirations and college-going self-efficacy (CGSE) of Latinx immigrant and U.S.-born students. Outcomes showed that participants' feelings of how others perceived their ethnic group (public regard) influenced their CGSE in that affirmation of their identity from others at school was associated with increased confidence in the college planning process. Participants also demonstrated a bicultural identity in that they maintained a connection to their Latinx culture and also identified with American cultural norms (e.g., speaking English, listening to English music, watching TV in English). Participants' perceptions of barriers related to educational aspirations included concerns about college acceptance, paying for college, familial obligations, and not feeling smart enough to attend college. This study highlights how educators can support CGSE and aspirations through validating and supporting immigrant students' ethnic identity and cultural background. Also, this study centers the need for educators to demystify college-going barriers by providing resources related to scholarships, financial aid, college options and type (e.g., full-time versus part-time attendance, 2- versus 4-year institutions), overcoming low-efficacy beliefs, and involving families in discussions on managing familial obligations.

Undocumented Immigrant Students

Though all students are entitled to attend public school for free (*Plyler v. Doe,* 1982), undocumented immigrant youth may face barriers as early as their initial enrollment into K–12 schools. In violation of federal or state law related to *Plyler v. Doe* (1982), some states require a social security number as a prerequisite for enrollment and others require families to show a passport, visa, or green card (Ofer, 2011; Sulkowski & Wolf, 2020). Some schools also request information during the enrollment process that would force a disclosure of one's immigration status (Ofer, 2011; Sulkowski & Wolf, 2020) and as a result compromise feelings of safety.

Undocumented immigrant youth further encounter unique challenges on the pathway to college and career access due to inconsistent and exclusionary policies across the United States. For example, in most states, undocumented students are ineligible for federal financial aid and in-state tuition rates, which creates significant financial challenges in paying for college. To address this significant financial barrier to college enrollment and persistence, 21 states and the District of Columbia have "tuition equity" laws that allow undocumented students to pay in-state tuition rates under certain conditions, including attending a high school for a certain number of years and graduating from a high school or obtaining a GED within the specific state (NILC, 2020). Some of these states with tuition equity laws also offer state financial aid and/or private aid or scholarships to undocumented students meeting certain criteria. Policies such as tuition equity laws increase college access for undocumented students, which otherwise would not be possible given the high cost of college attendance; therefore, educators must be aware of their state policies when addressing CCR for this population.

Limited data have been gathered on college enrollment among undocumented students; however, a recent report shows that undocumented students represent approximately 2%, and students who are DACA recipients, which provides reprieve from deportation, a social security number, and work authorization, comprise approximately 1% of all students in higher education (Feldblum et al., 2020). Additional data show many undocumented students are enrolled in 2- and 4-year public institutions (82%), while 18% are enrolled in private institutions. Similarly, 84% of students with DACA are enrolled in public institutions and 16% in private universities and colleges (Feldblum et al., 2020).

A study by Nienhusser et al. (2016) examined experiences with microaggressions among undocumented students during their college choice process. This qualitative study included 15 undocumented students who graduated from high school in New York, a state with tuition equity policies, but at the time of this study did not authorize eligibility for state financial aid. Findings revealed that all participants experienced microaggressions that permeated their college choice process. Participants discussed microaggressions in various forms including discriminatory financial aid policies making them ineligible for financial aid, counselors' lack of college-specific knowledge related to undocumented students, being told they cannot attend college due to their undocumented status, inappropriate and insensitive comments and jokes, and low expectations regarding their potential for college success. Schools should be a safe space for undocumented students and educators must be aware of policies and resources to ensure these students are college and career ready and prepared to meet their goals. Educators must also examine their biases and create a school climate that is supportive of undocumented students' well-being.

Disclosure of one's undocumented status is fear-inducing due to the potential legal consequences and social stigma. Murillo (2017) utilized ethnographic methods to explore the contexts in which undocumented students revealed their status to school staff and how educators responded to this information and protected students. This study took place in California, a state which has policies in place to support postsecondary enrollment and persistence of undocumented students. In 2011, California became the second state to permit undocumented students to receive in-state tuition, and enacted the California Dream Act in 2011, which provides undocumented students access to state financial aid and scholarships (Murillo, 2017). Participants included 13 educators and 14 undocumented students, of which seven also were DACA recipients. Student participants indicated that they revealed their legal status to educators with whom they built trusted relationships and felt truly cared about them when seeking assistance to apply for college. Educators in the study, particularly teachers and counselors, discussed the need to know students' legal status to provide targeted supports but they understood the sensitive nature of this status and maintained discretion when conversations about students' status arose. Educators reported that they generally did not share this information with others and if they did, they asked students for permission. This study highlights the significance of strong relationships between students and educators, in general, and also as a means to support undocumented students in CCR activities. In addition, educators should discuss confidentiality with undocumented students and the situations in which it might be necessary to disclose the student's status to another educator.

Lauby (2017) examined the barriers 60 undocumented Latinx adults faced in navigating college access and the strategies they utilized to overcome these obstacles. In this retrospective study, the adult participants' ages ranged between 18 and 29 years old and the majority were either enrolled in or graduated from a 2- or 4-year institution or were enrolled in graduate school; six participants never enrolled in a postsecondary institution. Similar to Murillo's (2017) findings, some of the participants reported positive relationships with school staff and as a result, felt comfortable disclosing their immigration status. Additionally, participants found that revealing their undocumented status or DACA status resulted in increased information about opportunities such as advanced courses, college tuition policies, and college options. Lauby (2017) noted that discussing one's status with educators was a necessity for participants to access information to become college ready rather than a choice. This speaks to the need for educators to make more information accessible without students having to reveal their status.

The participants also shared that they were excluded from some school activities because of their status, such as out of state trips and internships. They also reported having to educate school staff on the limitations of their status such as when directed to apply for financial aid or being told they cannot attend college. This type of poor guidance does not demonstrate to undocumented students that they can rely on school staff, particularly counselors, to assist them in becoming college ready. In spite of these experiences, the participants discussed strategies and supports that assisted them in attending college. Some of the participants reported school counselors went above and beyond to help them navigate the bureaucracy and intricate policies of colleges and universities. Also, educators' experiences with former students who were undocumented helped increase their knowledge to assist current students navigating the college choice process. Outside of school, some participants highlighted their reliance on family members who attended college and community and immigrant organizations to gain information about college access when their school staff were not able to assist them. Undocumented students can go to college and would significantly benefit from educators who are properly informed about college access. When educators lack accurate information, they contribute to the barriers undocumented students experience throughout their educational journey.

Romo et al. (2019) also conducted a retrospective study to explore the college choice process of undocumented Mexican-origin college graduates who attended a prestigious and highly-selective state institution. The sample of eight high-achieving participants included those who attended well-resourced and affluent schools and identified as gifted and talented. Due to their undocumented status, participants worried about reaching their goals of attending college despite hard work and high achievement. Moreover, they experienced challenges in completing college paperwork when educators told them that since they did not have a social security number, they would not be able to attend college. Despite these challenges, the participants were determined to find a way to attend college and engaged in their own research to learn about college admissions and financial aid. This again stresses the need for educators who can support undocumented students' college readiness and encourage college enrollment from an informed perspective versus erroneously telling students they cannot attend college.

Refugee Students

The number of refugees and forcibly displaced people has nearly doubled from 37.5 million to 79.5 million in the last decade; approximately half are under the age of 18 (UNHCR, 2020a). Though refugee students' enrollment in schools overall has increased, it is estimated that less than 1% of refugee youth between 18–35 years of age had access to postsecondary education in 2019 (UNHCR, 2020a). Though high school dropout rates have considerably declined for most racial groups in the United States, foreign-born youth have a dropout rate that is almost double that of their native-born peers (Child Trends, 2018). Even more concerning is that high school graduation is just one of the minimum qualifications for college readiness and does not guarantee adequate preparation for postsecondary education. Further, there is an unignorable paucity of research regarding refugee students and their access to career preparation and higher education (McWilliams & Bonet, 2016; Yi & Kiyama, 2018).

Refugee students face a multitude of barriers to CCR. A major barrier to accessing K–12—and subsequently higher education—is disrupted or limited access to formal education before coming to the United States. Refugee students may not have had this access due to war, persecution, multiple relocations, and years spent in refugee camps without educational resources (Capps et al., 2015; Dryden-Peterson, 2015). For example, Bang (2017) found that Iraqi refugee students' educational gaps negatively predicted school adjustment and positively related to marginalization. Bang and Collet (2018) further examined reasons for educational gaps and their consequences; major themes for educational gaps included trauma from war zones, greater trauma among girls, being of a minority and persecuted religious group, and lack of educational infrastructure. Even students who have received formal education in refugee camps or countries of origin may not have the documentation or proof of attendance, further complicating grade placements. This results in students being unable to graduate or graduating unprepared for tertiary education (McWilliams & Bonet, 2016).

Another major barrier for refugee students' access to higher education and vocational aspirations exist in the very systems meant to educate and empower them: schools. Schools are often the first acculturative institution that refugee students come into contact with in their host nation (Naidoo et al., 2015). Given that many refugees are resettled into communities with limited resources, this further impacts their access to quality education (Koyama, 2015). The literature reflects less than ideal educational experiences that pose barriers to students' access to furthering their education due to state- and school-level policies. For example, in a qualitative study with refugee high school students from the Vietnamese Central Highlands, Dávila (2012) described how refugee placements in remedial tracks prevented students from accessing resources. The structural policies of the school had refugee learners not only depicted by school personnel as reliant, passive, and unmotivated, but students were also expected to assimilate through learning English, following rules, and completing academic content. Unfortunately, refugee students placed in remedial classrooms often do not receive the linguistic supports needed for academic success (Short & Boyson, 2012). Linguistic instruction is often also structured in ways that segregate refugee students and institutionally label students as English language learners to delineate a novice status (Yi & Kiyama, 2018), which may impact students' abilities to access higher education.

Despite the aforementioned barriers, both refugee students' and their families' aspirations for higher education remain high (Dryden-Peterson et al., 2017; Isik-Ercan, 2012). In addition to placing high value on education, refugee students and their families exhibit resilience and persistence across the literature. For example, students who have experienced trauma and subsequent mental health difficulties continue to strive for educational mobility (Bang & Collet, 2018; Ellis et al., 2008; Naidoo et al., 2018). Beyond their resilience and aspirations, refugee students cultivate and maintain meaningful relationships with peers and educators (Dryden-Peterson et al., 2017; Roxas, 2016). Students also are appreciative of the efforts and sympathy some of their teachers have provided them (Bang & Collet, 2018), indicating the impact that educators can have to facilitate protective factors and strengths. Educators and schools that use refugee students' strengths, backgrounds, and experiences to empower students' personal narratives and thus learning processes have been widely shown to be impactful and meaningful for students (Roxas, 2016; Stewart, 2015).

SCHOOL PSYCHOLOGIST AND SCHOOL COUNSELOR COLLABORATION TO SUPPORT CCR

School Psychologists and College and Career Readiness

School psychologists have training and skills to address students' academic, behavioral, and social-emotional needs. Their many responsibilities include, but are not limited to, assessment, intervention, and consultation (National Association of School Psychologists [NASP], 2020). School psychologists' roles usually vary based on the population served in their school, but many remain at the forefront of providing services to a variety of students to address a wide array of components that influence their development. From an ecological perspective, school psychologists are trained to address the individual needs of students by examining all factors germane to a student's success in adapting to the school environment (Gutkin, 2012). With this lens, school psychologists are in a position to adequately provide individualized services to students, families, and other stakeholders in the school setting. However, and notably, there is a critical shortage of school psychologists (NASP, 2019). For best practice, the National Association of School Psychologists (2019) recommends a ratio of one school psychologist per 500 students. Current data estimates more than double this recommendation (i.e., one school psychologist to 1,211 students) with some states approaching 10 times that (NASP, 2019). In practice, this shortage can limit school psychologists' ability to provide comprehensive and individualized services, like those associated with CCR.

In considering how school psychologists may contribute to CCR in their school communities, it is first important to consider that CCR is not one in the same despite the terms typically being conflated by stakeholders (Mokher et al., 2018). In preparing youth for life after secondary education, factors as simple as how programs are branded can be critical. For example, courses and/or programs titled "College Readiness" may be alienating for both students whose aspirations do not include college and those who see college as beyond their reach (Mokher et al., 2018). Thus, school-based programs need to provide youth with access to both preparation for college (e.g., entry exams, tips for success) as well as practical and/or vocational skills for those planning to enter the workforce. Within the scope of school psychologists' practice, this should involve teacher collaboration, community partnerships, and strong relationships with the students they serve in order to understand their aspirations and individualize their access to preparation for postsecondary life.

Broadly, school psychologists are involved in assessing students' transition skills (Kellems et al., 2016). This may begin with a needs assessment. Based on these data, school psychologists may provide interventions to address the vocational skills needed for a student's successful transition into the workforce (Lillenstein et al., 2006; Walden et al., 2020). Thus, the school psychologist's role in addressing students' career readiness should be highly individualized. This is perhaps even more crucial for immigrant and refugee youth. For example, when conducting a needs assessment, school psychologists must consider the unique skills, strengths, and knowledge of immigrant and refugee youth. Vocational interventions should support maintaining one's home culture and language while also balancing the development of the skills and knowledge necessary for success in the United States (NASP, 2015). Related, youth and families from other countries may have different views about education and/or career involvement. To this end, it is imperative that school psychologists deliver culturally-informed vocational interventions that meaningfully engage both immigrant and refugee youth and their families. Schools can work with cultural liaisons to find ways to connect with and empower immigrant and refugee families (NASP, 2015).

Due mostly to the expectations of their position, school psychologists tend to interact with students receiving special education and related services, while school counselors tend to interact with those in the general education setting. As such, school psychologists may be directly involved in the postsecondary transition of young adults with disabilities (Walden et al., 2020) as dictated by their individualized education program. Thus, assisting youth with CCR is a task already within a school psychologist's purview. In collaboration with other stakeholders, particularly school counselors, expanding this assistance to all youth within a given school is not necessarily an unreasonable ask. Involvement may be direct or indirect and can include interventions to build students' academic, social, and/or behavioral skills (Lillenstein et al., 2006; Walden et al., 2020), as well as consultation/collaboration with other professionals, parents, and/or community members (Walden et al., 2020). School psychologists can foster greater partnerships within the communities they serve, possibly working in conjunction with a school-community liaison, in order to create partnerships with local colleges/universities, technical schools, and/or community agencies that offer opportunities for internships or vocational positions. Additionally, as part of their role, school psychologists have the opportunity to engage with students' families, and this collaboration may be an important correlate for college and career readiness (Hines et al., 2019).

To fulfill some of these services, there are manualized, evidence-based curricula available that school psychologists may consider implementing in accordance to the National Association of School Psychologists' Domains of Practice (2020) recommendations. These curricula may support students universally (e.g., "Making My Future Work") or more specific populations (e.g., students with disabilities; "Paths 2 the Future") and can be used in collaboration with a variety of stakeholders (e.g., teachers, school counselors; Walden et al., 2020). Notably, school psychologists' training in data-based decision-making, in delivering intervention across domains (e.g., academic, social-emotional), and in consultation/collaboration is invaluable with regard to helping youth feel prepared for college and/or careers. However, one important global consideration is how one's status as an immigrant or refugee may impact transition plans. For example, acculturation, emerging identities, social-emotional factors, and systemic barriers to education may be important in one's ability to plan for the future and/or their perceived self-efficacy in attending college or obtaining a career (Gonzalez et al., 2013). Thus, the onus to consider cultural implications embedded within attempts for college and career preparation (universal or individual) lies ultimately with the school psychologist and other personnel to ensure that the programming is equitable for all youth.

School Counselors and College and Career Readiness

A student's well-being and academic success in school is largely determined by the stakeholders involved. School counselors are critical to the postsecondary success of youth as they are trained to prepare students for CCR by aiding in their social-emotional, academic, and transitional goals through data-based decision-making, collaboration, and a focus on improving student outcomes (American School Counselor Association [ASCA], 2019). Throughout a student's educational experience, school counselors may directly and indirectly influence that student's overall educational trajectory. For example, school counselors may collaborate with other stakeholders (e.g., school psychologists, teachers, parents) to ensure that a child at the elementary level is meeting their developmental milestones. These interventions can appear in the form of individual or group counseling, wherein the school counselor employs different techniques to encourage autonomy and identity exploration needed for the later stages of development (Hines et al., 2019). Additionally, a school counselor may prepare elementary students for CCR by implementing system-wide interventions aimed at reaching equitable academic outcomes for a diverse student body, through the active participation of teachers, parents, and community members (The College Board National Office for School Counselor Advocacy [NOSCA], 2010).

Guided by the ASCA's standard of developing curriculum that is developmentally appropriate for students to achieve CCR, middle school counselors can implement, monitor, and individualize data-informed interventions to ensure that all students can access resources and information necessary for CCR (ASCA, 2019; NOSCA, 2010). For example, a middle school counselor may engage in direct one-on-one interventions with a teenager to help develop social skills, which may aid in making meaningful connections that can provide the social capital that is needed for CCR (NOSCA, 2010). Additionally, given that at this stage of development, students may experience additional hardships (such as exposure to illicit substances, violence, bullying, and self-harm), school counselors are well positioned to address any of these concerns directly with the student and by collaborating with relevant parties in order to properly address these barriers to personal and academic growth. In a study by Shtapura-Ifrah and Benish-Weisman (2019), the authors emphasize the importance of involving parents in the CCR process. For example, by collaborating with parents and informing them of the value of school counseling services, school counselors may promote parental involvement in the process of the CCR of their adolescent child. Furthermore, during this time, middle school counselors begin to more largely impact a student's academic trajectory by gathering information on students that may be falling behind (e.g., through analysis of GPA and attendance), implementing early interventions to promote academic growth, advocating for curriculum that aligns with a student's interests, and connecting students to mentors or other sources that may help them continue down the path toward CCR (NOSCA, 2011b).

In continuing onto high school, students may receive additional guidance from school counselors to help with their postsecondary transition. Depending on the need, school counselors may continue to provide direct, intensive services to students (e.g., social-emotional counseling and intervention) or they can take on a more active role in specifically preparing students to achieve a smooth transition out of high school. Based on the eight components of CCR, a high school counselor's focus may center heavily on the latter (i.e., college and career admission processes and the transition from high school graduation to college enrollment). In this case, school counselors may guide students to discovering postsecondary opportunities by meeting with them directly and going over the student's future goals, while providing resources on concepts such as college selection (e.g., 2- vs. 4-year institution), financial aid, and the application process (NOSCA, 2010). By increasing students' social capital, school counselors may play a pivotal role in the number of students who will consider and/or apply to postsecondary institutions (Bryan et al., 2011). Thereafter, the counselor may help the student strategize postsecondary goals (e.g., summer transition tasks) and help them understand what challenges may arise (e.g., adjustment to a new environment) and what can be done to address them (NOSCA, 2011a). The school counselor may play an active role by connecting the student to resources and helping that student delineate a plan of action for the next steps in their journey, considering the student's context and individual factors to ensure equitable positive outcomes (NOSCA, 2010). Additionally, school counselors at the high school level may have control over the master schedule, thereby indirectly shaping the education that students receive in the years leading up to postsecondary outcomes (Hines et al., 2019). Ultimately, including high school counselors in students' postsecondary planning may result in an increase in college enrollment numbers (Hurwitz & Howell, 2014).

Because of the ubiquitous influence that school counselors may have on all students, it is important that the counselors who are working with students take on a holistic approach to services (NOSCA, 2010; Wambu & Nkabinde, 2019). Specifically, when working with immigrant and refugee populations, for example, counselors ought to consider various contextual factors involved in a student's path to CCR. For instance, parents without knowledge of the U.S. educational system may hold onto their view of their own formal and/or informal learning experiences from their native country. In many African cultures, for example, caregivers are likely to leave a student's education in the hands of the teacher, believing that teachers are the sole experts in that area (Wambu & Nkabinde, 2019). This can lead to misunderstandings in how teachers view the quality of family involvement and may, in turn, affect the child's educational experiences (Wambu & Nkabinde, 2019). Along with cultural factors, it is important for counselors to acknowledge the differences between students and to meet them where they are in terms of development, knowledge, and access to resources (NOSCA, 2010). In doing so, school counselors may provide services that utilize a student's current experiences to build from and advocate for each student's personal growth throughout their educational career.

Collaboration to Support College and Career Readiness

As previously mentioned, school psychologists regularly collaborate with other educators and professionals. Given their training in counseling and the domain of consultation, along with the knowledge of education and psychology, school psychologists may collaborate effectively with school counselors in particular. Similar to school psychologists, school counselors are driven to provide comprehensive, evidence-based services that are unique to the student being served in order to ensure that students are progressing with their academic and personal goals (Hines et al., 2019). Therefore, school psychologists may find that consulting with school counselors is a seamless process. With a shared vision and similar training backgrounds, school psychologists can engage with school counselors in collaborative consultation to individualize services for students and other relevant parties.

For this process to begin, it is imperative that school counselors and school psychologists understand each other's roles and responsibilities in the school setting (Dahir et al., 2010). Often, both personnel are limited by the roles that their school or district requires of them, not utilizing the full scope of knowledge and training they have obtained in other areas (Hines et al., 2019). Together, school counselors and school psychologists can use their skill sets to develop interventions to prepare students for college and the workforce. This may come in the form of both parties designing an intervention after collecting data from a needs assessment. Thereafter, they may divide tasks based on which skill set each party is more familiar with. For example, the school psychologist may offer to track data of the student, while the counselor may take a primary role in leading group CCR sessions. The ultimate goal, however, would be for both parties to complement each other's roles with their unique skills and experience. In some areas, like social justice, for example, the counselor may add to the school psychologist's role by providing more insight and expertise in the subject given that social justice has not been as integrated into school psychology as in counseling (Miranda & Radliff, 2015). Similarly, the school psychologist may contribute by supplying information about the student's abilities and related contextual factors that may be hindering or propelling a student's CCR. From all of this, both can successfully work together to design, implement, and evaluate the progress of students—individually or in groups—offering expertise drawn from school psychologists' and school counselors' respective training and practice models.

An emergent consideration in extant literature is limited educator knowledge about access to postsecondary opportunities, particularly for undocumented students. School counselors and school psychologists may find it beneficial to partner with community organizations to access the most up-to-date information related to immigration policies and laws. They may also collaborate to provide in-service training to school staff on topics such as supporting undocumented students' educational and career aspirations, protecting their privacy if students disclose their legal status, and understanding immigration policy and law. Acquiring this knowledge can enable educators to advocate for immigrant students' CCR needs.

In addition, school counselors and school psychologists can engage in CCR activities to increase immigrant and refugee students' knowledge of college and career options by hosting career day and college fairs. They may consider inviting immigrant and refugee professionals and immigrant and refugee college students and graduates to share their journeys. Representation matters and this can assist in boosting students' self-efficacy beliefs and aspirations. School counselors and school psychologists should also collaborate with immigrant and refugee families, who are strong sources of support for their children, through parent informational sessions, groups, and one-on-one sessions, to help increase knowledge about the range of postsecondary opportunities and how to integrate parents into students' planning for postsecondary goals (Watkinson & Hersi, 2014).

RECOMMENDATIONS

Research

Current research on the CCR of immigrant and refugee youth has implications for future research. However, there are still gaps in the literature in various areas. For example, future research should disaggregate the experiences of immigrant, undocumented immigrant, and refugee students to better understand how school personnel including school psychologists and school counselors can meet their distinct needs. As previously stated, immigrants are not a monolith and their experiences may vary based on factors such as country of origin, migration processes, language proficiency, social-emotional status, race, and parent's educational background. Even students from the same national, regional, religious, racial, ethnic, or linguistic backgrounds have different life experiences. Therefore, at a minimum, research must include immigrant demographic information if we are to generalize their needs. Perhaps even more powerful would be to center immigrant and refugee voices about their experience with migration and its associated impacts via qualitative research methods such as phenomenological inquiry or case studies.

Additionally, research has not examined the extent to which school psychologists and school counselors collaborate in the area of CCR. Future research can examine the collaborative efforts between these personnel to ensure that immigrant and refugee youths' needs are met (e.g., collaboration to create culturally appropriate transition plans). The integration of these personnel's knowledge and skills can provide more insight into how they can and do increase immigrant and refugee students' workforce and postsecondary institution preparedness.

Related, research efforts to understand the implicit and explicit traits of the school climate immigrant and refugee students are nested within could be important for many reasons. For example, is educators' ultimate goal acculturation? Are efforts made to infuse the students' culture into their educational experience? Are there laws around the language students are able to use at school (i.e., English-only laws)? Do educators believe immigrant and refugee students can attend college? Do educators have the necessary training to work with immigrant and refugee students? Moreover, there is a need for research, which examines how educators such as school counselors, school psychologists, and/or teachers' implicit bias and stereotypical beliefs about immigrant and refugee populations impact their interactions with immigrant and refugee families and students. These areas are certainly not exhaustive, but are indicative of the critical thinking needed to create school climates that are welcoming for immigrant and refugee students while also helping them be successful in both the K–12 and postsecondary settings.

Practice

As highlighted throughout the chapter, both research and practice emphasize barriers over the strengths and perspectives that immigrant and refugee students have to offer. Thus, it is imperative for educators to dismantle deficit-based rhetoric regarding these students and focus on their strengths to advance their educational outcomes. Moreover, the literature has shown how detrimental it is to students' learning when the very educators serving them do not try to understand or empathize with their lived experiences (Dávila, 2012). Learning about students' backgrounds within the current and global contexts will deepen educators' abilities to connect and facilitate learning. Educators can demonstrate their commitment to socially just and anti-racist practices in many ways including through advocacy for inclusive policies and addressing racial/ethnic disparities in access and opportunities (García-Vázquez et al., 2020). School psychologists and school counselors are well-equipped and trained to spread such understanding and knowledge with colleagues through training and consultation. For example, many students and their families have gone through the onerous processes of applying for refugee status, citizenship, or resettlement; such efforts should be known to those working most closely with students who have overcome challenges (Naidoo et al., 2018). Particularly in navigating college and career counseling, Abkhezr and McMahon (2017) have advocated for narrative career counseling techniques that attend to students' processes in meaning making and agency. By having students explore and reflect upon their personal lives, they are able to account for life experiences that can further empower them to make decisions.

It is important for educators to listen to students and affirm immigrant and refugee students' identities and experiences. Naidoo et al. (2018) found that educators may be overwhelmed by students' previous experiences and feel uncomfortable or unequipped to engage in such conversations. However, they also found that this reticence was not reciprocated by students; in fact, students seemed eager to share their stories with the researchers and wanted more understanding from school staff. School psychologists and school counselors are trained in such listening and processing skills, and may further facilitate such conversations or support teachers in connecting with students and their histories.

Policy

Educators, particularly school leaders who set the tone in a school building, should make an explicit commitment to social justice to influence both approach and practice for supporting immigrant and refugee students (Taylor & Sidhu, 2012). Additionally, due to constantly changing immigration policies and practices, it is important to stay up-to-date and affirm the school's role in sensitive locations policy as it relates to Immigrations and Customs Enforcement (Teaching Tolerance, 2017). Immigrant and refugee students and families must know that school is a safe place for them and educators are committed to their safety.

Advocacy beyond the school setting is also important. School staff can build solidarity in supporting students undergoing difficulties due to policies that directly affect them and their families; such supports could be in the form of accompanying families to immigration hearings or contacting media regarding inaccurate representations of populations (Taylor & Sidhu, 2012; Teaching Tolerance, 2017). They may also advocate for equitable policies in accessing postsecondary opportunities for immigrant and refugee students. Particularly for undocumented students, states must re-examine their in-state tuition and financial aid policies by implementing tuition equity laws. There is a misconception that federal law prohibits states from allowing undocumented students to pay in-state tuition rates, however, that is untrue (NILC, 2020). Thus, states can and should allow undocumented students to pay in-state tuition rates. Additionally, states can enable access to state financial aid and scholarships to further support undocumented students' college completion. These policy changes would tremendously benefit undocumented students, and also benefit the institution and the economy by having more college-educated persons to contribute to the workforce (NILC, 2020; Nienhusser et al., 2016).

At the federal level, funding to increase the number of school psychologists and school counselors would be extremely beneficial in effectively and comprehensively addressing the CCR needs of immigrant and refugee youth. Funding to systematically support implementation of culturally responsive curricula and school programming to support the college and career development of such youth is also important. Many of the policies planned or already implemented by the Biden administration appear to be needed as well (e.g., a pathway for immigration), but there is room for more explicit policy. For example, Cortes (2013) examined the effect of legal status on postsecondary educational access of immigrant youth in the United States following the implementation of the Immigration Reform and Control Act (IRCA) of 1986, which granted amnesty to immigrants entering the United States before 1982. College enrollment increased by 15.8% for immigrant youth who were granted legal status under IRCA. This finding is similar to other research that supports more college enrollment when undocumented students are provided in-state tuition (e.g., Chin & Juhn, 2010), and supports that immigrant youth are more likely to enroll in college when legal barriers are removed and financial barriers are lowered (Cortes, 2013). Previous research has also shown IRCA's positive effects on the labor market and earnings for immigrant adults (e.g., Rivera-Batiz, 1999). Thus, similar federal policy centered on creating a feasible and non-persecutory pathway to citizenship for immigrant populations already residing in the United States is needed. Additionally, recent backlash occurred due to Biden's decision to maintain the previous administration's cap on refugee admissions into the United States at 15,000. However, Biden changed course and increased the cap to 62,500 through September 30, 2021. While this is a move in the right direction, it is significantly below the refugee admission cap of 110,000 from when Obama was in office, and fails to meet the dire needs of refugees living in substandard and unsafe conditions. Therefore, the cap needs to be reevaluated and more equitable entry policies for refugees need to be implemented.

CONCLUSION

The educational inequities faced by immigrant and refugee students presents a social justice issue and calls for educators to better provide CCR opportunities. The additional stressors from restrictive and discriminatory immigration policies combined with the COVID-19 global pandemic has presented new challenges to enable equitable CCR access. This requires educators, including school psychologists and school counselors, collaborating to create spaces for immigrant and refugee students to receive support tailored to their unique backgrounds and needs.

DISCUSSION QUESTIONS

1. What, if any, current district/school policies and practices exist to support students from different migrational backgrounds? How will knowing these policies assist in working with students and families?
   a. If there are no policies directly addressing needs of students from different migrational backgrounds, what steps can be taken to address this?
2. With the increasing demand for attaining a college degree in the United States, how can school counselors and/or school psychologists navigate conversations of diverse postsecondary opportunities available to immigrant and refugee students, while taking into consideration their background and values?
3. How can school psychologists and school counselors incorporate caregivers and the local community to connect immigrant and refugee students to resources that can increase their CCR?
4. What are some policies that school counselors and school psychologists should be aware of when working with students from undocumented, DACA, or mixed family status backgrounds?
   a. What precautions and considerations should be made for students and families from undocumented/DACA/mixed family status backgrounds?

ACTIVITIES

1. Get to know and understand your school culture and outcomes for students.
   a. Given the difficulty of collecting data around students' migration status, how has your school used data collection efforts to understand the needs of students from undocumented, DACA, refugee, or mixed family status backgrounds?
   b. What are outcomes and postsecondary options that students in your school pursue?
2. You are the school psychologist or school counselor in a district with a large population of immigrant and refugee students. Your administration asks you to create a handout to share and present to other school stakeholders (i.e., teachers, staff, and parents). Using the information presented in this chapter, create a one-page document highlighting specific barriers students experience related to CCR, action steps for stakeholders, and resources.
3. Community Gems: Reflect on the demographics of your student body. Place a particular emphasis on the group(s) of students that

may be thought of as needing more intensive services to achieve CCR. With that in mind, answer the following questions on a piece of paper:

   a. What are some aspects of this demographic that may make them more likely to need intensive services to prepare them for positive postsecondary outcomes?

   b. What services may be provided to help them reach CCR?

   c. List the unique knowledge, experiences, and skills these individuals possess that currently help them navigate school.

   d. How can drawing on students' strengths prepare them to reach higher levels of CCR?

AUTHOR NOTE

Desireé Vega https://orcid.org/0000-0003-1865-9164

We have no known conflicts of interest to disclose.

Correspondence concerning this chapter should be addressed to Desireé Vega, University of Arizona, 1430 E. Second Street, Tucson, AZ 85721. Email: dvega2@arizona.edu

REFERENCES

Abkhezr, P., & McMahon, M. (2017). Narrative career counselling for people with refugee backgrounds. *International Journal for the Advancement of Counselling, 39*(2), 99–111.

Alba, R., & Nee, V. (1997). Rethinking assimilation theory for a new era of immigration. *International Migration Review, 31*(4), 826–874. https://doi.org/10.2307/2547416

American School Counselor Association. (2019). *ASCA national model: A framework for school counseling programs.*

Bacallao, M. L., & Smokowski, P. R. (2013). Obstacles to getting ahead: How assimilation mechanisms impact undocumented Mexican immigrant families. *Social Work in Public Health, 28*(1), 1–20. https://doi.org/10.1080/19371910903269687

Bang, H. (2017). Iraqi refugee high school students' academic adjustment. *Diaspora, Indigenous, and Minority Education, 11*(1), 45–59. https://doi.org/10.1080/15595692.2016.1202232

Bang, H., & Collet, B. A. (2018). Educational gaps and their impact on Iraqi refugee students' secondary schooling in the greater Detroit, Michigan area. *Research in Comparative & International Education, 13*(2), 299–318. https://doi.org/10.1177/1745499918779258

Bryan, J., Moore-Thomas, C., Day-Vines, N. L., & Holcomb-McCoy, C. (2011). School counselors as social capital: The effects of high school college counseling on college application rates. *Journal of Counseling & Development, 89*(2), 190–199. https://doi.org/10.1002/j.1556-6678.2011.tb00077.x

Budiman, A. (2020). *Key findings about U.S. immigrants.* https://www.pewresearch .org/fact-tank/2020/08/20/key-findings-about-u-s-immigrants/

Capps, R., Newland, K., Fratzke, S., Groves, S., Auclair, G., Fix, M., & McHugh, M. (2015). *The integration outcomes of U.S. refugees: Successes and challenges.* Migration Policy Institute. https://www.migrationpolicy.org/sites/default/files/publications/UsRefugeeOutcomes-FINALWEB.pdf

Child Trends. (2018). *High school dropout rates.* https://www.childtrends.org/?indicators =high-school-dropout-rates

Chin, A., & Juhn, A. (2010). Does reducing college costs improve educational outcomes for undocumented immigrants? Evidence from state laws permitting undocumented immigrants to pay in-state tuition at state colleges and universities. In D. L. Leal & S. J. Trejo (Eds.), *Latinos and the economy: Integration and impact in schools, labor markets, and beyond* (pp. 63–94). Springer.

Cholera, R., Falusi, O. O., & Linton, J. M. (2020). Sheltering in place in a xenophobic climate: COVID-19 and children in immigrant families. *Pediatrics, 146*(1), 1–8.

Cortes, K. E. (2013). Achieving the DREAM: The effect of IRCA on immigrant youth postsecondary educational access. *American Economic Review, 103*(3), 428–432. https://doi.org/10.1257/aer.103.3.428

Crosnoe, R. (2012). Studying the immigrant paradox in the Mexican-origin population. In C. T. García Coll & A. K. Marks (Eds.), *The immigrant paradox in children and adolescents: Is becoming American a developmental risk?* (pp. 61–76). American Psychological Association.

Cross, F. L., Rivas-Drake, D., Rowley, S., Mendez, E., Ledon, C., Waller, A., & Kruger, D. J. (2019). Documentation-status concerns and Latinx parental school involvement. *Translational Issues in Psychological Science, 5*(1), 29–41. https:// doi.org/10.1037/tps0000184

Dahir, C. A., Burnham, J. J., Stone, C. B., & Cobb, N. (2010). Principals as partners: Counselors as collaborators. *NASSP Bulletin, 94*(4), 286–305. https://doi.org/ 10.1177/0192636511399899

Dávila, L. T. (2012). 'For them it's sink or swim': Refugee students and the dynamics of migration, and (dis)placement in school. *Power and Education, 4*(2), 139–149. http://dx.doi.org/10.2304/power.2012.4.2.139

Dryden-Peterson, S. (2015). *The educational experiences of refugee children in countries of first asylum.* Migration Policy Institute. https://www.migrationpolicy.org/ sites/default/files/publications/FCD_Dryen-Peterson-FINALWEB.pdf

Dryden-Peterson, S., Dahya, N., & Adelman, E. (2017). Pathways to educational success among refugees: Connecting locally and globally situated resources. *American Educational Research Journal, 54*(6), 1011–1047.

Ellis, B. H., MacDonald, H. Z., Lincoln, A. K., & Cabral, H. J. (2008). Mental health of Somali adolescent refugees: The role of trauma, stress, and perceived discrimination. *Journal of Consulting and Clinical Psychology, 76*(2), 184–193.

Federal Register. (n.d.). *Presidential Documents.* https://www.federalregister.gov/presidential-documents

Feldblum, M., Hubbard, S., Lim, A., Penichet-Paul, C., & Siegel, H. (2020). *Undocumented students in higher education: How many students are in U.S. colleges and universities, and who are they?* https://www.presidentsalliance.org/report-undocumented-students-in-higher-education-how-many-students-are-in-u-s-colleges-and-universities-and-who-are-they/

Fillmore, L. W. (2000). Loss of family languages: Should educators be concerned? *Theory Into Practice, 39*(4), 203–210. https://doi.org/10.1207/s15430421tip3904_3

García-Vázquez, E., Reddy, L., Arora, P., Crepeau-Hobson, F., Fenning, P., Hatt, C., Jimerson, S., Malone, C., Hughes, T., Minke, K., Radliff, K., Raines, T., Song, S., & Strobach, K. V. (2020). School psychology unified antiracism statement and call to action. *School Psychology Review, 49*(3), 209–211.

Gellat, J., & Zong, J. (2018). *Settling in: A profile of the unauthorized immigrant population in the U.S.* Migration Policy Institute. https://www.migrationpolicy.org/research/profile-unauthorized-immigrant-population-united-states

Gonzalez, L. M., Stein, G. L., & Huq, N. (2013). The influence of cultural identity and perceived barriers on college-going beliefs and aspirations of Latino youth in emerging immigrant communities. *Hispanic Journal of Behavioral Sciences, 35*(1), 103–120.

Grant, A. (2020). Coronavirus, refugees, and government policy: The state of US refugee resettlement during the coronavirus pandemic. *World Medical & Health Policy, 12*(3), 291–299.

Gutkin, T. B. (2012). Ecological psychology: Replacing the medical model paradigm for school-based psychological and psychoeducational services. *Journal of Educational and Psychological Consultation, 22*(1–2), 1–20.

Hines, E. M., Vega, D., Mayes, R. D., Harris, P. C., & Mack, M. (2019). School counselors and school psychologists as collaborators of college and career readiness for students in urban school settings. *Journal for Multicultural Education, 13*(3), 190–202. https://doi.org/10.1108/jmc-02-2019-0015

Hurwitz, M., & Howell, J. (2014). Estimating causal impacts of school counselors with regression discontinuity designs. *Journal of Counseling and Development, 92*(3), 316–327.

Hussar, B., Zhang, J., Hein, S., Wang, K., Roberts, A., Cui, J., Smith, M., Bullock Mann, F., Barmer, A., & Dilig, R. (2020). *The Condition of Education 2020* (NCES 2020-144). U.S. Department of Education, National Center for Education Statistics. https://nces.ed.gov/pubsearch/pubsinfo.asp?pubid=2020144

Isik-Ercan, Z. (2012). In pursuit of a new perspective in the education of children of refugees: Advocacy for the "family." *Educational Sciences: Theory & Practice, 12*(4), 3025–3038.

Kellems, R. O., Frandsen, K., Hansen, B., Gabrielsen, T., Clarke, B., Simons, K., & Clements, K. (2016). Teaching multi-step math skills to adults with disabilities via video prompting. *Research in Developmental Disabilities, 58*, 31–44.

Koyama, J. (2015). Learning English, working hard, and challenging risk discourses. *Policy Futures in Education, 13*(5), 608–620. https://doi.org/10.1177/1478210315579547

Lauby, F. (2017). "Because she knew that I did not have a social": Ad hoc guidance strategies for Latino undocumented students. *Journal of Hispanic Higher Education, 16*(1), 24–42.

Lillenstein, D. J., Levinson, E. M., Sylvester, C. A., & Brady, E. E. (2006). School psychologist involvement in transition planning: A comparison of attitudes and perceptions of school psychologists and transition coordinators. *The Journal for Vocational Special Needs Education, 29*(1), 4–16.

Loweree, J., Reichlin-Melnick, A., & Ewing, W. (2020). *The Impact of COVID-19 on noncitizens and across the US immigration system.* American Immigration Council. https://www.americanimmigrationcouncil.org/research/impact-covid-19 -us-immigration-system

Marks, A. K., Ejesi, K., & García Coll, C. (2014). Understanding the U.S. immigrant paradox in childhood and adolescence. *Child Development Perspectives, 8*(2), 59–64. https://doi.org/10.1111/cdep.12071

McWilliams, A., & Bonet, S. W. (2016). Continuums of precarity: Refugee youth transitions in American high schools. *International Journal of Lifelong Education, 35*(2), 153–170. https://doi.org/10.1080/02601370.2016.1164468

Mendenhall, M., Bartlett, L., & Ghaffar-Kucher, A. (2017). "If you need help, they are always there for us": Education for refugees in an international high school in NYC. *The Urban Review, 49,* 1–25. https://doi.org/10.1007/s11256-016-0379-4

Miranda, A. H., & Radliff, K. M. (2015). Consulting with a social justice mindset. In A. H. Miranda (Ed.), *Consultation across cultural contexts* (pp. 13–22). Routledge.

Mokher, C. G., Rosenbaum, J. E., Gable, A., Ahearn, C., & Jacobson, L. (2018). Ready for what? Confusion around college and career readiness: A program that conflates college and career readiness may unnecessarily discourage students without college aspirations. *Phi Delta Kappan, 100*(4), 40–43.

Murillo, M. A. (2017). The art of the reveal: Undocumented high school students, institutional agents, and the disclosure of legal status. *The High School Journal, 100*(2), 88–108.

Naidoo, L., Wilkinson, J., Adoniou, M., & Langat, K. (2018). *Refugee background students transitioning into higher education: Navigating complex spaces.* Springer.

Naidoo, L., Wilkinson, J., Langat, K., Adoniou, M., Cunneen, R., & Bolger, D. (2015). *Case study report: Supporting school-university pathways for refugee students' access and participation in tertiary education.* University of Western Sydney.

National Association of School Psychologists. (2020). *National Association of School Psychologists: Model for comprehensive and integrated school psychological services.* https://www.nasponline.org/standards-and-certification/nasp-practice-model

National Association of School Psychologists. (2015). *Supporting refugee children & youth: Tips for educators.* https://www.nasponline.org/resources-and-publications/ resources-and-podcasts/school-climate-safety-and-crisis/mental-health -resources/war-and-terrorism/supporting-refugee-students

National Association of School Psychologists. (2019). *NASP policy playbook.* https:// www.nasponline.org/research-and-policy/advocacy/policy-playbook

National Immigration Forum. (2020). *Fact sheet: U.S. refugee resettlement.* https:// immigrationforum.org/article/fact-sheet-u-s-refugee-resettlement/

National Immigration Law Center. (2020). Basic facts about in-state tuition for undocumented immigrant students. https://www.nilc.org/issues/education/basic-facts-instate/

Nienhusser, H. K., Vega, B. E., & Saavedra Carquin, M. C. (2016). Undocumented students' experiences with microaggressions during their college choice process. *Teachers College Record, 118*(2), 1–33.

Ofer, U. (2011). Protecting Plyler: New challenges to the right of immigrant children to access a public school education. *Columbia Journal of Race and Law, 1*(2), 187–226. https://doi.org/10.7916/cjrl.v1i2.2245

Passel, J. S., & Cohn, D. (2016). *Children of unauthorized immigrants represent rising share of K–12 students.* https://www.pewresearch.org/fact-tank/2016/11/17/children-of-unauthorized-immigrants-represent-rising-share-of-k-12-students/

Pierce, S., & Selee, A. (2017). *Immigration under Trump: A review of policy shifts in the year since the election.* Migration Policy Institute. https://www.migrationpolicy.org/research/immigration-under-trump-review-policy-shifts

Rivera-Batiz, F. L. (1999). Undocumented workers in the labor market: An analysis of the earnings of legal and illegal Mexican immigrants in the United States. *Journal of Population Economics, 12*(1), 91–116. https://doi.org/10.1007/s001480050092

Romo, E., Ozuna-Allen, T., & Martinez, M. A. (2019). "It was kind of a dream come true": Undocumented college students' testimonios of cultural wealth in the college choice process. *Journal of Hispanic Higher Education, 18*(4), 389–409.

Roxas, K. (2016). Creating communities: Working with refugee students in classrooms. *Democracy & Education, 19*(2), 1–8.

Salas-Wright, C. P., Robles, E. H., Vaughn, M. G., Cordova, D., & Perez-Figueroa, R. E. (2015). Toward a typology of acculturative stress: Results among Hispanic immigrants in the United States. *Hispanic Journal of Behavioral Sciences, 37*(2), 223–242.

Short, D. J., & Boyson, B. A. (2012). *Helping newcomer students succeed in secondary schools and beyond.* Center for Applied Linguistics.

Shtapura-Ifrah, M., & Benish-Weisman, M. (2019). Seeking the help of school counselors: Cross-cultural differences in mothers' knowledge, attitudes, and help-seeking behavior. *International Journal of Intercultural Relations, 69*, 110–119.

Soutullo, O. R., Smith-Bonahue, T. M., Sanders-Smith, S. C., & Navia, L. E. (2016). Discouraging partnerships? Teachers' perspectives on immigration-related barriers to family-school collaboration. *School Psychology Quarterly, 31*(2), 226.

Stewart, M. (2015). "My journey of hope and peace": Learning from adolescent refugees' lived experiences. *Journal of Adolescent & Adult Literacy, 59*(2), 149–159. https://doi.org/10.1002/jaal.445

Stoehr, A., Benders, T., Van Hell, J. G., & Fikkert, P. (2017). Second language attainment and first language attrition: The case of VOT in immersed Dutch-German late bilinguals. *Second Language Research, 33*(4), 483–518. https://doi.org/10.1177/0267658317704261

Suárez-Orozco, C., Onaga, M., & De Lardemelle, C. (2010). Promoting academic engagement among immigrant adolescents through school–family–community collaboration. *Professional School Counseling, 14*(1), 15–26. https://doi.org/10.1177/2156759x1001400103

Sulkowski, M. L., & Wolf, J. N. (2020). Undocumented immigration in the United States: Historical and legal context and the ethical practice of school psychology. *School Psychology International, 41*(4), 388–405. https://doi.org/10.1177/0143034320927449

Taylor, S., & Sidhu, R. K. (2012). Supporting refugee students in schools: What constitutes inclusive education? *International Journal of Inclusive Education, 16*(1). 39–56. https://doi.org/10.1080/13603110903560085

Teaching Tolerance. (2017). *Immigrant and refugee children: A guide for educators and school support staff.* https://www.tolerance.org/magazine/spring-2017/immigrant-and-refugee-children-a-guide-for-educators-and-school-support-staff

The College Board National Office for School Counselor Advocacy. (2010). *Eight components of college and career readiness counseling.* https://secure-media.collegeboard.org/digitalServices/pdf/nosca/11b_4416_8_Components_WEB_111107.pdf#:~:text=Eight%20Components%20of%20College%20and%20Career%20Readiness%20Counseling,and%20Career%20Assessments%206.%20College%20Affordability%20Planning%207

The College Board National Office for School Counselor Advocacy. (2011a). *High school counselor's guide.* https://secure-media.collegeboard.org/digitalServices/pdf/nosca/11b-4151_HS_Counselor_Guide_web.pdf

The College Board National Office for School Counselor Advocacy. (2011b). *Middle school counselor's guide.* https://secure-media.collegeboard.org/digitalServices/pdf/advocacy/nosca/11b-4382_MS_Counselor_Guide_WEB_120213.pdf

The White House. (2021). *Fact sheet: President Biden sends immigration bill to congress as part of his commitment to modernize our immigration system.* https://www.whitehouse.gov/briefing-room/statements-releases/2021/01/20/fact-sheet-president-biden-sends-immigration-bill-to-congress-as-part-of-his-commitment-to-modernize-our-immigration-system/

United Nations High Commissioner for Refugees. (2020a). *Global trends: Forced displacement in 2019.* https://www.unhcr.org/en-us/statistics/unhcrstats/5ee200e37/unhcr-global-trends-2019.html

United Nations High Commissioner for Refugees. (2020b). *IOM, UNHCR announce temporary suspension of resettlement travel for refugees.* https://www.unhcr.org/en-us/news/press/2020/3/5e7103034/iom-unhcr-announce-temporary-suspension-resettlement-travel-refugees.html

U.S. Bureau of Labor Statistics. (2020). *Foreign-born workers made up 17.4 percent of labor force in 2019.* https://www.bls.gov/opub/ted/2020/foreign-born-workers-made-up-17-point-4-percent-of-labor-force-in-2019.htm

Van Geel, M., & Vedder, P. (2009). The role of family obligations and school adjustment in explaining the immigrant paradox. *Journal of Youth and Adolescence, 40*(2), 187–196. https://doi.org/10.1007/s10964-009-9468-y

Van Lancker, W., & Parolin, Z. (2020). COVID-19, school closures, and child poverty: A social crisis in the making. *The Lancet Public Health, 5*(5), 243–244.

Vega, D., Lasser, J., & Plotts, C. (2015). Global migration: The need for culturally competent school psychologists. *School Psychology International, 36*(4), 358–374. https://doi.org/10.1177/0143034315587011

Walden, E. D., Leve, L. D., & Lindstrom, L. E. (2020). Paths 2 the future college and career readiness curriculum: Recommendations for school psychologists.

Journal of Applied School Psychology, 1–13. https://doi.org/10.1080/15377903 .2020.1799130

Wambu, G. W., & Nkabinde, Z. P. (2019). Supporting immigrant children in college and career readiness: Implications for teachers and school counselors. In G. Onchwari & J. Keengwe (Ed.), *Handbook of research on engaging immigrant families and promoting academic success for English language learners* (pp. 246–268). IGI Global.

Waslin, M. (2020). The use of executive orders and proclamations to create immigration policy: Trump in historical perspective. *Journal on Migration and Human Security, 8*(1), 54–67.

Watkinson, J. S., & Hersi, A. A. (2014). School counselors supporting African immigrant students' career development: A case study. *The Career Development Quarterly, 62*(1), 44–55.

Wickham Schmidt, P. (2019). An overview and critique of US immigration and asylum policies in the Trump era. *Journal on Migration and Human Security, 7*(3), 92–102.

Wilson, F. A., & Stimpson, J. P. (2020). US policies increase vulnerability of immigrant communities to the COVID-19 pandemic. *Annals of Global Health, 86*(1), 1–2.

Yi, V., & Kiyama, J. M. (2018). *Failed educational justice: Refugee students' postsecondary realities in restrictive times.* Association for the Study of Higher Education and the National Institute for Transformation and Equity. https://cece.sitehost.iu.edu/ wordpress/wp-content/uploads/2017/02/Failed-Educational-Justice-FINAL -2.pdf

Zong, J., & Balatova, J. (2019). *How many unauthorized immigrants graduate from U.S. high schools annually?* Migration Policy Institute. https://www.migrationpolicy .org/research/unauthorized-immigrants-graduate-us-high-schools

CHAPTER 10

FACILITATING CAREER AND COLLEGE READINESS FOR STUDENTS WITH DISABILITIES

Amy Milsom
Appalachian State University

Allyson Murphy
Central Wilkes Middle School

ABSTRACT

Despite 30 years of protections under the Americans With Disabilities Act of 1990, individuals with disabilities consistently have less positive employment and postsecondary educational outcomes than their peers without disabilities. P–12 counselors and educators are well-positioned to help students develop the knowledge, skills, and dispositions requisite for postsecondary success. In this chapter, data regarding postsecondary outcomes for students with disabilities are presented along with foundational theories, student-focused interventions, and systemic practices that can facilitate successful career and college transitions for students with disabilities.

In P–12 schools, students are identified as having a disability in accordance with criteria outlined by either the Individuals With Disabilities Education

Equity-Based Career Development and Postsecondary Transitions, pages 247–272
Copyright © 2022 by Information Age Publishing
www.infoagepub.com

Act (IDEA, 2004) or Section 504 of the Rehabilitation Act of 1973. IDEA delineates 13 categories of disabilities: autism, deaf-blindness, deafness, emotional disturbance, hearing impairment, intellectual disability, multiple disabilities, orthopedic impairment, other health impairment, specific learning disability, speech or language impairment, traumatic brain injury, and visual impairment, including blindness. In contrast, Section 504 defines a disability broadly, including students who have a condition that leads to challenges with academic or educational activities such as reading or concentrating. Common conditions that would fall under the Section 504 definition include attention deficit hyperactivity disorder, medical conditions such as asthma, or mental health disorders including depression and anxiety, to name a few.

A large percentage of P–12 students with disabilities in the United States receive special education services. In fact, data from 2018–2019 reveal 14.1% of school-age children being served through IDEA (National Center for Education Statistics [NCES], 2020). The majority of these students were American Indian/Alaskan Native (18%), followed by Black (16 %), White (14%), students of two or more races (14%), Hispanic (13%), Pacific Islander (11%), and Asian (7%). Additionally, 18% of males received special education services compared to only 10% of females. Finally, an average of 1.5% of P–12 students receive services through Section 504 (The Advocacy Institute, 2015). In college settings, however, a slightly higher percentage of students identify with disabilities, as data from 2015–2016 revealed 19.5% of undergraduate students reportedly having a disability (NCES, 2019b).

In postsecondary educational and work settings, individuals qualify for disability services based on the Americans With Disabilities Act (ADA, 1990) as well as Section 504. Conditions that negatively affect major life functions such as hearing, walking, working, or learning, for example, could lead to a diagnosis of disability. Individuals who seek support services in college or employment settings may or may not have received special educational services previously. For example, 33% of P–12 students with disabilities who receive services under IDEA have a diagnosis of learning disability (NCES, 2020). In contrast, 40% of college students with disabilities have a mental health diagnosis, 26% have ADHD, and only 3.5% have a learning disability (NCES, 2019b). These differences might be due to some college students not self-identifying as a person with a disability, or others who were not formally identified as having a disability in high school (Thompson-Ebanks & Jarman, 2018).

CAREER AND COLLEGE OUTCOMES
FOR INDIVIDUALS WITH DISABILITIES

Career and postsecondary educational outcomes for individuals with disabilities tend to be less positive in comparison to their peers without disabilities.

Career-related data points that are important to consider include employment and unemployment rates as well as type of occupation and salary outcomes. With regard to postsecondary education, outcomes such as level of education, enrollment in advanced courses, and college graduation rates reveal gaps. Additionally, although long-term effects of the COVID-19 pandemic on learning are unknown, potential disruptions to learning resulting from the pandemic could impact career and college outcomes for students with disabilities. For example, Nadworny (2020) indicated that although some teachers have been able to hold individualized sessions for students with disabilities online, others send work home and are not able to provide the accommodations or modifications students typically receive. Lederer et al. (2021) suggested that similar challenges likely are occurring at the college level, as university instructors struggled to shift to online teaching and also address diverse learning needs. Additionally, Soria et al. (2020) reported that college students with disabilities have been negatively impacted at higher rates than their peers without disabilities. Although unknown, the financial hardships and mental health challenges they faced could result in long-term impacts related to career or college outcomes.

Focusing on career outcomes, 2019 data showed that of working-age individuals (16–64), 8% of individuals with disabilities were unemployed, compared to only 3.6% of individuals without disabilities (Office of Disability Employment Policy, 2020). In December 2020, those rates increased to 11.5% and 6.4% respectively, likely as a result of the COVID-19 pandemic. As far as work type, data reveal that workers with disabilities are more likely to be employed part time and to work in the service industry, production, transportation, and material moving occupations, and are less likely to work in management, professional, and related occupations when compared to workers without disabilities (Bureau of Labor Statistics, 2020). Further, with adjusted inflation rates, the median earnings of individuals ages 16 and older with disabilities during 2019 was $25,270 as compared to $37,262 for individuals without disabilities (U.S. Census Bureau, n.d.).

With regard to educational opportunities for students with disabilities, approximately 95% of students with disabilities attend regular public schools and of those, only 72% complete their P–12 education (Hurwitz et al., 2020). In terms of high school graduation rates, while 5.8% of individuals without disabilities between the ages of 16–24 do not have a high school diploma or equivalent certificate, this number doubles to 12.4% in regards to individuals with disabilities (McFarland et al., 2018). High school students with disabilities face barriers to participation in advanced math and sciences courses such as algebra, physics, and chemistry as well as Advanced Placement (AP) courses (Schultz, 2012; U.S. Department of Education Office for Civil Rights, 2016). For instance, participants in Schultz's study indicated that teachers in some schools decided which students could enroll in their courses, introducing the opportunity for bias. Also, some school policies for enrollment eligibility fail to consider students with disabilities who might be more likely to excel in one subject and struggle in another due to specific learning disabilities, which can inadvertently prevent those students from participating in advanced coursework.

Postsecondary educational outcomes also reveal differences between students with and without disabilities. The National Center for Educational Statistics (2017) reported higher percentages of individuals with disabilities associated with lower educational status. For example, 11% of people ages 25 to 64 years old whose highest level of education was high school had disabilities, while only 4% of people with 4-year college degrees had disabilities. In fact, data reveal that at 20.8%, a slightly higher percentage of students pursuing 2-year degrees report having one or more disabilities as compared to 17.7% of students pursuing 4-year degrees who report having one or more disabilities (NCES, 2019b). The disparity increases in graduate school, with data suggesting approximately 11.9 % of individuals have disabilities, compared to 19.4% at the undergraduate level (NCES, 2019a).

The types of outcomes discussed above reveal a need for school counselors and educators to examine P–12 policies and practices. By identifying potential barriers and supports, they can better identify ways to assist with postsecondary transition planning for students with disabilities. A few theories and models relevant to career and college readiness are important to highlight as a foundation for this work.

FOUNDATIONAL COMPONENTS OF CAREER AND COLLEGE READINESS FOR STUDENTS WITH DISABILITIES

Numerous personal and environmental factors play a role in student development. Various models and frameworks exist to help explain how those factors affect career-related development and college readiness. In this section, career and college readiness (CCR) are defined, a framework for understanding college readiness is shared, and select counseling and career development theories are highlighted. This content will serve as the foundation for many recommendations presented later in this chapter.

Definitions of Career and College Readiness

Career readiness skills are important for all students, whether they plan to enter the workforce right away or after completing postsecondary education. The Association for Career and Technical Education (ACTE, n.d.)

defines career readiness in relation to three sets of skills: academic, employability, and job-specific skills. According to ACTE, the ability to apply academic skills to occupation-specific tasks makes someone career ready, it is not simply the acquisition of knowledge in various subject areas. In reference to employability skills, ACTE focuses on critical thinking, oral and written communication, adaptability, collaboration and teamwork, and professionalism, to name a few. Although packaged differently, the National Association of Colleges and Employers (NACE, 2020), defines career readiness similarly. Specifically, they define career readiness as inclusive of skills in the following areas: (a) critical thinking and problem solving; (b) oral and written communication; (c) collaboration and teamwork; (d) digital technology; (e) leadership; (f) professionalism and work ethic; (g) career management (e.g., self-awareness, ability to job search, self-advocacy); and (h) global/intercultural fluency, or possessing value for and the ability to interact respectfully with diverse individuals.

In comparison, college readiness refers to individuals possessing academic skills necessary to successfully complete college courses as well as knowledge and dispositions to navigate college. In that vein, Conley (2010) outlined four key areas of focus that are critical to college readiness. The first two, cognitive strategies and content knowledge, refer mainly to skills needed to understand and critique academic course content, relationships among content in specific course topics, and attitudes toward learning. It could be argued that classroom teachers have the most direct impact on the development of cognitive strategies and content knowledge, as they provide direct instruction related to those areas.

The third area of focus Conley (2010) discussed is learning skills and techniques. This area includes characteristics and skills related to feeling a sense of ownership over learning as well as developing techniques for effective learning. Goal setting, help seeking, and self-awareness are examples of the former, while test-taking and time management skills are examples of the latter. Collaborative efforts among educators and school counselors is important in relation to facilitating student development in this focus area.

Finally, Conley (2010) identified transition knowledge and skills as the fourth area of focus, and this area is particularly relevant for students with disabilities. He distinguished among five types of transition knowledge and skills: contextual, procedural, financial, cultural, and personal. Contextual refers to the development of aspirations or the influences from one's own culture that help determine available options for students, while procedural is about the logistics of how to move forward (e.g., how to apply to college or choose a major). Financial includes possessing knowledge about types of financial aid as well as understanding how to pay for college. Cultural knowledge and skills, according to Conley, refers to learning about the culture and norms of the postsecondary institutions and how to navigate them. Finally, personal transition knowledge and skills include self-advocacy and a sense of personal agency. Addressing transition knowledge and skills often involves collaborative efforts, including partnerships with and among school counselors, special education teachers, vocational rehabilitation (VR) counselors, and representatives from postsecondary institutions (e.g., college admissions or disability services offices).

Educators will find that students with disabilities are capable of attaining skills and knowledge in accordance with the CCR definitions above, with adequate support and accommodations. Those definitions provide a foundation for assessing potential areas of strength or growth in relation to individual goals. For example, oral and written communication skills might look different for someone wanting to pursue work as a mechanic in comparison to someone desiring to pursue a graduate degree in higher education administration. Similarly, requisite academic content knowledge might vary depending on the postsecondary major or degree someone desires to pursue. In essence, educators can use those definitions to help students with disabilities identify knowledge and skill areas that might need attention in order to achieve their future career goals. They also might use those definitions as a framework to help ensure relevant resources and accommodations are in place to support students in becoming career and college ready.

Researchers examining CCR specifically in relation to students with disabilities have reported findings that align with the definitions presented above. For example, Milsom and Dietz (2009) conducted a Delphi study to operationalize college readiness for students with learning disabilities. Their participants included special educators, directors of college disability services offices, school counselors, and student affairs professionals. The resulting list of factors included personal characteristics and dispositions (e.g., persistence, self-advocacy, adaptability), self and college awareness (e.g., knowledge of how their disability affects them as well as disability supports and resources available at college), and academic skills and strategies (e.g., time management, critical thinking), all of which align with employability skills (ACTE, n.d.) as well as learning skills and techniques, and transition knowledge and skills (Conley, 2010).

To clarify and refine a CCR framework for individuals with disabilities, Morningstar et al. (2017) conducted focus groups with state education agency representatives who possessed expertise related to transition services for students with disabilities. They found support for the importance of academic and nonacademic factors as well as for a model that included the following six domains: academic engagement, mindsets, learning processes, critical thinking, interpersonal engagement, and transition competencies. Their participants also emphasized the transferability of numerous skills across both work and educational settings.

Legislative Requirements for Career and College Planning

Variation occurs in the types of services schools provide to assist students in planning for careers and college, not only in relation to what services are offered and when they begin, but also in relation to which staff are involved. Individual states often mandate the incorporation of student individualized learning plans (ILPs) in middle and high schools as a way of facilitating CCR (Office of Disability Employment Policy [ODEP], 2016). These plans typically require students to identify career and college goals, map high school courses and activities to those goals, and engage in career development activities focused on self-exploration, career exploration, and career or college planning.

For students who receive special education services through IDEA, schools are required to provide transition services as part of the individualized education program (IEP) before students reach age 16. Transition planning must include an examination and consideration of student interests, strengths, and skills relevant to careers and college as well as development of postsecondary goals and the services and supports needed to help the student pursue those goals (Office of Special Education and Rehabilitation Services [OSERS], 2017). The IEP transition plan requirement could occur independent of or in conjunction with an ILP, but in states that do not require an ILP, this requirement ensures students with disabilities receive targeted attention related to CCR.

Relevant Counseling Theories

In addition to models of CCR, counseling and career development theories offer useful frameworks for understanding and supporting students with disabilities in relation to career and college planning. In particular, Bronfenbrenner's (1979) ecological systems theory illustrates the importance of students' environments on their preparation for college and career. Additionally, social cognitive career theory (SCCT; Lent et al., 1994) is a learning theory that explains how people develop occupational interests and aspirations and make vocational choices, and it has been applied to individuals with disabilities in a number of research studies (e.g., Hutchinson et al., 2008; Ochs & Roessler, 2004; Smith & Milsom, 2011; Waghorn et al., 2007). Interventions that will be discussed later in this chapter align with these theories, but a brief overview of important concepts is offered here.

In his theory, Bronfenbrenner (1979) identified various environments and described how they can shape our development. According to Bronfenbrenner, microsystems refer to an individual's immediate surroundings and include settings like family and school. He believed relationships within microsystems to have the most direct influence on individuals, suggesting peers, parents, teachers, and school counselors can play important roles in students' CCR. Bronfenbrenner also indicated that indirect influences occur in relation to the other environments. For example, mesosystems refer to interactions between microsystems, and an example would be that the degree and type of interaction between parents and teachers can indirectly affect students in relation to opportunities that might be communicated from school to home. Exosystems include interconnections between settings that do not directly involve the student. For example, a parent who works at a job where they talk all day might come home and have little energy to interact with their child. Finally, the macrosystem refers to cultural beliefs, values, and practices that affect every environment previously discussed.

Environmental influences also are reflected in SCCT (Lent et al., 1994), which offers models demonstrating how various factors interact to explain the development of occupational interests and goals as well as level of performance. Lent et al. suggested that personal and environmental factors as well as learning experiences influence self-efficacy and outcome expectations, which in turn affect interests, aspirations, and goals. They also discussed the role of persistence in relation to goal achievement. Interventions aligned with SCCT focus on enhancing self-efficacy, both through personal experiences as well as feedback from and interaction with others.

Every student with a disability is unique, and these theories encourage educators to identify and examine the role of personal, environmental, and systemic factors in relation to student development. More specifically, the intersection of various characteristics and identities (e.g., Black, high socioeconomic status, learning disability versus White, low socioeconomic status, hearing impairment) could result in different opportunities and barriers for each student. Although these theories are broad and do not pinpoint specific factors or characteristics on which to focus when working with students with disabilities, this can be a benefit in that the frameworks they provide are useful to educators working to identify both strengths and barriers and to conceptualize individual and systemic interventions with a diverse group of learners.

Recommendations

This section is broken into three subsections focusing on practice, research, and policy. Within each subsection, a review of some empirical and conceptual literature specific to students with disabilities and related to foundational content is presented. Recommendations based on this reviewed literature are then offered to assist the reader in gaining awareness and practical application knowledge with regard to supporting students with disabilities in CCR.

Practice

Numerous implications for transition planning practice for students with disabilities are offered in the literature. Although specialized services and interventions can be implemented to address the unique CCR needs of this population, students with disabilities can benefit from participation in the same kinds of services that are universally available to all P–12 students. In fact, Newman et al. (2019) explained that even in postsecondary educational settings, students with disabilities who used support services like writing centers or tutoring that were available to every student on campus experienced increased levels of success over their peers who did not access those services. Nevertheless, this section focuses on services that address some of the unique needs of students with disabilities.

Systemic Considerations

The definitions of CCR shared previously serve as a foundation for examining systemic practices in P–12 schools specifically in relation to students with disabilities. Recall that academic and critical thinking skills were included in the career readiness definitions shared previously, and that Conley (2010) identified content knowledge and cognitive strategies as important components of his model of college readiness. Additionally, job-specific and other employability skills were identified as important to career readiness. Educators can examine current practices to identify if and how they offer comprehensive and targeted CCR interventions for students with disabilities.

P–12 educators can also target specific educational and experiential opportunities associated with postsecondary success. For example, Theobald et al. (2019) found that students with disabilities who participated in clusters of career and technical education (CTE) courses during high school had higher employment rates than their peers who completed fewer of those courses. Theobald et al. (2019) also found that the more general education courses students with disabilities completed, the better their career and college outcomes; higher percentages of students attended college and were employed. Similarly, Lombardi et al. (2012) found participation in general education reading and math courses predicted college attendance. Finally, Jun et al. (2015) reported that student involvement in VR services was associated with better employment outcomes (i.e., salary and work hours) and that student participation in formal school transition programs and program involvement from a younger age also led to better employment outcomes. Educators are encouraged to offer these types of courses and learning opportunities to help students with disabilities develop job-specific and employability career readiness skills as well as the content knowledge and cognitive strategies important to college readiness.

Unfortunately, researchers have identified some disparities in these areas. Students with disabilities often complete less academically rigorous courses than their peers without disabilities (Gregg, 2007). Additionally, Lombardi et al. (2015) reported students with disabilities rated themselves lower on critical thinking skills than did their peers without disabilities. In relation to those outcomes, schools should examine existing practices related to course selection and enrollment. That is, they might start by collecting and disaggregating data to examine if students with disabilities have the same level of access to CTE education courses as their peers without disabilities (or, based on the statistics previously shared, participation in advanced math and science as well as AP courses). They also might review current practices to determine if any barriers exist that limit access for students with disabilities to those courses. Regarding enrollment in general education, IEP teams should identify if and when completion of general education courses is an important aspect of students meeting their postsecondary goals, and to ensure completion of rigorous general education courses when possible.

P–12 educators also should ensure that courses are accessible, or that students are afforded adequate opportunities to learn in each class. Although a detailed explanation is beyond the scope of this chapter, using a universal design for learning (UDL) approach can increase the likelihood students with disabilities will achieve success in general education courses (Fowler et al., 2014). Simplistically, UDL involves teaching in multiple ways, allowing students to demonstrate learning in different ways, and designing classes that will keep students engaged. For students with disabilities, this kind of approach helps ensure students can tap into their learning style strengths and that any limitations they have are more easily accommodated. School administrators can work to ensure general education and CTE education teachers are prepared to instruct in ways that support students with disabilities.

In addition to school-wide practices that create opportunities or barriers for students with disabilities, Bronfenbrenner's (1979) theory offers an important framework for understanding the importance of school and home environments on CCR. Milsom (2007) highlighted how postsecondary transitions involve students moving from a microsystem they are familiar with (e.g., P–12 school) to one they will need to learn to navigate; one that will require them to develop new relationships in order to be successful. Additionally, new mesosystems will emerge during the transition as family and P–12 school microsystems interact with workplace or college microsystems. Milsom (2007) suggested that a successful transition requires a strong mesosystem, one, for example, where the P–12 microsystem is familiar with requisite career or college readiness knowledge and skills students need to be successful and where opportunities are available to help students gain those identified factors. In this vein, systemic practices might include developing formal procedures whereby P–12 school personnel communicate with personnel affiliated with postsecondary career or college settings.

Transition Knowledge and Skill Development

As discussed previously, numerous knowledge and skill areas are important for career and college transitions, and research reveals students with disabilities lacking in many of these areas (e.g., Collier et al., 2017; Lombardi et al., 2015; Milsom & Sackett, 2018). To address these needs, broad recommendations exist regarding how to prepare students for career and college transitions. For example, Grigal et al. (2019) suggested that implementing career and college transition planning interventions for students with disabilities in middle school can help set students up for success. They also offered recommendations that schools ensure the materials and interventions used are relevant to the student population (e.g., cultural or socioeconomic factors) and accessible both in terms of disability-specific needs (e.g., closed captioning) and in relation to resources (e.g., access to technology or Internet services).

Further, Lombardi et al. (2020) offered guidance with regard to implementing interventions targeting transition knowledge and skills. They implemented an online career readiness curriculum for students in Grades 9–12 with disabilities and found positive academic and social postsecondary outcomes associated with participation. Notably, they identified significant differences based on fidelity of intervention implementation. As such, schools are cautioned to ensure the individuals implementing interventions are trained in relation to procedures used and that implementation is monitored and documented. With this approach, schools will have the data available to determine if variations in implementation might be relevant to consider in relation to student outcomes.

In addition to general recommendations, some specific transition knowledge and skill content areas appear frequently in disability literature. First, interventions targeting knowledge and skills related to self-advocacy or self-determination have been replete. Newman and Madaus (2015) reported 35% of students who received special education services while in high school disclosed their disability in college. Additionally, while 95% of students with disabilities received some accommodation in P–12, only 23% received accommodations in college. Interestingly, Mamboleo et al. (2020) recommended high schools target self-advocacy skills as an important goal area since they found that students who had experience requesting accommodations were more likely to do so later in college. Keenan et al. (2019) suggested self-advocacy skill development should occur through practice via role play. Others have identified self-advocacy curricula that incorporate self and disability awareness as well as instruction in self-advocacy skills as useful (Lingo et al., 2018). In fact, Sanderson and Goldman (2020) found that participating in a self-advocacy curriculum led to increased student involvement in IEP meetings. This outcome aligns with SCCT, in that students who practice or experience success in an activity likely develop positive self-efficacy, and are likely more apt to continuing engaging in that activity. Sanderson and Goldman (2020) recommended schools implement self-advocacy curricula and facilitate opportunities for students to actively participate in IEP meetings.

Student participation in IEPs is the second prominent transition content area in disability literature. In their research, Burnes et al. (2018) defined this participation as students being able to describe their present level of performance, share postsecondary goals, and explain how the IEP will facilitate goal attainment. They found that active participation in their IEP predicted students' future employment in a career of interest as well as participation in postsecondary education. A SCCT approach to intervention that helps students prepare for active IEP participation could target self-efficacy through (a) vicarious learning—having them watch a video of a student actively participating in their IEP meeting; (b) emotional arousal—preparing students for what to expect, clarifying information they would be asked to contribute, and helping them manage any anxious feelings before the meeting; (c) mastery experience—providing opportunities for students to develop and demonstrate self-advocacy skills prior to the meeting; and (d) verbal persuasion—offering supportive words.

A third area that appears frequently in the disability literature aligns clearly with the transition knowledge component of Conley's (2010) college readiness model. Mamboleo et al. (2020) discussed the importance of helping students become aware of their rights under the ADA (1990) and of college disability accommodation policies and procedures. They suggested high schools consider inviting current college students with disabilities to share their experiences and helping students find and review information about disability services on college websites. Milsom et al. (2004) implemented a psychoeducational group in which students with disabilities had opportunities to learn about college disability support services and the types of accommodations available in college. They found the small group format was effective in increasing students' transition knowledge. As discussed previously, Bronfenbrenner's (1979) theory supports P–12 personnel making time to connect with postsecondary staff to ensure they have accurate knowledge about requisite disability transition knowledge and skills as they help students with disabilities identify relevant transition goals.

Finally, interpersonal and social skills are identified in disability literature as important in relation to CCR. Interacting with others through group projects or in general at either home or in school is related to the teamwork and collaboration skills identified in the CCR definitions. Burnes et al. (2018) found that high scores on a measure of interacting with others predicted both employment and participation in postsecondary education. Schools can offer interventions to help students with disabilities develop confidence and comfort in interacting with diverse individuals. For example, Morningstar et al. (2017) suggested involvement in extracurricular or community activities can facilitate this kind of skill development. Schools might consider identifying IEP goals and corresponding interventions related to interpersonal or social skills that tap into students' existing or future social networks. One goal could involve students contacting personnel from career or college settings to practice asking relevant questions they might ask in the future. Finally, IEP teams also might consider how they do or do not model effective communication and collaboration within the team itself.

Finally, the recent shift to online learning due to effects of the COVID-19 pandemic has left P–12 and postsecondary educators considering the potential benefits of online learning. As such, students with disabilities might need to be prepared to complete some P–12 or college courses online. Buchnat and Wojciechowska (2020) discussed the importance of digital competence to their success with online courses and identified organizational skills as well as skills to work independently and maintain attention as ones some students with disabilities might struggle with. Also, students whose disabilities affect their written or verbal communication or comprehension might experience challenges if they cannot effectively identify and use accommodations. Given the uniqueness of how their disability is manifested, each student will need to be able to assess the types of online learning environments (e.g., synchronous versus asynchronous) that would be best suited to them while also making sure they advocate for appropriate accommodations and support.

Collaborative Efforts

As discussed previously, Bronfenbrenner's (1979) theory supports the idea that mesosystems can greatly influence student development and achievement. That is, the frequency and type of communication occurring across microsystems might be where intervention needs to occur. Schools can pay attention to family involvement in the transition planning process as one important area. Parents and guardians of students with disabilities report experiencing a number of barriers that prevent them from effectively supporting their students. To illustrate, Cavendish and Connor (2018) found parents reported being asked to attend IEP meetings at times they were not available and discouraged that IEP meetings mainly focused on deficits rather than strengths. Also, many parents said that although the school asked for parent input into IEP goals, they felt the school did not seem to take their feedback into consideration in the end.

In fact, culturally and linguistically diverse families often experience difficulties resulting from educators who lack cultural competence, and

Rossetti et al. (2017) offered numerous suggestions for engaging these parents. First, they encouraged educators to practice cultural humility, or to be open to worldviews that might differ from their own. Also, Rosetti et al. recommended educators learn about the family's expectations for and perceptions of their children and consider identifying someone who could serve as a cultural broker. They also discussed the importance of frequent and meaningful communication that takes into consideration family communication preferences and needs (e.g., time of day, method, use of interpreters) and ensures families have the background information needed to understand how they can more fully engage with the school. These suggestions also align with findings from a study by Tucker and Schwartz (2013), who indicated parents appreciated schools that communicated often, were responsive to their needs, and valued their input. Families must feel a sense of trust, which can be fostered by educators demonstrating genuine care and concern for students and their families, treating all students and families with respect, and following through with agreed upon responsibilities (Rossetti et al., 2017).

Best practice recommendations suggest educators should work with a variety of stakeholders in order to ensure effective transition planning. In fact, the 2016 Council for Accreditation of Counseling and Related Educational Programs (CACREP) Standards (CACREP, 2015) identifies consultation with community agencies and postsecondary school personnel as an important role for school counselors. With regard to community agencies, school counselors should consult with VR counselors. Funded by the federal government, VR is designed to provide career-related services to individuals with disabilities, focusing on helping people find or return to work. Most interventions they provide focus on employability skills. Although their services vary from state to state, VR counselors typically are involved in some way with high school students with disabilities.

Studies reveal positive outcomes associated with VR services. For example, students with disabilities who participate in VR services while in high school have been found to develop greater career awareness, skills, and knowledge, and more successfully enter the workforce than peers that do not (Jun et al., 2015; Lee et al., 2019). Additionally, the earlier students received VR services, the better their employment outcomes (Jun et al., 2015). Interestingly, many professionals (e.g., VR counselors, school counselors, special educators, school administration) note a lack of collaborative efforts between VR and school staff (Herbert et al., 2010). In fact, Collier et al. (2017) indicated that VR services often are overlooked as part of transition planning. They also indicated many students lack awareness of VR, with students of color and those with learning disabilities reporting less awareness. Collier et al. (2017) recommended schools help ensure students with disabilities become informed about the services VR counselors can provide as well as how they can seek support from VR counselors.

In relation to college, school counselors should engage in efforts to collaborate with postsecondary educational staff, such as college admissions counselors and directors of disability services offices. Through communication with these types of individuals, school counselors can ensure they have accurate knowledge of key transition knowledge and skills as well as policies and procedures for accessing and navigating services. Also, with this information, they can make certain transition goals and interventions that are relevant and meaningful. Additionally, Lautz et al. (2012) discussed the benefits of college admissions personnel visiting high schools, and they suggested having students serve as greeters. By selecting students with disabilities and helping them prepare for that role, school counselors can facilitate opportunities for them to practice self-advocacy skills.

Cultural Considerations

Students with disabilities differ not only in the unique ways in which their disabilities are manifested, but also in relation to any number of personal and cultural factors. Gender, race, ethnicity, and socioeconomic status are just a few factors that have been identified by researchers as important to consider when working with these students. As such, intentional efforts to examine intersectionality will help ensure educators holistically provide support to students with disabilities who have more than one marginalized identity.

Differential treatment among diverse students with disabilities has been discussed by many researchers. For example, Lombardi et al. (2012) revealed disparities where racial minority peers were more likely to be placed in restrictive learning environments as compared to their nonminority peers. Likewise, lower income peers with disabilities were also more likely to be placed in restrictive learning environments in comparison to their peers from higher income families. Further, Trainor et al. (2019) found that although the postsecondary transition experiences of students with disabilities for whom English is a second language were similar to their peers, they differed in a few ways. For example, these students and their parents attended IEP meetings at similar rates to their peers, but they and their parents were less likely than their peers to provide input into the IEP goals and plans. Limited access to translators during IEP meetings or during information workshops designed to educate parents and students about career and college-related topics such as how to apply for financial aid left parents uninformed and limited in their ability to play an active role in the transition planning process. Trainor et al. (2019) reported that most of these parents lived in poverty and did not graduate from high school, suggesting additional factors might need to be taken into consideration when identifying how to support these students.

Educators have a responsibility to address inequitable practices they see occurring, and Wang (2018) offered some guidance regarding how to do so from his qualitative study of school leaders. Proactively, educators should involve all stakeholders, including parents, and students, in discussions around school policy to help ensure diverse voices are considered. Also, professional development opportunities can help in cultivating a collaborative staff committed to social justice. By proactively creating a climate that focuses on equitable and inclusive practices, educators can more easily garner support to address related problems that arise and hold each other accountable.

Recommendations for addressing cultural factors when working with students with disabilities range from general to specific. Suk et al. (2020) offered a broad recommendation when they discussed the importance of not imposing personal beliefs. They also specifically highlighted the importance of ensuring transition goals are generated based on transition assessments and/or based on interviews with students and families. By using data gathered in a way that offers students and their families an opportunity to share their beliefs and preferences, educators decrease the likelihood of offering biased suggestions or ignoring salient cultural factors. Suk et al. also suggested educators consider how incorporating mentors and community role models in interventions could be important for some students. Finally, they suggested proactively considering ways to accommodate families to ensure their involvement (e.g., offering child care or flexibility with how and when meetings are scheduled).

Creating affinity groups for marginalized students with intersectional identities where they can communally share their unique perspectives in a safe space could be beneficial in supporting twice-marginalized populations. For instance, Lindstrom et al. (2018) found that the high school and college females with disabilities who participated in their girls-only transition curriculum realized a number of benefits. In addition to conveying appreciation for the opportunity to have a space where they felt safe to speak openly about experiences, they also reported increased self-confidence and disability awareness as well as a sense of personal agency. These results suggest that targeted psychoeducational group interventions may potentially be a safe space to develop transition knowledge and skills, receive support, and improve self-confidence. The incorporation of affinity groups as a format for transition intervention could be beneficial for other twice marginalized student groups.

Research

Many of the recommendations for practice shared above have been evaluated empirically or were based on research findings, but additional research in the area of postsecondary transitions for students with disabilities is needed. To start, limited research exists regarding the applicability of CCR models in relation to students with disabilities. In fact, Morningstar et al. (2017) suggested research involving students with disabilities is needed to validate CCR models in relation to their applicability specifically for that population. Given the diversity that exists within the disability population, further examination, such as by type of disability or in relation to intersectional identities, could help further hone these models.

The importance of focusing on student characteristics was one of six areas recommended for further research by Trainor et al. (2020). They suggested not only that researchers consider how and which student characteristics are salient to interventions, but also that they examine student strengths related to postsecondary transitions and intentionally conduct research with populations that are less represented in the literature. For example, an abundance of research exists related to students with learning disabilities or autism, but less for students who have visual impairments. Trainor et al. also suggested researchers examine if and how outcomes differ as a result of the intersection of disability and factors including race, gender, socioeconomic status, and language or origin.

Two other target areas for research noted by Trainor et al. (2020) are important as they relate to the content presented above. The first relates to assessing transition programs and interventions. They recommended research questions related to programming should focus on identifying which program or intervention components are the most impactful as well as what degree of implementation fidelity is needed to ensure desired outcomes are achieved. With that type of information, educators can ensure they identify and use interventions that can be implemented with fidelity. Trainor et al. also advised that research be conducted to examine collaborative efforts. This could include examining how P–12 and postsecondary work or educational settings can effectively work together to facilitate transitions. It also might involve examining existing practices to determine how effectively various entities can integrate services that support students with disabilities (e.g., high schools and VR services). For example, when it comes to participating in school transition programs in conjunction with VR services, students with noncognitive disabilities were found to experience better outcomes (i.e., work hours and salary) than students with cognitive impairments (Jun et al., 2015). Additional research could be conducted to better understand the nuances of integrated efforts that might lead to greater success for one subgroup of students with disabilities over another.

Finally, the COVID-19 pandemic has resulted in an increase in the number of students participating in online learning. As of 2017, however, the majority of states (84%) had unclear policies regarding the implementation of IEPs for students learning online (Tindle et al., 2017). Currently, outcomes connected to this shift to online learning are unknown. Research examining the effects of various online learning strategies for students with disabilities is needed to help identify best practices and inform future policy development.

Policy

Recommendations for policy that have emerged in the disability literature focus on three main areas: conceptualizing CCR, implementing services, and preparing personnel. First, Morningstar et al. (2017) suggested that individual state definitions of CCR can affect the types of services and interventions schools offer since they strive to align their services with those definitions. For this reason, and given the content shared throughout this chapter, educators should advocate for CCR definitions that are comprehensive. Definitions that incorporate academic and nonacademic skills, such as those identified by ACTE (n.d.) and NACE (2020) in relation to career readiness as well as by Conley (2010) in relation to college readiness, will help ensure schools approach postsecondary transition planning for students with disabilities holistically.

With regard to implementation of services, schools are encouraged to develop policy and processes around course enrollment and to monitor implementation via data. Recall that enrollment in general education as well as in CTE education courses was associated with more positive postsecondary outcomes for students with disabilities. Those students also need access to rigorous coursework, including AP courses and advanced math and science courses. School-level policy should be developed to ensure procedures for determining enrollment eligibility in those types of courses do not create barriers for students with disabilities. Ongoing examination of course enrollment data, including disaggregation by disability as well as type of disability, could help educators monitor outcomes, identify potential gaps, and make adjustments accordingly.

Additionally, school policy around personnel preparation can help ensure high quality instruction and interventions are offered to students with disabilities. Harvey et al. (2020) reviewed recommendations for ensuring all personnel, including general education teachers as well as CTE teachers, were prepared with strategies to teach students with disabilities in their classrooms. Training these teachers in UDL (Fowler et al., 2014) is one way to help them develop the skills to effectively teach students with diverse learning needs. Schools could consider developing policy that mandates regular professional development in the area of disability. They also could consider incorporating accountability systems where teachers are required to demonstrate and reflect on how they are effective across student subgroups.

Finally, recommendations to be made at the state and/or federal level can include creating policies that identify best practice recommendations for supporting students with disabilities in a virtual world (Smith, 2020; Tindle et al., 2017). These policies also might include guidelines for educator preparation. Also, states could be encouraged to examine their allocation of funding to schools to ensure culturally and linguistically diverse students have equitable access to opportunities and resources related to CCR (Harris et al., 2016).

CONCLUSION

This chapter offered an introduction to and brief overview of factors relevant to CCR for students with disabilities. Collaborative efforts among P–12 counselors, administrators, teachers, and other professionals who work with students in P–12 settings are critical to the development and implementation of comprehensive services. These individuals should ensure not only that students with disabilities are active participants in CCR interventions and programs that are available to all students, but also that they have access to interventions that amplify their strengths while targeting their unique needs. Counselors, administrators, and educators should seek information regarding relevant federal and state legislation related to disability and career development as well as college readiness. They also should engage in professional development to increase their cultural competence and awareness of disability as it relates to CCR. Collaborative and advocacy efforts can be enhanced through intentional partnerships with families as well as with other professionals, including VR services, college admissions, and disability services offices.

DISCUSSION QUESTIONS

1. As discussed in this chapter, Conley (2010), outlined four key areas of focus that are critical to college readiness: cognitive strategies, content knowledge, learning skills and techniques, and transition knowledge and skills. In your current (or future) professional role, describe the ways in which you can support students with disabilities in relation to each of these areas.

2. In your current (or future) professional role, explain your involvement in developing and implementing career and college readiness interventions for students with disabilities. Who do you (or

could you) collaborate with in order to support students with disabilities in relation to career and college readiness, and in what way do you collaborate with them? Try to identify at least two individuals within your school as well as two who represent organizations outside your school.

3. Think of the personal strengths and areas of growth you bring to your professional role in education. Which of those strengths will help you support students with disabilities in learning to advocate for themselves? What areas of growth do you have in relation to supporting the career and college readiness of students with disabilities? How will you work to improve these areas?

ACTIVITIES

1. Interview someone with a disability. Ask the questions below and come up with two of your own. Explain that you are particularly interested in their experiences in relation to having a disability, but inquire about any other salient aspects of their identity they want to share and that might have affected their experiences. Be sure to note their age, educational level, and work experience.
   - You identify as someone with a disability, tell me how your disability affects you.
   - Did you receive special education services at any point during your K–12 school experience? If so, what did those services look like?
   - What was your educational experience like in the K–12 education setting, particularly in relation to having a disability (but feel free to talk about any other salient aspects of your identity)? What barriers did you face? What support were you given?
   - Who was the most influential person in your K–12 education experience at school when it came to supporting your future educational and work-related goals? Who outside of school was most influential?
   - On a scale of 1 to 10 (1 being least, 10 being most) how confident were you in your ability to advocate for your own educational needs by the time you turned 16? How confident do you feel now in your ability to advocate for your work-related needs?
   - Did you attend college? If so, did you access additional student services to accommodate your disability? What was that experience like?
   - What do you think educators should know about working with K–12 students with disabilities in relation to helping them prepare for careers and college?

2. Spend some time learning about the types of career and college-related programs and services that exist for students with disabilities outside of the K–12 school system.
   - Conduct an Internet search using terms or phrases such as "career readiness disability" or "college transition disability" and review some of the websites that come up. Use search terms that help you hone in on your local community, or keep it broad so you can learn about programs that exist elsewhere.
   - Contact your local vocational rehabilitation office and talk with a counselor to learn what types of services they provide to K–12 students and to adults.
   - Search college websites to locate information about the types of services they can offer students with disabilities as well as what students need in order to receive services. Make some notes about how easy or difficult it was to find that information. Be sure to explore different types of colleges (e.g., 2-year versus 4-year, public versus private). Then, follow up by contacting one of those offices and ask if you can talk to someone about what recommendations they have for helping students with disabilities prepare for college.

AUTHOR NOTE

Amy Milsom https://orcid.org/0000-0001-6324-2048

Correspondence concerning this chapter should be addressed to Amy Milsom, Appalachian State University, 151 College Street Room 304A, Boone, NC 28608. milsomas@appstate.edu

REFERENCES

The Advocacy Institute. (2015). *Public school students overall and those served solely under Section 504 by race/ethnicity, students with disabilities under IDEA, by state: School year 2011–12.* https://www.advocacyinstitute.org/resources/Overall.504 StudentsCRDC2012.pdf

Americans With Disabilities Act of 1990, Pub. L. No. 101-336, 104 Stat. 328 (1990).

Association for Career and Technical Education. (n.d.). *What is "career ready"?* https://www.acteonline.org/wp-content/uploads/2018/03/Career_Readiness _Paper_COLOR.pdf

Bronfenbrenner, U. (1979). *The ecology of human development: Experiments by nature and design.* Harvard University Press.

Buchnat, M., & Wojciechowska, A. (2020). Online education of students with mild intellectual disability and autism spectrum disorder during the COVID-19 pandemic. *Interdisciplinary Contexts of Special Pedagogy, 29*(1), 150–171. https://doi.org/10.14746/ikps.2020.29.07

Bureau of Labor Statistics. (2020). *Persons with a disability: Labor force characteristics—2019* (USDL-20-0339). U.S. Department of Labor. https://www.bls.gov/news.release/archives/disabl_02262020.pdf

Burnes, J. J., Martin, J. E., Terry, R., McConnell, A. E., & Hennessey, M. N. (2018). Predicting postsecondary education and employment outcomes using results from the transition assessment and goal generator. *Career Development and Transition for Exceptional Individuals, 41*(2), 111–121. https://doi.org/10.1177/2165143417705353

Cavendish, W., & Connor, D. (2018). Toward authentic IEPs and transition plans: Student, parent, and teacher perspectives. *Learning Disability Quarterly, 41*(1), 32–43. https://doi.org/10.1177/0731948716684680

Collier, M., Griffin, M., & Yonghua, W. (2017). Learning from students about transition needs: Identifying gaps in knowledge and experience. *Journal of Vocational Rehabilitation, 46*(1), 1–10. https://doi.org/10.3233/JVR-160837

Conley, D. (2010). *College and career ready: Helping all students succeed beyond high school.* Jossey-Bass.

Council for Accreditation of Counseling and Related Educational Programs. (2015). *2016 CACREP Standards.* http://www.cacrep.org/wp-content/uploads/2018/05/2016-Standards-with-Glossary-5.3.2018.pdf

Fowler, C. H., Test, D. W., Cease-Cook, J., Toms, O., Bartholomew, A., & Scroggins, L. (2014). Policy implications of high school reform on college and career readiness of youth with disabilities. *Journal of Disability Policy Studies, 25*(1), 19–29. https://doi.org/10.1177/1044207313518072

Gregg, N. (2007). Underserved and unprepared: Postsecondary learning disabilities. *Learning Disabilities Research & Practice, 22*(4), 219–228. https://doi.org/10.1111/j.1540-5826.2007.00250.x

Grigal, M., Cooney, L., & Hart, D. (2019). Promoting college and career readiness with middle school youth with disabilities: Lessons learned from a curriculum development project. *Career Development and Transition for Exceptional Individuals, 42*(1), 64–71. https://doi.org/10.1177/2165143418814246

Harris, P., Hines, E. M., Mayes, R. D., & Vega, D. (2016). Reaching higher: College and career readiness for African American males with learning disabilities. *Journal of African American Males in Education, 7*(1), 52–69. https://doi.org/10.1007/978-94-6351-134-6_13

Harvey, M. W., Rowe, D. A., Test, D. W., Imperatore, C., Lombardi, A., Conrad, M., Szymanski, A., & Barnett, K. (2020). Partnering to improve career and technical education for students with disabilities: A position paper of the division on career development and transition. *Career Development and Transition for Exceptional Individuals, 43*(2), 67–77. https://doi.org/10.1177/2165143419887839

Herbert, J., Trusty, J., & Lorenz, D. (2010). Career assessment practices for high school students with disabilities and perceived value reported by transition personnel. *Journal of Rehabilitation, 76*(4), 18–26. https://gseuphsdlibrary.files.wordpress.com/2013/03/career-assessment-practices-for-high-school-students-with-disabilities-and-perceived-value-reported-by-transition-personnel.pdf

Hurwitz, S., Perry, B., Cohen, E. D., & Skiba, R. (2020). Special education and individualized academic growth: A longitudinal assessment of outcomes for students with disabilities. *American Educational Research Journal, 57*(2), 576–611. https://doi.org/10.3102/0002831219857054

Hutchinson, N. L., Versnel, J., Chin, P., & Munby, H. (2008). Negotiating accommodations so that work-based education facilities career development for youth with disabilities. *Work: A Journal of Prevention, Assessment and Rehabilitation, 30*(2), 123–136. https://pubmed.ncbi.nlm.nih.gov/18413928/

Individuals with Disabilities Education Act, 20 U.S.C. § 1400 (2004).

Jun, S., Osmanir, K., Kortering, L., & Zhang, D., (2015). Vocational rehabilitation transition outcomes: A look at one state's evidence. *Journal of Rehabilitation, 81*(2), 47–53. https://www.thefreelibrary.com/Vocational+rehabilitation+transition+outcomes%3A+a+look+at+one+state%27s . . .-a0421907258

Keenan, W. R., Madaus, J. W., Lombardi, A. R., & Dukes, L. L. (2019). Impact of the Americans With Disabilities Act amendments act on documentation for students with disabilities in transition to college: Implications for practitioners. *Career Development and Transition for Exceptional Individuals, 42*(1), 56–63. https://doi.org/10.1177/2165143418809691

Lautz, J., Hawkins, D., & Perez, A. B. (2012). The high school visit: Providing college counseling and building crucial K–16 links among students, counselors and admission officers/response. *Journal of College Admission, 214,* 108–116. https://files.eric.ed.gov/fulltext/EJ992759.pdf

Lederer, A. M., Hoban, M. T., Lipson, S. K., Zhou, S., & Eisenberg, D. (2021). More than inconvenienced: The unique needs of U.S. college students during the COVID-19 pandemic. *Health Education & Behavior 2021, 48*(1), 14–19. https://doi.org/10.1177/1090198120969372

Lee, E., Black, M. H., Tan, T., Falkmer, T., & Girdler, S. (2019). "I'm destined to ace this:" Work experience placement during high school for individuals with autism spectrum disorder. *Journal of Autism and Developmental Disorders, 49*(8), 3089–3101. https://doi.org/10.1007/s10803-019-04024-x

Lent, R., Brown, D., & Hackett, G. (1994). Towards a unifying social cognitive theory of career and academic interest, choice, and performance. *Journal of Vocational Behavior, 45*(1), 79–122. https://doi.org/10.1006/jvbe.1994.1027

Lindstrom, L., Hirano, L., Ingram, A., DeHarmo, D., & Post, C. (2018). "Learning to be myself": Paths 2 the future career development curriculum for young women with disabilities. *Journal of Career Development, 6*(4), 472–486. https://doi.org/10.1177/0894845318776795

Lingo, M. E., Williams-Diehm, K. L., Martin, J. E., & McConnell, A. E. (2018). Teaching transition self-determination knowledge and skills using the ME! bell ringers. *Career Development and Transition for Exceptional Individuals, 41*(3), 185–189. https://doi.org/10.1177/2165143417753582

Lombardi, A., Doren, B., Gau, J., & Lindstrom, L. (2012). The influence of instructional settings in reading and math on postsecondary participation. *Journal of Disability Policy Studies, 24*(3), 169–179. https://doi.org/10.1177/1044207312468766

Lombardi, A., Kowitt, J., & Staples, F. (2015). Correlates of critical thinking and college and career readiness for students with and without disabilities. *Career*

Development and Transition for Exceptional Individuals, 38(3), 141–151. https://doi.org/10.1177/2165143414534888

Lombardi, A., Rifenbark, G., Tarconish, E., Volk, D., Monahan, J., Buck, A., Izzo, M., & Murray, A. (2020). Main and moderating effects of an online transition curriculum on career readiness. *Career Development and Transition for Exceptional Individuals, 43*(3), 146–156. https://doi.org/10.1177/2165143419900952

Mamboleo, G., Dong, S., & Fais, C. (2020). Factors associated with disability self-disclosure to their professors among college students with disabilities. *Career Development and Transition for Exceptional Individuals, 43*(2), 78–88. https://doi.org/10.1177/2165143419893360

McFarland, J., Cui, J., Rathbun, A., & Holmes, K., (2018). *Trends in high school dropout and completion rates in the United States: 2018.* National Center for Education Statistics. https://nces.ed.gov/pubs2019/2019117.pdf

Milsom, A. (2007). Interventions to assist students with disabilities through school transitions. *Professional School Counseling, 10*(3), 273–278. https://doi.org/10.1177/2156759X0701000309

Milsom, A., Akos, P., & Thompson, M. (2004). A psychoeducational group approach to postsecondary transition planning for students with learning disabilities. *Journal for Specialists in Group Work, 29*(4), 395–411. https://doi.org/10.1080/01933920490516170

Milsom, A., & Dietz, L. (2009). Defining college readiness for students with learning disabilities: A Delphi study. *Professional School Counseling, 12*(4), 315–323. https://doi.org/10.1177/2156759X0901200405

Milsom, A., & Sackett, C., (2018). Experiences of students with disabilities transitioning from 2-year to 4-year institutions. *Community College Journal of Research and Practice, 42*(1), 20–31. https://doi.org/10.1080/10668926.2016.1251352

Morningstar, M. E., Lombardi, A., Fowler, C., & Test, D. W. (2017). A college and career readiness framework for secondary students with disabilities. *Career Development and Transition for Exceptional Individuals, (40)*2, 79–91. https://doi.org/10.1177/2165143415589926

Nadworny, E. (2020, March 27). *With schools closed, kids with disabilities are more vulnerable than ever.* National Public Radio. https://www.npr.org/2020/03/27/821926032/with-schools-closed-kids-with-disabilities-are-more-vulnerable-than-ever

The National Association of Colleges and Employers. (2020). *What is career readiness?* https://www.naceweb.org/career-readiness/competencies/career-readiness-defined/

National Center for Education Statistics (2017). *Disability rates and employment status by educational attainment.* https://nces.ed.gov/programs/coe/pdf/coe_tad.pdf

National Center for Education Statistics. (2019a). *Percentage distribution of students enrolled in postsecondary institutions, by level disability status, and selected student characteristics: 2015–2016.* https://nces.ed.gov/fastfacts/display.asp?id=60

National Center for Education Statistics. (2019b). *Profile of undergraduate students: Attendance, distance, and remedial education, degree program and field of study, demographics, financial aid, financial literacy, employment, and military status: 2015–16.* https://nces.ed.gov/pubs2019/2019467.pdf

National Center for Education Statistics. (2020). *Students with disabilities.* https://nces.ed.gov/programs/coe/indicator/cgg

Newman, L., & Madaus, J. (2015). Reported accommodations and supports provided to secondary and postsecondary students with disabilities: National perspective. *Career Development and Transitions for Exceptional Individuals, 38*(3), 173–181. https://doi.org/10.1177/2165143413518235

Newman, L., Madaus, J., Lalor, A., & Javitz, H. (2019). Support receipts: Effect on postsecondary success of students with learning disabilities. *Career Development and Transition for Exceptional Individuals, 42*(1), 6–16. https://doi.org/10.1177/2165143418811288

Ochs, L., & Roessler, R. (2004). Predictors of career exploration intentions: A social cognitive career theory perspective. *Rehabilitation Counseling Bulletin, 47*(4), 224–233. https://doi.org/10.1177/00343552040470040401

Office of Disability Employment Policy. (2016). *ILPs across the US.* https://www.dol.gov/sites/dolgov/files/odep/pdf/2014-ilp-map.pdf

Office of Disability Employment Policy. (2020). *Disability employment statistics.* https://www.dol.gov/agencies/odep/research/statistics

Office of Special Education and Rehabilitation Services. (2017). *A transition guide to postsecondary education and employment for students and youth with disabilities.* https://sites.ed.gov/idea/files/postsecondary-transition-guide-may-2017.pdf

Rossetti, Z., Story, J. S., Bui, O., & Ou, S. (2017). Developing collaborative partnerships with culturally and linguistically diverse families during the IEP process. *Teaching Exceptional Children, 49*(5), 328–338. https://doi.org/10.1177/0040059916680103

Sanderson, K. A., & Goldman, S. E. (2020). A systematic review and meta-analysis of interventions used to increase adolescent IEP meeting participation. *Career Development and Transition for Exceptional Individuals, 43*(3), 157–168. https://doi.org/10.1177/2165143420922552

Schultz, S. (2012). Twice-exceptional students enrolled in advanced placement classes. *Gifted Child Quarterly, 56*(3), 119–133. https://doi.org/10.1177/0016986212444605

Section 504 of the Rehabilitation Act of 1973, 34 C.F.R. Part 104.

Smith, A., & Milsom, A. (2011). Social cognitive career theory and adults with psychiatric disabilities: Bringing theory to practice. *Journal of Applied Rehabilitation Counseling, 42*(3), 20–25. https://connect.springerpub.com/content/sgrjarc/42/3/20

Smith, C. (2020). Challenges and opportunities for teaching students with disabilities during the COVID-19 pandemic. *International Journal of Multidisciplinary Perspectives in Higher Education, 5*(1), 167–173. https://www.ojed.org/index.php/jimphe/article/view/2619/1185

Soria, K. M., Horgos, B., Chirikov, I., & Jones-White, D. (2020). *The experiences of undergraduate students with physical, learning, neurodevelopmental, and cognitive disabilities during the COVID-19 pandemic.* SERU Consortium, University of California–Berkeley and University of Minnesota. https://conservancy.umn.edu/handle/11299/216715

Suk, A. L., Sinclair, T. E., Osmani, K. J., & Williams-Diehm, K. (2020). Transition planning: Keeping cultural competence in mind. *Career Development and*

Transition for Exceptional Individuals, 43(2), 122–127. https://doi.org/10 .1177/2165143419890308

Theobald, R. J., Goldhaber, D. D., Gratz, T. M., & Holden, K. L. (2019). Career and technical education, inclusion, and postsecondary outcomes for students with learning disabilities. *Journal of Learning Disabilities, 52*(2), 109–119._https:// doi.org/10.1177/0022219418775121

Thompson-Ebanks, V., & Jarman, M. (2018) Undergraduate students with nonapparent disabilities identify factors that contribute to disclosure decisions. *International Journal of Disability, Development and Education, 65*(3), 286–303. https://doi.org/10.1080/1034912X.2017.1380174

Tindle, K., East, B., & Mellard, D. (2017). *Online learning for students with disabilities: Considerations for SEA policies and procedures.* Center on Online Learning and Students with Disabilities, University of Kansas. http://www.centerononline learning.res.ku.edu/wp-content/uploads/2017/04/SEA_Resource_Document _February2017.pdf

Trainor, A. A., Newman, L., Garcia, E., Woodley, H. H., Traxler, R. E., & Deschene, D. N. (2019). Postsecondary education-focused transition planning experiences of English learners with disabilities. *Career Development and Transition for Exceptional Individuals, 42*(1), 43–55. https://doi.org/10.1177/2165143418811830

Trainor, A. A., Carter, E. W., Karpur, A., Martin, J. E., Mazzotti, V. L., Morningstar, M. E., Newman, L., & Rojewski, J. W. (2020). A framework for research in transition: Identifying important areas and intersections for future study. *Career Development and Transition for Exceptional Individuals, 43*(1), 5–17. https://doi .org/10.1177/2165143419864551

Tucker, V., & Schwartz, I. (2013). Parents' perspectives of collaboration with school professionals: Barriers and facilitators to successful partnerships in planning with students with ASD. *School Mental Health, 5*(1), 3–14. https://doi .org/10.1007/s12310-012-9102-0

U.S. Census Bureau. (n.d.). *Median earnings in the past 12 months (in 2019 inflationadjusted dollars) by disability status by sex for the civilian noninstitutionalized population 16 years and over with earnings* [Table]. https://data.census.gov/cedsci/ table?q=Table%20B18140&tid=ACSDT1Y2019.B18140&hidePreview=false

U.S. Department of Education Office for Civil Rights. (2016). *Key data highlights on equity and opportunity gaps in our nation's public schools.* https://www2.ed.gov/ about/offices/list/ocr/docs/CRDC2013-14-first-look.pdf

Waghorn, G. R., Chant, D. C., & King, R. (2007). Work-related subjective experiences, work-related self-efficacy, and career learning among people with psychiatric disabilities. *American Journal of Psychiatric Rehabilitation, 10*(4), 275–300. https://doi.org/doi:10.1080/15487760701680521

Wang, F. (2018). Social justice leadership-theory and practice: A case of Ontario. *Educational Administration Quarterly, 54*(3), 470–498. https://doi.org/10.1177/ 0013161X18761341

CHAPTER 11

"WE NEED SUPPORT TOO"

College and Career Readiness Needs of Gifted Students

Renae D. Mayes
University of Arizona

Lia D. Falco
University of Arizona

Alyssa F. Begay
University of Arizona

Cassandra L. Hirdes
University of Arizona

ABSTRACT

Current literature highlights the many roles of educators and counselors in promoting college and career readiness for all students. However, often missing from the literature are the unique needs of gifted students. This is likely due to stereotypical beliefs and limited understanding about their unique needs. For example, educators and counselors often believe that gifted

Equity-Based Career Development and Postsecondary Transitions, pages 273–299
Copyright © 2022 by Information Age Publishing
www.infoagepub.com

students have greater knowledge and understanding about future careers and postsecondary opportunities such that they are not in need of support (Greene, 2006; Smith & Wood, 2020). Further, gifted students are often perceived as not having any challenges to their holistic growth and development. As such, these perceptions place gifted students as having to navigate school experiences, social-emotional development, and college and career readiness in isolation. In this chapter, authors will discuss the strengths and challenges to college and career readiness for gifted students, with particular attention to the intersecting identities of gifted students. Additionally, authors will provide a framework to guide strategies and activities that can be used to support the holistic development and successful transition to postsecondary opportunities for gifted students.

College and career readiness has become an important policy goal for education in the United States which has led to added accountability measures with regard to postsecondary readiness, especially for high school students. High school graduates in the United States must gain a solid foundation of core content knowledge in academic areas as well as other skills such as critical thinking, goal setting, and decision-making in order to successfully complete high school and make a postsecondary transition to college or the world of work (Falco & Steen, 2018). This is also reflected in national initiatives like Reach Higher (Reach Higher, 2020) and the Better Make Room (Better Make Room, 2020) campaigns which focus specifically on future college and career planning for high school students. The Reach Higher initiative had a particular focus on the school counselor's role to help students think past high school towards some sort of postsecondary educational education or training opportunity (Reach Higher, 2020). It brought with it a call for collaboration at local, state, and national levels to develop practices and strategies to support postsecondary readiness (Reach Higher, 2020). The Better Make Room campaign is an extension of the Reach Higher Initiative with a specific focus on directly providing resources to Generation Z (individuals born between the years 1995–2016; Better Make Room, 2020). Further, it is an avenue to celebrate success stories through traditional and new social media platforms. It is perhaps no surprise that policy makers and leaders have this focus, and occupational outlooks often include projections that connect future jobs with the need for postsecondary education (Carnevale et al., 2013). Further, pursuit and completion of postsecondary education is often connected with other benefits for individuals, their families, and society more broadly (College Board, 2019). For example, higher rates of postsecondary education are linked to greater economic stability, increased civic involvement, higher rates of voting, and more opportunities for individuals to engage in educational activities with their children (College Board, 2019). It's clear that the pursuit and completion of postsecondary education has implications for present and future generations to come.

Interestingly, often left out of conversations regarding college and career readiness are the needs and experiences of gifted students. Gifted students, students who are more likely to exhibit high achievement in one or more areas, such as intellectual, creative, artistic, or leadership capacity, or in specific academic fields, are often seen as having the skills and capabilities to do postsecondary planning on their own (Greene, 2006; Smith & Wood, 2020). In fact, they are often seen as rarely needing any holistic support in their school lives (Peterson, 2006, 2015). As a result, gifted students are left to chart their paths independently without adequate support and often lacking the skills to even do such (Greene, 2006; Smith & Wood, 2020). In order to support their successful transition to postsecondary institutions, more is needed to understand gifted students' unique needs and experiences, not only as a group, but also as unique individuals with intersecting identities. This holistic understanding can be incorporated into comprehensive approaches school personnel, including school counselors, can use to foster postsecondary preparedness and readiness for gifted students.

WHAT IS COLLEGE AND CAREER READINESS?

It is important to understand that college and career readiness is a multidimensional developmental process. College and career readiness are often reduced specifically as content knowledge, however, it incorporates skills, knowledge, and behaviors that students should have upon high school graduation. Conley (2012) defines four areas of college and career readiness to include (a) cognitive strategies, (b) content knowledge, (c) learning skills and techniques, and (d) transition knowledge and skills. Cognitive strategies refer to the ways in which students process, interrogate, and apply information. Content knowledge refers to the foundational knowledge students engage in core academic subjects which also includes their attitudes toward learning and how they are structuring knowledge. Learning skills and techniques are those that enable students to own their learning experience through goal setting, persistence, while acquiring skills like time management, test taking skills, collaboration skills, and so forth. Finally, transition knowledge and skills refer to the skills and experiences needed to make a successful transition to postsecondary opportunities which may include identifying and applying for opportunities and securing financial resources.

In addition to defining college and career readiness, it is important to understand that it is a developmental process as well (ASCA, 2017). College and career readiness is not something that solely happens in high school but is a sequential process that occurs throughout students' K–12 experience and beyond. As such, activities that happen in elementary school are foundational where students build aspirations about their future careers. Middle school allows for more exploration of careers and connections between those careers and themselves. High school is typically where students begin to make concrete plans on future careers.

Challenges to College and Career Readiness

Current literature helps clarify the challenges and successes of college and career readiness for high school students along with the role of school personnel like school counselors. In particular, students who struggle with planning for postsecondary educational opportunities are less likely to make a successful transition (Britton & Spencer, 2020).This may mean that students have vague plans and ideas about their postsecondary educational pursuits but fail to make specific plans related to the networks and resources (i.e., tutoring, the office of financial aid, the office of disability support services, etc.) that may be helpful to their success. Further, students may be underprepared in terms of content specific knowledge and critical thinking skills. As such, while they may enroll and attend their postsecondary courses, they may struggle academically as they are trying to address the mismatch between their skills and the expectations of the course (Wahleithner, 2020). These challenges may cause students, especially those with minoritized identities, to pursue postsecondary educational opportunities or persist to graduation.

The current context, both locally and nationally can also bear an impact on college and career readiness. For example, the onset of the COVID-19 global pandemic resulted in a subsequent health and economic crisis. Many families experienced financial strain and economic instability with reduced wages and job loss. Further, families with children also were likely thrust into a world of virtual learning as most schools finished the 2019–2020 academic year remotely and many are having similar experiences in the 2020–2021 academic year (Dorn et al., 2020). While new models of hybrid and virtual learning are aimed at maximizing student and staff safety, it also means that academic content along with college and career readiness activities are likely implemented in new ways, which could mean that while content is potentially the same, it's more likely to be reduced or missing in an effort to streamline new learning models. This, of course, has an impact on student learning and college and career readiness, as some students may not have access to the typical supports and activities that would be available to them under normal circumstances.

Currently it is estimated that a cumulative K–12 learning loss during COVID-19 pandemic could be as much as 9 months; with students of Black,

Indigenous, and students of color (BISOCs) at risk of falling 6 to 12 months behind compared to 4 to 8 months for White students (Dorn et al., 2020). It's important to note that these estimates are related to academic content, but in no way capture the social-emotional learning loss that may be happening as well. However, what we do know is that the COVID-19 pandemic along with related economic instability and limited access to health care has led to increased mental health concerns for all ages (Center for Disease Control [CDC], 2021). For K–12 students in particular, prolonged crisis learning coupled with changes to routines, not only in face to face and remote learning, but also extracurricular activities and general opportunities for socialization are contributing to higher rates of anxiety, depression, and post-traumatic symptoms (Marques de Miranda et al., 2020).

In addition to challenges in academic and social-emotional development, there is also a growing impact on college and career readiness. With the onset of the COVID-19 pandemic, college enrollment fell dramatically for Spring 2020 high school graduates (National Student Clearinghouse Research Center [NSCRC], 2020). Further, while direct high school to college enrollment fell overall, it declined the most for low-income students and BISOCs. Further, while at this particular point it is difficult to ascertain the total impact in the 2020–2021 school year, there are already fewer college applications being completed and fewer students are applying for Federal student aid via FAFSA (Watson & Pananjady, 2020).These changes in direct college enrollment and applications along with financial aid are likely related to the impact of the pandemic, in particular, the ways in which the pandemic exacerbates preexisting systemic issues making those who are already vulnerable (i.e., low-income, BISOCs, etc.) even more vulnerable.

Despite the challenging terrain, students can, indeed, be prepared and ready for postsecondary educational opportunities. First, having detailed individual learning plans (ILPs) which include information regarding postsecondary educational opportunities can allow for students to adequately plan and gather resources needed for their successful transition (Britton & Spencer, 2020). As a part of that process school personnel, and school counselors in particular, can support the preparedness of students for postsecondary opportunities. More specifically, students who work with the school counselor to obtain college information and postsecondary assistance are more likely to apply for college (Bryan et al., 2011). This may be that school counselors are uniquely positioned to help students gain human and social capital needed to successfully plan for postsecondary opportunities. Said differently, school counselors' training in academic, social-emotional, and career development lends itself for more holistic postsecondary planning that can be tailored to the unique needs of individual students.

GIFTED STUDENTS

It is estimated that 6–10% of K–12 students in the United States are gifted and could use additional educational supports (National Center for Education Statistics [NCES], 2018). This number is likely conservative as there are challenges in the identification process related to the various definitions of giftedness along with bias in identification methods. First, giftedness and gifted education is not included in federal guidance or requirements, which allows for individual states and districts to develop their own definition and approaches (or lack thereof) towards gifted education (NAGC, n.d.). This means that giftedness varies from state to state where some states may take broad definitions and others may be narrow. Further, school districts may identify giftedness broadly but serve students narrowly. For example, this may mean that states may define giftedness as including leadership, performing/visual arts, specific academic areas but they may only serve students in academic areas (NAGC, n.d.).

As previously mentioned, estimates of the gifted K–12 population may also relate to biases in the identification process. Scholars have noted that often the identification process begins with teacher referral, which is inherently dependent on their worldview and understanding of giftedness which, in turn, can often be stereotypical and biased (Ford, 2013; Mayes et al., 2018; Mayes & Moore, 2016) As such, teachers are less likely to see BISOC students from low SES backgrounds, students with disabilities, and girls as being gifted; thus, less likely to make those referrals to gifted education (Bianco et al., 2011; Mayes & Moore, 2016). This bias is reflected in the disproportionality of the gifted population, but also in research concerning this population as it relates to understanding the unique experiences of gifted students holistically including their postsecondary readiness. More specifically, this bias means that BISOCs, students from low SES backgrounds, students with disabilities, and girls are underrepresented in gifted education across all school settings.

Gifted Students and College and Career Readiness

As we consider postsecondary decision-making, it's important to understand that college and career readiness is a multidimensional concept. Academic preparedness is important, but it is not the sole determining factor for readiness (Smith & Wood, 2020). Other indicators such as retention and postsecondary planning skills are necessary for students to be college and career ready. Further, motivation, social support, and self-efficacy each contribute to overall postsecondary readiness (Conley, 2014). For gifted students in particular, giftedness may be seen as both an advantage and a challenge as a part of the postsecondary readiness process. Knowledge of these potentially contradictory paradigms can help school personnel better support gifted students.

Multipotentiality and Career Indecision

Multipotentiality refers to the ability to engage in many activities with a high level of competence and enjoyment. Gifted students in particular may possess a high level of competencies across several academic areas and activities. Gifted students may possess capabilities that help them to persist and cope with stressors as a part of their school experience. They may have a distinct ability to navigate adversity as a part of problem-solving which can lead to greater self-awareness and self-confidence (Peterson, 2006, 2015). These skills may allow for gifted students to have a high-level of involvement in school which can include the pursuit of special interests and hobbies in addition to developing interests and achievements in academic subjects. While these capabilities can be viewed as advantages when it comes to postsecondary success, it may also impact their future career trajectory. In other words, gifted students may have the ability and interest to do many things at high levels of competence or even enjoyment but may also struggle to pinpoint which interest to pursue as a part of postsecondary planning (Greene, 2006; Smith & Wood, 2020). The latter, called career indecision, can make it easier to identify postsecondary opportunities, but more difficult to select a college major or specific career path to pursue. Multipotentiality often means more options for certain students, but more options may be accompanied by fear of making the wrong choice (fear of failing and perfectionism; Smith & Wood, 2020). This indecision may be particularly difficult for gifted students as they may be experiencing internal conflict as a part of the decision-making process. Specifically, career decision-making may seem more personal and high stakes in that gifted students may internalize this process as a question of personal calling and moral concern (Greene, 2006). As such, a career decision may be difficult as it must be reflective of a tension between the need, that many gifted students express, for a career to have a sense of purpose or meaning while also being socially desirable or lucrative (Smith & Wood, 2020).

Early Emergence and Career Foreclosure

While career indecision is a distinct possibility for gifted students, being gifted may also engender overconfidence and a tendency to make career decisions early. When giftedness is identified early, gifted students are more likely to explore talents and interests in particular subjects or activities. This leads to the development of strong self-efficacy and academic achievement in particular areas and with it can come a greater confidence to pursue postsecondary educational opportunities in preparation for future careers

(Kim, 2014; Smith & Wood, 2020). While this can be a great motivator for gifted students, a narrow focus or intense concentration in one or few areas can create challenges as well. More specifically, when this focus comes too soon or happens too quickly, especially with external social reinforcement, gifted students may lose interest to pursue if they no longer experience the intrinsic pleasure in the task or topic (Green, 2006). On the other hand, insistence on gifted children to be "well-rounded" may also diminish their passion and interest in developing any particular area of talent. In addition to early emergence, gifted students may also experience early career foreclosure. As a part of typical development, children and adolescents experience changes in their environment and new experiences which can expose them to new possibilities and options. For example, students may typically engage in career assessments, career fairs, and other opportunities that allow them to make connections to a broad range of future careers. However, early emergence and narrow focus for gifted students may push them to commit to a career or career trajectory before really exploring options, taking risks, and having new experiences (Greene, 2006; Smith & Wood, 2020). As such, they experience an early career foreclosure as they engaged minimally in exploration and committed to a career early with limited self-knowledge (Gottfredson, 2005).

Intersectionality and Gifted Students

In addition to the aforementioned advantages and challenges, it is important to understand that gifted students don't exist in a vacuum. They possess multiple identities (e.g., race, gender, disability status, class) which contribute to their worldview and the ways in which they navigate school and community experiences, including postsecondary decision-making. As such, there is a need to understand different aspects of identity and how intersecting identities shape how gifted students engage in postsecondary planning. In particular, it is important to highlight how gifted students with minoritized, marginalized, or multi-marginalized identities may experience additional challenges and barriers to navigate as a part of the decision-making process.

Intersectionality (Crenshaw, 1989, 1991, 2015) is a framework that can be used to understand overlapping issues around inequality, power, and politics as it relates to identity. Intersectionality brings to the forefront the complexities and marginalization that oppressed groups may have to navigate due to intersecting planes of oppression. Rather than viewing individuals one-dimensionally (i.e., race, gender, or class), intersectionality invites a multidimensional understanding of individuals to see that membership in multiple minoritized identity categories has sociopolitical and developmental implications (Crenshaw, 1989, 1991, 2015). This framework, especially as it relates to gifted students with minoritized identities, can help educators, administrators, school counselors, and so forth, see students more holistically which, in turn, can enhance their ability to be more effective in their practice. The following sections provide descriptions of identity categories along with relevant experiences and challenges that are relevant to postsecondary readiness for gifted students. While they are presented singularly, these identities can be seen in combination with each other to create a deeper understanding of gifted students with minoritized or multi-marginalized identities.

Race and Culture

The racial disparities in students receiving gifted education services is well-known and documented in research (Ford, 2013; Grissom & Redding, 2015). While there has been some improvement in the number of BISOCs in gifted education, race remains one of the most glaring discrepancies in many education services. According to 2015–2016 school year data from the Office of Civil Rights (OCR), White and Asian identifying students made up about 55% (48.9% and 5% respectively) of the total student population and represented almost 70% of those receiving gifted services (U.S. Department of Education, 2016). Meanwhile, out of the total student population identifying as Hispanic or Latino (25.8%) and Black (15.4%), only about 18% were enrolled in gifted programs (U.S. Department of Education, 2016). These recent numbers continue to reflect previous research that White and Asian students are more likely to be nominated for gifted education screening (McBee, 2006; Yoon & Gentry, 2009).

There has been work towards expanding the view of giftedness to include more than traditional considerations (i.e., academic achievement). However, the process often requires a student nomination or referral be made by a teacher or parent. These nominations have shown to be influenced by teacher biases, which includes, but is not limited to, race and ethnicity (Ford, 2013; Yoon & Gentry, 2009; Irizarry & Cohen, 2019). Additionally, many teachers, even those with years of experience, may not perceive or even understand how giftedness emerges in a cultural context unique to BISOCs (Neumeister et al., 2007). The lack of consideration for culturally-relevant giftedness could be particularly hindering to Native American students, as they are often grouped as one population and not distinguished by the more than 500 culturally and linguistically diverse tribes. However, for all BISOCs, this lack of consideration could convey that their racial and cultural identity is not recognized or acknowledged as even existing outside of academic achievements. Also, when they do occur, teacher nominations are less accurate (i.e., students do not complete screening) for Black and Hispanic identifying students, than for White or Asian students (McBee, 2006).

Unfortunately, when BISOCs are identified for gifted services, many leave these programs (Ford, 2013), especially those that lack peers and teachers from similar racial or cultural backgrounds (Gentry & Fugat, 2012). The presence of influential, leadership figures from the same racial or cultural background is key to BISOCs' success not only at the high school level, but in postsecondary settings as well. Although gifted services are not necessary to attend college, students that participate in gifted services are more likely to be familiar with college-level coursework (Spencer & Dowden, 2014). From these findings, it would seem supporting BISOCs' college and career readiness should include experiences in structured academic rigor, collaboration with peers from similar backgrounds, and exploration of identity in the academic setting.

Gender Identity

Gender refers to individual judgments about masculinity and femininity based on culture and context (Priess et al., 2009) and gender role identity refers to the image or feeling that each person has about their masculine and feminine characteristics. Most individuals view themselves as either having primarily feminine or primarily masculine characteristics (e.g., gender as binary), but many individuals identify as being both masculine and feminine or neither. Both socialization and aptitude can and do influence gender identity and the formation of gender schemas, also known as organized networks of knowledge about what it means to be male or female (Woolfolk, 2004). Some research has addressed gender differences in children and youth, but less has focused on gender in the context of giftedness, and gender and giftedness are often examined as one variable in larger studies (i.e., giftedness is not differentiated by gender). However, it is important to understand the factors that may differentially affect the development of giftedness in students of all genders. Given that most research views gender as binary, the following section focuses primarily on differences between boys and girls.

Gender Differences in Career Aspirations. Recent research examining differences in career aspirations among gifted boys and girls is relatively limited. Those studies that do exist, however, suggest that strong adherence to gender-role stereotypes in career aspirations may be declining for gifted girls. During the 1980s, business replaced education as the top choice of college majors for gifted girls. Additionally, Reis et al. (1996) found the top four career choices for gifted early adolescent males and females to be identical (i.e., doctor, scientist, lawyer, and business owner), although they were ranked differently for boys and girls. It appears from the literature that the increased similarity in the career aspirations of gifted boys and girls is attributable to girls becoming more interested in male-dominated occupations, rather than vice versa. Gifted boys are more likely to only consider traditionally male or masculine professions, while gifted girls are more likely to consider both traditionally female-dominated and traditionally male-dominated professions. And, no differences appear to exist in the prestige levels of career aspirations for gifted boys and girls. It has been noted by several researchers that there is greater pressure for boys than for girls to adhere to traditional gender-role stereotyped behavior (Wharton, 2012). Within the context of career development, this phenomenon can manifest in the perceived options available to gifted boys versus girls as well as the types of occupations that students are explicitly or implicitly encouraged to pursue (Kerr et al., 2012). For example, gifted boys are more likely to identify a narrower set of career options based on gender stereotypes (e.g., scientist, doctor, lawyer) than gifted girls. Likewise, in recent decades, gifted girls are more likely than their predecessors to identify a range of career aspirations that do not conform to traditional gender-role stereotypes. This appears to be related to the fact that masculine behaviors, preferences, and interests are more socially valued while feminine behaviors, preferences, and interests are often devalued (Mendez & Crawford, 2002). It is important to note that aspirations do not yet correspond strongly with attainment. In other words, gender differences in career aspirations among gifted students are diminishing; yet gender differences persist in many careers—especially those that are socially valued and highest paid. Women continue to be underrepresented in the upper echelons of business, medicine (e.g., anesthesiology, surgery, oncology), and STEM (Apaydin et al., 2018; Chen & Wong, 2013; Gupta et al., 2018).

Gifted Adolescent Girls.   The current generation of students coming of age in the wake of No Child Left Behind (2002) and other policies that focus on academic achievement and accountability are experiencing unique pressures and stressors. Socially, smart "Gen Z girls" have more pressure to be pretty, popular, and have boyfriends as soon as possible (Guthrie, 2020a). These challenges may intensify as gifted girls of the 21st century enter middle and high school when both the academic and social terrains of school become more rigorous and complex.

As gifted adolescent girls enter secondary school, they may start to experience a stigma related to being gifted (Coleman & Cross, 2014). They learn various social coping strategies in order to manage how their giftedness influences their experiences of social interactions including denying their giftedness, hiding their giftedness, conforming to the social norm, and more. In general, gifted adolescents may begin to define themselves in relation to how they compare to their peers, which is typical for the developmental period of adolescence in general. Yet, this can also complicate their individual identity development as they attempt to integrate advanced intellect, high creativity, and talents (Delisle & Galbraith, 2002).

Gifted adolescent girls, in particular, have had unique social-emotional, academic, and career development experiences and needs (Kerr et al., 2012). Gifted adolescent girls tend to downplay their abilities to conform to the social standards of their peers and are more likely to feel pressure to conform (Guthrie, 2020b). Compared to gifted boys, gifted adolescent girls are more likely report underconfidence in their abilities (Reis, 2002), and this is particularly true for math and math-related subjects. They often feel as though they have to be everything to everybody, and in turn, may suffer from over commitment and physical illness related to stress and exhaustion (Kerr, 2012). This phenomenon is often referred to as the *superwoman syndrome*. Callahan (1994) described the superwoman syndrome as a gifted female's tendency to "do it all" (e.g., take a rigorous course load, earn high grades, participate in multiple extra-curricular activities, hold a class office, speak multiple languages, earn awards and scholarships, and be a support to the family). The superwoman syndrome can leave many gifted adolescent girls feeling overwhelmed and overextended as they try to balance and manage multiple roles (Guthrie, 2020a). The superwoman syndrome may have a disproportionately negative impact on gifted Black girls and other students with marginalized identities as they contend with microaggressions alongside their professional identity development.

Special Education/Disability Status

Despite common misconceptions, gifted students can also have disabilities. These students, often referred to as twice exceptional (2E) students, possess the strengths and challenges associated with both giftedness and disability. This subpopulation is seemingly small due to challenges with masking, where their giftedness masks their disability or their disability masks their giftedness (Foley-Nicpon et al., 2012). Additionally, misconceptions and bias about giftedness may contribute to the under-identification of students with disabilities who are also gifted. This may be because educators may have a limited and biased view of what giftedness is and who can be gifted which may render students with disabilities as not having the capacity to be gifted as well (Mayes & Moore, 2016). As such, 2E students might only be identified as being gifted or as having a disability rather than both.

As previously mentioned, disability and giftedness interact in ways that bring in the strengths and challenges of both identities. For example, a gifted student with autism spectrum disorder (ASD) may struggle with short-term memory and deficits in the ability to process information but excel in areas related to verbal ability (Foley-Nicpon et al., 2012). Another gifted student with ADHD may exhibit an inability to concentrate while in class but excel in areas related to mathematics. Some students may have a propensity for creative endeavors but have an emotional disorder which affects their ability to regulate strong feelings in school. These strengths and challenges also contribute to the social-emotional development of 2E students. A systematic review examining noncognitive abilities among these students with identified learning disabilities noted similar experiences (Beckmann & Minnaert, 2018). Of note, these students indicated frustration with the discrepancy between their potential and their academic performance along with often having negative opinions about school and withdrawing socially (Beckmann & Minnaert, 2018). However, these students were also motivated, resilient, and possessed strong coping skills. When viewing 2E students holistically, educators can begin to see how to best support postsecondary planning and decision-making for individual students.

In looking towards the college and career readiness of 2E students, there are important considerations. First, 2E students often receive more attention for their disability than their giftedness (Shaunessy-Dedrick & Lazarou, 2020). This may influence the type of advice and expectations placed upon these students, negatively impacting their self-efficacy and understanding of their potential. They may have limited opportunities to explore their gifts through rigorous coursework and activities as they may be seen as solely a student in need of special education services (Mayes & Moore, 2016). Further, 2E students may already feel marginalized and uncertain about their inclusion in gifted education coursework (Reis et al., 2014) and suffer from further imposter syndrome if not properly assured of their belonging. This may stunt their college and career readiness and mismatch them with postsecondary opportunities despite their potential. As such, if 2E students are only seen for their disability, they may be likely to be encouraged to pursue vocational opportunities. However, if 2E students are seen for their giftedness and disability, they need support tailored towards their specific abilities, difficulties, and personality characteristics as it relates to college and career readiness (Mayes et al., 2019).

Socioeconomic Status

When considering the complex identity and experience of gifted students from a low-income background (low socioeconomic status or low SES), it is necessary to discuss the variety of influences on their career and college readiness. These influences include potential barriers for success due to the nature of gifted programming in addition to the strengths they possess in navigating the K–12 educational landscape.

Much of the research focused on students from low-income backgrounds concentrates on the inequitable identification and screening process for placing these students in gifted programming. This is important as students who are not identified are impeded in making strong advancements in their educational and professional careers. For example, a student may not have access to an accelerated math sequence of coursework starting as early as middle school (Olszewski-Kubilius & Corwith, 2017) or have fewer opportunities to enroll in Advanced Placement (AP) courses in high school (Crabtree et al., 2019). Losing out on such opportunities can have lasting impacts on college-access and in turn lifelong earnings and career stability.

Even for students from low-income backgrounds who are accurately placed in gifted programming, there is a lack of information about how they receive career and college readiness information. Perhaps because these students are still an underrepresented group in gifted education (Ford, 2013) little has been done to provide information about how to support these students; however, due to their specific needs, more research and focus must be done to ensure they are receiving appropriate scaffolding as the knowledge and support for college and career readiness may not be provided equitably. For example, when looking at those who apply to selective colleges or universities, only a small percentage of those who are identified as high-achieving and low income go through the application process (Hoxby & Avery, 2012). This indicates that even when students could attend these schools, they either choose not to apply or are not provided the information about the opportunity.

As stated previously, intersectionality of individual identities provides a more complete and holistic picture that allows for greater insight into gifted students' experiences. In this case, it is notable to state that many of the students from low-income backgrounds also identify with underrepresented racial/ethnic groups. In the Condition for Education Report (McFarland et al., 2019) the rates for children under 18 living in poverty were such: American Indian/Alaska Native and Black (32% each); Hispanic and Pacific Islander (26% each); two or more races (17%); White (11%); Asian (10%). These numbers indicate many of the students living in low-income households not only contend with the challenges of financial insecurity but also face the systematic racism noted in the race and culture section above. Educators need to acknowledge that although being in gifted programming might be advantageous in many ways, the cultural and historical challenges of classism and racism will persist and must be addressed proactively; even if a student completes some honors or gifted courses, they are not immune to the explicit and implicit messaging of their peers, counselors, and teachers, some of whom will have stereotyped or biased beliefs about their ability to succeed.

It is also important to recognize and consider some of the positive characteristics that influence these students and their academic progression. In an analysis investigating how giftedness, race, and poverty are discussed and represented in gifted academic journals from 2000 to 2015, the authors found that a large portion of articles also discuss the benefits that many BISOCs experience due to familial or other adult support which often pushes these children to strive for excellence (Goings & Ford, 2017). If capitalized upon, this can be extremely advantageous for students as they prepare for college and beyond. Having the support of social systems is considered influential in getting students from economically disadvantaged backgrounds to aspire and prepare for college (Buckley et al., 2011) in addition to influencing individuals' overall college success (Sandoval-Lucero et al., 2014). VanTassel-Baska (2017) also notes that students coming from historically marginalized backgrounds may want to focus on improving the world and utilize this as motivation to further themselves academically.

RECOMMENDATIONS FOR PRACTICE AND POLICY

The policies and practice that gifted students engage in the K–12 schooling system can either serve to bolster or inhibit their educational progression for college and career readiness including preparedness. Gifted students need equitable college and career counseling which is supported by comprehensive practices and policies. Each aspect of services provided must take into account the whole child including the intersectionality of their identities. Utilizing the College Board National Office for School Counselor Advocacy (NOSCA) eight components of college and career readiness counseling (College Board, 2010) ideas are suggested for practice below to ensure that the college and career readiness support from counselors is comprehensive and addresses the needs of students highlighted in previous sections:

1. College Aspirations Goal: Build a college-going culture based on early college awareness by nurturing in students the confidence to aspire to college and the resilience to overcome challenges along the way. Maintain high expectations by providing adequate supports, building social capital and conveying the conviction that all students can succeed in college.
   a. In regard to gifted students, VanTassel-Baska (2017) notes that

   > school psychologists and/or counselors need to assist students in improving skills that are critical for academic success in college, including test-taking skills, study strategies, and managing time effectively. Students also need to be supported in developing aspirations for their careers. (p. 77)

   Building aspirations begins as early as kindergarten with encouraging students to engage in career conversations (i.e., "What would you like to be when you grow up? What problem would you like to solve when you grow up?"). Even subtleties in language like referring to students as the class of 202x to denote that they will be graduating from high school and engaging in some kind of postsecondary opportunity is important.

b. As gifted programs in particular can start as early as elementary school, it would be important to think of a developmental approach to building aspirations systemically. This may include helping gifted students engage in mentorship with those who are further along in their college and career readiness, who can provide support and insight as a part of building aspirations. For example, gifted elementary school students can be paired with gifted middle and high school students who can share about their respective journeys, support academic and social-emotional development, while engaging in career conversations that relate to aspirations, age appropriate activities, and the planning process they have engaged thus far. Further, the creation of partnerships with community college and 4-year universities where students can find mentors would help to alleviate some of the fears often associated with college going. Participation in college preparation programs that are organized by institutions (e.g., Upward Bound) is particularly important, especially for underrepresented students, as they are structured to provide insight and experience in college life and research opportunities, while also allowing underrepresented students to interact and collaborate with peers from similar backgrounds with similar experiences.

2. Academic Planning for College and Career Readiness Goal: Advance students' planning, preparation, participation, and performance in a rigorous academic program that connects to their college and career aspirations and goals.

   a. Ensure that students understand their ability to take challenging courses. High school would be the time for example, for a twice-exceptional student to take honors or AP courses because within a high school setting, scaffolding and support could be consistent and ongoing, providing a safe environment for the student to build self-efficacy. This in turn may influence their perception of their college-going ability.

   b. It is also for these reasons that gifted students from underrepresented backgrounds should take advanced coursework so they can begin to build self-efficacy and translate this confidence to their college experience and beyond. For example, if high school counselors can connect their gifted BISOC to rigorous coursework that builds their interest in areas related to a potential career field, such as engineering or psychology, this may encourage students to pursue challenging areas of study during their higher education career.

3. Enrichment and Extracurricular Engagement Goal: Ensure equitable exposure to a wide range of extracurricular and enrichment

opportunities that build leadership, nurture talents and interests, and increase engagement with school.

    a. Teachers, school counselors, and support staff should all be a part of different teams, including grade level, content, and extra-curricular focus. These teams should continuously collaborate throughout the school year to provide students with the most opportunities.

4. College and Career Exploration and Selection Processes Goal: Provide early and ongoing exposure to experiences and information necessary to make informed decisions when selecting a college or career that connects to academic preparation and future aspirations.

    a. Each student needs to have conversations and support tailored to their situation. Considering both the pinch points and positives of every student will help benefit all gifted students, no matter their background. A good example of a planning process for a twice-exceptional student is provided by Foley-Nicpon and Assouline (2015),

> A gifted student with ADHD may be mathematically talented, which could suggest a propensity for the field of accounting, but aspects associated with this diagnosis (e.g., an inability to focus for long periods of time) may preclude pursuing a career in which the daily work is fairly routine. (p. 205)

5. College and Career Assessments Goal: Promote preparation, participation, and performance in college and career assessments by all students.

    a. School counselors are also key in this goal as they are often the ones that plan and facilitate these assessments. School counselors should have the most up-to-date information on relevant college and career assessments and should be able to provide the materials and space necessary for student study and preparation (with the support of the school).

6. College Affordability Planning Goal: Provide students and families with comprehensive information about college costs, options for paying for college, and the financial aid and scholarship processes and eligibility requirements, so they are able to plan for and afford a college education.

    a. Educators must understand and then communicate that for individuals who are capable of attending highly selective universities (often those within the gifted community) the costs associated are actually almost lower than other less competitive universities or colleges. In addition, typically the retention and graduation of students (no matter their background or experience) is actually *higher* for students who attend the more selective schools.

7. College and Career Processes Goal: Ensure that students and families have an early and ongoing understanding of the college and career application and admission processes so they can find the postsecondary options that are the best fit with their aspirations and interests.

    a. School counseling programs should include curriculum aimed at supporting student's preparation for postsecondary life. Students should be engaged in activities that are aimed at grade-level and age-appropriate content relevant to academic, social, and professional growth. For example, Arizona's 9–12 students are required to complete an Education and Career Action Plan, which is a set of activities given each school year to help students complete the following: plan future high school courses, complete interest and skill surveys, learn to budget, and engage in a number of other activities that prepare students for life after graduation. This type of student portfolio should be compiled in congruence with other programming aimed at building student's academic skills, supporting and validating their racial/cultural identity, and engagement in nonacademic experiences.

8. Connect students to school and community resources to help the students overcome barriers and ensure the successful transition from high school to college.

    a. Knowing that low-income students and BISOCs who are also gifted may not receive the appropriate support when considering their college-going potential and preparing for the transition from high school to college, there is a great need to create a network of support. As previously indicated, much of college-going extends beyond having academic skills, but also being connected with the appropriate resources (Britton & Spencer, 2020). It would be important to help gifted students cultivate the community they need to provide holistic support which may include cultural centers, offices of disability support services, tutoring and academic retention services, and so forth. This may be done as an extension of mentoring connections with current college students and gifted students. Mentors may share insights to campus and professional resources that they have found helpful to their success while highlighting that success in college means collaboration and networking to gain holistic support. As a part of this process, it would be important for educators to think about ways to intentionally include family members and caregivers. They are also an incredible support for their gifted students that would be important to cultivate for this transition. Further, family members and caregivers may also need to know and understand the kinds of support available to their gifted student as a part of the college-going process as they can reinforce their students' need to develop a campus community geared towards their support.

It's important that the eight components of college and career readiness counseling (NOSCA, 2010) be operationalized through a comprehensive, systemic, and anti-racist approach. An anti-racist approach to school counseling centers wholeness and humanness of students, families, and communities while working to resist and dismantle racist ideologies, policies, and practices (Holcomb-McCoy et al., 2020; Sharp & Mayes, 2020). As such, school counselors work directly with students through individual and group counseling along with classroom guidance to intentionally create spaces of joy and resistance while growing college and career readiness (Hines et al., 2022; Sharp & Mayes, 2020). At the same time, school counselors are also working at the schoolwide, district, community, state, and federal levels to interrogate and dismantle oppressive systems and policies related to college and career readiness while readily building partnerships to build better, supportive systems (Hines et al., 2022). More specifically, when considering specific policies (and related practices), three major areas need to be addressed to ensure that the college and career readiness of gifted students is provided effectively and adequately.

1. Change the way in which students are placed into gifted programming. More equity in determining who is placed into gifted programs is of utmost importance for students. For example, if all identified students in a district have to be recommended for testing, many students may be missed. If educators are the only ones responsible for making initial referrals for gifted education, implicit (or overt) biases are likely to occur allowing for the exclusion of individuals based upon racial, gender, and disability characteristics. More expansive models of identification that extend beyond standardized testing are also important as it allows for more BISOCs, girls, students with disabilities, and so forth to be evaluated more fairly and holistically (Mayes et al., 2018; Mayes & Moore, 2016; Reis et al., 2014).
2. Ensure that school counselors are present and staffed at recommended ratios for student to counselor. Current recommendations suggest a ratio of 250 students to 1 school counselor (ASCA, 2019). This ratio may serve as a baseline to work from, while also recognizing that the unique needs of the students and the school may require a lower ratio. This particular area involves multilevel

advocacy at the school/district, local, and state level as this not only relates to school funding, hiring practices, and role definition for school counselors. This involves understanding how schools are funded and how such funds are allocated in ways that may meet or overlook student needs. With the effects of the COVID-19 pandemic along with the ways that anti-Blackness, racism, sexism, classism, and so forth have been perpetuated in schools and communities over time, there is a great need for anti-racist school counselors to be present in schools but also allowed to engage in the full scope of comprehensive school counseling.

3. Provide teaching and support staff with training on anti-racism, cultural sensitivity and inclusion, and differences in cultural strengths and skills in order to broaden the understanding of giftedness. As previously mentioned, educator bias plays a role in the identification process for students which contributes to disproportionality in the identified gifted population (Ford, 2013; Mayes & Moore, 2016). Moreover, these biases find their way in gifted education services as well, which can also impact the development of gifted students from a range of backgrounds. In order to address this bias and enhance the experience of all gifted students, it would be important to engage in ongoing training and professional development to increase cultural sensitivity, humility, and inclusion for all educators including those focused on gifted education.

RECOMMENDATIONS FOR RESEARCH

Current literature helps to illuminate the experiences and needs of gifted students in regard to postsecondary readiness. However, there are significant gaps as it relates to gifted students from an intersectional lens. More research is needed to understand how gifted minoritized students make meaning of and experience the process of postsecondary readiness. For example, how do twice exceptional BISOCs develop career aspirations and identities? What are critical incidents in the successful transition to college for gifted Black students? How does participation in rigorous courses facilitate interest in STEM for gifted Latinx girls? This would help practitioners understand similarities and uniquenesses that gifted minoritized students may share with the general K–12 population and gifted population. Building on this, more research is needed in the area of effective practices, interventions, and policies that support the postsecondary readiness of gifted minoritized students.

CONCLUSION

Giftedness is often overlooked within the broader context of career development. Because most gifted students are high ability, they are often perceived as not having unique academic, social, or career needs and, therefore, may not receive the necessary supports to ensure their college and career readiness. In this chapter, we aimed to describe how giftedness impacts the academic experience including the ways in which it intersects with other facets of identity decision-making. As a general summary, gifted students may face a number of challenges throughout their academic careers. Gifted students may narrow their career interests to conform to high status, prestigious occupations. This may result in career foreclosure in which they have limited their options that may potentially have resulted in higher career satisfaction. Perfectionism among gifted students may restrict career development as they attempt to conform to the career aspirations of their parents/peers or experience anxiety and believe that they must find that one, perfect career. Lastly, gifted students may find themselves restricted by gender-based ideals regarding career development where, especially for girls, their aspirations and opportunities suffer in order to meet societal expectations and in their effort to balance multiple roles.

Despite their academic potential, gifted students may experience unique barriers and challenges in their career exploration and planning. As such, this group of students needs support when it comes to career development and in the school setting. Being cognizant of this reality, this chapter attempts to draw attention to the complexity of giftedness to ensure the college and career readiness needs of gifted students are met.

DISCUSSION QUESTIONS

1. How does your school approach identifying gifted students? What are related district, state, federal policies to identifying gifted students? How does that have an impact on who participates in gifted education?
2. What are the current college and career readiness practices for gifted students in your school? How do these practices take into account the intersectional identities of gifted students?

ACTIVITIES

1. Using school data, identify the profile of a successful gifted student in your school. What is their cultural background, gender identity,

class, disability status, and so forth? What school experiences does that student have (i.e., involvement in extracurricular activities including leadership opportunities, discipline referrals, engagement in school counseling services including academic, social-emotional supports, etc.)? What courses does that student take (i.e., advanced placement, honors, international baccalaureate, dual credit, etc.)? What experiences does that student typically have related to college and career readiness (i.e., college entrance exam test prep, access to college entrance exam cost waivers, college visits, mentoring with college students and professionals in their area of interest, support completing FASFA, etc.)?

2. Interview a district level administrator responsible for gifted education. What are the ways they see policies impact the ways schools can identify and serve gifted students? What are key issues they see at the school and district level impacting gifted students' college and career readiness? What are ways they believe schools can better school gifted students holistically, including specifically regarding college and career readiness?

AUTHOR NOTE

Renae D. Mayes ORCID https://orcid.org/0000-0001-7999-456X

We have no known conflict of interest to disclose.

Correspondence concerning this chapter should be addressed to Renae D. Mayes, Dept of Disability & Psychoeducational Studies, University of Arizona College of Education, P.O. Box 210069, Tucson, AZ 85721

REFERENCES

American School Counselor Association. (2017). *The school counselor and career development.*

American School Counselor Association. (2019). *The ASCA national model: A framework for school counseling programs* (4th ed.).

Apaydin, E. A., Chen, P. G., & Friedberg, M. W. (2018). Differences in physician income by gender in a multiregion survey. *Journal of General Internal Medicine, 33*(9), 1574–1581.

Beckmann, E., & Minnaert, A. (2018). Non-cognitive characteristics of gifted students with learning disabilities: An in-depth systematic review. *Frontiers in psychology, 9,* 504. https://doi.org/10.3389/fpsyg.2018.00504

Better Make Room. (2020). https://www.bettermakeroom.org

Bianco, M., Harris, B., Garrison-Wade, D., & Leech, N. (2011). Gifted girls: Gender bias in gifted referrals. *Roeper Review, 33*(3), 170–181. https://doi-org.ezproxy2.library.arizona.edu/10.1080/02783193.2011.580500

Britton, T., & Spencer, G. (2020). Do students who fail to plan, plan to fail? Effects of individualized learning plans on postsecondary transitioning. *Teachers College Record, 122*(5), 1–16.

Bryan, J., Moore-Thomas, C., Day-Vines, N. L., & Holcomb-McCoy, C. (2011). School counselors as social capital: The effects of high school college counseling on college application rates. *Journal of Counseling and Development, 89,* 190–199. https://doi.org/10.1002/j.1556-6678.2011.tb00077.x

Buckley, J. A., Kuh, G. D., Kinzie, J., Bridges, B. K., & Hayek, J. C. (2011). *Piecing together the student success puzzle: Research, propositions, and recommendations* (ASHE Higher Education Report). Wiley.

Callahan, C. M. (1994). Foundations for the future: The socio-emotional development of gifted, adolescent women. *Roeper Review, 17,* 99–105. https://doi.org/10.1080/02783199409553634

Carnevale, A. P., Smith, N., & Strohl, J. (2013). Postsecondary education and economic opportunity. In L. Perna (Ed.), *Preparing today's students for tomorrow's jobs in metropolitan America* (pp. 93–120). University of Pennsylvania Press.

Center for Disease Control. (2021). *Anxiety and depression: Household pulse survey.* https://www.cdc.gov/nchs/covid19/pulse/mental-health.htm

Chen, C. P., & Wong, J. (2013). Career counseling for gifted students. *Australian Journal of Career Development, 22*(3), 121–129.

Coleman, L. J., & Cross, T. L. (2014). Is being gifted a social handicap? *Journal for the Education of the Gifted, 37*(1), 5–17.

College Board (2019). *Education pays: The benefits of higher education for individuals and society.* https://research.collegeboard.org/pdf/education-pays-2019-full-report.pdf

College Board. (2010). *The eight components of college and career readiness.* http://nosca.collegeboard.org/eight-components

Conley, D. T. (2012). *A complete definition of college and career readiness.* Educational Policy Improvement Center.

Conley, D. T. (2014). *Getting ready for college, careers and the Common Core: What every educator needs to know.* Jossey-Bass.

Crabtree, L. M., Richardson, S. C., & Lewis, C. W. (2019). The gifted gap, STEM education, and economic immobility. *Journal of Advanced Academics, 30*(2), 203–231. https://doi-org.ezproxy3.library.arizona.edu/10.1177/1932202X19829749

Crenshaw, K. W. (1989). Demarginalizing the intersection of race and sex: A Black feminist critique of antidiscrimination doctrine, feminist theory and antiracist politics. *University of Chicago Legal Forum, 1989,* 138–167.

Crenshaw, K. (1991). Mapping the margins: Intersectionality, identity politics, and violence against women of color. *Stanford Law Review, 43,* 1241–1299.

Crenshaw, K. (2015, September 24). Why intersectionality can't wait. *The Washington Post.* https://www.washingtonpost.com/news/in-theory/wp/2015/09/24/why-intersectionality-cant-wait/

Delisle, J., & Galbraith, J. (2002). *When gifted kids don't have all the answers: How to meet their social and emotional needs.* Free Spirit Publishing Inc.

Dorn, E., Hancock, B., Sarakatsannis, J., & Viruleg, E. (2020, June 1). *COVID-19 and student learning in the United States: The hurt could last a lifetime.* McKinsey & Company. https://www.mckinsey.com/industries/public-and-social-sector/our -insights/covid-19-and-student-learning-in-the-united-states-the-hurt-could -last-a-lifetime#

Falco, L. D., & Steen, S. (2018). Using school-based career development to support college and career readiness: An integrative review. *Journal of School-Based Counseling Policy and Evaluation, 1,* 51–67. https://doi.org/10.25774/v1t4-c816

Foley-Nicpon, M., Assouline, S. G., & Stinson, R. D. (2012). Cognitive and academic distinctions between gifted students with autism and Asperger syndrome. *Gifted Child Quarterly, 56*(2), 77–89. https://doi.org/10.1177/0016986211433199

Foley-Nicpon, M., & Assouline, S. G. (2015). Counseling considerations for the twice-exceptional client. *Journal of Counseling & Development, 93*(2), 202–211. https://doi.org/10.1002/j.1556-6676.2015.00196.x

Ford, D. Y. (2013). Recruiting and retaining culturally different students in gifted education. Prufrock Press.

Gentry, M., & Fugate, C. M. (2012). Gifted, Native American students: Underperforming, under-identified, and overlooked. *Psychology in the Schools, 49,* 631–646. http://dx.doi.org/10.1002/pits.21624

Goings, R. B., & Ford, D. Y. (2017). Investigating the intersection of poverty and race in gifted education journals: A 15-year analysis. *Gifted Child Quarterly, 62*(1), 25–36. https://doi.org/10.1177/0016986217737618

Gottfredson, L. S. (2005). Applying Gottfredson's theory of circumscription and compromise in career guidance and counseling. In S. D. Brown & R. W. Lent (Eds.), *Career development and counseling: Putting theory and research to work* (p. 71–100). John Wiley & Sons, Inc.

Greene, M. J. (2006). Helping build lives: Career and life development of gifted and talented students. *Professional School Counseling, 10*(1), 34–42.

Grissom, J. A., & Redding, C. (2015). Discretion and disproportionality: Explaining the underrepresentation of high-achieving students of color in gifted programs. *Aera Open, 2*(1). https://doi.org/10.1177/2332858415622175

Gupta, V. K., Mortal, S. C., & Guo, X. (2018). Revisiting the gender gap in CEO compensation: Replication and extension of Hill, Upadhyay, and Beekun's (2015) work on CEO gender pay gap. *Strategic Management Journal, 39*(7), 2036–2050.

Guthrie, K. H. (2020a). The weight of expectations: A thematic narrative of gifted adolescent girls' reflections of being gifted. *Roeper Review, 42*(1), 25–37.

Guthrie, K. H. (2020b). Exploring Kerr and McKay's beehive of smart girls: Understanding the challenges facing gifted adolescent females. *Gifted Child Today, 43*(2), 108–115.

Holcomb-McCoy, C., Mayes, R. D., Savitz-Romer, M., Cheatham, C. B., & Sharp, S. (2020). *Antiracist school counseling: A call to action* [Webinar]. American University. https://youtu.be/JEjNaB2L3Vc

Hines, E. M., Harris, P. C., Mayes, R. D., & Owen, L. (2022). Using an antiracist approach to ensure college and career readiness for students of color. In C. Holcomb-McCoy (Ed), *Antiracist counseling in schools and communities* (pp. 81–101). American Counseling Association.

Hoxby, C. M., & Avery, C. (2012). *The missing "one-offs": The hidden supply of high-achieving, low income students* (No. w18586). National Bureau of Economic Research.

Irizarry, Y., & Cohen, E. D. (2019). Of promise and penalties: How student racial-cultural markers shape teacher perceptions. *Race and Social Problems, 11*(2), 93–111.

Kerr, B. A. (2012). Developmental issues for gifted and creative girls: Milestones and danger zones. In T. L. Cross & J. R. Cross (Eds.), *Handbook for counselors serving students with gifts and talents: Development, relationships, school issues, and counseling needs/interventions* (pp. 315–331). Prufrock Press.

Kerr, B. A., Vuyk, M. A., & Rea, C. (2012). Gendered practices in the education of gifted girls and boys. *Psychology in the Schools, 49*(7), 647–655.

Kim, M. (2014). Family background, students' academic self-efficacy, and students' career and life success expectations. *International Journal for the Advancement of Counselling, 36*, 395–407. https://doi.org/10.1007/s10447-014-9216-1

Marques de Miranda, D., da Silva Athanasio, B., Sena Oliveira, A. C., & Simoes-E-Silva, A. C. (2020). How is COVID-19 pandemic impacting mental health of children and adolescents? *International Journal of Disaster Risk Reduction, 51.* https://doi.org/10.1016/j.ijdrr.2020.101845

Mayes, R. D., Hines, E. M., Bibbs, D. L., & Rodman, J. (2019). Counselors and psychologists mentoring gifted Black males with disabilities to foster college and career readiness. *Gifted Child Today, 42*(3), 157–164.

Mayes, R. D., Jones, S. G., & Hines, E. M. (2018). Diverse gifted students: Intersectionality of cultures. In S. M. Wood & J. S. Peterson (Eds.), *Counseling gifted students: A guide for school counselors.* (pp. 47–64). Springer.

Mayes, R. D., & Moore, J. L., III. (2016). The intersection of race, disability, and giftedness: Understanding the education needs of twice-exceptional, African American students. *Gifted Child Today, 39*(2), 98–104.

McBee, M. T. (2006). A descriptive analysis of referral sources for gifted identification screening by race and socioeconomic status. *Journal of Secondary Gifted Education, 17*(2), 103–111.

McFarland, J., Hussar, B., Zhang, J., Wang, X., Wang, K., Hein, S., Diliberti, M., Cataldie, E. F., Mann, F. B., & Barmer, A. (2019). *The Condition of Education 2019 (NCES 2019-144).* U.S. Department of Education, National Center for Education Statistics. https://nces.ed.gov/pubs2019/2019144.pdf

Mendez, L. M. R., & Crawford, K. M. (2002). Gender-role stereotyping and career aspirations: A comparison of gifted early adolescent boys and girls. *Journal of secondary gifted education, 13*(3), 96–107.

National Association for Gifted Children. (n.d.). *The national picture: Gifted education in the U.S.* http://www.nagc.org/index.aspx?id=532

National Center for Education Statistics. (2018). *Percentage of public school students enrolled in gifted and talented programs, by sex, race/ethnicity, and state: Selected years, 2004 through 2013–14.* https://nces.ed.gov/programs/digest/d18/tables/dt18_204.90.asp

National Student Clearinghouse Research Center. (2020). *2020 high school benchmarks with covid-19 special analysis: National college progression rates.* https://nscresearchcenter.org/wp-content/uploads/2020_HSBenchmarksReport.pdf

Neumeister, K. L. S., Adams, C. M., Pierce, R. L., Cassady, J. C., & Dixon, F. A. (2007). Fourth-grade teachers' perceptions of giftedness: Implications for identifying and serving diverse gifted students. *Journal for the Education of the Gifted, 30*(4), 479–499.

Olszewski-Kubilius, P., & Corwith, S. (2017). Poverty, academic achievement, and giftedness: A literature review. *Gifted Child Quarterly, 62*(1), 37–55. https://doi.org/10.1177/0016986217738015

Peterson, J. S. (2006). Addressing counseling needs of gifted students. *Professional School Counseling, 10*(1), 43–51. https://doi-org.ezproxy2.library.arizona.edu/10.5330/prsc.10.1.b76h32717q632tqn

Peterson, J. S. (2015). School counselors and gifted kids: Respecting both cognitive and affective. *Journal of Counseling & Development, 93*(2), 153–162. https://doi-org.ezproxy2.library.arizona.edu/10.1002/j.1556-6676.2015.00191.x

Priess, H. A., Lindberg, S. M., & Hyde, J. S. (2009). Adolescent gender-role identity and mental health: Gender intensification revisited. *Child Development, 80*(5), 1531–1544.

Reach Higher. (2020). https://obamawhitehouse.archives.gov/reach-higher

Reis, S. M. (2002). Internal barriers, personal issues, and decisions faced by gifted and talented females. *Gifted Child Today, 25*(1), 14–28. https://doi.org/10.4219/gct-2002-50

Reis, S. M., Baum, S. M., & Burke, E. (2014). An operational definition of twice-exceptional learners: Implications and applications. *Gifted Child Quarterly, 58*(3), 217–230. https://doi-org.ezproxy3.library.arizona.edu/10.1177/0016986214534976

Reis, S. M., Callahan, C. M., & Goldsmith, D. (1996). Attitudes of gifted adolescents toward their achievement, education and future. In K. D. Arnold, K. D. Noble, & R. F. Subotnik (Eds.), *Remarkable women: Perspectives on female talent development* (pp. 209–224). Hampton Press.

Sandoval-Lucero, E., Maes, J. B., & Klingsmith, L. (2014). African American and Latina(o) community college students' social capital and student success. *College Student Journal, 48*(3), 522–533.

Sharp, S., & Mayes, R. D. (2020). *Antiracist opportunity: Examining education careers thru antiracist lens* [Conference session]. Unpacking Bias and Systemic Racism Virtual Conference, Capital Area Intermediate Unit.

Shaunessy-Dedrick, E., & Lazarou, B. (2020). Curriculum and instruction for the gifted: The role of school psychologists. *Psychology in the Schools, 57*(10), 1542–1557. https://doi.org/10.1002/pits.22379

Smith, C. K., & Wood, S. M. (2020). Supporting the career development of gifted students: New role and function for school psychologists. *Psychology in Schools 57*, 1558–1568.

Spencer, N. F., & Dowden, A. (2014). Racial identity development and academic achievement of academically gifted African American students: Implications for school counselors. *Georgia School Counselor Association Journal, 21*(1).

U.S. Department of Education, Office for Civil Rights, Civil Rights Data Collection, 2016, available at http://ocrdata.ed.gov. Data notes are available at https://ocrdata.ed.gov/Downloads/Data-Notes-2015-16-CRDC.pdf

VanTassel-Baska, J. (2017). Achievement unlocked: Effective curriculum interventions with low-income students. *Gifted Child Quarterly, 62*(1), 68–82. https://doi.org/10.1177/0016986217738565

Wahleithner, J. M. (2020). The high school–college disconnect: Examining first-generation college students' perceptions of their literacy preparation. *Journal of Adolescent & Adult Literacy, 64*(1), 19–26. https://doi-org.ezproxy2.library.arizona.edu/10.1002/jaal.1057

Watson, A., & Pananjady, K. (2020, December 11). College financial aid applications down 16% this school year. *Ct Mirror.* https://ctmirror.org/2020/12/11/college-financial-aid-applications-down-16-this-school-year/

Wharton, A. S. (2012). *The sociology of gender: An introduction to theory and research* (2nd ed.). John Wiley & Sons.

Woolfolk, A. E. (2004). *Educational psychology.* Allyn & Bacon.

Yoon, S. Y., & Gentry, M. (2009). Racial and ethnic representation in gifted programs: Current status of and implications for gifted Asian American students. *Gifted Child Quarterly, 53*(2), 121–136.

CHAPTER 12

PREPARING LGBTQ+ STUDENTS FOR POSTSECONDARY TRANSITIONS THROUGH CAREER DEVELOPMENT

Eunhui Yoon
Florida State University

Michael Morgan Jr.
Florida State University

Viola May
Florida State University

ABSTRACT

LGBTQ+ students face distinct challenges and need assistance in preparing for and navigating the postsecondary transition. However, due to limited research in this area, counselors lack adequate preparation and tools for supporting this population. The purpose of this chapter is to explore the environmental and developmental issues for LGBTQ+ students and ways in which school, career, and mental health counselors can support their postsecond-

Equity-Based Career Development and Postsecondary Transitions, pages 301–324
Copyright © 2022 by Information Age Publishing
www.infoagepub.com

ary transition. The chapter includes a discussion of the cognitive information processing (CIP) theory and the psychology of working theory (PWT) to offer identity-affirming career services and evidenced-based interventions grounded in theory.

High school students need to receive appropriate support to have smooth transitions into the next stage of their lives whether they choose to pursue higher education, enter the workforce, or pursue other options. Successful completion of high school and career development planning are key tasks with which they often receive postsecondary transition support. Unfortunately, LGBTQ+ students often experience the high school environment as neither safe nor affirming, and this negatively affects their school experience and attendance (Kosciw et al., 2018). Negative school experiences, such as microaggression, school bullying, and unaffirming policies, also impact LGBTQ+ students through relationships with lower academic achievement (Bontempo & D'Augelli, 2002), mental health issues like depression and suicidality, and substance abuse (Birkett et al., 2009; Bontempo & D'Augelli, 2002; Higa et al., 2014; Russell et al., 2011). Importantly, some concerns specific to LGBTQ+ students can become barriers to career development (Gedro, 2009; House, 2004); for example, both gender identity and sexual orientation are associated with occupational stereotypes that artificially limit choice (Hancock et al., 2020).

This chapter will outline unique issues and needs of LGBTQ+ students that can affect their high school completion and career. There will be an emphasis on ways mental health counselors and school counselors can help and advocate for LGBTQ+ students because counseling can be a powerful avenue for marginalized students to address their issues and receive support for optimal development (McKinney et al., 2020). The chapter will conclude with an actionable model for career counseling with LGBTQ+ students grounded in cognitive information processing theory (CIP) and psychology of working theory (PWT).

LGBTQ+ STUDENTS' ISSUES RELATED TO HIGH SCHOOL COMPLETION AND CAREER DEVELOPMENT

Generally, LGBTQ+ students do not experience school as a place of safety. According to the Gay, Lesbian, and Straight Education Network (GLSEN), 87% of the LGBTQ+ students have experienced school bullying and harassment, 98% of the LGBTQ+ students heard negative remarks about gender and sexual identity from peers or authority figures like teachers and administrators (Kosciw et al., 2018). Many LGBTQ+ students (60%) also report that the adult figures in school responded to reports of harassment and assault by either doing nothing at all or telling the student to ignore it (Kosciw et al., 2018, p. 31). Even though strong evidence suggests that pervasive experiences of discrimination related to gender identity and sexual orientation negatively impact LGBTQ+ students' mental health (Birkett et al., 2009; Bontempo & D'Augelli, 2002; Higa et al., 2014; Russell et al., 2011) and academic achievement (Bontempo & D'Augelli, 2002), current efforts to create gender and sexual identity affirming policies and school-based interventions are not fully addressing these problems.

The interventions currently being used in school settings by staff and administration often leave gaps in meeting the safety and inclusion needs of LGBTQ+ students. Anti-bullying policies in schools do not consistently ban aggression based on sexual/affectional orientation or gender identity/expression (Kosciw et al., 2018). The results of Kosciw et al. (2018) also observed that many students experience school policies that: (a) mandated dress codes enforced a gender binary system, (b) did not respect preferred name and pronouns, (c) disallowed students' usage of locker room and restroom based on preferred gender identity, and (d) discouraged participation in certain sports. Unsafe and non-affirming school environments often lead LGBTQ+ students to absenteeism that can negatively impact their graduation (Kosciw et al., 2018).

High school students who identify as LGBTQ+ are also less likely to have psychological energy to invest in their career development compared to their peers because of challenges in their sexual or gender identity development (Lonborg & Phillips, 1996; Schmidt & Nilsson, 2006). In comparison to cisgender heterosexual adolescents, LGBTQ+ high school students expend more energy in the development of their gender or sexual identities (Schmidt & Nilsson, 2006; Tomlinson & Fassinger, 2003) because of a variety of discrimination-related obstacles like heteronormativity enforced through familial expectations or peer pressure (Gedro, 2009) and internalized homophobia caused by non-affirming communities (Barnes & Meyer, 2012; Heiden-Rootes et al., 2020). Also, rather than focusing on their individual career interests, LGBTQ+ students might be forced by societal messages to expend additional energy to determine whether their career decision is acceptable to their gender or sexual identity (Gottfredson, 1981; Hancock et al., 2020; Lindley, 2006). These discrimination related barriers to career planning might be one reason whyLGBTQ+ students are much less likely to report a desire to pursue higher education compared to cis-gender-heterosexual peers (Goodrich & Luke, 2009).

Occupational stereotypes based on gender and sexual orientation are likely to influence LGBTQ+ student's perceptions of freedom to choose their career path. Both gender and sexual orientation stereotypes influence career decision-making (Gottfredson, 1981; Hancock et al., 2020). Sexual and affectional orientation stereotyping often influences the job-seeking process for LGBTQ+ individuals (Cech & Rothwell, 2020; Clarke & Arnold, 2018). For example, gay males are more likely perceived to fit in occupations traditionally considered as more feminine and less masculine (Cech & Rothwell, 2020; Clarke & Arnold, 2018; Kite & Deaux, 1987), whereas lesbian females are more likely perceived to fit traditionally more masculine and less feminine occupations (Pope et al., 2004). Not only can stereotypes influence students' independent career planning, but counselors who lack awareness of these societal biases might unwittingly reinforce job-related sexual orientation stereotypes while providing career services. Additionally, career assessments and psychological scales developed and normed based on cisgender binary and heteronormativity are additional roadblocks to affirmative career counseling because they do not reflect diverse sexual and gender identities (Pope et al., 2004).

Finally, students who identify as LGBTQ+ have fewer role models that inform career aspirations (Goodrich & Luke, 2009). Role models who identify as LGBTQ+ could increase awareness of possibilities in career choice (Hetherington et al., 1989). Role models can also offer guidance to manage sexual/affectional orientation and gender identity/expression in the context of career (Barber & Mobley, 1999). It can also be highly beneficial for LGBTQ+ students to have exposure to role models who are in occupations that contradict stereotypes (Pope, 1996). When compared to the past, the visibility of LGBTQ+ population in media and the workplace has increased significantly (Magrath, 2019). School counselors should provide LGBTQ+ students with greater exposure to role models to improve the poor perception that LGBTQ+ students report about school counselor's ability to understand their unique career-related concerns (Varjas et al., 2006). In addition to providing LGBTQ+ students with examples of role models, these students should also receive information about how to find queer-friendly environments, knowing their legal rights, and openness in job interviews (Ng & Rumens, 2017; Rumens, 2011).

The current climate of societal unrest associated with public displays of systemic injustice (e.g., creation of flagrantly oppressive laws directed at transgender individuals, incessant displays of police brutality directed at African Americans, etc.) and the global pandemic have created an inflection point in working with LGBTQ+ students. Highly salient social justice movements enable the development of critical consciousness (Diemer et al., 2021) and community connectedness (Perrin et al., 2020) in LGBTQ+ students by engaging them in critical conversations and connecting them with resources and opportunities for participation in various aspects of advocacy. Not only can both critical consciousness and community connectedness mitigate the effect of systemic oppression on well-being (Heberle et al., 2020), they can both contribute meaningfully to academic outcomes and career development.

The COVID-19 pandemic has been characterized as a "career shock" by Akkermans et al. (2020). This means that the pandemic has been an event that causes individuals to reevaluate their careers because it is disruptive, extraordinary, and uncontrollable. Career theorists predict the pandemic will causes radical changes to the world of work (Autin et al., 2020), but effective career interventions that increase hope for employment, address mental health concerns, build critical consciousness, and provide students with strong career-decision making skills can create a growth opportunity out of this crisis. Importantly, the strongest support for career development with LGBTQ+ students by school counselors should emphasize both individual services and advocacy efforts at the system level (Autin et al., 2020).

WHAT CAN COUNSELORS DO FOR LGBTQ+ STUDENTS' POSTSECONDARY TRANSITION AND CAREER DEVELOPMENT?

School Counselors

School counselors can respond to the needs of LGBTQ+ students and develop school environments that are safe and inclusive for LGBTQ+ students through their pivotal role as system changers (West-Olatunji et al., 2020). School counselors can advocate for LGBTQ+ students by proposing improvements to non-affirming/non-inclusive school policies. For example, they can suggest strengthening school-wide anti-bullying policies through the addition of distinctive language that prohibits both physical and verbal aggression based on sexual/affectional orientation and gender identity/expression (Abreu et al., 2016; Gower et al., 2018; Kull et al., 2016). School counselors can also offer reviews of school policies based on traditional gender-binary systems (e.g., dress codes, bathroom and locker usage, sports inclusion) to better ensure students are able to access basic school facilities and school activities based on their gender identity. School counselors can cultivate a LGBTQ+ embracing school and community atmosphere by offering workshops, classroom guidance, and diversity appreciation events for students, teachers, staff members, administrators, and families that are designed to increase stakeholder's knowledge and awareness of LGBTQ+ issues.

At an individual level, school counselors develop sexual and gender development support plans that assist with gender/sexual orientation identity exploration, access to resources, and other forms of support to promote growth and well-being. For example, school counselors can create a LGBTQ+ library with inclusive books and other media (e.g., books that highlight the history of the LGBTQ+ rights movement, books written about historical figures who were sexual or gender minorities/expansives, etc.); this would help students, see their issues and themselves be included in school and the world. School counselors should increase their accessibility to LG-BTQ+ students to facilitate this process, which can be accomplished with an action as simple as displaying a rainbow flag in their office or putting LG-BTQ+ pride or ally-ship stickers on their personal belongings. Counselors and teachers who practice visible ally-ship are perceived as more approachable by LGBTQ+ students (Kosciw et al., 2018).

Career and Mental Health Counselors

The American Counseling Association (ACA, 2014) and the National Career Development Association (NCDA, 2015) mandate counselors to practice cultural competence. The Association for Lesbian, Gay, Bisexual, and Transgender Issues in Counseling (ALGBTIC) Competencies for Counseling with Lesbian, Gay, Bisexual, Queer, Questioning, Intersex and Ally Individuals (ALGBTIC, 2009) and the American Counseling Association (2010) Competencies for Counseling With Transgender Clients also emphasize guidelines for working with LGBTQ+ individuals in a culturally competent manner.

A large part of cultural competence is counselor self and other awareness. Counselors should explore their own biases and prejudices related to the LGBTQ+ population through reflective practices and supervision (Scott et al., 2011). Self-awareness allows the counselor to examine their views, beliefs, and implicit biases that may inform their practice. Counselors must also expand their knowledge and expose themselves to diverse populations through literature, training, workshops, and community events, broadening their practice and advocacy efforts. Greater emphasis on knowledge, skills, and awareness of LGBTQ+ specific diversity issues should also be incorporated in graduate level training; for example, social justice immersion projects have been found to greatly enhance cultural competence in counselors in training (Goodman & West-Olatunji, 2009).

Career exploration and identity transition add a significant amount of stress for LGBTQ+ students. LGBTQ+ students endure the tension of finding a job and the fear of how their unveiled identity may influence their career development and therapeutic relationship (Scott et al., 2011). Additionally, past experiences of discrimination can impact LGBTQ+ students and their academic and career decision-making process (Schneider & Dimito, 2010) potentially causing many students to delay or avoid planning. Counselors must be cognizant of the intersectionality of oppression, biases, and discrimination transgenders face in both the workplace and community (ALGBTIC, 2009; Scott et al., 2011) and be open to discussing the impact of these and other societal and institutional factors.

Helpers should strive to create a safe and nonjudgmental environment for students to explore and define their career goals (Scott et al., 2011). Rapport building is essential when establishing a safe space for students, and this includes being informed of significant LGTBQ+ terminology. Therapist should be knowledgeable of LGBTQ+ language such as transgender, gender identity, gender nonconforming, transsexuals, transvestites, and sexual orientation. Staying current on terms and civil rights legislation and organizations like the Human Rights Campaign and Out of Work (ALGBTIC, 2009; Scott et al., 2011) also enhance one's ability to understand the struggles LGBTQ+ students face and identify ways to advocate for them.

Counselors can also become an ally of the LGBTQ+ population by advocating for campus-wide trans-inclusive practices, laws, and policies, and informing other professionals and employers of LGBTQ+ issues and needs, whether career or mental health focused or the intersection of the two. Some students need resources and referrals for health care, social support, advocacy organizations, and financial aid while others need work on self-esteem (Sangganjanavanich & Headly, 2016). In general, counselors should be prepared to explore various topics with students including sessions focused on resume building and interview preparation. Counselors may also prepare a resource/service list that is nondiscriminatory and inclusive and supports both the developmental and career identities of LGBTQ+ students (Beck et al., 2016).

Counselors can further advocate for LGBTQ+ individuals by supporting guidelines and policies that will benefit LGBTQ+ students (i.e., gender transitions, name changes, using appropriate pronouns, and handling transphobic expressions and bullying; Sangganjanavanich & Headly, 2016). Additionally, practitioners can encourage and facilitate more ally and safe space trainings for all students, staff, and employees.

Finally, counselors can engage in more research to increase awareness of the issues the LGBTQ+ population face and to provide insight into training programs with best practices for supporting LGBTQ+ students as they matriculate and transition into postsecondary education and careers (Beck et al., 2016). With further research and support, practitioners can better assist LGTBQ+ individuals as they explore their identity and postsecondary options that enhance their overall career, college, and lifestyle development.

AN INTEGRATED, THEORY GROUNDED MODEL FOR CAREER COUNSELING WITH LGBTQ+ STUDENTS

In general, there is a lack of research specific to evidence-based career interventions with LGBTQ+ clients (Prince, 2013). The dearth of research in this area deteriorates further when attempting to identify research on efficacy of interventions for LGBTQ+ students in the K–12 school environment; to the authors knowledge, no such studies exist. In contrast to research on career interventions with this population, research on both evidence-based career interventions for youth and barriers to career development for LGBTQ+ individuals have strong support. This section will endeavor to assist school counselors with providing career and college readiness interventions by integrating two popular theories of career development to offer identity affirming career services with evidence-based interventions grounded in theory.

Rationale for Theories Discussed

Given the lack of research on effective interventions with gender and sexual minority/expansive (GSM) students, this section needs some form of foundation to offer evidence-based suggestions. First, Whiston et al. (2017) reported that career services are most effective when they possess the following aspects: (a) counselor support, (b) psychoeducation, (c) written exercises, (d) values clarification, (e) dialogue about assessment results, and (f) career exploration. Second, the interventions should be grounded in theory to support high quality service provision based on reliable research. Third, to best meet the needs of GSM students, the interventions and theories discussed should be modifiable to offer identity affirming counseling.

The CIP theory (Sampson et al., 2020) offers a model of career decision-making and career service delivery that is often preferred by school counselors (Osborn et al., 2004). This theory has been successfully adapted into a tiered service model, workshops, and a college career course that feature interventions meeting all the critical ingredients of effective career services outlined by Whiston et al. (2017). The model has also been successfully used in K–12 settings to facilitate career development in adolescents (Hughes, 2017), including adolescents of marginalized backgrounds (Osborn & Reardon, 2006), and it is a general theory so it can be modified to meet the needs of specific populations. Finally, the CIP model of service delivery allows more students to be given assistance than through individualized services alone and, therefore, meets a social justice need by reducing the cost associated with offering evidence-based career services (Sampson et al., 2011).

The PWT (Duffy et al., 2016) has revitalized vocational psychology by integrating an emphasis on social justice advocacy in career development with marginalized individuals. Key components of the PWT include the constructs of decent work and work volition. Decent work is defined by the International Labor Organization ([ILO], 2012) as work that provides an individual with "(a) physically and interpersonally safe working conditions (e.g., absent of physical, mental, or emotional abuse), (b) hours that allow for free time and adequate rest, (c) organizational values that complement family and social values, (d) adequate compensation, and (e) access to adequate health care" (p. 130). When an individual attains decent work, they are more likely to experience positive mental and physical health because their biopsychosocial needs are supported (Duffy et al., 2019). Work volition can be defined as the extent to which an individual believes they have freedom to choose their own career path (Duffy et al., 2016). Importantly, individuals of marginalized backgrounds experience deficits in work volition that often undermines their ability to attain decent work (Duffy et al., 2019). For example, research on PWT with GSM has identified that experiences of discrimination in this population is negatively associated with both work volition and decent work, and work volition has been observed to mediate a portion of the relationship between discrimination and decent work (Allan et al., 2019). Given the direct applicability of PWT to the needs of GSM individuals and the successful use of CIP in the K–12 setting, integration of these theories offers an excellent way to offer career counseling to LGBTQ+ students.

Cognitive Information Processing Theory

The CIP Pyramid

The Pyramid of Information Processing Domains (Sampson et al., 2020) represents the core knowledge components an individual draws upon to make a career decision (see Figure 12.1). It comprises four subsections: (a) knowledge of the self, (2) knowledge of options, (c) decision-making skills, and (d) executive processing. In its most basic and ideal form, a career decision is made when an individual identifies an option with acceptable fit to their knowledge of themselves.

The knowledge domains are the foundation of CIP. The self-knowledge domain includes, at a minimum, knowledge of one's interests, values, skills, and employment preferences. In the options knowledge domain, the individual stores information related to specific options from which they can choose as an outcome of a career decision (e.g., jobs, education, occupations, etc.). In the CIP framework, individuals must understand how their interests, values, and skills are either congruent or incongruent with their potential options under consideration.

The domain of decision-making includes generic information processing skills and strategies, this can be viewed as a toolkit from which an individual can select, either consciously or unconsciously, a way of interacting with information for comprehension, assimilation, and accommodation for the purpose of decision-making. In CIP theory, the CASVE cycle is explicitly taught as a method of decision-making conducive to high-quality decisions.

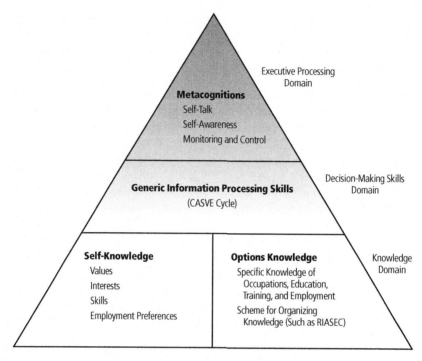

Figure 12.1 Pyramid of information processing domains in career decision-making. *Source:* Adapted from *Career development and services:* A cognitive approach (p.28), by G. W. Peterson, J. P. Sampson, and R. C. Reardon, Copyright 1991 by Brooks/Cole. Adapted with permission.

The executive processing domain is concerned with metacognition that acts as a governor of the decision-making process. At a minimum, the executive processing domain includes self-talk, self-awareness, and monitoring and control. Self-talk represents the common patterns and habits an individual has while thinking to themselves. Self-awareness refers to the amount and quality of the thoughts and feelings an individual has during their decision-making process. Monitoring is the experience an individual has of their internal states while engaging in a task and control refers to the ways an individual changes their thinking and actions to move themselves toward a desired state.

The CASVE Cycle
The CASVE cycle is a model career decision-making that outlines a series of decision-making phases (Sampson et al., 2020). This model offers career service providers and clients a scaffold for identifying the tasks a decider must accomplish during decision-making to help facilitate the selection of

interventions best suited to advancing through the cycle. The name for CASVE is an acronym that represents the five phases: (a) communication, (b) analysis, (c) synthesis, (d) valuing, and (e) execution (see Figure 12.2).

The *communication* phase begins when the individual determines there is a gap between their current career state and their desired career state. The *analysis* phase is characterized by information seeking and is marked by behaviors associated with career exploration. The purpose of this phase is to acquire sufficient information in the four domains of information processing for the individual to make an informed career decision. In the *synthesis* phase, the student engages in a process of matching the information in the self-knowledge domain to the information in the options knowledge domain, first by an expansion of the number of potential matches (elaboration) followed by a reduction of potential options to a manageable number of attractive options for simultaneous comparison (crystallization). During the *valuing* phase, the individual reviews the options with regards to themselves, their significant others, their cultural groups, their community, and society at large. Finally, the main goal of the *execution* phase is to create an actionable plan by which the student can achieve their first choice.

When using CIP theory to work with clients, whether in groups or individually, psychoeducation on the CIP Pyramid and CASVE are essential. The

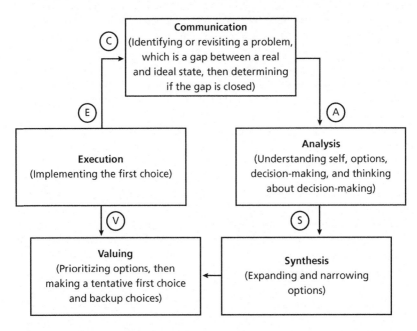

Figure 12.2 The CASVE cycle of career decision-making. *Source:* Adapted from Peterson et al., 1991, p. 28. Adapted with permission.

career service provider begins by informing the client(s) that, "In making a career choice, there are things you need to *know* and things you need to *do*" (Sampson et al., 2020, p. 12). When talking about "knowing," the service provider outlines the CIP Pyramid. When talking about "doing," the service provider outlines the CASVE cycle. Handouts with the CIP Pyramid and the CASVE cycle are very helpful during this process. Finally, the student is told that this system is designed to help them arrive at an informed and careful choice. Ideally, the use of this process will transfer such that the students will be able to reuse the process independently (Sampson et al., 2020).

Career Readiness

An assumption of CIP theory is the humanistic ideal that individuals can independently and consistently arrive at a high-quality career decision under ideal circumstances (Morgan et al., 2020). The word "ideal" in this case is key to understanding successful career services, as a variety of factors both internal and external to the client can act as barriers to this process. Therefore, when working with clients, it is vital to determine what level of services they might benefit from most.

The best practice for initial determination of the level of services most likely to assist a client in making a career decision is through assessment of career readiness (Sampson et al., 2004). Career readiness can be defined as "a person's preparation for engaging in the learning activities necessary to explore and decide between options" (Sampson et al., 2020, p. 16). Importantly, readiness changes over time and improvements in career readiness are an important outcome of career interventions based on CIP theory. Career readiness changes in response to an interaction of components of career readiness: capability and complexity. Capability is defined as the internal factors (e.g., mental health concerns) that either facilitate or hinder career problem-solving and decision-making. Complexity is defined by external factors (e.g., systemic discrimination) that either complicate or support career decision-making.

When an individual has internal factors that support career decision-making (i.e., high capability) and little external factors that complicate the situation (i.e., low complexity), then they are most appropriate for self-help services because this individual exists in the ideal state whereby decision-making will evolve independently. When an individual has an unfavorable disposition in either their capability or their complexity, then they would most likely benefit from some form of brief assistance. Brief assistance can be defined as a short-term intervention (i.e., no more than a few sessions that last 30 minutes or less) that terminates with the creation of a set of concrete goals through which an individual can complete the rest of the decision-making process independently. Finally, a student who presents with low capability and high complexity (e.g., a GSM student, with a mental health diagnosis, and parents who overtly express sexual orientation

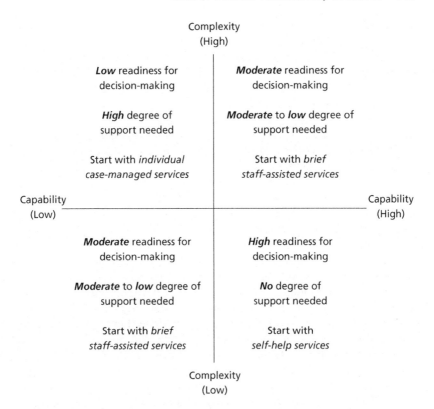

Figure 12.3 A two-dimensional model of decision-making readiness. *Source:* Adapted from Sampson et al., 2000, p. 161. Adapted with permission.

prejudices) is the least likely to overcome their career concern without individual career counseling.

Applying Needs of LGBTQ+ Students to the CIP Framework

The CIP framework has been used internationally to help students with career development (Osborn, 2020). The CIP model for service delivery (Sampson et al., 2004) can be broken down into seven steps: (a) initial interview, (b) preliminary assessment, (c) define problem and analyze causes, (d) formulate goals, (e) develop an individual learning plan (ILP), (f) execute the ILP, and (g) review and generalize.

1. Initial Interview

The initial interview is the entry into providing a career intervention and it has the dual purpose of developing a career-specific helping relationship and gaining contextual information about the client's career concern (Sampson et al., 2004). It is essential that basic practices associated with individual counseling (e.g., rapport building, the core conditions of therapy, behavioral observations, etc.) are integrated into this stage. Additionally, the data gathered in this step can give the attuned service provider initial ideas for areas of assessment.

We encourage the use of a nonspecific, open-ended question to begin this process such as, "What brings you in today?" This question allows the client to direct the course of the session while accepting a measure of responsibility for their choice and progress (Sampson et al., 2004). A specific, career-related statement or question (e.g., "Where can I find information on junior colleges in the state of Iowa?") is often an indication that the client has moderate to high career readiness, while an ambiguous response (e.g., "My mom said I need to talk about college.") might suggest a lower level of career readiness.

In working with LGBTQ+ students, it is essential to attend to personal assumptions associated with gender and sexual orientation or rapport could be damaged (Beck et al., 2016; Wada et al., 2019). Inappropriately labeling a client with incongruent gender pronouns or offering insensitive responses to a client who is questioning or conflicted about their sexual or gender identity can exacerbate a student's distress and negatively influence career readiness (American Psychological Association [APA], 2000). Importantly, do not assume that an individual of GSM status, or a student who is engaged in gender or sexual identity development, signifies low career readiness; an ethical career service provider will always engage in an assessment process while attending to personal biases before deciding the level of service provision.

2. Preliminary Assessment

A two-step process is best when assessing a client's career readiness in a quantitative manner (Sampson et al., 2004). A brief readiness screening is suggested first, followed by either more in-depth readiness assessment or directing the student toward resources they could use for independent career exploration and decision-making. In-depth career assessment should attend to both capability dimensions and complexity dimensions of the career problem (Sampson et al., 2020). Once readiness has been determined, the provider helps the client navigate into an appropriate level of service (Sampson et al., 2020).

Brief screening.   The Career State Inventory (Leierer et al., 2020) is a brief-screening instrument that can assist a helping professional in identifying whether a client should undergo more in-depth assessment. The instrument is constructed of three sets of questions that assess certainty, satisfaction, and clarity. The certainty item asks the client to list the number of options they are currently considering and whether they can rank their first choice. The satisfaction item uses a Likert scale to rank the client's level of satisfaction they feel for their preferred option identified in the certainty item. The clarity section consists of three true/false items that further identify whether the client has a sense of confidence related to their other responses. The open-access instrument can be obtained through the website for the Florida State University Career Center (see Leierer et al., 2020). The manual located at the provided link suggests that a cutoff score can be easily used to identify whether a client could benefit from additional screening.

In-depth assessment. Numerous career assessments can be meaningfully integrated during this phase. Sampson et al. (2015) identified 48 career-related assessments that are appropriate for this phase. The most common assessment associated with CIP that belongs in this session is the Career Thoughts Inventory ([CTI]; Sampson et al., 1996). Several instruments have also been developed in relation to PWT, but we will focus on the Work Volition Survey ([WVS]; Duffy et al., 2012). Ethical considerations are essential in the selection and interpretation of assessments with LGBTQQ+ clients (APA, 2000).

The CTI is a valid and reliable instrument that assesses negative career thoughts with 48 Likert-scaled items that represent thoughts that can impede the process of career decision-making (Sampson et al., 1996). In addition to a total score (i.e., overall level of negative career thoughts), the CTI includes subscales that assess decision making confusion (DMC), commitment anxiety (CA), and external conflict (EC). The DMC subscale measures difficulty with decision-making associated with distressing emotions and/or insufficient understanding of the decision-making process (Sampson et al., 1996). The CA scale measures anxiety that contributes to indecision because of worry about real or imagined consequences of making a specific choice. Finally, the EC scale can identify reluctance to assume responsibility for making a career decision caused by an imbalance in the importance of personal beliefs and values in comparison to beliefs and values of significant others.

In the career readiness model, the presence of negative career thoughts suggests low capability. The CTI total score is positively correlated with career indecision, career commitment, state-trait anxiety, and depression symptoms. Bullock-Yowell et al. (2012) observed significant correlations between the CTI subscales and environmental exploration measured with the CES (Stumpf et al., 1983), and self-appraisals and problem-solving as assessed with the Career Decision Making Self-Efficacy Scale (Betz & Luzzo, 1996). The CTI and the cognitive-behavioral therapy inspired CTI workbook can be acquired from PAR, Inc.

The WVS is a valid and reliable assessment that uses 15 Likert-scaled items to assess whether an individual perceives they have the freedom to choose their career path (Duffy et al., 2012). The instrument has a total score and two subscales. The first subscale ("Constraints") measures the extent to which individuals perceive barriers reducing their potential career options, the second subscale ("Volition") measures the confidence an individual has in their ability to choose an occupation. The WVS total score is positively correlated to career decision-making self-efficacy, core self-evaluations, career locus of control, and negatively correlated with career barriers and neuroticism. The WVS can be accessed open source through a website hosted by the creator of the instrument Dr. Ryan Duffy (www.drryanduffy.com). Research strongly suggests that scores on the WVS are highly sensitive to experiences of marginalization and financial strain (Duffy et al., 2019), therefore the WVS can be viewed as a quantitative measure of complexity.

3. Define the Problem and Analyze Causes

In adopting an approach with both CIP and PWT in mind, it is essential that the service provider and client collaborate to develop a mutual understanding of the problem (Blustein et al., 2019; Sampson et al., 2004). It is also important not to frame the problem in terms that pathologize the client, it is better to review the problem areas as opportunities for learning and growth that are associated with specific behaviors the client can either start or stop to help the client develop a sense of power (Sampson et al., 2004). Avoidance of pathologizing and building a sense of agency is vital when working with marginalized clients because doing otherwise could reinforce systemic oppression and internalized stigma (Blustein et al., 2019; Wynn & West-Olatunji, 2009). It is recommended that the service provider outline the concepts of the CIP Pyramid, the CASVE cycle, and decent work as an attainable goal during this phase.

4. Formulate Goals

It is useful to use the language of career readiness during goal creation with GSM students to help identify capability and complexity dimensions that align with (a) critical consciousness, (b) proactive engagement, and (c) social support and community engagement (Blustein et al., 2019). This process can be supported through the application of a strengths-based approach to understanding growth and well-being because it will further reduce a tendency to pathologize and support the development of client agency (Perrin et al., 2020). All goals should be structured to help the client strive toward greater independence in future career decision-making (Sampson et al., 2004).

5. Develop an Individual Learning Plan

An ILP is a structured worksheet that helps the service provider and the client develop a clear set of actionable steps (i.e., concrete and obtainable) that will help the client achieve their goals (Sampson et al., 2004). The specific form for the ILP can be found on the Florida State University Career Center website (https://career.fsu.edu/sites/g/files/upcbnu746/files/Individual%20Career%20Learning%20Plan.pdf). Collaboration remains the bedrock of ILP development, at the end of this process the student should view the service provider as (a) a supportive and caring advocate, (b) capable of offering them meaningful assistance, and (c) knowledgeable of resources that can be used to achieve their goals (Sampson et al., 2004). At minimum, an ILP should include: (a) reiteration of the collaborative goals, (b) identification of relevant activities/resources, (c) connecting activities to outcomes, (d) estimating time to completion, (e) connecting activities to goals, and (f) prioritizing activities. Clients sign that document as a symbol of ownership and their status as an equal partner in creation and completion of the plan (Sampson et al., 2004).

6. Execute the ILP

This phase of service provision is designed to further support client agency and growth (Sampson et al., 2004). The service provider should offer the minimal necessary support for the completion of the plan based on the client's readiness as identified during the assessment phase. When reviewing progress, it is useful to use the constructs of PWT and CIP to help the client ground and generalize their successes and what they have learned. This is an iterative process and additional activities can be planned as the client completes their plan.

7. Review and Generalize

The purpose of this phase is to reinforce the client's development of agency associated with successful completion of the ILP (Sampson et al., 2004). At a minimum, the process should include: (a) review of progress made, (b) identify client strengths and barriers overcome during the process, (c) process the emotional nature of termination, and (d) identify plans to continue client growth. In the context of CIP, there should be review of the client's learning and application of the CIP Pyramid and CASVE cycle to reinforce learning and support future independent problem solving (Sampson et al., 2004). In the context of PWT, there should be a review of how social engagement and proactive behaviors can be used to challenge and overcome systemic barriers to career development (Blustein et al., 2019).

CONCLUSION

Due to the various environmental, social, and developmental issues LGBTQ+ individuals encounter, school, career, and mental health counselors must consider several factors when assisting LGBTQ+ individuals in post-secondary transition. The outstanding societal challenges LGBTQ+ individuals face intensifies when encountering helpers unprepared or ill equipped to assist them. Limited resources and support of career and college readiness in K–12 settings may delay LGTBQ+ individuals' career, college, and lifestyle development (Beck et al., 2016). Therefore, it is essential that helping professionals are trained and equipped to assist LGBTQ+ individuals throughout the career development and exploration phases. CIP and PWT are presented as two evidence-based approaches effective for informed career decision-making, offering step by step guidelines for working with LGBTQ+ students.

The information and systematic approach to career services with LGBTQ+ youth outlined in this chapter can offer a way to meet the challenges currently posed by societal unrest caused by systemic oppression and the COVID-19 pandemic. Specifically, these crises have created a transformational inflection point and, if school counselors meet this challenge by providing support that builds critical consciousness and community connectedness, then LGBTQ+ students can develop skills to support their transition into the next phase of their lives. The CIP-based, structured approach to providing students with career services offers a step-by-step process for assessing a student's career readiness and integrating critical consciousness into career plans that build student's independence and hope for the future.

DISCUSSION QUESTIONS AND ACTIVITIES

1. What policies would you implement at your school to better support LGBTQ+ students?
2. Identify current (or past) LGBTQ+ legislation and its impact from an ecological systems approach (individual to community).
3. What is decent work? How can decent work be integrated into the CIP Pyramid and CASVE cycle to advocate for GSM students during career decision-making?
4. List and describe the seven stages of the CIP Model?
5. A lesbian student has a goal of finding an identity-affirming university for college. What are some activities you could list on an ILP to help this student reach her goal?

AUTHOR NOTE

Eunhui Yoon https://orcid.org/0000-0001-5085-0669
Michael Morgan, Jr. https://orcid.org/0000-0001-9820-7912

We have no known conflict of interest to disclose.

Correspondence concerning this book chapter should be addressed to Eunhui Yoon, Florida State University, 1114 W. Call street, Tallahassee, FL 32306. Email: eyoon@fsu.edu

REFERENCES

Abreu, R. L., Black, W. W., Mosley, D. V., & Fedewa, A. L. (2016). LGBTQ youth bullying experiences in schools: The role of school counselors within a system of oppression. *Journal of Creativity in Mental Health, 11*(3–4), 325–342.

Akkermans, J., Richardson, J., & Kraimer, M. L. (2020). The Covid-19 crisis as a career shock: Implications for careers and vocational behavior. *Journal of Vocational Behavior, 119*(May), 1–5. https://doi.org/10.1016/j.jvb.2020.103434

Allan, B. A., Tebbe, E. A., Bouchard, L. M., & Duffy, R. D. (2019). Access to decent and meaningful work in a sexual minority population. *Journal of Career Assessment, 27*(3), 408–421. https://doi.org/10.1177/1069072718758064

American Counseling Association. (2010). Competencies for counseling with transgender clients, *Journal of LGBT Issues in Counseling, 4*(3–4), 135–159. https://doi.org/10.1080/15538605.2010.524839

American Counseling Association. (2014). *ACA code of ethics.*

American Psychological Association. (2000). Guidelines for psychotherapy with lesbian, gay, and bisexual clients. *American Psychologist, 55*(12), 1440–1451. https://doi.org/10.1037/0003-066x.55.12.1440

Association of Lesbian, Gay, Bisexual, and Transgender Issues in Counseling. (2009). *Competencies for counseling with transgender clients.* American Counseling Association. https://www.counseling.org/docs/default-source/competencies/algbtic _competencies.pdf?sfvrsn=d8d3732f_12

Autin, K. L., Blustein, D. L., Ali, S. R., & Garriott, P. O. (2020). Career development impacts of COVID-19 : Practice and policy recommendations. *Journal of Career Development, 47*(5), 487–494. https://doi.org/10.1177/0894845320944486

Barber, J. S., & Mobley, M. (1999). Counseling gay adolescents. In A. M. Horne & M. S. Kiselica (Eds.), *Handbook of counseling boys and adolescent males: A practitioner's guide* (pp. 161–178). SAGE Publications. https://doi.org/10.4135/9781452220390.n10

Barnes, D. M., & Meyer, I. H. (2012). Religious affiliation, internalized homophobia, and mental health in lesbians, gay men, and bisexuals. *American Journal of Orthopsychiatry, 82*(4), 505–515. https://doi.org/10.1111/j.1939-0025.2012.01185.x

Beck, M. J., Rausch, M. A., Lane, E. M., & Wood, S. M. (2016). College, career, and lifestyle development with students who are LGBQQ: Strategies for school counselors. *Journal of LGBT Issues in Counseling, 10*(4), 197–210. https://doi.org/10.1080/15538605.2016.1233838

Betz, N. E., & Luzzo, D. A. (1996). Career assessment and the career decision-making self-efficacy scale. *Journal of Career Assessment, 4*(4), 413–428. https://doi.org/10.1177/106907279600400405

Blustein, D. L., Kenny, M. E., Autin, K., & Duffy, R. (2019). The psychology of working in practice: A theory of change for a new era. *Career Development Quarterly*, 67(3), 236–254. https://doi.org/10.1002/cdq.12193

Bontempo, D. E., & D'Augelli, A. R. (2002). Effects of at-school victimization and sexual orientation on lesbian, gay, or bisexual youths' health risk behavior. *Journal of Adolescent Health*, 30(5), 364–374. https://doi.org/10.1016/S1054-139X(01)00415-3

Birkett, M., Espelage, D. L., & Koenig, B. (2009). LGB and questioning students in schools: The moderating effects of homophobic bullying and school climate on negative outcomes. *Journal of Youth and Adolescence*, 38(7), 989–1000. https://doi.org/10.1007/s10964-008-9389-1

Bullock-Yowell, E., Katz, S. P., Reardon, R. C., & Peterson, G. W. (2012). The roles of negative career thinking and career problem-solving self-efficacy in career exploratory behavior. *The Professional Counselor*, 2(2), 102–114. https://doi.org/10.15241/eby.2.2.102

Cech, E. A., & Rothwell, W. R. (2020). LGBT workplace inequality in the federal workforce: Intersectional processes, organizational contexts, and turnover considerations. *ILR Review*, 73(1), 25–60. https://doi.org/10.1177/0019793919843508

Clarke, H. M., & Arnold, K. A. (2018). The influence of sexual orientation on the perceived fit of male applicants for both male-and female-typed jobs. *Frontiers In Psychology*, 9, 656 https://doi.org/10.3389/fpsyg.2018.00656

Diemer, M. A., Pinedo, A., Bañales, J., Mathews, C. J., Frisby, M. B., Harris, E. M., & McAlister, S. (2021). Recentering action in critical consciousness. *Child Development Perspectives*, 15(1), 12–17. https://doi.org/10.1111/cdep.12393

Duffy, R. D., Blustein, D. L., Diemer, M. A., & Autin, K. L. (2016). The psychology of working theory. *Journal of Counseling Psychology*, 63(2), 127–148. https://doi.org/10.1037/cou0000140

Duffy, R. D., Diemer, M. A., Perry, J. C., Laurenzi, C., & Torrey, C. L. (2012). The construction and initial validation of the work volition scale. *Journal of Vocational Behavior*, 80(2), 400–411. https://doi.org/10.1016/j.jvb.2011.04.002

Duffy, R. D., Gensmer, N., Allan, B. A., Kim, H. J., Douglass, R. P., England, J. W., Autin, K. L., & Blustein, D. L. (2019). Developing, validating, and testing improved measures within the psychology of working theory. *Journal of Vocational Behavior*, 112, 199–215. https://doi.org/10.1016/j.jvb.2019.02.012

Gedro, J. (2009). LGBT career development. *Advances in Developing Human Resources*, 11(1), 54–66. https://doi.org/10.1177/1523422308328396

Goodrich, K. M., & Luke, M. (2009). LGBTQ responsive school counseling. *Journal of LGBT Issues in Counseling*, 3(2), 113–127. https://doi.org/10.1080/15538600903005284

Goodman, R. D., & West-Olatunji, C. A. (2009). Applying critical consciousness: Culturally competent disaster response outcomes. *Journal of Counseling & Development*, 87(4), 458–465. https://doi.org/10.1002/j.1556-6678.2009.tb00130.x

Gottfredson, L. S. (1981). Circumscription and compromise: A developmental theory of occupational aspirations. *Journal of Counseling Psychology*, 28(6), 545–579. https://psycnet.apa.org/doi/10.1037/0022-0167.28.6.545

Gower, A. L., Forster, M., Gloppen, K., Johnson, A. Z., Eisenberg, M. E., Connett, J. E., & Borowsky, I. W. (2018). School practices to foster LGBT-supportive climate: Associations with adolescent bullying involvement. *Prevention Science, 19*(6), 813–821.

Hancock, A. J., Clarke, H. M., & Arnold, K. A. (2020). Sexual orientation occupational stereotypes. *Journal of Vocational Behavior, 119*(June 2019), 103427. https://doi.org/10.1016/j.jvb.2020.103427

Heberle, A. E., Rapa, L. J., Farago, F., & Austin, S. F. (2020). Supplemental material for critical consciousness in children and adolescents: A systematic review, critical assessment, and recommendations for future research. *Psychological Bulletin, 146*(6), 525–551. https://doi.org/10.1037/bul0000230.supp

Heiden-Rootes, K., Wiegand, A., Thomas, D., Moore, R. M., & Ross, K. A. (2020). A national survey on depression, internalized homophobia, college religiosity, and climate of acceptance on college campuses for sexual minority adults. *Journal of Homosexuality, 67*(4), 435–451. https://doi.org/10.1080/00918369.2018.1550329

Hetherington, C., Hillerbrand, E., & Etringer, B. D. (1989). Career counseling with gay men: Issues and recommendations for research. *Journal of Counseling & Development, 67*(8), 452–454. https://doi.org/10.1002/j.1556-6676.1989.tb02115.x

Higa, D., Hoppe, M. J., Lindhorst, T., Mincer, S., Beadnell, B., Morrison, D. M., Wells, E. A., Todd, A., & Mountz, S. (2014). Negative and positive factors associated with the well-being of lesbian, gay, bisexual, transgender, queer, and questioning (LGBTQ) youth. *Youth & Society, 46*(5), 663–687. https://doi-org.proxy.lib.fsu.edu/10.1177/0044118X12449630

House, C. (2004). Integrating barriers to Caucasian lesbians' career development and super's life-span, life-space approach. *Career Development Quarterly, 52*, 246–255. https://doi.org/10.1002/j.2161-0045.2004.tb00646.x

Hughes, C. (2017). *Career work in schools: Cost-effective career services.* Australian Academic Press Group Pty. Ltd.

International Labor Organization. (2012). *Decent work indicators: Concepts and definitions.* https://www.ilo.org/wcmsp5/groups/public/—dgreports/—integration/documents/publication/wcms_229374.pdf

Kite, M. E., & Deaux, K. (1987). Gender belief systems: Homosexuality and the implicit inversion theory. *Psychology of Wmen Quarterly, 11*(1), 83–96. https://doi.org/10.1111%2Fj.1471-6402.1987.tb00776.x

Kosciw, J. G., Greytak, E. A., Zongrone, A. D., Clark, C. M., & Truong, N. L. (2018). *The 2017 national school climate survey: The experiences of lesbian, gay, bisexual, transgender, and queer youth in our nation's schools.* Gay, Lesbian, and Straight Education Network (GLSEN). https://eric.ed.gov/?id=ED590243

Kull, R. M., Greytak, E. A., Kosciw, J. G., & Villenas, C. (2016). Effectiveness of school district antibullying policies in improving LGBT youths' school climate. *Psychology of Sexual Orientation and Gender Diversity, 3*(4), 407.

Leierer, S. J., Peterson, G. W., Reardon, R. C., & Osborn, D. S. (2020). *The career state inventory (CSI) as a measure of the career decision state and readiness for career decision making: A manual for assessment, administration, and intervention* (2nd edition). https://career.fsu.edu/sites/g/files/upcbnu746/files/TR-60.pdf

Lindley, L. (2006). The paradox of self-efficacy: Research with diverse populations. *Journal of Career Assessment, 14*(1), 143–160. https://doi.org/10.1177/1069 072705281371

Lonborg, S. D., & Phillips, J. M. (1996). Investigating the career development of gay, lesbian, and bisexual people: Methodological considerations and recommendations. *Journal of Vocational Behavior, 48*(2), 176–194. https://doi.org/ 10.1006/jvbe.1996.0017

Magrath, R. (Ed.). (2019). *LGBT athletes in the sports media.* Palgrave Macmillan. https://link.springer.com/book/10.1007%2F978-3-030-00804-8

McKinney, R., Desposito, M., & Yoon, E. (2020). Promoting identity wellness in LG-BTGEQIAP+ adolescents through affirmative therapy. *Journal of LGBT Issues in Counseling, 14*(3), 176–190. https://doi.org/10.1080/15538605.2020.1790464

Morgan, M. J., Langford, Z. D., & Osborn, D. A. (2020). A novel approach to modeling career decision making. *Proceedings of the 24th World Multi-Conference on Systemics, Cybernetics, and Informatics* (WMSCI 2020), 1–6. www.iiis.org/CDs2020/ CD2020Summer/papers/CK673YZ.pdf

National Career Development Association. (2015). *2015 NCDA code of ethics.* https:// www.ncda.org/aws/NCDA/asset_manager/get_file/3395

Ng, E. S., & Rumens, N. (2017). Diversity and inclusion for LGBT workers: Current issues and new horizons for research. *Canadian Journal of Administrative Sciences/Revue Canadienne des Sciences de l'Administration, 34*(2), 109–120. https://doi .org/10.1002/cjas.1443

Osborn, D.S. (2020). International use of CIP theory in career interventions [Special Issue]. *Career Development Network Journal, 35*(4), 1–124.

Osborn, D. S., & Baggerly, J. N. (2004). School counselors' perceptions of career counseling and career testing: Preferences, priorities, and predictors. *Journal of Career Development, 31*(1), 45–59. https://link.springer.com/article/10.1023/B:JOCD .0000036705.02911.df

Osborn, D. S., & Reardon, R. C. (2006). Using the self-directed search: Career explorer with high-risk middle school students. *Career Development Quarterly, 54*(3), 269–273. https://doi.org/10.1002/j.2161-0045.2006.tb00158.x

Perrin, P. B., Sutter, M. E., Trujillo, M. A., & Henry, R. S. (2020). The minority strengths model: Development and initial path analytic validation in racially/ ethnically diverse LGBTQ individuals. *Journal of Clinical Psychology, 76*(1), 118–136. https://doi.org/10.1002/jclp.22850

Peterson, G. W., Sampson, J. P., & Reardon, R. C. (1991). *Career development and services: A cognitive approach.* Thomas Brooks/Cole Publishing.

Pope, M. (1996). Gay and lesbian career counseling: Special career counseling issues. *Journal of Gay & Lesbian Social Services, 4*(4), 91–106. https://doi.org/10 .1300/J041v04n04_06

Pope, M., Barret, B., Szymanski, D. M., Chung, Y. B., Singaravelu, H., McLean, R., & Sanabria, S. (2004). Culturally appropriate career counseling with gay and lesbian clients. *The Career Development Quarterly, 53*(2), 158–177. https://doi .org/10.1002/j.2161-0045.2004.tb00987.x

Prince, J. N. (2013). Career development of lesbian, gay, bisexual, and transgender individuals. In S. D. Brown & R. W. Lent (Eds.), *Career development and counseling: Putting theory and research to work* (2nd ed., pp. 275–298). John Wiley & Sons.

Rumens, N. (2011). Minority support: Friendship and the development of gay and lesbian managerial careers and identities. *Equality, Diversity and Inclusion: An International Journal, 30*(6), 444–462. https://doi.org/10.1108/0261 0151111157684

Russell, S. T., Ryan, C., Toomey, R. B., Diaz, R. M., & Sanchez, J. (2011). Lesbian, gay, bisexual, and transgender adolescent school victimization: Implications for young adult health and adjustment. *The Journal of School Health, 81*(5), 223–230. https://doi-org.proxy.lib.fsu.edu/10.1111/j.1746-1561.2011.00583.x

Sampson, J., Dozier, V., & Colvin, G. (2011). Translating career theory to practice: The risk of unintentional social injustice. *Journal of Counseling and Development, 89*(3), 326–337. https://doi.org/10.1002/j.1556-6678.2011.tb00097.x

Sampson, J. P., Jr., Hou, P. C., McClain, M.-C., Musch, E., & Reardon, R. C. (2015). *A partial listing of measures that can be used as a component of readiness assessment.* Florida State University, Center for the Study of Technology in Counseling and Career Development. https://career.fsu.edu/sites/g/files/imported/storage/original/application/f2b70a88a287c1ce0f6b0d2563d6b288.pdf

Sampson, J. P., Osborn, D. S., Bullock-Yowell, E., Janet, G., Peterson, G. W., Reardon, R. C., Dozier, V. C., Leierer, S. J., Hayden, S. C. W., & Saunders, D. E. (2020). *An introduction to CIP theory, research, and practice* (Technical Report No. 62). Florida State University Libraries. http://fsu.digital.flvc.org/islandora/object/fsu%3A749259

Sampson, J. P., Jr., Peterson, G. W., Lenz, J. G., Reardon, R. C., & Saunders, D. E. (1996). *Career thoughts inventory: Professional manual.* Psychological Assessment Resources.

Sampson, J. P., Peterson, G. W., Reardon, R. C., & Lenz, J. G. (2000). Using readiness assessment to improve career services: A cognitive information processing approach. *The Career Development Quarterly, 49*(2), 161. https://doi.org/10.1002/j.2161-0045.2000.tb00556.x

Sampson, J. P., Reardon, R. C., Peterson, G. W., & Lenz, J. G. (2004). *Career counseling and services: A cognitive information processing approach.* Brooks Cole.

Sangganjanavanich, V. F., & Headly, J. A. (2016). Career development of transgender college students pursuing gender transition. *Career Planning and Adult Development Journal. 16*(1). 161–168.

Schmidt, C. K., & Nilsson, J. E. (2006). The effects of simultaneous developmental processes: Factors relating to the career development of lesbian, gay, and bisexual youth. *The Career Development Quarterly, 55*(1), 22–37. https://doi.org/10.1002/j.2161-0045.2006.tb00002.x

Schneider, M., & Dimito, A. (2010). Factors influencing the career and academic choices of lesbian, gay, bisexual, and transgender people. *Journal of Homosexuality, 57*(10), 1355–1369. https://doi.org/10.1080/00918369.2010.517080

Scott, D. A., Belke, S. L., & Barfield, H. G. (2011). Career development with transgender college students: Implications for career and employment counselors. *Journal of Employment Counseling, 48*(3). https://doi.org/10.1002/j.2161-1920.2011.tb01116.x

Stumpf, A., Colarelli, S. M., & Hartman, K. (1983). Development of the career exploration survey (CES). *Journal of Vocational Behavior, 226*(2), 191–226. https://doi.org/10.1016/0001-8791(83)90028-3

Tomlinson, M. J., & Fassinger, R. E. (2003). Career development, lesbian identity development, and campus climate among lesbian college students. *Journal of College Student Development, 44*(6), 845–860. https://doi.org/10.1353/csd .2003.0078

Varjas, K., Mahan, W. C., Meyers, J., Birckbichler, L., Lopp, G., & Dew, B. J. (2006). Assessing school climate among sexual minority high school students. *Journal of LGBT Issues in Counseling, 1*(3), 49–75. https://doi.org/10.1300/ J462v01n03_05

Wada, K., Mcgroarty, E. J., & Amundsen-Dainow, E. (2019). Affirmative career counselling with transgender and gender nonconforming clients: A social justice perspective orientation professionnelle affirmative auprès de clients transgenres et transsexuels: Une perspective de justice sociale. *Canadian Journal of Counselling and Psychotherapy, 53*(3), 255–275. https://orcid .org/0000-0002-2138-5670

West-Olatunji, C., Yoon, E., Shure, L., Pringle, R., & Adams, T. (2020). Exploring how school counselor position low-income African American girls as mathematics and science learners: Findings from year two data. In B. Polnick, J. Ballenger, B. J. Irby, & N. Abdelrahman (Eds.), *Girls and women of color in STEM: Navigating the double bind in K–12 education* (pp. 207–228). Information Age Publishing.

Whiston, S. C., Li, Y., Goodrich Mitts, N., & Wright, L. (2017). Effectiveness of career choice interventions: A meta-analytic replication and extension. *Journal of Vocational Behavior, 100* (June 2017), 175–184. https://doi.org/10.1016/j .jvb.2017.03.010

Wynn, R., & West-Olatunji, C. (2009). Use of culture-centered counseling theory with ethnically diverse LGBT Clients. *Journal of LGBT Issues in Counseling, 3*(3–4), 198–214. https://doi.org/10.1080/15538600903317218

CHAPTER 13

BLACK STUDENT ATHLETES

Readiness Versus Eligibility

Paul C. Harris
The Pennsylvania State University

Joseph M. Williams
University of Virginia

Chauncey Smith
University of Virginia

Miray D. Seward
University of Virginia

Liana Elopre
University of Virginia

Ellie C. Wengert
University of Virginia

Joshua Rauguth
Ball State University

Equity-Based Career Development and Postsecondary Transitions, pages 325–344
Copyright © 2022 by Information Age Publishing
www.infoagepub.com
All rights of reproduction in any form reserved.

ABSTRACT

What does it mean to be college and career ready? How do we ensure that Black student athletes are not just eligible for intercollegiate athletic competition, but ready for college and career upon graduation from high school? The National Collegiate Athletic Association (NCAA) has incrementally increased the academic standards that graduating high school seniors needed to meet in order to participate in intercollegiate athletics. However, despite the NCAA's best efforts and intentions, such eligibility criteria do not always equate to college and career readiness, especially for Black student athletes. Black student athletes are disproportionately socialized to identify exclusively with athletics, which ultimately precludes them from forming a multidimensional sense of self, a critical indicator of college and career readiness (Baker & Hawkins, 2016). To be clear, the problem is not sports participation, but instead a system that exploits the labor of Black student athletes (Cooper, 2019). As such, cultivating identity development for Black student athletes using an anti-racist framework can lead to sports being added value to their educational experience and ultimately aiding their thriving in and out of sport. The authors describe the difference between being eligible for NCAA competition and being ready for college and career. Further, the authors emphasize identity formation as a critical indicator for college and career readiness, and detail the ways in which targeted attention to Black student athlete identity development can contribute to more positive educational outcomes. An anti-racist paradigm is introduced to inform the efforts of all educators, and particularly school counselors. Future research, policy, and practice recommendations are provided.

College and career readiness (CCR) has long been a focus of state and national dialogue (Conley, 2010; Roderick et al., 2009; Harris et al., 2016).

> A student who is ready for college and career can qualify for and succeed in entry-level, credit bearing college courses leading to a baccalaureate or certificate, or career pathway-oriented training programs without the need for remedial or developmental coursework. (Conley, 2012, p. 1)

The racial dispatiy in such readiness is readily apparent in part by only 80% of Black students completing high school, versus 89% of their White counterparts (The U.S. Department of Commerce, 2021). Further, such disparities are only exacerbated when athletics is considered (Beamon & Bell, 2006; Cooper, 2016; McDougle & Capers, 2012). As Black male student-athletes, in particular, move from junior varsity to varsity sports in high school or varsity in high school to college, college enrollment and college graduation is adversely affected, especially in basketball and football where they are overrepresented (Harper, 2018; Harris et al., 2014; McDougle & Capers, 2012). Black student athletes are more likely to enroll in college with lower high school GPAs and lower pre-college admission test scores, whether that be the SAT or ACT (Cooper, 2016). These students also earn lower GPAs in college and are much less likely to graduate than their White teammates (Cooper, 2016). Specifically, 55.2% of Black male student athletes graduate from college within 6 years as compared to 69.3% of student athletes overall (Harper, 2018).

To be clear, racial disparities in CCR are not due to a lack of capability of Black students. Rather, it reflects the long-standing issue of systemic racism that permeates all of society, including education (Holcomb-McCoy, 2007). Whether low teacher expectations, biased gifted and talented program selection processes, culturally insensitive disciplinary practices, or inappropriate gatekeeping for advanced course access, Black students and their families are challenged with navigating a system that is not set up for them to thrive (Cooper, 2016; Holcomb-Mccoy, 2007). In order for meaningful change to occur, educators must work intentionally to disrupt the status quo and dismantle these racist systems. Moreover, Black student athletes may fall prey to being eligible for intercollegiate athletic competition without being ready for the rigors of college and career if their unique needs are not served through an anti-racist framework.

AN ANTI-RACIST LENS FOR EDUCATORS

Black student athletes' CCR are often explained in terms of student deficits (e.g., lack of individual effort, motivation, interest, and devalue of education; ACT, 2016; Harper, 2018; Harris, 2014). However, such explanations are not grounded in an understanding of the historical, economic, sociopolitical, and moral decisions and policies that contribute to racial inequalities in academic achievement and educational attainment for Black and Latinx students (Ladson-Billings, 2006). In contrast, viewing the same phenomenon through an anti-racist lens allows us to see how the use of power by individuals, schools, and institutions has led to the steady decline in CCR of Black K–12 students, particularly Black student athletes.

Anti-Racism is defined as the practice of identifying, challenging, and changing the values, structures, and behaviors that perpetuate systemic racism and its residual effects (Kishimoto, 2018). These structures contribute to inequitable education outcomes for Black student athletes (Harper, 2018). An anti-racist lens leads us to look at the historical roots for both explanations and solutions to the steady decline in Black student athletes' CCR. Whether we are aware of it or not, we all look through a particular set of lenses. We encourage educators to use this lens when promoting the CCR of Black student athletes. When looking through an anti-racist lens, educators can see how race influences college and career opportunities and aspirations; access to resources, and the representation and respect that Black student athletes receive.

Moreover, an anti-racist lens helps bring a historical, social, and political perspective to understanding and solving Black student-athletes' plight. Asking the following questions can open a useful discussion on the significance of race and racism in athletics, its harmful impact on Black student athletes, and potential areas to intervene. What was the political, social, economic, and racial context in the United States and the world as Black athletes integrated collegiate and professional sports? How do those challenges parallel the current struggles of Black student athletes (e.g., formal and informal rules that either precluded or severely limited Black students' participation in sports at predominantly White colleges and universities)? Who has historically profited from revenue generated by sports? How has sports promoted racist ideologies in U.S. society? How has racism in sports contributed to the marginalization of the academic, social, and psychological well-being of the Black student athlete? How do past and current racial ideologies influence how Black athletes are assessed in society and science (e.g., the myth that Black athletes' achievements are due to biology and natural physical abilities)? How do sports mirror America's attitude toward race? How does the current COVID-19 pandemic exacerbate the educational challenges experienced by Black student athletes and why? What does the negative reaction to Black athletes' protests about the multiple killings of unarmed Black men say about society's view of Black athletes? How might the increasing economic concerns due to the pandemic highlight and perpetuate the exploitative nature of sports for Black males? The most important feature of an anti-racist lens is that it helps educators see how situations can be transformed and how injustices can be reversed. It draws attention to how power can be used and is used at the individual, schools, and institutional levels for change (Lee et al., 1997).

COLLEGE AND CAREER READINESS

To ensure that Black student athletes are ready for college and career and not just eligible for athletic participation, an anti-racist paradigm must be superimposed on all traditional CCR models, most of which have been developed and conceptualized through White norms. Conley's (2010) four keys to CCR, for example, is a useful lens through which to view CCR, in general: are relevant for effectively preparing Black student athletes: (a) key content knowledge, (b) key cognitive strategies, (c) key learning skills and techniques, and (d) key transition knowledge and skills. The American School Counselor Association also designed a set of 35 K–12 CCR standards for every student (American School Counselor Association [ASCA], 2014).

These frameworks should first provoke our beginning to understand how Black student athletes' acquisition of such skills are greatly compromised by systemic racism throughout their educational experiences. The National Office for School Counselor Advocacy's (2010) 8 components of CCR counseling, geared specifically toward underrepresented students, add to these frameworks in meaningful ways: (a) college aspirations, (b) academic planning for college and career readiness, (c) enrichment and extracurricular engagement, (d) college and career exploration and selection processes, (e) college and career assessments, (f) college affordability planning, (g) college and career admissions processes, and (h) transition from high school graduation to college enrollment.

A thread through each of these and other approaches to CCR that is particularly critical for Black student athletes, though, is the importance of identity development. It is particularly important for Black student athletes to develop a multi-dimensional sense of self in order for them to thrive in and out of their athletic endeavors. While sports participation is not inherently problematic, its potential to be exploitive is more prevalent in the lives of Black student athletes than other groups (Cooper, 2019; Harper, 2018; Harris, 2020; Rhoden, 2006). Certainly, all education stakeholders can play a role in embracing an anti-racist framework to ensure that sports participation can be the useful mobilizing mechanism it can be for Black student athletes. School counselors, in particular, can play a crucial role, given their training in and emphasis on CCR and particular training in human development and multicultural counseling (ASCA, 2014). For example, school counselors can conduct faculty in-service training where they highlight the importance of reinforcing more than just the athletic identity of Black male student athletes in their engagement of them in the classroom. Given the unique presence of school counselors in the lives of all students as they navigate the college-going process, and NCAA eligibility requirements as appropriate for student athletes, school counselors can also facilitate the empowerment of Black student athletes in high school through individual counseling and group counseling as well.

BLACK STUDENT ATHLETE PARTICIPATION AND SUCCESS

Researchers advocate for underserved students to participate in athletics because of the potential academic benefits that can come through the experience, including but not limited to confidence and resilience on the field and in the classroom (Beamon & Bell, 2006; Jordan, 1999; Gawrysiak et al., 2015; Lee, 1983). According to Lumpkin and Favor (2012), 81% of all high school student athletes report a GPA of 3.0 or higher compared to 70.9% of non-athletes achieving the same GPA. However, the reality is that this potential is not always realized with Black student athletes and has not been for decades (Jordan, 1999; Lumpkin & Favor, 2012; May, 2004). The NCAA enacted Proposition 48 in 1986 which outlined certain requirements for student athletes to be eligible to play Division 1 college sports. At that time, according to a comprehensive study by the NCAA, 46% of Black males and 51% of Black females met those requirements while 91% of White males and 91% of White females met the same requirements (Baumann & Henschen, 1986; Nwadike et al., 2016). Researchers (Harris, 2014; Harper 2018) contend that such disparities persist in many forms, not the least of which included college enrollment and graduation. Educators must redress such inequities with intentional and purposeful interventions.

Comeaux and Harrison's (2011) model for college student athlete academic success suggests that sports can create a way for students to find community within their educational journey by creating a sense of belonging and personal involvement (Comeaux & Harrison, 2011). While this specific model pertains more to the college student athlete, it also considers individual pre-college experiences, making its relevance to the high school athlete clear. Athletic involvement can expose student athletes to a new, supportive environment that can enrich not only their passion for their sport but also their interest and success in their education (Jordan, 1999). It can be a space within which Black students can build their skills to succeed in and out of the classroom as they navigate their secondary school experience (Eide & Ronan, 2001; Gawrysiak et al., 2015; Jordan, 1999). In short, athletics can bring meaning to a student's time at school on an academic level (Beamon & Bell, 2006; Jordan, 1999). However, this should be a collective effort from all stakeholders involved in a student's education. Black student athletes feeling that they matter in all aspects of their time at school is crucial to their academic success (Tucker et al., 2010).

BLACK STUDENT IDENTITY FORMATION

As we discuss the current status and potential of Black student athletes as it relates to their achievements in classrooms and athletic venues, on college campuses and in their future careers, it is imperative that we attend to a central question present in their minds: Who am I? This question and all of its associated answers refer to identity, which shapes how adolescents and emerging adults experience the world. The answers to it also undergird decisions that inform performance across multiple social contexts. As we center the humanity of Black student athletes, it is important to note the special ways that they understand and negotiate their identity—especially across academic and athletic contexts.

For more than half a century, scholars have examined how Black citizens in the United States make meaning of their identity in a country that has dehumanized Black people centuries prior to its declaration of independence (Byrd, 2011). In particular, scholars have noted that Black children and the families that support them are tasked with developing a racial identity that assesses their self-worth, appraises how Black people are viewed as a group, and imagines a path toward progress. Racial identity matters for the survival of Black children and is linked to mental health, physiological health, and academic outcomes among other dimensions of well-being (Willis & Neblett, 2019; Yip et al., 2019).

Unfortunately, Black students report racial discrimination from their peers, teachers, and other school staff as a normal and mundane element of their daily experiences in school (Leath et al., 2019; Smith & Hope, 2020). From disciplinary gaps to opportunity gaps, aspects of the school context can be toxic to Black students' well-being (Gale & Dorsey, 2020; Gray et al., 2020). It is also important to note the role of gender in Black students' school experiences. For example, Black boys and girls negotiate the weights of different stereotypes (Mims & Williams, 2020; Smith & Hope, 2020) and the role of racial identity can function differently across gender (e.g., Butler et al., 2018). Although Black students are rendered vulnerable, scholars have noted the role of racial identity in mitigating some of the harmful effects of racial discrimination in the school context (e.g., Butler et al., 2018; Leath et al., 2019). For example, it is expected that there is a negative relationship between Black students' school-based racial discrimination and favored academic outcomes (e.g., motivation, curiosity, engagement, performance); however, students' positive beliefs and appraisals around being Black tend to dampen the magnitude of that negative relationship. Beyond the statistics associated with these studies, let us imagine a Black student who hears negative comments about Black people or witnesses references to harmful stereotypes about Black people at least once a week at school. That creates a harmful school environment and may impact their motivation to achieve, their engagement or sense of belonging at school, their confidence, and eventually their grades and test scores. The hope of racial identity applied to the school context is that in the face of those harmful messages, they can remember and access their positive beliefs and histories about being Black—and that the harmful messages would lose their power in driving their academic outcomes.

In addition to the role of racial identity, Black student athletes are also tasked with making sense of: What does it mean to be a Black student athlete? As athletes, Black youth must contend with how much they identify with their role as athletes (Brewer et al., 1993). Athletic identity has been linked with athletic performance (Horton & Mack, 2000), academic performance (Bimper, 2014; Huml et al., 2019), career readiness (Lally & Kerr,

2005; Moiseichik et al., 2019), and the transition out of sport (Beamon, 2012). In particular, Black student athletes with high athletic identity centrality report lower levels of racial identity centrality, suggesting that athletics has the potential to downplay the salience of race for student athletes (Brown et al., 2003). While this work examined Black student athletes more broadly, it does not speak to the different ways athletic and racial identity may be functioning for Black male and female student athletes.

Athletics provides a potentially positive context for Black youth's development. Offering an environment that leads to the development of teamwork, time management, leadership skills, working under pressure and more, participation in athletics offers a lot of benefits to Black youth. However it is imperative that Black youth are socialized in environments that foster and support their multiple identities. If Black youth are only praised for their athletics pursuits, they have the potential to become identity foreclosed (i.e., high identity commitment with little identity exploration) as a result of their environment only presenting one path to success (Anthony & Swank, 2018; Beamon, 2012; Beamon & Bell, 2006; Fuller et al., 2020; Harrison et al., 2011). Inherently, athletics are not detrimental for the development of Black student athletes. Without support for other identities and outlets, Black youth may over-prioritize athletics. Previous work has pointed to an inverse relationship between athletic identity and racial identity, where those with high athletic identity centrality had low racial identity centrality (Brown et al., 2003; Jackson et al., 2002). This high centrality speaks to the deep immersion and indoctrination into sports that Black student athletes can experience at the expense of the centrality of their race.

Influential others (e.g., school counselors, coaches, teachers, parents/guardians) can help Black female student athletes to effectively negotiate their intersecting identities (Black and female) and face simultaneous barriers (racism, sexism, classism, poor media coverage, lack of exposure, geographic perceptions; Bruening et al., 2008). Thus, those working closely with Black student athletes must intentionally work to foster the development and exploration of multiple identities (e.g., academic identity, racial identity) for Black youth in addition to just sport. This more holistic development will allow Black student athletes to not only arrive at college eligible, but ready.

NCAA ELIGIBILITY VS. READINESS

Even when prospective student athletes are eligible to play college sports according to the NCAA Eligibility Center standards, they are not necessarily prepared to succeed in college and beyond (Harris, 2020). The unfortunate reality is that when athletic development is prioritized, academics are often compromised (Carodine et al., 2001; Hosick & Sproull, 2012). The landscape of education has become more equity-focused in recent decades, with issues of racial justice and educational opportunity becoming "complementary cornerstone values of American life"; nevertheless, there is ample evidence to say that athletics have risen to take equal or greater priority in the landscape of higher education (Bruton, 2001). Especially considering that the college athletics industry is worth close to 16 billion dollars, it is unsurprising that the role of athletics has become outsized, allowing academic and college outcomes for student athletes to fall to the wayside (Harper, 2018; Harris, 2020). As the revenue streams and the role in mass culture have ballooned, athletic departments inflate athletic priorities in the lives of student athletes, leaving their academic and college outcomes underdeveloped (Harris, 2020).

There are serious and negative consequences of overemphasizing athletics, including demonstrably lower academic achievement (Beamon, 2012). Importantly, there are racial equity gaps within the student athlete population. Black student athletes, especially male basketball and football players, have persistently lower academic achievement compared to their athlete peers (Baker & Hawkins, 2016; Cooper, 2019). It would be inaccurate to say that these students are simply underprepared for the rigor of college-level academics: In reality, there is an array of variables involved in Black student athletes' underachievement that stem from their experiences on campus including athletic exploitation, hostile campus climate, racial discrimination, and inadequate student development supports aimed at Black students' personal and academic needs (Baker & Hawkins, 2016). Harris (2020) argues that many Black student athletes, particularly males, are being encouraged towards athletic pursuits without receiving similar encouragement as scholars. Thus, Black student athletes are often reinforced for their efforts as athletes during their college years and do not always reap the benefits of holistic student development that universities promise. Such occurrences are unacceptable, particularly given the academic missions of colleges and universities and the persistent underrepresentation of Black students at prestigious institutions (Harper, 2018).

When considering the relationship between athletics and CCR, it is important to acknowledge the history of initial eligibility requirements set by the NCAA. In the organization's early history, NCAA academic standards were determined and enforced at an institutional level, and there was no standardization or governing body to ensure accountability (Petr & McArdle, 2012). Also, for the first 7 decades of its existence, the NCAA could not make data-driven decisions about student-athlete outcomes because it did not collect academic data on its players (Petr & McArdle, 2012). The first minimum high school GPA requirement for initial eligibility—a modest

1.6—came about in the 1960s, which was followed by a minimum of 2.0 in the early 1970s (Bruton, 2001; Petr & McArdle, 2012). Even with these early provisions in place, there were still multiple high-profile academic scandals revealing student athletes who were essentially illiterate, without any expectation or realistic likelihood of graduating from the institution (Bruton, 2001; Petr & McArdle, 2012). Related to "A Nation at Risk" and the general education climate in the mid-1980s, Proposition 48 named three distinct academic requirements for college-bound student athletes: (a) graduate high school with at least a 2.0 GPA; (b) complete core courses including three English, two math, two history, and two science classes; and (c) achieve at least a combined score of 700 on the Scholastic Aptitude Test (SAT) or a 15 composite score on the American College Test ([ACT]; McKenna, 1987). Proposition 48, well-intended as it was, was also controversial due to the lack of evidence at the time, particularly in regards to its potential impact on low-income and minority populations (Hosick & Sproull, 2012).

NCAA eligibility requirements have been renegotiated over time, with minimums for GPA, number of core courses, and standardized test scores on the rise (Hosick & Sproull, 2012). This is due in large part to the major shift in NCAA decision-making in the mid-1980s and beyond, when the NCAA commissioned the Academic Performance Study (APS) and committed to making data-driven policy decisions (Hosick & Sproull, 2012; Petr & McArdle, 2012). Nevertheless, the eligibility requirements remain quite modest and flexible, especially with the sliding scale for GPA and test scores. There are multiple purposes for this, and multiple stakeholders are involved. For example, a modest bar for eligibility can help promote college access for prospective student athletes (PSAs) coming from disadvantaged backgrounds who are disproportionately Black, a population that remains underrepresented at elite colleges and universities (Hosick & Sproull, 2012; Harper, 2018; Petr & McArdle, 2012).

The NCAA has recognized the challenges that student athletes face in balancing athletic and academic pursuits, and has made some strides to promote the holistic development of student athletes (Carodine et al., 2001; Hosick & Sproull, 2012). Nevertheless, we contend that the NCAA eligibility standards leave gaps between eligibility and CCR, allowing many student athletes to enter college eligible to play while remaining unprepared for academic success and career transitions beyond athletics. This is especially problematic given that over 98% of student athletes will have to transition into careers outside of athletics when they leave college (Harper, 2018; Schafer, 2018). It is the responsibility of educators at both the K–12 and college levels to promote the CCR of student athletes.

It is important for K–12 educators to challenge Black student athletes academically, encouraging them to aim not just for eligibility, but for CCR, which involves making substantive postsecondary plans that go beyond sport. High school counselors, in particular, have several opportunities to promote equitable college and career outcomes for Black student athletes. Unfortunately, high school counselors have been shown to reinforce the stereotype that Black student athletes are more athletically endowed, encouraging them to pursue their athletic development while inadvertently downplaying their chance of success in academics and other career fields (Czopp, 2010). Preservice school counselor training and professional development of in-service school counselors focused on disrupting the historic exploitative nature of sports in the lives of Black student athletes through strengths-based, anti-racist efforts can go a long way to reversing this trend. Without such targeted training and development, school counselors are likely to advise students in ways that confirm positive athletic stereotypes of their Black students, thus perpetuating race-based differences in academic planning (Czopp, 2010). And unfortunately, the overemphasis on sport means that students spend significantly less time on academic tasks like studying, and have underdeveloped long-term academic and career plans (Czopp, 2010).

Black student athletes face a perfect storm that can lead them to be unprepared for college and career transitions: With overdeveloped athletic aspirations and well-meaning school counselors that perpetuate positive athletic stereotypes, it is no wonder that Black student athletes can be eligible to play at the college level, but not ready for major life transitions beyond their sport. At the college level, there is ample evidence that Black student athletes face exploitative systems, experience an array of challenges related to campus climate, and ultimately see little pay-off in terms of career opportunities (Baker & Hawkins, 2016; Harper, 2018; Harris, 2020). Intimately acquainted with equity data, Harper (2018) advises Black student athletes and their families to "resist the seductive lure of choosing a university because it appears to be a promising gateway to careers in professional sports" (p. 19). School counselors, equipped with an equity lens and the skills to assist students in academic and career planning, are strategically positioned to help Black student athletes resist the temptation of having short-sighted postsecondary plans. For example, high school counselors can provide small group counseling for Black male student athletes with an emphasis on career exploration and college decision-making, using personality and career interest inventories to generate conversations about college and career goals beyond sports (Hines et al., 2020). Applying an anti-racist lens, school counselors can create spaces for consciousness raising and dialogue around Black male identity, the complex world of college athletics, and athletic stereotypes that can have a pernicious impact on students' college and career outcomes.

School counselors can also apply insights from racial equity scholars like Harper (2018) to advise Black student athletes and their families during the recruitment process in high school. One critical recommendation is that while being recruited, student athletes should ask coaches a more expansive and comprehensive set of questions that address data such as: graduation rates for Black student athletes on their teams, opportunities for pursuing internships or study abroad opportunities, sample careers of student athletes who do not go professional after college, and career preparedness after college (Harper, 2018). Harper (2018) highlights, "Spending all their time on athletics-related activities is unlikely to yield a portfolio of educational experiences that make them competitive for rewarding post-college options beyond the NFL or NBA" (p. 19). School counselors should be a guiding voice as Black student athletes navigate the athletic recruitment process, encouraging them to ask critical and specific questions about the ways coaches promote the holistic development of their student athletes. In addition to supporting their recruitment process, school counselors can also encourage students to weigh other important factors of the college decision-making process including location, public vs. private, available majors, and so forth. The myth that athletics are a reliable means of upward social mobility, even when the reality is that this is true for only a small fraction of student athletes, is particularly salient in the Black community (Baker & Hawkins, 2016; Harris, 2020; Harper, 2018; Hosick & Sproull, 2012). In fact, the proportion of high school athletes who "go pro" is only a fraction of 1%—more specifically, .03% for men's basketball and .08% for football (NCAA data). With this exceedingly small chance of high school athletes becoming professional athletes, high school counselors should be intentional about working with Black high school student athletes to develop substantive plans for a college experience and career trajectory that leverage the utility of athletics, but do not hinge on athletics (Harper, 2018; Meyer, 2005).

School counselors can work with their committed collegiate student athletes on developing these plans by connecting these students with their respective university's resources. Colleges offer student athletes a plethora of resources for their career advancement and development through the career center and student athlete support services. These services work with students and help them succeed outside their sport through academic and career advising. School counselors are encouraged to reach out to university student athlete support services to connect college bound students to services offered at their chosen institutions.

IMPLICATIONS

In order to redress the racial inequities in CCR, educators, researchers, and policy-makers must first increase their awareness of such inequities and why they persist. Black student athletes have historically been underserved by a system designed to benefit from their athletic talent while virtually ignoring their other identities (Cooper, 2019; Holcomb-McCoy, 2007). Given the persisting disparities in educational success between Black student athletes and their White counterparts, we present considerations for practice, policy, and future research.

First, for school counselors and other education stakeholders we present a cluster of questions and actions that can be adapted for use in practice and shaping policy. These questions help look through anti-racist lens to critically analyze and act upon situations in schools that might impede the CCR of Black high school student athletes (Lee et al., 1997). It is important to note that educators can also apply other lenses when looking at issues of equity in schools.

1. *What is the specific problem being addressed?* Who is affected by the problem in terms of race, gender, class (etc.), and how are they affected?
2. *How did things get to be the way they are?* Who gains (benefits) from the situation the way it is now? Who loses? Who sees this as a problem? Who might feel threatened by an attempt to erase this problem? Who is doing something about the problem, and what are they doing? What are some of the needs and strengths identified? How will eliminating this problem help the group mentioned above?
3. *What are some of the beliefs (prevailing ideologies) that have led to this situation?* What are the beliefs by those in power and those without, regarding the ability and worth of Black student athletes? What are the explanations presented to justify actions and the positions of privilege or disadvantage Black student athletes enjoy or endure?
4. *What are some things that keep the situation the way it is?* Has there been a conscious examination of the experiences of Black student athletes concerning the issue? Where and how are the voices and views of Black student athletes represented or excluded in this present situation? Has there been an examination of the impact of school policies and practices on the CCR of Black student athletes? How has the school's silence on these matters helped to maintain the status quo? How has the lack of material, financial, or human resources contributed to the situation?
5. *What would the school have to change in order for the situation to be different?* How can we institutionalize this change? How can we prevent this situation from reoccurring? What power/leverage/influence do I have within the affected school? How does my current professional role interact with the specific problem I have targeted for change? How committed am I to stay the course during this journey? What am I willing to sacrifice to ensure the success of this endeavor?

6. *How will I cultivate allies?* Where can I find allies? What credibility do I have, or can I establish to represent this cause authentically? How will I handle objections and naysayers? How will I communicate my level of commitment? How will I make space for others to participate with me?

7. *How can I commit to ongoing learning and unlearning colonial ways of being/thinking?* How can I rigorously attack internalized oppression? How can I interrogate my biases and stereotypical thinking? How can I continually ask myself whether my actions demonstrate an anti-racist standpoint?

Lastly, CCR research from an anti-racist perspective places Black student athletes at the center of analysis by focusing on their lived experiences and the simultaneity of their oppressions (Brewer, 1993). Such research can deepen our understanding of how various forms of oppression help to construct and constrain the various identities (race, gender, class, athletic status) of Black student athletes (Dei, 2005). Black students experience oppression in a way that is different both in substance and intensity. Milner (2007) encourages researchers to become aware of their social position and critically reflect on it. Self-reflection of the researchers' social position includes understanding that we possess both privileged and oppressed identities and that our socialization and intersecting identities (including internalized racial superiority or inferiority) can have an impact on our research and work within the Black community (Kishimoto, 2018). As Kumashiro (2003) reminds us, "It is often difficult for researchers to acknowledge their own complicity with other forms of oppression, especially when they are trying to challenge multiple forms of oppression" (p. 63).

CONCLUSION

We have drawn attention to the ways that disparities can persist for Black student athletes in the area of CCR, despite the measures included in NCAA eligibility. The unfortunate reality is that high school athletes can be eligible, yet underprepared to succeed in college and careers beyond their sport. Fortunately, high school counselors can play a critical support role in promoting CCR. School counselors are ethically obligated to provide "critical, timely information on college, career and postsecondary options" to students and help them "understand the full magnitude and meaning of how college and career readiness can have an impact on their educational choices and future opportunities" (ASCA, 2016, p. 1). Especially in advocating for Black student athletes, it is critical for school counselors to promote equitable college and career development opportunities. Receiving interventions at the high school level, student athletes can be more prepared for college and beyond—and not only prepared for academic rigor, but also prepared with the self-knowledge necessary to pursue meaningful academic and career pathways. It is the responsibility of school counselors to create a culture of CCR for *all* students (ASCA, 2014). This culture, however, is not created by school counselors alone. Administrators, teachers, coaches, and all staff are needed to ensure that a school environment is conducive to helping Black student athletes thrive in the classroom and in sport. School counselors should absolutely develop interventions in the context of NCAA eligibility and the ways it may fall short of promoting CCR for Black student athletes, but should be doing so in concert with all education stakeholders, including parents. When all educators hone their craft and deliver their services through an anti-racist paradigm, Black student athletes' potential to thrive is that much greater. All educators have a role to play ensuring Black male student athletes. This is best accomplished through an anti-racist paradigm.

DISCUSSION QUESTIONS

1. What does it mean to be a Black student athlete?
2. In what ways can K–16 educators hinder or enhance Black student-athletes' racial identity development?
3. What does it mean to be college and career ready?

ACTIVITIES

1. Look at the Eligibility Center's website and note the various paths toward eligibility that the NCAA has created over time. Which of the paths comes the closest to mapping on to typical college and career readiness indicators? Where are the gaps, if any?
2. Considering the definition of anti-racism that the authors provided, analyze all of the NCAA eligibility requirements and determine what specific aspects of the eligibility process are congruent with the anti-racism paradigm. Why?

AUTHOR NOTE

Paul C. Harris ORCID https://orcid.org/0000-0002-2140-8393

We have no known conflict of interest to disclose.

Correspondence concerning this chapter should be addressed to Paul C. Harris, Department of Educational Psychology, Counseling, and Special Education, State College, PA 16801. Email: paulharris917@gmail.com

REFERENCES

ACT. (2016). *The condition of college and career readiness 2015: African American students.* https://equityinlearning.act.org/wp-content/uploads/2016/06/2015 -african-american.pdf

American School Counselor Association. (2016). *ASCA ethical standards for school counselors.*

American School Counselor Association. (2014). *Mindsets and behaviors for student success: K–12 college- and career-readiness standards for every student.*

Anthony, C. E., & Swank, J. M. (2018). Black college student-athletes: Examining the intersection of gender, and racial identity and athletic identity. *Journal for the Study of Sports and Athletes in Education, 12*(3), 179–199.

Baker, A. R., & Hawkins, B. J. (2016). Academic and career advancement for Black male athletes at NCAA Division I Institutions. *New Directions for Adult and Continuing Education, 2016*(150), 71–82.

Baumann, S., & Henschen, K. (1986). A cross-validation study of selected performance measures in predicting academic success among collegiate athletes. *Sociology of Sport Journal, 3*(4), 366–371.

Beamon, K. (2012). 'I'm a baller': Athletic identity foreclosure among African-American former student-athletes. *Journal of African American Studies, 16*(2), 195–208. https://doi.org/10.1007/s12111-012-9211-8

Beamon, K., & Bell, P. A. (2006). Academics versus athletics: An examination of the effects of background and socialization on African American male student-athletes. *The Social Science Journal, 43*(3), 393–403. https://doi.org/10.1016/j.soscij.2006.04.009

Bimper, A. Y. (2014). Game changers: The role athletic identity and racial identity play on academic performance. *Journal of College Student Development, 55*(8), 795–807. https://doi.org/10.1353/csd.2014.0078

Brewer, R. M. (1993). Theorizing race, class and gender: The new scholarship of Black feminist intellectuals and Black women's labor. In S. James, & A. Busia (Eds.), *Theorizing Black Feminisms* (pp. 13–30). Routledge.

Brewer, B. W., Van Raalte, J. L., & Linder, D. E. (1993). Athletic identity: Hercules' muscles or Achilles heel? *International Journal of Sport Psychology, 24*, 237254. https://doi.org/10.1037/t15488-000

Brown, T. N., Jackson, J. S., Brown, K. T., Sellers, R. M., Keiper, S., & Manuel, W. J. (2003). There's no race on the playing field: Perceptions of racial discrimination among white and black athletes. *Journal of Sport and Social Issues, 27*, 162–183. https://doi.org/10.1177/0193732502250715

Bruening, J., Borland, J., & Burton, L. (2008). The impact of influential others on the sport participation patterns of African American female student-athletes.

Journal for the Study of Sports and Athletes in Education, 2, 379–417. https://doi
.org/10.1179/ssa.2008.2.3.379

Bruton, D. P. (2001). At the busy intersection: Title VI and NCAA eligibility standards. *JC & UL, 28,* 569.

Butler-Barnes, S. T., Leath, S., Williams, A., Byrd, C., Carter, R., & Chavous, T. M.
(2018). Promoting resilience among African American girls: Racial identity as
a protective factor. *Child Development, 89*(6), e552–e571.

Byrd, C. M. (2011). The measurement of racial/ethnic identity in children. *Journal
of Black Psychology, 38*(1), 3–31. http://doi.org/10.1177/0095798410397544

Carodine, K., Almond, K. F., & Gratto, K. K. (2001). College student athlete success
both in and out of the classroom. *New directions for student services, 93,* 19–33.

Comeaux, E., & Harrison, C. K. (2011). A conceptual model of academic success
for student–athletes. *Educational Researcher, 40*(5), 235–245. https://doi.org/
10.3102/0013189X11415260

Conley, D. T. (2010). *College and career ready: Helping all students succeed beyond high
school.* Jossey-Bass.

Conley, D. T. (2012). A complete definition of college and career readiness. *Educational Policy Improvement Center, 1–4.*

Cooper, J. N. (2016). Excellence beyond athletics: Best practices for enhancing
Black male student-athletes' educational experiences and outcomes. *Equity
& Excellence in Education, 49*(3), 267–283.

Cooper, J. N. (2019). *From exploitation back to empowerment: Black male holistic (under)
development through sport and (mis) education.* Peter Lang.

Czopp, A. M. (2010). Studying is lame when he got game: Racial stereotypes and the
discouragement of Black student-athletes from schoolwork. *Social Psychology of
Education, 13*(4), 485–498.

Dei, G. J. S. (2005). Critical issues in anti-racist research methodologies: An introduction. In G. J. S. Dei & G. S. Johal (Eds.), *Critical issues in anti-racist research
methodologies* (pp. 1–27). Peter Lang.

Eide, E. R., & Ronan, N. (2001). Is participation in high school athletics an investment or a consumption good? Evidence from high school and beyond. *Economics of Education Review, 20*(5), 431–442. https://doi.org/10.1016/S0272
-7757(00)00033-9

Fuller, R. D., Harrison, C. K., Bukstein, S. J., Martin, B. E., Lawrence, S. M., &
Gadsby, P. (2020). That smart dude: A qualitative investigation of the African
American male scholar-baller identity. *Urban Education, 55*(5), 813–831.

Gale, A., & Dorsey, M. (2020). Does the context of racial discrimination matter for
adolescent school outcomes? The impact of in-school racial discrimination
and general racial discrimination on Black adolescents' outcomes. *Race and
Social Problems, 1–15.* http://doi.org/10.1007/s12552-020-09286-0

Gawrysiak, E. J., Cooper, J. N., & Hawkins, B. (2015). The impact of baseball participation on the educational experiences of black student-athletes at historically
black colleges and universities. *Race Ethnicity and Education, 18*(5), 696–722.
https://doi.org/10.1080/13613324.2013.792795

Gray, D. L., Hope, E. C., & Byrd, C. M. (2020). Why Black adolescents are vulnerable at school and how schools can provide opportunities to belong to fix

it. *Policy Insights From the Behavioral and Brain Sciences, 7*(1), 3–9. http://doi
.org/10.1177/2372732219868744

Harper, S. (2018). *Black male student athlete and racial inequities in NCAA Division I
college sports* (2018 ed.). The USC Race and Equity Center.

Harris, P. C. (2014). The sports participation effect on educational attainment of
Black males. *Education and Urban Society, 46*(5), 507–521. https://doi.org/
10.1177/0013124512446219

Harris, P. C., Mayes, R. D., Vega, D., & Hines, E. M. (2016). Reaching higher: College and career readiness for African American males with learning disabilities. *Journal of African American Males in Education, 7*(1), 52–69.

Harris, P. C., Hines, E. M., Kelly, D. D., Williams, D. J., & Bagley, B. (2014). Promoting the academic engagement and success of Black male student-athletes. *The High School Journal, 97*(3), 180–195. https://doi.org/10.1353/hsj.2014.0000

Harris, P. C. (2020). Healing hate: Promoting readiness over eligibility. *Virginia Journal of Social Policy & the Law, 27*, 59.

Harrison, L., Sailes, G., Rotich, W. K., & Bimper, A. Y. (2011). Living the dream or awakening from the nightmare: Race and athletic identity. *Race Ethnicity and Education, 14*(1), 91–103.

Hines, E. M., Hines, M. R., Moore, J. L., III., Steen, S., Singleton, P., Cintron, D., Golden, M. N., Traverso, K., Wathen, B.-J., & Henderson, J. (2020). Preparing African American males for college: A group counseling approach. *The Journal for Specialists in Group Work*, 1–17. Routledge.

Holcomb-McCoy, C. (2007). *School counseling to close the achievement gap: A social justice framework for success.* Corwin Press.

Horton, R. S., & Mack, D. E. (2000). Athletic identity in marathon runners: Functional focus or dysfunctional commitment? *Journal of Sport Behavior, 23*, 101–110.

Hosick, M. B., & Sproull, N. (2012). NCAA: Eligibility and success. *Journal of College Admission, 217*, 31–33.

Huml, M. R., Hancock, M. G., & Hums, M. A. (2019). Athletics and academics: The relationship between athletic identity sub-constructs and educational outcomes. *Journal of Issues in Intercollegiate Athletics, 2019*(12), 46–62.

Jackson, J.S., Keiper, S., Brown, K.T., Brown, T.N., & Manuel, W. (2002). Athletic identity, racial attitudes, and aggression in first-year black and white intercollegiate athletes. *Paradoxes of Youth and Sport*, 159–172.

Jordan, W. J. (1999). Black high school students' participation in school-sponsored sports activities: Effects on school engagement and achievement. *The Journal of Negro Education, 68*(1), 54–71. https://doi.org/10.2307/2668209

Kishimoto, K. (2018). Anti-racist pedagogy: From faculty's self-reflection to organizing within and beyond the classroom. *Race, Ethnicity and Education, 21*, 540–554.

Kumashiro, K. K. (2003). Against repetition: Addressing resistance to anti-oppressive change in the practices of learning, teaching, supervising, and researching. In A. Howell & F. Tuitt (Eds.). *Race and higher education: Rethinking pedagogy in diverse college classrooms* (pp. 45–67). Harvard Educational Review.

Ladson-Billings, G. (2006). From the achievement gap to the education debt: Understanding achievement in U.S. schools. *Educational Researcher, 35*, 3–12.

Lally, P. S., & Kerr, G. A. (2005). The career planning, athletic identity, and student role identity of intercollegiate student-athletes. *Research Quarterly for Exercise and Sport, 76*(3), 275–285. https://doi.org/10.1080/02701367.2005.10599299

Leath, S., Mathews, C., Harrison, A., & Chavous, T. (2019). Racial identity, racial discrimination, and classroom engagement outcomes among black girls and boys in predominantly Black and predominantly White school districts. *American Educational Research Journal, 56*(4), 1318–1352. http://doi.org/10.3102/0002831218816955

Lee, C. C. (1983). An investigation of the athletic career expectations of high school student athletes. *The Personnel and Guidance Journal, 61*(9), 544–547. https://doi.org/10.1111/j.2164-4918.1983.tb00096.x

Lee, E., Menkart, D., & Okazawa-Rey, M. (1997). *Beyond heroes and holidays: A practical guide to K–12 anti-racist, multicultural education and staff development.* Network of Educators on the Americas.

Lumpkin, A., & Favor, J. (2012). Comparing the academic performance of high school athletes and non-athletes in Kansas in 2008–2009. *Academic Performance of Athletes and Non-Athletes, 4(1),* 41–62.

May, R. A. (2004). Of mice, rats, and men: Exploring the role of rodents in constructing masculinity within a group of young African-American males. *Qualitative Sociology, 27*(2), 159–177.

McDougle, L., & Capers, Q., IV. (2012). Establishing priorities for student-athletes: Balancing academics and sports. *Spectrum: A Journal on Black Men, 1*(1), 71–77.

McKenna, K. M. (1987). A proposition with a powerful punch: The legality and constitutionality of NCAA proposition 48. *Duq. L. Rev., 26,* 43.

Meyer, S. K. (2005). NCAA academic reforms: Maintaining the balance between academics and athletics. *Phi Kappa Phi Forum 85*(3), 15–19. Honor Society of Phi Kappa Phi.

Milner, H. R. (2007). Race, culture, and researcher positionality: Working through dangers seen, unseen, and unforeseen. *Educational Researcher, 36*(7), 388–400

Mims, L. C., & Williams, J. L. (2020). "They told me what I was before I could tell them what I was" Black girls' ethnic-racial identity development within multiple worlds. *Journal of Adolescent Research, 35*(6), 754–779. https://doi.org/10.1177/0743558420913483

Moiseichik, M., Stokowski, S., Hinsey, S., & Turk, M. R. (2019). Athletic identity and career maturity of women's basketball student-athletes. *The Journal of Sport, 7*(1), 2.

Nwadike, A. C., Baker, A. R., Brackebusch, V. B., & Hawkins, B. J. (2016). Institutional racism in the NCAA and the racial implications of the "2.3 or take a knee" legislation. *Marquette Sports Law Review. 26*(2), 523–543.

Petr, T. A., & McArdle, J. J. (2012). Academic research and reform: A history of the empirical basis for NCAA Academic Policy. *Journal of Intercollegiate Sport, 5*(1), 27–40.

Rhoden, W. (2006). *Forty million dollar slaves: The rise, fall, and redemption of the Black athlete.* Three Rivers Press.

Schafer, J. W. (2018). NCAA Division I transfers are now basically screwed. *Buffalo Law Review, 66,* 481.

Smith, C. D., & Hope, E. C. (2020). "We just want to break the stereotype" Tensions in Black boys' critical social analysis of their suburban school experiences. *Journal of Educational Psychology, 112*(3), 551–566. http://doi.org/10.1037/edu0000435

Tucker, C., Dixon, A., & Griddine, K. (2010). Academically successful African American male urban high school students' experiences of mattering to others at school. *Professional School Counseling, 14*(2), 135–145.

United States Department of Education. (n.d.). *Public high school graduation rates.* Institute of Education Sciences, National Center for Education Statistics. https://nces.ed.gov/programs/coe/indicator/coi

Willis, H. A., & Neblett, E. W. (2019). Racial identity and changes in psychological distress using the multidimensional model of racial identity. *Cultural Diversity and Ethnic Minority Psychology,* 1–12. http://doi.org/10.1037/cdp0000314

Yip, T., Wang, Y., Mootoo, C., & Mirpuri, S. (2019). Moderating the association between discrimination and adjustment: A meta-analysis of ethnic/racial identity. *Developmental Psychology, 55*(6), 1274–1298. http://doi.org/10.1037/dev0000708

CHAPTER 14

MEETING THE UNIQUE NEEDS OF FIRST-GENERATION COLLEGE STUDENTS

An Exploration of Psychosocial Theory, Postsecondary Transition, and Career Development

Jonique R. Childs
University of Massachusetts–Amherst

Jennifer Sánchez
Florida Atlantic University

Grace Wambu
New Jersey City University

ABSTRACT

This chapter examines the unique needs of first-generation college students that can be useful for providing academic support and counseling services

Equity-Based Career Development and Postsecondary Transitions, pages 345–375
Copyright © 2022 by Information Age Publishing
www.infoagepub.com

to promote positive career development and facilitate healthy social identity development at American postsecondary institutions. The authors aim to elucidate the effects of psychosocial barriers on career development for these marginalized students. Erickson's psychosocial theoretical framework is used to analyze barriers and needs of first-generation college students, including those of color. Understanding how personal experiences and environmental expectations interact and the influence on postsecondary transition is critical for successful academic matriculation and career attainment. This chapter begins with a review of the literature pertaining to first-generation college students, including those of color, and their representation in various postsecondary education settings. Information about demographics, enrollment, and graduation rates are provided. Next, the authors describe psychosocial theory, focusing on two stages: Stage 5—identity vs. role confusion and Stage 6—intimacy vs. isolation. The major emphasis of the chapter includes postsecondary options for first-generation college students, including those of color; barriers to postsecondary transition and career development; and needs of first-generation college students, including those of color to promote equitable navigation through postsecondary transition and career development. Given the recent COVID-19 outbreak, relevant academic and career development impacts for first-generation college students, including those of color, brought on by the pandemic are infused throughout the chapter. Finally, the authors provide recommendations for research, practice, and policy.

The alarming growth of first-generation college students (FGCS) and students of color (SOC) enrollment in U.S. postsecondary institutions requires imminent attention. The need to recognize the influence of equity-based barriers on career development and decision-making of this population is urgent. Complex barriers hinder successful postsecondary transition and career attainment for these unique students (Stebleton & Soria, 2012). The attention to inequities within high school and college environments underscores that monumental actions are required to enhance college readiness and completion rates for first-generation college students of color (FGC-SOC). The systemic barriers impeding degree attainment needs to be addressed (Bilton, 2002). FGCSOC represent students from racial and ethnic backgrounds who have oftentimes been marginalized in higher education (Callan, 2018). Issues of disparity and inequity facing FGCSOC manifest within areas of socioeconomic status, family background, race and ethnicity, gender, sexual orientation, and disability (Engle & Tinto, 2008; Owens et al., 2010; Tate et al., 2015). The successful transition of FGCSOC hinges on the early identification of academic needs and the provision of counseling services during this pivotal time to promote healthy social and identity development. Moreover, the implementation of high impact practices to promote positive career development must occur within postsecondary institutions (Conefrey, 2018).

Recently, postsecondary institutions have implemented significant changes in education, training, and associated programming safety protocol requirements due to the outbreak of the novel coronavirus (COVID-19) pandemic (Smalley, 2020). COVID-19 has illuminated societal racial inequities in housing, employment, and health access (Lederer et al., 2021), which in turn negatively impacts career development for FGCSOC. Specifically, attention to racial tensions coupled with the heightened awareness of educational injustices, has reignited interest in social activism, including calls for equitable practices and demands for anti-racist policies to remove oppressive racist systemic barriers and improve unwelcoming academic cultural environments.

CURRENT EVENTS

Anti-Racism

The COVID-19 pandemic has resulted in the realization of profound racial inequalities and systemic inequities impacting marginalized communities that include Black indigenous people of color (BIPOC). The push to identify and eradicate racist actions and polices has created the growth of anti-racism/anti-racist education practices. Attention to issues of economic and health disparities has created a call to action within education to increase fair practices. The amplification of challenges faced by first-generation SOC representing low-income backgrounds includes support and access to postsecondary education. The pandemic has also highlighted the racial equity gap which impacts the career development for SOC. For anti-racism work means acknowledging that racist beliefs and structures exist and are pervasive in all aspects of society including education policies and structures. Examining the inequities created by racism is the responsibility of every educational institution. In particular, predominately White Institutions (PWI) have an ethical responsibility to provide culturally relevant pedagogy focused on diversity and equity-based issues related to postsecondary access and transitions for marginalized students.

Minoritized students need anti-racism education especially vulnerable populations like FGCS and SOC. The urgency for anti-racist work means acknowledging that racist beliefs and structures exist in society and within educational institutions, then actively trying to tear down those beliefs and structures (Pollock, 2006). Institutional malpractice or racist mindsets that prevail in schools and colleges can have detrimental effects on the learning of students, especially FGCOC. Pollock (2006) asserts that anti-racism in education calls for educators to make strategic self-conscious everyday moves to counter tendencies ingrained in people's minds. This entails rejecting false notions of human difference, and actively treating all people as equally human, worthy, intelligent, and with full potential (Pollock, 2006). Furthermore, everyday anti-racism in education involves acknowledging and engaging in lived experiences along racial lines. Racialized groups in the United States today bring different experiences to the table, with differences in educational resources, opportunity, and success (Pollock, 2006). Anti-racism in education will require equipping oneself and others to challenge racial inequalities. Such efforts should include proactively reminding SOC that they are equally intelligent and have potential to succeed.

Escayg (2018) espouses anti-racism education as the means by which institutions need to draw attention and criticize institutional racism. This will involve addressing how racist beliefs and ideologies structure micro relations and also examine how institutions support and maintain advantage and disadvantage along racial lines (Berman & Paradies, 2010). Anti-racist education is critical particularly in order to address the barriers that FGSOC face on a daily basis and which hinder their academic and career progression. The impact of institutional discrimination cannot be overemphasized. Mirza (2018), revealed some of the inequities experienced by SOC in higher education. Studies have shown that SOC are less likely to be admitted in elite schools even when they have similar qualifications with their White peers. Furthermore, students who manage to get in will likely select less competitive majors with a lower market value and are less likely than their White counterparts to be awarded honorary degrees or find jobs commensurate with their qualifications when they graduate (Mirza, 2018).

Anti-Blackness

Institutions of learning must take proactive measures to engage in systemic and intentional efforts to combat racism at the macro and micro levels. A practical step in addressing the racism menace that has prevailed in the school system for so long may require the teachers to re-evaluate their curriculum. Students from BIPOC communities need to see themselves depicted in the literature and history they study. Similarly, White students need to hear those perspectives just as the straight and cisgender students need to hear and read LGBQ+ issues (Pollock, 2004).

Indeed, FGCSOC require well-intentioned support and advocacy for academic and postsecondary transitions. For anti-Blackness that includes the covert, structural, and systemic policies, institutions, and ideologies to be examined. With the growing recognition of reinforcing racial hierarchies and racism tenets within PWIs, the urgency to promote an anti-Blackness coalition has become the focus in higher education. Racial inequities such as the denying of status and rights to African Americans can be classified as anti-Blackness (Learning Scientists for Racial Justice [LSRJ], 2020). Moreover, anti-Blackness, encompasses the lack of human decency for fair treatment, has increased since post COVID-19 based on systemic barriers plaguing African

Americans. Such issues like housing discrimination, corrupt criminal justice system, and healthcare disparities call for disrupting anti-Blackness. Specifically, the recognition that White supremacy policies and practices create unequal access to financial resources favoring nonminority students. Laybourn and Pine (2020) explain that examining anti-Blackness does includes the experiences with racism, microaggressions, and internalized anti-Blackness for individuals. Academic environments such as PWIs have the highest occurrence where students encounter anti-Blackness messages. Combating racism with the overlapping political and social change has resulted in identification of complicity and the need for accountability standards in postsecondary institutions (Buchanan et al., 2020).

Asian-American

The occurrence of anti-Asian violence and discrimination has increased since the onset of the COVID-19 pandemic (Lee & Waters, 2021). Stigma and discrimination against people of Asian descent contributes to the psychological and physical well-being being at risk (Akiba, 2020). FGCSOC that also identify as Asian American descent require equity-based advocacy for anti-racist practices due to societal racial stereotypes and minority threat idealization (Li & Lalani, 2020). This marginalized group of first-generation SOC has experienced changes to increased barriers to postsecondary education such as microaggressions, discrimination, and racism. In a study conducted on Asian Americans regarding self-reported discrimination in relation to mental physical health outcomes, over 40% reported an increase in anxiety and depressive symptoms (Lee & Waters, 2021). The increase in microinvalidations and environmental microaggressions has increased within the diverse cultures and ethnicities of Asian American and Asian international students (Yeo et al., 2019). Sawchuk and Gewertz (2021) reported that Asian representation and creating safe spaces while maintaining support are key components to working with these populations.

First-Generation College Students

FGCS have been described in the literature using broad and narrow definitions. Students who are the first in their family to go to college (i.e., whose parents have not attained a degree higher than a high school diploma) are considered "first generation" (Choy, 2001; Thayer, 2000; Ward et al., 2012). FGCS can also include students who lack a primary parent (or guardian) with a higher education (i.e., 4-year college) degree (Bui, 2002). In fact, eight different definitions of "first-generation" commonly used by researchers were used to examine data from the *Education Longi-tudinal Study of 2002*, with FGCS ranging from 22% to 77%, depending on the definition used (Toutkoushian et al., 2018). However, the most used is the federal definition (developed to determine program eligibility), which states a FGCS is a student: (a) neither of whose natural or adoptive parents received a baccalaureate degree; (b) who, prior to the age of 18, regularly resided with and received support from only one parent and whose sup-porting parent did not receive a baccalaureate degree; or (c) who, prior to the age of 18, did not regularly reside with or receive support from a natural or an adoptive parent (Student Support Services Program [SSSP], 2011).

The higher education literature highlights issues related to enrollment, retention, achievement, socioeconomic status, parental influence, campus engagement, and social networks for FGCS (Covarrubias et al., 2015; Kat-revich & Aruguete, 2017; Longwell-Grice et al., 2016). Specifically, FGCS have reported issues related to financial concerns, needing to work while at-tending school, and feeling less connected to their peers due to the limited time available to engage in college-related activities resulting from their first-generation and socioeconomic statuses (Pratt et al., 2019). Compared to their non-FGCS peers (i.e., those whose parents achieved a 4-year col-lege degree), FGCS lack postsecondary support networks (Choy, 2001; Pas-carella et al., 2004). The multiple discrepant institutional, socioeconomic, and personal barriers faced by FGCS are some reasons they are less likely to persist and graduate (Ishitani, 2006; Pike & Kuh, 2005). Given their recent proliferation since the turn of the century, FGCS are a new student popula-tion and worthy of understanding (Ward et al., 2012; Wildhagen, 2015).

First-Generation College Students of Color

Whereas FGCS refer to generational status, SOC refer to identifying with nondominant racial/ethnic (i.e., non-White) minoritized groups repre-sented in U.S. society and on most college campuses (Bensimon, 2018). As explained by Harper (2010) and Shange (2019), SOC are subjected to dis-crimination and subordination in relation to their non-White racial/ethnic identity. SOC may identify as Hispanic/Latino, Black/African American, Alaskan Native/Pacific Islander, and/or American Indian/Native Ameri-can (Santa-Ramirez et al., 2020). Students who are the first in their family to attend college with the goal of achieving a 4-year degree, and come from racial/ethnic minoritized groups are classified as FGCSOC (Bui, 2002; Pas-carella et al., 2004).

When attending a PWI, FGCSOC have reported difficulty in their pur-suit of higher education due to high familial expectations, lack of knowl-edge about the admissions process, challenges with transition and "culture shock in a sea of whiteness" (McCoy, 2014, p. 164). Many FGCSOC revealed not being encouraged by family to attend college, but deciding to do so to achieve a better life for themselves (Blackwell & Pinder, 2014). Thus, FGCSOC share all the same barriers as FGCS, and issues specific to race/ethnicity. Specifically, FGCSOC reported difficult experiences and feelings of "otherness" related to their racial/ethnic identity, first-generation, and socioeconomic statuses (Havlik et al., 2020).

Student Enrollment in the United States

FGCS (i.e., were not raised by parents who completed a 4-year degree) make up over 50% of the student population at 2-year colleges (U.S. Department of Education [USDOE], 2014). Studies have shown that FGCS tend to enroll in 2-year colleges after graduating high school at higher rates than their non-FGCS peers (Engle, 2007). According to a recent study, about 43% of students at 4-year colleges are FGCS (Whitley et al., 2018), a significant increase from 32% reported a few years prior (USDOE, 2014). Currently, one-third of undergraduates are FGCS (Cataldi et al., 2018). Results from national postsecondary data revealed that 42% of all SOC (i.e., racial/ethnic minority students) were first-generation, making them FGCSOC (Redford & Hoyer, 2017). Rates vary by racial/ethnic group; for example, Black students made up 14% of all FGCS compared to 27% who were Hispanic (Redford & Hoyer, 2017).

Postsecondary options for high school graduates include community colleges, 4-year universities, trade schools, military enlistments, apprenticeships, and certification programs, all play a huge role in increasing employable skills for job opportunities. Postsecondary institutions can be broadly categorized into two groups, PWIs and minority-serving institutions (MSIs). MSIs are those meeting Title III and Title V criteria, based on mission or student enrollment, comprised of majority (50% or greater) low-income, and significant percentage of racial/ethnic minoritized group membership ranging from not less than 40% Black, to 25% Hispanic, to 10% for the rest (e.g., Native American; Higher Education Opportunity Act [HEOA], 1965). There are seven types of MSIs, including Hispanic-serving institutions (HSIs). However, historically Black colleges and universities (HBCUs) were established before 1964 (i.e., pre-Civil Rights Act) to educate African American students. According to the National Center for Education Statistics (n.d.), there were 101 HBCUs in 2018, a slight decrease from 107 in 1991 (USDOE, 1991). Meanwhile, HSIs have grown over the years from 137 in 1990 to 425 as of 2014 (Vela & Gutierrez, 2017).

Conversely, there is no official designation for PWI, and the term is often used without thought allotted to the fact that these institutions were founded on racism, operate in structurally racialized spaces, and perpetuate systems of privilege and power based on race (Hughes, 2014). Research indicates that White students perceive campus climate at PWIs to be "'non-racist,' 'friendly,' and 'respectful'" whereas SOC perceive the campus climate at PWIs as "'racist,' 'hostile,' and 'disrespectful'" (Rankin & Reason 2005, p. 52). Whites have marginalized, dominated, and oppressed racial/ethnic minorities at varying levels at different times depending on their particular needs, one minoritized group may even be allowed to occupy a space of privilege over another based on the perceived value of their contribution to the labor market or their efforts to assimilate to White society (Bourke, 2016). For example, at the University of Iowa, "The Iowa Way" represents "how one must run their program," it is assumed "that The Iowa Way is the *right* way to do anything," while neglecting "the racial discrimination that [SOC] may have experienced on the Iowa campus" (TePoel, & Narcotta-Welp, 2020, p. 9).

Postsecondary Education Enrollment by Setting Type

Retention rates for these postsecondary settings demonstrate that FGCS and SOC face barriers to successful completion. In particular, only about 72% of FGCS continue a second year of college compared to 88% of non-FGCS, reflecting difficulty during the transition process (Radunzel, 2018). Conversely, between 50% and 70% of FGCS are expected to drop out before obtaining a degree or transferring to a 4-year university (Ishitani, 2006; Warburton et al., 2001). One-half of community college students are women, 25 years of age or older, work full time, have dependents, and belong to a minority racial/ethnic group (Pascarella et al., 2004).

FGCSOC have been attending various institutions in pursuit of higher education. The attrition rates for SOC at PWIs are increasing, while matriculation rates steadily decrease (Postsecondary National Policy Institute, 2021). These rates vary significantly based on type of postsecondary education setting, such as PWIs. For example, a national study reported that while only 12.9% of all Black undergraduate students attend HBCUs, HBCUs graduate 21.5% (nearly double) of all Black undergraduates (Provasnik & Shafer, 2004). In comparison, the remaining 87.1% of Black undergraduates who attend PWIs, graduate at a rate of 78.5%, and an estimated 41% will not complete their degrees within a 6-year time period (McClain & Perry, 2017).

THEORETICAL FRAMEWORK

Erickson's Psychosocial Theory

Based on Freud's psychoanalytic theory of individual and psychosexual development, Erikson created a theoretical framework with age-linked sequential stages for healthy human identity development (Erikson,

1950/1963, 1959/1980, 1968; Orenstein & Lewis, 2020). According to Erikson's theory of psychosocial development, individuals are balancing individual psychological needs with societal pressures to develop identity through awareness and self-reflection across the life span (Batra, 2013; Erikson, 1959/1980). Through coping skills that are influenced by the individual's culture, developmental tasks arise that require progression and growth. A balanced healthy personality is constructed by moving through the eight stages of the human life cycle (Batra, 2013). Each stage presents issues and developmental tasks that must be resolved based on the interactions from internal, biological, psychological, and environmental demands (Erikson, 1959/1980). Demands are influenced by social norms and roles individuals are expected to resolve based on a turning point or crisis (Erikson, 1968). The eight human life cycle stages include: trust vs. mistrust, autonomy vs. shame/doubt, initiative vs. guilt, industry vs. inferiority, identity vs. role confusion (prolonged), intimacy vs. isolation, and generativity vs. stagnation (Erikson, 1950/1963). Researchers have demonstrated the interconnection between psychosocial development and career development, linking issues for college students to include autonomy, sense of purpose, vocational identity, and occupational information (Bowers et al., 2001; Floerchinger, 1989; Long et al., 1995).

Application of Stages 5 and 6 of Erikson's Theory

Erikson's psychosocial theory aids in the analysis of FGCSOC postsecondary transition and career development with connections to issues of racial identity, identity diffusion, identity crisis, intimacy, and isolation. According to Erikson, the psychosocial crisis of identity vs. role confusion (Stage 5) occurs between the age of 13 to 19 years, and intimacy vs. isolation (Stage 6) between the ages of 20 and 39. This theory is applicable to FGCSOC based on the critical period of how societal practices and influences may positively or negatively influence the emergence of adulthood and overall identity development. Furthermore, psychosocial theory can be used to explore the postsecondary transition and career development with analysis of situations that influence the experimentation stage of career exploration, choices, and formation during college (Zuschiag & Whitbourne, 1994). Examining the development of FGCSOC in identity vs. role confusion and intimacy vs. isolation provides insight for assisting through the influences of social norms and practices and social maturity for postsecondary career transition and decision-making. While these are critical developmental periods for FGCSOC, resolution through these stages can provide information to assist with the growth of healthy career identity.

The psychological needs of college students including recognition of values, beliefs, aspirations, self-determination, and motivation (Pascarella & Terenzini, 1991) influence postsecondary readiness and career development. Coupled with societal demands and expectations, college students search for a place in society that provides acceptance of career choices and job-seeking skills. The intersection of school and homelife based on individual guidance about postsecondary options can be linked to the overall psychosocial crisis FGCSOC encounter during these stages. While this is a crucial developmental period, identity formation may lead to role confusion that may be applicable to FGCS and SOC. Erikson's theory articulates the importance of personal development through self-reflection and personal freedom while balancing social norms during the identity process in comparison to global expectations (Batra, 2013; Friedman, 2000). These stages are relevant to understanding how societal crises manifest into systemic barriers influencing the postsecondary transition and career development.

Some issues affecting the psychosocial stages of career development for FGCSOC include imposter syndrome, racial trauma, perceived discrimination, financial burden, social capital, mental health, cultural mismatch, self-concept, motivation, anxiety, support systems, persistence level, and family involvement (Chang et al., 2020; McClain et al., 2016; Stebleton et al., 2014). Psychosocial theory can be used to help explain the unique challenges and crises that impede FGCSOC's ability to successfully matriculate and transition into postsecondary career development and attainment (Soria & Stebleton, 2012). Considering the potential impact on the cognitive, social, and emotional development of FGCSOC, a sense of identity affects their ability to understand the postsecondary transition process (Orbes, 2008). Furthermore, psychosocial theory explains how the processes of career choices are influenced by factors related to social class, context of family, school, peers, mentors, and the neighborhood with societal influences that present limited choices (Allan et al., 2016). Thus, social and class inequalities during postsecondary transition for career development of FGCSOC must include an analysis of factors influencing career choices, goals, aspiration, maturity, beliefs, and decision-making (Harlow & Bowman, 2016; Jury et al., 2015; Raque-Bogdan & Lucas, 2016; Tate et al., 2015).

POSTSECONDARY BARRIERS AND NEEDS

Barriers to Postsecondary Transition and Career Development

Although colleges and universities have made progress by increasing enrollment rates for FGCS, these students still face barriers to successfully navigate, matriculate, and complete their educational goals (Stebleton & Soria, 2012). In order to promote positive career development and facilitate healthy social identity formation, it is necessary to identify psychosocial barriers in order to address them in a timely manner. Precollege factors (e.g., K–12 school, academic preparation, family constellation, peer group, personality, temperament) disproportionately affect FGCSOC's educational access and trajectories for postsecondary options (Portnoi & Kwong, 2011). Common barriers include the opportunity gap, lack of awareness on navigating the college environment, and achievement gaps with educational disparities, which impact academic performance and educational attainment.

Institutional Barriers

Literature on the topic of FGCS and SOC navigation through postsecondary education highlights the inequalities that begin in K–12 education. Issues that manifest into barriers include limited school funding for impoverished, low performance schools, which limit students' access to educational resources that would aid their academic preparation. Poor academic preparation has been sighted as a major barrier to college access and success (Katrevich & Aruguete, 2017). However, many practices implemented to reduce education disparities and improve achievement gaps, such as the integration of White teachers with SOC (Fergus, 2017), the group placement of students by "ability" (Hansen et al., 2018), and the use of punitive strategies for behavior management (Mallett, 2016), actually disproportionately impact FGCSOC's academic performance and subsequently hinder postsecondary preparation compared to their White peers (Cataldi et al., 2018; Katrevich & Aruguete, 2017).

FGCS are more likely to be less prepared to qualify for college admission (Barry et al., 2009; Pascarella et al., 2003, 2004). Even when academically qualified, FGCS are less likely to attend college within their first year of graduating high school (Cataldi et al., 2018). Furthermore, FGCS are less likely to be enrolled in college preparation classes, lowering their chances of being admitted to high-quality schools. Studies show that if students are enrolled in more rigorous curriculum such as advanced math courses, it increases the chances that FGCS will attend college (Horn & Nuñez, 2000; Katrevich & Aruguete, 2017). Yet, parental involvement in student choice of high school courses is lacking; noncollege educated parents are less informed about the value of taking rigorous curriculum. When FGCS do enroll in college, they are more likely to enroll in remedial coursework compared to their continuing-generation peers (Jenkins et al., 2009; Riehl, 1994). Moreover, FGCS who attend community colleges experience disparate benefits from institutional services due to failed access and negligent service programming efficacy (Shumaker & Wood, 2016).

Additionally, institutional historical legacy of inclusion or exclusion, compositional diversity, psychological and behavioral climate, and structural diversity are social factors that affect the career development and postsecondary readiness and retention of FGCSOC (Hurtado et al., 1999; McCallen & Johnson, 2019). The negative academic success and postsecondary performance for FGCSOC at PWIs can be attributed to experiences of microaggressions (Ellis et al., 2019; Gray Benson, 2020; Keels et al., 2017). In a recent study of FGCSOC, more than half (52%) reported experiencing a racial microaggression while attending a PWI; most believed that racial microaggressions would lead to stress (86%), affect their mental well-being (74%), affect their ability to make career-related decisions (60%), and had impacted their self-efficacy (52%); yet only a minority stated they would attend university-sponsored personal counseling (41%) or career services (42%) for racial microaggressions experienced on campus (Childs, 2018). Yet many institutions, despite claiming to be committed to diversity, equity, and inclusion continue to engage in institutional racist practices, preserving the "social stratification" (Tamargo, 2021).

Socioeconomic Barriers

FGCS tend to have more work and family obligations compared to their peers (Kuh, 2008; Stebleton & Soria, 2012). Research has shown that FGCS and SOC have limited access to financial aid (Sy et al., 2011). FGCS tend to work for longer hours, consequently limiting the amount of time spent on campus (Stebleton & Soria, 2012). Working full time, leaves students with less time to participate in high-impact educational opportunities, such as learning communities, service-learning, and study abroad programs (Kuh, 2008). Failure to engage in such learning opportunities puts these students at a disadvantage for academic and social integration. Given their low academic preparation and lack of social integration, it is not surprising that one-fourth (26%) of all FGCS drop out during their first year of college, compared to only 7% of their non-FGCS peers (Engle & Tinto, 2008).

FGCS report less support from parents compared to their peers whose parents have a college degree (Pascarella et al., 2003). Some students even report being discouraged from going to college (Engle, 2007). Parents who are of lower income ranges may expect their children to start working immediately after graduating high school (rather than go to college) so that they can contribute to the family's financial needs. Due to their own lack of postsecondary experience, parents may not understand the value of attending college, may have misconceptions about college processes, especially about the actual cost and financial aid opportunities and requirements. Consequently, parents of FGCS may discourage their children from attending college (Vargas, 2004).

Recently, Childs (2018) found prominent socioeconomic barriers reported by FGCSOC included financial stress (91%), lack of family assistance or support (70%), and lack of friend/mentor support system (50%).

Results from a qualitative study of Black male FGCS attending community college revealed similar issues: complexities of being a first-generation student (e.g., family pressure to be the first to graduate), difficulties of college (e.g., entry-level class difficulty), and facing racism (e.g., being profiled and stereotyped; Kirkman, 2018).

Personal Barriers

Precollege disadvantages experienced by FGCS include a basic lack of understanding about college (Pascarella et al., 2003). FGCSOC reported prominent personal barriers, including personal self-efficacy stress (65%), loneliness (62%), and academic concerns (57%; Childs, 2018). Similarly, Black male FGCS reported issues such as: questioning the value of higher education (e.g., community college often viewed as a last option), difficulties of college (e.g., feeling all alone), and facing the reality of racism (e.g., no one of color with whom they could identify; Kirkman, 2018). FGCS are less confident of their academic abilities and also less likely to ask for help from faculty compared to their classmates (Jenkins et al., 2009; Riehl, 1994).

COVID-19 Factors

The sudden shift to online and remote learning during COVID-19, has increased the disparate burdens confronting FGCSOC. Compared to their White peers, SOC experienced greater difficulty due to not knowing where to get help with courses, conflicts with home and family responsibilities, and feeling too unwell to participate (Means & Neisler, 2020). A recent study found students negotiated their identities differently in virtual (vs. face-to-face) classrooms, acknowledgment of COVID-19 impact created a sense of community in virtual classrooms, and incorporation of self-care practices fostered empowerment for students and educators (Sequeira & Dacey, 2020). The remote instruction during COVID for SOC was as good as or better than instruction as usual in terms of feeling included as a member of the class, being kept interested in the course, and having opportunities to collaborate with other students (Means & Neisler, 2020).

Current Events

Anti-racism. The pivotal moments of racial reckoning in the United States coupled with the #BlackMindsMatters and #BlackOnCampus movements call for equity and advocacy (Anderson et al., 2020; Casey, 2020). Using intersectionality to promote marginalized college students' healthy psychosocial development requires a social justice dialogue about institutional practices for equity and access. The current educational climate calls for an intersectionality lens for the deconstruction of barriers within physical, intellectual, social, and emotional development for marginalized college students. Specifically, the needs of minority student populations create a heightened awareness of educational injustice, racism, and inequalities within the education systems resulting in disenfranchised students (Hilton & White, 2017; Lampinen, 2020).

Higher education can arguably be described as a place that facilitates inequity and stress among students with marginalized identities that include students with disabilities; first-generation, low-income students; and LGBTQ+ students' (Bowling et al., 2020; Glick et al., 2018). The Black Lives Matter movement and COVID-19 calls attention to the intersectionality of race, class, and economic barriers and the need for social justice practices on college campuses (Li & Lalani, 2020). Furthermore, attention to racial discrimination is highlighted as a common occurrence to police brutality, but current dialogue has also expanded to examine the impact of systemic racism within college spaces and policies (Flaherty, 2020; Hargons et al., 2017). Illuminating the racial inequities and disparities at PWIs calls for social action and change for the healthy postsecondary transition and career attainment of FGCSOC.

Ash et al. (2020) recommended that higher education can move towards an anti-racist model for creating change by incorporating anti-racist models and intervention at the institutional level. Furthermore, Carr (2016) argues for the acknowledgment of Whiteness and White privilege being inextricably linked to building an equitable and transformative educational experience within institutions of higher education. The myriad levels of White supremacy have contributed to the permeances of various forms of racism and oppression entered by individuals from underrepresented backgrounds. In fact, these acts can have profound consequences for positive postsecondary transition for career development (Gillborn, 2015).

Career Development and Postsecondary Transition Needs

Considering the economic growth and recession influences on job availability patterns, government programs that provide support for FGCS are required. Furthermore, the COVID-19 pandemic has left in its wake far-reaching implications into the future outlook of the workforce (i.e., how people work and where they work). According to a series of recent articles published in Forbes, remote employment models might be the permanent future of the work world. The year 2020 transformed the business world overnight, from identifying and providing technology equipment to enable telework to considering and establishing accommodations and policies to meet the evolving personal and family needs of their employees (Robinson, 2020). While COVID-19 thrust remote work into hyperdrive in 2020, the percentage of telework is expected to double in 2021 (Castrillon, 2020).

This may have significant implications on how institutions of higher education train and prepare students for the job market, specifically FGCSOC who might already be disadvantaged in terms of access and skills level in technology use. Expected lasting impacts from COVID-19 include the following: (a) telework models, including hybrid models which combine in-person with remote work practices; (b) videoconferencing, including video chat which is proving more valuable than traditional phone and conference calls; and (c) virtual conferences and events due to their cost-saving benefits, and because people are more reluctant to leave their homes, and have become more "sensitive to social interaction" (Stahl, 2021, n.p.).

Attending to societal influences that play a role in postsecondary transition for FGCSOC is warranted. Career and educational advancement have been linked to the benefits derived from access to various resources including career counseling, assessment, and academic advising based on informed choices. Thus, identifying postsecondary transition needs of FGCS, including SOC that may foster successful academic matriculation and career attainment is paramount. FGCSOC are often underrepresented on college campuses and face various barriers including financial strain, culture shock, discrimination, systemic role-related inequities, and psychological distress (Choy et al., 2000; Hurd et al., 2018; Inkelas et al., 2007; Smith et al., 2007). Moreover, FGCSOC experience culture conflict between their working-class backgrounds and the middle-class culture of higher education (Covarrubias & Fryberg, 2015; Covarrubias et al., 2015). Effective use of brief interventions provides transitional support to address social class differences while navigating college (Stephens et al., 2015). Furthermore, interventions that promote culture capital and normalization of their unique backgrounds by uncovering their hidden strengths and identities may support FGCS's ability to cope with stress and subsequent health outcomes. To support the career development and transition of FGCS, including SOC, the assessment of family capital, priorities, belief system, family involvement, and values can assist with postsecondary transition (Gofen, 2009; McCarron & Inkelas, 2006). In addition, the support and guidance received from school and career counselors to aid and assist with college information has been found to play a key role (Bryan et al., 2011; Gibbons & Shoffner, 2004; Roderick et al., 2011).

Despite considerable efforts made to increase postsecondary access and participation among underrepresented populations, FGCS are still at a clear disadvantage (Engle, 2007). Several barriers persist which hinder FGCS from attending and graduating from college. However, there are several interventions that could be put in place to help these students gain access and be successful in college. Engle (2007) posited that interventions aimed at improving access and subsequent completion of college by FGCS should target the following:

Improving pre-college preparation: This could be achieved by exposing students to a more rigorous academic curriculum at the high school level including advanced math. Greater access to college preparatory courses will give students an upper edge in college admission.

Forming early college aspirations: Providing college information to both students and parents early on will help increase chances for college attendance and persistence.

Increasing access to financial aid: Knowledge on how and when to apply for financial aid would be helpful. Increased financial aid will help lessen the burden on the students, reduce the number of working hours, and engage more with academic and social activities on campus (Katrivich & Aruguete, 2017). Knowledge about different scholarship options would also be helpful, and such funding sources could increase financial stability of the students and give them more time to focus on academic and social integration (Katrivich & Aruguete, 2017).

Support during transition: FGCS need a lot of support as they make academic, social, and cultural transitions to college. Bridge programs can help socialize students to the academic environment. Involving parents will orient them to the demands of college and hence be more supportive of their children. Advising, tutoring, and mentoring by faculty and peers can help maintain the needed support throughout the college experience. However, FGCSOC revealed that developmental education programs negatively affected their self-efficacy (Murphy, 2018).

Exposure to and engagement with the college environment: FGCS tend to spend a limited amount of time on campus as they must balance school, work, and sometimes family life obligations. Schools should offer additional opportunities, such as work-study to help students remain on campus much longer while meeting their financial needs. Faculty should increase interaction and engagement in the classrooms given that this is the most time students spend on campus (Engle, 2007). Since FGCS are always reluctant to engage with faculty, structured interaction in the class may increase participation (Katrivich & Aruguete, 2017).

RECOMMENDATIONS

Implications for Research

With the surge of research pertaining to FGCS, a more comprehensive understanding of the experiences and career development of those who are SOC is warranted. There is a need for more empirical research to assist in understanding the growing personal, social, and emotional barriers and needs of this unique population. Future research should focus on the intersectionality of accessibility to mental health services tailored to this population of students that consequently focuses on their career development and decision-making opportunities at PWIs. Additionally, research related to the specific types of support programs and services that are offered at the various types of postsecondary institutions and their efficacy in enhancing career development and educational attainment would be useful. Qualitative studies could help reveal the talents, resilience, and strengths that FGCSOC bring with them and which could be tapped to increase their persistence and ultimate completion of college.

Future research should also examine the career development needs of FGCSOC enrolled within the science, technology, engineering, and math (STEM) fields. Research should examine whether instructors' behaviors (e.g., focusing on students' assets rather than deficits, affirming students' potential as scientists) cultivate equitable and inclusive environments (White et al., 2021). Investigating social positioning as it pertains to enrollment in college majors connected to STEM disciplines may provide crucial information for supporting completion in the various types of institutions (McCoy et al., 2020). Vital to the ultimate academic and career success of FGCSOC is more research focused on the middle and high school years to include increasing college access, career exploration activities, and service-learning opportunities (Brown, 2020).

Implications for Practice

An important factor to consider when supporting FGCSOC is establishing early interventions to counteract microaggressions during primary and secondary school. Keels and colleagues (2017) suggested that prior academic achievement such as high school GPA and racial-ethnic identity status share a relationship between microaggressions and depressive symptoms. Thus, exposure to racial microaggressions may stunt the students' academic, emotional, and identity development leading up to college entry as they are less prepared for both academic and social adjustment. This can be linked to the depressive symptoms experienced at the start of college that may further create barriers for mental health help-seeking and supports. However, previous positive experiences in academic advising and career guidance can lead to both short-term and long-term outcomes, and willingness to seek out these services if and when needed in the future. A recent study found that teachers and school counselors strongly influenced female FGCSOC decisions to pursue higher education (Portnoi & Kwong, 2019).

Additionally, the heightened vulnerability and psychological distress produces greater stressors that may require formal mentoring programs and intervention strategies (Hurd et al., 2016). Institutions can create programs for FGCSOC that support natural mentoring relationships through the use of faculty, student book clubs, and community engagement events (Schwartz et al., 2018). Recommendations include the promotion of clear messages about the benefits derived from utilizing campus support services and intentional engagement efforts to alert, attract, and retain FGCSOC throughout their college-going experience. The use of outreach programming and policies to increase resilience and increase motivation for college completion would serve to assist this vulnerable population. Peer support programs that demonstrate the journey of faculty and staff who identify as first-generation would create a sense of community, comradery, and engagement for FGCSOC (Mishra, 2020). Another recommendation is to support FGCSOC transition to college early through the implementation of comprehensive and integrative programs (Kezar et al., 2020). The use of appraisal support from natural mentors using social networks could serve to promote healthy development for FGCSOC (Hurd et al., 2018). Focusing on the cultural capital skills for navigating the college environment, while paying attention to the college readiness framework was recommended for assisting FGCSOC (White et al., 2020). Building academic literacy in high school, with attention to college communication styles can help establish norms for successful postsecondary transition (White et al., 2020).

Implications for Policy

Public policy that addresses FGCSOC career development and postsecondary readiness must incorporate the needed investment in higher education grant aid and support programs. McFadden (2015) recommends that first-generation community colleges reexamine campus policies that strengthen student support services. Policies that consider the importance of health, social, and cultural capital for academic success should be implemented (WHO, 2014). For example, adopting a paradigm shift from trying to increase trust among racial/ethnic minoritized groups to working to improve trustworthiness among academic, health, and employment institutions throughout the United States (Best et al., 2021). Thus, changing narratives, advocating for policies, and investing in

> institutional resources that facilitate cultural health can push back against monoculturalism and anti-Blackness by valuing the cultures of Black students and students of color and by building communities in which students can generate a wellspring of pride and resilience in their cultural backgrounds. (Grier-Reed et al., 2021, p. 13)

Increasing opportunities with federal financial assistance at the state and local levels would promote higher education access and retainment. Creating tuition-caps with reduced expenses for housing and living costs would also reduce the number of FGCSOC having to work multiple jobs. Future policies can also include support for the hiring and retention of faculty that identify as first-generation and members from racial and ethnic minoritized groups. Unfortunately, recent policies, such as the former President's Executive Order on Combating Race and Sex Stereotyping (Exec. Order No. 13950, 2020), could be in stark contrast to those that would reduce racial/ethnic disparities and promote equitable success among FGCSOC.

CONCLUSION

In this chapter we explored the psychosocial theoretical framework for the examination into FGCS' career development needs. According to Erikson's psychosocial framework the identification of barriers within the identity vs. role confusion and intimacy vs. isolation, Stages 5 and 6 respectively, facilitate healthy postsecondary transition for successful academic matriculation and career attainment. Furthermore, we elucidated how current events including antiracism, ant-Asian hate and violence, and anti-Blackness significantly impact the career choice and career development of FGCSOC. The recent incidents of social injustice directed towards minority groups will have significant implications in the choice of where graduating SOC might choose to work. Additionally, we discussed major factors that influence academic matriculation and career attainment for postsecondary transition of FGCS, including those who identify as persons of color. Further, we provided recommendations of appropriate interventions to be integrated in American postsecondary institutions in order to best assist this unique and growing population. Areas for future research and policy changes to promote equitable navigation through postsecondary transition and career development were also included. In conclusion, it is imperative to promote positive career development for FGCSC within the United States.

DISCUSSION QUESTIONS

1. Identify and describe the impact of current racial climate on advocacy efforts at the local, state, and national levels to deconstruct and reform higher education practices for this unique population?
2. How can higher education institutions promote the intersectionality of multiple identities held by first-generation students of color

and healthy psychosocial development in lieu of racism, discrimination, and oppression?

3. Identify empowerment and strength-based interventions at the individual, institutional, and cultural levels for postsecondary transition and career development for this population?

4. What do you think are the future implications of the pandemic (COVID-19) on career planning and career development of FGCSOC?

ACTIVITIES

1. *Psychosocial Assets Exploration.* Using an anti-deficit lens, identify and compare first-generation college students of color assets within Erikson psychosocial Stage 5 and Stage 6.

2. *Resiliency and Advocacy Tools.* Conduct an online search and identify evidence-based interventions and programs for the development of resiliency techniques and tools for use with this population. Describe advocacy efforts for implementation.

AUTHOR NOTE

We have no known conflict of interest to disclose.

Correspondence concerning this chapter should be addressed to Jonique R. Childs, S170 Furcolo, Department of Student Development, University of Massachusetts Amherst, 813 North Pleasant Street, Amherst, MA, 01003. Email: jrchilds@umass.edu

REFERENCES

Akiba, D. (2020). Reopening America's schools during the COVID-19 pandemic: Protecting Asian students from stigma and discrimination. *Frontiers in Sociology, 5.*

Allan, B. A., Garriott, P. O., & Keene, C. N. (2016). Outcomes of social class and classism in first- and continuing-generation college students. *Journal of Counseling Psychology, 63*(4), 487–496. https://doi.org/10.1037/cou0000160

Anderson, R. M., Heesterbeek, H., Klinkenberg, D., & Hollingsworth, T. D. (2020). How will country-based mitigation measures influence the course of the COVID-19 epidemic? *The Lancet, 395*(10228), 931–934. https://doi.org/10.1016/s0140-6736(20)30567-5

Ash, A. N., Hill, R., Risdon, S., & Jun, A. (2020). Anti-racism in higher education: A model for change. *Race and Pedagogy Journal: Teaching and Learning for Justice, 4*(3). https://soundideas.pugetsound.edu/rpj/vol4/iss3/2

Barry, L. M., Hudley, C., Kelly, M., & Cho, S. J. (2009). Differences in self-reported disclosure of college experiences by first-generation college student status. *Adolescence, 44*(173), 55–68.

Batra, S. (2013). The psychosocial development of children: Implications for education and society—Erik Erikson in context. *Contemporary Education Dialogue, 10*(2), 249–278. https://doi.org/10.1177/0973184913485014

Bensimon, E. M. (2018). Reclaiming racial justice in equity. *Change: The Magazine of Higher Learning, 50*(3–4), 95–98. https://doi.org/10.1080/00091383.2018 .1509623

Berman, G., & Paradies, Y. (2010). Racism, disadvantage and multiculturalism: Towards effective anti-racist praxis. *Ethnic and Racial Studies, 33*(2), 214–232. https://doi.org/10.1080/01419870802302272

Best, A. L., Fletcher, F. E., Kadono, M., & Warren, R. C. (2021). Institutional distrust among African Americans and building trustworthiness in the COVID-19 response: Implications for ethical public health practice. *Journal of Health Care for the Poor and Underserved 32*(1), 90–98. https://doi.gov/10.1353/hpu.2021.0010

Bilton, P. D. (2002). Strategies to support degree attainment for first-generation college students (Publication No. 192407550). *NAAAS Conference Proceedings.* ProQuest.

Blackwell, E., & Pinder, P. J. (2014). What are the motivational factors of first-generation minority college students who overcome their family histories to pursue higher education? *College Student Journal, 48*(1), 45–56.

Bourke, B. (2016). Meaning and implications of being labelled a predominantly white institution. *College & University, 91*(3), 12–21.

Bowers, P. J., Dickman, M. M., & Fuqua, D. R. (2001). Psychosocial and career development related to employment of graduating seniors. *NASPA Journal, 38,* 326–347.

Bowling, J., Miller, R. A., & Mather, N. (2020). Making campus-based LGBTQ climate assessments matter. *Journal of Student Affairs Research and Practice, 57*(2), 197–211. http://dx.doi.org/10.1080/19496591.2019.1631837

Brown, C. W. (2020). *College access for prospective first-generation high school students: Parent perceptions* (Publication No. 27832648) [Doctoral dissertation, Southern Illinois University]. ProQuest Dissertations and Theses Global.

Bryan, J., Moore-Thomas, C., Day-Vines, N. L., & Holcomb-McCoy, C. (2011). School counselors and social capital: The effects of high school college counseling on college application rates. *Journal of Counseling & Development, 89*(2), 190–199. https://doi.org/10.1002/j.1556-6678.2011.tb00077.x

Bui, K. V. T. (2002). First-generation college students at a four-year university: Background characteristics, reasons for pursuing higher education, and first-year experiences. *College Student Journal, 36*(1), 3–11.

Buchanan, L., Bui, Q., & Patel, J. K. (2020, July 3). Black lives matter may be the largest movement in U.S. history. *The New York Times.* https://www.nytimes .com/interactive/2020/07/03/us/george-floyd-protests-crowd-size.html

Callan, R. D. (2018). *Black, female, first-generation college students: Perceptions of academic persistence* (Publication No. 10808686) [Doctoral dissertation, University of Miami]. ProQuest Dissertations and Theses Global.

Carr, P. R. (2016). Whiteness and White privilege: Problematizing race and racism in a color-blind world and in education. *International Journal of Critical Pedagogy, 7*(1), 51–74

Casey, N. (2020). College made them feel equal. The virus exposed how unequal their lives are. *The New York Times, 4.* https://www.nytimes.com/2020/04/04/us/politics/coronavirus-zoom-college-classes.html

Castrillon, C. (2020, December 27). This is the future of remote work in 2021. *Forbes.* https://www.forbes.com/sites/carolinecastrillon/2021/12/27/this-is-the-future-of-remote-work-in-2021/?sh=309c4f3b1e1d

Cataldi, E. F., Bennett, C. T., & Chen, X. (2018). *First-generation students: College access, persistence, and postbachelor's outcomes* (Stats in Brief No. NCES 2018-421). U.S. Department of Education, National Center for Educational Statistics. https://nces.ed.gov/pubs2018/2018421.pdf

Chang, J., Wang, S.-W., Mancini, C., McGrath-Mahrer, B., & Orama de Jesus, S. (2020). The complexity of cultural mismatch in higher education: Norms affecting first-generation college students' coping and help-seeking behaviors. *Cultural Diversity & Ethnic Minority Psychology, 26*(3), 280–294. https://doi.org/10.1037/cdp0000311

Childs, J. R. (2018). *First-generation college students of color attending PWIs in the midwest relationship among help-seeking behaviors for racial microaggressions, academic self-efficacy, academic stress, mental well-being, and career decision-making difficulties: Using social cognitive career theory (SCCT)* [Doctoral dissertation, The University of Iowa]. Iowa Research Online. https://ir.uiowa.edu/etd/6394/

Choy, S. (2001). *Students whose parents did not go to college: Postsecondary access, persistence, and attainment* (Report No. NCES 2001-126). U.S. Department of Education, National Center for Education Statistics. https://nces.ed.gov/pubs2001/2001126.pdf

Choy, S. P., Horn, L. J., Nuñez, A.-M., & Chen, X. (2000). Transition to college: What helps at-risk students and students whose parents did not attend college. *New Directions for Institutional Research, 2000*(107), 45–63. https://doi.org/10.1002/ir.10704

Conefrey, T. (2018). Supporting first-generation students' adjustment to college with high-impact practices. *Journal of College Student Retention: Research, Theory & Practice.* Advance online publication. https://doi.org/10.1177/1521025118807402

Covarrubias, R., & Fryberg, S. A. (2015). Movin' on up (to college): First-generation college students' experiences with family achievement guilt. *Cultural Diversity and Ethnic Minority Psychology, 21*(3), 420–429. https://doi.org/10.1037/a0037844

Covarrubias, R., Romero, A., & Trivelli, M. (2015). Family achievement guilt and mental well- being of college students. *Journal of Child and Family Studies, 24*(7), 2031–2037. https://doi.org/10.1007/s10826-014-0003-8

Ellis, J. M., Powell, C. S., Demetriou, C. P., Huerta-Bapat, C., & Panter, A. T. (2019). Examining first-generation college student lived experiences with microaggressions and microaffirmations at a predominately White public research university. *Cultural Diversity and Ethnic Minority Psychology, 25*(2), 266–279. https://doi.org/10.1037/cdp0000198

Engle, J. (2007). Postsecondary access and success for first-generation college students. *American Academic, 3,* 25–48. https://www.voced.edu.au/content/ngv%3A64786

Engle, J., & Tinto, V. (2008). *Moving beyond access: College success for low-income, first generation students.* The Pell Institute for the Study of Opportunity in Higher Education.

Erikson, E. H. (1963). *Childhood and society.* W. W. Norton & Company. (Original work published 1950)

Erikson, E. H. (1980). *Identity and the life cycle.* W. W. Norton & Company. (Original work published 1959)

Erikson, E. H. (1968). *Identity: Youth and crisis.* W. W. Norton & Company.

Escayg, K. A (2018). The missing links: Enhancing anti-bias education with anti-racist education. *Journal of Curriculum, Teaching, Learning and Leadership in Education, 3*(1), 4. https://digitalcommons.unomaha.edu/ctlle/vol3/iss1/4

Exec. Order No. 13950, 3 C.F.R. (2020). https://www.govinfo.gov/content/pkg/FR-2020-09-28/pdf/2020-21534.pdf

Fergus, E. (2017). The integration project among white teachers and racial/ethnic minority youth: Understanding bias in school practice. *Theory Into Practice, 56*(3), 169–177. https://doi.org/10.1080/00405841.2017.1336036

Flaherty, C. (2020). *Making sense of the senseless.* https://www.insidehighered.com/news/2020/06/03/academics-called-help-interpretguide-national-response-police-violence-and-related

Floerchinger, D. S. (1989). Bereavement: Applying Erikson's theory of psychosocial development to college students (Publication No. ED312577). *ERIC.* https://eric.ed.gov/?id=ED312577

Friedman, L. J. (2000). *Identity's architect: A biography of Erik H. Erikson.* Harvard University Press.

Gibbons, M. M., & Shoffner, M. F. (2004). Prospective first-generation college students: Meeting their needs through social cognitive career theory. *Professional School Counseling, 8*(1), 91–97.

Gillborn, D. (2015). Intersectionality, critical race theory, and the primacy of racism: Race, class, gender, and disability in education. *Qualitative Inquiry, 21*(3), 277–287. https://doi.org/10.1177/1077800414557827

Glick, J. L., Theall, K. P., Andrinopoulos, K. M., & Kendall, C. A. (2018). The role of discrimination in care postponement among trans-feminine individuals in the U.S. national transgender discrimination survey. *LGBT Health, 5*(3),171–179. https://doi.org/10.1089/lgbt.2017.0093

Gofen, A. (2009). Family capital: How first-generation higher education students break the intergenerational cycle. *Family Relations, 58*(1), 104–120. https://doi.org/10.1111/j.1741-3729.2008.00538.x

Gray Benson, A. C. (2020). *An exploration of factors influencing first-generation college students' ability to graduate college: A Delphi study* [Doctoral dissertation, Antioch University]. Antioch University Repository and Archive. https://aura.antioch.edu/cgi/viewcontent.cgi?article=1563&context=etds

Grier-Reed, T., Said, R., & Quiññones, M. (2021). From antiblackness to cultural health in higher education. *Education Sciences, 11*(2), Article 57. https://doi .org/10.3390/educsci11020057

Hansen, M., Levesque, E., Valant, J., & Quintero, D. (2018). *The 2018 Brown Center Report on American education: How well are American students learning?* Brown Center on Education Policy at Brookings.

Hargons, C., Mosley, D., Falconer, J., Faloughi, R., Singh, A., Stevens-Watkins, D., & Cokley, K. (2017). Black lives matter: A call to action for counseling psychology leaders. *The Counseling Psychologist, 45*(6), 873–901. https://doi.org/ 10.1177/0011000017733048

Harlow, A. J., & Bowman, S. L. (2016). Examining the career decision self-efficacy and career maturity of community college and first-generation students. *Journal of Career Development, 43*(6), 512–525. https://doi.org/10.1177/ 0894845316633780

Harper, S. R. (2010). An anti-deficit achievement framework for research on students of color in STEM. *New Directions for Institutional Research, 2010*(148), 63–74. https://doi.org/10.1002/ir.362

Havlik, S., Pulliam, N., Malott, K., & Steen, S. (2020). Strengths and struggles: First-generation college-goers persisting at one predominantly white institution. *Journal of College Student Retention: Research, Theory & Practice, 22*(1), 118–140. https://doi.org/10.1177/1521025117724551

Higher Education Opportunity Act of 1965, Pub. L. No. 110-315, 122 Stat. 3078 (1965). https://www.govinfo.gov/content/pkg/PLAW-110publ315/pdf/PLAW-110 publ315.pdf

Horn, L., & Nuñez, A.-M. (2000). *Mapping the road to college: First-generation students' math track, planning strategies, and context of support* (NCES 2000-153). U.S. Department of Education, National Center for Education Statistics.

Hughes, R. L. (2014, May 29). *10 signs of institutionalized racism.* Diverse Issues in Higher Education. https://diverseeducation.com/article/64583/

Hurd, N. M., Albright, J., Wittrup, A., Negrete, A., & Billinglsey, J. (2018). Appraisal support from natural mentors, self-worth, and psychological distress: Examining the experiences of underrepresented students transitioning through college. *Journal Youth and Adolescence. 47*(5), 1100–1112. http://doi. org/10.1007/s10964-017-0798-x

Hurd, N. M., Tan, J. S., & Loeb, E. L. (2016). Natural mentoring relationships and the adjustment to college among under-represented students. *American Journal of Community Psychology, 57*(3–4), 330–341. https://doi.org/10.1002/ajcp.12059

Hurtado, S., Milem, J., Clayton-Pederson, A., & Allen, W. (1999). *Enacting diverse learning environments: Improving the climate for racial/ethnic diversity in higher education.* (Publication No. ED 430-514) [ASHE-ERIC Higher Education Report] . The George Washington University, Graduate School of Education and Human Development.

Inkelas, K. K., Daver, Z. E., Vogt, K. E., & Leonard, J. B. (2007). Living–learning programs and first-generation college students' academic and social transition to college. *Research in Higher Education, 48*(4), 403–434. https://doi.org/ 10.1007/s11162-006-9031-6

Ishitani, T. T. (2006). Studying attrition and degree completion behavior among first-generation college students in the United States. *The Journal of Higher Education, 77*(5), 861–885. https://doi.org/10.1353/jhe.2006.0042

Jenkins, A. L., Miyazaki, Y., & Janosik, S. M. (2009). Predictors that distinguish first-generation college students from non-first generation college students. *Journal of Multicultural, Gender and Minority Studies, 3*(1), 1–9.

Jury, M., Smeding, A., Court, M., & Darnon, C. (2015). When first-generation students succeed at university: On the link between social class, academic performance, and performance-avoidance goals. *Contemporary Educational Psychology, 41*, 25–36. https://doi.org/10.1016/j.cedpsych.2014.11.001

Katrevich, A. V., & Aruguete, M. S. (2017). Recognizing challenges and predicting success in first-generation university students. *Journal of STEM Education: Innovations and Research, 18*(2), 40–44.

Keels, M., Durkee, M., & Hope, E. (2017). The psychological and academic costs of school-based racial and ethnic microaggressions. *American Educational Research Journal, 54*(6), 1316–1344. https://doi.org/10.3102/0002831217722120

Kezar, A., Hypolite, L., & Kitchen, J. A. (2020). Career self-efficacy: A mixed-methods study of an underexplored research area for first-generation, low-income, and underrepresented college students in a comprehensive college transition program. *American Behavioral Scientist, 64*(3), 298–324. https://doi.org/10.1177/0002764219869409

Kirkman, S. D. (2018). *Persisting to graduation: Experiences of degree-seeking, first-generation, African-American males at a community college* [Doctoral dissertation, University of Dayton]. OhioLINK. https://etd.ohiolink.edu/apexprod/rws_olink/r/1501/10?clear=10&p10_accession_num=dayton1542727688823316

Kuh, G. D. (2008). *High-impact educational practices: What they are, who has access to them, and why they matter.* Association of American Colleges and Universities.

Lampinen, A. (2020). *Tweeting for change: How Twitter users practice hashtag activism through #blacklivesmatter and #metoo.* http://jultika.oulu.fi/files/nbnfioulu-202005262182.pdf

Laybourn, S., & Pine, S. (2020, June, 6). Examining anti-blackness in TRA & Asian American communities. *KAAN.* https://www.wearekaan.org/post/examining-anti-blackness-in-tra-asian-american-communities

Learning Scientists for Racial Justice (2020, November 18). *Dear professor: On anti-Blackness and learning.* Inside Higher Ed. https://www.insidehighered.com/views/2020/11/18/group-non-black-scholars-invites-other-professors-help-strengthen-teaching-support

Lederer, A. M., Hoban, M. T., Lipson, S. K., Zhou, S., & Eisenberg, D. (2021). More than inconvenienced: The unique needs of U.S. college students during the COVID-19 pandemic. *Health Education & Behavior, 48*(1), 14–19. https://doi.org/10.1177/1090198120969372

Li, C., & Lalani, F. (2020, April 29). *The COVID-19 pandemic has changed higher education forever. This is how* [Online forum post]. World Economic Forum. https://www.weforum.org/agenda/2020/04/coronavirus-education-global-covid19-online-digital-learning/

Lee, S., & Waters, S. F. (2021). Asians and Asian Americans' experience of racial discrimination during the COVID=19 pandemic: Impacts on health outcomes and the buffering role of social support. *Stigma and Health, 6*(1), 70–78. https://doi.org/10.1037/sah0000275

Long, B. E., Sowa, C. J., & Niles, S. G. (1995). Differences in student development reflected by the career decisions of college seniors. *Journal of College Student Development, 36*(1), 47–52.

Longwell-Grice, R., Adsitt, N. Z., Mullins, K., & Serrata, W. (2016). The first ones: Three studies on first-generation college students. *NACADA Journal, 36*(2), 34–46.

Mallett, C. A. (2016). The school-to-prison pipeline: A critical review of the punitive paradigm shift. *Child and Adolescent Social Work Journal, 33*(1), 15–24. https://doi.org/10.1007/s10560-015-0397-1

McCallen, L. S., & Johnson, H. L. (2019). The role of institutional agents in promoting higher education success among first-generation college students at a public urban university. *Journal of Diversity in Higher Education, 13*(4), 320–332. https://doi.org/10.1037/dhe0000143

McCarron, G. P., & Inkelas, K. K. (2006). The gap between educational aspirations and attainment for first-generation college students and the role of parental involvement. *Journal of College Student Development, 47*(5), 534–549. https://doi.org/10.1353/csd.2006.0059

McClain, K. S., & Perry, A. (2017). Where did they go: Retention rates for students of color at predominantly white institutions. *College Student Affairs Leadership, 4*(1), Article 3. http://scholarworks.gvsu.edu/csal/vol4/iss1/3

McClain, S., Beasley, S. T., Jones, B., Awosogba, O., Jackson, S., & Cokley, K. (2016). An examination of the impact of racial and ethnic identity, impostor feelings, and minority status stress on the mental health of Black college students. *Journal of Multicultural Counseling and Development, 44*(2), 101–117. https://doi.org/10.1002/jmcd.12040

McCoy, D. L. (2014). A phenomenological approach to understanding first-generation college students' of color transitions to one "extreme" predominantly white institution. *College Student Affairs Journal, 32*(1), 155–169.

McCoy, D. L., Luedke, C. L., Lee-Johnson, J., & Winkle-Wagner, R. (2020). Transformational mentoring practices: Students' perspectives on practitioner-educators' support during college. *Journal of Student Affairs Research and Practice, 57*(1), 28–41. https://doi.org/10.1080/19496591.2019.1614934

McFadden, D. L. H. (2015). Health and academic success: A look at the challenges of first-generation community college students. *Journal of the American Association of Nurse Practitioners, 28*(4), 227–232. https://doi.org/10.1002/2327-6924.12345

Means, B., & Neisler, J. (2020). *Unmasking inequality: STEM course experiences during the COVID-19 pandemic.* Digital Promise Global.

Mirza, H. S. (2018). Decolonizing higher education: Black Feminism and the intersectionality of race and gender. *Journal of Feminist Scholarship, 7*, 1–12.

Mishra, S. (2020). Social networks, social capital, social support and academic success in higher education: A systematic review with a special focus on 'underrepresented' students. *Educational Research Review, 29*, Article 100307. https://doi.org/10.1016/j.edurev.2019.100307

Murphy, M. (2018). *An analysis of the meaning, barriers, and value of developmental education for first-generation minority students at a community college* [Master's thesis, Eastern Illinois University]. The Keep. https://thekeep.eiu.edu/theses/3580

National Center for Education Statistics. (n.d.). *Historically Black colleges and universities*. Institute of Education Sciences. https://nces.ed.gov/fastfacts/display .asp?id=667

Orbes, M. P. (2008). Theorizing multidimensional identity negotiation: Reflections on the lived experiences of first-generation college students. *New Direction for Child and Adolescent Development, 2008*(120), 81–95. https://doi.org/10.1002/ cd.217

Orenstein, G. A., & Lewis, L. (2020). *Eriksons stages of psychosocial development*. StatPearls. https://www.ncbi.nlm.nih.gov/books/NBK556096/#!po=7.14286

Owens, D., Lacey, K., Rawls, G., & Holbert-Quince, J. (2010). First-generation African American male college students: Implications for career counselors. *The Career Development Quarterly, 58*(4), 291–300. https://doi.org/10.1002/ j.2161-0045.2010.tb00179.x

Pascarella, E. T., Pierson, C. T., Wolniak, G. C., & Terenzini, P. T. (2004). First-generation college students: Additional evidence on college experiences and outcomes. *The Journal of Higher Education, 75*(3), 249–284. https://doi.org/10.1080/ 00221546.2004.11772256

Pascarella, E. T., & Terenzini, P. T. (1991). *How college affects students: Findings and insights from twenty years of research* (Vol. 1). Jossey-Bass.

Pascarella, E. T., Wolniak, G. C., Pierson, C. T., & Terenzini, P. T. (2003). Experiences and outcomes of first-generation students in community colleges. *Journal of College Student Development, 44*(3), 420–429. https://doi.org/10.1353/csd .2003.0030

Pike, G. R., & Kuh, G. D. (2005). First- and second-generation college students: A comparison of their engagement and intellectual development. *The Journal of Higher Education, 76*(3), 276–300. https://doi.org/10.1080/00221546.2005 .11772283

Pollock, M. (2004). Race wrestling: Struggling strategically with race in educational practice and research. *American Journal of Education, 111*(1), 25–67.

Portnoi, L. M., & Kwong, T. M. (2011). Enhancing the academic experiences of first-generation master's students. *Journal of Student Affairs Research and Practice, 48*(4), 411–427. https://doi.org/10.2202/1949-6605.6268

Portnoi, L. M., & Kwong, T. M. (2019). Employing resistance and resilience in pursuing K-12 schooling and higher education: Lived experiences of successful female first-generation students of color. *Urban Education, 54*(3), 430–458. https://doi.org/10.1177/0042085915623333

Postsecondary National Policy Institute. (2021). *Factsheets: First-generation students*. https://pnpi.org/first-generation-students/

Pratt, I. S., Harwood, H. B., Cavazos, J. T., & Ditzfeld, C. P. (2019). Should I stay or should I go? Retention in first-generation college students. *Journal of College*

372 ■ J. R. CHILDS, J. SÁNCHEZ, and G. WAMBU

Student Retention: Research, Theory & Practice, 21(1), 105–118. https://doi .org/10.1177/1521025117690868

Provasnik, S., & Shafer, L. L. (2004). *Historically Black colleges and universities, 1976 to 2001* (Publication No. NCES 2004–062). U.S. Department of Education, National Center for Education Statistics. http://purl.access.gpo.gov/GPO/ LPS54090

Radunzel, J. (2018). *They may be first but will they last? Retention and transfer behavior of first-generation students* (Working paper No. 2018-5). ACT.

Rankin, S. R., & Reason, R. D. (2005). Differing perceptions: How students of color and white students perceive campus climate for underrepresented groups. *Journal of College Student Development, 46*(1), 43–61.

Raque-Bogdan, T. L., & Lucas, M. S. (2016). Career aspirations and the first generation student: Unraveling the layers with social cognitive career theory. *Journal of College Student Development, 57*(3), 248–262. https://doi.org/10.1353/ csd.2016.0026

Redford, J., & Hoyer, K. M. (2017). First-generation and continuing-generation college students: A comparison of high school and postsecondary experiences (Stats in Brief No. NCES 2018-009). U.S. Department of Education, National Center for Education Statistics. https://nces.ed.gov/pubs2018/2018009.pdf

Riehl, R. J. (1994). The academic preparation, aspirations, and first-year performance of first-generation students. *College and University, 70*(1), 14–19.

Robinson, B. (2020, May 4). How remote working is reshaping a future new world of work. *Forbes.* https://www.forbes.com/sites/bryanrobinson/2020/05/04/ how-remote-working-is-reshaping-a-future-new-world-of-work/?sh=5f075 27627bf

Roderick, M., Coca, V., & Nagaoka, J. (2011). Potholes on the road to college: High school effects in shaping urban students' participation in college application, four-year college enrollment, and college match. *Sociology of Education, 84*(3), 178–211. https://doi.org/10.1177/0038040711411280

Santa-Ramirez, S., Wells, T., Sandoval, J., & Koro, M. (2020). Working through the experiences of first-generation students of color, university mission, intersectionality, and post-subjectivity. *International Journal of Qualitative Studies in Education.* https://doi.org/10.1080/09518398.2020.1783012

Sawchuk, S., & Gewertz, C. (2021). Anti-Asian violence: What schools should start doing about it. *Education Week.* https://www.edweek.org/leadership/anti -asian-violence-what-schools-should-start-doing-about-it/2021/03

Schwartz, S. E. O., Kanchewa, S. S., Rhodes, J. E., Gowdy, G., Stark, A. M., Horn, J. P., Parnes, M., & Spencer, R. (2018). "I'm having a little struggle with this, can you help me out?" Examining impacts and processes of a social capital intervention for first-generation college students. *American Journal of Community Psychology, 61*(1–2), 166–178. https://doi.org/10.1002/ajcp.12206

Sequeira, L., & Dacey, C. M. (2020). The COVID-19 diaries: Identity, teaching, and learning at a crossroads. *Frontiers in Education, 5,* Article 586123. https://doi .org/10.3389/feduc.2020.586123

Shange, S. (2019). *Progressive dystopia: Abolition, antiblackness, + schooling in San Francisco.* Duke University Press.

Shumaker, R., & Wood, J. L. (2016). Understanding first-generation community college students: An analysis of covariance examining use of, access to, and efficacy regarding institutionally offered services. *Community College Enterprise, 22*(9), 9–17.

Smalley, A. (2020). *Higher education responses to coronavirus (COVID-19).* National Conference of State Legislatures. https://www.ncsl.org/research/education/higher-education-responses-to-coronavirus-covid-19.aspx

Smith, W. A., Allen, W. R., & Danley, L. L. (2007). "Assume the position...You fit the description": Psychosocial experiences and racial battle fatigue among African American male college students. *American Behavioral Scientist, 51*(4), 551–578. https://doi.org/10.1177/0002764207307742

Soria, K. M., & Stebleton, M. J. (2012). First-generation students' academic engagement and retention. *Teaching in Higher Education, 17*(6), 673–685. https://doi.org/10.1080/13562517.2012.666735

Stahl, A. (2021, February 1). 5 lasting changes to expect in the workplace post-Covid. *Forbes.* https://www.forbes.com/sites/ashleystahl/2021/02/01/5-lasting-changes-to-expect-in-the-workplace-post-covid/?sh=4219658d213d

Stebleton, M. J., & Soria, K. M. (2012). Breaking down barriers: Academic obstacles of first-generation students at research universities. *The Learning Assistance Review, 17*(2), 7–19. https://nclca.wildapricot.org/tlar_issues

Stebleton, M. J., Soria, K. M., & Huesman, R. L., Jr. (2014). First-generation students' sense of belonging, mental health, and use of counseling services at public research universities. *Journal of College Counseling, 17*(1), 6–20. https://doi.org/10.1002/j.2161-1882.2014.00044.x

Stephens, N. M., Brannon, T. N., Markus, H. R., & Nelson, J. E. (2015). Feeling at home in college: Fortifying school-relevant selves to reduce social class disparities in higher education. *Social Issues Policy Review, 9*(1), 1–24. https://doi.org/10.1111/sipr.12008

Student Support Services Program, 34 C.F.R. § 646 (2011). https://www.ecfr.gov/cgi-bin/text-idx?node=sp34.3.646.a&rgn=div6

Sy, S. R., Fong, K., Carter, R., Boehme, J., & Alpert, A. (2011). Parent support and stress among first-generation and continuing-generation female students during the transition to college. *Journal of College Student Retention: Research, Theory & Practice, 13*(3), 383–398. https://doi.org/10.2190/CS.13.3.g

Tamargo, E. J. (2021). The changing exasperations of higher education. In K. R. Roth, & Z. S. Ritter (Eds.), *Whiteness, power, and resisting change in US higher education* (pp. 179–192). Palgrave Macmillan. https://doi.org/10.1007/978-3-030-57292-1_9

Tate, K. A., Caperton, W., Kaiser, D., Pruitt, N. T., White, H., & Hall, E. (2015). An exploration of first-generation college students' career development beliefs and experiences. *Journal of Career Development, 42*(4), 294–310. https://doi.org/10.1177/0894845314565025

TePoel, D., & Narcotta-Welp, E. (2020). The white moderate, sport and black lives matter: Echoes from Martin Luther King Jr.'s "letter from Birmingham Jail" at the University of Iowa. *Sport in Society.* https://doi.org/10.1080/17430437.2020.1828767

Thayer, P. B. (2000). Retention of students from first generation and low income backgrounds. *Opportunity Outlook: The Journal of the Council for Opportunity in Education, 3*(1), 2–9.

Toutkoushian, R. K., Stollberg, R. A., & Slaton, K. A. (2018). Talking 'bout my generation: Defining "first-generation college students" in higher education research. *Teachers College Record, 120*(4), 1–38. https://www.tcrecord.org/Content.asp?ContentId=22042

U.S. Department of Education. (1991). *Historically Black colleges and universities and higher education desegregation.* Office for Civil Rights. https://www2.ed.gov/about/offices/list/ocr/docs/hq9511.html

U.S. Department of Education. (2014). *Profile of undergraduate students: 2011–2012* (Web Tables Publication No. NCES 2015-167). National Center for Education Statistics. https://nces.ed.gov/pubs2015/2015167.pdf

Vargas, J. H. (2004). *College knowledge: Addressing information barriers to college.* The Education Resources Institute.

Vela, M., & Gutierrez, P. (2017). The Hispanic population and Hispanic serving institutions. *eJournal of Education Policy, 18*(2). https://in.nau.edu/wp-content/uploads/sites/135/2018/08/Vela_Gutierrez-ek.pdf

Warburton, E. C., Bugarin, R., & Nuñez, A.-M. (2001). *Bridging the gap: Academic preparation and postsecondary success of first-generation students.* U.S. Department of Education, National Center for Education Statistics. https://nces.ed.gov/pubs2001/2001153.pdf

Ward, L., Siegel, M. J., & Davenport, Z. (2012). *First-generation college students: Understanding and improving the experience from recruitment to commencement.* Jossey-Bass.

White, J. W., Pascale, A., & Aragon, S. (2020). Collegiate cultural capital and integration into the college community. *College Student Affairs Journal, 38*(1), 34–52. https://doi.org/10.1353/csj.2020.0002

White, K., & Hilton, A. A. (2017). Introduction to special issue: From #BlackLivesMatter to#BlackMindsMatter. *Journal of African American Males in Education, 8*(2), 1–4.

White, K. N., Vincent-Layton, K., & Villarrea, B. (2021). Equitable and inclusive practices designed to reduce equity gaps in undergraduate chemistry courses. *Journal of Chemical Education, 98*(2), 330–339. https://doi.org/10.1021/acs.jchemed.0c01094

Whitley, S. E., Benson, G., & Wesaw, A. (2018). *First-generation student success: A landscape analysis of programs and services at four-year institutions.* Center for First-Generation Student Success, NASPA–Student Affairs Administrators in Higher Education, and Entangled Solutions. https://firstgen.naspa.org/2018-landscape-analysis

Wildhagen, T. (2015). "Not your typical student": The social construction of the "first-generation" college student. *Qualitative Sociology, 38*(3), 285–303. https://doi.org/10.1007/s11133-015-9308-1

World Health Organization. (2014). *Health in all policies: Framework for country action.* https://www.afro.who.int/publications/health-all-policies-framework-country-action

Yeo, H. T., Mendenhall, R., Harwood, S., & Huntt, M. B. (2019). Asian international student and Asian American student: Mistaken identity and racial microaggressions. *Journal of International Students, 9*(1), 39–65. https://doi.org/10.32674/jis.v9i1.278

Zuschiag, M. K., & Whitbourne, S. K. (1994). Psychosocial development in three generations of college students. *Journal of Youth and Adolescence, 23*(5), 567–577. https://doi.org/10.1007/BF01537736

CHAPTER 15

USING HIP-HOP PRACTICES TO FOSTER COLLEGE AND CAREER READINESS

Ian P. Levy
Manhattan College

Justis Lopez
University of Pennsylvania

Erik M. Hines
Florida State University

ABSTRACT

While federal calls exist advocating for all students to receive postsecondary education, research notes large disparities in college and career support services for Black and Latinx students. Hip-hop based practices in education and school counseling have emerged as promising strategies to both challenge existing educational structures that create disparities, while affirming Black and Latinx youth and their communities as asset-rich. However, hip-hop strategies are underexplored in college and career readiness work. This chapter pulls from a particular approach to hip-hop and counseling work, dubbed Hip-

Equity-Based Career Development and Postsecondary Transitions, pages 377–391
Copyright © 2022 by Information Age Publishing
www.infoagepub.com
All rights of reproduction in any form reserved.

Hop and Spoken Word Therapy (HHSWT), that draws from the myriad ways the hip-hop community has used collective gatherings and artistic expression as healing to reimagine how school counselors meet the College Board National Office of School Counselor Adovocacy's *Eight Components of College and Career Readiness.*

While federal calls exist advocating for all students to receive postsecondary education, research notes large disparities in college and career support services for Black and Latinx students. Some of these inequities are found in the under placement of Black and Latinx youth in AP courses and gifted education programs (Johnson & Larwin, 2020), inadequate services for students with disabilities (Shapiro, 2020), or the significantly lower college enrollment and retention rates (Grooms et al., 2021). All too often college and career readiness interventions and initiatives are deployed with a specific focus on addressing gaps through the frame of offering student knowledge they are assumed to lack, evidencing the ways in which education and counseling endorse a deficit lens that undermines Black and Latinx students' internal capacities to actualize. Thus, there is a distinct need within the area of college and career readiness to highlight and foster the joy, resilience, and systems of empowerment that already exist within youth intrapersonally and in their communities. Hip-hop based practices in education and school counseling have emerged as promising strategies to both challenge existing educational structures that create disparities, while affirming Black and Latinx youth and their communities as asset-rich (Love, 2016; Travis, 2015). However, hip-hop strategies are underexplored in college and career readiness work. Drawing from the College Board National Office of School Counselor Adovocacy's (NOSCA) *Eight Components of College and Career Readiness,* this chapter will explore how hip-hop based practices can draw on youth's internal knowledge, capacities, and their rich community resources, to reimagine how school counselors deliver college and career readiness services.

HIP-HOP PRACTICES IN SCHOOL COUNSELING

Aiming to integrate asset-rich and culturally responsive practices, contemporary school counseling research has explored the intersections of hip-hop and school counseling (Levy, 2019; Washington, 2018). Hip-hop and school counseling work builds on a larger line of research that has found hip-hop song analysis, lyric composition, beat making an engaging and preferable alternative to traditional talk therapy (Elligan, 2004; Gonzalez & Hayes, 2009; Travis et al., 2019; Tyson, 2002). This chapter pulls from a particular approach to hip-hop and counseling work, dubbed Hip-Hop and Spoken Word Therapy (HHSWT), that draws from the myriad ways the hip-hop community has used collective gatherings and artistic expression as healing (Chang & Cook, 2021; Levy, 2021).

Salient HHSWT practices focus on the coupling of community defined practices with traditional counseling methodologies that lack cultural responsiveness. This includes lyric writing as cognitive and emotive journaling (Levy, 2019), capitalizing on lyric writing as a cultural mechanism to make sense of one's lived experiences, where school counselors prime youth with keeping a lyric journal about specific thoughts, feelings, and experiences between sessions. Mixtape making, as a larger guide to group process where youth construct a series of emotionally themed songs around a shared group goal, is modeled after the ways that mixtapes have been used by the hip-hop community to collect and disseminate research about systemic inequities (Ball, 2011). As a multimodal and malleable approach to group work, mixtape making is found effective in reducing stress, depression, and anxiety symptoms (Levy & Travis, 2020).

Paired with lyric writing and mixtape making, school counselors have youth share within hip-hop cyphers—again pulling from the value of the cultural cypher as a place for unity and cohesion, with norms that allow for equal airtime, deep listening, and the validation of vulnerabilities (Levy, Emdin, & Adjapong, 2018). The creation of school recording studios as therapeutic environments draws from the hip-hop community's use of studios for identity development and transformation (Harkness, 2014). Youth have described school studios as welcoming peer support, personal development, authenticity, and a sense of comfort and belonging (Levy & Adjapong, 2020).

Hip-Hop Sensibilities

Hip-hop practices in schools are framed as culturally sustaining because they call on the intricate balance of hip-hop's five elements: b-girling (breakdancing), emceeing, graffiti, DJing, and knowledge of self (Love, 2013). Through acknowledging the culture of hip-hop, educators enable hip-hop sensibilities to be cultivated, which spark creativity, critical thinking, and communication (Petchauer, 2015). Beneath the engagement of various hip-hop elements, is the unearthing of hip-hop mindsets like resistance, knowledge of self, and self-determination (Petchauer, 2012), which are not only alive in hip-hop culture but are invaluable for the college and career process. These mindsets/sensibilities are part of the collective identity of Black and Latinx students navigating educational spaces. Integrating hip-hop approaches in school counseling are humanizing, critical, and creative pedagogical (re)interventions and sensibilities that foster self-determination, self-knowledge, and acts of resistance with young people (Love, 2016).

The aesthetics of hip-hop are rooting in ways of "doing and being" (Petchauer, 2015). Hip-Hop sensibilities cultivate a consciousness that allow youth to navigate the institution of schooling beyond college and career and into the action of their everyday lives. Much like leading scholars in counseling calls for the infusion of irreducibility (Hannon & Vareern, 2016) or intersectionality (Singh, 2020) to support Black and Latinx youth in expressing and becoming all of who they are—hip-hop advocates for this same complex authenticity to be projected out into the world. For this complex personhood (self-determination, self-knowledge, and acts of resistance) to be cultivated, it is essential to have these school counselors allow hip-hop sensibilities to flourish. Like the five elements working in balance together to create the foundation to hip-hop culture, educators are responsible for not only allowing hip-hop sensibilities to come to the surface, but to be thoughtfully merged with their academic identities to propel authentic development (Emdin, 2021).

COLLABORATION ON COLLEGE AND CAREER READINESS AND HIP HOP PRACTICES

Educator collaboration has been seen to improve academic outcomes (Erford, 2019). Moreover, the phrase, "It takes a village to raise a child" is very applicable to assisting underserved students as every school personnel is needed to aid in the college and career readiness of this particular population. Specifically, school counselors and teachers can collaborate by creating classroom guidance curriculum related to both hip-hop and the educational pedagogy to align with postsecondary preparation (Emdin et al., 2016). Also, teachers can consult with school counselors on which students need more support around college and career readiness to provide equitable resources to achieve success in that area. Moreover, Hines et al. (2020) suggested school counselors collaborate with educators in higher education to create a bridge with high schools to prepare underserved students for college.

School counselors can use a school–family–community partnership approach (Bryan, 2005; Bryan & Henry, 2012) to merge hip-hop practices with college and career readiness. In particular, school–family–partnerships have shown to improve academic achievement, student engagement, student retention, and parent involvement (National Center on Safe and Supportive Learning Environments [NCSSLE], n.d.). Moreover, school–family–community partnerships provide school counselors with an ecosystem of parents, community stakeholders, and educators (Hines et al., 2021) to use hip-hop practices to aid in the college and career readiness of underserved students. Moreover, school counselors and other educators can positively impact underserved youth by using a systemic, comprehensive approach to college and career readiness coupled with innovative hip-hop practices.

EIGHT COMPONENTS OF COLLEGE AND CAREER READINESS AND HIP-HOP PRACTICES

Conley (2011) defined college and career readiness as "the level of preparation a student needs to enroll and succeed in a credit-bearing general education course at a post-secondary institution, without remediation" (as cited in Hines et al., 2020, p. 1). Therefore students, especially ones from underrepresented backgrounds must have the skills and knowledge needed to do college-level work. Further, educators, in particular school counselors, must understand how to engage students in various ways to increase the likelihood of college and career readiness; therefore, we created an integrated approach in using NOSCA's *Eight Components of College and Career Readiness* with hip-hop practice to use as an innovative approach to achieve this goal. The eight components (College Board, 2010, p. 3; Perusse et al., 2015) along with the hip-hop practices are:

1. College Aspirations
    a. *Goal:* Build a college-going culture based on early college awareness by nurturing in students the confidence to aspire to college and the resilience to overcome challenges along the way. Maintain high expectations by providing adequate support, building social capital, and conveying the conviction that all students can succeed in college.
    b. *Hip-Hop Practice:* Various hip-hop practices can be leveraged to support the cultivation of college aspirations amongst students. First, we recommend the creation of graffiti murals with images of various hip-hop practitioners (deejays, emcees, visual artists, breakdancers, etc.) with their degrees and affiliation (e.g., a mural of two Chainz and Virginia State University). These murals can be created by youth themselves, or in collaboration with artists within the community. Bulletin boards can also be utilized for this purpose, where homerooms engage in friendly competition to research and create the best representation of hip-hop practitioners and their college/university affiliations. School counselors should intentionally use this hip-hop artist mural intervention to promote intersectionality, allowing rotation murals monthly to adequately portray ravenous racial groups, gender and sexual identities.

2. Academic Planning for College and Career Readiness
   a. *Goal:* Advance students' planning, preparation, participation, and performance in a rigorous academic program that connects to their college and career aspirations and goals.
   b. *Hip-Hop Practice:* School counselors are required to understand the complex identities of students on their caseload so they can encourage a college planning process that connects to their aspirations and goals. To accomplish this, lyric writing can be used as an assessment, where school counselors co-select an instrumental beat with youth, and have them reflect lyrically on their strengths, areas of growth, and then goal setting. For example, students might construct a song titled "5-year plan" where they set long-term and short-term goals. This inherently narrative and aspirational verse can illuminate myriad student assets that can be used in the college and career planning process. This intervention should not be limited to song creation, as a poem or a visual representation of this same 5-year is also useful.
3. Enrichment and Extracurricular Engagement
   a. *Goal:* Ensure equitable exposure to a wide range of extracurricular and enrichment opportunities that build leadership, nurture talents and interests, and increase engagement with school.
   b. *Hip-Hop Practice:* Enrichment and extracurricular engagement can be ascertained through various hip-hop based practices. For example, the development of an extensive multi-element internship program where deejays, emcees, graffiti/graphic/visual artists, and breakdancers from the community allow youth to apprentice with them. This would entail working with them on their art, and attending public events/showcases/performances where the art is displayed. Myriad practical skills can be developed through these partnerships that support robust extracurricular activities that can be reported to colleges. Furthermore, there are possibilities that some of the hip-hop practitioners are parents within the school community, or individuals in the local community, which strengthens school–family–community partnerships and affirms students, community, and families as asset-rich.

   Another option is connecting youth, perhaps through the internship experiences, to formal initiatives like the First Wave Program at the University of Wisconsin–Madison. Administered by the Office of Multicultural Arts Initiatives (OMAI), the First Wave Learning Community is the first university program in the country centered on urban arts, spoken word, and hip-hop culture. The goal of First Wave is to provide innovative, culturally relevant hip-hop art programs to inspire engagement, learning, and activism for diverse communities. This program is available to high school seniors across the country. Students that are selected for this program receive a full tuition 4-year scholarship and participate in a summer college bridge experience, a supportive studio learning community, an internship, study abroad, and a culminating capstone seminar project.

4. College and Career Exploration and Selection Processes

   a. *Goal:* Provide early and ongoing exposure to experiences and information necessary to make informed decisions when selecting a college or career that connects to academic preparation and future aspirations.

   b. *Hip-Hop Practice:* Immersive college tours can follow the creation of student-made mixtapes. School counselors deploying hip-hop-informed college and career readiness must form partnerships with college campuses, prior to college visits, to carve out opportunities for students to share their work. For example, a school counselor might identify a Black student union on a college campus to collaboratively hold an open-mic event where college students and high school students can perform. Then, in addition to the normal tour activities, an experiential/immersive open-mic event can occur where students share their rhymes about retention, transitions, and/or 5-year plans, while also building community within otherwise potentially isolating campuses. Much like a post-tour reflection that artists engage in, a post-college tour reflection can be facilitated by school counselors. Here school counselors guide youth though processing their college visit, reflection on the open-mic event, but also fit. The immersive nature of the tour should increase the depth of the reflections, as students are offered a genuine opportunity to assess feelings of connectedness or lack thereof. Pictures or documents from the college-tour performances can then be displayed across the school building to create a college-going culture that looks and feels relevant to students.

   Ultimately, These immersive college visit experiences provide for the opportunity in communal collaboration between high school educators, high school counselors, and college student orgs that embody hip-hop sensibilities. For example, The organization Leadership in Diversity (LID) at the University of Connecticut is a mentoring program that is focused on maintaining and encouraging confidence and success in students of color as they pursue careers in the field of education. Each year through intentional programing educators, counselors, high school students of color, and college student members of LID host an annual, day-long, multicultural education conference. These conferences always feature sessions and programming on open-mic and hip-hop where students, educators, and counselors have the opportunity to co create pieces together and co perform during a communal open-mic. Opportunities such as these allow for the space for school counselors to gain a unique perspective to colleges that embody hip-hop sensibilities.

5. College and Career Assessments
    a. *Goal:* Promote preparation, participation, and performance in college and career assessments by all students.
    b. *Hip-Hop Practice:* There are numerous possibilities for the coupling of hip-hop practices and college and career assessments. An initial activity might be administering traditional career assessment (MBTI, Strong Interest Inventory, Skills Assessments, or a Value-card Sort)—but to then distill those to lyrics, a poem, a short video, or a visual representation. Here the hope is to transcend the, often short-sighted, quantitative assessments with a bit more of a nuanced processing/discussion. Building on this, students might consider submitting their work as a supplemental/project component to a college application. For example, having students write a poem about why you want to be a nurse—and create a video clip that sits alongside their statement of purpose. This practice calls school counselors to see students abilities beyond quant methods. Further, can they teach the rest of the school to see the same?

6. College Affordability Planning
    a. *Goal:* Provide students and families with comprehensive information about college costs, options for paying for college, and the financial aid and scholarship processes and eligibility requirements, so they are able to plan for and afford a college education.
    b. *Hip-Hop Practice:* Burt (2020) explored the creation of a financial literacy small-group curriculum that utilized hip-hop practices. This preventive, psychoeducational group engaged youth in analyzing lyrics for popular rap songs which explore the role money plays in people's lives, engaging youth in both discussion and reframing the perspectives on money to plan how to navigate a capitalist society. While there are a plethora of hip-hop songs that might glamorize or glorify money in unhealthy ways, it is important to remember hip-hop is simply a reflection of society at large. Returning to hip-hop sensibilities, hip-hop preaches authenticity and ownership which encourage us to consider how our financial planning work with youth is focused on highlighting assets and developing entrepreneurial skills. This type of

small-group work might look like youth learning how to create podcasts, engage in fashion design, or develop social media campaigns that help them ascertain social capital in the field of their desired careers but also set and monetize their own value. Youth possess many of the social media skills that we lack, so strategically integrating various digital platforms into our financial planning work could be quite beneficial to their college and career development.

7. College and Career Admission Processes
   a. *Goal:* Ensure that students and families have an early and ongoing understanding of the college and career application and admission processes so they can find the postsecondary options that are the best fit with their aspirations and interests.
   b. *Hip-Hop Practice:* To propel the college and career admission process, schools can integrate hip-hop based practices into their already established college and career fairs. This can be done in at least two ways. Frist, a bevy of schools exist nationally that have programming in support of students who identify with hip-hop. Organizations like *Digging in the Crates* guided by Craig Arthur and Dr. Freddy Page through the library at Virginia Tech University have established and maintained a robust student-led community that invites hip-hop practitioners to lead workshops and campus-wide events rooted in self-expression. Skyline College, Harvard University, Trinity College, and various others hold similar space for youth and hip-hop. If school counselors are truly focused on ensuring that their students enter colleges that are the right fit for them, then calling on colleges with hip-hop programming to be represented at their college fairs is paramount.

   Second, given the pervasiveness of hip-hop as a social entrepreneurial tool, various careers can be promoted as well. For example, Bartholomew Jones started a hip-hop and coffee company out in Memphis Tennessee which uses hip-hop lyric writing events, in conjunction with coffee roasting and brewing, as an act of reclaiming distinctly Black and Brown narratives. Michael Ford, AKA the Hip-Hop Architect, began workshops infusing hip-hop sensibilities and architecture and is now playing an integral role in the design of the forthcoming Universal Hip-Hop Museum in the Bronx, NY. School counselors can consult with various professionals who have used hip-hop in their career development, and bring together a career and hip-hop panel as part of their career fairs. Parents should be encouraged to attend these events as well.

   As a final event of a career fair, students can host a listening party, video screening, or art gallery where they share their 5-year art plan with their families and larger community. Effectively, this culminating event functions as an opportunity for youth to share their goals and aspirations with family, in an experiential way that might help communicate the passion and value of using hip-hop in their college and career process.

Schools can also create core classes that focus on the college and career admissions process for their ninth grade freshman. For example, Imagine College and Career Readiness Class (ICC9) is a core class designed for students in CT that focuses on preparing first-generation college students, students of color, and low-income students with the college and career selection process. Teachers and counselors have led, "For the Culture Fridays" that focuses on bringing in local and professional hip-hop practitioners that have gone to college from the various elements (breakdancing, emceeing, graffiti, DJing, knowledge of self), each Friday to talk with students and lead a session on their expertise.

8. Transition From High School Graduation to College Enrollment
   a. *Goal:* Connect students to school and community resources to help the students overcome barriers and ensure the successful transition from high school to college.
   b. *Hip-Hop Practice:* While the aforementioned college/career fair may help to aid the transition process, to some degree, there are also ways to leverage classroom instruction or small-group counseling towards this goal. Classroom or small-group lessons that support youth in analyzing hip-hop lyrics, songs, videos, art, to generate reflections about upcoming transitions are recommended. Once concerns about college transitions are generated, youth can process them together as a group and then creatively develop solutions in the form of hip-hop projects. The authors have included a full lesson plan in the appendix of this paper detailing these practices in more depth (Appendix A).

RECOMMENDATIONS IN A POST-PANDEMIC ERA

The approaches described above pervade school counselors' roles and responsibilities. The authors recommend that the aforementioned be used as a guide for implementation in small-group counseling, classroom instruction, collaboration and consultation work with all educational stakeholders, and via school-wide initiatives. However, the strategies shared in this paper are not prescriptive. Meaning, the approach described as a classroom lesson can be adjusted for a school-wide initiative, and the like. Also, given the complexity of hip-hop, it is possible that one strategy (like the immersive college tour) has the potential to impact multiple NOSCA standards. With access to music, videos, and multi-modal editing software for free online (e.g., see Canva.com), it is entirely possible to carry out these interventions virtually.

While our hope is that this chapter encourages school counselors to integrate hip-hop based approaches into their work, it should be noted that prerequisites to implementations exist. First, school counselors must believe that youth's words, and hip-hop, are valuable and deserve time and space in counseling sessions. Oftentimes, youth are engaging with hip-hop already, but we (as school counselors) fail to actively listen to the thoughts and feelings expressed via "nontraditional" modes of communication. School counselors must be ready to listen, deeply, to what lies beneath the content that youth create. Furthermore, given the COVID-19 pandemic and the aftermath of racial tension in this country, now more than ever, school counselors must use creativity and "thinking outside of traditional counseling methods" to engage students! Second, it is likely that school counselors implementing these strategies will receive pushback from other educational stakeholders. This is to be expected, as we are intentionally pushing back against the ways in which college and career readiness minimize the experiences and voices of Black and Brown youth. The answer to this is, evaluate your practice, gather research articles that support your use of these practices, and prepare to present those to naysayers. Lastly, this work must be done authentically. While this concept requires an entire chapter in and of itself, school counselors must trust that youth who identify with the culture have the tools to use it for their development. Finding authentic ways to tap into local instances of hip-hop culture is encouraged—visiting open mic night, venues, and/or listening to local artists.

DISCUSSION QUESTIONS AND ACTIVITIES

Below are reflective questions, and recommended activities, to support school counselors' readiness.

1. What types of messaging are your students receiving, with regards to their college and career process, from the music they listen to?
   a. *Activity:* School counselors can work with students to create a college and career playlist of songs that they listen to to "feel motivated about their future." The school counselor can then listen to those songs to deepen their understanding of students' mindsets.
2. How able are you to listen to the thoughts and feelings that sit beneath hip-hop songs, beyond your own biases?

a. *Activity:* Make it a regular practice to listen to hip-hop music. Print out lyrics, highlight text, and work to identify thoughts and feelings. In groups, school counselors might discuss the meaning behind songs together. This collective practice of honing our ability to understand and hear the complex ways identities and lived experiences are communicated via hip-hop is essential.

3. What are the ways in which your school community is connected to the local hip-hop scene?

a. *Activity:* Akin to community asset-mapping, school counselors can deliver surveys, or form a student/parent/community hip-hop advisory committee whose express purpose is to assess current connections to local hip-hop and explore new avenues for collaboration. The goal here would be to build out opportunities for new after-school programming, support with in-school events (career fairs, workshops, etc.), and local field trips.

APPENDIX

Classroom Guidance Lesson Plan

Title of Lesson: Crown

Grade Level: 12

Outcome or Standard:

B-SS 1. Use effective oral and written communication skills and listening skills.

B-SMS 10. Demonstrate ability to manage transitions and ability to adapt to changing situations and responsibilities.

Learning Objective(s):

Students will learn to anticipate inter- and intra-personal challenges they might face on college campuses.

Materials:

Chart paper, CROWN song lyrics, notebook, pencils, highlighters, speakers

Developmental Learning Activities:

Introduction: The lesson will begin with a group song-analysis, looking at the song *Crown* by CHIKA. Crown is a song about perseverance, specifically in moments when we feel others do not believe in our potential. The following is needed for this intro:

- The school counselor will stream Crown, by CHIKA (https://www.youtube.com/watch?v=6ljSbN0Pg28);
- while listening, students will highlight lyrics that stick out to them; and
- students share and process reactions in a large group.

Activity: Lyric Writing About College Transitions

For this activity, students engage in the process of creating a collective 16-bar verse about their upcoming college transition. First, they will brainstorm potential concerns and then they will create their verse.

- Small groups, using chart paper, students will generate a list of responses to the following questions:
  - What is one worry you have about going to college next year?
  - What are solutions to these worries?
- After the list is developed, the group will collaborate on a 16-bar verse that integrates the worries and solutions they generated.
- School counselors should play the following beat while students write: https://youtu.be/ldpCeoWb_3Q

Conclusion: Sharing out of Verses

- This lesson concludes with students sharing their verses.

Assessment/Evaluation:

- As a brief *Exit Ticket* students should write two sentences, one describing their worry about transitioning to college and one describing a solution to said transition.

Follow-up:

AUTHOR NOTE

Ian P. Levy ORCID https://orcid.org/0000-0002-4798-0224
Erik M. Hines ORCID https://orcid.org/0000-0002-6025-0779

Ian P. Levy is now an assistant professor of school counseling at Manhattan College, The Bronx, NY. We have no conflict of interest to disclose. Correspondence concerning this chapter should be addressed to Dr. Ian P. Levy of Manhattan College, Department of Counseling and Therapy, 4513 Manhattan College Pkwy, Bronx, NY 10471. Email: Ian.Levy@manhattan.edu

REFERENCES

Ball, J. A. (2011). I mix what I like! In defense and appreciation of the rap music mixtape as "national" and "dissident" communication. *International Journal of Communication, 5*, 20.

Bryan, J. (2005). Fostering educational resilience and achievement in urban schools through school-family-community partnerships. *Professional School Counseling,* 219–227.

Bryan, J., & Henry, L. (2012). A model for building school–family–community partnerships: Principles and process. *Journal of Counseling & development, 90*(4), 408–420.

Chang, J., & Cook, D. (2021). *Can't stop won't stop (young adult edition): A hip-hop history.* Wednesday Books.

College Board. (2010). *Eight components of college and career readiness counseling.* https://secure-media.collegeboard.org/digitalServices/pdf/nosca/11b_4416_8_Components_WEB_111107.pdf

Conley, D. T. (2011). *Redefining college readiness.* Educational Policy Improvement Center.

Emdin, C. (2021) Ratchetdemic: Reimagining academic success. Beacon Press.

Emdin, C., Adjapong, E., & Levy, I. (2016). Hip-hop based interventions as pedagogy/therapy in STEM. *Journal for Multicultural Education. 10*(3), 307–321.

Elligan, D. (2004). *Rap therapy: A practical guide for communicating with youth and young adults through rap music.* Kensington Books.

Erford, B. T. (2019). *Transforming the school counseling profession* (5th ed.). Merrill Prentice Hall.

Gonzalez, T., & Hayes, B. G. (2009). Rap music in school counseling based on Don Elligan's rap therapy. *Journal of Creativity in Mental Health, 4*(2), 161–172.

Grooms, A. A., Mahatmya, D., & Johnson, E. T. (2021). The retention of educators of color amidst institutionalized racism. *Educational Policy, 35*(2), 180–212.

Hannon, M. D., & Vereen, L. G. (2016). Irreducibility of Black male clients: Considerations for culturally competent counseling. *The Journal of Humanistic Counseling, 55*(3), 234–245.

Harkness, G. (2014). Get on the mic: Recording studios as symbolic spaces in rap music: Get on the mic. *Journal of Popular Music Studies, 26*(1), 82–100. https://doi.org/10.1111/jpms.12061

Hines, E. M., Fletcher, E., Moore J. L., III., & Ford, D. Y. (2021). *Culturally responsive postsecondary readiness outcomes for Black males: Practice and policy recommendations for school counselors* [Manuscript submitted for publication].

Hines, E. M., Hines, M. R., Moore, J. L., III., Steen, S., Singleton, P., II., Cintron, D., Traverso, K., Golden, M. N., Wathen, B., & Henderson, J. A. (2020). Preparing African American males for college: A group counseling approach. *The Journal for Specialists in Group Work, 45*(2), 129–145. https://doi.org/10.1080/01933922.2020.1740846

Johnson, L., & Larwin, K. H. (2020). Systemic bias in public education: The exception of African American males enrolled in gifted and Advanced Placement courses. *Journal of Organizational & Educational Leadership, 6*(2), 3.

Levy, I., Emdin, C., and Adjapong, E. S. (2018). Hip-hop cypher in group work. *Social Work with Groups, 41*(1–2), 103–110. https://doi.org/10.1080/01609513.2016.1275265

Levy, I., & Travis, R. (2020). The critical cycle of mixtape creation: Reducing stress via three different group counseling styles. *Journal for Specialists in Group Work, 45*(4), 307–330. https://doi.org/10.1080/01933922.2020.1826614

Levy, I. P. (2019). Hip-hop and spoken word therapy in urban school counseling. *Professional School Counseling, 22.* https://doi.org/10.1177/2156759X19834436

Levy, I. P. (2021). *Hip-hop and spoken word therapy in school counseling: Developing culturally responsive approaches* (1st ed.). Routledge. https://doi.org/10.4324/9781003023890

Levy, I. P., & Adjapong, E. S. (2020). Toward culturally competent school counseling environments: Hip-hop studio construction. *Professional Counselor, 10*(2), 266–284.

Love, B. L. (2013). Black girlhood, embodied knowledge, and hip hop feminist pedagogy. *Engaging culture, race, and spirituality in education: New visions,* 167–173.

Love, B. L. (2016). Complex personhood of hip hop & the sensibilities of the culture that fosters knowledge of self & self-determination. *Equity & Excellence in Education, 49*(4), 414–427. https://doi.org/10.1080/10665684.2016.1227223

National Center on Safe and Supportive Learning Environments. (n.d.). *Family-School-Community Partnerships.* American Institutes for Research. https://safe-supportivelearning.ed.gov/training-technical-assistance/education-level/early-learning/family-school-community-partnerships

Perusse, R., Poynton, T. A., Parzych, J. L., & Goodnough, G. E. (2015). The importance and implementation of eight components of college and career readiness counseling in school counselor education programs. *Journal of College of Access, 1*(1), 29–41. https://scholarworks.wmich.edu/jca/vol1/iss1/4/

Petchauer, E. (2012). *Hip-hop culture in college students' lives: Elements, embodiment, and higher edutainment.* Routledge.

Petchauer, E. (2015). Starting with style: Toward a second wave of hip-hop education research and practice. *Urban Education, 50*(1), 78–105.

Shapiro, A. (2020). Over diagnosed or over looked? The effect of age at time of school entry on students receiving special education services (EdWorkingPaper No. 20-259). *Annenberg Institute for School Reform at Brown University.* ERIC.

Singh, A. A., Appling, B., & Trepal, H. (2020). Using the multicultural and social justice counseling competencies to decolonize counseling practice: The important roles of theory, power, and action. *Journal of Counseling & Development, 98*(3), 261–271.

Travis R., Jr. (2015). *The healing power of hip hop.* ABC-CLIO.

Travis, R., Jr., Gann, E., Crooke, A. H., & Jenkins, S. M. (2019). Hip hop, empowerment, and therapeutic beat-making: Potential solutions for summer learning loss, depression, and anxiety in youth. *Journal of Human Behavior in the Social Environment, 29*(6), 744–765.

Tyson, E. H. (2002). Hip hop therapy: An exploratory study of a rap music intervention with at-risk and delinquent youth. *Journal of Poetry Therapy, 14.*

Washington, A. R. (2018). Integrating hip-hop culture and rap music into social justice counseling with Black males. *Journal of Counseling & Development, 96*(1), 97–105. https://doi.org/10.1002/jcad.12181

CHAPTER 16

THE ROLE OF THE SCHOOL COUNSELOR IN CREATING EQUITABLE OPPORTUNITIES FOR POSTSECONDARY SUCCESS THROUGH SELF-AWARENESS, CAREER EXPLORATION, AND ACADEMIC RIGOR

Clifford Mack Jr.
Trinity International University

Laura J. Cohen
Nova Southeastern University

Randi Schietz
Nova Southeastern University

Equity-Based Career Development and Postsecondary Transitions, pages 393–429
Copyright © 2022 by Information Age Publishing
www.infoagepub.com
All rights of reproduction in any form reserved.

ABSTRACT

In this chapter, the authors discuss the fundamental components of a college and career education framework to help students construct, clarify, correct, and confirm a suitable career path and trajectory. School counselors and educators implement programs that encourage students to develop self-awareness, explore and examine skills, interests, gifts, and talents that lead to rigorous academic experiences, goal setting, and postsecondary education and career fit. The authors will explore career development through the use of various self-assessment tools and inventories to examine personality types, skills and interests, and other career exploration activities throughout the K–12 school experience. Furthermore, the authors address issues of inequity and access to ensure all students have access to postsecondary and career options regardless of sexual gender identity, gender expression, national origin, race, religion, sex or sexual orientation. The authors provide appendices to describe specific college and career development activities and experiences for students at the primary and secondary levels that promote self-awareness, rigorous postsecondary planning, and equitable access and participation.

THE SCHOOL COUNSELOR
AND POSTSECONDARY PREPARATION

The role of school counselors in preparing students for college and future careers has been the flagship role for over a century (Gysbers, 2013). This role might be more obvious when working with high school students who are in the final stages of their K–12 educational experiences before they enter life after high school. Students are focused on grades, college applications, financial aid and scholarship opportunities, and are ready to launch their futures. High schools work to promote a college-going and career-ready school culture supported by school counselors, teachers, and families (Curry & Milson, 2017). The role of preparing students for postsecondary education and career success is undeniable in the secondary educational environment.

However, creating that college-going and career-ready school culture no longer rests solely on the shoulders of high school counselors but begins as early as kindergarten. It is in these younger formative (Erikson, 1963) years that the foundation is established through early awareness of careers; academic rigor (College Board National Office of School Counselor Advocacy [NOSCA], 2010); and through the development of social-emotional, self-management, and learning skills needed for success (American School Counselor Association [ASCA], 2019). These social-emotional learning (SEL) soft skills and other general career skills will be presented in this chapter, in addition to strategies to assist students to identify their own strengths and interests to match their future academic and career choices that will influence their trajectory over the course of their K–12 educational experience.

It is also important to note it is not only worth considering WHEN students begin preparing through school counseling initiatives that promote awareness, exposure, exploration, and assessment but HOW can we best prepare students for the future. Truly preparing students for the future involves looking at the world that they will be entering in 5 to 15 years and evolving daily. It is believed that 85% of the jobs that will be available in 2030 have not even been invented yet (as cited in the McKinsey Global Institute Report, Manyika et al., 2017) and more than 60 % of the careers that students have traditionally learned about will become fully automated and might no longer exist (Manyika et al., 2017). Much of the job training will be "on-the-job" training that will occur as quickly as the technology advances. It is therefore imperative that in order to meet the college and career preparation needs of the 21st century learners and digital citizens, it will become important to teach "skills" that will be applicable in all areas of the workforce.

Social-Emotional Skill Development and Postsecondary Preparation: K–12

A key role of the school counselor is to assist K–12 students with social-emotional skill acquisition and development (ASCA, 2017; Paolini, 2019; VanVelsor, 2009) that will ensure that they will be prepared with a particular set of "soft" skills needed for college and career success. To facilitate this skill development, school counselors implement SEL curricula and interventions (ASCA, 2017; Bowers et al., 2017). As leaders in the school climate and culture, the school counselor will function as an advocate, collaborator, consultant, and facilitator of SEL (ASCA, 2017; Paolini, 2019; VanVelsor, 2009). It is imperative for school counselors to establish evidence-based strategies that support noncognitive, SEL development and its impact on college and career readiness (Warren & Hale, 2016).

SEL is defined as the practice through which students can acquire and effectively apply the knowledge, attitudes, and skills necessary to understand and manage emotions, set and achieve positive goals, feel and show empathy for others, establish and maintain positive relationships, and make responsible decisions (Mahoney et al., 2018). According to Collaborative for Academic, Social, and Emotional Learning (Collaborative for Academic, Social, and Emotional Learning [CASEL], 2015), SEL is the process through which students understand and manage emotions, set and achieve positive goals, feel and show empathy for others, establish and maintain positive relationships, and make responsible decisions.

The CASEL model (2005), as introduced in the elementary section, has become prominent in social and emotional competency studies. The five competencies and structure of this model are (a) self-management, or the ability to regulate thoughts, emotions, and behaviors; (b) self-awareness, or the ability to recognize one's emotions and accurately assess one's strengths and weaknesses; (c) social awareness or awareness of the culture, beliefs, and feelings of the people and world around them; (d) relationship skills or the ability to effectively communicate, work well with peers, and build meaningful relationships; and (e) responsible decision-making or the ability to make plans for the future, follow moral/ethical standards, and contribute to the well-being of others (Ross & Tolan, 2018). The CASEL model provides guard rails for students to acquire key skills for the long haul of college, career, and lifelong success. The school counselor is in a position and posture to provide collaborative leadership for SEL implementation and execution. Their role is pivotal for providing awareness of the key competencies and to provide consultation with teachers, administration, parents, and stakeholders.

ELEMENTARY SCHOOL: DEVELOPMENTAL OVERVIEW AND IMPLICATIONS

The process of child development encompasses everything from sensory awareness, motor skills, language, and socialization. Beginning to prepare students for a college and career ready future starts early but must be appropriate based on the developmental maturity of the students and how they perceive the world around them. Some of the experiences will involve bringing awareness to the world of work around them and others may provide deliberate and intentional exposure to jobs that may not be easily observed in their own families or communities.

Prekindergarten

The purpose of prekindergarten is to promote school readiness. The assumption is that students who engage in an organized learning program prior to kindergarten will possess the linguistic and social-emotional skills to fully engage in the K–12 academic environment. As gaps in school readiness have received national attention, states and local districts have attempted to create prekindergarten programs to create an equitable field for all students (Slicker & Hustedt, 2020). In fact, President Biden's American Family

Plan (2021) introduces the importance of offering 2 years of prekinder-garten learning. As stated in his speech to a joint session of congress, "The research shows that when a young child goes to school—not day care—they are far more likely to graduate from high school and go on to college" (Biden, 2021, April 28). While the focus of prekindergarten is on academic readiness, the school counselor can provide leadership in the area of social skills development. In addition, when the prekindergarten is part of the elementary school, the counselor can include these youngest students in career oriented school-wide activities. To learn more about workers in the community, prekindergarten teachers can introduce students to the vocabulary and provide experiential opportunities like dress-up and imaginary play within the classroom.

Grades K and 1

Students in these grades are learning and mastering basic academic skills and a sense of self confidence. They are more keenly aware of themselves and how they compare to their peers in areas such as likability and intelligence (Erikson, 1963). Cognitively, these young learners are learning through fantasy play, magical thinking, and require more hands-on practice and repetition in learning (Piaget, 1977). They tend to interact with the world with a sense of obedience and are likely to "tattle" when they see peers breaking rules. Given this worldview, students in kindergarten and first grade are more likely to categorize careers into "good" and "bad" based on this internal moral compass (Kohlberg, 1981). Social interactions become more influential as children enter elementary school and for the first time they are developing their own awareness of their strengths and weaknesses. It is during this time that students will start to see a connection between what they are learning and how it relates to careers.

Grades 2 and 3

Children who are starting to recognize their own competence in areas like social relationships, physical and athletic skill development, and academic skills, are beginning to develop a stronger self-concept (Piaget, 1977). Visualizing themselves as successful adults seems attainable and this is amplified by their innate sense of curiosity and wonder (Erikson, 1963). Students who have experienced deficits and challenges in comparison to their peers are also more aware of these shortcomings and might be developing a sense of inferiority. Bandura (1986) highlights particular social tasks that enable students to develop intrinsic motivation, understand social norms, and develop friendships. Children are learning how to overcome obstacles, failures, and how to cooperate with their peers. These are all vital skills needed as future members of the workforce and the basic competencies outlined in *ASCA Mindsets and Behaviors for Student Success* (ASCA, 2014) that serves as the key standards of the core counseling curriculum and comprehensive school counseling programs.

Grades 4 and 5

As students transition from early to late childhood and approach adolescence, they are developing social skills like assertiveness and conflict resolution. Popularity and social acceptance have significant importance and children are developing positive social skills like empathy, positive relationships, and responsible decision-making. Self-regulation (Bandura, 1977) can lead to goal setting and a desire and capacity to work towards achieving goals. Again, this is a mindset that should be promoted with students in these grades through the core curriculum. Most notably, students in fifth grade are preparing to transition to middle school and a more rigorous and socially challenging environment. Developing meaningful relationships and a sense of belonging, as well as the ability to stay self-disciplined and focused, will help ease this transition to adolescence. This involves a shift from the awareness, explorative, and play-focused career development activities provided in elementary school to the middle school where activities will be more driven by self-awareness and aim to deepen college and career knowledge for academic planning and goal setting (NOSCA, 2010).

Role of the School Counselor: Elementary

School counselors in elementary school are tasked with developing a systemic and developmental approach to design a curriculum that promotes social-emotional growth and the development of mindsets and behaviors that build a bridge between learning and college and career readiness (ASCA, 2019). This is optimally achieved through classroom lessons, use of technology, and school-wide initiatives and activities. Through this curriculum and career experiences, school counselors can focus on career skills such as problem-solving, communication, critical thinking skills, creativity, flexibility, and entrepreneurial skills. These skills are important in all grade levels as students develop more maturity and college and career readiness (Savitz-Romer & Bouffard, 2012)

Ideally, a school counselor can partner with local businesses, parents, and other stakeholders to provide resources, support, and participation in school-wide career activities. This can be particularly challenging in communities that have less access to these resources and successful community members. Developing a comprehensive and equitable program might involve more family outreach and the use of technology to bring in more virtual opportunities to help reduce the disparities that might exist in less affluent communities. Developing community partnerships is another effective way of collaborating with community and families to meet the needs of students and reduce the achievement and access gap (Bryan & Henry, 2012). It is also essential that curriculum and planning of activities is done in a culturally responsive manner.

In addition to the ASCA (2014) mindsets and behaviors that provide standards to guide the school counselor core curriculum, school counselors are promoting college and career readiness through the five SEL core competencies (CASEL, 2015)—responsible decision-making, relationship skills, social awareness, self-awareness, and self-management—and through the *Eight Components of College and Career Readiness* (NOSCA, 2010). These components are addressed throughout the K–12 pipeline but an elementary school counselor can create a college-going and career ready school campus through the inclusion of the following components in the counseling core curriculum: (1) college aspirations, (4) college and career exploration and selection processes, and even some simplified versions of (5) college and career assessments.

Career Exploration and Equitable Access: Elementary School

In following *ASCA Mindsets and Behaviors for Student Success* (ASCA, 2014), the CASEL (2014) SEL core competencies, and the NOSCA (2010) *Eight Components of College and Career Readiness*, the elementary school counselor can develop a curriculum with a potentially distinct set of learning objectives and activities for each grade level focusing on college and career readiness. The 35 standards included in *ASCA Mindsets and Behaviors for Student Success* align with each of the competencies and domains of a comprehensive school counseling program, including the career development domain. The school counselor would develop classroom lessons or experiences that help students develop competencies based on these standards. With younger students, the lessons might engage students using stories, art projects, and play activities like exploring "Tools of the Trade." Older students can participate in online and abbreviated and modified versions of traditional career inventories based on the six career personalities (Holland, 1973) to see how their strengths and interests align with potential career paths or learn about "career clusters." Developing family "genograms" is a way that students can compare their own interests, skills, aspirations, and talents to those of their family members. This can be an interesting way for students to learn about what the adults in their lives do for work, their educational experiences, and compare this with their own goals. Students can share these with each other or complete the activity independently based on their own comfort level.

Counselors use several forms of data to determine the specific needs of their schools. The American School Counselor Association (2019) recommends that all school counseling programs begin with a needs assessment to ensure alignment of the school counselor's interventions to the needs of the individual school and the community it serves. In addition to this survey data, school counselors rely on student specific data such as behavioral referrals, academic progress, and standardized achievement tests. Using these data points helps in the development of a career development program that addresses the needs at the school. The use of posttest assessments from the school counseling core curriculum lessons can help to further determine whether particular students are in need of additional interventions. The mindsets and behaviors which are the foundation of the school counseling core curriculum (ASCA, 2014) provide a rationale for integrating these areas of need into the educational program.

Career Days and School-Wide Events

Even more impactful than classroom instruction and activities is the opportunity to meet people who can describe their work. Schools often host career day events to bring in outside guest speakers. These are sometimes presented as a "career fair" with different guest attendees at a table or booth or through more elaborate "career week" activities and classroom presentations. In Appendix 16.A (located at the end of the chapter), a school counselor describes the process of planning and facilitating a school-wide career week event in an elementary school, including a school-wide career-themed "vehicle day," where students can explore a variety of vehicles used in jobs like construction, animal control, agriculture, law enforcement, fire and rescue, and even limousines. Through events like this, students are exposed to careers that they would not normally learn about and able to interact and ask questions related to the field and the required training.

Other school-wide events include student driven career fairs that could provide students in upper elementary grades to research careers and present the career in a format similar to a science fair with tri-fold boards to exhibit for students. In this scenario, the student becomes the "expert" to share their knowledge about the career, including a job description, training and education needed, and any other unique aspects of the job. Schools might promote a college and career ready campus environment with other activities like "Dress like your future." Such an event would allow students to dress for the career that they aspire to gain as an adult.

Many programs are now providing digital programs to help elementary students learn about the Holland Codes (1997) and other career-related interest inventories. A career gallery walk is a unique approach to involve students in sharing their interests and learning more about careers within each personality code. One counselor wrote about a program that the fourth grade students participate in each year after they complete interest inventories (School, 2020). The personality codes are each given a color and students dress in that color on the day of their "gallery walk" through the hallways that are decorated with posters and information about each career within each interest and trait. The school partners with the local career technical education (CTE) program and hosts guest speakers and hands-on activities in each area. This annual event increases exposure to professions to meet the needs of all students and can be a springboard for learning more about potential careers and opportunities in CTE and not just the traditional college path.

Legos are another great tool for elementary school counselors with various uses. Using play-based approaches helps students develop social skills, communication, and leadership skills (Tulluck, 2021). One career-focused use of these popular toys involves the creation of an "architect group" or team and students use the Lego blocks to design a theme park or other place of interest. The teams must use cooperative, problem-solving, and leadership skills to set goals and complete the design. Lego blocks are also easy to clean and can be provided to students in separate containers for extra precautions in an age of social distancing and safety.

Equitable Access and the 21st Century Digital Citizens

While school-wide events might be highly engaging for students, they are not always easy to plan. Schools might not be geographically close to many of these presenters and many schools do not have as many working parents or parents that are able to take time away from their jobs to come and present at a school. One way to increase accessibility and access is through the use of technology. One simple approach to use technology in school-wide programming is through the use of broadcasted morning news shows that are very common in elementary schools. Guest speakers from a variety of careers in the community can submit pre-recorded video clips of their workplace or be interviewed in the studio to be shared throughout the school.

This format allows one presenter to easily connect with an entire student population in a short amount of time and also reach schools that might not have the same highly involved parent volunteer resources.

In 2020, many school counselors were charged with bringing their comprehensive programs to the world of distance learning due to the COVID-19 school closures (Hecht-Weber, 2021). While this did limit some of the activities that might have previously occurred, it also opened up a door to a delivery model that can be easily accessed by all and even shared among schools. Many schools are now discovering how to turn these obstacles into opportunities. In one school district, the school counselors collaborated to develop a Google Classroom or Google Site online career week. Members of the community and even around the country were able to record videos of themselves that were then compiled to create a "virtual career week." In this model, the short segments were pre-recorded or guest speakers could join live in Google Meet or Zoom meetings to deliver live and interactive presentations. These events are recorded so they can be collected and shared on one website. The website can also include interactive activities, such as using programs that allow students to record their own videos to share their future aspirations with their peers.

In the future, schools could plan virtual classroom visits from guest speakers who can be from all over the city, state, or country to share their career experiences with students. This is one way school counselors can narrow the disparities among schools and access quality career programming. Virtual career experiences also expose students to careers beyond those that can be found in their local communities like the more traditional professions in medicine, law, and other community helping professions. The delivery approach is convenient for the presenters, who might otherwise not be able to leave work. It also offers students a peek into their work environment beyond what they might be able to share in a traditional slide show and classroom presentation. The possibilities are endless when professionals are invited to interact with students through the various web conferencing platforms. When inviting professionals to log in virtually, students can interact with high-interest careers like YouTubers, video game designers, Disney Imagineers, and more.

Today's technology is so innovative that there are schools that can even offer "virtual reality expeditions" using virtual reality goggles. These limitless opportunities will really bridge the gap between students and prepare all 21st century learners for a world where careers are now more automated and the need for many careers will no longer exist (Manyika et al., 2017). It begins with our youngest of students and continues through to adolescence when aspirations lead to actions and choices.

MIDDLE SCHOOL: DEVELOPMENTAL OVERVIEW
AND IMPLICATIONS

As typical students enter middle school, change is a pervasive force. Physical changes introduced by puberty can bring about conflicts associated with body image and sexuality. In addition, the major educational transition from elementary to secondary school is often stressful. In most cases, this represents the first time a child experiences working with more than one or two teachers at a time. This barrage of change can thwart a student's sense of identity which in turn can lead to confusion and ambiguity about future goals.

Psychosocial Perspective

According to Erikson (as cited in Newman & Newman, 2018), students at this point of development are either experiencing or just completing the psychological conflict of industry vs. inferiority. Industry refers to an eagerness to learn a skill or perform a task. The other side of this conflict, inferiority, refers to a child's belief that he or she is incapable of performing to the degree of his or her peers. These feelings of worthlessness or inadequacy are usually based on external sources such as peers who appear to complete new tasks with ease, or others in their social communities who appear to achieve more easily. Students who master this conflict successfully create a self-concept focused on competence. Those who fail to manage this conflict successfully are faced with the core pathology of inertia and might find it difficult to engage in meaningful or challenging work.

The Role of the School Counselor: Middle School

The middle school counselor can play a pivotal role in guiding a child's career planning at this point of development. The role of the counselor at this point will be to provide praise and acceptance through this turbulent stage, while at the same time helping the student to discover his or her strengths, interests, and preferences for the world of work. The middle school counselor also acts as a liaison for the transition to high school which typically involves choosing courses and electives that will prepare the student for postsecondary goals. While the transition to high school is a difficult time for all students, it can be even more so for students of color, particularly African American male students (Holcomb-McCoy, 2007b). The middle school counselor can serve as an equalizer by ensuring that each and every student has the tools needed to manage this transition effectively, creating opportunities for postsecondary success.

By focusing on the ASCA (2014) mindsets and behaviors, the middle school counselor can help each student navigate the transition to middle school while at the same time focusing on self-knowledge that will help students to shape positive self-concepts. The counselor can target college and career readiness by addressing the behavior standards that align to learning strategies, self-management skills, and social skills. These standards provide the backdrop that allow the counselor to introduce a school culture that values postsecondary education as well as readiness for the world of work. By using various inventories, the counselor can facilitate students' understanding of their own personal values, aptitudes, and interests. According to ACT (2008), an eighth grader's level of preparation for college and career can be more significant than anything the student will gain academically while in high school. The ACT further asserts that for students who are not properly prepared for college and career readiness by the end of eighth grade the "impact may be nearly irreversible" (p. 2). As middle school counselors begin to understand their own potential to impact all aspects of a student's life through college and career counseling, there could be a shift in the delivery of comprehensive school counseling plans to include more career counseling at the middle school level (Anctil et al., 2012).

Assessment and Inventory Tools

Various assessments are available to middle school counselors to help students examine their fit for specific careers or college majors. Several states include a requirement that students engage in career education for promotion from middle school. Virginia, for example, requires all students to develop an academic and career plan (ACP) beginning in seventh grade (Association for Career and Technical Education [ACTE], 2018). In Florida, State Statute requires that all students complete a course in career education and planning where students are guided to create an individualized plan prior to promotion to high school (FLA. STAT., §1003.4156 (1,e), (2020)). School counselors assist students in the process of career exploration by providing opportunities for students to learn about the world of work, helping engage students in inventories that allow them to identify potential career choices and helping students to connect their own personal attributes to the world of work. Through this self-exploration model, counselors help students make preliminary decisions that are open for change as they progress through middle and high school. One evidence-based program that counselors can use is the ACT Explore (ACT, 2014). This program assesses students to determine their likelihood of becoming college ready by the end of high school. While not every student will attend college, it is important that counselors introduce postsecondary education as an option that is available to all students, regardless of gender, race, ethnicity, or socioeconomic status. When students are assured that college is accessible, and when a culture of college readiness is established within a school, students are more likely to reach their academic potential (ACT, 2008).

At the same time, the ACT Explore assessment allows students to complete various inventories to assess their own interests and work preferences. The results of these assessments can be used as a tool for the middle school counselor to help each student understand his or her personal career trajectory. While the ACT Explore results provide a detailed analysis of each student's profile (ACT, 2014), it is up to the counselor to help the student interpret these results and to help the student understand the important connection between middle school and postsecondary success. Another important tool for students is a value sorter. Value sorters allow students to become aware of their own personal work values while developing a sense of respect for the diversity of values among their peers. School counselors can use value sorters to help students select careers and majors that are consistent with their self-discovery. The U.S. Department of Labor offers various online self-assessments that students can complete at school or at home. These free inventories help students to explore careers and also to understand how their own interests can help them to choose a career cluster. The online inventory tool uses Holland's (1973) RIASEC model to identify personality types that align to specific categories of work. While there are several free inventories available online, one evidence-based protocol that can be used in schools is the Knowdell's (2005) Career Values Card Sort. This assessment is available as a physical deck of cards or as an online sorting tool. School counselors can use these cards to add hands-on manipulatives to the career planning process and cannot only pinpoint those work values their students see as important, but they can also use the activity to celebrate the diversity among students in order to foster respect for the values of their peers. When students understand the impact that personal values have on college and career choices, they gain valuable insight aimed at maximizing their future success.

Equity and Accessibility

While activities such as inventories and value sorters do help students to choose careers and majors, the school counselor must aim to help students avoid obstacles based on preconceived notions or stereotypes based on gender, race, ethnicity, or socioeconomics. According to Jones (2010), career counseling at the middle school level can help to lessen the impact of these barriers (ASCA, 2018). School counselors must act as advocates for all students and must provide equitable access to futures that supersede preconceived notions (ASCA, 2019). As counselors strive to help students identify their postsecondary goals, they must be sensitive to the racial and ethnic development of students at this stage. As students begin to differentiate their understanding of self, they become increasingly aware of racial and ethinic differences. The constructs of racial inequity and prejudice can become central to a student's development at this stage. For many middle school students, this period represents an introduction to majority versus minority cultures. Students of color, for example, might find healthy racial identity more difficult to develop than their White counterparts (Akos & Ellis, 2008; Holcomb, 2017b). This can create a potential risk for a sense of inadequacy or inferiority. When working with marginalized students, the middle school counselor must consider the impact that cultural, social, economic, and other discrimination influences have on their education and career aspirations (Jackson & Nutini, 2002).

A study to determine students entering fields of science, technology, engineering, and mathematics (STEM) found that females and minority students were less likely to select careers than their White male counterparts (Mau & Li, 2018). This disparity can be lessened by the intervention of a middle school counselor who is willing to engage all students in a culture of equitable access. Through career counseling in middle school, each student must be encouraged and convinced that all options are available and accessible. The middle school counselor may not necessarily solidify a student's career choice, but rather open doors through self-exploration with the assurance that all students can overcome barriers to future success.

HIGH SCHOOL: DEVELOPMENTAL OVERVIEW AND IMPLICATIONS

Adolescents between the age of 14–18 face essential cognitive and psychosocial prerequisites that aid in their ability to identify their path and impact their trajectory for postsecondary college and career success. From a cognitive development perspective, metacognition is a key skill for students to possess and utilize as they assess their identity and navigate postsecondary plans. Metacognition is defined as "cognition of cognition" for the purpose of monitoring and controlling cognition (Flavell, 1979). From a metacognitive perspective, a student can be aware of the outcome of the monitoring process and gains an ability to be "mindful of their feelings of knowing, feelings of confidence, feeling of satisfaction, awareness of not understanding and of the beliefs about their own cognition" (Efklides, 2008, p. 278). Lemberger & Clemons (2012) noted that metacognition and executive function are operative factors of self-regulation that contribute to academic and constructive school engagement. Furthermore, Efklides highlighted that metacognition offers students specific skills for success to connect to the "deliberate use of strategies in order to control cognition" (Efklides, 2008, p. 280).

Philosophically, this cognitive skill development is composed of strategies such as orientation, forethought, performance control, regulation, monitoring, evaluation of cognitive process, self-reflection, executive planning, and task processing (Savitz-Romer & Bouffard, 2012; Veenman & Elshout, 1999). As students plan for postsecondary life, the school counselor is well positioned to promote the benefits of metacognition for it allows students to be self-reflective, assess, and evaluate the potential outcomes of their choices and to use that information to make solid and well thought out decisions (Savitiz-Romer & Bouffard, 2012).

From a psychosocial perspective as outlined by Erikson (1963), high school students are in the stage of identity versus role confusion. They are focused on developing and cultivating relationships with key figures in their lives that will provide positive role models and experiences to equip and empower them to gain a better understanding of self, temperament, values, interests, and abilities. These components aid the student to construct their self-concept. The consequence of negative role models and corrosive experiences may lead to role confusion.

School counselors are in a prime position to use their knowledge of adolescent developmental stages to help optimize overall student success. The awareness and understanding of student growth and development can certainly be understood through recognizing the diversity among high school students in their personal interactions. Based on cognitive and social emotional stages of development, students' capacities to learn and interact vary greatly throughout secondary education. The basis of human growth and development can be thought of as the foundation for understanding the connection to their college and career development. In order to successfully assist students with postsecondary success, school counselors must understand the nuances of students from diverse backgrounds, cultural context, and their unique stage of development; if they are solid in their identity or if they are confused. Using the student's personal narrative and journey can aid in developing positive postsecondary plans and potential outcomes. Using the students' current stage of development and projecting the potential growth trajectory can be tools for students to be victors and not victims of their negative socio-economic status (SES) or family context. Helping students dissect and decipher their current dilemmas for the sole purpose of developing a growth over fixed mindset is imperative in assisting high school students navigate the steps from late adolescence through young adulthood.

Practically, school counselors working with students who, based on their development and context are marginalized, vulnerable, or lack economic and social resources to succeed may stand to serve as a bridge to success or a blockade to success. School counselors may strategically serve in minimizing educational inequalities due to SES, and other vital demographic variables (Auwarter & Aruguete, 2008; Cox & Lee, 2007; Holcomb-McCoy, 2007a). Understanding the nuisances conceptualizing a student's background, development and its current impact is essential in assisting students to understand who they are and who they can become.

Role of the School Counselor in Postsecondary Preparation

School counselors provide personal and individualized assistance aligned and rooted in cultural intentionality and competency (ASCA, 2016). They must evaluate their own cultural awareness and be prepared to engage and be mindful of the student's cultural context and personal narrative. In context of the 2020–2021 Covid-19 pandemic, racial injustice events, and a political divide—the need for the school counselor to be a "cultural sustainer" and be cognizant of many cultures and subcultures is vital to service the essential needs of students' postsecondary planning (ASCA, 2020). Utilizing a case conceptualization format (Butler & Constantine, 2006), the school counselor will formulate a view of each student. Based on key information, the following factors can be considered when using this approach. First, family context is considered (i.e., as discussed previously, use a family genogram to understand the family system, work life, and backstory). Second, academic record review provides key information (i.e., reviewing the students high school transcript, standardized test scores, and informal and formal assessments). Third, personal narrative provides relevant information by having a brief conversation with the student regarding their own journey through elementary to secondary, highlighting any significant mile markers as well as the student's vision of self. Fourth, provide students with career assessments (a battery of inventories, if possible) to gauge and measure interest, strength, areas of potential growth, and skills. By conceptualizing the student successfully provides the school counselor a foundation to understand the student's personal narrative/story, academic context and their potential postsecondary trajectory. Having depth of knowledge about the student will provide a base and keen insight to be more prepared to assist the student with constructing a sound plan, clarify goals and objectives, confirm steps needed to take, and possibly correct postsecondary plan assumptions and mindsets.

School counselors have an ethical and moral obligation to provide equal access, opportunity, and availability to all students regardless of race, greed, color, or immigration status (ASCA, 2016; ASCA, 2018). An equal platform of support to students means that regardless of a student's cultural background, they will assist all students by providing individual and personalized postsecondary planning. They will support student success by facilitating intentional and culturally responsive conversations. Helping the student connect the dots of who they are to what they want to become is critical. The ASCA High School Career Conversations (ASCA, n.d.) is a useful tool for school counselors to assist, stimulate, and facilitate critical postsecondary dialogue. Exploring with the student, their interest, skills, strengths, abilities, and talents helps them to understand their opportunity to manage their own talent and make linkages to a well-matched college major and career path. Career conversations can propel students to engage in constructive experiential learning opportunities (i.e., volunteering or internships) that can enlighten students about possible career paths. School counselors can encourage high school students to volunteer with an organization that is aligned with their interest, skills, and ability (rather than just for fulfilling mandatory community service hours for graduation requirements). Sanctioning an environment for students to develop a portfolio (i.e., engaging experiences, building a resume and interest inventories/assessments) can be a capstone of their high school experience and propel students for postsecondary success.

Career Exploration and Equitable Access: High School

Students having optimum career exploration and equitable access is important to building school culture of exposure and experience to possible career paths. Career exposure and experiences put students in a posture of learning about potential career paths in different fields of study, vocation, and industry. Constructive career exposure and experiences can be facilitated through the promotion of intentional internships. Internship or volunteer opportunities provided by community stakeholders (businesses, organizations, or civic groups) that link with the student's interest, skills, abilities, and talents may pave the way for students to either confirm, clarify, correct, and possibly construct a career path. For minority and marginalized students, the use of internships and mentorship relationships are vital to career planning (Glenn et al., 2012). Students fully engaged in a robust internship or volunteer program may inform and inspire decisions for postsecondary decisions. Counseling students via classroom presentations, small group discussions, or individually will provide an opportunity to facilitate and stimulate dialog based on the ASCA Career Conversations.

Based on the impact of the COVID-19 pandemic that forced schools to go virtual, school counselors needed to use technology to provide lessons via webinar style presentations and discussions. In a post-pandemic society, the school counselor will remain positioned to engage students by providing on-demand lessons to educate and enlighten students.

Consulting and collaborating with key individuals associated with the school and community is critical to providing an equity-based culture of assisting students in identifying a major, vocation, and career path. Brigman (2005) addressed the integral role of the school counselor as possessing specific skills for working effectively with key career path influencers. Developing a plan to assist students and aid in linking strong allies is essential in creating and cultivating a climate that fosters equity-based college and career planning. School counselors are challenged to realize that the consultation and collaboration process is focused on advocating for students' success (i.e., minority women in STEM-related fields or careers that don't require a college degree). School counselors are leaders in consulting and collaborating and by utilizing skill, exhibiting multifaceted competency in linking key persons, students and parents, and empowered with insight to guide students in making informed decisions regarding postsecondary life, gather information, explore options, and listen to suggestions and recommendations (Baker et al., 2009; Brigman, 2005). Teachers, administrators, community stakeholders (organizational leaders and business owners), college staff (Admission reps and professors), and military recruiters comprise some of the members in this consultation and collaboration approach. Teachers and administrators based on their area of study and subject matter can point to and facilitate areas of further research for students to consider (i.e., resources, organizations, and summer programs). By connecting with community stakeholders, students will have access to possible experiential learning and enlightenment (through internships or apprenticeships) in their area of interest. College representatives and military recruiters will be able to assist with informing schools and other community leaders about unique programs that are available to interested students and the information shared can provide vital insight on what steps students need to take.

Equitably Access: Assessments and Opportunities

School counselors play a critical role in providing equitable access to assessments and opportunities that can provide key insight to students about what they can consider and contemplate their postsecondary options. The College Board offers a suite of assessments including the PSAT 8/9, PSAT 10, PSAT/NMSQT, and SAT. These assessments provide an opportunity for students in 8th–12th grade to assess their knowledge and skill for college preparation. Uniquely for the 11th grade PSAT/NMSQT, the College Board has partnered with organizations that focus on equity and access to college planning. Hinging on PSAT/NMSQT performance, students may garner scholarship and internship opportunities (i.e., Jackie Robinson Foundation, Hispanic Scholarship Fund, and DREAMers.us). The ACT organization offers the PreACT 8/9, PreACT, and ACT as assessments that prepare students in appropriate grades for the ACT that is taken in the 11th and 12th grade. The ACT version for 11th and 12th will gauge the students' readiness for college. While these assessments are available for all students, the cost of these assessments may prohibit a student's ability to take these assessments. By using and evaluating school data, a school counselor can determine which students may be eligible for fee waivers based on SES. Removing barriers and issuing test fee waivers for each respective test will pave the way to opportunity and provide access and equity. This is essential and further provides a platform for scholarships and other college and career opportunities.

The Advanced Placement (AP) program, sponsored by the College Board, enables willing and academically prepared students to pursue college-level studies while still in high school. AP courses offer students the opportunity to gain college credit while in college while being exposed to a nationally normed curriculum and end of course assessment. Students engaged in these courses have the opportunity to study and identify potential career paths and opportunities of enlightenment. School counselors can utilize the College Board's computer-based AP Potential program, to align PSAT achievement to specific subject areas. The program uses an algorithm to determine AP courses where specific students would likely succeed. The proper use of AP Potential information can attract students who may not have been inclined otherwise to take an AP course. This can remove the school counselor's role of "gatekeeper" by creating opportunities for all students based upon their individual areas of strength. Investigating equity gaps and providing opportunities to close those gaps is critical and vital to marginalized students such as the observed underrepresentation of women of color in the computer and hard sciences fields of study. Using the AP Potential information can aid in being able to identify students and linking them to opportunities that can help them identify a career path.

Dual Enrollment (DE) are courses that are offered by colleges and community colleges for students to receive high school credit as well as college credit. DE provides an opportunity for students to engage with college level curriculum and exposure. Students are able to take entry level courses that can provide an environment for students to take courses at a free or reduced cost and be exposed to experiences and opportunities that can aid in helping students identify a major and career path.

The Armed Services Vocational Aptitude Battery (ASVAB) is another assessment and is commonly used for military placement but can also be used as an exploratory tool to gauge student ability, interest, skill, and talents regardless of military service aspirations. Career interest assessments and surveys are designed to uncover, measure normal personality, and to assess strengths, skills, and motivation (Harrington & Long, 2013). The purpose of implementing such instruments is self-discovery and are another tool to reveal personality, strengths, and their potential vocational interests, skills, and values. In the Curry and Milsom (2017) text, the authors highlight a wide range of informal and formal assessments and surveys. A clear sense of vocational interests may facilitate high school students' capacity to connect current interests to congruent educational and occupational environments. This is particularly important for youth who are marginalized and experience external constraints on career development (Diemer et al., 2010). Using all resources available to review and research for implementation with students, increases access to tools that can assess the students' gifts, talents, and abilities. Assisting students in identifying their strengths and areas of growth equips the student to understand their own skill set, talent, limitations, and be informed about potential career paths.

While collaboration with community stakeholders was previously addressed, collaborating with community colleges, technical colleges, and universities to host campus visits, tours, and sessions with current students to provide exposure opportunities is another way to bridge the gap for students. Whether taking students to a campus or hosting a college fair at the high school, the school counselor promotes an outreach culture through these events that will aid in providing equity access to information, resources, and experiences. Assisting students in casting vision and providing a space to have honest dialog about hopes and holdups (i.e., authentic conversations) is essential. The school counselor sanctioning space for open dialogue and vision casting is a vital vehicle for college and career planning (Conrad, 2020). College and career planning artifacts to use with students during advisement sessions and consultation with students are provided in Appendices 16.C and 16.D (located at the end of this chapter). Additionally, a case vignette of college planning and advisement is provided in Appendix 16.E.

DISCUSSION

From a data driven practice perspective, school counselors must seek to evaluate and measure gains to validate the SEL implementation and impact. The advocacy for these essential skills must not be minimized or trivialized as an add-on to a school counselor's duties within the school. Social-emotional skill intervention must be baked and ingrained into the role and service delivery of school counselors. The College Career Student Skills (CCSS) is a data driven SEL intervention that teaches students critical skills in the areas of content knowledge, transition knowledge and skills, learning skills and techniques, and cognitive strategies (Villares & Brigman, 2019). Teaching these skills is documented as strengthening and firming a student's success in college and career (Conley, 2010).

As students prepare and plan for future college admissions and career placement, SEL skills are significant and essential. A critical component of the school counselor's role is to provide assistance to all students (e.g., gender identification, cultural heritage, geographical region, or SES) in becoming college and career ready. In their evaluation of prospective and incoming students, college admissions representatives look for students who will exhibit the skills and lifestyle that will deem them as positive contributors to the campus culture (Jones et al., 2016). Under a holistic college admissions review, students can be evaluated not just based on grade point average, test scores, or rigor of schedule. Students who are able to present themselves as socially and emotionally skillful will be better equipped.

The 21st century workplace will require specific technical and philosophical skills for specific occupations, careers, and jobs (that exist today) but also be equipped and prepared for future careers that don't currently exist today (Manyika et al., 2017). The acquisition of these hard skills are essential for appropriate career placement, engagement, and success. Technical, hard, and specific skills are needed, required, and essential to obtain specific jobs and careers. The need for soft skills (social-emotional skills) are and will continue to be needed even more so, as they are essential and necessary to preserve, retain, and maintain employment. Furthermore, SEL skill proficiency is deemed significant to prospective employers and supervisors (Mitchell et al., 2010). Cunningham and Villaseñor (2014) emphasized the notion that skills such as problem-solving and communicating clearly are equal to or more important than technical skills.

In a 2015 study by Columbia University Teacher College that highlighted the economic benefits of SEL skill development, it was determined that this may help students progress further in their education and may also enhance personal, economic, and social well-being in development and transition to adulthood (Belfield et al., 2015). Interpersonal and intrapersonal skills, solution-seeking, collaboration, and respectful engagement—all universally known as skills for success—are essential skills for the current and future workplaces. Job and career-specific skills learned through college, university, or technical institutions change over time, but the skills taught via SEL interventions are unending and do not expire. Developing an SEL foundation in primary and secondary education has a healthy end game, focused not just on the primary and secondary students, but ensures that youth learn skills for life that are transferable and adaptable to any situation or vocation in life. School counselors with this clear vision and mission, will promote a positive outcome for students evidenced by workplace readiness skills and techniques needed to succeed professionally.

Assisting K–12 students in the area of social-emotional attentiveness and comprehension is essential in helping students understand themselves and the gifts and tools they must possess. Those SEL skills possessed by students during their time in elementary and secondary schools will aid in students being equipped for college and career success by having self-awareness. Knowledge is power and the power of SEL must be afforded to students to make powerful decisions for their own success. As students prepare for college and career, SEL skills will be portable and transferable to any career path a student selects. An example of a college and career week for students in Grades 6–12 including a "soft skill fair" and student activities is included in Appendix 16.B.

Recommendations for Policy

Policy must be enacted to ensure all students have access to the benefits of a school counselor. This means that all schools should be funded sufficiently to reach the maximum caseloads recommended by the American School Counseling Association of 250:1 (ASCA, 2014). Only when school counselors' caseloads are manageable can they create and deliver a comprehensive school counseling program that focuses on the mindsets and behaviors that lead to college and career readiness (2014). When all schools have a sufficient number of school counselors, then all students can learn in a culture of postsecondary readiness based on evidence-based programs and delivered by a professional with the proper training and expertise.

Several states require that students initiate a college and career plan in middle school. It is imperative that this plan not remain stagnant after middle school. It should be required that all middle school students develop this prior to high school and that the high school counselor facilitate the revision and review of the plan annually.

Recommendations for Practice

According to the American School Counselors Association (2014), students must receive a curriculum based on the ASCA (2014) mindsets and behaviors delivered by a professional school counselor. School counselors must be accessible to all students regardless of their race, ethnicity, socioeconomic level, sex, gender, gender identity, or sexual preference. This is an ideal that can only be accomplished when administrators prioritize school counselors in their operating budget. In addition, this only happens when counselor education programs "help prepare school counselors in training to identify and address racism and bias while working within the ASCA Ethical Standards for School Counselor Education Faculty" (ASCA, 2020, p. 9). Every student deserves the very best school counselor and a culture that respects college and career readiness as its top initiative.

School counselors are charged with the responsibility of providing comprehensive school counseling services and programs that include direct services to address the three domains: academic development, social-emotional development, and college and career readiness (ASCA, 2019). Often school counselors struggle to balance their direct and indirect services to focus on all three of these domains, but it is critical for students to be prepared for college and career success through the intentional and targeted, competency-based school counselor interventions. This involves the collaboration and consultation with stakeholders and administrators to deliver a culturally responsive approach that ensures equity and access, and encourages ALL students to cross-cultural and gender stereotypical boundaries, and engages in all possible postsecondary outcomes.

School counselors will need to adapt their approach to provide equitable service taking into consideration that students have witnessed racial inequities, protests, violence, political tensions, and insurrections, in a year that the world has been struggling with the economic and social impacts of a world-wide pandemic. The American School Counselor Association (2020) asserts in it's preamble that all students should "be respected, be treated with dignity and have access to a school counseling program that advocates for and affirms all students from diverse populations" (p. 5). It is imperative as school counselors develop their framework for career education and experiences, that special attention be given to the educational materials used, such as books that feature characters from diverse backgrounds, sociopolitical concepts, and historical events (Susko, 2021). Guest speakers who are invited to speak about their careers in the events outlined in this chapter should also be representative of diverse cultures.

Recommendations for Further Research

A series of longitudinal studies indicating the effectiveness of college and career planning that spans the K–12 education experience would further support the need for school counselors to implement a comprehensive school counseling curriculum that includes college and career development. More empirical research is needed to demonstrate a clear causal relationship between the delivery of a college and career school counseling curriculum and future success in postsecondary studies and in the world of work. Furthermore, there is a need for more research on the effectiveness of evidence-based college and career planning activities, assessments, and inventories. Finally, it is important to expand this body of research to explore the impact of these interventions on closing the equity and achievement gaps.

CONCLUSION

Educators must contend with turbulent political unrest, the current Co-vid-19 pandemic, and violence in schools, while striving for academic achievement and maintaining a safe and secure environment. Teachers and administrators must depend on school counselors now more than ever before. School counselors are educators with specialized training in social-emotional health, academic achievement, and postsecondary readiness. In order to perform these tasks effectively, school counselors must understand the impact of race and ethnicity on each student's ability to succeed. The American School Counselor Association calls on all educators to recognize the state of our education system as well as the racial divide faced by our youth. ASCA notes that recent events are impactful on the lives of all students and must be addressed within the educational setting. Recent events including the deaths of Ahmaud Arbery, Breonna Taylor, George Floyd, and countless other Black Americans have tragically revealed the racial divisions that persist in the United States. "Educators have an obligation to end racism and bias in schools and school counselors have the unique opportunity to be part of this commitment through the implementation of a school counseling program that promotes equity and access for all students within a school culture free of systemic racism and bias." (ASCA, 2020, n.p.). When considering Bandura's (1986) theory of self-efficacy, counselors must understand that students who have been marginalized, who have faced discrimination, or who have felt less valuable than their White peers may be less likely to engage in opportunities that lead to increased achievement and possibilities for the future. School counselors have a responsibility to understand this construct in order to serve the needs of every student. Educators who attempt to use a one-size-fits-all approach will fail to meet the needs of an entire generation and will essentially perpetuate rather than ameliorate the racial and ethnic achievement gaps that exist. As counselors perform their duties, they must be open to learning about the cultural differences of the students they serve. School counselors must be attuned to the social and political perception of their students and must respond as social justice warriors, fighting to create equity and justice for all students.

DISCUSSION QUESTIONS

1. Describe the ways school counselors create a culture of college and career readiness for all students? How would this be different with younger and older students?
2. In what ways can school counselors work with community stake-holders to model opportunities for all students, including those

from marginalized groups whose historicity might lead them to believe that certain careers are out of their reach?

3. How can school counselors help students understand the links between their academic achievement and their postsecondary success?
4. How do the impacts of cultural, social, economic, and other biases influence students' education and career aspirations.
5. How can the school counselor encourage marginalized students to participate in rigorous coursework such as Advanced Placement and Dual Enrollment?
6. Consider your own K–12 experience. Discuss how your own ethnic or racial background created advantages or disadvantages for you.

ACTIVITIES

1. Create a list of five classroom lesson topics aligned with the ASCA (2014) mindsets and behaviors that school counselors can deliver to increase a culture of college and career readiness. Create one lesson plan and student activity to deliver in an elementary, middle, or high school.
2. Create a list of ten small businesses in your area that are owned or operated by minority individuals who can serve as role models or mentors for your students.
3. Create a calendar of activities for an entire school year. Incorporate activities each month that help students explore careers, develop self-knowledge, understand rigor, and plan for the future.
4. Find 2–3 children's books that show characters from different cultures and highlight career opportunities or job skills. How might you use these books in your career education program?

APPENDIX 16.A
Planning a Career Week Event in Elementary

Format of the Event: Some school counselors plan "Career Days" where all of the speaking is done in one day throughout the campus. However, when planning the "week" format, the school counselor can be better positioned to greet the guest speakers and facilitate the event. In the week format, each day can be for a different grade level or pair of grade levels.

Scheduling and Facilitating: Presenters tend to prefer the first 2 hours of the day so they can return to work and this usually helps school counselors avoid student lunch schedules when planning the event. Depending on the size of the school and number of classes per grade level, the students will see 4–5 guest speakers. Each speaker will speak for 20 minutes about their job and the students rotate to different rooms to hear each speaker. Given this speaker rotation style, each speaker will be speaking 4 or 5 times. Some prepare interactive role plays, bring in uniforms or gear related to their job, and others prepare videos and slideshows to teach about their jobs. Speakers are asked to prepare an age-appropriate presentation that includes information about their daily experiences and training.

Upper Elementary "Conference Style": For the more mature students on an elementary campus, there could be as many speakers as there are classrooms. For example, if there are 9 fifth grade classrooms, 9 speakers could be invited to speak. Alternatively, the day could be divided into more than one shift and speakers could speak 2 or 3 times each but there could be a second shift of speakers to fill the rooms. In this format, the students would have a schedule of the event and who is speaking in each room. They would choose their own sessions to attend based on their interest in the career. For example, Student A might choose to hear a veterinarian, mechanical engineer, and pilot, while Student B is attending the sessions for the firefighter, baseball player, and photographer. Classroom teachers assist with the supervision in each room and the transitions to each session but the students have more independence and self-direction with this model. (Note: This model would work well in a MS campus, as well.)

Guest Speaker Recruitment: Speakers can be recruited from parents at school through flyer/registration forms. By hosting this as an annual event, many parents will be eager to participate and it is a great way to encourage parent involvement in the school. Parents are usually given first priority to fill speaking slots. School business partners make up the next group that can be recruited to participate. By sending flyers out 6–8 weeks prior to the event, the school counselor can then see how many additional speakers are needed to fill the four to five speakers per grade level. Extra speakers needed could be from local businesses, community organizations, military, city employees, and so forth. Using technology could allow for some "virtual" career presentations from guest speakers anywhere.

School-Wide Vehicle Day: This is a 3+ hour event where vehicles representing a variety of careers are parked on campus (bus loop or parking lot) and students can walk around and view mini-presentations by the drivers. While learning about their job, they are also able to explore the vehicle and any related gear and equipment on the vehicle. This event might include animal rescue, fire and rescue, construction, agricultural, police, and even horses.

APPENDIX 16.B
College and Career Week (CCW)
for Secondary (6–12) Students

Secondary school counselors work every day to create a college and career readiness culture within their schools. All of the ASCA (2014) mindsets and behaviors standards are designed to promote college and career readiness for every student. When school counselors spearhead an annual week to spotlight this effort, they make tremendous strides in advocacy for their students as well as for the school counseling profession itself. The college and career week (CCW) must be a team effort that incorporates school personnel and community stakeholders. The following are some ideas for this exciting annual event.

1. School Staff College Posters: This activity must be started a few weeks before the college and career week in order to prepare the final product for staff to display.
   a. Create an online questionnaire such as a Google Form where staff can input information about their own college experiences. Sample questions can include:
      i. staff member's name;
      ii. name of college;
      iii. city and state of the college;
      iv. college major;
      v. Why did I choose this college?;
      vi. Did I live at home, college dorm, apartment, other?;
      vii. Did I participate in a sorority or fraternity?; and/or
      viii. one great memory from college.
   b. The school counselor sends an email to all staff encouraging them to participate in this survey.
   c. Once all of the data is collected, the counselor creates a document that merges this information into an 8×10 poster (see sample, Exhibit A). With a little creativity, the counselor can also include a graphic of the college or university for each poster.
   d. Staff members receive the poster prior to the first day of CCW. They display the posters in their classrooms or in their office for students to enjoy!
2. The Soft Skills Fair (see sample worksheet, Exhibit B)
   a. The school counselor collaborates with the School Advisory Counsel and Parent Teacher Association (PTA, PTSA, PTO or PTSO) to solicit participation from community stakeholders.

b. Many times, community members are reluctant to make a commitment to volunteer in a school. However, with this program, the commitment is for 1 hour, one time plus a $10.00 gift card as a prize. The $10.00 prize can be to a local fast food restaurant or a movie theater or a retail store. Usually the community member will bring a gift card from their own business.

c. On the day of the fair, students are encouraged to come to school "dressed for success." They should come to school in business attire.

d. During lunch period, students will move through stations depending on the number of volunteers. Each station might have as many as five volunteers. Some examples of stations include:

    i. How is my outfit? (Volunteers will help the student determine if the outfit is business appropriate and if not, what the student might do to improve.

    ii. The Handshake: Students will practice shaking hands with the volunteer while establishing eye contact and introducing him/herself.

    iii. The Interview: Students will practice answering basic interview questions.

    iv. Review my resume: Students will bring their resumes to be reviewed and critiqued.

    v. Hopes and Dreams: Students will have a chance to share their hopes and dreams for the future with a community partner.

e. Students will have a prepared worksheet for each of the stations. As they complete the stations, the volunteer will sign the space for their station (see sample). Worksheets will be handed to the counselor when completed.

f. At the end of the school day, the counselor will randomly select students who have completed the worksheet to win the prizes provided by the volunteer.

3. College Attire Day: All students and staff come to school dressed in attire from their favorite college or university!

4. College Fair Day: The counselor coordinates with local colleges and military recruiters to set up tables during lunch for students to visit and receive information.

5. Campus Visit: The counselor coordinates a field trip to a local community college or a local university. Students tour the campus and speak to an admissions counselor. In order to make the tour more meaningful, students will use a worksheet to ask questions. Students can also use this worksheet (Exhibit C) when taking virtual tours of colleges through the campus websites.

Sample Poster (Appendix 16.B, Exhibit A)

Central High School
College and Career Week 2020

Mrs. Tammy Jones

The University of Miami
Coral Gables, Florida
Major: Education

I chose this college because
it was close to home, and it had a great football team.

I lived at home for all four years.

I did not join a sorority.

Great memory: I remember being at the football game
when we beat Nebraska for the national championship.

Sample Soft Skills Worksheet (Appendix 16.B, Exhibit B)

Student Name _____ Grade level _____

Student ID _____

To enter the drawing for a prize at the end of the day, you must visit each station and you must have a community volunteer sign the blank for their station. Once your form is complete, you must turn it in to your school counselor. Prizes will be announced at the end of the day.

Station	Signature
1—My dress for success	
2—My handshake	
3—My practice interview	
4—My resume	
5—My hopes and dreams	

Sample College Tour Worksheet
(Appendix 16.B, Exhibit C)

Name of School _____

School Mascot _____

City and State of School _____

How many undergraduate students attend? _____

What is the average SAT/ACT score for admission _____

What are the average Weighted/Unweighted GPAs? _____

Does the application include a student essay? _____

Does the school accept teacher/counselor recommendations? _____

What are your most popular majors _____

How can students get academic support/tutoring? _____

Is there a writing center on campus? _____

What are the most popular sports? _____

Are there clubs and activities? _____

Do all Freshmen live on campus? _____ Can I have a car? _____

What are the meal plan options? _____

How are roommates assigned and what if I don't like mine? _____

About how much time per day do Freshmen spend studying? _____

How many students are in most classes? _____

Are there opportunities for study abroad? _____

Will I need to attend any summer semesters? _____

Are there opportunities for internships? _____

APPENDIX 16.C
Sample College Consultation
Interview Worksheet (Juniors)

Date:

Name:

Cell Number:

Personal Email:

What perspective do your parents provide? Are you a "First Generation College student"? Are there siblings /relatives in college? Have you faced any adverse situations? **(Family Context)**

What are your career interests and goals? What are you passionate about? Have you taken a career assessment? Have you taken a spiritual gifts inventory? What information would be important to know about your potential career path? **(College and Career Path Objectives)**

As you consider your career path, what types of post-high-school education/ training have you already explored? What colleges/universities are you interested in? What are your vision, hopes and dreams? **(Learning Venue)**

Have you registered for the SAT or ACT? Have you taken either of these and what can you do to maximize your score? What is your current grade point average and have you taken any courses that are considered more rigorous? **(Admission Criteria)**

What are your academic reflections (9th, 10th and 11th)? What is your vision for 12th? **(Transcript)**

How will you fund your college experience? **(Stewardship)**

How are you impacting and contributing to our community? **(Volunteering)**

APPENDIX 16.D
Sample College Consultation
Interview Worksheet (Seniors)

Name: Cell Phone:

What did you do during the summer?

What experiences did you have this summer that helped clarify your gifts, abilities and talents?

Desired Major/

Application/Transcript request procedures: **Area of Study:**
  • What schools will receive an application from you?   _____

    – _____

    – _____

    – _____

    – _____

Review recommendation procedures:
  • Do you have a resume prepared? Will you need recommenders? Who are they?

College and Career Path:
  • What information would be important to know about your potential career path?
  • As you consider your career path, what types of post-high-school education/training have you already explored?

Standardized Testing:
  • Have you taken an ACT or SAT? If so, what was your score? Are you retaking? What steps are you taking to improve your score?

Financial Aid:
  • How recent has the family discussed college funding plans? Have you started/completed a scholarship search? Have you searched specific college/university scholarships? What is the family view on college debt? Have you completed your FAFSA?

Community Service:

How did your service benefit the community?

Personal Attributes:

What can you offer to the college or university? What makes you special as an applicant?

APPENDIX 16.E
Arianna's Journey

Arianna and her mother met with her school counselor for her junior meeting. They conducted an hour-long consultation (see Junior Year Worksheet). During this meeting, Arianna expressed her desire to attend a 4-year college and major in journalism. During that meeting, Arianna shared her hesitancy and resistance when the counselor inquired about her potentially attending a community college. This recommendation was based on her low GPA and low test scores. These factors would make her local college a reach school and cost prohibitive. Arianna expressed concern associated with the stigma of attending a community college, as her friends had plans to leave the area, and she desired to leave the area as well. Based on an already well established rapport and relationship with the school counselor, the parent and student were able to discuss the merits and benefits of attending her local community college. Throughout the junior year, the SC and student continued the conversation on college planning and took a career assessment to confirm, clarify, correct, and confirm her interests.

As Arianna transitioned to her senior year, her resistance to attending a community college remained, yet she began to understand the benefits. As Arianna drew closer to graduation, she made plans to attend her local community college and obtain her Associates of Arts degree. The SC remained in contact with Arianna post-graduation and obtained updates about her development and engagement with her community college. Using the results from her career assessment, Arianna had confidence to seek out internship opportunities related to journalism and communication, thriving via those opportunities. Arianna's time at her community college was well spent and a wise investment of time and energy. She garnered self-confidence and developed a strong network of support. She now plans to attend a rigorous college of communications.

AUTHOR NOTE

Clifford H. Mack, Jr. ORCID https://orcid.org/0000-0001-7499-2784
Laura J. Cohen ORCID https://orcid.org/0000-0002-0981-8074
Randi Schietz ORCID https://orcid.org/0000-0002-0560-7501

We have no known conflict of interest to disclose.

Correspondence concerning this chapter should be addressed to Clifford Mack Jr., Dept of Mental Health Counseling, 2065 Half Day Road, Deerfield, IL 60015. Email: cmack@tiu.edu

REFERENCES

ACT. (2008). *The forgotten middle: Ensuring that all students are on target for college and career readiness before high school.* College Readiness. https://www.act.org/content/dam/act/unsecured/documents/ForgottenMiddle.pdf

ACT. (2014). *Using your ACT Explorer results.* https://www.act.org/content/dam/act/unsecured/documents/Explore-UsingYourResults.pdf

Association for Career and Technical Education. (2018). *Career education in middle school: Setting students on the path to success* [Executive Summary]. https://www.acteonline.org/career-exploration-in-middle-school-setting-students-on-the-path-to-success/

Akos, P., & Ellis, C. M. (2008). Racial identity development in middle school: A case for school counselor individual and systemic intervention. *Journal of Counseling & Development, 86*(1), 26–33. https://doi.org/10.1002/j.1556-6678.2008.tb00622.x

American School Counselor Association. (n.d.). *High school career conversations.* https://www.schoolcounselor.org/getmedia/abecfeda-566d-4bea-874c-5a57681518ec/Career-Conversations-High-School.pdf

American School Counselor Association. (2014). *ASCA mindsets and behaviors for student success: K–12 college- and career-readiness standards for every student.* https://www.schoolcounselor.org/getmedia/7428a787-a452-4abb-afec-d78ec77870cd/Mindsets-Behaviors.pdf

American School Counselor Association. (2016). *Ethical standards for school counselors.* https://www.schoolcounselor.org/getmedia/f041cbd0-7004-47a5-ba01-3a5d657c6743/Ethical-Standards.pdf

American School Counselor Association. (2017). *The school counselor and social/emotional development* [Position Statement] https://www.schoolcounselor.org/Standards-Positions/Position-Statements/ASCA-Position-Statements/The-School-Counselor-and-Social-Emotional-Developm

American School Counselor Association. (2019). *The ASCA national model: A framework for school counseling programs* (4th ed.).

American School Counselor Association. (2020). *Standards in practice: Eliminating racism and bias in schools: The school counselor's role.* https://www.schoolcounselor.org/getmedia/542b085a-7eda-48ba-906e-24cd3f08a03f/SIP-Racism-Bias.pdf

American School Counselor Association. (2020). *Eliminating racism in schools: The school counselor's role.* Standards in Practice. https://www.schoolcounselor.org/getmedia/542b085a-7eda-48ba-906e-24cd3f08a03f/SIP-Racism-Bias.pdf

American School Counselor Association. (2018). *The school counselor and equity for all students* [Position statement]. https://www.schoolcounselor.org/Standards-Positions/Position-Statements/ASCA-Position-Statements/The-School-Counselor-and-Equity-for-All-Students

Anctil, T. M., Smith, C. K., Schenck, P., & Dahir, C. (2012). Professional school counselors' career development practices and continuing education needs. *The Career Development Quarterly, 60*(2), 109–121. https://doi.org/10.1002/j.2161-0045.2012.00009.x

Auwarter, A. E., & Aruguete, M. S. (2008). Counselor perceptions of students who vary in gender and socioeconomic status. *Social Psychology of Education: An International Journal, 11*(4), 389–395.

Baker, S., Robichaud, T., Dietrich, V., Wells, S., & Schreck, R. (2009). School counselor consultation: A pathway to advocacy, collaboration, and leadership. *Professional School Counseling, 12(3)*, 200.

Bandura, A. (1977). *Social learning theory.* Prentice Hall.

Bandura, A. (1986). *Social foundations of thought and action: A social cognitive theory.* Prentice Hall.

Belfield, C., Bowden, A. B., Klapp, A., Levin, H., Shand, R., & Zander, S. (2015). The economic value of social and emotional learning. *Journal of Benefit-Cost Analysis, 6*(3), 508–544.

Biden, J. (2021). *Remarks by President Biden in address to a joint session of congress* [Transcript]. https://www.whitehouse.gov/briefing-room/speeches-remarks/2021/04/29/remarks-by-president-biden-in-address-to-a-joint-session-of-congress/

Bowers, H., Lemberger-Truelove, M. E., & Brigman, G. (2017). A social-emotional leadership framework for school counselors. *Professional School Counseling, 21*(1b), 2156759X18773004

Brigman, G. (2005). *School counselor consultation: Developing skills for working effectively with parents, teachers, and other school personnel.* J. Wiley & Sons.

Bryan, J., & Henry, L. (2012). A model for building school-family partnerships: Principles and and process. *Journal of Counseling and Development, 90*, 408–420.

Butler, S. K., & Constantine, M. G. (2006). Web-based peer supervision, collective self-esteem, and case conceptualization ability in school counselor trainees. *Professional School Counseling, 10*(2), 146.

Collaborative for Academic, Social, and Emotional Learning. (2015). *2015 CASEL guide: Effective social and emotional learning programs.* https://casel.org/middle-and-high-school-edition-casel-guide/

College Board National Office of School Counselor Advocacy. (2010). *The eight components of college and career readiness counseling.* https://www.wacac.org/wp-content/uploads/2014/07/NOSCAs-Eight-Components-of-College-and-Career-Readiness-Counseling.pdf

Conley, D. T. (2010). *College and career ready: Helping all students succeed beyond high school.* John Wiley & Sons

Conrad, S. (2020, September–October). College admissions in the Covid era. *ASCA School Counselor, 58*(1), 1–15.

Cox, A. A., & Lee, C. C. (2007). Challenging educational inequities: School counselors as agents of social justice. In C. C. Lee (Ed.), *Counseling for social justice* (2nd ed., pp. 3–14). American Counseling Association.

Curry, J., & Milsom, A. (2017). Career and college readiness counseling in P–12 schools (2nd ed.). Springer Publishing.

Cunningham, W., & Villasenor, P. (2014). Employer voices, employer demands, and implications for public skills development policy. *B World Bank Research Observer, 31*(1), 102–134. https://openknowledge.worldbank.org/handle/10986/27700

Diemer, M. A., Wang, Q., & Smith, A. V. (2010). Vocational interests and prospective college majors among youth of color in poverty. *Journal of Career Assessment, 18*(1), 97–110.

Efklides, A. (2008). Metacognition: Defining its facets and levels of functioning in relation to self-regulation and co-regulation. *European Psychologist, 13*, 277–287.

Erikson, E. H. (1963) *Childhood and society* (2nd ed.). W.W. Norton.

Flavell, J. H. (1979). Metacognition and cognitive monitoring: A new area of cognitive development inquiry. *American Psychologist, 34*, 96, 906–911.

Glenn, M., Esters, L. T., & Retallick, M. S. (2012). Mentoring perceptions and experiences of minority students participating in summer research opportunity programs. *NACTA Journal, 56*(1), 35–42.

Gysbers, N. (2013). Career-ready students: A goal of comprehensive school counseling programs. *The Career Development Quarterly, 61*(3), 283–288.

Harrington, T., & Long, J. (2013), The history of interest inventories and career assessments in career counseling. *The Career Development Quarterly, 61*, 83–92. https://doi.org/10.1002/j.2161-0045.2013.00039.x

Hecht-Weber, K. (2021, January–February). Proactive SEL: During the current pandemic, social/emotional learning is vital, yet it requires innovation to deliver. *ASCA School Counselor, 57*(3), 29–30.

Holcomb-McCoy, C. (2007a). *School counseling to close the achievement gap: A social justice framework for success.* Corwin Press.

Holcomb-McCoy, C. (2007b) Transitioning to high school: Issues and challenges for African-American students. *Professional School Counseling, 10*(3), 253–360. https://doi.org/10.1177/2156759X0701000306

Holland, J. L. (1973). *Making vocational choices: A theory of careers.* Prentice Hall.

Holland, J. L. (1997). *Making vocational choices: A theory of vocational personalities and work environments* (3rd ed.). Psychological Assessment Resources, Inc.

Jackson, M., & Nutini, C. (2002). Hidden resources and barriers in career learning assessment with adolescents vulnerable to discrimination. *The Career Development Quarterly, 51*, 56–77.

Jones, M., Baldi, C., Philips, C. & Wakar, A. (2016). The hard truth about soft skills: What recruiters look for in business graduates. *College Student Journal*, 422–428.

Jones, V. R. (2010). Virginia's academic and career plan emphasizes middle school. *Guidance and Career Development, 85*, 24–27.

Knowdell, R. (2005). *Motivated skills: Card sort card deck.* Career Research & Testing.

Kohlberg, L. (1981). *The philosophy of moral development.* Harper & Row.

Lemberger, M., & Clemens, E. (2012). Connectedness and self-regulation as constructs of the student success program in inner city African American elementary school students. *Journal of Counseling and Development, 90*, 450–458.

Mahoney, J. L., Durlak, J. A., & Weissberg, R. P. (2018). An update on social and emotional learning outcome research. *Phi Delta Kappan, 100*(4), 18–23.

Mau, W., & Li, J. (2018). Factors influencing STEM career aspirations of underrepresented high school students. *The Career Development Quarterly, 66*, 246–258. https://doi.org/10.1002/cdq.12146

Manyika, J., Lund, S., Chui, M., Bughin, J., Woetzel, J., Batra, P., Ko, R., & Sanghvi, S. (2017). *Jobs lost, jobs gained: What the future of work will mean for jobs, skills, and wages.* McKinsey Global Institute Report.

Mitchell, G. W., Skinner, L. B., & White, B. J. (2010). Essential soft skills for success in the twenty-first century workforce as perceived by business educators. *Delta Pi Epsilon Journal, 52*(1).

Newman, B. M., & Newman, P. R. (2018). *Development through life: A psychosocial approach.* Cengage.

Paolini, A. C. (2019). School counselors promoting college and career readiness for high school students. *Journal of School Counseling, 17*(1–23), 1–21.

Piaget, J. (1977). *The development of thought: Equilibrium of cognitive structure.* Viking Press.

Ross, K., & Tolan, P. (2018), Social and emotional learning in adolescence: Testing the CASEL model in a normative sample. *The Journal of Early Adolescence, 38*(8), 1170–1199. https://doi.org/10.1177/0272431617725198

Savitz-Romer, M., & Bouffard, S. (2012). *Ready, willing and able: A developmental approach to college access and success.* Harvard Education Press.

School, R. (2020, November–December). Build career interest early: Through a career gallery walk focusing on CTE programs, elementary students connect learning to earning. *ASCA School Counselor, 58*(2), 31–34.

Slicker, G., & Hustedt, J. (2020, December). Children's school readiness in socioeconomic pre-K classrooms. *Early Childhood Development and Care. 190*(15), 2366–2379. https://doi.org/10.1080/03004430.2019.1582527

Susko, J. (2021, January–February). Books as mirrors and windows. *ASCA School Counselor, 57*(3), 22.

The White House. (2021). *The American Families Plan* [Fact Sheet]. https://www.whitehouse.gov/briefing-room/statements-releases/2021/04/28/fact-sheet-the-american-families-plan/

Tulluck, D. (2021, January–February). Brick-based school counseling. *ASCA School Counselor, 57*(3), 27.

Warren, J. M., & Hale, R. W. (2016). Fostering non-cognitive development of underrepresented students through rational emotive behavior therapy: Recommendations for school counselor practice. *The Professional Counselor, 6*(1), 89–106.

Van Velsor, P. (2009). School counselors as social-emotional learning consultants: Where do we begin? *Professional School Counseling.* https://doi.org/10.1177/2156759X0901300106

Veenman, M. V. J., & Elshout, J. J. (1999). Changes in the relation between cognitive and metacognitive skills during the acquisition of expertise. *European Journal of Psychology of Education, XIV*, 509–523.

Villares, E., & Brigman, G. (2019). College/career success skills: Helping students experience postsecondary success. *Professional School Counseling.* https://doi.org/10.1177/2156759X19834444

CHAPTER 17

EQUITY-BASED CAREER DEVELOPMENT AS AN INTEGRAL COMPONENT OF A COMPREHENSIVE SCHOOL COUNSELING PROGRAM

Julie A. Cerrito
Bloomsburg University of Pennsylvania

Richard Joseph Behun
Millersville University of Pennsylvania

ABSTRACT

The American School Counselor Association ([ASCA], 2019) identifies career development as one of three essential domains of a comprehensive, inclusive, and equitable school counseling program. However, research suggests that career development initiatives in schools are often fragmented in comparison to the other two domains of academic and social/emotional development (Anctil et al., 2012; Schenck et al., 2012). School counselors, while tasked with a plethora of daily demands, are called upon to find innovative ways to

Equity-Based Career Development and Postsecondary Transitions, pages 431–461
Copyright © 2022 by Information Age Publishing
www.infoagepub.com
431

narrow the achievement gap by assisting all students to make informed decisions regarding their future career goals. Because school counselors are in prime positions to facilitate college and career readiness for PK–12 students, it is necessary that they are guided by the principles of inclusivity, equity, and advocacy, which help form the cornerstone of their work. This chapter will provide context regarding the need for equity-based career development with all students who may lack the resources and support to successfully navigate the transition from school to work, especially those students who are representative of minoritized populations. School counselors will gain awareness regarding how they might better equip, support, and encourage students in reaching their postsecondary pathways and career opportunities.

Choosing a career is an important developmental milestone that often takes shape as middle and high school students begin their transition to the postsecondary and career opportunities that lie before them. Throughout their school experience, students are positively influenced by many educators and administrators on a daily basis (Alcott, 2017). However, there is no educator in a better position to influence a student's postsecondary decision-making than the professional school counselor (PSC). PSCs serve as leaders, advocates, collaborators, and systemic change agents (ASCA, 2019) who assist all students in PK–12 schools in their transition to the college and career pathways for which they are best suited. The successful completion of this vital transition is best achieved when PSCs implement a comprehensive school counseling program.

Ensuring that all students are able to thrive during the critical transition from high school to a postsecondary institution, or a career, has come to the forefront of national priorities and has garnered recent, widespread, public attention (Lapan et al., 2012). During the Obama administration, the former president called for students to continue their education past high school during his delivery address to the Joint Session of Congress (Obama, 2009). Former president Obama envisioned that the United States would have the highest proportion of college graduates in the world. As an outgrowth of that goal, Michelle Obama, the former first lady, created the National Reach Higher Initiative (Obama, 2014). The National Reach Higher Initiative aimed to help high school students understand the value of obtaining a college degree or postsecondary credential. The initiative also cited the important role that PSCs have in assisting historically underrepresented and underserved students to gain access to postsecondary pathways.

It is important to acknowledge that PSCs provide career support services to all students as part of their essential job functions. However, it is of utmost importance to recognize that certain vulnerable populations (i.e., minoritized members of racial and ethnic groups, students of a lower socioeconomic status, and first-generation college students) frequently experience disparities in equity and access with respect to receiving college and career information

(Curry & Milsom, 2017). PSCs need to be cognizant of these disparities so they can approach their work diligently through an inclusive lens. This is especially notable, as issues surrounding equity have been present throughout the history of career education (Schenck et al., 2012).

This chapter will focus on the PSCs role of promoting inclusivity, equity, and advocacy in career development with minoritized populations through a comprehensive school counseling program designed to assist all students in reaching their postsecondary and career potential. For the purpose of this chapter, minoritized student populations will refer to students who have been historically marginalized and underserved including racial and ethnic groups, those from a lower socioeconomic status, and those representing the first generation in their families to attend college.

Career development is defined as "the lifelong psychological and behavioral processes as well as contextual influences shaping a person's career over the life span" (Niles & Harris-Bowlsbey, 2017, p. 12). Career development is thought to begin as early as the preschool years and extend well into adulthood (Cerrito et al., 2018; Curry & Milsom, 2017; Magnuson & Starr, 2000). Therefore, the formative years of school (PK–12) provide many opportunities for PSCs to assist students in postsecondary planning and decision making (Cerrito & Behun, 2020; Curry & Milsom, 2017). This represents a call for school counseling to return to its roots in career guidance (Schenck et al., 2012).

Arguably, career development is needed for all students as part of a comprehensive and developmental school counseling program, but it is even more critical for marginalized student populations who may lack the resources and role models to assist them in making informed decisions regarding their future career and postsecondary opportunities (McKillip et al., 2012). Certain minoritized groups (low income, first generation, African American, and Hispanic) are underrepresented in colleges thus indicating an increased need for assistance from PSCs and other educators within school settings (Cholewa et al., 2018).

DEMOGRAPHICS

Irrespective of the demographic makeup of the future population in higher education, the transition for any high school student into college, or other postsecondary pathway, could be met with a number of complex obstacles (Aud et al., 2010; Kim, 2009; Lee & Barnes, 2015; McKillip et al., 2012). High school students often feel inadequately prepared to make the kinds of career decisions that are needed as they emerge into working adults (Morgan et al., 2014). While all students have some degree of adjustment to the psychological, academic, social, and cultural demands of college, a significant stressor for many minoritized students is feeling the need to conform to, or adapt to, the majority culture of a university (Anguinaga & Gloria, 2015; Kim, 2009). Additionally, underrepresented students may experience perceived discrimination and may lack a sense of belonging, or feeling welcome, at postsecondary institutions (Cohen & Garcia, 2008; Smith et al., 2007; Yeager et al., 2014).

Students From Underrepresented Racial and Ethnic Groups

Based on data from the National Center for Education Statistics ([NCES], 2019a), about 3.7 million students on average are expected to graduate high school each year through 2030. According to the U.S. Census Bureau (2015), the racial and ethnic minority population in the United States is expected to consistently increase, while the majority population of non-Hispanic Whites will decrease. By 2044, the U.S. population is expected to experience a majority-minority crossover in which the current minority will represent the majority (U.S. Census Bureau, 2015). By 2060, roughly 20% of the U.S. population will consist of foreign-born immigrants (U.S. Census Bureau, 2015). The results from the decreasing majority population and the increasing ethnic minority and immigrant population will be directly reflected in the number of students graduating from high school (NCES, 2019a) and transitioning to college (NCES, 2019b), as predicted by the NCES.

According to these predictions, the composition of students in higher education will be much more diverse in the coming years. A similar trend can be found in the increasing racial and ethnic diversity among the enlisted ranks of military service members (Barroso, 2019). PSCs will likely need to respond to these changing demographics by rethinking how they assist students in navigating their impending transitions from high school into college, career, or other postsecondary pathway. Thus, the college and career process can no longer be representative of norms and experiences associated with the belief and value structures of a majority population (Castillo et al., 2004; Guiffrida, 2006; Pyne & Means, 2013; Torres, 2003). It is important to consider that the challenges that racial and ethnic minority students face are often amplified when that student is also from a lower socioeconomic status (Brown & Lent, 2016; Eshelman & Rottinghaus, 2015) or a first-generation college student (Garza et al., 2014; Pascarella et al., 2004).

Students From a Lower Socioeconomic Status

The majority of students who are educated through the public school system come from families whose economic situations are below, at, or just above the poverty line (Suitts, 2015). Among this marginalized population, many potential barriers exist such as lacking information or receiving inaccurate information with respect to college and career planning (Robinson & Roksa, 2016). For example, students from lower socioeconomic backgrounds may be limited by the number and types of occupations available or attainable to them (Brown & Lent, 2016). In comparison to peers with more financial or social capital, students living in poverty are more likely to demonstrate lower educational and occupational aspirations (Brown & Lent, 2016; Eshelman & Rottinghaus, 2015). As a result, many students coming from lower socioeconomic backgrounds may represent higher high school dropout rates and lower college enrollment rates (Williams et al., 2016).

As part of a comprehensive school counseling program, PSCs who are contributing to equity and equality in career readiness for all students, must give careful focus to students of lower socioeconomic status. PSCs must become important allies and advocates for assisting minoritized populations traverse through the decision-making process that comes along with choosing a college and a career. PSCs should challenge their own personal biases with economically disadvantaged students and understand the importance of being visible and accessible within their schools and for their students (Williams et al., 2016). Students from a lower socioeconomic status want to know that the PSC cares, which can be demonstrated through relationship building (Williams et al., 2016).

First Generation College Students

Many minoritized students entering college are likely to be the first generation in their families to attend college (Terenzini et al., 1996; Zalaquett, 1999) or are students whose parents or guardians have not obtained a college degree (Garza et al., 2014; Pike & Kuh, 2005). These students represent a large percentage of individuals who are enrolling in higher education in the United States, however they often struggle academically and do not persist at rates similar to their peers (Tate et al., 2015). In general, these first-generation college students may be less prepared to enter college, or lack the academic, personal, and social supports needed to ensure success (Dennis et al., 2005; Garza et al., 2014; Pascarella et al., 2004).

External influences on career development, understanding the career development process, and self-concept were examined in a study involving first generation college students (Tate et al., 2015). This study found that external influences on career development included the following: family influences, lack of a professional career network, and support programs. Understanding the career development process reflected how students would navigate barriers and challenges such as building a professional network and feelings surrounding marginalization. Self-concept was centered around the identity of students and noted unique strengths and dispositions that first generation college students possessed. These included being persistent and motivated, being appreciative and not entitled, being self-reliant and responsible, and being adaptable. Based on this research, PSCs should acknowledge the need to assist first-generation students with developing opportunities to help them network and form connections with others. Furthermore, they should approach their work from a strengths perspective and offer hope and encouragement to students regarding the assets they are bringing to higher education and their future career.

ROLE OF THE PSC IN WORKING WITH VULNERABLE POPULATIONS

Based on the stressors that minoritized students encounter, PSCs are well positioned to provide support and guidance to students as they make critical postsecondary, career, and life decisions and navigate the many unknowns of their future (McKillip et al., 2012). When schools increase the amount of counseling services being provided, students experience a higher likelihood of attaining more positive outcomes as a result (Dimmitt & Wilkerson, 2012). For example, when PSCs are able to provide more career counseling services, their students will experience an increase in positive college and career outcomes. A mechanism to achieve such positive outcomes is to encourage PSCs to provide more career services to students. However, it is imperative that these services are inclusive of all students and that access to the PSC is equitable. Students who attend large, high poverty schools with less PSCs are less likely to visit the PSC for college information (Bryan et al., 2009). Additionally, the number of PSCs in a school has a positive effect on students applying to two or more colleges (Bryan et al., 2011). Students who had more contact with a PSC also had more career competencies than students who did not meet with a PSC (Whiston & Aricak, 2008). Thus, research concludes that school counseling services matter when it comes to student outcomes. Furthermore, school counseling outcomes are connected to the PSCs implementation of a comprehensive school counseling program.

ASCA NATIONAL MODEL AND COMPREHENSIVE SCHOOL COUNSELING PROGRAMS

ASCA, which is the professional organization that supports and guides PSCs, proposed a model, known as the ASCA national model, to guide the work that PSCs do in their positions. According to ASCA (2019), "School counseling programs need to be comprehensive in scope, results-oriented in design, and developmental in nature" (p. x). The ASCA national model encourages PSCs to develop programs that

> are based on data informed decision making, are delivered to all students systematically, include a developmentally appropriate curriculum focused on the mindsets and behaviors all students need for postsecondary readiness and success, close achievement and opportunity gaps, and result in improved student achievement, attendance, and discipline. (ASCA, 2019, p. xii)

Represented in the model, there are three domains: academic, social/emotional, and career development. The *ASCA National Model* (4th ed.) reinforces "the idea that school counselors help every student improve academic achievement, navigate social/emotional learning, and prepare for successful careers after graduation" (ASCA, 2019, p. x). Additionally, there are four quadrants forming a diamond graphic (see Figure 17.1) which are

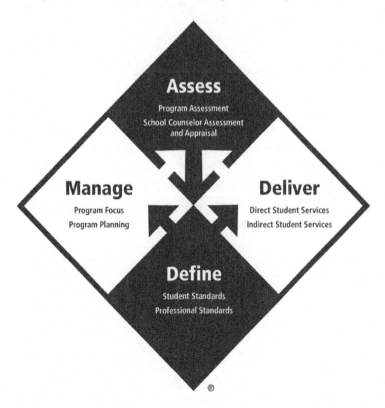

Figure 17.1 ASCA National Model, fourth edition.

described using the following action words: define, manage, deliver, and assess. These four quadrants further describe the tasks in which PSCs engage as part of comprehensive programming.

In the domains of academic, social/emotional, and career development, and in the components of define, manage, deliver, and assess, there are four embedded themes. These themes consist of leadership, advocacy, collaboration, and systemic change and are woven throughout the ASCA model and are considered an integral part of a comprehensive school counseling program (ASCA, 2019). Leadership refers to how PSCs use thoughtful and intentional approaches in the strategies, activities, and interventions they employ to promote the *ASCA Student Standards: Mindsets & Behaviors for Student Success K–12 College-, Career-, and Life-Readiness Standards for Every Student* (ASCA, 2021). PSCs are school leaders and must ensure that they are serving as advocates for all students, especially those who have been historically underserved. Advocacy is an essential role of a comprehensive school counseling program and refers to how PSCs explain the work that they do as they stand up for the profession and the students they serve (ASCA, 2019). Collaboration refers to individuals working together for a common goal (ASCA, 2019). ASCA (2019) identifies situations involving collaboration which include teams/partners, school/district committees, parent workshops, community partnerships, and crisis response. Systemic change refers to how PSCs show the impact of cultural, social, and environmental influences on student success and opportunities (ASCA, 2019). Each of these four themes will be considered throughout this chapter so that PSCs can begin to understand how these themes relate to creating a comprehensive school counseling program and supporting a college going culture in schools specifically with underserved student populations.

ASCA DOMAINS (ACADEMIC, SOCIAL/EMOTIONAL, AND CAREER DEVELOPMENT)

Historically, PSCs have given a significant amount of attention to the domains of academic and social/emotional development with less emphasis placed on career development (ASCA, 2019; Anctil et al., 2012; Osborn & Baggerly, 2004). However, it is fundamental that PSCs consider how the domains compliment and relate to each other as they are not entirely discrete and separate categories. It should be emphasized that effective academic and social/emotional development ultimately lead to successful career development and postsecondary transitions (Anctil et al., 2012; Gysbers & Lapan, 2009). PSCs who are reflective and responsive in their practices incorporate inclusivity into each of the three domains of academic, social/emotional, and career development as they advocate for educational equity for all students in a nontraditional, non-status quo manner (Mitcham et al., 2009). The importance of each of these domains will be addressed as they relate to the career development progression of students who are underserved.

Academic Development

Academic development and career development are intricately related. PSCs should assist students in creating academic plans that align with their postsecondary and career aspirations (Anctil et al., 2012). In addition, PSCs should promote academic factors, because a solid academic background will contribute to a successful adjustment to college (Kirby et al., 2007). PSCs can greatly influence certain academic factors such as study skills, test-taking skills, writing skills, communication skills, and time management skills through a variety of delivery methods including individual counseling, small group counseling, and core curriculum. PSCs can help students find the vital, but often missing, link to the work they are doing now and the work they will be doing in their future careers or work settings.

Minoritized students often struggle in the area of academic achievement (Williams et al., 2016; Bodenhorn et al., 2010; Savitz-Romer, 2012). Academic factors (grade point average, standardized test results, class rank) and socio-economic status (parents' occupations, need for financial aid) were predictors of academic success among White and non-White students (Kirby et al., 2007). Academic factors appeared to be good predictors for academic success and achievement for all students, but especially for White students. With non-White students, grade point average and class rank in high school were better predictors of college success than standardized test scores.

As social justice advocates and change agents, PSCs have an obligation to close the achievement gap and address cultural, racial, and socioeconomic disparities among underserved students (Mitcham et al., 2009). PSCs can close the achievement gap in several ways. They can encourage students to focus on their academic preparation by maintaining strong grade point averages. They can advocate that teachers grade equitably and keep in mind how students' diverse backgrounds may impact language and writing skills. PSCs can also help students to make the connection that academic success often leads to career and postsecondary success. In their collaborative roles with other educators, PSCs can create and sustain a college going culture, create an academic rigorous environment, distribute college advisement, and encourage youth to participate in cocurricular activities (Knight-Diop, 2010).

When examining academic factors leading to the completion of a bachelor's degree, it was found that the factors with the strongest effects included academically intensive science and math courses that students took in high school (Trusty, 2004), such as Advanced Placement (AP) courses. In addition, intensive science and math courses completed in high school were more important to bachelor's degree completion than levels of academic ability in high school. These findings indicate that the experience and exposure to intensive academic curriculum that middle and high school students have will greatly impact their later success in college. With minoritized students, they may not have access to opportunities for intense and rigorous coursework offerings or may not be encouraged to enroll in such offerings (Kolbert et al., 2016). Due to minoritized students being underrepresented in gifted and enrichment programs within schools, educators must do more to both recruit and retain those students (Moore et al., 2005). PSCs need to acknowledge their role in equity and advocacy and make concerted efforts to ensure that all students are afforded equally challenging and enriching academics as part of their school experiences.

In combination with the academic factors described above, dual enrollment is another factor to consider when examining minoritized populations. Dual enrollment refers to students participating in college level courses while still in high school. Minoritized populations, especially those from low-income families, who participate in dual enrollment courses, are more likely to graduate high school, enroll and persist in college, accrue college credits, and complete college in comparison to those students who are not enrolled in dual enrollment courses (Barnett et al., 2015). It is important to consider, however, that not all school districts offer dual enrollment options and some students may be disadvantaged in their opportunities for participation. Even schools that do offer dual enrollment may only provide limited information to parents and students about the availability of courses and it may be difficult for families to ascertain the benefits that can be derived from participation (Barnett et al., 2015). PSCs should consider developing relationships with admissions personnel from local colleges and universities who can visit high schools to promote the benefits of dual enrollment. They may also want to establish articulation agreements with neighboring colleges. By doing so, this may ensure that students gain a sense of self-efficacy regarding the college-going process.

Social/Emotional Development

Positive personal qualities in students (e.g., a positive attitude, perseverance, and help seeking) appear to be substantial factors that can be promoted by educators, such as PSCs (Curtin et al., 2016). This promotion of personal factors may lead to greater adjustment in college or a future career. When examining the extent to which PSCs address resiliency factors with students in school settings, traits of self-worth, problem-solving, communication skills, care for others, locus of control, school success and competency, self-understanding, conviction of being loved, self-efficacy, and not following the crowd were found as those most frequently addressed by PSCs (Taylor & Thomas, 2002). In addition to these, fostering hopeful and optimistic attitudes for students, especially for at-risk students, can include addressing a positive outlook, self-confidence, and self-esteem (Curtin et al., 2016). African American women who had greater confidence in their ability to succeed were also more motivated toward acquiring knowledge and reported higher levels of academic adjustment (Thomas et al., 2009). Positive personal qualities should include persistence, goal-oriented qualities, adaptability, appropriate social skills, and motivation (Burnham, 2009).

Students will make the decision to attend college either based on individual (e.g., personal expectations) or collectivist motivators (e.g., expectations of others) and these motivational characteristics combined with environmental supports have an impact on academic outcomes (Dennis et al., 2005; Thomas et al., 2009). Personal/career related motivation to attend college was a positive predictor for college adjustment (Dennis et al., 2005). PSCs should work toward understanding the motivation, or perceived sense, or ability, of minoritized students to achieve academically, as this may impact their transition to college or other postsecondary opportunities.

An influential factor leading to successful college transitions with respect to positive personal qualities include assessing the reasons why students want to attend college in the first place (Phinney et al., 2006). For most upper-middle-class White American high school students, college is the expectation after graduation (Garza et al., 2014; Phinney et al., 2006). For White middle-class America, college is not necessarily a question about whether to go but where to go; for ethnic minority groups, this dilemma is much more complex (Phinney et al., 2006). Many minoritized students consider education as a way to improve their quality of life (Lopez, 2001). Frequently, immigrant populations consider a college education to be paramount to achieving socioeconomic advancement and as a primary means for assimilation (Kim, 2009). Phinney et al. (2006) found that the top three reasons for students to attend college were to help one's family, to prove one's self-worth, and because of encouragement.

PSCs can encourage social/emotional development with minoritized students by acknowledging how promotion of the aforementioned factors may contribute to academic and career success. Williams et al. (2016) examined the perspectives of low-income middle school students to determine what PSCs can do to promote their academic achievement and determined the themes of building meaningful relationships, building on the cultural wealth of students, and providing mental health services in schools as factors of utmost importance for this particular demographic. Students in this study viewed meaningful relationships with the PSC as essential in order to learn about the challenges of low-income students, help students navigate those challenges, and show how much counselors care about the students' well-being.

Career Development

Curry and Milsom (2017) acknowledge that in order for postsecondary opportunities to be realized by students, PSCs must first create a sustained culture of career and college readiness. Research supports the need to provide a supportive school environment and school climate (Curtin et al., 2016; Williams & Portman, 2014). PSCs play a key role in influencing the school climate (Taylor & Karchner, 2009) and schools allow for plenty of opportunities for healthy relationships with positive adults and peers (Masten et al., 2008). A positive school experience or staff member can make a significant difference in a young person's life (Thomsen, 2002). For minoritized students specifically, they are often able to find support for their academic goals through a positive school environment with community involvement (Reddick et al., 2011). Bryan et al. (2018) found that college related interactions with PSCs, teachers, and coaches had a modest impact on students' college enrollment. School professionals should embrace having adult role models available to help establish connections with youth and can include family members, mentors, teachers, coaches, clergy, or employers (Curtin et al., 2016).

PSCs who recognize the broader context of stigma that often faces minoritized populations in their transition to college can indeed be advocates for positive social conditions as well (McKillip et al., 2012). Perceived stigma and perceived discrimination among minoritized students in their transition to college was examined (Huynh & Fuligni, 2012). Perceived stigma refers to the extent in which individuals believe they are viewed negatively, or undervalued, by society. This may include internalized prejudices that lead to shame or embarrassment (i.e., based on skin color, underlying concern about being viewed as unintelligent by college professors). Perceived discrimination is the extent to which individuals believe they were treated differently in society (i.e., based on socioeconomic status, belief that one was discouraged by their high school counselor from applying to more selective colleges). Huynh and Fuligni (2012) found that perceived discrimination decreased over time, however, perceived devaluation by society increased (Huynh & Fuligni, 2012). Perceived discrimination was associated with depressive and somatic symptoms for all participants however perceived societal devaluation had consequences only for minoritized students.

Because effective career development often hinges on satisfactory academic and social/emotional development, it is important to consider how the three domains of the ASCA national model work in tandem when examining career development specifically. An essential task for PSCs' work with transitioning students is to help those students understand the importance of maintaining strong social support networks after leaving high school, because these types of networks are associated with an overall positive college adjustment (Chhuon & Hudley, 2008; Eunyoung, 2009). Specifically, peer networks impact the way in which minoritized students negotiate acculturative stress, social integration, cultural values, and academic engagement (Eunyoung, 2009). Ethnic peer network membership plays a positive role in helping minority students adjust and persist in college (Eunyoung, 2009). A student's sense of academic belonging, being directly related to a sense of personal connection, may aid with a successful adjustment to college (Chhuon & Hudley, 2008). School connectedness was shown to promote prosocial behaviors and academic success (Bryan et al., 2012). A lack of peer support negatively influenced college adjustment and GPA (Dennis et al., 2005). Because academic and social/emotional factors serve as predictors in college adjustment and career success, it is essential that PSCs consider a holistic view of students as they aim to assist them in their career journeys and destinations.

Because not all students will pursue a 4-year college degree, it is important to recognize that PSCs also assist students who may be interested in pursuing a career in the military, obtaining some form of career-technical education, or entering the workforce (ASCA, 2019; Grimes et al., 2017). PSCs serve as advocates for students choosing alternative paths to entering work (Grimes et al., 2017). Based on the varied goals of students, PSCs need to be well equipped with the knowledge and resources to help students sort through the many career options that are presented before them (Cerrito et al., 2018). Although career advising via the PSC is taking place during the high school years, research suggests that many PSCs lack awareness and comfort regarding the different kinds of technical careers that are available to students (Ferguson et al., 2019). Specifically, PSCs have a greater degree of familiarity with technical careers in health or medicine as opposed to engineering, or other forms of science (Ferguson et al., 2019). This lack of understanding is also present in STEM careers, pathways, and opportunities (Byars-Winston, 2014). PSC's, who also serve as career advisors, can increase diversity and access for underrepresented groups, especially in STEM careers (Byars-Winston, 2014). Students need to know that these careers exist before they can consider them as career options. Knowledgeable PSCs in the areas of career-technical education can greatly influence students' career decision-making by presenting them with a range of options that are available to them (Ferguson et al., 2019).

ASCA DIAMOND QUADRANTS (DEFINE, MANAGE, DELIVER, AND ASSESS)

The four quadrants that comprise the ASCA diamond (define, manage, deliver, and assess) can be found in Figure 17.1. Increased emphasis will be placed on the *ASCA Student Standards: Mindsets & Behaviors for Student Success K–12 College-, Career-, and Life-Readiness Standards for Every Student* (2021) found in Figure 17.2. Because this chapter is primarily focused

ASCA Student Standards: Mindsets & Behaviors for Student Success K-12 College-, Career- and Life-Readiness Standards for Every Student

Each of the following standards can be applied to the academic, career and social/emotional domains.

Category 1: Mindset Standards
School counselors encourage the following mindsets for all students.

M 1. Belief in development of whole self, including a healthy balance of mental, social/emotional and physical well-being
M 2. Sense of acceptance, respect, support and inclusion for self and others in the school environment
M 3. Positive attitude toward work and learning
M 4. Self-confidence in ability to succeed
M 5. Belief in using abilities to their fullest to achieve high-quality results and outcomes
M 6. Understanding that postsecondary education and life-long learning are necessary for long-term success

Category 2: Behavior Standards
School counselors provide culturally sustaining instruction, appraisal and advisement, and counseling to help all students demonstrate:

Learning Strategies		Self-Management Skills		Social Skills	
B-LS 1.	Critical-thinking skills to make informed decisions	B-SMS 1.	Responsibility for self and actions	B-SS 1.	Effective oral and written communication skills and listening skills
B-LS 2.	Creative approach to learning, tasks and problem solving	B-SMS 2.	Self-discipline and self-control	B-SS 2.	Positive, respectful and supportive relationships with students who are similar to and different from them
B-LS 3.	Time-management, organizational and study skills	B-SMS 3.	Independent work	B-SS 3.	Positive relationships with adults to support success
B-LS 4.	Self-motivation and self- direction for learning	B-SMS 4.	Delayed gratification for long-term rewards	B-SS 4.	Empathy
B-LS 5.	Media and technology skills to enhance learning	B-SMS 5.	Perseverance to achieve long- and short-term goals	B-SS 5.	Ethical decision-making and social responsibility
B-LS 6.	High-quality standards for tasks and activities	B-SMS 6.	Ability to identify and overcome barriers	B-SS 6.	Effective collaboration and cooperation skills
B-LS 7.	Long- and short-term academic, career and social/emotional goals	B-SMS 7.	Effective coping skills	B-SS 7.	Leadership and teamwork skills to work effectively in diverse groups
B-LS 8.	Engagement in challenging coursework	B-SMS 8.	Balance of school, home and community activities	B-SS 8.	Advocacy skills for self and others and ability to assert self, when necessary
B-LS 9.	Decision-making informed by gathering evidence, getting others' perspectives and recognizing personal bias	B-SMS 9.	Personal safety skills	B-SS 9.	Social maturity and behaviors appropriate to the situation and environment
B-LS 10.	Participation in enrichment and extracurricular activities	B-SMS 10.	Ability to manage transitions and adapt to change	B-SS 10.	Cultural awareness, sensitivity and responsiveness

Figure 17.2 ASCA student standards.

on promoting equity in comprehensive school counseling programs, the mindsets and behaviors are seen as essential in enhancing student learning and creating a culture of college and career readiness (ASCA, 2019).

Define

The Define quadrant contains standards for students and for professional practice (ASCA, 2019). These standards are defining documents for the profession of school counseling. A specific document we will focus on in this chapter is the *ASCA Student Standards: Mindsets & Behaviors for Student Success K–12 College-, Career-, and Life-Readiness Standards for Every Student* (ASCA, 2021). These standards are used to describe the knowledge, skills, and attitudes students need to achieve academic success, college and career readiness, and social/emotional development (ASCA, 2019). The standards are separated into two categories. Category 1 includes mindset standards (beliefs students have about themselves in relation to their academic work) and Category 2 includes behavior standards (visible behaviors associated with being a successful student). Within Category 2, the behaviors are separated into three subcategories and include learning strategies, self-management skills, and social skills (see Figure 17.2).

Mindset Standards

Mindsets Standards focus on how PSCs can encourage student development of the whole self (mental, social/emotional, and physical well-being), an ability to succeed, a sense of belonging, an understanding of the connection of postsecondary education/lifelong learning with career success, belief in one's abilities, and an overall positive attitude toward learning (ASCA, 2019). Mindset Standards can be addressed by PSCs to include skills such as assertiveness, perseverance, coping skills, and setting and accomplishing goals (Curtin et al., 2016). Help seeking can be focused on by the PSC through stressing the importance of students reaching out to others, especially for those students who may lack support or social confidence. Positive social aspects, such as a supportive environment and adult role models, are substantial factors that influence career success among students and are traits that can be promoted by the PSC (Curtin et al., 2016).

Behavior Standards

Behavior Standards indicate the standards that students will demonstrate through classroom lessons, activities, and individual or small group counseling (ASCA, 2019). Self-esteem building activities in individual counseling, group counseling, and classroom guidance are simple ways for PSCs to gain an understanding of student motivations and to help support students in their adjustment to life after college. PSCs can adopt culturally responsive practices to include developing a strong knowledge of students' backgrounds and cultures, designing small group interventions and classroom lessons tailored to the needs of diverse students, and strengthening school and family partnerships (Watkinson & Hersi, 2014). Positive language, specific therapeutic approaches, skill building activities, direct teaching, games, social learning theory techniques, consultation, and questioning can be implemented through classroom lessons, individual counseling, or group counseling (Taylor & Thomas, 2002).

Manage

The Manage quadrant provides a program focus and program planning tools to help PSCs design and implement a school counseling program (ASCA, 2019). The program focus includes beliefs, vision statement, and mission statement. Program planning includes the following: school data summary, annual student outcome goals, action plans (for classroom, group, and closing the gap), lesson plans, annual administrative conference, use of time, calendars (annual and weekly), and an advisory council.

With a program focus, PSCs need to self-reflect upon their individual beliefs about students, families, and the educational process because unexamined beliefs can unintentionally contribute to inequality (ASCA, 2019). By examining their own personal biases, PSCs can ensure that they are managing programs that are inclusive and equitable for minoritized populations with an eye toward social justice. This is of the utmost importance because PSCs are ideally situated in schools to serve as advocates for social justice by ensuring success for historically underserved and underrepresented students (Dahir & Stone, 2009). Social justice advocacy is an important role of the PSC in closing the achievement gap (Dahir & Stone, 2009; Kolbert et al., 2016; ASCA, 2019) and PSCs historically have reported moderate to high social justice advocacy attitudes and beliefs (Feldwisch & Whiston, 2016).

These beliefs should inform the PSC's vision of where they hope to see students in the future (ASCA, 2019). As leaders, advocates, and systemic change agents, PSCs must promote a vision where all students are successful as an outcome of a comprehensive school counseling program. How that vision is reached should be stated as part of the school counseling programs' mission (ASCA, 2019). As leaders, PSCs must create a mission statement for their comprehensive school counseling program that is representative and reflective of the demographics of the student population and one that is inclusive, equitable, and accessible for all.

Deliver

The Deliver quadrant addresses the importance of PSCs delivering developmentally appropriate activities through both direct and indirect services (ASCA, 2019). ASCA (2019) recommends that "a minimum of 80% of a school counselor's time be spent in direct and indirect student services" (p. xiii). Direct services include personal interactions between PSCs and students (ASCA, 2019). Examples of these direct delivery methods include instruction, appraisal, advisement, and counseling. These kinds of activities are instrumental in helping students attain the *ASCA Student Standards: Mindsets & Behaviors for Student Success K–12 College-, Career- and Life-Readiness Standards for Every Student* (ASCA, 2021). PSCs examine data related to achievement, attendance, and discipline to help guide the programmatic decisions they make using the direct delivery methods described (ASCA, 2019).

Indirect services are provided to students via the PSC collaborating with other school personnel. PSCs should never feel the need to act in isolation in their role. Rather, they should leverage the knowledge and expertise of other individuals in the school and community who may be able to assist them in reaching defined goals. Collaboration in school counseling brings individuals together and unites them to focus on the needs of all students as part of a comprehensive school counseling program. As leaders, advocates, and systemic change agents, PSCs utilize indirect services to provide equity and access for all students as they collaborate with a variety of different stakeholders such as teachers, parents, administrators, school board members, and school staff. When PSCs share their knowledge and expertise with others, students become the beneficiaries.

Mentoring and peer networking opportunities are two examples of collaboration within schools that may benefit all students, including those who are underserved. PSCs may wish to include mentors and mentoring programs as part of their collaborative efforts for comprehensive programming. Teachers, counselors, community members, and peers were identified as supportive individuals in helping students achieve their postsecondary goals (Reddick et al., 2011). Mentoring programs and faculty-student activities may be particularly useful in pairing students with adult members inside or outside the community to provide individual attention, to monitor academic and social performance, to advocate, and to provide opportunities for school engagement (Curtin et al., 2016; Taylor & Karchner, 2009). PSCs should consider having students identify key individuals who may serve as supports during middle and high school years and the transition to college or a career.

PSCs may also help students identify supportive peer networking opportunities, such as clubs, organizations, and associations, at their chosen colleges and universities so that they are familiar with various offerings based on their interests. As high school juniors and seniors begin to visit college campuses, they should be encouraged to seek out opportunities for strong social support networks in advance of their actual arrival on campus. This will allow for networking opportunities and relationship building to take place throughout the transition period and enable students to become connected to the campus and college life prior to move-in day.

Assess

The Assess quadrant identifies the importance of assessment to show program effectiveness, inform improvements needed to programs, and to show how students are different because of a school counseling program (ASCA, 2019). The quadrant has two major categories including program assessment and PSC assessment and appraisal. These categories focus on accountability measures centered around data driven decision-making. Program assessment includes school counseling program assessment and annual results reports. PSC assessment and appraisal includes several elements such as a PSC self-assessment, a formal assessment by a school administrator, and a reflection on the data used to inform the assessment. PSCs need to show data indicating how the school counseling program impacts student success and achievement and share this data with relevant stakeholders.

It is essential that PSCs are engaged in data collection and analysis to determine how they can assist in closing information, opportunity, and attainment gaps (ASCA, 2019). This is particularly important when it comes to equity and access opportunities for minoritized students. By observing data over time, PSCs can uncover trends within schools and identify systemic issues, or barriers, that need to be prioritized. For example, achievement gaps or equity gaps may become apparent after examining aggregated and disaggregated data within a school (ASCA, 2019). PSCs may then develop specific interventions, or strategies, targeted at improving student outcomes as they relate to academic, social/emotional, and career development.

Strengthening the ASCA Model

The ASCA Ethical Standards represented in the ASCA national model require PSCs to "monitor and expand personal multicultural and social-justice advocacy awareness, knowledge and skills to be an effective culturally competent school counselor" (ASCA, 2019, p. 26). Further, it requires that PSCs

> understand how prejudice, privilege and various forms of oppression based on ethnicity, racial identity, age, economic status, abilities/disabilities, language, immigration status, sexual orientation, gender, gender identity expression, family type, religious/spiritual identity, appearance and living situations (e.g., foster care, homelessness, incarceration) affect students and stakeholders. (ASCA, 2019, p. 26)

One of the greatest strengths of the ASCA National Model is its ability to address all students through a multicultural lens. However, placing all minoritized students in a single category is an area requiring deeper consideration. When referring to diverse populations and social justice advocacy, multiculturally competent PSCs must be able to discuss more specifically the different lived experiences of individual students (i.e., systemic racism, anti-Black racism, classism).

RECOMMENDATIONS

Research

Because most of the research regarding career development focuses on middle class populations with more levels of choice for occupations than minoritized groups (Blustein, 2011), research with middle and high school student populations who are marginalized, disenfranchised, or oppressed should be at the forefront of national priorities. If career professionals are to form a deeper understanding of the needs of working individuals, populations who have been overlooked in the past need to become future focus (Blustein, 2011). PSCs and school counselor educators must engage in evidence-based practice and scholarly research within school settings to truly understand the struggles that are unique to minoritized populations. Additionally, most research is focused on college-bound students with less emphasis placed on other postsecondary trajectories (military, career-technical education, workforce) that may be available and accessible to students.

PSCs should consider conducting action research with all students regarding college and career counseling interventions to determine how students respond to such interventions. Upon the disaggregation of data, PSCs can examine different demographic variables and plan interventions accordingly. Little research exists regarding specific interventional approaches that can be employed with minoritized students and can guide PSCs competency level in career development practices with students. It is well understood that the needs of underserved students who are transitioning from high school to a college, or a career, are unique, but there is much more guidance needed regarding how PSCs can specifically equip students for success during this critical career and life transition.

Practice

Given the connection of academic predictors to success in college, PSCs should have focused discussions with students about how learning and grades achieved in high school, as well as the study and organizational skills acquired, may have bearing on success in college and a future career. The more students can develop effective time management, study, and organizational strategies, the easier it will be for them to employ those strategies in a new academic setting, such as college or other postsecondary endeavors. These strategies may further contribute to a more positive adjustment to college and increased retention and completion rates for minoritized students.

As PSCs do essential work in preparing students for successful and meaningful careers, they should consider some of the factors surrounding the outcomes and successes of working with minoritized students. Because enriched academics leads to greater success in college, PSCs should advocate for dual enrollment and advanced placement course offerings, if they are not already part of the school district's academic curriculum. This task can be accomplished through grant writing and collaborating with local and online colleges and universities to create pathways between high schools and colleges. PSCs can be information gatherers and disseminators of information to make sure that all students and parents are well informed with respect to how dual enrollment and AP classes may positively impact students' academic experiences in college.

A working understanding of the military is a tool every PSC should have in their toolbox. To qualify for a military enlistment in the United States, a citizen or permanent resident must have earned a high school diploma (or its equivalent in some cases) and be at least 17 years old (NCES, 2018). PSCs should understand that serving in the Armed Forces can be an excellent option for high school students with a wide array of future ambitions. With both active duty (full-time) or reserve (part-time) enlistment opportunities, the military can be a great option for students seeking college enrollment, career readiness, and other postsecondary pathways. Enlistment in the military comes with a wide range of incentives including money for college and job skills training. High school students with the ambition of attending college but without the financial means to do so, can enroll in an enlistment package containing educational benefits designed to greatly alleviate or completely cover the cost of a 4-year college degree. There are also options to attend college while serving simultaneously through an officer preparation (i.e., ROTC). PSCs must equally understand that for many high school students who do not plan to receive a college degree, the Armed Forces can be an incredible postsecondary pathway to a future career. Many enlisted service members can receive paid on-the-job training of certain skills (i.e., medic, cook, truck driver, mechanic, law enforcement, etc.) that may be transferred into the civilian workforce. For some, the military can potentially be a career.

Increased focus in school counselor training regarding career technical education options available to students is essential. Training and education for PSCs regarding STEM careers and the underrepresentation of minoritized students should be a priority. PSCs should consult with industry experts and secondary education programs regarding possible STEM careers (Ferguson et al., 2019). New Skills for Youth Initiative (2018) recommends providing professional development resources for PSCs to ensure career advising is effective, to make career advising a school- and community-wide effort, to emphasize forming collaborative partnerships with secondary and postsecondary schools, and to apply broad career advising practices to benefit students in guiding them toward their chosen career path.

Because PSCs collaboration with stakeholders is essential, the relationship with the administrator in charge of a school counseling program should be underscored. PSCs should consider using an annual administrative conference to help guide conversations between the PSC and the administrator (i.e., principal or assistant principal). When there is agreement on program priorities, implementation strategies, and school counseling program organization, desired results for students are achieved (ASCA, 2019). Given the importance of the relationship between PSCs and administrators, conversations surrounding program priorities are critical and should be based on data collection and assessment. The plan should be reviewed on an annual basis. Conversations that include access and equity initiatives are recommended as an integral component of a comprehensive school counseling program.

As part of an equity-based, comprehensive school counseling program, PSCs should have a program mission statement and program goals that reflect diversity initiatives. The program mission statement and program goals should include the needs and priorities of the school building and include access and equity initiatives to benefit underserved populations. As leaders, advocates, collaborators, and systemic change agents (ASCA, 2019), PSCs are responsible for seeing the mission become a reality. Specifically, as data-driven decision makers, PSCs must find achievement, opportunity, and attainment gaps and implement systemic interventions aimed at closing such gaps. PSCs must be involved in creating equitable policies and seeing that existing policies that create barriers are removed. PSCs should also ensure that the school-wide curriculum is rigorous and accessible for all. In addition, creating an advisory council by bringing together key stakeholders will allow for varied perspectives to be realized. PSCs can lead stakeholder presentations to educate individuals, such as faculty and members of the community, on numerous topics including those of diversity, inclusion, and equitable practices in education and counseling. All of these examples show how PSCs, in collaboration with other professional educators, can lead the charge on anti-discriminatory practices and eliminating bias in order to provide rigorous and equitable career pathways to students.

Policy

Educational policy makers have indicated the need for an increase in students from the United States to earn some type of postsecondary credential or college degree in order to compete for jobs in the 21st century (McKillip et al., 2012; Obama, 2009). Schenck et al. (2012) stated, "The call for a return of school counseling roots based in career guidance has never been louder" (p. 221). It is apparent that the work that PSCs do each day provides great impact for all students, including minoritized students, as they navigate the transition from high school to college to a career. However, challenges exist regarding the large caseloads that many PSCs assume. Although ASCA recommends a ratio of 250:1, that is a caseload of 250 students for every 1 PSC, many states have much higher ratios than the current recommendation (ASCA, 2019). Students in schools with PSCs who have smaller caseloads benefit more with respect to navigating the high school to college pipeline and have access to key college preparation resources (Woods & Domina, 2014). Too many students leave their high schools not having received the true benefits of a PSC (Lapan, 2012). Therefore, it is recommended that states adopt mandated ratios for PSCs to accomplish the current call to action by educational policy makers.

Because PSCs are typically responsible for large numbers of students, the efficacy of comprehensive school counseling programs may be diminished due to such large caseloads (Anctil et al., 2012). PSCs assume a plethora of tasks and daily demands and may not be able to focus their time and attention on career development needs as their other professional roles and responsibilities take precedence. When PSCs lack clarity in their job description, other roles and duties stand in the way of college counseling (McKillip et al., 2012). If PSCs regarded career development as important, they were also more likely to engage in career development tasks to support students (Anctil et al., 2012). When examining the attitudes counselors in training had regarding their perceptions of career counseling, it was found that they regarded themselves as not competent, or confident, regarding their career counseling practices (Lara et al., 2011). We recommend that significant attention is given to the area of career development in school counselor preparation programs so that PSCs exit their graduate studies with a firm understanding of how career development is linked with academic and social/emotional development and how, when the three are combined, they can contribute greatly to career and life success for all students, especially minoritized students who may benefit from increased support and guidance.

CONCLUSION

There are distinct benefits to students when PSCs are able to implement comprehensive school counseling programs (Lapan, 2012). However, schools with a high number of economically disadvantaged students and those with a high percentage of minority students have less comprehensive counseling services in comparison to other schools (Dimmit & Wilkerson, 2012). A comprehensive school counseling program, implemented by a PSC, ensures that all students are prepared for the postsecondary pathways ahead of them. The comprehensive school counseling program must be grounded in the principles of inclusivity, equity, and advocacy, to ensure that all students are future career ready to meet the work demands of the 21st century.

DISCUSSION QUESTIONS

Discussion Question 1:

1. In what ways do standardized tests (i.e., SAT, ACT) serve as potential hurdles for minoritized students in the college admissions process? Many colleges and universities are now test optional, meaning that standardized tests are not required for admission. How might this benefit minoritized student populations?
2. What considerations should be given to minoritized students as they apply for college, career technical schools, the military, or the workforce?
3. How can PSCs collaborate with other educators (teachers, principals, superintendents, and other administrators) to build a culture of college and career readiness and other postsecondary pathways?
4. What role does the PSC have in making sure that all students receive equitable learning experiences and access to supports? How does this translate into creating a comprehensive school counseling program?

ACTIVITIES

Activity 1

1. Visit the following websites that include career planning systems commonly used in school throughout the United States:
   a. Kuder—www.kuder.com
   b. Naviance—www.naviance.com
   c. Xello—https://xello.world/en/

   Compare and contrast the career planning systems, considering how these systems provide opportunities or obstacles for minoritized students. How might these systems serve as compliments to a comprehensive school counseling program? How can these systems assist PSCs in their responsibilities when it comes to career programming in schools?

2. Imagine you are working as a high school counselor in a low socioeconomic school district with a high proportion of minoritized students who will soon be first generation college students. Your principal asks you to create a guidance curriculum in which you will deliver six career planning lessons to 12th grade students over the course of 6 weeks. What will you include in your lessons? What needs should be addressed given the demographics within your school? How might you involve other key stakeholders to assist you in delivering these lessons? Create six different lesson plans using the *ASCA Student Standards: Mindsets & Behaviors for Student Success*

3. *K–12 College-, Career-, and Life-Readiness Standards for Every Student* (ASCA, 2021). Each lesson plan should align with one of the six mindsets. Be sure to group the lessons together to form a career planning unit.

AUTHOR NOTE

Julie A. Cerrito https://orcid.org/0000-0002-3511-1080
Richard Joseph Behun https://orcid.org/0000-0003-4167-0433

We have no known conflict of interest to disclose.

Correspondence concerning this chapter should be addressed to Julie A. Cerrito, Bloomsburg University of Pennsylvania, 400 East Second Street, Bloomsburg, PA 17815. Email: jcerrito@bloomu.edu.

REFERENCES

Alcott, B. (2017). Does teacher encouragement influence students' educational progress? A propensity-score matching analysis. *Research in Higher Education, 58*, 773–804. https://doi.org/10.1007/s11162-017-9446-2

American School Counselor Association. (2019). *The ASCA national model: A framework for school counseling programs* (4th ed.).

American School Counselor Association. (2021). *ASCA student standards: Mindsets and behaviors for student success.*

Anguinaga, A., & Gloria, A. M. (2015). The effects of generational status and university environment on Latina/o undergraduates' persistence decisions. *Journal of Diversity in Higher Education, 8*(1), 15–29. https://doi.org/10.1037/a0038465

Anctil, T. M., Smith, C. K., Schenck, P., & Dahir, C. (2012). Professional school counselors' career development practices and continuing education needs. *The Career Development Quarterly, 60*, 109–121. https://doi.org/10.1002/j.2161-0045.2012.00009.x

Aud, S., Fox, M., & KewalRemani, A. (2010). *Status and trends in the education of racial and ethnic groups* (NCES 2010-015). U.S. Department of Education, National Center for Education Statistics. U.S. Government Printing Office.

Barnett, E., Maclutsky, E., & Wagonlander, C. (2015). Emerging early college models for traditionally underserved students. *New Directions for Community Colleges, 169*, 39–49. https://doi.org/10.1002/cc.20131

Barroso, A. (2019). *The changing profile of the U.S. military: Smaller in size, more diverse, more women in leadership.* https://www.pewresearch.org/fact-tank/2019/09/10/the-changing-profile-of-the-u-s-military/

Blustein, D. L. (2011). Vocational psychology at the fork in the road: Staying the course or taking the road less traveled. *Journal of Career Assessment, 19*(3), 316–322. https://doi.org/10.1177/1069072710395537

Bodenhorn, N., Wolfe, E. W., & Alren, O. E. (2010). School counselor program choice and self-efficacy: Relationship to achievement gap and equity. *Professional School Counseling, 13*, 165–174.

Brown, S. D., & Lent, R. W. (2016). Vocational psychology: Agency, equity, and well-being. *Annual Review of Psychology, 67*, 541–565. https://doi.org/10.1146/annurev-psych-122414-033237

Bryan, J., Farmer-Hinton., R., Rawls, A., & Woods, C. S. (2018). Social capital and college-going culture in high schools: The effects of college expectations and college talk on students' postsecondary attendance. *Professional School Counseling, 21*, 95–107. https://doi.org/10.5330/1096-2409-21.1.95

Bryan, J., Moore-Thomas, C., Day-Vines, N. L., Holcomb-McCoy, C. (2009). Who sees the school counselor for college information? A national study. *Professional School Counseling, 12*, 280–291. https://doi.org/10.5330/1096-2409-21.1.95

Bryan, J., Moore-Thomas, C., Day-Vines, N. L., Holcomb-McCoy, C. (2011). School counselors as social capital: The effects of high school college counseling on college application rates. *Journal of Counseling and Development, 89*, 190–199. https://doi.org/10.1002/j.1556-6678.2011.tb00077.x

Bryan, J., Moore-Thomas, C., Gaenzle, S., Kim, J., Lin, C., & Na, G. (2012). The effects of school bonding on high school seniors' academic achievement.

Journal of Counseling & Development, 90, 467–480. https://doi.org/10.1002/j.1556-6676.2012.00058.x

Burnham, J. J. (2009). Contemporary fears of children and adolescents: Coping and resiliency in the 21st century. *Journal of Counseling & Development, 87,* 28–35. https://doi.org/10.1002/j.1556-6678.2009.tb00546.x

Byars-Winston, A. (2014). Toward a framework for multicultural STEM-focused career interventions. *The Career Development Quarterly, 62,* 340–357. https://doi.org/10.1002/j.2161-0045.2014.00087.x

Castillo, L., Conoley, C., & Brossart, D. (2004). Acculturation, white marginalization, and family support as predictors of perceived distress in Mexican American female college students. *Journal of Counseling Psychology, 51,* 151–157. https://doi.org/10.1037/0022-0167.51.2.151

Cerrito, J. A., & Behun, R. J. (2020). Online career guidance systems for PK–12 school students: Compliments to a comprehensive school counseling program. In L. Waller (Ed.), *Education at the intersection of globalization and technology* (1st ed). IntechOpen. https://doi.org/10.5772/intechopen.95084

Cerrito, J. A., Trusty, J., & Behun, R. J. (2018). Comparing web-based and traditional career interventions with elementary students: An experimental study. *Career Development Quarterly, 66*(4). https://doi.org/10.1002/cdq.12151

Cholewa, B., Burkhardt, C. K., & Hull, M. F. (2018). Are school counselors impacting underrepresented students' thinking about postsecondary education? A nationally representative study. *Professional School Counseling, 19*(1), 144–154. https://doi.org/10.5330/1096-2409-19.1.144

Chhuon, V., & Hudley, C. (2008). Factors supporting Cambodian American students' successful adjustment into the university. *Journal of College Student Development, 49*(1), 15–30. https://doi.org/10.1353/csd.2008.0005

Cohen, G. L., & Garcia, J. (2008). Identity, belonging, and achievement: A model, interventions, implications. *Current Directions in Psychological Science, 17,* 365–369. https://doi.org/10.1111/j.1467-8721.2008.00607.x

Curtin, K. A., Schweitzer, A., Tuxbury, K., & D'Aoust, J. A. (2016). Investigating the factors of resiliency among exceptional youth living in rural underserved communities. *Rural Special Education Quarterly, 35*(2), 3–9. https://doi.org/10.1177/875687051603500202

Curry, J., & Milsom, A. (2017). *Career and college readiness counseling in P–12 schools* (2nd ed). Springer Publishing Company.

Dahir, C. A., & Stone, C. B. (2009). School counselor accountability: The path to social justice and systemic change. *Journal of Counseling and Development, 87,* 12–20. https://doi.org/10.1002/j.1556-6678.2009.tb00544.x

Dennis, J. M., Phinney, J. S., & Chuateco, L. I. (2005). The role of motivation, parental support, and peer support in the academic success of ethnic minority first-generation college students. *Journal of College Student Development, 46*(3), 223–236. https://doi.org/10.1353/csd.2005.0023

Dimmitt, C., & Wilkerson, B. (2012). Comprehensive school counseling in Rhode Island: Access to services and student outcomes. *Professional School Counseling, 16,* 125–135. https://doi.org/10.1177/2156759X0001600205

Eshelman, A. J., & Rottinghaus, P. J. (2015). Viewing adolescents' career futures through the lenses of socioeconomic status and social class. *The Career Development Quarterly, 63,* 320–332. https://doi.org/10.1002/cdq.12031

Eunyoung, K. (2009). Navigating college life: The role of peer networks in first-year college adaptation experience of minority immigrant students. *Journal of the First-Year College Adaptation Experience of Minority Immigrant Students, 21*(2), 9–34.

Feldwisch, R. P., & Whiston, S. C. (2016). Examining school counselors' commitments to social justice advocacy. *Professional School Counseling, 19,* 166–175. https://doi.org/10.5330/1096-2409-19.1.166

Ferguson, S. L., Kluttz-Drye, B., & Hovey, K. A. (2019). Preparing students for a bright outlook: Survey of the preparation for high school counselors for advising on technician careers. *Journal of Research in Technical Careers, 3*(1), 66–82. https://doi.org/10.9741/2578-2118.1046

Garza, K. K., Bain, S. F., & Kupczynski, L. (2014). Resiliency, self-efficacy, and persistence of college seniors in higher education. *Research in Higher Education, 26,* 1–19.

Grimes, L. E., Bright, S., & Whitley, N. C. (2017). Why we work: School counselors and their role in helping P–12 students learn about the world of work. *Career Planning and Adult Development Journal, 33*(2), 26–31.

Guiffrida, D. A. (2006). Toward a cultural advancement of Tinto's theory. *The Review of Higher Education, 29*(4), 451–472. https://doi.org/10.1353/rhe.2006.0031

Gysbers, N. C., & Lapan, R. T. (2009). *Strengths-based career development for school guidance and counseling programs.* Counseling Outfitters.

Huynh, V. W., & Fuligni, A. J. (2012). Perceived ethnic stigma across the transition to college. *Journal of Youth and Adolescence, 41*(7), 817–30. https://doi.org/10.1007/s10964-011-9731-x

Kim, E. (2009). Navigating college life: The role of peer networks in first-year college adaptation experience of minority immigrant students. *Journal of the First-Year Experience & Students in Transition, 21*(2), 9–34.

Kirby, E., White, S., & Aruguete, M. (2007). Predictors of white and minority student success at a private women's college. *College Student Journal, 41*(2), 460–465.

Knight-Diop, M. G. (2010). Closing the gap: Enacting care and facilitating Black students' educational access in the creation of a high school college-going culture. *Journal of Education for Students Placed at Risk, 15,* 158–172. https://doi.org/10.1080/10824661003635192

Kolbert, J. B., Williams, R., Morgan, L., Crothers, L. M., & Hughes, T. (2016). *Introduction to professional school counseling: Advocacy, leadership, and intervention.* Routledge.

Lapan, R. T. (2012). Comprehensive school counseling programs: In some schools for some students but not in all schools for all students. *Professional School Counseling, 16*(2), 84–88. https://doi.org/10.1177/2156759X1201600201

Lapan, R. T., Turner, S., & Pierce, M. E. (2012). College and career readiness policy and research to support effective counseling in schools. In N. A. Fouad (Ed.), *APA handbook of counseling psychology* (pp. 57–73). American Psychologist Association.

Lara., T. M., Kline, W. B., & Paulson, D. (2011). Attitudes regarding career counseling: Perceptions and experiences of counselors-in-training. *The Career Development Quarterly, 59*, 428–440. https://doi.org/10.1002/j.2161-0045.2011.tb00969.x

Lee, J. A., & Barnes, A. R. (2015). Predominantly white institutions. Transition programs to address academic underpreparedness and experiences of discrimination. *Translational Issues in Psychological Science, 1*(4), 401–410. https://doi.org/10.1037/tps0000043

Lopez, G. (2001). The value of hard work: Lessons on parent involvement from an (im)migrant household. *Harvard Education Review, 71*(3), 416–438. https://doi.org/10.17763/haer.71.3.43x7k542x023767u

Magnuson, C. S., & Starr, M. F. (2000). How early is too early to begin life career planning? The importance of the elementary school years. *Journal of Career Development, 27*(2), 89–101. https://doi.org/10.1177/089484530002700203

Masten, A. S., Herbers, J. E., Cutuli, J. J., & Lafavor, T. L. (2008). Promoting competence and resilience in the school context. *Professional School Counseling, 12*(2), 76–84. https://doi.org/10.1177/2156759X0801200213

McKillip, M. E., Rawls, A., & Barry, C. (2012). Improving college access: A review of research on the role of high school counselors. *Professional School Counseling, 16*(11), 49–58. https://doi.org/10.1177/2156759X1201600106

Mitcham, M., Portman, T. A. A., & Dean, A. A. (2009). Role of school counselors in creating equitable educational opportunities for students with disabilities in urban settings. *Urban Education, 44*, 465–482. https://doi.org/10.1177/0042085909341042

Moore, J. L., Ford, D. Y., & Milner, H. R. (2005). Recruitment is not enough: Retaining African American students in gifted education. *Gifted Child Quarterly, 49*(1), 51–67. https://doi.org/10.1177/001698620504900106

Morgan, L. W., Greenwaldt, M. E., & Gosselin, K. P. (2014). School counselors' perceptions of competency in career counseling. *The Professional Counselor, 4*, 481–496. https://doi.org/10.15241/lwm.4.5.481

National Center for Education Statistics (2018). *Military service and education attainment of high school sophomores after 9/11.* https://nces.ed.gov/pubs2019/2019427.pdf

National Center for Education Statistics. (2019a). *High school graduates, by sex and control of school; Public high school averaged freshman graduation rate (AFGR); And total graduates as a ratio of 17-year-old population: Selected years, 1869–70 through 2029-30.* https://nces.ed.gov/programs/digest/d19/tables/dt19_219.10.asp

National Center for Education Statistics. (2019b). *Fall enrollment of U.S. residents in degree-granting postsecondary institutions, by race/ethnicity: Selected years, 1976 through 2029.* https://nces.ed.gov/programs/digest/d19/tables/dt19_306.30.asp

New Skills for Youth Initiative. (2018). *The state of career technical education: Career advising and development.* Advance CTE. https://cte.careertech.org/sites/default/files/files/resources/State_of_CTE_Career_Advising_Development_2018.pdf

Niles, S. G., & Harris-Bowlsbey, J. (2017). *Career development interventions* (5th ed). Pearson.

Obama, B. (2009). *Remarks of president Barack Obama—As prepared for delivery address to joint session of congress.* https://obamawhitehouse.archives.gov/the-press-office/remarks-president-barack-obama-address-joint-session-congress

Obama, M. (2014). *The White House—Reach higher initiative.* Reach Higher. https://obamawhitehouse.archives.gov/reach-higher

Osborn, D. S., & Baggerly, J. N. (2004). School counselors' perceptions of career counseling and career testing: Preferences, priorities, and predictors. *Journal of Career Development, 31,* 45–59. https://doi.org/10.1177/089484530403100104

Pascarella, E. T., Pierson, C. T., Wolniak, G. C., & Terenzini, P. T. (2004). First-generation college students: Additional evidence on college experiences and outcomes. *Journal of Higher Education, 75*(3), 249–284. https://doi.org/10.1080/00221546.2004.11772256

Phinney, J. S., Dennis, J., & Osorio, S. (2006). Reasons to attend college among ethnically diverse college students. *Cultural Diversity and Ethnic Minority Psychology, 12*(2), 347–366. https://doi.org/10.1037/1099-9809.12.2.347

Pike, G. R., & Kuh, G. D. (2005). First- and second-generation college students: A comparison of their engagement and intellectual development. *The Journal of Higher Education, 76*(3), 276–300. https://doi.org/10.1080/13562517.2012.666735

Pyne, K. B., & Means, D. R. (2013). Underrepresented and in/visible: A Hispanic first-generation student's narratives of college. *Journal of Diversity in Higher Education, 6*(3), 186–198. https://doi.org/10.1037/a0034115

Reddick, R. J., Welton, A. D., Alsandor, D. J., Denyszyn, J. L., & Platt, C. S. (2011). Stories of success: High minority, high poverty public school graduate narratives on accessing higher education. *Journal of Advanced Academics, 22*(4), 594–618. https://doi.org/10.1177/1932202X11414133

Robinson, K. J., & Roksa, J. (2016). Counselors, information, and high school college-going culture: Inequalities in the college application process. *Research in Higher Education, 57,* 845–868. https://doi.org/10.1007/s11162-016-9406-2

Savitz-Romer, M. (2012). The gap between influence and efficacy: College readiness training, urban school counselors, and the promotion of equity. *Counselor Education and Supervision, 51,* 98–111. https://doi.org/10.1002/j.1556-6978.2012.00007.x

Schenck, P. M., Antcil, T. M., Smith, C. K., & Dahir, C. (2012). Coming full circle: Reoccurring career development trends in schools. *The Career Development Quarterly, 60,* 221–230. https://doi.org/10.1002/j.2161-0045.2012.00018.x

Smith, W. A., Allen, W. R., & Danley, L. L. (2007). "Assume the position . . . you fit the description": Psychosocial experiences and racial battle fatigue among African American male college students. *American Behavioral Scientist, 51,* 551–578. https://doi.org/10.1177/0002764207307742

Suitts, S. (2015). *A new majority: Low income students now a majority in the nation's public schools.* Southern Education Foundation. https://www.southerneducation.org/wp-content/uploads/2019/02/New-Majority-Update-Bulletin.pdf

Tate, K. A., Caperton, W., Kaiser, D., Pruitt, N. T., White, H., & Hall, E. (2015). An exploration of first-generation college students' career development beliefs and experiences. *Journal of Career Development, 42,* 294–310. https://doi .org/10.1177/0894845314565025

Taylor, E. R., & Karcher, M. (2009). Cultural and developmental variations in the resiliencies promoted by school counselors. *Journal of Professional Counseling: Practice, Theory & Research, 37*(2), 66–87. https://doi.org/10.1080/15566382 .2009.12033861

Taylor, E. R., & Thomas, C. (2002). The application of resilience processes by school counselors in Texas. *TCA Journal, 30*(2), 56–67. https://doi.org/10.1080/155 64223.2002.12034604

Terenzini, P. T., Springer, L., Yaeger, P. M., Pascarella, E. T., & Nora, A. (1996). First-generation college students: Characteristics, experiences, and cognitive development. *Research in Higher Education, 37*(1), 1–22. https://doi.org/ 10.1007/BF01680039

Thomas, D. M., Love, K. M., Roan-Belle, C., Tyler, K. M., Brown, C. L., & Garriott, P. O. (2009). Self-efficacy, motivation, and academic adjustment among African American women attending institutions of higher education. *The Journal of Negro Education, 78*(2).

Thomsen, K. (2002). *Building resilient students: Integrating resiliency into what you already know and do.* Corwin.

Torres, V. (2003). Influences on ethnic identity development of Latino college students in the first two years of college. *Journal of College Student Development, 44*(4), 532–547. https://doi.org/10.1353/csd.2003.0044

Trusty, J. (2004). *Effects of students' middle-school and high-school experiences on completion of the bachelor's degree.* Center for School Counseling Outcome Research, School of Education, University of Massachusetts.

U.S. Census Bureau. (2015). *Projections of the size and composition of the U.S. population: 2014–2060.* Current Population Reports. https://www.census.gov/content/ dam/Census/library/publications/2015/demo/p25-1143.pdf

Watkinson, J. S., & Hersi, A. A. (2014). School counselors supporting African immigrant students' career development: A case study. *The Career Development Quarterly, 62*(1), 44–55. https://doi.org/10.1002/j.2161-0045.2014.00069.x

Whiston, S. C., & Aricak, O. T. (2008). Development and initial investigation of the school counseling program evaluation scale. *Professional School Counseling, 11*(4), 253–261. https://www.jstor.org/stable/42732831

Williams, J. M., & Portman, T. A. A. (2014). "No one ever asked me": Urban African American students' perceptions of educational resilience. *Journal of Multicultural Counseling and Development, 42,* 13–30. https://doi.org/10.1002/ j.2161-1912.2014.00041.x

Williams, J., Steen, S., Albert, T., Dely, B., Jacobs, B., Nagel, C., & Irick, A. (2016). Academically resilient, low-income students' perspectives of how school counselors can meet their academic needs. *Professional School Counseling, 19,* 155–165. https://doi.org/10.5330/1096-2409-19.1.155

Woods, C. S., & Domina, T. (2014). The school counselor caseload and the high school-to-college pipeline. *Teachers College Record, 116,* 1–30.

Yeager, D. S., Purdie-Vaughns, V., Garcia, J., Apfel, N., Brzustoski, P., Master, A., Hesset, W. T., Williams, M. E., & Cohen, G. L. (2014). Breaking the cycle of mistrust: Wise interventions to provide critical feedback across the racial

divide. *Journal of Experimental Psychology: General, 143*(2), 804–824. https://doi
.org/10.1037/a0033906

Zalaquett, C. P. (1999). Do students of noncollege-educated parents achieve less
academically than students of college-educated parents? *Psychological Reports,
85*, 417–421. https://doi.org/10.2466/PR0.85.6.417-421

CHAPTER 18

EQUITY-FOCUSED GROUP COUNSELING STRATEGIES

Preparing African American Males for Their First Year in College

Sam Steen
George Mason University

Dantavious Hicks
Johns Hopkins University

Norma L. Day-Vines
Johns Hopkins University

ABSTRACT

In this chapter, the authors describe the experiences of many African American[1] youth and explain how group counseling interventions can help Black students navigate the transition from high school to their first year in college. In order to prepare African American young men, the sociocultural and identity aspects of college topics such as toxic masculinity, mentoring, social capital, identity development, and healthy relationships are discussed. The

Equity-Based Career Development and Postsecondary Transitions, pages 463–492
Copyright © 2022 by Information Age Publishing
www.infoagepub.com
463

authors use research, a case illustration, and personal and professional experiences to provide the reader with ideas to build upon within group counseling settings. Implications for innovative and creative practice, future research and bolder policy are provided.

As the current cohort of high school seniors prepare to attend college, they will matriculate in the wake of a global pandemic that has taken the lives of several hundred thousand Americans, an economic crisis that has left many African Americans on the brink of financial ruin, an unprecedented insurrection that has threatened the fabric of our democracy, and a racial crisis following the high-profile arrest and murder of an unarmed African American man who pleaded mercilessly for his life as former police officer Derek Chauvin repositioned his knee on Floyd's motionless neck. According to the American Academy of Pediatrics, the rapid succession of social and racialized stressors has had a profound impact on their social and psychological sense of well-being (Trent et al., 2019). Chronic exposure to racism, discrimination, and implicit bias are associated with diminished socio-emotional functioning, mental health, certain physical diseases (e.g., autoimmune), and reduced levels of academic performance (Pascoe & Richman, 2009). As school counselors and others helping professionals provide mechanisms of support to assist students in acclimating successfully to college life, it is important to remember the symbiotic relationship between stress, socio-emotional functioning, and academic performance. That is, students may struggle to manage their academic life when they do not experience a sense of socio-emotional well-being, especially given the onslaught of social, racial, and political upheaval in the nation. Moreover, as students leave the security of their homes and communities they will have to navigate new social supports. One such support involves group counseling. This article describes strategies for working effectively with African American males to help them examine and explore nonacademic concerns that may impinge on their academic functioning.

VARIABILITY WITHIN THE AFRICAN AMERICAN COMMUNITY

A large corpus of scholarship documents the needs and challenges of African American males in particular, and devotes far less attention to the strengths, resources, and resilience of African American males (American Psychological Association [APA], 2008). Regrettably, much of this literature base relies heavily on negative tropes, stereotypes, distortions, and deficit paradigms that treat African Americans as one, indistinct monolith. Robinson (2010) captured the vast heterogeneity of African American people.

He argued in particular, that prior to the Civil Rights Movement, African Americans had a shared political agenda—liberation. Robinson asserted that following the Civil Rights Movement many African origin people became estranged from one another. He identified four specific groupings of African Americans: (a) transcendent Blacks, (b) mainstream Blacks, (c) abandoned Blacks, and (d) emergent Blacks.

Transcendent Blacks refer to those individuals that are so rich and powerful that we know them on a first name basis, Barack and Michelle, Will and Jada, Oprah and Steadman. Moreover, these individuals are materially privileged in ways that even White people struggle to achieve comparable levels of wealth and prestige. Robinson identified *mainstream* Blacks as those individuals who are working to achieve middle-class American dreams and sensibilities. It could be presumed that many Black Americans fit into this category. Robinson described *abandoned* Blacks as those African Americans who confront the attendant consequences of intergenerational poverty, inequality, and limited access to quality housing, education, healthcare, economic growth, and so forth. *Emergent* Blacks, according to Robinson (2010), reflect those individuals classified as African and Caribbean émigrés, and biracial individuals. Robinson argues that these individuals have limited interactions with one another, different social and political agendas, and are often at odds with one another philosophically. Yet, media portrayals characterize African Americans as one indistinct group, predominantly members of individuals Robinson classifies as members of the abandoned class (Martin, 2008; Robinson, 2010). Educational scholarship often takes a similar stance by not focusing enough attention on the attributes of successful African American students (Morris, 2001; U.S. Department of Education Office for Civil Rights, 2006).

Robinson's (2010) taxonomy serves as a useful heuristic for recognizing within group differences among African Americans and precludes school counseling professionals from essentializing or reducing African American males to pernicious stereotypes. That being said, there are a myriad of ideas and creative interventions that can be used to serve our African American youth. The purpose of this chapter is to describe a series of group counseling sessions designed expressly for African American males in ways that account for some of the challenges they encounter as they prepare for their freshman year in college. Due to the emphasis on sociocultural and identity aspects of college preparation, the group topics will cover discussions suchs as toxic masculinity, mentoring, social networks, healthy relationships, and so forth. We begin with examining the strengths of Black youth. In the section that follows, we review a small body of group counseling interventions that focus on African American young men. Afterwards, we present in detail a group counseling program designed for these scholars. We conclude with implications for practice, research, and policy, but first we discuss strengths of African American students and families.

STRENGTHS OF AFRICAN AMERICAN STUDENTS AND FAMILIES

Regrettably, far too much media attention and scholarly literature utilizes deficit paradigms to characterize African American students. Such frameworks ignore important social, historical, and ecological contexts of African American children and families. Conceptual models that focus on deficits and pathology fail to account for the sources of strength and resilience that African American families and communities enlist as they work to surmount numerous obstacles (Perry et al., 2003). Hill (1998) identified five specific strengths associated with African American families that include: (a) a strong achievement orientation, (b) strong work orientation, (c) flexible family roles, (d) strong kinship bonds, and (e) a religious orientation. Taken together, these traits help African American communities persist despite the odds and have insulated Black communities during both slavery and more contemporary times, given intense and unrelenting exposure to varying forms of institutional and structural racism and discrimination.

More recently, scholars have devoted more consistent attention to the success attributes of high achieving African American students. Williams and Bryan (2013) identified areas that contributed to the success of students in his study: (a) home factors, (b) school factors, and (c) community factors. Home factors that contributed to students' success included parents who used praise and encouragement, high expectations, supervision of school work, physical discipline as a response to poor grades, and behavior. School factors included the presence of a warm, caring adult in ways that contributed to students' investment and engagement in school, quality teaching, and meaningful extracurricular activities. Community factors included social ties with community members that provided nurturing and support, including church involvement.

Code-switching refers to one's ability to move fluidly between cultural contexts, that is one's own culture and a dominant culture as it pertains to speech, dress, gait, and a host of other domains (Hudley et al., 2020). Considerable research attention has been devoted to code-switching as students shift linguistically between standardized varieties of English and African American English (Baker-Bell, 2020). African American students may communicate one way with peers and family members and in more formal ways when they interact with teachers and other authority figures. Although many youth code-switch, African American youth also must learn to understand White culture. Historically, code-switching has been used to help Black students navigate interactions with non-Black people in order to ensure well-being, success, and survival (Hudley & Mallinson, 2015). Black students may be compelled to adjust their appearance, behavior, communication style, and expressiveness to ensure that those around them are comfortable and more likely to treat them fairly or at least not set up barriers. An emerging body of research suggests that code-switching may exact a hefty psychological price on students, because they are trying to contort themselves in order to curry favor with people who may have little regard for them. School counselors can facilitate efforts to teach Black youth that they can be academically oriented without sacrificing their ability to fully express and embrace their African American identity and language expression (Steen et al., 2015).

Successful African American students have also learned, either directly or indirectly, the politics of respectability (Kerrison et al., 2018). This concept is defined here as a set of beliefs holding that conformity to prescribed mainstream standards of appearance, language, and behavior will protect a Black person from prejudices and systemic injustices. In this context, Black students are pressured to maintain temperance, sexual restraint, neat appearance, conservative dress, thereby preventing them from claims of right to certain behaviors (Cooper, 2018; Harris, 2003). However, Cooper highlights there is not one way to be Black and shares her experiences reflecting deeper into what it means to be a Black, feminist who is overweight, full of rage, and full of power. She contends that rage, "focused with precision," can fuel change and progress (Cooper, 2018, p. 5). Cooper argues the politics of respectability; wherein young people are no longer beholden to rigid dictates about appearance and behavior arguing that they should be able to present themselves in a way that implies, "Do you boo, cuz I'm gonna do me!"

Next, many African American students also have the agency and strength to navigate politics associated with intra-racial group attributes (Hunter, 2005). Within the Black community there are cultural connotations associated with skin complexion, hair texture, and other phenotypic traits. For instance, lighter or fairer skin tones are seen more favorably. Furthermore, tightly curled or nappy hair has a negative connotation, however, if one's skin complexion is light brown or one's hair is long, straight or more closely appearing like a White woman's, these traits are considered attractive (Tate, 2007). The politics of skin tone, hair texture, facial features and expressions, and so forth, also impact Black masculinity (Carrington, 2017). Taking a deeper look into what it means individually for a young Black man during their school experiences can help them begin to give and receive validation to each other as they prepare for what to expect after high school.

Successful identity development for African American boys includes overcoming the stress of racism coupled with hegemonic masculinity which may pressure them to exhibit certain characteristics and performative behaviors meant to demonstrate manhood (Allen, 2016). Additionally, toxic masculinity, which intersects with hegemonic masculinity, fosters traits such as homophobia and emotional restriction as positive and manly (Levant & Wong, 2017). These ideological traditional gender roles can be detrimental to self and others (Marasco, 2018). Moreover, boys learn misogynistic tendencies including displaying prejudices against women or those would behave in ways that is considered gay or girly. While some features of hegemonic masculinity are harmful, not all characteristics of masculinity are detrimental (Dixon, 2017). For instance, courage, loyalty, and caballerismo translated as respect and chivalry within Latin communities are integral to a healthy development, however, striving to act and behave in ways that cause homophobic thoughts and emotionally restricted expressions can cause psychological, emotional, or physical destruction (Marasco, 2018). These ideals of manhood may prevent Black young men from accessing mental health services, especially if the goal of the interventions is to express one's emotions. Unfortunately, many Black and Hispanic boys have the added conflict when demonstrating what it means for them to be young men because they are limited in the opportunities afforded them to develop positive, platonic and romantic relationships with other boys. This is important to note as healthy sexual expression and positive mental health outcomes have been linked (Ratner, 2011).

The deleterious consequences of toxic masculinity within the African American community may have stemmed from efforts to emasculate Black men in slave times. It is presumed the perpetuation of Black men having uninterrupted access to a woman's body can be linked to the depictions that Black men are rapists and constantly on the prowl to engage in sexual deviance with White women. This notion of deviance was supported historically by Jim Crow laws and more recently during the Clinton administration when Black young men were claimed to be lustful black savages (Sager, 2010). Furthermore, commercialized rap and other popular genres of music/movies fuel notions of masculinity that embodies misogyny and genderphobia, essentially gender discrimination based on one's behavior rather than their choice in sexual partners or dress (Stephens, 2005).

GENDER ROLE CONFLICT

College campuses have rates of African American women outnumbering the number of African American males (Roach, 2001). These discrepancies may cause some tension between Black men and women in light of the pressure for men to espouse Black hegemonic masculinity. For instance, this conflict may include the need to conform to a stereotypical image of a Black man as strong and heterosexual and interracial dating could result in ridicule. In other examples, men who choose to have sex with men might not openly share their experiences for fear of being ostracized or socially excluded by others. In some cases, Black men may keep some less socially acceptable relationships secret (also known as "keeping it on the down low") for fear of scrutiny or retaliation.

Wilkins (2006) examined the experiences of African American male college students by having them share factors related to their challenges and opportunities both prior to and after entering college. Salient findings consistent with the impact of race and gender on their academic path included social and economic conditions including the perpetuation of negative or inaccurate portrayals throughout various media of Black boys and men in particular. Other experiences included lack of pre-college educational support, limited assistance with college transition, unwelcoming spaces, and limited Black faculty at predominantly White institutions (PWIs; Wilkins, 2006).

Gender role conflict intersects with deciding how and when to code switch (e.g., use different language, postures, dress, and attitudes) in order to win the respect and approval of peers (Ford, 2011) or not. There can be a psychological conflict related to gender identity and expression that many young Black men have to contend with well before college that may further be exploited once entering a campus. For example, the Black male scholar will be forced to decide whether to be considered an obedient, happy go lucky Sambo or Uncle Tom, a hypersexualized Black athletic hero, a saggy pants wearing thug, or even some variation of a gangster or drug dealer. All too often, the numerous stereotypes and conflicting messages are born from outside socio-political forces, as well as internal negotiations of one's true feelings, experiences, and desires (Swanson et al., 2003). The contrasting street and decent behaviors young Black men exhibit is fluid, subtle, and more complicated than the binary and simplified category (Ford, 2011). For instance, in college Black men will actively have to decide physically and behaviorally how to "do" Black masculinity in order to embrace or challenge their socially constructed racialized selves as Black men in White public spaces. Helping Black male youth explore, cultivate, and accept all that it means to be a Black man and how this could impact one's experiences navigating higher education institutions can help with future transitions (Ford, 2011).

RATIONALE FOR COLLEGE AND CAREER READINESS FOCUSED GROUP

There are a number of articles discovered in the group counseling literature that support African American youth in various aspects of college readiness (Belgrave et al., 2011; Bruce et al., 2009; Goicoechea et al., 2014; Shin et al., 2010). For example, Belgrave et al. (2011), facilitated a group intervention helping Black students discuss the value of education and learn to set short term and long-term academic goals that could later help them as they transition from elementary to middle and middle to high school. Examples of these goals include asking for help when necessary and making a commitment to striving for good grades. These goals could lead to a strong foundation for students as they begin to explore postsecondary options. This group intervention increased the students' identity development and fostered critical consciousness so that they could seek positive relationships with others, more confidence in their ethnic identity, and higher expectations for future accomplishments. Belgrave et al.'s (2011) group topics included African and African American culture, responsibility to others, health and fitness, education, life choices, and handling conflict.

Other researchers created innovative groups for African American males that infused topics such as racial pride, ethnic and racial identity, as well as academically related topics (Bruce et al., 2009; Day-Vines & Day-Hairston, 2005; Malott & Paone, 2013; Steen, 2009). Groups like these can help Black youth in particular draw upon their own individual and collective strengths when exploring their needs and concerns about the academic pipeline together (Williams et al., 2014). Groups like these can be useful when creating innovative college and career focused groups for Black males. Even though there are group related research studies for some students of color, there remains a large dearth of group counseling programs that foster college and career preparation in particular for Black youth.

Two exceptions include Malott et al. (2019) and Hines et al. (2020). Malott et al. (2019) acknowledges that it is important to help Black students understand the career process overtime and this process should start as early as elementary school. The group leaders in Malott's study created safe and culturally responsive spaces to discuss these concerns with Black high school seniors which helped the students release anxiety that they had about being the first in their families to get accepted to attend college. However, whenever students begin exploring postsecondary options, the questions below are useful for students to reflect upon and can be used as prompts within a small group setting especially for Black male students:

1. What are some options for you after high school?
2. What impact does what you do now have on what you may be doing in the years to come?
3. Where do you see yourself and your family relationships in the near and far future?
4. How do the choices you make impact the career path you take?
5. Are there external forces that you are aware of that could be a barrier to accomplishing your goals?

6. What are some of your individual strengths and interests related to your identity as Black young men that can be harnessed in fostering your future success?

Questions like these posed above, can help the Black youth focus on cultivating aspirations, hopes, and dreams.

Most recently, Hines et al.'s study (2020) provides a strong prototype for the intervention proposed in the present chapter. Essentially these researchers used a structured group counseling program to prepare African American males for college through group counseling. These researchers created an intervention aimed at high school sophomores to facilitate the process of intentional college planning. The group intervention was based on the Eight Components of College and Career Readiness endorsed by the College Board. Additionally, Hines et al. worked to increase the participants' cultural capital, a theory that posits high schools emphasize assets and welfare of White middle class students and families as the norm for academic success and college attainment (Welton & Martinez, 2014). To do this, Hines et al. (2020) offered an intervention in a culturally relevant manner that afforded Black youth opportunities to explore their perceptions, hopes, and dreams while also developing knowledge, skills, and strategies that they may build upon when transitioned to college.

For example, Hines et al. (2020) helped the students acquire college knowledge defined as an understanding of the complex college admission and selection process, learning options available to help with postsecondary selection, and understanding academic requirements for college level coursework and the differences between high school and college (Welton & Martinez, 2014). In order to accomplish this, the group facilitators and participants engaged in discussions about differences between 2-year and 4-year colleges, Historically Black colleges and universities (HBCU's) and PWI's, and pursuing scholarships and seeking financial aid. The ultimate goal was to use the group format to help Black males become college ready, signifying they have the quality of education and level of preparation needed to succeed without remediation (Conley, 2007). Specific factors associated with this readiness are cognitive strategies, content knowledge, academic behaviors, and contextual skills and knowledge.

Some of the barriers to Black students gaining access to the college enterprise include the hidden curriculum which consists of unwritten and unofficial rules, expectations, values, and perspectives that do not align closely with Black culture (Preston, 2017). Black students are often not privy to unwritten rules in high school or information that would help connect them to college preparation resources. In order to help Black males in particular, counselors, helping professionals and laypersons may find the proposed group intervention below useful. The purpose is to help the Black youth increase their college knowledge, while also including discussions about sociopolitical aspects of the present and future experiences when transitioning from high school to college.

Group interventions can help African American students successfully build aspirations to go to college, make the necessary academic preparations to be qualified to attend college, and sign up and follow through on taking the necessary college entrance exams and applications (Hines et al., 2020). Social capital, described as social networks that impact a student's college pathway, is only valuable when this social connection leads to institutional support, privileged status or information, or addresses a student's individual need (Welton & Martinez, 2014). In small group settings guest speakers who hold identities that intersect with that of other Black men are important sources of said capital especially as it relates to sharing the understanding of pursuing their own college and career aspirations. For those who are interested in helping Black youth explore college and career options in small group settings, consider making a plan that includes some of the things we believe will help our students to be successful in these academic and career pursuits. It will be important to capitalize on the resources and structures available to you in these groups. In the examples that we provide below, we are aiming to offer helpers with examples of strategies, important concepts, session topics, group activities, and case illustrations highlighting skills and group leadership behaviors. The ensuing suggestions offered below are based on the literature and our collective professional expertise found to be useful when offering groups to support Black male students in their college transitioning. We provide detailed ideas and strategies to consider below.

GROUP COUNSELING PROPOSED INTERVENTION

Group Leaders

There are a variety of individuals who can help African American youth in a group setting.

These include:

- mental health practitioners,
- clinicians from community agencies (e.g., social workers),
- church and other community leaders,
- boys and girls club staff,
- school counselors, and
- paraprofessionals.

Group leaders ideally would match the Black young men in terms of their racial, gender, and other cultural aspects of their identities (Holcomb-McCoy, 2005; Muller, 2012). That being said, the intersection of identities and the impact these dynamics have on groups are still not fully understood (Steen et al., 2021). However, it is assumed that having a group leader that identifies with members in the group and vice versa can increase the likelihood of success. It is important to note that all Black youth do not feel comfortable with all of the Black counselors and educators they encounter (Steen et al., 2014).

Co-Leadership

Other considerations include co-leadership defined as involving the pairing of two group leaders. Many times one of the leaders has more experience (Luke & Hackney, 2007). When possible, coleading with others can help to create cohesion faster because it eliminates the need to cancel sessions when one adult cannot make it. Co-leadership relationships allow an expanded understanding of the interactions between two functioning adults as well. Co-leadership also helps the adults hold each other accountable and share the workload in order to offset the potential for burnout or taking on too much of the responsibility alone.

GROUP SCREENING, PLANNING, AND GOALS

Overall, the number of sessions recommended within school settings is a range from 6 to 20, with 10 being the average (Steen et al., 2021). The session duration will depend on the time allotted to this intervention if occurring in schools. However, 45 and 60 minutes should be sufficient to afford time to engage in delivering any material related to the topics for discussion and processing the information. When selecting the participants, meeting with students individually before group sessions begin to screen them and again at the end to garner their feedback would be considered best practice outlined by the Association for Specialists in Group Work (Thomas & Pender, 2008). The number of students selected will vary, but one group leader to no more than nine students is reasonable. If there is a co-leader, then the number of students should not exceed 12 (Steen et al., 2021). Other preparation will include determining goals and objectives for the group to ensure the students are clear as to the purpose of the group. These goals can be co-created with the participants during the screening and/or earlier stages of the intervention. In addition to a group goal, it will be important to have the youth each determine their own individual respective goals at the time. The goals must include one long-term goal related to attending a college or university. Exploring academic and social goals for attending college will

474 ▪ S. STEEN, D. HICKS, N. L. DAY-VINES

help students explicitly understand what their goals are once they actually enter the campus. For example: Is the primary reason for them wanting to attend college to prepare for a career path that requires graduate school, medical school, law school, or the such? Is the main reason in order to start a business or play professional sports? Or rather, is it to accomplish something of a more personal nature, like finding a life partner or starting a family? Regardless, group leaders are encouraged to help Black youth identify very clearly and often their goals and aspirations for pursuing postsecondary education. It will also be important to help the students understand the necessity of using these same skills in college such as setting goals and identifying people and various communities where they can get support once that journey begins.

Group Leadership Skills and Responding to Students in Session

There are numerous skills that can be used when responding to comments from students in groups. These include but are not limited to:

- making encouraging remarks;
- inviting peer to peer interactions;
- using personal and appropriate self-disclosures;
- offering constructive feedback;
- sitting in silence intentionally; and
- broaching race, ethnicity, culture, and the intersection of identities.

Broaching

Day Vines and scholars (2007) coined *broaching* as a set of skills that an ethically sound practitioner uses by considering the impact sociopolitical factors (e.g., race) have on the presenting concerns. The ethically sound helper learns and recognizes the cultural meaning each unique client attaches to their stories and uses this cultural knowledge and insight to foster client empowerment, a strong therapeutic alliance, and enhanced counseling experiences. In groups, counselors who broach can foster conversations and engage in activities that encourage Black youth to critically examine current daily experiences with popular literature, movies, and music in order to critique faulty standards of beauty, and help students know and understand their racial identity (Wilkins et al., 2013). Popular and classic movies and other media can be used as illustrations or as an activity within the sessions (e.g., *Moonlight, Color of Fear*).

Group Evaluation

Evaluation of a group is a necessary component to examine any aspects of the group program that was successful or not as successful. Short quantitative (e.g., like yes/no, true/false, scale of 1 to 10, etc.) tools can be used to gather useful information to evaluate the groups success collectively or individually. Qualitatively, simple questions, prompts, and other sentence stems can be helpful in learning what information may have been retained by the students following the intervention. For instance, group leaders can ask some of the following questions before, during, and even after the completion of the intervention:

Pre-Group
- What do you hope to gain from these experiences?
- What are some of your concerns about the group overall?
- What are some things you would like to accomplish in our sessions?
- What are some of your strengths?
- What are some areas for improvement?

During Group
- What are you learning from these experiences?
- What are some concerns you are having about the group overall?
- What are some things you would still like to accomplish in our sessions?
- What are some new strengths you can identify?
- What are some other areas you still see for improvement?

Post Group
- What if any, did you gain from these experiences?
- What remaining concerns did you have about the group overall?
- What are some things you did accomplish in our sessions?
- What are some strengths that you discovered in our sessions?
- What areas of improvement have you discovered during our sessions that you still need to address?

Final Participant Reflections
The students can be asked to share some of their thoughts and feelings in a written manner in order to provide another platform to understand their experiences. Group journaling is a useful tool used in groups with students to allow them to process their experiences without others' input. Group leaders can read and/or respond to journal prompts, or may just review them for a deeper understanding that might not be captured using other similar strategies mentioned above.

CASE ILLUSTRATION

Group counseling is a promising approach to exploring postsecondary college and career concerns and dynamics with students (Malott et al., 2020; Muller, 2002; Steen et al., 2014). Professional school counselors are often the only professions in elementary and secondary school settings with the training and skills to lead counseling groups (Kulic et al., 2004). However, collaboration and consultation with community organizations truly allows the school counselor to meet the diverse needs of students. For example, the professional school counselor might collaborate with community agencies, churches, nonprofit organizations, and so forth to enhance the group process.

While school counselors are often at the lead of designing and implementing these groups, many organizations (e.g., College Board, AVID, Achieve, etc.) are devoted to college and career development. Consequently, group processes may vary from district to district and even school to school. Regardless, group leaders are tasked with the duty of developing a group that is data-informed and responsive to the cultural needs of the group participants. As mentioned, the development of a group program or plan is an intention process that is responsive to specific student needs. Group leaders can devise a group based on either quantitative data, qualitative data, or a combination of the two.

Quantitative data, also referred to as discrete or continuous data, is expressed in some measurable, numeric form. Group leaders can draw from data sources such as needs-based assessments, trends specific to the setting they are serving, and/or national postsecondary college and career trends. Professional school counselors are likely to rely on quantitative data to develop their group interventions to demonstrate the effectiveness of their interventions (Young & Kaffenberger, 2018).

Qualitative data, contrarily, is defined as non-numerical sources (Ary et al., 2014). Qualitative data is collected through observations, one-on-one interviews, focus groups, and other similar methods. Group leaders utilizing qualitative data might develop a group in response to conversation(s) with or the experience(s) of one particular student. One of the benefits of utilizing the qualitative approach might be the potential to address concerns that are more student-centered and responsive to specific needs. Elevating and responding to specific students' needs will likely lead to an engaging, interactive group process.

Consider the following case illustration and the use of both quantitative and qualitative data to inform group implementation:

Devin is a 17-year-old, African American male in an urban school district who is now seeing his professional school counselor as he prepares to graduate. Devin has participated in the data-driven interventions that his school counselor has implemented since his freshman year in preparation for college. Now at his final decision—which college to attend—Devin has come to his school counselor concerned about "making the right decision."

Devin is an only child and has grown up in a single-parent household with his mother since 4th grade. Through his high school career, Devin has excelled and maintained a 4.0 GPA. His academic achievement has earned him several scholarships and acceptances.

As the school counselor broaches the subject of race, ethnicity, and culture, he notices themes in Devin's decision-making process. Devin has repetitively referenced concerns related to the culture of the university he chooses—specifically racism, the impacts on his personal and collective identities, and overall school belonging. In his own words, Devin has expressed "not wanting to forget where he comes from and who he really is." He added, "people either leave and forget who they are, or stay when they had so many other options... I don't want to do either."

While the school counselor was engaging in individual services with Devin, he considered how other students in the larger school community might benefit from the opportunity to process similar concerns. In this regard, Devin's case provided the counselor with insight and motivation to explore if there was a larger need within the school context.

The school counselor developed a school-wide needs-based assessment to determine high school seniors' concerns about selecting and attending college. The needs-based assessment provided the school counselor with quantitative data that could also be used to develop group curriculum. The disaggregated data, from the assessment, indicated 90% of all male students of African descent also had concerns related to racism and school belonging. The professional school counselor now had both qualitative and quantitative data to reference when designing the group. The result from the needs-based assessment also assisted the group leader, in this scenario the school counselor, in recruiting participants for the group. The school counselor identified eight students with very similar concerns (Devin and seven other male students of African descent) and began the recruitment process.

Aware of the gender and racial dynamics of the group members (first-generation African American males), the school counselor could engage in research on specific trends and postsecondary concerns that are unique to this population. The school counselor might collaborate/consult with community organizations, local college/university diversity committees, review current literature or elicit feedback from recent students enrolled in postsecondary settings to become more informed. As the school counselor utilizes a combination of Devin's personal accounts (qualitative data), results from the needs-based assessment (quantitative data), and national data from postsecondary surveys (quantitative data) to develop group curriculum, he is more prepared to facilitate the group process.

The following serves as an outline for group curriculum responsive to the specific needs of this case study. While this outline can serve as a guide for potential topics that a group leader might cover, group curriculum should be designed based on students' needs (emotionally, culturally, developmentally, socially, and academically). Although students might share racial or minoritized identities, it is critical to explore within group differences that exist (i.e., differences in geographies, classes, nationalities, etc.). For example, Black students across the diaspora have varying cultural experiences that will likely need unique focus; an African American, U.S. slave descendant student from a middle-class, rural community will have different needs than a second-generation, Nigerian-American student from an upper class, suburban background. Exploring these nuances not only require that the group leader(s) have cultural awareness, knowledge about the historical and present factors related to the population(s) they are serving, group facilitation skills and cultural humility, but also sophisticated self-awareness. Specifically, group leaders need an awareness of how their own social identities inform the power/privilege dynamics within the group. While specific identities are not a prerequisite for facilitating a group, awareness of the privileges and power associated with specific and intersecting identities certainly is. Again, group leaders might collaborate with community organizations/leaders to best meet the needs of students. Consider the following curriculum outline:

Session 1: Toxic Masculinity

Session Objectives: Students will (a) define toxic masculinity, (b) explore how they've internalized toxic masculine traits/behaviors, and (c) commit to actively working against toxic masculinity.

Session Question(s): What is toxic masculinity? What examples of toxic masculinity have I seen in my personal life and/or the media? How do I work against it now and as I make the transition to college? Considering the previous discussions, how do you shape your own identity as an African American male going to college?

Kofi, one of the group members, is an 18-year-old Ghanaian male who engages in the group process by sharing his personal experiences with toxic masculinity. Kofi and his parents moved to Baltimore from Houston his ninth grade year after his maternal grandfather passed. Kofi had a very close relationship with his grandfather and struggled through the grieving process. He shared that he was scared to even cry, because he'd "appear too weak and men aren't supposed to be weak." The group leader captured Kofi's experience and invited other participants to share by responding:

"I'm hearing you had to suppress your emotions, because of the societal expectations of how a man is supposed to act and behave ... have any other group members had experiences similar to Kofi?" The leader's attempt to link members enhanced the process by building cohesion. The leader eventually returned to Kofi to explore his plans to avoid restricting his emotions during college. Kofi responded,

> I feel like I don't need to let things build up. There's already too much you have to think about as a Black man—the pressure to be successful and challenge statistics, worrying about police, staying focused ... I can't afford to let all that build up. I really feel like it's important to have people to talk to because the work from college will add even more stress.

It is important for group leaders to provide students with psychoeducation on resources available to them during their college career. For this scenario, the leader might educate Kofi and other members on the process of seeking counseling services at a university's counseling center, finding a mentor, and developing a social network.

Session 2: Sexual Health

Session Objectives: Students will (a) explore internalized messages about sexual health and (b) develop a plan to maintain sexual health in the future.

Session Question(s): What message(s) did you get about becoming sexually active?; Where can you seek reliable knowledge on sexual health?; What is your plan to maintain sexual health in the future?

Ty'Quan, a 17-year-old, native Baltimorean senior, has been less engaged in the group process during Session 2. The group leader is unsure whether he is nervous to discuss the topic of sexual health or just engaging as a listener. He utilizes the skill of immediacy (a discussion, grounded in the here and now that explores the therapeutic relationship; Hill, 2014), to discuss Ty'Quan's experience with the group process. "Ty'Quan, I'm noticing you haven't had the chance to share yet ... I want to check in with you. How are you processing today's group and what you've heard so far?" he asked. Ty'Quan's replies,

> I mean ... to be honest I've heard all of this from older friends, uncles, and all ... most of what everyone has said. It's really only half of the sexual health that I need to hear. Everyone knows I'm bisexual, but they choose to ignore it. For example, in our health class everything we learn is for straight people. It's kind of frustrating because I'm never fully included in these conversations.

It was important that group leaders respond by acknowledging Ty'Quan's frustration and naming the heteronormativity that exists (both in the group and society at large). The leader acknowledged Ty'Quan's experience by responding:

> Ty'Quan, first thank you for sharing with the group. You're describing what's called heteronormativity—which is basically the assumption that straightness is the default or "normal" mode of sexuality. One of the consequences, much like you've described, is LGBT people feel isolated. I want to apologize and acknowledge that I didn't invite people to share their unacknowledged experiences earlier. The other message that heteronormativity communicates is that your sexual health—as a young, Black, bisexual, male—isn't important. That is not true. What other conversation have we not had that would make you feel heard and included in our group today?

The group leader's response acknowledges Ty'Quan's emotional response, names heteronormativity, and embodies cultural humility. This exchange highlights the importance of exploring intersectionality and using immediacy during the group process. The group leader has an ethical and moral responsibility to direct Ty'Quan to appropriate sexual health resources that are aligned with his sexuality. The leader can do so either during the group process or as a follow-up.

Session 3: Title IX—Sexual Violence and Date Rape

Session Objectives: Students will (a) define Title XI and (b) understand their responsibility when engaging in sexual encounters.

Session Question(s): What is Title IX? How do you engage in responsible sexual encounters?

Psychoeducation will be an essential component of Session 3. At the conclusion of the session, students should be able to define Title IX and understand the process of engaging in responsible sexual encounters. Emphasis should be placed on the process of obtaining consent before any sexual interactions. Education about the consent process prepares students to engage in safe sexual encounters as they transition into college settings.

Group leaders might consider collaborating with Title IX coordinators at local universities to design and facilitate the group process. Group leaders should educate students about the severe consequences of sexual misconduct, assault, and harassment. Regardless of approach, it is important to broach the subject of race, ethnicity, and gender during the Title IX session. Acknowledging the discrepancies in consequences for African

American males and their White male counterparts is essential. Giving students the space to discuss and process during the group can facilitate healthy awareness.

In the present case, the group leaders invited students to share their responses after the psychoeducation. Cory—one of the five group members—shares that he's had these conversations with his parents but not at this depth. He added, "My mom always tells me that I have to be smart because Black men can't afford to make any mistakes." The group leader asks other members if they heard similar things, they all nod in agreement. The leader then poses the question, "What information have you learned about Title IX to have responsible sexual encounters and avoid sexual misconduct?" Cory responded,

> Well first I need to make sure it is somebody I have a healthy relationship with like we talked about last time. I think what I've learned today—that I didn't know before—was the importance of consent. I've never really heard the specific information about what sexual harassment and misconduct is.

Collaborating with a Title IX coordinator during this session might be beneficial for specific student questions. Prior to the session, develop your session objectives with your coleader(s) to maximize student outcomes. Group leaders can check that objective(s) were met by administering an exit ticket at the conclusion of the session.

Session 4: Combating Anti-Black Racism

Session Objectives: Students will (a) identify examples of anti-Black racism, (b) develop the skills to respond to microaggressions, (c) develop self-advocacy and assertiveness skills.

Session Question(s): What is anti-Black racism? How might I respond to microaggressions and anti-Black racism? How do I advocate for myself (and others) when I experience or witness racism?

Students of color experience covert, overt, institutional, and/or individual acts of racism well before their college experience. However, the college setting warrants a unique focus on equipping Black male students with tools to respond to institutional racism and racial microaggressions. These self-advocacy skills will be particularly important as students are developing a sense of independence outside of their familiar support networks (i.e., family, friends, teams, etc.).

Racial microaggressions are defined as brief and commonplace daily verbal, behavioral, or environmental indignities, whether intentional or unintentional, that communicate hostile, derogatory, or negative racial slights and insults toward people of color (Sue et al., 2007, p. 271). During Session 4, students should be presented with specific examples of behavioral microaggressions. It is also important to give them the space to process and discuss prior instances where they've experienced microaggressions. Group leaders should exercise active listening skills to not only assess how students either responded or did not respond, but also the underlying emotional/behavioral consequences. Consider the following example as Marquese, one group member, shares a microaggression he experiences from a current teacher. Marquese shares,

> My math teacher keeps calling me "Mark" because she says I should prepare to present as a professional now that I'm an adult. I didn't really get what she meant at first... I was offended because my name isn't "Mark," it's Marquese. But I didn't want to say anything because I couldn't tell whether she was trying to be rude or not... plus she's my teacher.

Oftentimes people of color are left carrying the emotional burden of wondering whether they've responded correctly or should have responded to a microaggression. Marquese's example captures the emotional consequences of microaggressions. In the group leader's response, he captures that emotional response and invites Marquese to think about how he might respond. He responds,

> Marquese the experience you've shared is a specific type of microaggression— known as a microinsult. The message that the teacher is sending, regardless of whether it is intentional or not, is that your name isn't professional. I sense that you are aware of that but might not yet know how to respond to that. Is that correct?

After Marquese confirmed the leader's interpretation, he invited the group to offer suggestions of their own before providing examples of what *might* be appropriate responses. Eventually, the leader should provide specific examples of language to use. "When I hear you say that, I feel like you are saying I can't be a professional because of my name," might be a specific example to share with Marquese. When providing students with examples for how they *might* respond to microaggressions and anti-Black racism, it is important to communicate that they should exercise their own judgment on when and how to respond. The emotional burden of either choosing to respond, or preserving energy, during each experience can both be deleterious to psychological health. Sue and colleagues (2007) refer to this as the catch-22 of responding to microaggressions. Nevertheless, students should leave the session with a plan for how they can exercise self-advocacy and assertiveness skills *should* they decide to as they encounter anti-Black racism and microaggressions. Examples of ways to respond to microaggressions might include but aren't limited to:

- asking for clarity,
- acknowledging the feelings behind the statement,
- sharing your own process, and
- expressing your feelings (Goodman, 2011).

RECOMMENDATIONS FOR PRACTICE, RESEARCH AND POLICY

Practice

The following recommendations provided to school personnel and lay-persons will help glean the benefits from group counseling interventions created for African American students. First, school personnel can develop group interventions with the help of collaborative partners, community stakeholders, and other advocates desiring to help Black students be successful after high school (Williams et al., 2014). These group programs can draw upon the caring and supportive adults that will help Black students feel connected in school and could lead to positive student outcomes (Williams et al., 2014). Second, Black students can cultivate close relationships with peers and motivate one another (Williams et al., 2014), especially in small group settings (Steen, 2009). In the case illustrated above, Kofi's group facilitator aimed to link him with other members during the sessions in order to build cohesion. These efforts paid off as Kofi felt connected to others in these groups. Third, school personnel, mentors, and positive peers can use a group format to discuss information about college, the college application process, scholarships, financial aid, and campus life (Hines et al., 2020). In Devin's case, the school counselor worked diligently to use national research and trends and school related data to inform the sessions. Additionally, a panel of former high school students who have attended college or contemporary film can be used to augment the discussions in session. Fourth, school personnel can help Black students explore gender roles and conflict as well as time management skills before heading to college (Reid & Moore, 2008; Marasco, 2018). Ty'Quan's self-disclosures in session suggest that the group leader was effective in facilitating the group process by drawing him in with the questions posed as an invitation. The group leader willingly broached with intentionality and often throughout these sessions.

The role that anti-Black racism plays in the educational experiences of all students has implications for all stakeholders (e.g., teachers, administrators, district-level leaders, etc.). Strategic session plans can unveil both strengths and areas of growth for the larger school community; students will likely engage in meaningful discussions about the way anti-Black racism has impacted their educational experiences when the topic is broached. Group facilitators should exercise leadership skills to create professional development for other school personnel based on these group discussions. In that regard, the findings from group practices can serve as rich data to bring about meaningful, transformative change that is aligned with student-reported needs/concerns.

Research

Research concerning African American children in general suffers from a number of limitations including the lack of cultural contexts in child development, narrowly focused theoretical frameworks, and comparisons to White middle-class samples (Harris & Graham, 2014). One prominent scholar argued that the interrelated nature of African American culture highlights the necessity for an expanded conceptual and research framework that more fully captures the within group differences of Black people especially within the educational enterprise (Tillman, 2002). She offers that researchers and the targeted participants can work together to use the cultural knowledge and experiences that they share to inform more rigorous and culturally appropriate research. In group counseling practice infusing relevant and important cultural considerations is imperative when working with Black students as well. The body of research about Black children and adolescents participating in group counseling interventions is scarce. The group counseling literature targeting Black students in particular is even more dismal (Steen & Hines, 2020). That being said, Black youth who participate in small group experiences can learn about postsecondary options and college preparatory information (e.g., social capital, college selection, transition skills; Malott et al., 2019). Nevertheless, exploring the extent to which group counseling interventions are efficacious when serving Black students is sorely needed within the literature.

Policy

Bold policies targeting the strengths and talents of Black children and adolescents in schools are not widespread. The policies that do exist concerning Black youth focus on deficits (e.g., special education services, attendance policies, remediation, alternative schools, etc.; Dumas, 2016). Schools need policies that afford personnel the capacity and resources to help African American students understand the importance of college preparation (e.g., signing up for rigorous course selections including advanced level math in high school) signifying the ability to handle college material (Davis et al., 2019; Reid & Moore, 2008). However, policies that only focus on academic related issues concerning Black students is not enough. School personnel need tools and resources to raise the critical consciousness of Black males by helping them to become aware of, recognize, and dissect inequities in their lives. As a result, school personnel can help Black students learn how to act against these systems (Hale, 2002). Prior research demonstrated that Black teenagers are attuned to the vast array of unjust structural forces operating in their communities, in society, and in their schools, however, schools are failing at directly addressing these racist environments (El-Amin, 2017). Research also suggests that learning a critical consciousness about racism can motivate Black students to resist oppressive forces through persisting in school and achieving in academics (Carter, 2008). Therefore, policies can be created to support Black youths' ability to recognize and address the sociopolitical forces they will face while pursuing their academic ambitions after high school. In addition, offering opportunities for school personnel (i.e., school counselors, educators, administrators) to reflect on anti-racist curricula, teaching practices, and mentorship experiences with Black students could address some of the inequities within school environments. Specifically, professional development on how to create inclusive and affirming educational environments would be most helpful. Additionally, offering equity audits of current policies that are colorblind or too generalized towards diversity and multiculturalism without taking a focused view of the impact on Black scholars could mitigate current inequities that exist in schools. Finally, learning about implicit bias and participating in professional conferences, workshops, and webinars to expose one's own anti-Black racist mindsets and behaviors within their personal and professional lives position school practitioners and leaders to reflect on current understanding and gain practical strategies unique to their role and responsibilities.

CONCLUSION

African American students in our nation's schools can be successful when transitioning from high school to college if given chances to learn important college knowledge and other sociopolitical issues facing many of their Black peers. Group interventions created specifically for Black students to ensure college success are necessary and these programs would be helpful prior to leaving high school. Helping Black male youth succeed in college beyond gaining admissions is of vital importance. Innovative group counseling programs can become an essential tool in helping Black male youth prepare for postsecondary endeavors.

DISCUSSION QUESTIONS

1. What are some ways in which a school counselor could encourage Black boys to express their emotions in a healthy manner, while keeping in mind that hegemonic masculinity and traditional gender roles may have influenced the way they view emotional expression? How would you go about starting a conversation on their notions of masculinity?
2. Who might a school counselor partner or collaborate with to promote college and career readiness to Black male students, particularly those who might be first generation college students? How might you utilize a group counseling model for these students similar to the one mentioned in the text?
3. How would you broach the topics of race, ethnicity, culture, and the intersection of identities when facilitating groups with Black male students? How might you engage students who have not had the space to discuss these issues in schools previously?

ACTIVITIES

Activity 1: Intersecting Identities

In a group with your peers or co-workers, consider exploring your most salient identities and jot them down on an index card. In pairs of two, share one of your identities with your partner and describe how this identity has caused you to experience privilege or oppression. Take turns sharing. Next, on the back, ask all of your peers or co-workers to jot down strengths associated with these identities and challenges. Switch pairs and share one of your identities with your partner detailing a strength and challenge associated with this identity respectively. Following these small pair/share activities, reconvene as a larger group for further discussion and to identify common themes that arise.

Consider reflecting on this activity using the following prompts:

1. What messages did you receive regarding your identities?
2. Who did you hear these messages from?
3. How did this influence the way you interact with others?
4. Have your most important identities changed over the years? How so?

5. What impact do these identities have when interacting with others (e.g., peers and colleagues) within educational spaces, work, community, and so forth?
6. How do you anticipate your identities impacting the way in which you might work with Black males in school settings? What about with Black males aspiring to attend college? What about Black scholars who are less interested in going to college, but perhaps pursuing other career options?

Activity 2: Notions of Masculinity

With your classmates, imagine you are a school counselor facilitating a group for Black high school males. In this role, you have asked students to anonymously list words they associate with masculinity on sticky notes during one of your group sessions. Following this, you collect these notes and then read the words to the group. Pay attention to how the group members react when the words are repeated aloud. Facilitate a discussion on the messaging students have received regarding masculinity. Explore these questions below for reflection:

1. How did your group mates choose which words to write down?
2. What did you as the group leader notice when these words were shared with the group?
3. What were some of the outliers that were used? What were some of the common themes?
4. After reflecting, what do you anticipate the participants saying regarding masculinity?
5. Has this discussion challenged any of the views you as a group leader or participant hold on masculinity?

NOTE

1. Authors' note: We use the terms *African American* and *Black* interchangeably throughout this chapter.

AUTHOR NOTE

Sam Steen ORCID https://orcid.org/0000-0003-0917-0543
Dantavious Hicks ORCID https://orcid.org/0000-0002-9518-8688
Norma L. Day-Vines ORCID https://orcid.org/0000-0003-4889-8289

We have no known conflict of interest to disclose.

Correspondence concerning this chapter should be addressed to Sam Steen, PhD, Counseling and Development Program, George Mason University, Fairfax, VA 22030. Email: ssteen@gmu.edu

REFERENCES

Allen, Q. (2016). "Tell your own story": Manhood, masculinity and racial socialization among Black fathers and their sons. *Ethnic and Racial Studies, 39*, 1831–1848. https://doi.org/10.1080/01419870.2015.1110608

American Psychological Association. (2008). *Resilience in African American children and adolescents: A vision for optimal development.*

Ary, D., Jacobs, L., Sorensen, C., & Walker, D. (2014). *Introduction to research in education.* Wadsworth Cengage Learning.

Baker-Bell, A. (2020). Dismantling anti-Black linguistic racism in English language arts classrooms: Toward an anti-racist Black language pedagogy. *Theory Into Practice, 59*(1), 8–21.

Belgrave, F. Z., Allison, K. W., Wilson, J., & Tademy, R. (2011). *Brothers of Ujima: A cultural enrichment program to empower adolescent African-American males.* Research Press Publishers.

Bruce, A. M., Getch, Y. Q., & Ziomek-Daigle, J. (2009). Closing the gap: A group counseling approach to improve test performance of African-American students. *Professional School Counseling, 12*, 450–457. https://doi.org/10.1177/2156759X0901200603

Carrington, A. M. (2017). Spectacular intimacies: Texture, ethnicity, and a touch of Black cultural politics. *Souls, 19*, 177–195.

Carter, D. J. (2008). Cultivating a critical race consciousness for African-American school success. *Educational Foundations, 22*(1–2), 11–28.

Conley, D. T. (2007). *Redefining college readiness.* Educational Policy Improvement Center (NJ1). https://files.eric.ed.gov/fulltext/ED539251.pdf

Cooper, B. (2018). *Eloquent rage: A Black feminist discovers her superpower.* St. Martin's Press.

Davis, J., Anderson, C., & Parker, W. (2019). Identifying and supporting black male students in advanced mathematics courses throughout the K–12 pipeline. *Gifted Child Today, 42*, 140–149.

Day-Vines, N. L., & Day-Hairston, B. O. (2005). Culturally congruent strategies for addressing the behavioral needs of urban, African American male adolescents. *Professional School Counseling, 8*(3), 236–243.

Day-Vines, N. L., Wood, S. M., Grothaus, T., Craigen, L., Holman, A., Dotson-Blake, K., & Douglass, M. J. (2007). Broaching the subjects of race, ethnicity, and culture during the counseling process. *Journal of Counseling & Development, 85*(4), 401–409. https://doi.org/10.1002/j.1556-6678.2007.tb00608.x

Dixon, P. (2017). *African American relationships, marriages, and families: An introduction.* Taylor & Francis.

Dumas, M. J. (2016). Against the dark: Antiblackness in education policy and discourse. *Theory Into Practice, 55*, 11–19.

El-Amin, A., Seider, S., Graves, D., Tamerat, J., Clark, S., Soutter, M., Johannsen, J., & Malhotra, S. (2017). Critical consciousness: A key to student achievement. *Phi Delta Kappan, 98*(5), 18–23. https://doi.org/10.1177/0031721717690360

Ford, K. (2011). Doing fake masculinity, being real men: Present and future constructions of self among Black college men. *Symbolic Interaction, 34*(1), 38–62. https://doi.org/10.1525/si.2011.34.1.38

Goicoechea, J., Wagner, K., Yahalom, J., & Medina, T. (2014). Group counseling for at-risk African American youth: A collaboration between therapists and artists. *Journal of Creativity in Mental Health, 9*(1), 69–82. https://doi.org/10.1080/15401383.2013.864961

Goodman, D. (2011). *Promoting diversity and social justice.* Routledge.

Hale, J. E. (2002). *Learning while Black: Creating educational excellence for African American children.* Johns Hopkins University Press. https://jhupbooks.press.jhu.edu/title/learning-while-black

Harris, P. J. (2003). Gatekeeping and remaking: The politics of respectability in African American women's history and Black feminism. *Journal of Women's History, 15*(1), 212–220.

Harris, Y. R., & Graham, J. A. (2014). *The African American child: development and challenges.* Springer Publishing Company.

Hill, C. E. (2014). *Helping skills: Facilitating exploration, insight, and action* (4th ed.). American Psychological Association.

Hill, R. B. (1998). Understanding Black family functioning: A holistic perspective. *Journal of Comparative Family Studies, 29*, 15–25.

Hines, E. M., Hines, M. R., Moore J. L., III., Steen, S., Singleton, P., Cintron, D., & Henderson, J. (2020). Preparing African American males for college: A group counseling approach. *The Journal for Specialists in Group Work,* 1–17.

Holcomb-McCoy, C. (2005). Ethnic identity development in early adolescence: Implications and recommendations for middle school counselors. *Professional School Counseling, 9*(2), 120–127. https://doi.org/10.1177/2156759X0500900204

Hudley, A. H. C., & Mallinson, C. (2015). *Understanding English language variation in US schools.* Teachers College Press.

Hudley, A. H. C., Mallinson, C., Berry-McCrea, E. L., & Muwwakkil, J. (2020). Empowering African-American student voices in college. In A. Kibler, G. Valdés, and A. Walqui (Eds.), *Reconceptualizing the role of critical dialogue in American classrooms* (pp. 157–184). Routledge.

Hunter, M. (2005). *Race, gender and the politics of skin tone.* Routledge.

Kerrison, E. M., Cobbina, J., & Bender, K. (2018). "Your pants won't save you": Why Black youth challenge race-based police surveillance and the demands of Black respectability politics. *Race and Justice, 8*(1), 7–26. https://doi.org/10.1177/2153368717734291

Kulic, K. R., Horne, A. M., & Dagley, J. C. (2004). A comprehensive review of prevention groups for children and adolescents. *Group Dynamics: Theory, Research, and Practice, 8*(2), 139–151. https://doi.org/10.1037/1089-2699.8.2.139

Levant, R. F., & Wong, Y. (2017). *The psychology of men and masculinities.* American Psychological Association.

Luke, M., & Hackney, H. (2007). Group coleadership: A critical review. *Counselor Education and Supervision, 46*(4), 280–293. https://doi.org/10.1002/j.1556 -6978.2007.tb00032.x

Malott, K. M., Havlik, S., Gosai, S., Diaz Davila, J., & Steen, S. (2019). College readiness and first-generation college goers: Group impacts with students from an urban, predominantly African-American population. *Journal of Child and Adolescent Counseling, 5*(3), 256–274. https://doi.org/10.1080/23727810.2019 .1672241

Malott, K., Havlik, S., Gosai, S., & Davila, J. D. (2020). A group intervention for prospective first-generation college students: Application with an urban, African American population. *Professional School Counseling, 24*(1). https://doi. org/10.1177/2156759X20957297

Malott, K. M., & Paone, T. R. (2013). Mexican-origin adolescents' exploration of a group experience. *Journal of Creativity in Mental Health, 8*(3), 204–218.

Marasco, V. M. (2018). Addressing hegemonic masculinity with adolescent boys within the counseling relationship. *Journal of Child and Adolescent Counseling, 4*, 226–238.

Martin, A. C. (2008). Television media as a potential negative factor in the racial identity development of African American youth. *Academic Psychiatry, 32*(4), 338–342. https://doi.org/10.1176/appi.ap.32.4.338

Morris, J. E. (2001). African American students and gifted education: The politics of race and culture. *Roeper Review, 24*(2), 59–62. https://doi.org/10 .1080/02783190209554130

Muller, L. E. (2002). Group counseling for African American males: When all you have are European American counselors. *Journal for Specialists in Group Work, 27*(3), 299–313. https://doi.org/10.1177/0193392202027003005

Pascoe, E. A., & Richman, L. S. (2009). Perceived discrimination and health: A meta-analytic review. *Psychological Bulletin, 135*(4), 531–554.

Pascoe, E. A., & Smart, R. L. (2009). Perceived discrimination and health: A meta-analytic review. *Psychological Bulletin, 135*, 531–554. https://doi.org/10.1037/ a0016059

Perry, T., Steele, C., & Hilliard, A. G. (2003). *Young, gifted, and Black: Promoting high achievement among African-American students.* Beacon Press.

Preston, D. (2017). *Untold barriers for Black students in higher education: Placing race at the center of developmental education.* Southern Education Foundation.

Robinson, E. (2010). *Disintegration: The splintering of Black America.* Random House.

Ratner, E. S., Erekson, E. A., Minkin, M. J., & Foran-Tuller, K. A. (2011). Sexual satisfaction in the elderly female population: A special focus on women with gynecologic pathology. *Maturitas, 70*(3), 210–215. https://doi.org/10.1016/j .maturitas.2011.07.015

Reid, M. J., & Moore, J. L., III. (2008). College readiness and academic preparation for postsecondary education: Oral histories of first-generation urban college students. *Urban Education, 43*(2), 240–261. https://doi.org/10.1177/ 0042085907312346

Roach, R. (2001). Where are the Black men on campus? *Diverse Issues in Higher Education, 18*, 18.

Sager, H. R. (2010). *The Ku Klux Klan's portrayal of African Americans in mass media technology* [Master's thesis, West Virginia University]. The Research Repository at WVU. https://doi.org/10.33915/etd.3002

Shin, R. Q., Rogers, J., Stanciu, A., Silas, M., Brown-Smythe, C., & Austin, B. (2010). Advancing social justice in urban schools through the implementation of transformative groups for youth of color. *The Journal for Specialists in Group Work, 35*(3), 230–235. https://doi.org/10.1080/01933922.2010.492899

Steen, S. (2009). Group counseling for African American elementary students: An exploratory study. *The Journal for Specialists in Group Work, 34*(2), 101–117. https://doi.org/10.1080/01933920902791929

Steen, S., & Hines, E. M. (2020). Introduction to group work with African American children and adolescents. *The Journal for Specialists in Group Work, 45*(1), 1–2. https://doi.org/10.1080/01933922.2019.1704115

Steen, S., Kotsoeva, L., & Kotsoev, D. (2015). Promoting African American male students' success through group work: Research and practice implications for professional school counselors. In M. S. Henfield, & A. R. Washington (Eds.), *Black male student success in 21st century urban schools: School counseling for equity, access and achievement* (pp. 99–124). Information Age Publishing.

Steen, S., Shi, Q., & Hockersmith, W. (2014). Group counseling for African Americans: Research and practice considerations. In J. L. DeLucia-Waack, C. R. Kalodner, & M. T. Riva (Eds.), *Handbook of group counseling and psychotherapy* (pp. 220–230). SAGE Publications.

Steen, S., Shi, Q., & Melfie, J. (2021). A systematic literature review of school-counsellor-led group counselling interventions targeting academic achievement: Implications for research and practice. *Journal of School-Based Counseling Policy and Evaluation, 3*(1), 6–18. https://doi.org/https://doi.org/10.25774/sgvv-ta47

Stephens, V. (2005). Pop goes the rapper: A close reading of Eminem's genderphobia. *Popular Music, 24*(1), 21–36.

Sue, D. W., Capodilupo, C. M., Torino, G. C., Bucceri, J. M., Holder, A. M. B., Nadal, K. L., & Esquilin, M. (2007). Racial microaggressions in everyday life: Implications for clinical practice. *American Psychologist, 62*(4), 271–286. https://doi.org/10.1037/0003-066X.62.4.271

Swanson, D. P., Spencer, M. B., Harpalani, V., Dupree, D., Noll, E., Ginzburg, S., & Seaton, G. (2003). *Psychosocial development in racially and ethnically diverse youth: Conceptual and methodological challenges in the 21st century.* http://repository.upenn.edu/gse_pubs/2

Tate, S. (2007). Black beauty: Shade, hair and anti-racist aesthetics. *Ethnic and racial studies, 30,* 300–319.

Thomas, R. V., & Pender, D. A. (2008). Association for specialists in group work: Best practice guidelines 2007 revisions. *The Journal for Specialists in Group Work, 33*(2), 111–117. https://doi.org/10.1080/01933920801971184

Tillman, L. C. (2002). Culturally sensitive research approaches: An African-American perspective. *Educational Researcher, 31*(9), 3–12. https://doi.org/10.3102/0013189X031009003

Trent, M., Dooley, D. G., & Dougé, J. (2019). The impact of racism on child and adolescent health. *Pediatrics, 144*, e20191765. https://doi.org/10.1542/peds.2019-1765

U.S. Department of Education Office for Civil Rights. (2006). *Elementary and secondary school civil rights survey.*

Welton, A. D., & Martinez, M. A. (2014). Coloring the college pathway: A more culturally responsive approach to college readiness and access for students of color in secondary schools. *The Urban Review, 46*(2), 197–223. https://doi.org/10.1007/s11256-013-0252-7

Williams, J. M., & Bryan, J. (2013). Overcoming adversity: High-achieving African American youth's perspectives on educational resilience. *Journal of Counseling & Development, 91*(3), 291–300.

Williams, J. M., Greenleaf, A. T., Albert, T., & Barnes, E. F. (2014). Promoting educational resilience among African American students at risk of school failure: The role of school counselors. *Journal of School Counseling, 12*(9), 1–34.

Wilkins, E. J., Whiting, J. B., Watson, M. F., Russon, J. M., & Moncrief, A. M. (2013). Residual effects of slavery: What clinicians need to know. *Contemporary Family Therapy, 35*(1), 14–28. https://doi.org/10.1007/s10591-012-9219-1

Wilkins, R. D. (2006). *Swimming upstream: A study of Black males and the academic pipeline* (Dissertation, Georgia State University). https://scholarworks.gsu.edu/eps_diss/1

Young, A., & Kaffenberger, C. (2018). *Making DATA work*. American School Counselor Association.

CHAPTER 19

CAREER ACADEMIES AS AN EXEMPLARY MODEL OF PREPARING STUDENTS OF COLOR TO BE COLLEGE AND CAREER READY

Edward C. Fletcher Jr.
The Ohio State University

ABSTRACT

Preparing students to be college and career ready upon graduation are top priorities for secondary schools in the United States. While college and career readiness are the major aims of secondary schools across the country, there remains little consensus of what this commitment entails. In this book chapter, I examine the literature on career academies as an exemplary high school reform initiative aimed at preparing students to be college and career ready. I then highlight areas of opportunities that the academy model might address related to educational inequities. I also discuss implementation, research, and best practices in equity-based college and career development of students to provide them with opportunities to successfully transition into

Equity-Based Career Development and Postsecondary Transitions, pages 493–515

postsecondary education and the workforce, specifically for economically disadvantaged and ethnically and racially diverse learners. I conclude the book chapter with recommendations for research, practice, and policy for ensuring students have access to equity-based college and career preparation.{/ABS}

Preparing students to be college and career ready upon graduation are top priorities for secondary schools in the United States (Fletcher et al., 2018). While college and career readiness are the major aims of secondary schools across the country, there remains little consensus of what this commitment entails. Many educational stakeholders believe college and career readiness translates into increasing the rigor and standards of the secondary education curricula as well as focusing on more student core academic (e.g., English, mathematics, and science) course taking (Chester, 2018; Conley, 2005; McClarty et al., 2018). Others define college and career readiness as the preparation of students for college—without the need for remediation (National Center on Education and the Economy, 2007). The predominant perspectives seem to equate college ready with career ready (Stone & Lewis, 2012). These perspectives exist mainly because of the emphasis on "college for all." The mindset of many educators is that all students will pursue a baccalaureate degree, but fails to account for those who follow other pathways. It also does not recognize that even students who plan to earn baccalaureate degrees still need to explore careers to help them decide on their majors. Stone and Lewis (2012) provided an alternate and comprehensive definition for college and career readiness. Their definition encompassed the need for high school students to graduate with proficient academic knowledge as well as employability and technical skills.

The struggles of urban schools to ensure that students become college and career ready in the midst of challenging conditions have been well documented (Green & Godden, 2014; Milner, 2013). Many urban schools lack resources and supports (e.g., a network of business, postsecondary, and community partners) to offer a wide array of college (e.g., college tours) and career (e.g., job shadowing, internships) readiness activities for their students. It is also widely understood that inadequate college and career readiness often prevents youth from seamless transitions into postsecondary education and the workforce (Loera et al., 2013). To be sure, it is quite difficult for schools to deliver curricula that meet the needs of diverse learners to promote their success. Under these conditions, what can urban schools operating in economically disadvantaged settings do to promote student college and career readiness? In alignment with the new college and career readiness paradigm, many urban school administrators have sought to recalibrate their curricula to better prepare students to be college and career ready by garnering resources and various supports from their local business, postsecondary, and community members oftentimes by developing advisory boards. The Strengthening Career and Technical Education for the 21st Century Act of 2018—known as Perkins V—is a reauthorization of over 100 years of legislation and $1.3 billion in funding for career and technical education (CTE) programs at the middle, secondary, and 2-year college levels. Perkins V "focuses on improving the academic and technical achievement of CTE students, strengthening the connections between secondary and postsecondary education and improving accountability of CTE programs" (Advance CTE, 2020, p. 2). The goal of the legislation is to provide

> individuals with rigorous academic content and relevant technical knowledge and skills needed to prepare for further education and careers in current or emerging professions, which may include high-skill, high-wage, or in-demand industry sectors or occupations. (Strengthening Career and Technical Education for the 21st Century Act, 2018, p. 4)

The legislation also emphasizes the need for schools to establish programs of study (e.g., career academies), provide students with work-based learning experiences, and increase their chances of obtaining a postsecondary credential through advanced placement and/or dual enrollment opportunities.

THE EMERGENCE OF HIGH SCHOOL CAREER ACADEMIES

In response to the challenges in preparing students to be college and career ready, career academies have emerged as promising programs, after decades of implementation and documented positive outcomes (Stern et al., 2010). There is extensive evidence documenting the impact of participation in career academies regarding reduced dropout rates; improved attendance; increased academic course-taking, engagement, and interpersonal skills; and positive labor market outcomes (Fletcher et al., 2012; Kemple, 2008; Stern et al., 2010). The key components of the academy approach involve integrated and contextualized academic and career-related curricula, work-based learning experiences, and partnerships with business and industry (Fletcher et al., 2012; Stern et al., 2010). Career academies are one of the most popular high school reform initiatives with over 8,000 high schools—including area regional career centers, charter, magnet, and traditional comprehensive high schools (school-within-a-school model)— serving over 1 million students across the nation (Lanford & Maruco, 2019; National Career Academy Coalition [NCAC], 2019). Career academies are programs of study featuring small learning communities found within high schools. They focus on providing students with a college-preparatory curriculum integrated within a career theme. Thus, curricula in career academies feature the integration of academic and technical content to increase rigor and relevance to students' career interests. The academy model also emphasizes partnerships with employers and postsecondary institutions (Kemple & Snipes, 2000). The aims of career academies align both with the provisions of the Perkins V legislation—related to establishing programs of study—as well as Stone and Lewis (2012) three-part definition of college and career readiness. First, academic knowledge in and of itself is not sufficient. Instead, high school graduates need to be able to apply what they learn through the "occupational expression" of academic knowledge. In essence, "graduates should know how to use mathematics or science to solve real workplace problems (Stone & Lewis, 2012, p. 15)." Second, many refer to employability skills as "21st century skills" or "soft skills." These skills include capabilities such as responsibility, critical thinking/problem-solving, and technology proficiency. Third, technical skills are specific competencies needed for each occupational area.

NAF ACADEMIES

With the growing popularity of the career academy concept, the quality of implementation has varied greatly as schools and districts have rushed to join the bandwagon. To this end, there have been efforts to inform related implementation with the development of standards of practice by school networks such as NAF (formerly known as the National Academy Foundation). NAF has supported the implementation of the career academy model beginning in 1982 (Stern et al., 2010). NAF provides curricular support, professional development, and technical assistance to a national network of high school career academies in five career themes: engineering, finance, health sciences, hospitality and tourism, and information technology (National Academy Foundation [NAF], 2014). For nearly 40 years, NAF has refined a model that provides youth access to industry-specific curricula, work-based learning experiences, and relationships with professionals. Over 5,000 business professionals serve as mentors, engage NAF students in paid internships, and serve on local advisory boards. During the 2019–2020 school year, over 120,000 students attended 620 NAF academies across 38 states, including District of Columbia, Puerto Rico, and the U.S. Virgin Islands. NAF academies serve an increasingly large diverse set of students: currently 42% Latinx, 28% African American, 20% White, 6% Asian, and 3% multi-racial. In addition, 67% of NAF students qualify for free and/or reduced lunch. NAF academies reported that 97% of seniors graduated on time. In terms of student selection, NAF academies operate under an open enrollment policy. Therefore, any student may enroll and participate in a NAF academy. While some schools require that students apply to gain entry, students are not selected based on prior academic achievement. For magnet schools who are oversubscribed, students may enter a lottery system and then may be selected at random.

Despite the documented benefits of student participation in career academies, the general public is still reticent to embrace related programs given the lingering negative views regarding CTE. Some of the stigma stems from tracking students into differentiated curricular programs based on ethnic and racial backgrounds and socioeconomic status (Fletcher & Zirkle, 2009; Gamoran, 1989). To change this stigma, CTE educators and administrators have attempted to provide high-quality programs that are integrated with rigorous academic courses and are aligned with high-demand, high-skilled, and high-wage occupations. Yet, many parents still view CTE from the vantage point of their own K–12 schooling experiences, associating CTE programs with noncollege bound students and preparation for entry level, low-wage jobs. Further contributing to this misconception is the "college for all" mindset, which has taught administrators, educators, school counselors, parents, and students that a 4-year baccalaureate degree is the only pathway to prosperity (Fletcher & Cox, 2012). Another issue is that career academies demand greater resources in terms of equipment and software, and require access to worksites and employer support in the community to provide work-based learning opportunities to students.

A NEED TO FOCUS ON EDUCATIONAL EQUITY

While the NAF academy model has squarely focused on addressing common challenges of connecting schools to business and industry leaders for the purpose of supporting students and preparing them to be college and career ready, much of the educational literature within the past 3 decades has emphasized the need for schools to solve the complex challenges of addressing inequities (Fletcher et al., 2020a, 2020b). The achievement gap (what is now termed the opportunity gap) has not narrowed and a large proportion of diverse learners are being left behind in schools (Verstegen, 2015). To that end, NAF has an opportunity to contribute to solving some of the great challenges of education. It is important to note that educational equity differs from educational equality where the former concept requires that students are provided access to educational opportunities that are calibrated and customized based on need (including customizing and tailoring resources and supports), whereas the latter concept emphasizes equal distribution of resources and services regardless of need.

In this chapter, I examine the literature based on career academies, and highlight areas of opportunities that the academy model might address related to inequities. I also discuss implementation, research, and best practices in equity-based college and career development of students to provide them with opportunities to successfully transition into postsecondary education and the workforce, specifically for economically disadvantaged and ethnically and racially diverse learners. I conclude the book chapter with recommendations for research, practice, and policy for ensuring students have access to college and career supports.

SETTING THE CONTEXT: RACISM IN SOCIETY

It is important to acknowledge that racial discrimination is inherently common for African American/Black, Latinx, Native American, and other ethnically and racially diverse individuals in our society, and will likely result in physiological and psychological issues during youth and into adulthood (Benner & Graham, 2013; Hope et al., 2015). Racism permeates our society and can occur at all levels: individual, institutional, and cultural (Jones, 1997; Pincus, 1996). At the individual level, youth and adults alike encounter racial discrimination in the forms of bigotry, prejudice, and micro-aggressions (Jones, 1997; Saleem & Lambert, 2016). At the institutional level, African Americans/Blacks, Latinx, Native American, and other ethnically and racially diverse individuals live and work under laws and policies that are inherently racist and oppressive (Jones et al., 2014). At the cultural level, historical discrimination has led to division among the dominant group (White males) and has left marginalized individuals at a disadvantage (Jones, 1997; Utsey & Ponterotto, 1996). Racial prejudice is ingrained in our everyday practices, and has become the norm in our society.

Recent events, such as the murder of George Floyd (one of many) by police officers and the Black Lives Matter movement, have garnered international attention to the racial injustices that linger in the United States as well as the urgent need for dismantling systemic racism, implicit biases, and implementing anti-racists actions in all aspects of society, including education. Thus, it is imperative that schools continue to seek relevance and continually transform to improve the education and potential success of its student populations. To that end, schools must deconstruct anti-racist language, curricula, policies, and practices.

The lack of a holistic approach to provide diverse learners and their families with needed services to help them stay and finish school has been a lingering issue in the United States (Fries et al., 2012). In urban settings, like the majority of NAF schools, with large concentrations of ethnically and racially diverse and economically disadvantaged families, school staff face a daunting task of helping students succeed amidst personal and family challenges (Levin et al., 2007). Providing support services to students and their families in these communities is a critically important challenge for our society. In 2016–2017, according to the National Center for Education

Statistics (National Center for Educational Statistics [NCES], 2019), high school completion in low-income and ethnically and racially diverse communities was 77.3% compared to an overall national graduation rate of 84.6%. Completing high school has been a challenge in urban settings with limited economic resources, where the dropout rate of African American/ Black and Latinx students is higher than their White peers (NCES, 2018). Many schools in low-income communities are considered "dropout factories" as they account for over half of the students not completing school every year (Balfanz & Legters, 2004). Addressing this problem in schools is not easy because limited resources often interface with low student motivation to learn. These challenges stem from a lack of engaging curricula, health concerns, family issues, and limited school supports (Fitzpatrick et al., 2015; Fries et al., 2012). The career academy model is a high school reform initiative that has the potential to transform the college and career preparatory approach for students across the country as well as help to ensure educational equity. NAF supports the largest network of high school career academies in the nation The NAF academy model features—*academy development and structure, integrated curriculum and structure, work-based learning,* and *advisory boards.*

ELEMENTS OF THE NAF ACADEMY MODEL

Academy Development and Structure

The first element of the NAF academy model is the academy development and structure component, which focuses on small learning communities using student cohorts, career-themed and sequenced coursework, and career themed guidance. Academies are either organized as schools-within-schools or as whole school/wall-to-wall (where all students in the school participate) programs, and emphasize block scheduling for students. The idea is to break down larger high schools into a small family-like atmosphere where students are assigned to the same teachers for 4 years—enabling students to form a community of learners as well as a close knit and caring environment (Stern et al., 2010). Teachers receive instructional supports and technical assistance using industry validated curricula provided by NAF. Through this structured support, teachers form deep relationships with their students and make stronger connections between their teaching practice and real-world applications. The structure of each academy is designed such that students interact with teachers and peers in a small learning community who share interests in a given occupational area, and are situated within a cohort. Students have the same peers and teachers throughout their 4 years in high school—forming a community. This allows for interdependent learning by which students learn from each other while simultaneously learning to work collaboratively.

Equity Issues Related to the Academy Structure

Researchers have found that the use of small learning communities is a contributing factor promoting a positive school culture (Fletcher et al., 2019). Fletcher et al. found that academy stakeholders described their schools as a laboratory of equity, safety, and inclusivity. Related research has revealed the challenges of building positive and supportive cultures in large, comprehensive, urban high schools—particularly those that serve low-income and ethnically and racially diverse youth (Letgers et al., 2002; Murphy, 2010). The difficulty of establishing a positive culture in comprehensive high schools typically stems from their relatively large student populations and fixed departmental silos. Hence, one major recommendation that addresses the issue of large schools is the idea of establishing small learning communities. The term "small learning communities" denotes a variety of school structures and configurations—including schools within a school, and magnet programs that are wall-to-wall (where all students participate in a given career theme; Kuo, 2010). Researchers have also found that students in small learning communities experience an increased sense of personalization and belonging, and lower levels of school vandalism (Page et al., 2002). Fletcher and Cox (2012) found that African American students believed participation in career academies was the most meaningful aspect of their schooling experiences and provided them an opportunity to gain a sense of community/belonging, acquire hands-on training, and explore their own individual interests. Thus, it is quite plausible that career academies have a positive impact on African American students. In addition, Fletcher et al. (2020a), using propensity score matching and structural equation modeling, compared academy and non-academy students on student engagement—behavioral, cognitive, and emotional. They found that academy students had significantly higher levels of emotional engagement and significantly lower levels of behavioral engagement than non-academy students. Emotional engagement is related to students' sense of belonging, safety, and their abilities to be themselves in school (and valued for it). They also found no statistically significant differences in the levels of cognitive engagement of academy students compared to comprehensive school students. Based on their findings, they believed the academy model has the promise of transforming the high school experience for students as it relates to their attachment to the school, their relationships with peers and teachers, and their sense of belonging and safety—all related to emotional engagement. However, academies need to work with students to create and develop co-curricular and extracurricular activities of interest to engage students in their schools at a higher level (Fletcher et al., 2020a). Based on related evidence, Kuo (2010) recommended that "policymakers and practitioners should continue to find opportunities to reduce the size of large high schools and increase the sense of personalization, belonging, and safety among students, teachers, and staff" (p. 395).

Integrated Curriculum and Instruction

The second component of NAF academies is the integrated curriculum and instruction, which promotes career and academic learning around a relevant career theme (e.g., business and finance, engineering, health sciences, hospitality and tourism, information technology) through project-based activities involving core academic content. Career academies integrate career themed curricula with college preparatory coursework to encourage students to learn core academic subjects in an applied career-oriented fashion. The term *curriculum integration* is referred to in a variety of ways—as a method or process to connect skills, themes, concepts, and topics across disciplines and between academic and technical education (Pierce & Hernández-Gantes, 2015). Teachers that integrate curriculum connect multiple content areas to break down overarching theories, concepts, and big ideas that help students and enhance learning from one subject to another (Klein, 2006). Teachers can implement curriculum integration around an occupational theme, such as IT, or may involve concept connections within single subjects such as arithmetic, algebra, geometry, or across two or more subjects, such as mathematics and CTE (Pierce & Hernández-Gantes, 2015). The purposeful integration of academic and technical education is a signature feature of successful programs bringing meaning and relevance to curriculum and instruction (Castellano et al., 2012). The occupational context serves as the source of relevant learning tasks and applications involving authentic representations of what employees do in the world of work (Hernández-Gantes & Brendefur, 2003). Findings from the math-in-CTE experimental study demonstrated that the integration of mathematical concepts in CTE courses—teaching math in an occupational context—resulted in statistically significant higher scores for students on 2 of 3 mathematical assessments. However, the assessment scores within the third examination did not produce significantly different achievement compared to the control group (Stone et al., 2008; Stone & Lewis, 2012).

EQUITY ISSUES RELATED TO AN INTEGRATED CURRICULUM AND INSTRUCTION

Tech-Equity

The COVID-19 pandemic has brought more attention and awareness to the digital divide across the nation. It is not only a matter of economically disadvantaged, ethnically and racially diverse, and female students having limited access to technologies at home (e.g., access to computers/ devices, Internet access), it is equally concerning regarding the lack of access to high quality technologies as well as rigorous computer science and engineering courses in schools. NAF academies concentrate on emerging and growing career areas (those that are high skilled, high waged, and in high demand) such as engineering and information technology (IT). All students need to know and be able to utilize Microsoft Office software applications and have computer literacy skills. Knowing Microsoft Office software applications and learning how to search for information on the Internet are not enough. Given that we are in a technological revolution, all students—particularly ethnically and racially diverse learners and those from economically disadvantaged backgrounds—need to have exposure to emerging technologies as well as associated industry-recognized certifications (e.g., Adobe Photoshop, InDesign, Illustrator, Microsoft Office User Specialist). These technologies include areas such as coding, cybersecurity, gaming, and robotics. Students also need to understand the ubiquitousness of technology as it traverses, and that technology is embedded in all industries, including business, finance, health sciences, and hospitality and tourism. It is also important to note that increasing access and student learning in computer science and engineering related courses aligns with the need to emphasize learning mathematics. Further, schools need to promote a shift from students as consumers and users of technologies to creators, developers, and entrepreneurs. Students need these emerging skills and mindsets to be competitive in our technology rich workforce. To that end, it is also important to note that teachers need professional development opportunities to ensure they are equipped with the knowledge and tools to teach rigorous and high-level computer science courses in schools. Thus, it is important to consider how technology has the potential to transform lives, particularly students coming from economically disadvantaged backgrounds. Ensuring that underserved students have access to emerging technologies and rigorous technologically advanced curricula has the potential to encourage them to pursue high-demand, high-skilled, and high-wage occupations.

An Underrepresentation of Diverse Learners in Accelerated Programs

Although many people believe that, as a nation, we have moved beyond racism, classism, and other discriminatory practices, the attitudes and beliefs of some regarding the intellectual and academic prowess of ethnically and racially diverse students continue to impede their access and opportunity to fully participate in accelerated learning options (e.g., advanced placement, dual enrollment, gifted, honors, international baccalaureate) as well as advanced STEM courses. Many contemporary scholars of gifted and talented education have challenged definitions and theories of giftedness, and unfair tests, checklists, policies, procedures, and practices that contribute to the persistent underrepresentation of ethnically and racially diverse (e.g., African American and Latinx) students in accelerated learning options. For example, current definitions of giftedness continue to place major emphasis on standardized intelligence tests reflective of White middle-class values and, therefore, discriminate against students of color who do not necessarily embrace such values; this results in untapped potential (Ford, 2013; Wright et al., 2017). Identifying gifted and talented as well as placing barriers for accelerated learning options based on narrow standards that reflect, represent, and enforce the languages, literacies, and cultural practices of the status quo are bound to marginalize much of what ethnically and racially diverse students learn in their homes and communities as irrelevant for school, substandard, and inferior. This practice of ranking and sorting students based on their skills to think, speak, and act in ways that represent White students undermines the cultural strengths, assets, and ethnic capital of ethnically and racially diverse students—what Yosso (2005) termed cultural community wealth. It is important to debunk the myth that ethnically and racially diverse families do not place a high value and priority on education when consideration is given to longstanding structural inequalities. The education of students of color is often compromised, which gives little opportunity for their gifts and talents to be recognized and cultivated at school. We must be sure that ethnically and racially diverse as well as economically disadvantaged students gain access to a highly rigorous curriculum, particularly related to accelerated programs.

Work-Based Learning

The third component of the NAF academy model is providing students with work-based learning experiences. Career academy students engage in successively progressive, work-based learning experiences from 9th through 12th grades that are developmentally and age-appropriate. It has been well documented that students often find learning as void of meaning and are prone to question the relevance of instructional tasks (Castellano et al., 2012; Hernández-Gantes & Brendefur, 2003). To address this disconnect in teaching and learning, career academies emphasize learning in specific occupational contexts to enhance the relevance of student experiences. The premise is that the authenticity of occupational contexts provides opportunities to make learning more meaningful for students (Newmann & Wehlage, 1995; Stipanovic et al., 2012). Through providing a range of work-based learning experiences, NAF academies address this call to encourage authentic learning in real-world contexts. Under the NAF model, work-based learning includes career awareness and exploration activities in 9th (e.g., field trips) and 10th (e.g., job shadowing) grades, and experiential opportunities (e.g., industry certifications, paid internships) in 11th and 12th grades. Kuh (2015) argued that students who participate in high-impact, work-based learning practices "invest substantial time and energy to educationally purposeful tasks, interact frequently with their teachers and peers, get feedback often, and apply what they are learning" (p. xi). That is, work-based learning enables students to apply what they know in real-world settings, while building exposure to, preparation for, and experience in their interested career path (Papadimitriou, 2014). In this regard, work-based learning experiences (particularly internships) should help students acquire both the employability and technical skills needed to be college and career ready (Hernández-Gantes, 2016; Stone & Lewis, 2012).

Equity Issues Related to Work-Based Learning

Because work-based learning experiences (in particular, internships) promote deeper understanding of students' career potential, students who participate in internships could have better opportunities to overcome their socioeconomic origins and move up the social ladder. They also have opportunities to build their 21st century skills (e.g., collaboration, critical thinking, problem-solving, and technological development) which are critical to compete in our knowledge-based technological economy. However, we know from social stratification theory that education reproduces existing social inequalities (Domina et al., 2017; Gamoran, 1987) and thus high school internships could be a part of the problem. It is critical that we develop strategies to ensure equal access to opportunities for underrepresented students in high school, as we know this is the foundation for long-term college and career success. However, there remains a dearth of research about the quality, access, and equity related to internships, particularly at the high school level (Alfeld et al., 2013). We have yet to study how internships influence student postsecondary outcomes, particularly for low-income students of color.

Schools should ensure that students have opportunities to participate in a host of work-based learning as well as college preparatory experiences (e.g., college tours, university research experiences). Effective schools ensure students are able to make seamless transitions to postsecondary education both through coursework (e.g., accelerated courses and programs) and a combination of work-based learning activities (e.g., resume writing, mock interviews, job shadowing, internships) and college preparatory experiences (e.g., college trips from a variety of institutional types—both in-state and out-of-state, college tours of ivy league institutions, research lab experiences at local colleges and universities). Students should be exposed to opportunities beyond their zip code and network with community members, business and industry representatives, and college/university faculty. It is important to provide economically disadvantaged students opportunities to go beyond their neighborhoods and see the potential that might lie ahead of them post high school. These opportunities represent transformative learning experiences for students and help them to form future ready college and career mindsets.

Advisory Boards

The fourth component of NAF academies is the advisory board comprising a diverse network of members representing business and industry, postsecondary institutions, parents, alumni, students, school personnel, and community members. The advisory board has a host of purposes, including curriculum support, mentoring programs for students, guest speakers, field trips, job shadowing, internships, and fundraising for scholarships and school equipment (Orr et al., 2004). The advisory board helps bridge and link social capital to promote work-based learning, provide various learner and academy supports, and acts as a vehicle to advance the goals of the academy (Ling & Dale, 2013). Academies work with an advisory board representing business partners in the occupation of interest who provide support and promote career awareness, exploration, and readiness (NAF, 2014).

THE ROLE OF THE ADVISORY BOARD
IN ADDRESSING EQUITY ISSUES

Wraparound Services

Living in poverty has far-reaching implications for student success. The practice of schools providing students with wraparound services is a promising initiative to meet the needs of youth in communities with limited resources (Fries et al., 2012). Typically, agencies pool funding from multiple sources to provide targeted wraparound services to individuals in need. However, there are instances where schools provide integrated wraparound services to students in collaboration with community partners. This practice is often referred to in the literature as community schools (Harris & Hoover, 2003; Melaville et al., 2006). Community schools utilize needs assessments, partnerships, coordinated supports, and data tracking, to improve students' educational attainment and academic achievement. Through community partnerships, schools become hubs of community learning for parents and families by providing trainings and skill classes, such as GED, English language, home-ownership, and parenting in the evenings and/or on the weekends (Harris & Hoover, 2003; Melaville et al., 2006). Community schools seek to wrap social, family, and health services around students and their families in ways that are unique to their locations (Peebles-Wilkins, 2004; Valli et al., 2016). The advisory board can have a unique role and opportunity to leverage its resources and capital to provide wraparound services for students, their families, and their broader communities. Fletcher et al. (in press) examined the benefits of a community school for students. They found that students, in a 98% African American STEAM academy with wraparound services, were provided equitable supports for economically disadvantaged students. These supports were instituted using a healing-centered mindset and enabled the school personnel and stakeholders to adopt a no excuse disposition. They also found that in comparison to students at a large comprehensive high school, the academy students had statistically significantly higher scores on behavioral engagement and cognitive engagement. There were no statistically significant differences in emotional engagement.

The Role of Advisory Boards to Address the Need
for Role Models

Because of the lack of ethnically and racially diverse teachers across the country, coupled with the issue of having a prevalence of fatherlessness in African American communities, many African American males in particular struggle with the lack of role models who look like them. Fatherlessnes contributes to poverty, crime, and adverse outcomes for youth (Blankenhorn, 1995; Popenoe, 1996). Randles (2019) emphasized the role of race-based sources of discrimination as substantial contributors to adverse outcomes of ethnically and racially diverse males. These race-based sources include targeting of African American males in the criminal justice system as well as a reduction of educational and workforce opportunities. All of these issues have undermined the abilities of low-income African American men to participate in caregiving roles (Edin & Nelson, 2013; Smeeding et al., 2011).

Given the lack of African American male (and other ethnically and racially diverse) role models in schools across the country, I recommend that advisory boards advocate and utilize their networks to recruit and retain ethnically and racially diverse staff and other role models (e.g., business/industry partners, college/university faculty, and community members that may serve as guest speakers) that reflect the student population within their schools. Schools could have African American/Black male alumni participate on these advisory boards to provide recommendations for implementation and special initiatives. It is critical that students coming from low-income families are aware of opportunities that lie beyond their neighborhoods. They need reinforcement so that they can reach their highest potential. When educational professionals create teaching and counseling spaces that are supportive and encouraging, African American males and other ethnically and racially diverse learners are more likely to be more academically engaged and motivated to learn.

RECOMMENDATIONS FOR ENSURING EQUITY-BASED COLLEGE AND CAREER READINESS

Recommendations for Research

While educators, school administrators, and policy makers tout the need for students to be "college and career ready," researchers have yet to reach a consensus on defining the terms. Hence, in this book chapter, I used Stone and Lewis' (2012) notion of college and career readiness as students' acquisition of academics, the occupational expression of academics, employability, and technical skills. However, the field of education could benefit from an agreed upon definition of the two constructs as well as a reliable and valid instrument to measure both college and career readiness, especially as it related to addressing inequities in schools.

Given the prevalence of career academies around the country (in 8,000 high schools, affecting over 1 million students), and the prescribed model designed by NAF, research is needed to understand the relationship between academy structure and development (e.g., the establishment of small learning communities and cohorting of students) and student engagement. Second, research is needed to examine how integrated curricula that focus on college preparatory coursework within a career themed context contributes to student achievement, rigorous course taking, and postsecondary outcomes. Third, investigations are needed to examine the influence of work-based learning experiences on the promotion of college and career readiness (e.g., 21st century skill sets, engagement college and career preparatory activities) for students and longitudinally track graduates' labor market outcomes. Fourth, research is needed to disentangle associated outcomes (e.g., course taking patterns, on time graduation, acceptance into college) for learners from diverse backgrounds.

Recommendations for Practice

It is important that schools develop an equity mindset when strategically implementing a college and career preparatory curriculum. School administrators need to promote a shift from students as consumers and users of technologies to creators, developers, and entrepreneurs by ensuring that economically disadvantaged and ethnically and racially diverse learners take high level computer science courses in schools with opportunities to earn industry certifications as well as preparing their teachers to provide this type of education for their students. It is also important for school counselors to ensure that diverse learners are exposed and encouraged to take a rigorous set of high school courses (e.g., accelerated courses) as well as participate in co-curricular activities (e.g., college tours, work-based learning, university research lab experiences) that will prepare them to be college and career ready. Ensuring that students have dual enrollment course options requires school personnel to collaborate with 2-year colleges (and possibly 4-year universities) to establish articulation agreements so that it is possible for a high school student to graduate with an associate's degree—based on taking dual enrollment courses in a particular program or in general education. Further, school administrators and teachers should create advisory boards to offer a variety of services and supports to students, including curricular development, mentoring, guest speaking, financial supports, and wraparound services.

Understanding whether academies promote college and career readiness (through school structures, integrated curricula, work-based learning, and advisory boards) will also have implications for traditional schools of all configurations across the United States in their quests to help students seamlessly transition through secondary schools into postsecondary education to gain competencies as well as enter careers that are high wage, high skilled, and in high demand—constructing a well-developed workforce development system.

Recommendations for Policy

While Perkins V advances ambitious goals for CTE programs, there have been few studies examining whether modern CTE programs are meeting the expectations set by the Perkins V legislation (Giani, 2019). According to the Perkins V legislation, a program of study is defined as "a coordinated sequence of academic and technical content at the secondary and postsecondary level" (Granovskiy, 2018, p. 20). However, few studies have examined whether modern career academies—a school reform initiative that utilizes a program of study model—are indeed fulfilling Perkins V obligations related to preparation of students for college and careers. Implications could help revise the language, expectations, and provisions of Perkins V to specify which types of activities (e.g., small learning communities, integrated curricula, work-based learning) may promote student preparedness for college and careers. In addition, implications could be useful in a broader sense, given that 85% of all high school students across the nation participate in CTE courses, and therefore, may benefit from participating in small learning communities, integrated curricula, and work-based learning activities (National Assessment of Career and Technical Education [NACTE], 2014).

At the school district level, I recommend that school district administrators consider becoming a member of national organizations, such as NAF, that will help provide supports and resources for implementing the best practices for equity based college and career readiness discussed in this book chapter. For example, NAF provides technical assistance, industry validated curricula, and access to national companies that help prepare students to be college and career ready through a variety of work-based learning activities.

CONCLUSION

A sole emphasis on preparing students for entry into a 4-year college/university, the "college for all" phenomenon in schools, is all too familiar and widespread in schools across the country. Nonetheless, efforts to ensure that schools are preparing students to be both college *and* career ready represents a pivotal and critical transition that has the potential to address some of the lingering issues related to equity and access to a high quality and individualized curriculum. It also aligns with the call to prepare students for a new knowledge based economy. In summary, this chapter provides a call to action for educators, school counselors, community, business, and postsecondary partners to unite under a shared vision: to prepare students to be college and career ready.

DISCUSSION QUESTIONS

1. Articulate how you define college and career readiness, and compare and contrast your understanding of these concepts to how it is defined in this book chapter. What unique supports might schools provide for diverse learners to address inequities and ensure their preparedness for college and careers?
2. Describe your comprehension of the role of career and technical education (CTE) in schools today. Do you believe CTE programs are different than when you were in K–12 schools? Why or why not?
3. Discuss how schools might operate to ensure diverse and underserved learners are not tracked into low status programs. What school policies would you recommend to prevent school personnel from tracking students?

ACTIVITIES

1. Identify a local high school and provide a detailed analysis of their student and school personnel demographics, curricula and programs offered, and supports (or lack thereof) for college and career readiness. Provide a strengths, weaknesses, opportunities, and threats (SWOT) analysis of the school. Then, develop a detailed improvement plan that emphasizes equitable practices to prepare students in the school to be college and career ready. The criteria for the improvement plan should emphasize access to college and career preparation activities for all students. The college preparation activities might include ensuring that students have a college going mindset through accelerated coursework (e.g., AP and dual enrollment), understanding of the college processes (e.g., college visits, financial aid information). The career preparation activities might include ensuring that all students have access to career-themed programs, work-based learning activities (e.g., job shadowing, internships), and industry certifications.
2. Interview school administrators, teachers, and school counselors on their definitions of college and career readiness. Upon completion of the interviews, write a report comparing and contrasting the viewpoints of each participant and compare and contrast it to other participants within the three categories (school administrators, teachers, and school counselors) as well as between the three constituent groups. In the conclusion section, discuss how the school personnel viewpoints align or diverge from your own thoughts on college and career readiness.

AUTHOR NOTE

Edward C. Fletcher Jr. is at the Workforce Development and Education program, Department of Educational Studies, The Ohio State University.

I have no known conflict of interest to disclose.

Correspondence concerning this chapter should be addressed to Edward C. Fletcher Jr., The Ohio State University, A456 PAES Building, 305 Annie and John Glenn Avenue, Columbus, OH 43210. Email: fletcher.158@osu.edu

REFERENCES

Advance CTE. (2020). *Federal policy: Strengthening career and technical education for the 21st century act.* https://careertech.org/perkins

Alfeld, C., Charner, I., Johnson, L., & Watts, E. (2013). *Work-based learning opportunities for high school students.* National Research Center for Career and Technical Education.

Balfanz, R., & Legters, N. (2004). *Locating the dropout crisis: Which high schools produce the nation's dropouts? Where are they located? Who attends them?* (CRESPAR, Report 70). Center for Research on the Education of Students Placed At Risk. The Johns Hopkins University.

Benner, A., & Graham, S. (2013). The antecedents and consequences of racial/ethnic discrimination during adolescence: Does the source of discrimination matter? *Developmental Psychology, 49*, 1602–1613.

Blankenhorn, D. (1995). *Fatherless America: Confronting our most urgent social problem.* HarperCollins.

Castellano, M., Sundell, K., Overman, L. T., & Aliaga, O. A. (2012). Do career and technical education programs of study improve student achievement? Preliminary analyses from a rigorous longitudinal study. *International Journal of Educational Reform, 21*, 98–118.

Chester, M. (2018). Foreword: "A toast to Sofia and Hector's future." In McClarty, K., Mattern, K., & Gaertner, M. (Eds.), *Preparing students for college and careers: Theory, measurement, and educational practice* (p. vii). Routledge.

Conley, D. T. (2005). *College knowledge: What it really takes for students to succeed and what we can do to get them ready.* Jossey-Bass.

Domina, T., Penner, A., & Penner, E. (2017). Categorical inequality: Schools as sorting machines. *Annual Review of Sociology, 43*(27), 1–27. https://doi.org/10.1146/annurev-soc-060116-053354

Edin, K., & Nelson, T. (2014). *Doing the best I can: Fatherhood in the inner city.* University of California Press.

Fitzpatrick, C., Gartner, L., & LaForgia, M. (2015, August 14). Failure factories: How the Pinellas County School Board neglected five schools until they became the worst in Florida. *Tampa Bay Times.* http://www.tampabay.com/projects/2015/investigations/pinellas-failure-factories/5-schools-segregation/

Fletcher, E. C., & Cox, E. (2012). Exploring the meaning African American students ascribe to their participation in high school career academies and the challenges they experience. *The High School Journal, 96*(1), 4–19. https://doi.org/10.1353/hsj.2012.0017

Fletcher, E. C., Dumford, A., Hernandez-Gantes, V., & Minar, N. (2020a). Examining the engagement of career academy and comprehensive high school students in the United States. *The Journal of Educational Research, 113*(4), 1–15. https://doi.org/10.1080/00220671.2020.1787314

Fletcher, E. C., Ford, D. Y., & Moore, J. L. (in press). From a bag lunch to a buffet: A case study of a low-income African American academy's vision of promoting college and career readiness. *College Access Journal.*

Fletcher E. C., Jr., & Haynes, D. (2020b). Traditional students as second-class citizens through modern day tracking. *Journal of Education for Students Placed at Risk*, 1–20. https://doi.org/10.1080/10824669.2020.1768857

Fletcher E. C., Jr., & Hernández-Gantes, V. (2020). They're moving in spaces they're not used to: Examining the racialized experiences of African American students in a high school STEAM Academy. *Education and Urban Society*, 1–20. https://doi.org/10.1177/0013124520928610

Fletcher, E. C., Jr., & Tan, T. (in press). Black lives matter: Examining an urban high school STEAM academy supporting African American students, families, and communities using a healing-centered approach. *International Journal of Multiple Research Approaches.*

Fletcher, E. C., Warren, N., & Hernandez-Gantes, V. (2019). The high school academy as a laboratory of equity, inclusion, and safety. *Computer Science Education, 29*(4), 382–406. https://doi.org/10.1080/08993408.2019.1616457

Fletcher, E. C., Jr., Warren, N., & Hernandez-Gantes, V. (2018). Preparing high school students for a changing world: College, career, and future ready learners. *Career and Technical Education Research, 43*(1), 77–97. https://doi.org/10.5328/cter43.1.77

Fletcher, E. C., & Zirkle, C. (2009). The relationship of high school curriculum tracks to degree attainment and occupational earnings. *Career and Technical Education Research, 34*(2) 81–102. https://doi.org/10.5328/CTER34.2.81

Ford, D. Y. (2013). *Recruiting and retaining culturally different students in gifted education.* Prufrock Press.

Fries, D., Carney, K. J., Blackman-Urteaga, L., & Savas, S. A. (2012). Wraparound services: Infusion into secondary schools as a dropout prevention strategy. *NASSP Bulletin, 96*(2) 119–136.

Gamoran, A. (1989). Measuring curriculum differentiation. *American Journal of Education, 97*(2), 129–143.

Gamoran, A. (1987). The stratification of high school learning opportunities. *Sociology of Education, 60*(3), 135–155.

Giani, M. (2019). Does vocational still imply tracking? Examining the evolution of career and technical education curricular policy in Texas. *Educational Policy, 33*(7), 1002–1046. https://doi.org/10.1177/0895904817745375

Granovskiy, B. (2018). *Reauthorization of the Perkins Act in the 115th congress: The strengthening career and technical education for the 21st century act.* Congressional Research Service. https://crsreports.congress.gov/

Green, T., & Gooden, M. (2014). Transforming out-of-school challenges into opportunities: Community school reform in the urban Midwest. *Urban Education, 49,* 930–954.

Harris, M. M., & Hoover, J. H. (2003). Overcoming adversity through community schools. *Reclaiming Children & Youth, 11,* 206–210.

Hernández-Gantes, V. M. (2016). *College and career readiness for all: The role of career and technical education in the U.S.* In D. Wyse, L. Hayward, & J. Pandya. (Eds.), *SAGE handbook of curriculum, pedagogy and assessment* (Vol. 2, pp. 674–689). SAGE Publications.

Hernández-Gantes, V. M., & Brendefur, J. (2003). Developing authentic, integrated, standards-based mathematics curriculum: [More than just] an interdisciplinary collaborative approach. *Journal of Vocational Education Research, 28*(3), 259–284.

Hope, E., Hoggard, L., & Thomas, A. (2015). Emerging into adulthood in the face of racial discrimination: Physiological, psychological, and sociopolitical consequences for African American youth. *Translational Issues in Psychological Science, 1,* 342–351.

Jones, J. (1997). *Prejudice and racism* (2nd ed.) McGraw Hill.

Jones, J., Dovidio, J., & Vietze, D. (2014). *The psychology of diversity: Beyond prejudice and racism.* Wiley Blackwell.

Kemple, J. J. (2008). *Career academies: Long-term impacts on labor market outcomes, educational attainment, and transitions to adulthood.* MDRC.

Kemple, J., & Snipes, J. (2000). *Career academies: Long-term impacts on labor market outcomes, educational attainment, and transitions to adulthood.* MDRC.

Klein, J. T. (2006). Platform for a shared discourse of interdisciplinary education. *Journal of Social Science Education, 6*(2), 10–18. http://www.jsse.org

Kuh, G. D. (2015). Foreword. In S. J. Quaye & S. R. Harper (Eds.), *Student engagement in higher education* (pp. ix–xiii). Routledge.

Kuo, V. (2010). Transforming American high schools: Possibilities for the next phase of high school reform. *Peabody Journal of Education, 85*(3), 389–401. https://doi.org/10.1080/0161956X.2010.491709

Lanford, M., & Maruco, T. (2019). When job training is not enough: The cultivation of social capital in career academies. *American Educational Research Journal, 55*(3), 617–648. https://doi.org/10.3102/0002831217746107

Letgers, N., Balfanz, R., & McPartland, J. (2002). *Solutions for failing high schools: Converging visions and promising models.* Office of Vocational and Adult Education.

Ling, C., & Dale, A. (2013). Agency and social capital: Characteristics and dynamics. *Community Development Journal, 49*(1), 4–20.

Loera, G., Nakamoto, J., Oh, Y., & Rueda, R. (2013). Factors that promote motivation and academic engagement in a career technical education context. *Career and Technical Education Research, 38*(3), 173–190. https://doi.org/10.5328/cter38.3.173

Levin, H., Belfield, C., Muennig, P., & Rouse, C. (2007). *The cost and benefits of an excellent education for all of America's children.* Columbia University.

Melaville, A., Berg, A. C., & Blank, M. J. (2006). *Community-based learning: Engaging students for success and citizenship.* The Coalition for Community Schools.

Milner, H. (2013). Analyzing poverty, learning, and teaching through a critical race lens. *Review of Research in Education, 37*(1), 1–53.

McClarty, K., Gaertner, M., & Mattern, K. (2018). Introduction. In K. McClarty, K. Mattern, & M. Gaertner's (Eds.), *Preparing students for college and careers: Theory, measurement, and educational practice* (pp. 1–8). Routledge.

Murphy, J. (2010). *The educator's handbook for understanding and closing achievement gaps*. Corwin Press.

National Assessment of Career and Technical Education. (2014). *Final report to Congress*. U.S. Department of Education.

National Academy Foundation. (2014). *Statistics and research: 2013–2014*. http://naf.org

National Career Academy Coalition. (2019). *Career academies change lives every day*. https://www.ncacinc.com/nsop/academies

National Center on Education and the Economy. (2007). *Tough choices or tough times: The report on the new commission on the new skills of the American workforce*. Wiley.

National Center for Education Statistics. (2019). *Public high school 4-year adjusted cohort graduation rate (ACGR), by race/ethnicity and selected demographic characteristics for the United States, the 50 states, and the District of Columbia: School year 2016–17*. https://nces.ed.gov/ccd/tables/ACGR_RE_and_characteristics_2016-17.asp

National Center for Education Statistics. (2018). *The condition of education 2018, status dropout rates* (NCES 2018-144). https://nces.ed.gov/programs/coe/indicator_coj.asp

Newmann, F. M., & Wehlage, G. G. (1995). *Successful school restructuring: A report to the public and educators*. Center on Organization and Restructuring of Schools.

Orr, M., Bailey, T., Hughes, K., Karp, M., & Kienzl, G. (2004). *The national academy foundation's career academies: Shaping postsecondary transitions. Institute on education and the economy* (IEE Working Paper No. 17). Teacher's College, Columbia University.

Page, L., Layzer, C., Schimmenti, J., Bernstein, L., & Horst, L. (2002). *National evaluation of smaller learning communities literature review*. Abt Associates.

Papadimitriou, M. (2014). High school students' perceptions of their internship experiences and related impact on career choices and changes. *Online Journal for Workforce Education & Development, 7*(1), 1–27.

Peebles-Wilkins, W. (2004). The full-service community school model. *Children and Schools, 26*(3), 131–133.

Pierce, K., & Hernández-Gantes, V. M. (2015). Do mathematics and reading competencies integrated into career and technical education courses improve high school student scores? *Career and Technical Education Research, 39*(3), 213–229.

Pincus, F. (1996). Discrimination comes in many forms: Individual, institutional, and structural. *American Behavioral Scientist, 40*, 186–194.

Popenoe, D. (1996). *Life without father: Compelling new evidence that fatherhood and marriage are indispensable for the good of children and society*. The Free Press.

Randles, J. (2019). Role modeling responsibility: The essential father discourse in responsible fatherhood programming and policy. *Social Problems, 67*(1), 1–17.

Saleem, F., & Lambert, S. (2016). Differential effects of racial socialization messages for African American adolescents: Personal versus institutional racial discrimination. *Journal of Child and Family Studies, 25*, 1385–1396.

Smeeding, T., Garfinkel, I., & Mincy, R. (2011). Young disadvantaged men: Fathers, families, poverty, and policy. *The ANNALS of the American Academy of Political and Social Science, 635*(1), 6–21. https://doi.org/10.1177/0002716210394774

Stern, D., Dayton, C., & Raby, M. (2010). *Career academies: A proven strategy to prepare high school students for college and careers.* University of California Berkeley Career Academy Support Network.

Stipanovic, N., Lewis, M. V., & Stringfield, S. (2012). Situating programs of study within current and historical career and technical educational reform efforts. *International Journal of Educational Reform, 21,* 80–97.

Stone, J. R., III, Alfeld, C., & Pearson, D. (2008). Rigor and relevance: Testing a model of enhanced math learning in career and technical education. *American Educational Research Journal, 45*(3), 767–795.

Stone, J. R., III., & Lewis, M. V. (2012). *College and career ready in the 21st century: Making high school matter.* Teacher's College Press.

Strengthening Career and Technical Education for the 21st Century Act 20 U.S.C. § 2301 (2018).

Utsey, S., & Ponterotto, J. (1996). Development and validation of the index of race-related stress (IRRS). *Journal of Counseling Psychology, 43,* 490–501.

Valli, L., Stefanski, A., & Jacobson, R. (2016). Topologizing school–community partnerships. *Urban Education, 51*(7), 719–720.

Verstegen, D. (2015). On doing an analysis of equity and closing the opportunity gap. *Education Policy Analysis Archives, 23,* 41. https://doi.org/10.14507/epaa.v23.1809

Wright, B. L., Ford, D. Y., & Young, J. L. (2017). Ignorance or indifference? Seeking excellence and equity for under-represented students of color in gifted education. *Global Education Review, 4*(1), 45–60.

Yosso, T. (2005). Whose culture has capital? A critical race theory discussion of community cultural wealth. *Race, Ethnicity and Education, 8*(1), 69–91.

AFTERWORD

Cheryl Holcomb-McCoy
American University

As we continue to cope with the effects of a global pandemic and a national reckoning of the country's "racism problem," career development for Black and Brown students should take front and center stage in education. First, consider that for 2020, the COVID-19 pandemic and the resulting lockdown caused 114 million people to lose their jobs. With tens of millions of people losing their jobs or seeing their working hours reduced, the ongoing crisis has disrupted labor markets around the world at an unprecedented scale. For Black and Brown people, employment during pre-pandemic and then *during* pandemic has been bleak. For instance, in 2020, 4 in 10 nonelderly Black adults belong to families in which someone lost a job, was furloughed or had hours cut, or lost work-related income because of COVID. Although the employment-related losses closely followed the national average (40.7% of Black adults compared with 41.5% of adults nationally), underlying structural factors, such as occupational segregation and less relative wealth, suggest families of color will face disproportionately more significant challenges as the COVID-19 crisis continues (Urban Institute, 2020). Moreover, at every education level (including college graduates!), Black workers have higher unemployment rates compared to their White counterparts (U.S. Bureau of Labor Statistics, n.d.).

So, when preparing students for future careers, school counselors must be accountable for how well they ready Black, Latinx, and Indigenous

Equity-Based Career Development and Postsecondary Transitions, pages 517–520
Copyright © 2022 by Information Age Publishing
www.infoagepub.com
All rights of reproduction in any form reserved.

students for the future workforce. This means preparing them for college, training them to receive high-quality credentials that lead to good jobs with good pay, and appropriately preparing them for work-based learning experiences, such as internships and apprenticeships. More critically, school counselors must ensure that Black, Latinx, and Indigenous students aren't relegated to lower academic tracks, pushed out of school via harsh discipline policies, or ignored when social and emotional issues plague them. School counselors must act to disrupt racist and oppressive systems in schools to achieve postsecondary success for all.

The chapters in this book, *Equity-Based Career Development and Postsecondary Transitions: An American Imperative,* offer a much-needed roadmap for school counselors to create equal and equitable postsecondary opportunities for students. While the authors presented evidence-based practices and precise strategies, the question is whether school counselors will follow their lead. *Why haven't school counselors disrupted the uneven access to postsecondary opportunities that they observe daily? Why do we continue to need a book like this to spell out to school counselors what they possibly already know?* The answer is simple—disrupting racist and oppressive policies and practices embedded in our schools is not easy. It's complicated and uncomfortable. School counselors are well-meaning people, but are they willing to "swim upstream" to ensure equity for all students and for students who don't look like them? I'm not so sure.

Two Stanford psychologists, Roberts and Rizzo (2021), provide a helpful framework for answering the above question. They outline seven factors, determined after an extensive review of interdisciplinary research, that contribute to American racism. I suspect that school counselors' willingness or unwillingness to disrupt racism in college and career readiness is based on several of these factors. The factors include (a) *categories,* which organize people into distinct groups by promoting essentialist and normative reasoning; (b) *factions,* which trigger ingroup loyalty and intergroup competition and threat; (c) *segregation,* which hardens racist perceptions, preferences, and beliefs through the denial of intergroup contact, (d) *hierarchy,* which emboldens people to think, feel, and behave in racist ways; (e) *power,* which legislates racism on both micro and macro levels; (f) *media,* which legitimizes overrepresented and idealized representations of White Americans while marginalizing and minimizing people of color; and (g) *passivism,* such that overlooking or denying the existence of racism obscures this reality, encouraging others to do the same and allowing racism to fester and persist. I argue that school counselors often align with this notion of passivism or silence. Thus, doing nothing seems like a safe way to act. When actually, silence perpetuates racist and oppressive behaviors and thoughts.

Also, with projections of people of color making up most of the U.S. population by 2044 (Colby & Ortman, 2014), White Americans often feel that their status is under threat and hence, show greater pro-White biases and support for conservative policies, parties, and political candidates (Craig & Richeson, 2018). This dynamic is evidenced now with the debate over critical race theory (CRT) in schools. School counselors are impacted by an increasingly tense and divisive racialized climate in schools. The question for school counselors in the foreseeable future will be, "How will school counselors navigate equity goals in an environment where so many feel threatened by the topic of racism?"

Again, this book gives a much-needed roadmap for school counselors to achieve equity in college and career readiness. But the roadmap must be implemented within an antiracist perspective. The literature on the psychology of American anti-racism is comparatively lacking, particularly among White Americans (Anyiwo et al., 2018). Thus, rather than attempting to map out what an anti-racist road might look like for school counselors, I suggest that school counselors begin reflecting on their own anti-racist journey within the context of ensuring equity in college and career readiness. Questions for reflection include: "How often is anti-racism socialized in one's school counseling program, and to what extent does this socialization vary as a function of race, class, experiences with racism, or other social realities?"; "How can school counselors—individually and as a profession, be mobilized toward anti-racism in their everyday work?"; "What cognitive frameworks lead to greater college and career awareness and antiracist thought?"; "Can those frameworks be effectively nurtured in school counseling programs?"; and "How can we promote anti-racism in our students and our schools?" Indeed, anti-racism can only be active, and to understand it, we must actively examine it. Thus, one of the essential steps for future school counseling research will be to shift our attention away from how people become racist toward the *contextual influences, psychological processes, and developmental mechanisms that help people become anti-racist*. I firmly believe that in the current state of school counseling, we will need to find future students and scholars well versed in creating anti-racist school counseling programs. This book is the beginning of the journey.

REFERENCES

Anyiwo, N., Banales, J., Rowley, S., Watkins, D., & Richards-Schuster, K. (2018). Sociocultural influences on the sociopolitical development of African American youth. *Child Development Perspectives, 12*, 165–170.

Colby, S. L., & Ortman, J. M. (2014). *Projections of the size and composition of the U.S. population: 2014 to 2060, current population reports* (P25-1143). U.S. Census Bureau.

Craig, M. A., & Richeson, J. A. (2018). Majority no more? The influence of neighborhood racial diversity and salient national population changes on Whites' perceptions of racial discrimination. *Journal of the Social Sciences, 4,* 141–157.

Roberts, S. O., & Rizzo, M. T. (2021). The psychology of American racism. *American Psychologist, 76*(3), 475–487.

Urban Institute. (2020, May 6). *How COVID-19 is affecting Black and Latino families' employment and financial well-being.* Urban Institute. https://www.urban.org/urban-wire/how-covid-19-affecting-black-and-latino-families-employment-and-financial-well-being

U.S. Bureau of Labor Statistics. (n.d.). *Table A.2. Employment status of the civilian population by race, sex, and age.* https://www.bls.gov/news.release/empsit.t02.htm

ABOUT THE CONTRIBUTORS

Sophia L. Ángeles is a doctoral candidate in the School of Education and Information Studies at the University of California, Los Angeles. Her research examines how immigration and language policies shape the educational trajectories of high school immigrant youth.

Alyssa Begay, MA, is a doctoral student at the University of Arizona in the counselor education and supervision program. She comes from the Hopi tribe in northern Arizona and has a background in education and research within rural reservation communities, including the Zuni Pueblo and Tohono O'odham Nation. She holds a master's degree in counseling with a school counseling emphasis and she currently serves as a teaching assistant and counselor in an alternative high school. She is also part of the mental health team that is aimed at improving mental health awareness and access to services. Her research interests include improving school counseling services for Native American students in reservation communities and her focus is on building collaborative relationships between school counselors and community-based mental health providers and those from off-reservation agencies.

Richard Joseph Behun, PhD, is a counselor educator at Millersville University of Pennsylvania. During his career, Dr. Behun has been employed as the principal of an international baccalaureate high school and has worked as a high school counselor in the private sector and as a middle school counselor in the public school system. He holds a PhD in counselor education and supervision from Duquesne University and has advanced degrees in school counseling, school administration, and school law. Dr. Behun is a li-

Equity-Based Career Development and Postsecondary Transitions, pages 521–536
Copyright © 2022 by Information Age Publishing
www.infoagepub.com
All rights of reproduction in any form reserved.

censed professional counselor, national certified counselor, approved clinical supervisor, and is a certified PK–12 school counselor in Pennsylvania.

Damian Brown Jr. is a fourth-year psychology student at Florida Agricultural & Mechanical University.

Julia Bryan, PhD, is a professor of counselor education at Penn State University. She researches school counselors' role in school–family–community partnerships and their influence on student outcomes. She has developed an antiracist equity-focused partnership process model for counselors, educators, and youth workers to foster access and equity for marginalized students. Dr. Bryan has written over 75 peer-reviewed publications and edited a special issue of *Professional School Counseling* journal on "Collaboration and Partnerships With Families and Communities." Dr. Bryan was recently awarded the American Counseling Association Extended Research Award and the Association of Counselor Education and Supervision Outstanding Mentor Award.

Diana Camilo, EdD, LCP, NCC, is an assistant professor at CSU San Bernardino. Her expertise is in school counseling, student services, and administration. As an administrator for Chicago Public Schools, she provides district-wide planning, management, and the evaluation of interventions and policies to support and sustain the implementation of school counseling programs. Her work predominantly explores culturally responsive practices, school counseling, and the college and career readiness of minoritized populations. She was also the founder and chair of the Supporting Access to Higher Education for Immigrant and Undocumented Students conference and is a member of the UndocuResearch Collaborative.

Julie Cerrito, PhD, is a counselor educator and coordinator of the school counseling graduate program at Bloomsburg University of Pennsylvania. She has been actively engaged in the school counseling profession for over 20 years. Dr. Cerrito spent the first 12 years of her career as a practicing school counselor in Pennsylvania public schools. She worked in higher education as a school counselor educator for the past 8 years. Dr. Cerrito earned a PhD in counselor education and supervision from the Pennsylvania State University and holds credentials including national certified counselor, national certified school counselor, and approved clinical supervisor.

Carla B. Cheatham, MEd, LCPC, NCC, GCDF, CSCDA, has been a high school counselor for 25 years. Carla is a doctoral candidate in the counselor education and supervision program at Governors State University. She has earned the certified school career development advisor credential through the National Career Development Association. Carla is the 2020–2021 president of the Illinois Association for Multicultural Counseling. Carla received a BS in journalism from Southern Illinois University at Carbondale, a MEd in school counseling from Georgia State University, and an EdM in global studies in education from the University of Illinois Urbana Champaign.

Jonique R. Childs, PhD, NCC, LPC, is an assistant professor in the College of Education, specifically, the student development program. She has completed her PhD in counselor education and supervision from the University of Iowa. Additionally, she has completed a graduate minor in multicultural education and cultural competency and is a licensed professional counselor (LPC) and nationally certified counselor (NCC). Jonique has also completed dual masters' degrees (MS/Eds) in school and clinical mental health counseling with an emphasis in career development. Dr. Childs has previous experiences as an at-risk school counselor, college career counselor and recruiter, and clinical mental health counselor on the national suicide prevention hotline.

Laura Cohen, PhD, entered the field of education in 1985. She has served as a teacher, school counselor, school counseling director, school-based administrator, and district supervisor of school counseling for Broward County Schools, Florida. She was recognized by the Broward School Counselors Association as School Administrator of the year in 2018 and as School Counseling Advocate of the Year by the Florida School Counselors Association in 2019. Dr. Cohen is a national certified counselor and school counselor. She completed her undergraduate studies at the University of Miami and her post-graduate studies at Florida Atlantic University. Currently, she serves as an adjunct professor of school counseling at Nova Southeastern University and Valdosta State University.

Norma L. Day-Vines, PhD, serves as associate dean for diversity and faculty development in the School of Education at Johns Hopkins University and maintains a faculty appointment as professor of counseling and human development. Prior to joining the faculty at Johns Hopkins University, she held tenured faculty positions at the College of William and Mary and Virginia Tech. Dr. Day-Vines' research agenda examines the importance of multiculturalism as an indispensable tool in the delivery of culturally competent counseling and educational services for clients and students from marginalized groups. More specifically, she specializes in the measurement of attitudes towards discussing the contextual dimensions of race, ethnicity, and culture with ethnic minority clients/students and the identification of strategies that reduce barriers to well-being. She has consulted with school districts across the country to address issues related to diversity, equity, and inclusion. Her scholarship has appeared in leading counseling journals such as the *Journal of Counseling and Development*, the *Journal of Multicultural Counseling* *and Development,* the *Journal of Measurement and Evaluation in Counseling and Development,* and *Professional School Counseling.* Dr. Day-Vines was recognized with an Exemplary Diversity Leadership Award in 2013 by the Association of Multicultural Counseling and Development. In 2018, she received an Excellence in Teaching Award at Johns Hopkins University, and in 2019, she was awarded a presidential citation from the American Counseling Association, in recognition of her scholarship on multiculturalism. Norma earned her bachelor's degree from the University of North Carolina at Chapel Hill and her master's and doctorate from North Carolina State University.

Mary Edwin, PhD, LPC, NCC, is an award-winning career development researcher and assistant professor of counseling at the University of Missouri–St Louis. She received her PhD in counselor education from the Pennsylvania State University, where she was also a career counselor. Prior to earning her doctoral degree, Dr. Edwin served as an elementary and middle school counselor. She received her BS in biology with a minor in psychology from the University of Texas at Arlington and her MS in counseling from Johns Hopkins University. Her research focuses on career development across the lifespan and fostering career development in K–12 schools.

Liana Elopre has her BA in psychology from George Mason University and is a current graduate student (2021) in the University of Virginia counselor education program. She is a Teach for America Alum and was a Jacksonville 2014 Corps Member. She has experience working in Title I schools as a high school mathematics teacher in Jacksonville, Florida, and as a family advocate in an elementary school in Henrico, Virginia. She has participated and led school interventions in school climate and culture, new teacher training, and parent empowerment.

Lia D. Falco, PhD, (educational psychology) is an assistant professor of counseling in the Disability and Psychoeducational Studies Department. She is a certified school counselor in the state of Arizona and worked as a middle school counselor in the Amphitheater School District prior to completing her doctorate. Her expertise is in the area of career development with research that explores how adolescents view themselves as future workers and how career issues are related to aspects of motivation and identity. Her specific focus is STEM career choice, and her scholarship seeks to identify and evaluate educational practices that are effective at supporting students who are underrepresented in STEM occupations.

Edward C. Fletcher Jr., PhD, is an EHE distinguished associate professor of workforce development and education in the College of Education and Human Ecology (EHE) at The Ohio State University. He serves as senior faculty fellow for the Center on Education and Training for Employment and co-editor for the *Journal of Career and Technical Education*. Dr. Fletcher's research focuses on the role of high school STEM themed career academies in promoting students' engagement and positive school experiences as well as postsecondary and labor market transitions, particularly for ethnically and racially diverse learners and those who come from economically disadvantaged backgrounds.

Beth Gilfillan, PhD, is an assistant professor in the Department of Counselor Education at Northeastern Illinois University. She has a doctorate in counselor education and supervision from Penn State University and a master's in counseling from DePaul University. She was a high school counselor for 10 years in Illinois. Her research and advocacy interests include training school counselors, college and career readiness, improving college access, and supporting first generation college students and their families.

Bobby B. Gueh, PhD, originally from Liberia, West Africa, is lead counselor at Lanier High School in Gwinnett County Public Schools. He has 18 years of school counseling experience across all K–12 levels. Dr. Gueh has dedicated his career to the mentoring and development of Black males in schools and juvenile systems. He has developed programs to support marginalized student populations and is a presenter and trainer at state, national, and international levels on topics including race and racism, multiculturalism, Black male achievement, and crisis response. Dr. Gueh is currently writing his own book, *Talking to Children and Teens About Race and Racism*.

Paul C. Harris, PhD, NCC, NCSC, is an associate professor of education in the Department of Educational Psychology, Counseling, and Special Education at Pennsylvania State University. Dr. Harris' research focuses on achieving three goals: (a) improving the college and career readiness process of underserved students, (b) promoting the development of a multidimensional sense of self for Black male student athletes, and (c) facilitating the empowerment of anti-racist school counselors. He currently serves on the editorial review board for the *Professional School Counseling* journal and on the senior advisory board for *The Professional Counselor* journal.

Latoya Haynes-Thoby, PhD, is an assistant professor of counselor education at the University of Florida. Her work explores the benefits of trauma-informed and culturally relevant counseling. As such, her research focuses on individual and community healing from trauma, including community-rooted factors that promote resilience. Her research agenda is brought forth through applied research methods and includes the exploration of culturally specific factors that contribute to resilience and success. Her research aims to broaden what we understand about resilience and to promote human thriving within community, school, and career counseling settings, especially through the training of new counselors.

Brent Henderson, PhD, NCC, NCSC, has been a school counselor for 19 years with Gwinnett County Public Schools. For 5 of those years, Dr. Henderson served as coordinator of school counseling in the Office of Advisement and Counseling. He is active in the Georgia School Counselor Association, having served in many roles, including president during 2015–2016. Dr. Henderson is a part-time counselor educator at Capella University and the University of Georgia. He is also a guest lecturer having delivered staff development for school counselors, principals, and central office personnel on working with LGBTQ+ students.

Dantavious Hicks, MS, is a licensed, school-based clinical mental health counselor in the state of Maryland. Before entering the counseling profession, Dantavious served as a middle school and adult education mathematics teacher in Hawai'i. He also has experience coaching and training novice teachers through a culturally relevant, anti-racist education framework. In Spring of 2020, Dantavious earned the Johns Hopkins University School of Education's Student Excellence Award for his research, service, and scholarship. Hicks's research interests include broaching, multicultural orientation, social justice, anti-racism in counselor education, and identity development. His future aspirations include pursuing his doctoral studies in counselor education and supervision.

Erik M. Hines, PhD, N.C.C., is an associate professor in the Department of Educational Psychology and Learning Systems at the Florida State University, where he also serves as the coordinator of the counselor education program and school counseling track. Dr. Hines prepares pre-service school counselors, and his research agenda focuses on (a) college and career readiness for African American males; (b) parental involvement and its impact on academic achievement for students of color; and (c) improving and increasing postsecondary opportunities for first generation, low-income, and students of color (particularly African American males). Additionally, his research examines career exploration in the fields of science, technology, engineering, and mathematics (STEM) for students of color. Over the years, he has secured major funding from the National Science Foundation to study the college readiness and persistence of African American males to improve their academic and career outcomes. Finally, he is a proud American Counseling Association (ACA) Fellow.

Mia R. Hines is an academic advisor in the School of Teacher Education at Florida State University, where she coordinates numerous recruitment and retention initiatives to increase the number of students of color entering the teacher profession. Mia also worked as a high school counselor and has her school administrator license in which she gained an extensive background in developing college and career readiness programs that assist students with matriculating through college. Mia is currently pursuing a doctoral degree in educational leadership and policy at Florida State University.

Cassandra Hirdes, MEd, is a first-year doctoral student in the counselor education and supervision program at the University of Arizona. She holds a master's degree in school counseling and has a background in higher education academic support programming. She currently serves as the director of Health and Wellness Initiatives at the University of Arizona. In this role, she provides administrative oversight for professionally licensed counselors and manages Wildcats R.I.S.E. (Resilience in Stressful Events), a peer-to-peer Psychological First Aid program. Her research interests include innovative models of mental health care and the influence of student support services on college students' mental wellness.

Cheryl Holcomb-McCoy, PhD, is an American Counseling Association (ACA) fellow with 30 years of experience as a former kindergarten teacher, elementary school counselor, family therapist, and most recently university professor and administrator, she has a wealth of knowledge, expertise, and wisdom. Dr. Holcomb-McCoy is currently the dean of the School of Education and a professor at American University (AU). She is also the author of the best-selling book *School Counseling to Close the Achievement Gap: A Social Justice Framework for Success* (Corwin Press, 2007) and her book, *Antiracist Counseling in Schools and Communities* (American Counseling Association, 2021). In her 5 years as dean, Dr. Holcomb-McCoy founded AU's Summer Institute on Education, Equity, and Justice, and the AU Teacher Pipeline Project, a partnership with the DC Public Schools and Friendship Charter Schools. She is also actively working to develop an anti-racist curriculum for teachers-in-training. Prior to leading the School of Education at AU, she served as vice provost for faculty affairs campus-wide and vice dean of academic affairs in the School of Education at Johns Hopkins University, where she launched the Johns Hopkins School Counseling Fellows program and The Faculty Diversity Initiative. Dr. Holcomb-McCoy has also been an associate professor in the Department of Counseling and Personnel Services at the University of Maryland College Park and director of the school counseling program at Brooklyn College of the City University of New York. Dr. Holcomb-McCoy's passion for school counseling, mental health and wellness, starts at home. As a proud mother of two, she knows firsthand the importance of systemic change to help students reach their full potential. A proud member of Delta Sigma Theta Sorority, Inc., Dr. Holcomb-McCoy holds her bachelor's and master's degrees from the University of Virginia.

She earned a doctorate in counseling and counselor education from the University of North Carolina at Greensboro.

Ian Levy, EdD, is an assistant professor of school counseling at Manhattan College, New York City native, former high school counselor. His research explores preparing school counselors to use hip-hop based interventions to support youth development. Most notably, Dr. Levy piloted the development, implementation, and evaluation of a hip-hop based counseling framework, which has been featured in *The New York Times,* CNN, and published in a variety of reputable academic journals. Ian is also the author of the research monograph, *Hip-Hop and Spoken Word Therapy in School Counseling: Developing Culturally Responsive Approaches,* published with Routledge (2021).

Justis Lopez (also known as DJ Faro) is the founder and chief enthusiasm officer (CEO) of Just Experience LLC, a start up company that strives to educate, entertain, and empower communities across the world. As a community organizer, he focuses on ways to create spaces of radical joy, justice, and possibility through the arts. He is currently pursuing his MSED degree in educational entrepreneurship at the University of Pennsylvania. He is an adjunct professor at Stephen F. Austin University teaching multicultural education, and strategic project consultant at the Council for Opportunity in Education where he focuses on supporting national efforts for first generation, low-income college students a part of the TRIO federal programs. Before this role, he was a social studies teacher in the Bronx and a guest lecturer at Teachers College, Columbia University focusing on incorporating hip-hop as a pedagogical practice in schools. When Justis isn't teaching, he can be found DJing or dancing down the street. He enjoys long hikes, funfetti cupcakes, and long walks on the beach.

Clifford Mack Jr., PhD, has been a high school counselor in the private sector since 2007. From 2017–2020 he served on the North American Christian College Admissions Professionals (NACCAP) board. Dr. Mack completed his undergraduate studies at Washington Bible College (Maryland), graduate work at Trinity International University (Florida), and PhD at Florida Atlantic University. Currently he serves as a school counselor at Calvary Christian Academy (Fort Lauderdale, FL), a current member of the Florida School Counselor Association (FSCA) Board (2nd term), and adjunct professor at Trinity International University and Florida Atlantic University.

Robert Martinez, PhD, is an assistant professor at University of North Carolina, Chapel Hill. Dr. Martinez is a Latinx researcher who was raised and attended public schools in Los Angeles, had immigrant parents who didn't graduate high school, and was an underserved/underresourced foster youth. Dr. Martinez was also a first-generation college graduate who lacked access information for postsecondary education throughout his education experience. As an early career Latinx scholar in the field of school counseling, he has begun to build a body of research on the college ready (CR) process specific to Latinx youth in the Southeast, and in particular, how they navigate postsecondary opportunities at school. Dr. Martinez reported that Latinx high schoolers experience their high schools as emotionally arousing, inequitable, and stressful learning environments. Furthermore, his research findings have demonstrated that school-based CR practices intended to support all students, including Latinx students, create CR stressors that Latinx adolescents must manage in order to be CR. At the same time, he has garnered insights into ways in which Latinx adolescents draw on aspects of their Latinx identity, their family and community resources, and other mechanisms, to manage the psychological and physiological arousal that results from their school, community, and environmental circumstances.

Erin Mason, PhD, LPC, CPCS, is an assistant professor at Georgia State University in Atlanta and formerly a faculty member at DePaul University in Chicago. She spent 13 years as a middle school counselor. Her research includes conceptual, quantitative, and qualitative work in the areas of school counselor professional identity development, leadership, advocacy, social justice, and antiracism, as well as technology and innovation in counselor education. Erin's greatest joys as a counselor educator come from teaching, mentoring, and collaborating, and she values most that students and colleagues provide her with ongoing opportunities to learn.

Viola Simone May, PhD, holds a Teaching Faculty I position in the Department of Educational Psychology and Learning Systems at the Florida State University. She pursued graduate studies at Auburn University earning a MEd in clinical mental health counseling in 2014 and a PhD in counselor education and supervision in 2017. Her clinical experience includes work with individuals who have experienced intimate partner and domestic violence, depression, anxiety, and interpersonal issues. May's research interests include higher education preparation, retention and success, and race-based trauma with an emphasis on women and adolescents of color.

Renae D. Mayes, PhD, NCC, is an associate professor in the Department of Disability and Psychoeducational Studies at the University of Arizona where she prepares masters and doctoral level students to be counselors and counselor educators. Dr. Mayes's research agenda centers around the academic success and college readiness for gifted Black students with dis/abilities and Black girls. Mayes' research details the experience of students and families navigating schools, while also providing recommendations for dismantling systems of oppression through policy and practice. Further, Dr. Mayes has extended this research to include implications for leadership, advocacy, and collaboration for school counselors and school administrators.

Amy Milsom, PhD, LPC-S, NCC, is a professor of counselor education, department chair at Appalachian State University, and a certified school counselor. She is a former middle and high school counselor who has worked with students transitioning to college in both P–12 and postsecondary settings. Her research centers around career and college readiness and postsecondary transition planning for students with disabilities, and she has numerous publications and presentations on this topic.

James L. Moore III, PhD, is the vice provost for diversity and inclusion and chief diversity officer at The Ohio State University, while currently serving as the first executive director of the Todd Anthony Bell National Resource Center on the African American Male. He is also the inaugural EHE Distinguished Professor of Urban Education in the College of Education and Human Ecology. Dr. Moore is internationally recognized for his work on African American males. He has published over 150 publications; obtained over $28 million in grants, contracts, and gifts; and given over 200 scholarly presentations and lectures throughout the United States and other parts of the world. From 2018 to 2021, Dr. Moore was cited by *Education Week* as one of the 200 most influential scholars and researchers in the United States, who inform educational policy, practice, and reform. Notably, he was selected as an American Council on Education fellow, American Counseling Association fellow, and Big Ten Committee on Institutional Cooperation Academic Leadership Program fellow.

Michael J. Morgan Jr. is a doctoral candidate in the combined counseling psychology and school psychology program in the College of Education at Florida State University. He is a nationally certified counselor. The focus of his research is on building the practical and theoretical knowledge base related to cognitive information processing theory, especially in relation to extending CIP theory to work with diverse groups and technology-enhanced career exploration. His clinical work is focused on the application of third wave CBT and person-centered approaches, and he loves guiding new graduate students through clinical supervision.

Allyson Murphy, MA, is a recent graduate of Appalachian State University's professional school counseling master's degree program and a certified school counselor. During her time in graduate school she interned as an elementary and middle school counselor and mentored low-income and first-generation college students. This chapter is one of her first publications and she hopes to continue researching and publishing on various topics in the counseling field as she enters the profession.

Laura Owen, PhD, is the executive director for the Center for Equity and Postsecondary Attainment at San Diego State University. A prior urban school counselor and district counseling supervisor, she is a passionate advocate for closing college opportunity gaps. Her research focuses on evaluating the impact of interventions and programs designed to address the systems, structures, and policies that drive equitable access to high quality postsecondary advising support. Laura has researched interventions targeting FAFSA completion, the high school to college transition, virtual advising, the use of technology in college counseling, and how students prefer to receive college and career information.

Tim Poynton, EdD, is a professor and counselor educator committed to improving the transition from high school into young adulthood. A former school counselor, Dr. Poynton is currently an associate professor at the University of Massachusetts Boston. Dr. Poynton has published several research articles and book chapters related to school counseling, career development, and college readiness, and was recognized in 2011 as the Counselor Educator of the Year by the American School Counselor Association. He is also an instructor for the facilitating career development program with the National Career Development Association, and has been invited to speak at conferences across the United States.

Diandra J. Prescod, PhD, is an associate professor and program coordinator of counselor education at the University of Connecticut. In her previous role, she spent 5 years as an assistant professor of counselor education and program coordinator of career counseling at Pennsylvania State University. Dr. Prescod received her bachelor's degree in psychology from Rutgers, The State University of New Jersey; her master's in mental health counseling from Monmouth University; and her PhD in counselor education from the University of Central Florida. Her research focuses on career development interventions for (a) STEM undergraduate students and (b) women/students of color in higher education.

Joshua Rauguth is a graduate student within the Department of Educational Psychology at Ball State University. His dissertation focuses on the integration of online programming into college counseling departments in an independent setting. His other work focuses on student-athlete identity development, leadership development, and college matriculation.

Adrianne Robertson, MEd, LPC, NCC, is a doctoral student at Georgia State University. She is a school counselor and licensed mental health counselor with experience at middle and high school and varied clinical settings. She has presented nationally and internationally and is currently an adjunct instructor at DePaul University where she earned her master's degree in school counseling. Adrianne is a 2021 Minority fellow of the National Board for Certified Counselors. Her research interests include mental health issues, systemic racism, and the impact of both on student success in K–12 schools.

Carol Robinson-Zañartu, PhD, is professor emerita, Department of Counseling and School Psychology at San Diego State University, where she served as department chair for 16 years and taught multiple classes in school psychology for some 30 years. Her work has been devoted to educational equity, with a strong commitment to and emphasis on culturally responsive work with Native American and Indigenous youth and multiple language learners, especially Spanish speakers. She also specialized in and taught classes in intervention-base dynamic assessment and mediated interventions, focusing on the development of critical thinking skills, their integration with culturally responsive practice. She currently directs the following federally funded projects: (a) PUEDE! A School Psychology-SLP Bilingual Collaboration; and (B) SHPA, Mental Health Specialization and Collaboration with School Psychology-School Counseling on behalf of Native and Indigenous youth and communities.

Jennifer Sánchez, PhD, CRC, LMHC, is an associate professor of rehabilitation and counselor education at The University of Iowa. She received her PhD in rehabilitation psychology from the University of Wisconsin–Madison and her MEd in rehabilitation and mental health counseling from Florida Atlantic University. Dr. Sánchez possesses over 15 years of clinical, teaching, and research experience. She has co-edited two special issues, published over 35 peer-reviewed articles, and delivered more than 75 professional presentations. Dr. Sánchez serves on the editorial boards of the *Journal of Counseling & Development, Counselor Education and Supervision,* and the *Journal of Rehabilitation Administration.*

Randi Schietz, PhD, has been an elementary school counselor in Palm Beach County, Florida since 1994. In 2015, she was recognized as school counselor of the year in Palm Beach County, and Florida school counselor advocate. She is currently working as an adjunct professor in the school counseling programs at Nova Southeastern and Valdosta State Universities. Dr. Schietz completed her undergraduate studies at University of Massachusetts, her graduate student at Northeastern University, and a PhD in counseling from Florida Atlantic University. She has served on the executive board of the Palm Beach School Counselor Association for over 10 years.

Miray D. Seward is a PhD student in educational psychology—applied developmental science at the University of Virginia. Her research examines the educational experiences of Black girls and women, with a focus on student athletes. In particular, her work examines how the socialization of Black female student athletes impacts their identity development.

Paul Singleton II is a fifth-year PhD candidate in the counselor education program, focusing on educational equity and social justice at the University of Connecticut's Neag School of Education. Paul is a certified school counselor and Crandall-Cordero fellow at the University of Connecticut, where he also serves as the assistant director for the Scholastic House of Leaders in support of African American Researchers and Scholars (ScHOLA²RS House). As part of this work, he offers academic, social-emotional, and behavioral counseling to Black and Brown college males. Paul's research interests surround African American male academic achievement and college readiness.

Tyron Slack is a doctoral student in the combined counseling psychology and school psychology program in the College of Education at Florida State University. Tyrone received his BA in psychology at Southeastern Louisiana University and Master's degree in social work at Florida State University. His clinical and research interests include, but not limited to, the impact of racial microaggressions on Black undergraduate students' academic self-concept, resilience, and mental health.

Chauncey D. Smith, PhD, is a community psychologist of education and an assistant professor of education at the University of Virginia School of Education and Human Development. His research examines Black youth's lived experiences at intersections of race, gender, class, community, and school. His most recent work is centered on Black boys' sociopolitical development via a youth participatory action research program. He is affiliated with Youth-Nex |The UVA Center to Promote Effective Youth Development and the Center for Race and Public Education in the South.

Sam Steen, PhD, an associate professor and licensed professional school counselor, specializes in group work and cultivating Black students' academic identity development. Dr. Steen was a school counselor for 10 years and these practitioner experiences shaped his research agenda, approach to teaching, and service. Dr. Steen is a fellow for the Association for Specialists in Group Work, a division of the American Counseling Association. Additionally, Dr. Steen received the Al Dye Research Award and the Professional Advancement Award both from ASGW recognizing his outstanding efforts advancing the field of group work through research and development of new and innovative strategies for schools, families, and communities.

Marie L. Tanaka is a fourth-year student in the school psychology program at the University of Arizona. She completed her BA in psychology and literary arts at Brown University. Marie worked as an English language instructor as part of the Fulbright program in Andorra and then subsequently in a sheltered English immersion program in a middle school for 2 years prior to beginning her graduate career. Her research and service seek to support culturally and linguistically diverse students from immigrant backgrounds.

Ayanna C. Troutman is a proud graduate of Spelman College and a current doctoral student in the school psychology program at the University of Florida. Her research interests include integrating social justice practices in graduate training programs, adapting social, emotional, and behavioral (SEB) interventions for Black youth, and examining how youth Black youth engage in resistance and radicalism in their communities and schools. Ayanna's ultimate goal is to become faculty at a Historically Black College or University (HBCU) to conduct research highlighting Black students' experiences in the education system.

Desireé Vega, PhD, is an associate professor in the school psychology program at the University of Arizona. She completed her BA in psychology at SUNY–Binghamton University and MA and PhD in school psychology at The Ohio State University. Dr. Vega worked as a school psychologist for the Omaha Public Schools district for 3 years prior to beginning her faculty career at Texas State University. Her research, teaching, and service intersect to focus on advancing the academic outcomes of culturally and linguistically minoritized students and preparing future school psychologists and researchers to engage in advocacy and implement culturally responsive practices.

César D. Villalobos is currently a doctoral student in the school psychology program at the University of Arizona. He received his MA in child, family, and school psychology from the University of Denver. Through his service, passion, and leadership, César hopes to inspire local and wide scale changes that will result in a more equitable society for students, families, and communities of color. César firmly believes that focusing more on the valuable assets already present within our students of color and within their community may allow us to better serve, advocate for, and empower them to reach higher levels of success.

Grace W. Wambu, EdD, LAC, NCC, is an associate professor of counseling in the Counselor Education Department at New Jersey City University. She obtained her doctorate in counselor education and supervision from Northern Illinois University. Dr. Wambu began her career as a high school teacher, school counselor, and currently as counselor educator. She has taught several courses including career counseling and development, school counseling courses, practicum, and internship over the last 8 years. Her research interests include career development and decision-making for immigrant youth, supervision, multicultural counseling, and international counseling.

Bobbi-Jo Wathen is a fourth-year PhD student at the University of Connecticut's Neag School of Education. For more than 9 years, she has worked as a practicing school counselor and is currently working at Middletown High School in Middletown, CT as college and career readiness counselor. Bobbi-Jo's research focuses on school counselors' readiness to offer comprehensive career counseling to African American boys. Over the years, she has worked as education consultant for the National Center for Women in Information Technology, where she works with Counselors 4 Computing to expand computer science access to women and people of color.

Ellie Wengert, MEd, is a graduate student (2021) in the University of Virginia Counselor Education program. Previously, she received an MEd in social foundations of education (UVA, 2019) with a focus on the ways that race, gender, culture, and social class shape students' experiences in K–12 schools and access to postsecondary opportunities. She has also worked in youth-serving positions in nonprofit, local government, summer camp, and after-school program settings.

Joseph M. Williams is an associate professor in the Counselor Education program at the University of Virginia. He earned his PhD in counselor education and supervision from the University of Iowa and his MS in clinical mental health counseling from Minnesota State University. His primary research line focuses on resilience-based interventions at the micro and macro levels that offset the detrimental effect of racism and poverty on the academic, personal/social, and career development of K–12 students. His secondary line of interest includes multicultural and social justice training practices for (K–12) counselors, educators, and other helping professionals.

Jaclyn N. Wolf is a doctoral candidate in the school psychology program at the University of Arizona. Jaclyn previously attended California State University, Northridge, where she earned a bachelor's degree in psychology with a minor in family studies and a master's degree in clinical psychology. Currently, Jaclyn is a doctoral intern at Casa Pacifica Centers for Children & Families in Camarillo, CA. Her broad research focus is on sociocultural factors related to the mental health and educational/academic outcomes of marginalized youth populations (e.g., Latinx youth, emergent bilinguals). Jaclyn has held positions in schools, private assessment practices, hospitals, and community-based settings.

Eunhui Yoon, PhD, is an assistant professor in the counselor education program at Florida State University. She is an active member of the Society for

Sexual, Affectional, Intersex, and Gender Expansive Identities (formerly ALGBTIC) and was awarded as an Emerging Leader in the year of 2017–2018. She also has been serving as an editorial board member of the *Journal of LGBTQ Issues in Counseling* since 2016. She has been conducting various studies on LGBTAIQ topics with her colleagues. Dr. Yoon has given invited lectures and workshops related to LGBTQAIQ+ counseling competencies at several state, national, and international conferences and universities.

Printed in Great Britain
by Amazon

49338669R00309